DANTE
THE MAKER

DANTE
THE MAKER

William Anderson

Crossroad · New York

1982
The Crossroad Publishing Company
575 Lexington Avenue, New York, NY 10022

Printed in the United States of America

Library of Congress Catalog Card Number: 81-70796

ISBN 0-8245-0414-3

In memory of Robert Symmons
1937–58
Manibus date lilia plenis

Contents

Contents

Illustrations

Preface and acknowledgments

I owe many debts to friends, colleagues, and kind helpers incurred during the several years it has taken to write this book and I must offer my thanks to the following: John Calmann, who first induced me to write the book; Dr I. Grafe, who read it at many stages and made many erudite and helpful suggestions; Dr Marjorie Reeves, who read an earlier draft and saved me from many errors; Peter Levi, who read it and saw the point; Charles Davis for his help; Alison Brown for her comments; Dr Peter Fenwick, who read and discussed with me the passages where I ventured into his field of neuro-physiology; Catharine Carver for her help and encouragement; Margaret and Adrian Lyttelton for taking me round the battlefields of Tuscany; and Sarah Codrington. I must also thank the librarian and staff of Chelsea College, London, for their help in obtaining books that I needed, the librarian of King's College, London, for allowing me to consult his shelves, and the librarian and staff of the London Library. I must also express my gratitude to James Hodgson, who drew the maps and diagrams for me, and to my publishers, Routledge & Kegan Paul, notably Stephen Brook and Elaine Donaldson.

I would like to thank the following publishers and owners of copyright material for their kindness in allowing me to quote from their editions, works and translations: Arnoldo Mondadori and the Società Dantesca Italiana for permission to use passages from the *Commedia*, ed. Giorgio Petrocchi (4 vols, 1966–7), and the edition of *De monarchia* ed. Pier Giorgio Ricci, Edizione Nazionale, vol. 5 (1965); Felice Le Monnier for passages from *De vulgari eloquentia*, ed. Marigo, 3rd edn, 1957, and from *Il Convivio*, ed. G. Busnelli and G. Vandelli, 2nd edn, 2 vols (1954 and 1964); Giunti Marzocco for passages from *La Vita Nuova*, ed. Michele Barbi (1932); Oxford University Press for passages from the Italian text of the *canzoni* and other lyric poems from Dante's *Lyric Poetry*, ed. K. Foster and P. Boyde, 2 vols (1967), for passages from the translation of the *Convivio* (*The Banquet*) by W. W. Jackson (1909), for passages from the text and translation of the letters in *Dantis Alagherii Epistolae*, ed. and tr. Paget Toynbee, 2nd edn, 1966, and for the translation on p. 296 from Hildegard of Bingen from Charles Singer's *From Magic to Science* (1928);

Preface and acknowledgments

Mrs Nicolete Gray and the Society of Authors, on behalf of the Laurence Binyon Estate, for permission to use the late Laurence Binyon's translation of the *Divine Comedy*; J. M. Dent & Sons Ltd for the extract on pp. 184–5 from A. G. Ferrers Howell's translation of *De vulgari eloquentia* from *The Latin Works of Dante Alighieri* (1904); Weidenfeld & Nicolson Ltd for the passages on pp. 44, 218, and 236 from Donald Nicholl's translation of the *Monarchia* in *Monarchy and Three Political Letters*, 1954; Faber & Faber Ltd and Harcourt Brace Jovanovich Inc. for the quotation from T. S. Eliot's *Four Quartets* on p. 5; Houghton Mifflin Co. and Constable & Co. Ltd for the passage from John Livingstone Lowes's *The Road to Xanadu* on p. 429; M. B. Yeats, Miss Anne Yeats, and the Macmillan Co. of London and Basingstoke for the passage from *Essays and Introductions* by W. B. Yeats on p. 430; Victor Gollancz Ltd for the passage from George Mackay Brown's *An Orkney Tapestry* on p. 431, Princeton University Press and Routledge & Kegan Paul Ltd for the passages from Erich Auerbach's *Literary Language and its Public in Later Latin Antiquity and in the Middle Ages* on pp. 85–6, and from Henry Corbin's *Avicenna and the Visionary Recital* on p. 111; Schocken Books Inc. and George Allen & Unwin (Publishers) Ltd for the material on pp. 88, 94, 95, 99, and 100 from *Songs of the Troubadours*, ed. and tr. by Anthony Bonner (copyright © 1972 by Schocken Books Inc.); Professor Clarence Brown for the passage from the translation from Osip Mandelstam's *Conversation about Dante* on p. 118; Eyre & Spottiswoode (Publishers) Ltd for the passages from the *Summa theologiae* of St Thomas Aquinas, tr. Thomas Gilby, O. P., on pp. 111 and 332; The Vedanta Society of Southern California for the passages from *The Upanishads : Breath of the Eternal*, tr. Swami Prabhavananda and Frederick Manchester, on p. 275, and from *The Song of God ; Bhagavad-Gita*, tr. Swami Prabhavananda and Christopher Isherwood, on p. 453; Penguin Books Ltd for the passage from Cicero, *On the Good Life*, tr. Michael Grant (© Michael Grant Productions Ltd, 1971), on p. 276; George Allen & Unwin (Publishers) Ltd for the extract from Mohammed Marmaduke Pickthall's *The Meaning of the Glorious Koran* on p. 277; Harcourt Brace Jovanovich Inc. for the passages from I. A. Richards's *Beyond* on pp. 313 and 450; Constable & Co. Ltd for the passage from Karl Vossler's *Medieval Culture*, tr. W. C. Lawton, on p. 451; the Bobbs-Merrill Company Inc. for the passage from St Bonaventure's *The Mind's Road to God*, tr. George Boas (copyright © 1953, by the Liberal Arts Press, Inc.), on p. 400; the Executors of C. Day Lewis, the Hogarth Press, and Harold Matson Company Inc. for the quotations from C. Day Lewis's translation of *The Aeneid*, © 1952 by C. Day Lewis, on pp. 420–2; New York University Press for the passage from *American Critical Essays on the Divine Comedy*, ed. Robert J. Clements, copyright © 1967 by New York University, on p. 294; Harper & Row, Publishers, Inc. for the passage from Raymond B. Blakney's *Meister Eckhart: A Modern Translation* on p. 126; Chicago University Press for the passage from Erich Auerbach's *Dante: Poet of the Secular World* on p. 50; and Yale University Press for the passage from Helen Flanders Dunbar's *Medieval Symbolism and its Consummation in the Divine Comedy* on p. 403.

INTRODUCTION

1

The central man of all the world

John Ruskin called Dante 'the central man of all the world' because he represents in perfect balance 'the imaginative, moral, and intellectual faculties all at their highest' and because in him the expression of the first function of the imagination—the apprehension of ultimate truth—reached 'the most distinct and the most noble development to which it was ever brought in the human mind'.[1] This eulogy arose out of Ruskin's long familiarity with the *Commedia*, the poem which has probably exerted a wider influence than any other great work of Western literature.

In the *Commedia* Dante introduced a new way of presenting human characters, a way that has permanently influenced all later forms of narrative, fiction, and drama. He invented modern literature by making contemporary characters and events the subject of art. He changed the course of Italian history by making the Italian language into a comprehensive vehicle for the expression of civilized thought and feelings and by providing Italian culture with standards and a model that no future generations could ignore. For this he is regarded as the father of the Italian nation;[2] the very colours of the Italian flag are those in which Beatrice appears to him in the Earthly Paradise. Furthermore his influence has been strong on the literature of every European country from England in the West to Poland and Russia in the East and, of course, on the literature of the United States. That wider influence has not been confined to art but also extends to political life; his *De monarchia* is now seen as the earliest statement of the idea of Europe as a political entity; and the mark of his thought has recurred throughout history, in the golden Bull of 1356, among the Elizabethan and Jacobean political and religious writers, and as one of the great inspirations of Gladstone's political life.[3] Art of the order of the *Commedia* may affect history directly as in these instances but it also has a wider and more profound effect in changing and enlarging attitudes of mind and understanding over generations. It does so not by subservience to an ideology, but by cutting across the divisions of an epoch and by offering men a new ideal to which they should aspire. The influence of the *Commedia* in this way goes back to one man who had a vision and remade his inner life in order to express it.

As the standards of our civilization depend for their maintenance and revivification on such art, then it should be a matter of universal and practical importance to study the creative processes of the makers of our civilization. Through such studies we can define, adapt, and nurture those qualities through which the creative processes work and enrich the traditions we have inherited. These are not illusory aims: the members of the Florentine academy, to whom the achievements of the Renaissance are largely owed, believed that philosophy was reborn in them as poetry had already been reborn in Dante.[4] A great part of that philosophy concerned the study of inspiration and creativity and thus they were able to bestow on the artists and writers about them a patronage that was, in every sense, enlightened. They, of course, interpreted their experience in terms of the knowledge available to them as we must make the fullest use of the knowledge of our own time.

When the study concerns the creative imagination of a man such as Dante, who changes the future by his reinterpretation of the past and whose art makes use of all the major social and intellectual currents of his time, then we must pay greater attention to the historical forces that made the environment into which he was born, than would be the case with an artist or writer more private or more limited in his themes. His ability to change the responses of his own and future generations depends, however, on the strength and power of his inner life, on his capacity for assimilating impressions, and his steadfastness in keeping true to his inspirations. Therefore throughout this book particular attention is paid to the ways in which Dante wrote, to the ways in which he received his inspirations, and to how he made use of them. His experience is compared with the experience of writers and poets of other periods and I have also drawn on certain recent psychological and neuro-physiological studies of creativity, on how the writer or artist receives impressions from the world and changes them into works of art. This approach to Dante is not as out of place or anachronistic as might at first appear; he and his friends had drawn on the medical and psychological systems of their time to make a much more extensive model of the inner processes of artistic creation than anything we can command today because they were able to relate creativity to their cosmology and their faith. (See Chapter 8.) Dante has left many indications of his own processes of writing. The number of these is surprising, given that we have no drafts of his work, not even an example of the hand-writing that an early biographer said was so finished with its thin, long, perfectly formed, letters.[5] Only ten examples of his correspondence survive that are generally regarded as authentic, and, of these, only three deal with poetry. The chief indications are in the works themselves. His authority for what he said depended on the truth of his inspiration and he desired to convince the readers of the *Commedia* that his inspirations were from the highest source. As he wrote, he would give his credentials for what he wrote, and it was the urgent desire to convince others of the inner truth of what he was saying that made him so aware of his readers, so tender of the need to evoke in them a great range of memories, so that they could respond to and share his marvellous and beautiful experiences.

Works of art are storehouses of psychic energy and they transmit this energy according to the quality of attention we bring to them. The effects of this energy can be described as happiness, awareness, tranquillity, or a willing surrender of our private concerns to a universal experience. This energy is extremely volatile and frequently we dissipate it the moment we receive it. Every now and then, we experience certain works of art so deeply that the memory of them returns again and again to persuade us the energy is not lost but has been transferred to us and stored in the depths of our nature. There is a certain point on coming into contact with a work of art when one seems suddenly to connect with its emotional or symbolic message. Unless there is this connexion which rivets attention upon the work, it makes no more than a shallow impression. A further stage follows which depends on the enjoyer surrendering himself to the impressions received and attending at the same time to the effect these impressions have on him. This is the equivalent of the discriminatory functions of interpreting and selecting which the artist brings to his inspiration. Beyond this is another stage, in which the barriers separating the inner life of the enjoyer and the essence of the work of art seem to dissolve, and the enjoyer is conscious of being united with the particular mood and insight out of which the work was created. This is the state described by T. S. Eliot as

> music heard so deeply
> That it is not heard at all, but you are the music
> While the music lasts.[6]

The enjoyer is only able to experience this deep unifying awareness if the artist has achieved a similar union between his subject and his execution of it, in the way that Dante described in his *canzone* on nobility:

Poi chi pinge figura,	For he who paints a face
se non può esser lei, non la può porre[7]	Cannot succeed unless he *is* it first.

Sometimes at the very beginning of a poem or a book the reader knows that he is going to make this connexion, that there is a symbiotic destiny awaiting him in the contact between his own nature and the mind of the writer. His nerve ends are stimulated immediately to recognize the power of feelings they can at first only anticipate—as the various parts of Dante's psychology cried out at the first sight of Beatrice and variously exulted in or lamented the events that awaited them. The reader is possessed by the mood of the work and so experiences something of what an artist goes through once he is possessed by an inspiration. Just as the reader finds his responses to life changed by the dominance of this mood, so by a magical working of synchronicity all kinds of unconnected

5

impressions in the artist's daily life arrange themselves into a pattern or reveal significances that connect with the inspiration and enrich the means at his disposal for its execution. With the higher emotion of the inspiration comes the higher order that guides his interpretation of his perceptions and impressions towards the one aim of making a work of art.

Seen in this way, the purpose of art is to change the state of being of the enjoyer, to awaken his sensitivity to the feelings of others, to reveal the unity underlying his own nature, and to fructify and refresh through the integration of his psychology his capacity for insight, understanding, and joy. This is how Dante desired his work to affect the lives of his readers. As he says in his letter to the lord of Verona, Can Grande della Scala, the aim of the *Commedia* is 'to remove those living in this life from a state of misery, and to bring them to a state of happiness'. He adds that the whole work and its parts were conceived 'not for speculation, but with a practical object'.[8]

In many widely different religions and traditions the ability of art to change people's psychological states is well recognized. The use of music and song in the Christian liturgy was probably originally intended to alter and exalt the mental state of the congregation and, more than that, to unify it, so that each member shared the same emotion as his neighbour. Very full descriptions of this state can be found in the writings of the Sufi mystics who made use of music and poetry as part of their spiritual exercises in the auditions known as *samā*.[9]

Thus Jalâl al-Dîn Rûmî, who died in 1272, says in his *Mathnawi*, a work comparable to the *Commedia* both for its mystical inspiration and for its encyclopaedic erudition:

> We have all been parts of Adam, we have heard these
> melodies in Paradise.
> Although the water and earth of our bodies have caused
> a doubt to fall upon us, something of those melodies
> comes back to our memory.[10]

The twelfth-century Persian philosopher and mystic Al Ghazzali, some of whose writings Dante knew and quoted in *Il Convivio*, wrote justifying the use of music for encouraging devotion against the complaints of orthodox Muslim puritans. He says of those whose hearts are consumed in the fire of God's love:

> If a form presents itself to their sight, their insight passes to Him that
> formed it; and if a melody strikes upon their ears, their secret thoughts
> pass hastily to the Beloved; and if there comes to them a voice dis-
> turbing or disquieting or moving or making to sorrow or making
> joyous or making to long or stirring up, that they are disturbed is only
> unto Him, and that they are moved is only by Him and that they are
> disquieted is only on account of Him; their sorrow is only in Him and
> their longing is only unto that which is within Him, and their being

aroused is only for Him, and their coming and going is only around Him.[11]

This is, I believe, very close to the effect that Dante desired his own works should have on his listeners. He describes something of this effect when the musician Casella sings Dante's *canzone* 'Amor che ne la mente mi ragiona' and the listening spirits on the shore of Mount Purgatory stand spellbound with no other thought in mind.[12] In Dante's time poetry was written, recited, and listened to as though it were a branch of music and he defined poetry as 'nichil aliud quam fictio rethorica musicaque poita' (nothing other than a work composed according to the rules of rhetoric and music).[13]

The relation between reader and poet may also be looked at in this way. A poet may write a poem for himself alone, for two or three other people, or for generations present and still unborn. It only comes to life when it is being read; it needs an audience to give it life, even if this consists only of one. Thus readers are constantly re-creating the poetry of others; according to their background and the depth of their own experience they are party to the poet's original act of making. To return to the analogy of art with energy, energy is always in the process of change from one of its forms to another. The technical name for the mediation between one form of energy and another is transduction and the mediating mechanism is a transducer. Extending this analogy, we can say that art is a transducer of energy of one order, the intense mental and emotional psychic energy of the inspiration, to energy of another order, stored in the physical artefact of the book or the object of art. What is known above has to be made known below and the agony of the artist lies in his certainty that, when he has made something, he has only told half and by telling only half he has told an untruth. The Russian poet Tyutchev put it very bluntly in his poem 'Silentium':

A thought once spoken is a lie.[14]

And Dante in the *Paradiso* faces the problem many times. In this passage he and Beatrice have just ascended into the sphere of the moon:

Beatrice tutta ne l'etterne rote
   fissa con li occhi stava; e io in lei
   le luci fissi, di là sù rimote.
Nel suo aspetto tal dentro mi fei,
   qual si fé Glauco nel gustar de l'erba
che 'l fé consorto in mar de li altri dèi.
	Beatrice was standing and held full in view
	   The eternal wheels, and I fixed on
	    her keen
	My eyes, that from above their gaze
	   withdrew.
	And at her aspect I became within
	   As Glaucus after the herb's tasting,
	    whence
	To the other sea-gods he was made
	   akin.

Trasumanar significar *per verba*
non si poria; però l'essemplo basti
a cui esperïenza grazia serba.[15]
	The passing beyond bounds of human
	  sense
	Words cannot tell; let then the example
	  sate
	Him for whom grace reserves the
	  experience.

Dante produces an answer to the problem in the last two lines. This idea was not Dante's own but derives from the tradition and experience of the poets of the *dolce stil nuovo*; only the man who possesses the *cor gentile* (the noble heart) can understand their poems because they write for those who share their experiences. Ultimately it is we as readers or enjoyers who must redeem what the artist lacks in expressing only part of the truth. Without our memory and experience the cycle of transduction is incomplete; and we are able to complete the cycle because we have in each one of our natures a poet or an artist. It is the poet in us who responds to and enjoys poetry.[16] Again it is the creative artist in each one of us that enables us to understand the creative processes in others. The means by which inspirations come to their recipients are common to the experience of the rest of humanity.[17] We all dream, we all experience the sudden and unbidden appearance in our minds of ideas fully expressed in words or images, we are all subject at times to overpowering emotions, we all acknowledge in love and grief the inability of words to communicate our feelings and find other ways to overcome the gap in expression; a high proportion of us experience brilliant mental pictures as we are drifting off to sleep (known as hypnagogic or hypnapompic images) or see waking visions,[18] hear chords of inner music or rhythms that have an unaccountable significance, or find memory restoring the past to us so overwhelmingly that we seem to live simultaneously in two times at once. These latter experiences, so different because of their emotional content from the umbrella label of hallucinations, under which they are generally lumped, are the very ways which great numbers of artists, thinkers, and scientists have described as the means through which they receive their inspirations. We are all capable of such inspirations; what divides the poet from his fellow men is his superior ability to attend to and remember such inspirations, to interpret their meaning, and to make the meaning intelligible to others. Just as we all know the experience of the sudden insight that explains and shows the way out of a difficult situation, or understand in a flash a problem that has exercised us over years, so the authors of many accounts of the act of creation stress the overwhelming mass of information that is contributed in an astonishingly short time.[19] Thus Blake says in his *Milton*:

Every Time less than a pulsation of the artery
Is equal in its period & value to Six Thousand Years,

For in this Period the Poet's Work is Done, and all The Great
Events of Time start forth & are conceiv'd in such a Period,
Within a Moment, a Pulsation of the Artery.[20]

In the course of writing about Dante, Ugo Foscolo, obviously drawing on his
own experience, speaks of the extreme speed and inconceivable mobility with
which the minds of certain geniuses work.[21] The inspirations containing this
concentrated information may appear as symbols, metaphors, images, chance
phrases dragging volumes of words behind them, or as a new experience of light,
in the course of dreams, sudden visions or thoughts intruding on the waking
state, and in the intermediate state in which hypnagogic images appear. These
waking visions and hypnagogic phenomena may consist of patterns of bright
mental visions, of voices or sounds and music; they included some of Dante's
most important sources of inspiration which he related to particular stages of
the mystic ascent and built into the formal arrangement of the *Purgatorio*.

Dante's imaginative life was frequently enriched by pictorial or eidetic
images, a faculty he possessed in common not only with other poets such as
Coleridge and Blake,[22] but with a scientist such as August von Kekulé whose
fundamental contribution to organic chemistry, the discovery of the structure
of the benzene ring, came to him as a hypnagogic image of a whirling snake
biting its tail as he was drifting off to sleep in front of his fire.[23] In describing this
experience in later years he said, 'Let us learn to dream, gentlemen, and we may
perhaps find the truth, but let us beware of publishing our dreams before they
have been tested by a discerning mind that is wide awake.' To take an earlier
example, the prophet Joachim of Fiore, whom Dante greatly admired,
described how, vexed by doubts about the Trinity and after long spiritual
exercises, he suddenly received a vision of a musical instrument, a psaltery. He
responded to the vision 'as if he himself were a musical instrument swept into
chords of harmony by the divine hand',[24] and was so full of his inspiration that
he needed an extra scribe, in addition to the two he already had, to take down
what became a work called the *Psalterium* whose first book rings with his sense of
jubilation.

Whatever the manifestations, whether visual or auditory, the inspirations are
compressed codes, microdots of information out of a different and far more
intensely lived time-world, and they have to be decoded or enlarged for their
messages to be apprehended. One of Dante's most wonderful images, that
conveys both the concentration of information present in an inspiration and the
different order of understanding from which it comes, appears in these lines
from the last canto of the *Paradiso*:

> Un punto solo m'è maggior letargo
> che venticinque secoli a la 'mpresa
> che fé Nettuno ammirar l'ombra d'Argo.[25]

A necessarily expanded translation might be:

> A single point [of that vision of eternity] is a greater weariness to me [to describe or recall] than the twenty-five centuries that have elapsed since the enterprise of the Golden Fleece made Neptune wonder at the shadow of the *Argo*.

In classical mythology the *Argo* was the first ship and it carried Jason and the Argonauts to Colchis in search of the golden Fleece and then back to Athens—just as Dante was carrying the memory of Heaven back to Earth. An atom of that vision has more experience crammed into it than the history of humanity in a period of two and a half thousand years. In the few syllables of the last line he gives a marvellous picture of Neptune the sea god, as bound to his element as Dante in normal life is bound to the Earth, looking up in amazement at the shadow of the first ship ever to sail upon the face of the sea. The very sound of *ombra* hangs below the quicker wavelike vowels earlier in the line like the weight of the keel beneath the waterline.

What makes these lines especially apposite is that Dante used this image to convey the insuperable difficulty of describing in words what he considered the highest experience known to man, the greatest level of integration possible, that is, the union of man with God. The image contrasts two different modes of existence, two levels of mind, the lower of which cannot understand and which generally misinterprets the higher. Only when the experience of the higher level is overpowering, as in this case, does the lower level of mind acknowledge its true position and act as the servant and not the master.

The sudden appearance of great inspirations reveals their power and authority as though the mind in a twinkling is ordered in another way, a way that opens infinitely greater possibilities of connexions between thoughts and images when compared to the state of the mind working at its ordinary efficiency. Dante described the way in which his first great poem came to him in the following example. It happened just after a period of rejection by Beatrice and when he had been made to understand how he had been at fault in his attitude to her:

> Avvenne poi che passando per uno cammino, lungo lo quale sen gia uno rivo chiaro molto, a me giunse tanta volontade di dire, che io cominciai a pensare lo modo ch' io tenesse; e pensai che parlare di lei non si convenia che io facesse, se io non parlasse a donne in seconda persona, e non ad ogni donna, ma solamente a coloro che sono gentili e che non sono pure femmine. Allora dico che la mia lingua parlò quasi come per se stessa mossa, e disse: *Donne ch'avete intelletto d'amore.*
> Queste parole io ripuosi ne la mente con grande letizia, pensando di prenderle per mio cominciamento; onde poi, ritornato a la sopradetta cittade, pensando alquanti die, cominciai una canzone con questo cominciamento. . . .[26]

It chanced that as I was walking one day along a road beside which flowed a river of very clear water, such a desire to speak came upon me that I began to think about the style that I should maintain; and it struck me that it would be wrong to speak of her [Beatrice] unless I addressed myself to other ladies in the second person; that is not to *any* other ladies, but to those who are noble and not merely women. At that moment, I say, my tongue spoke as though moved by itself and said 'Donne ch'avete intelletto d'amore'. I laid these words up in my mind with great joy, intending to make them my beginning; then after returning to the already mentioned city and reflecting for several days, I started a poem with this opening. . . .

This passage has much in common with other writers' descriptions of moments of inspiration. After a period of emotional turmoil Dante, in a relaxed state and alone, first conceived the desire to write and it was when he decided for whom he was writing it that the miraculous gift of the one line was granted him, the line that led him, like a vocation, to the praise of Beatrice. The energy present in him during the period of self-regard and reproach is transformed first in the biting of his conscience (see p. 137) and then in the course of planning the poem when he has to think of others when considering whom he should address, into the finer psychic energy of artistic inspiration experienced in a moment of heightened consciousness.

Frequently in constructing a poem the poet has to work backwards from his inspiration which provides the climax or finale of the work. This is how Dante would appear to have written the *Commedia*, working backwards from the vision of the Trinity of Easter, 1300. He had to nurse this vision within him for years before he could begin the poem, and his journey of return to that vision of perfection forced him to bring to the light of awareness all the horrors he had ever known of the imperfections of mankind. There is a parallel between his experience and that of the late-fifteenth-century Swiss mystic, Brother Klaus (St Nicholas of Flüe, the patron saint of Switzerland), who also saw a vision of the Trinity which appeared to him as a piercing light resembling a human face. It was an experience so terrifying that it altered his countenance to the extent that people were afraid of him. He took years to assimilate the vision and to bring it into harmony with the tenets of his faith. Nevertheless he was finally able to express it as a calm abstraction by painting it, or by having it painted to his direction, as a mandala of six parts with the crowned face of God at its centre.[27]

Henry James describes how the idea for a novel would come to him first of all as a nexus of relationships and how he would have to work backwards from that to find out how his characters had arrived at such a situation. In his preface to *The American* he speaks of how he dropped the first idea into 'the deep well of unconscious cerebration'. In this connexion it is important to remember, not only that there may be a gap of years between the gift of an inspiration and its execution, necessary for its incubation,[28] but also that the writer or poet may receive numerous subsidiary inspirations in this intervening period. These subsidiary inspirations declare themselves to be related to the main inspiration by mood, theme or images and they too may come in the same sudden and surprising manner to reveal some necessary information about the form or the construction of the work.

Taking into account both the gap in time between inspiration and execution and the subsidiary inspirations that relate to the main inspiration and remind the poet of his duty towards it, we can think of a great work of art like the *Commedia* as existing at right angles to the life of the poet. His life proceeds in a straight line from birth to death, but acting on it from this perpendicular direction is a living power, sending messages, instructions, inspirations, all imbued with a particular emotional flavour and with a sense of certainty and newness. In Dante's case this living power was the *Commedia*, preparing him, and prepared for him, as the fate that he had to remember, acting on him through his love of Beatrice in her lifetime, sending presages of itself in the early poems that treat of the afterlife of hell and heaven and in the visions mentioned in *La Vita Nuova*, offering itself as the end and height of the poem in the vision of 1300, and then providing numerous subsidiary inspirations until the moment some time between 1308 and 1313 when his interpretative powers had grown the equal of the inspiration and, by understanding the roles that Virgil and Beatrice should play in the poem, he was able to devote the rest of his life to writing it out. Another way of looking at this abiding and coterminous world of the creative imagination is Rilke's who once said that it seemed to him that he had just one thing to say and that successive poems were made provisional statements by the more adequate expression of later ones.[29]

The concentration of information and experience contained in an inspiration is carried over into the nature of the art form through which it is expressed. Thus in relation to the nature of poetry this concentration may be described as compression of meaning. Poetry communicates simultaneously through words, rhythms, images, and form. Communicating at once on several levels gives an extraordinary intensity to the amount of information that can be conveyed in a short space. This intensity of communication is, of course, a sign of efficiency and has a counterpart in the development of scientific language and mathematical techniques, where an equation expressing a physical law sums up in its symbols the concentrated labour of centuries of investigation and thought.

Compression of meaning is present in poetry in all its aspects. It is there in the aspect of poetry which is intensified speech. It is essential to the impact of rhythm, when rhythm is properly used as a dimension of the emotion or mood to be communicated. It is typical of sentences arranged in the formal structure of a stanza or *canzone* because the form narrows down the possible ways of expressing an idea and imposes clarity on it by defining it in one of those possibilities. It is present in the various levels of meaning that may coexist in a poem. Dante says in his letter to Can Grande[30] that for a poem to be of serious standing it must have four levels of meaning ranging from the literal to the anagogic (that is, beyond the level of the senses). Compression of meaning is also there in the formal structure as when the triple form of the canticles of the *Commedia* and the *terza rima* scheme of the lines are reflections of the journey to a vision of the Trinity which the poem celebrates.[31]

In his command of imagery, in his use of metaphor, simile, and symbol to concentrate meaning and to enlarge the understanding, Dante is unequalled by any European poet except for Shakespeare. In writing about Shakespeare, Pasternak produced this explanation of the need for metaphor:

> Man is driven to the use of metaphor owing to the fact that he is too short-lived to carry out his tremendous self-imposed task. It is this disparity between the brevity of his life and the greatness of his task which forces him to gaze eagle-eyed at all things, and to make his meaning clear by instantaneous flashes. That is what poetry is. Metaphor is the shorthand of a great individuality, the handwriting of the soul.[32]

Frequently it is in Dante's use of imagery that we come closest to understanding the nature of the creative process. In what follows two examples are given to demonstrate the range and beauty of his imagery.

Metaphors in poetry may be implicit in the style and the rhythm or they may be explicit as clearly stated similes and carefully described visual images. An example of implicit metaphor comes from the octet of Sonnet XV in the *Vita Nuova*.

Tanto gentile e tanto onesta pare
La donna mia quand'ella altrui saluta,
ch'ogne lingua deven tremando muta,
e li occhi non l'ardiscon di guardare.
Ella si va, sentendosi laudare,
benignamente d'umiltà vestuta;
e par che sia una cosa venuta
da cielo in terra a miracol mostrare.

So noble she seems and so full of grace,
My lady when she greets others nearby,
Their quivering tongues hush silently,
And their eyes dare not look on her face.
Hearing herself lauded, she goes her ways,
Benignly clothed in humility;
And seems a creature sent from heaven on high
To show a miracle on earth take place.

Here, in the original, nearly all the work of finding fitting resemblances to the experience of seeing Beatrice pass by is done by the subtle rhythm and the play on the ear of the delicate accord of vowel and consonant. The movement of the octet carries this vision past us with such a sense of wonder that we hardly notice the simile is buried in the ambiguous use of the word *pare*. Is she a sign from heaven or is she like one? The barely formulated question is part of the wonder itself, an evocation essential to the drama. This is an effect of the perfect relation between subject and style; and implicit metaphor is another name for style if style is regarded as a means of making the reader experience as directly as possible what the writer has experienced—and not as the signature or the expression of the writer's personality.

At the same time that metaphor compresses meaning, it also expands the understanding to comprehend greater depths of meaning, through webs of cross-association and clusters of related images. In the reader's mind it activates a higher level of integration so that his understanding is enlarged to take in the mass of new information. The appearance of the right image in the poet's mind has the same effect and in his case it deepens his control of the possible meanings of his inspiration. This effect of metaphor in poetry is closely akin to the effect that Berenson called 'space composition'[33] in painting. Metaphor has this expansive effect in at least two ways. The more obvious way is on the smaller scale, when an image of particular brilliance lights up our understanding of an idea or a situation. The other is on a much bigger scale, pervading both form and structure, when the form of the work is based on one all-inclusive image, as in the *Commedia*, on that of the journey from darkness to light.

How does this effect of expansion work? Here is one famous pair of examples from the eighth canto of the *Purgatorio* which begins:

Era già l'ora che volge il disio
  ai navicanti e 'ntenerisce il core
  lo dì c'han detto ai dolci amici addio;
e che lo novo peregrin d'amore
  punge, se ode squilla di lontano
  che paia il giorno pianger che si more;[34]

Now was the hour which longing backward bends
In those that sail, and melts their heart
  in sighs,
The day they have said farewell to their
  sweet friends,
And pricks with love the outsetting
  pilgrim's eyes
If the far bell he hears across the land
Which seems to mourn over the day
  that dies,

It is evening in the valley of the negligent rulers in the Ante-Purgatory and the hymn 'Te lucis ante' is about to be sung. The regret of the rulers for their omissions in life is implied in these two images of sea and land in that they did not guide the ship of state or govern their territories to the best of their abilities. This regret merges the sadness of their individual faults into the more universal nostalgia of their situation, condemned, as they are, to wait long years before they can ascend the mountain. The sadness of the sailors takes up the suggestion of the view from the valley out over the southern ocean and, as we feel their emotion winging back to the friends they left in port that morning, we too feel the growing stretch of distance separating them, for the image also recalls the vast waters of the hemisphere on which the sun in the story now sets. So, too, the heart-piercing sound of the compline bells re-creates not only the pilgrim's own remembered church at home but all the towers of town and village he has passed on his way. Both images recur in other parts of the poem, seafaring from the beginning of the *Inferno* and that of the pilgrim from the beginning of the

Purgatorio, and therefore achieve another kind of expansion through cross-association. But, most of all, the nostalgia of sailor and pilgrim relates to the nostalgia of the human soul for its origins and its longing to return home to God so that we, in being touched and melted by these lines, have our thoughts involuntarily expanded to a foretaste of the poem's ultimate object.

The part played by metaphor in enlarging understanding is related to the creative act on a wider scale by Arthur Koestler in his theory of bisociation.[35] It can also be related to our continual need to harmonize our experience and to reconcile the dualities of our psycho-physiological natures. Neurologists since Hughlings Jackson in the last century have come to look upon the brain as organized in a hierarchy of levels of awareness and control and crowned by the dual monarchy of the 'new brain', the part characteristic of man as a thinking animal. The new brain exhibits this dualism in the division of the cortex into the two cerebral hemispheres; the left-hand hemisphere being concerned with language and analytical thought, governs our relations with the external world, and the right-hand hemisphere, processing dreams and images and being particularly concerned with visual and spatial relationships, seems to be the road to our inner life. Much more is said on this subject as a contemporary approach to Dante's political thought and to his creative processes in Chapter 21. Here we are looking for the birthplace of metaphor—a manger so obscure that all the best accounts of it are themselves metaphorical. The subject forces writers back to images from their own childhood to explain the unreason of its reason; thus Edward A. Armstrong, writing about recurrent patterns or clusters of imagery in Shakespeare, speaks of the strange frolics of his images as they changed partners 'like children in a game or dance'[36] and Koestler notes that 'the capacity to regress, more or less at will, to the games of the underground, without losing contact with the surface, seems to be the essence of the poetic, and of any other form of creativity'.[37]

Many poets have described how they have found the ability to enter the realm of sleep and of dreams while retaining consciousness. Yeats described the state as a 'waking trance',[38] a paradoxical phrase that expresses the resolution of the opposites, and Edwin Muir, who gives a long description of his experience of waking visions in his autobiography, believed that 'poetic inspiration is a joining of the sleeping self with the conscious mind'.[39]

From the evidence of these reports and the frequent first appearance of symbols and metaphors as waking visions or hypnagogic images, it seems that the capacity for visual metaphor is an aspect of the cyclical labour of the master of dreams as the Talmudists called him. P. D. Ouspensky wrote of his observations of dreams that there was an artist in him, 'sometimes very naive, sometimes very subtle', who worked at his dreams and created them out of material he possessed but could never use in full measure while awake. This artist, which is in every man, is of extraordinary versatility, 'a playwright, a producer, a scene-painter, and a remarkable actor-impersonator.'[40] He points out that dreams in which people 'see their dead friends or relations strike their imagination so strongly because of this remarkable capacity for impersonation inherent in themselves' – a capacity, he says, that can sometimes function in a waking state. This is an observation which will be of great significance when we come to consider Dante's waking visions. As a result of his investigations Ouspensky thought that we have dreams continuously, both in sleep and in the waking state,[41] a thesis partly confirmed, though with modifications, by recent research,[42] which suggests that there are regular alternations in our waking consciousness throughout the day in which we tack from cognition in the dominant hemisphere to relaxed awareness in the non-dominant side, an alternation comparable to the now well-known rhythms of non-dreaming and dreaming in the sleeping state. This would mean, perhaps, that for a given person there would be times of day at which the gates of inspiration would be more likely to open than at others when they are shut. Dante, following the classical traditions in the evaluation and interpretation of dreams, believed that morning dreams were of especial validity and, probably following his own experience, set the two series of waking visions that flank the speeches of Marco Lombardo in the *Purgatorio* in the evening towards sunset. There are several great differences, though, between on the one hand most dreams and experiences of mental imagery and on the other hand the artistic and scientific inspirations even though they also may be experienced in dreams and related imagery. First of all, in most dreams the dreamer has no control over the actions he sees or takes part in or the emotions aroused in him; he is a helpless performer and his deeds in dream have no practical outcome. By contrast the inspiration, though it may arise in a dream or dreamlike state, brings with it a sense of order and a pure objective emotion which the poet notes and obeys but ultimately controls, and the inspiration does lead to a finished artefact. Thus Dante's skill in the portrayal of whole characters probably derives from the degree of control he learned to exert over the capacity for impersonation mentioned above, which nevertheless operated in the dream levels of his mind.

This difference between dreams and the matter of poetry was marvellously analysed by Charles Lamb in his essay on the 'Sanity of True Genius'. After pointing out the insubstantiality of most dreams, however vivid and fantastic they may be, and how nothing can be *made* of them, not only intellectually but in a practical sense, he says in a passage where he obviously has Dante and Milton in mind:

> the true poet dreams being awake. He is not possessed by his subject, but has dominion over it. In the groves of Eden he walks familiar as in his native paths. He ascends the empyrean heaven, and is not intoxicated. He treads the burning marl without dismay; he wins his flight without self-loss through realms of chaos 'and old night'.[43]

Our hidden artist who weaves such cluster patterns of images and associations, who mimics the laboratories of nature with his own invented landscapes and fauna, may work unseen but he prefers, like all of us, to be paid the right kind of attention. Though much has been written about the role of the unconscious workings of the mind in the preparation of works of art, and though, on a practical basis, numerous artists and writers realize the necessity of the period of incubation that often must precede the act of making, little has been said about how the hidden artist can be stirred into making more than dreams. Left to himself he works diligently at dreams but dreams, to quote the Talmudists again, are the unripe fruits of prophecy. He is like Robin Goodfellow who would work all night to scour the house and put it in order while the housewife slept, but only if she did not spy on him and if she had remembered to set out bowls of cream for him.

That is perhaps too Anglo-Saxon and too country-like an image for Dante the sophisticated townsman, but he too thought of inspiration in terms of youth. He presents the author of his dreams, the chief actor in them, and the dictator of his verse in the same character, the imperious youth whom he called Love. Love was his name for the state of heightened consciousness in which his conscience in relation to art and to life was stirred to action, and in whose presence the words of the left-hand hemisphere were married to the rhythms and mental pictures of the right-hand, a state comparable to Aquinas's definition of the intellect as the highest condition of knowing because what is known is present and does not have to be sought. When Dante is asked by the Tuscan poet of an earlier generation, Bonagiunta da Lucca, if he is the author of the new rhymes that begin with *Donne ch'avete intelletto d'amore'*, he replies:

> I' mi son un che, quando
> Amor mi spira, noto, e a quel modo
> ch'e' ditta dentro vo significando.[44]

I am one who, when Love breathes within me, takes note, and to the mode dictated within me, I set down the significance.

He is describing how in writing he surrenders himself to the level on which *amore* is manifested, and the key word is *noto*. He notes, he remembers, he makes himself subservient to the experience. The control and ordering that we have been speaking of, in his case, at any rate, appears not as a nervous worrying of unruly inspirations but as an effect of heightened awareness, as the stamp of the enhanced ordering of his own mind in the light of pure consciousness.

Experience of such states of consciousness gave him the standard by which he judged the characters of the *Commedia* as they rose up in his creative imagination. Thus the cast of the *Commedia* depicts the range between the lowest and the highest possibilities of men and women in the control and ordering of their own natures. These differences in the levels of mental control come out most clearly in the descriptions of the characters' physical control. As we descend with Dante through the levels of Hell, so we find the damned less and

17

less able to exercise control over their bodily movements. Some are impelled to run on burning sand like Brunetto Latini, some are fixed as stationary trees in the wood of the suicides, some undergo horrible transformations of their limbs, and some are fixed in ice. This inability to move as they could wish is a physical analogue of the decay of mental control. In the *Purgatorio* the souls also move under constriction but they agree to it because they know it leads to their purification. The exterior discipline is consciously followed because it will enhance their humanity, not debase it. In the *Paradiso* every movement of the blessed is transfigured into art. At will they follow the dance, the most rigorously controlled of human movements, or they come to rest as they need. Their full communication with one another and with the Highest Will is expressed figuratively by the grace and splendour of their movements.

Another way of finding correspondences between the *Commedia* and the levels of experience and integration in the brain is to use Indian terminology. René Guénon[45] is only one of several writers who have noted the correspondence of the three parts of the *Commedia*, Hell, Purgatory, and Paradise, with the three *gunas* of Indian philosophy, *tamas*, the principle of inertia, and the downwards tendency, *rajas*, the principle of expansion of being, and *sattva*, the principle of balance and happiness. The three *gunas*, of course, are related to psychological states as well as physical ones. Someone who is sunk in *tamas* is, psychologically speaking, in Hell. The man in whom *sattva* predominates is at the opposite pole of integration. He is a maker whether of his own life or of works of art.

There is an obvious and important relationship between self-knowledge and creative work, because of the constant watch an artist has to keep on his inner promptings. Out of his growth in self-knowledge Dante gained access to the memories of every experience that ever left a trace on him. He derived from his self-knowledge the objectivity towards himself and others and the universal human sympathy that have made his influence so profound. In his works too we can study the vital relationship between a man's sexual nature and his creative possibilities and the way in which these sides of himself can be brought into harmony. In *Felix Holt*, one of the many works deeply influenced by the *Commedia*, George Eliot makes her hero say:

> I wonder . . . whether the subtle measuring of forces will ever come to measuring the force there would be in one beautiful woman whose mind was as noble as her face was beautiful—who made a man's passion for her rush in one current with all the great aims of his life.[46]

Though we cannot measure the force there was in Beatrice, we can at least estimate something of its power because one of its effects is the greatest poem of Western literature. That force entered his life when Dante was still a child, and it is to the environment of his childhood by way of the early history of Florence and of the various movements dominating thirteenth-century Italy that we now turn.

PART I

THE MAKING OF A POET

2

Encounters on the road to Montaperti:
Florentine history to 1260

Florence, the birthplace of Dante Alighieri in 1265, was growing into the richest and one of the most populous cities in Europe. She was rich because of the industrial, technical, and commercial skills of her citizens: her trading connexions stretched far beyond the Mediterranean world and a few years before Dante's birth she had struck the famous gold florin, one of the first regular issues of gold coinage since Charlemagne had made silver the standard for an impoverished Western empire. She had long burst out of her Roman walls and was extending far beyond the circuit built in the later twelfth century, but her citizens kept the memory of their Roman origins and she inspired in them the most passionate devotion and civic pride.

Dante's contemporary and friend, the Florentine chronicler Giovanni Villani, says that Florence was founded after the neighbouring and older city of Fiesole had sheltered followers of Catiline and had been destroyed by Caesar in 72 BC.[1] According to this story, now regarded as fictitious, the Fiesolans had killed the consul Fiorinus in a battle beside the river Arno and Caesar chose the site of the battle for the new city which took its name either from the dead consul or from the abundance of flowers that grew in the river meadows. The Senate decreed that settlers chosen from the best and ablest of the Romans should populate the city and some Fiesolans were also allowed to live there. The extent of the Roman city is shown by the city walls in Figure 1. Christianity is thought to have reached Florence by the later first century through Levantine traders who brought with them the cult of the Syrian martyr St Reparata, to whom, later, the first cathedral was dedicated. Florence gained her own martyr during the Decian persecution in AD 250 in Miniatus who is still commemorated in the great church of San Miniato. Confused memories survived of the sack and destruction of the city either by Attila or by Totila, the last Ostrogothic king, though the evidence of excavations reveals continuity of occupation in the city throughout the Dark Ages, albeit on a greatly reduced scale.[2]

The survival of these legends gave the Florentines of Dante's time a historical perspective that extended past the time of the Crusades, of Charlemagne and

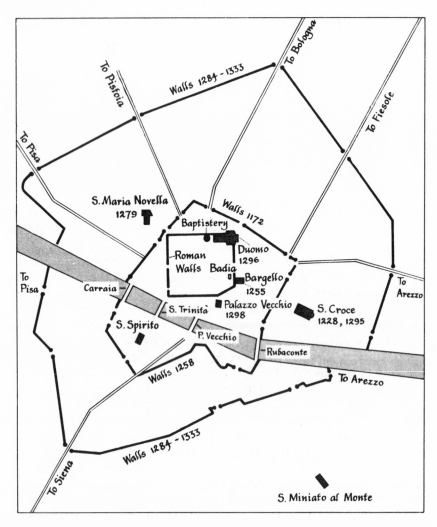

—Figure 1 Map of Florence, adapted and simplified from Paget Toynbee, *A Dictionary of Proper Names and Notable Matters in the Works of Dante* (Oxford, 1968)

his paladins, and of the first Christians, to the founding of Florence, and even beyond that, through Aeneas and his ancestors, to a time when Rome had not been built and the doom of Troy was being settled on the plains below her walls. Thus there was a tradition of lineal descent that not only conferred the honour of blood-relationship to the famous heroes of antiquity, but also gave to some Florentines a sense that they were the inheritors of the majesty of imperial Rome. Their patriotism and their pride in the exceptional achievements of their city were given justification by the belief they shared in the continuing destiny of the Roman tradition. When the palace of the captain of the *popolo* was completed in 1255 (now the Bargello), it was inscribed with a proud boast in Latin, resembling Florence to Rome in her lasting triumphs.[3]

Dante shared this profound historical sense and, though this is not the place for a full treatment of the early history of Florence,[4] we can study events on a wider scale that affected Italy in the Dark Ages through certain historical personages whom Dante introduced into the *Commedia*: Boethius, St Benedict, the emperor Justinian, Gregory the Great, the Prophet Mohammed, and the emperor Charlemagne.

The first two of these names complement one another in signifying the end of one era and the start of another. Not long after Romulus Augustulus, the last Emperor of the West, resigned to the barbarian ruler Odoacer in 476, Italy fell into the hands of the Ostrogothic invader Theodoric, who murdered Odoacer and ruled the peninsula from Ravenna, in name as the regent of the Eastern emperor and in fact as an independent monarch. Although an Arian Christian and therefore not acknowledging the pope as the spiritual leader of Christianity, he had the deepest admiration for Roman achievements and traditions. One way in which this admiration was shown was in the honours he poured on Boethius (*c.*480–524), the eminent philosopher and statesman, and head of one of the oldest Roman families. It was through Boethius' translations into Latin from the Greek and his commentaries that much of the substance of classical thought was transmitted to the Middle Ages—until the wider diffusion of Aristotle's works from Islamic sources came about in the thirteenth century. In his political career, especially after he was made consul in 510, he attracted enemies who persuaded Theodoric he was plotting with Byzantium against him. In 523 Theodoric had him thrown into prison where he wrote his greatest work, *De consolatione philosophiae*, a book that deeply influenced Dante. Then in 524 Theodoric had him horribly murdered—for which in the Middle Ages Boethius was regarded as a martyr. Dante celebrates him in the *Paradiso* as a doctor of the Church,[5] but he is also the type of the man who follows both the active life and the contemplative life, who accepts his responsibilities in the world and at the same time fulfils his highest spiritual needs, an ideal which only the revival of civilized city life in Dante's period was to make generally practicable again for laymen.

Civilization was on the retreat and it was Boethius' exact contemporary, Benedict of Nursia, who, as the founder of Western monasticism, devised the mode of life through which the learning and the educational ideals that Boethius had done so much to preserve could be transmitted. Benedict's monastery at Monte Cassino provided the model of the enclosed spiritual fortresses which were to spread throughout the Europe of the Dark Ages, playing a fundamental part in the reclamation and repossession of land and in the reorganization of society. One of his most revolutionary changes was his insistence that his monks should work with their hands—so that where the senators and educated classes of Rome had despised manual labour, like the Greeks whose example they followed, thinking it fit only for slaves, now the guardians of civilization regarded it as an integral part of their spiritual discipline. 'The monk was the first intellectual to get dirt under his fingernails,' says Lynn White[6] who points out that the monk in his very person destroyed the old artificial barrier between the empirical and the speculative, the manual and the liberal arts, and thus helped to create a social atmosphere favourable to scientific and technological innovations. Dante preserves this sense of the dignity of labour in the similes he draws from peasant life and from the trade and work of the towns. The revival of Florence was to owe much to her connexions with the foundations at Camaldoli and Vallombrosa outside the city and to the Badia close to her Roman walls. St Benedict appears twice in the *Paradiso*, in the heaven of the contemplatives where he describes to Dante the founding of his order and laments the corruption of his ideals in the Italy of Dante's time, and then again beside St Francis in the Celestial Rose.[7]

Benedict fulfilled his mission none too soon because the Eastern emperor, Justinian (527–65), unleashed on Italy the campaigns known as the Gothic Wars in order to win back the West.

One of Dante's most brilliant and extended examples of the compression of history into symbol is the speech delivered by Justinian on the course of the Roman empire.[8] Justinian announces his identity in these lines.

Cesare fui e son Iustiniäno,	Caesar I was, and am Justinian,
che, per voler del primo amor ch'i' sento,	Who by the will of Primal Love possessed
d'entro le leggi trassi il troppo e 'l vano.	Pruned from the laws the unneeded and the vain.

Concentrating on the vicissitudes of the Roman power from the time of Aeneas to the coming of Charlemagne, the whole passage is dominated by the emblem of the imperial eagle whose flights and wheelings signify the expansion and contraction of Roman rule. Sonorous with the poetry of heroic names and famous towns and battles, Justinian's language evokes the majesty of the past of Rome and finally swoops upon the warring parties of Dante's time: the Guelphs who oppose to the eagle standard the yellow lilies of France, and those Ghibellines who wrongly try to appropriate the eagle to themselves. Justinian, to Dante, was the emperor who ruled with the right relationship to the papacy, acknowledging its spiritual supremacy in his conversion from the Monophysite heresy by Pope Agapetus but retaining and exercising all his office's temporal rights, notably in his codification of the laws and in the campaigns of the Gothic Wars. Though the Gothic Wars were brilliantly successful in terms of crushing the enemy, the Byzantines could not hold the whole of Italy. They destroyed both the Ostrogothic dynasty and the last vestiges of Roman civic government in Italy and opened up Italy to the latest and most barbaric of her invaders, the Lombards. In 570 Florence fell to the Lombards when their leader Alboin conquered Tuscany and the Byzantines were driven back to the area surrounding Ravenna and to Southern Italy.

Under Pope Gregory the Great (590–604) the papacy began to assert itself as an independent force in international affairs. Gregory, a Roman nobleman by birth with experience of civil administration before he became a priest, launched the missionary movement which was to lead to the conversion, first, of the Anglo-Saxons and eventually of north-west Germany and Scandinavia. By instructing his missionaries to make use of the sites of holy places and shrines of the pagans, he ensured a strong element of continuity in the change from the older religions to the new faith. Through his doctrine of the treasury of intercession by which Christians were allowed to pray through the intermediary of a saint or saints, he provided a doctrine which filled the gap in men's hearts and minds caused by the decay of pagan cults of lesser and tutelary deities. Attachment to the cult of a local saint was to become one of the most fervent bonds uniting members of a community, whether rural or urban, in the early Middle Ages. He made special efforts to build up a papal state around Rome—for the same reasons of security that were to obsess many of his successors. He became the head of the most stable institution in a rapidly changing world though the authority he wielded depended largely upon his personal qualities rather than upon the powers allowed to the papacy in general estimation. He was the first pope to assume the temporal responsibilities abdicated by a collapsing civil government. The most dramatic mention of him in Dante's poem forms another striking example of poetic and mythical history. In *Paradiso*[9] he raises the emperor Trajan from the dead and baptizes him a Christian nearly 500 years after his death, so that Trajan now shines as a star above the eye of the eagle of justice—a popular medieval legend that accords with Gregory's own benign instructions to his missionaries to preserve all in the pagan religions that could be turned to the purposes of Christianity.

At the same time that Gregory was bringing Northern Europe into the Catholic fold and was enunciating the doctrines that led to the massive proliferation of saints' cults and images, the Prophet Mohammed was inaugurating the faith that was to remove most of the Middle East and North Africa from its Christian allegiance, and that, by its insistence on the unity of the One God, destroyed all lesser cults, broke the images, and eradicated all intercessors between man and the Deity. The Mediterranean world had already been polarized, first between the Eastern and Western empires, and then by the increasing differences between the Greek and Latin churches; now the tension was between two world faiths, each claiming mastery of men's souls by divine authority. This tension was kept at breaking-point until long after Dante's time, constantly leading to wars and battles but also to the most fruitful exchanges of ideas and insights. The great debt the *Commedia* owes to Islam is not acknowledged in the poem; the extent of the debt is a discovery only made in this century (see Chapter 16), and the Prophet appears in the *Inferno* as a 'seminator di scandolo e di scisma',[10] in a passage that most modern readers find tasteless and unpleasant though it serves to point the fear and antagonism of Christians to the followers of this rival faith whose superiority in so many branches of learning and in the arts of civilization both shamed them and stirred them to emulation for the honour of Christianity.

Fear and antagonism was what the Christians had every reason to feel in the first two centuries of Islam. The threat to Christianity in the West became most serious when the conquerors of Spain thrust across the Pyrenees and met the Christian allies under Charles Martel in the battle of Tours or Poitiers in about 732. It is generally thought that the force of the Islamic advance was largely expended by the time of the battle but the significance of the occasion lies in the victors—the Frankish nation which was soon to transform Northern Europe under Charles Martel's grandson Charlemagne. Charlemagne is mentioned three times in the *Commedia*, the last when he and his paladin Roland are shown as two of the shooting stars that make up the great cross of the fighting saints.[11] In 774 Charlemagne invaded Italy, took the Lombard capital, Pavia, after a long siege and, putting an end to the monarchy, absorbed the Lombard kingdom into his own realm.

The consequences of Charlemagne's invasion of Italy were many. Whether his coronation on Christmas Day, 800, by the pope was on Charlemagne's initiative or whether it was a clever papal move symbolizing the dependence of the empire on the Church, it began the tradition that all later emperors had to come to Italy to receive the crown from the pope. This was the cause of all those future descents from the north by Saxons, Salians, Hohenstaufens and, of immediate concern to Dante, by Henry of Luxemburg in 1310. North and Central Italy were henceforth regarded as integral parts of the empire and the emperor was the ultimate source of all authority. Another consequence was that with the destruction of the Lombard monarchy and the failure of a branch of Charlemagne's line, there was no native royal dynasty surviving in Italy round which a unified state could grow up. This was one of the most important directions in which the future development of Italy differed from that of the countries of Northern Europe. Only the papacy, itself an Italian creation, fulfilled something of this function and thus it became the natural ally of all the forces which were to resist the periodic invasions from the north. Charlemagne was remembered especially in Florence, because a popular tradition recorded by Villani[12] credited him with the refounding of the city in 801 after its destruction. Villani says that the old men of the city had claimed it could not be rebuilt unless the famous marble statue which had been dedicated by black arts to the god Mars, the first patron of the city, and flung into the river on the city's destruction, could be found again. The citizens had it dredged from the Arno and placed on a pillar by the Ponte Vecchio, where it stood until swept away in the great flood of 1333. Many superstitions connecting the welfare of the city with its preservation were current.

The Carolingian empire broke up in the course of the ninth century under the impact of great invasions from the Norse, the Magyars, and the Saracens.

With the abeyance of the monarchy in Italy, power passed to the local bishops and the nobility. Because the bishops were generally based in towns or what remained of towns, they became responsible for the towns alone; the surrounding countryside which, in Roman times, had always formed part of the administrative unit centred on the city, now fell into the hands of the nobility who broke up and took over the vast ecclesiastical estates the Church could no longer control. This separation of town and countryside was later of great significance when the new communes, to assure their security and their food supplies, were impelled to conquer the *contado* round their cities from the feudal nobility.

Each bishop was the guardian of the shrine of the local saint and so acted as the natural focus of civic patriotism in the tenth century and later when, under the influences of expanding trade, a growing population, and greater productivity on the land, town life was at last beginning—not just to survive, for that it had done untypically where most of Europe was concerned—but to grow and flourish. The first signs of expansion were shown by the coastal cities of Pisa and Genoa which launched naval campaigns against the Saracen corsairs so successfully that by the end of the eleventh century they virtually controlled the sea routes of the western Mediterranean and were poised for the important part they were to play in the Crusades. They also formed an alliance with the Norman adventurers who, between 1030 and 1090, took the South of Italy from Byzantium and Sicily from the Saracens, setting up a kingdom and increasing the division of Italy through the separate development of the South.

The inland towns such as Florence revived more slowly and the rise of the republics, involving a changeover from rule by the bishops to rule by the communes, took place under the shadow of an even mightier upheaval, the Investiture Contest. From the time of Otto I (962–73) and his intervention in Italy, the papacy had played a subservient role to the empire, partly because of a succession of theocratic emperors such as Otto III and Henry III who kept all higher ecclesiastical appointments in their hands, and partly because of the debasement of the papacy itself, especially in the first part of the eleventh century. The Reform movement, which had its origins in the monasteries, most notably Cluny with its many dependencies, was to smash this system to pieces. The aims of these stern monks were to give to the Church all power in the matter of ecclesiastical appointments, to restore and increase the authority of the pope, to impose on the parish clergy the monastic rule of celibacy, to improve standards of literacy and, by glorifying the Mass, to exalt the priesthood in the minds of believers. The most notable of the Reformers to appear in the *Commedia* is the religious leader and poet, St Peter Damian.

It was the reforming pope Gregory VII who was to break the longstanding domination of the empire over the Church by his quarrel with the emperor Henry IV, so cutting open the wounds that Dante and his contemporaries were still trying to heal two hundred years later. The quarrel arose over the investiture of bishops and the *regalia*, the right of the Crown to take the revenues of vacant benefices; the real quarrel, however, was over who should have supremacy in Christendom. The papacy found new and strong allies in the Norman kingdom of the South, which had become a papal fief, in the religious-political bodies known as the Patarini in the Lombard cities, in Countess Matilda of Tuscany who, though the emperor's aunt, supported the reformers, and in many German magnates and bishops. With these allies, Gregory and his successors managed to divide society throughout Germany and North and Central Italy, unleashing war and anarchy to an extent that permanently altered the forms of government. As the authority of the bishops in the cities was destroyed in the confusion, so private bodies of the wealthier and established citizens confronted the threat of anarchy by taking over the government of the cities. This was the beginning of the process that was to turn hundreds of small and large cities of North and Central Italy into self-governing republics.

The men who took over the government came from a small group of families and they formed what was frequently called a consulate. These families were not necessarily aristocratic in origin though well before this time many nobles kept town houses and understood that if they wished to keep close to the centre of power they had to take part in city life. Social fusion and intermarriage between the richer merchants and the nobility produced the new social class leading the communes. Merchants bought their way into the middle ranks of landowners by purchasing estates in the country, thus increasing the bonds between city and *contado*, and nobles, to an extent largely unheard of in Northern Europe, participated in trading either by investment or by active business. Earlier in the eleventh century the citizens had forced the emperor Conrad II to recognize their part in the feudal hierarchy.[13] Now at the end of the century they founded their communes, which were based on the joint exercise by elected consuls of feudal powers which were vested in their collective authority. The new class was not formed by a victory of businessmen over landowners but by an alliance between the two classes in which each took over the functions of the other and so produced the mixed and vital urban society in which the art of Dante and his contemporaries was to flourish.

Florence became the centre of the Reform movement in Tuscany, partly through the proximity of the monks of the new foundation at Vallombrosa and partly through the attachment of Countess Matilda to the papal cause. Two at least of the bishops of Florence in the eleventh century exemplified the corruption of which the reformers complained. One bishop used to hear cases in his court with his wife sitting beside him, and another who was accused of simony, i.e. of buying his office, was driven from Florence after a monk of Vallombrosa passed unscathed through the ordeal of fire before a large crowd in order to maintain the truth of this charge. Many of Dante's early commentators identify the lady Matelda who guides Dante through the Earthly Paradise with the stern, warlike countess, who would lead her troops into battle against the emperor's forces.[14] It was at her castle of Canossa in 1077 that Henry IV was made to stand three nights in the snow before Gregory VII who was staying there would receive his submission, and when in 1081 through a reversal of fortune Henry won back his position and deposed his aunt, only Florence of all the towns of Tuscany rallied to Matilda's support and successfully withstood an imperial siege. Matilda granted many privileges to the city and it was even before her death in 1115 without an heir that the first period of the city's expansion began. In 1125 Florence conquered and destroyed the town of Fiesole and she had already begun to assert herself over her noble neighbours.

The *contado* or country surrounding the city was dominated by the castles of the nobility, frequently in strategic positions that could hinder the trading of Florentine merchants. It is estimated that by 1100 there were 130 of these castles.[15] The commune made war on these castles and when the Florentines conquered their noble neighbours, they forced them to live in the city for part of the year and to build palaces and houses within the city. In this way they forced recognition of the city's suzerainty on the nobles and ensured that the military forces of the city were strengthened by a class devoted to war. At the same time they added greatly to the possible causes of division because these quarrelsome and proud new citizens built for their town dwellings what were virtually castles within the city, defensive stone houses with tall slim towers from which they attacked their neighbours or to which they fled for security. There must have been over a hundred of these towers in Florence in Dante's time though all had been shortened on the commune's orders well before his birth. Families would also make private treaties with other families for mutual defence and for sharing the cost of building these *casatorri* as they were called. A group of families bound together in this way was known as a *consorzeria*.

This early period of the Florentine commune was idealized by Dante in the description of his meeting with his Crusader ancestor, Cacciaguida, the subject of the central cantos of the *Paradiso*. Cacciaguida was knighted by the emperor Conrad III whom he followed to the Holy Land where he was killed in 1147. From Cacciaguida's knighthood derived the claim of Dante's family to nobility—though Dante has been accused of fabricating this ancestry to dissociate himself from the new families whom he, in common with many other writers, blamed for disorders in the republics.[16] The part Cacciaguida plays in the *Commedia* is dealt with in Chapter 20—a part so important that questions of social standing pale before it. Here we are more concerned with his depiction of Florence in the years before Barbarossa's invasions of the mid-twelfth century—a small tranquil town where social order was respected, with little or no immigration from the *contado*, where the wives of the leaders of the commune indulged in no outrageous expenditure on their persons, where fathers did not blench when a daughter was born because of the crippling dowries that were customary in later times, and where, above all, there was peace.[17] Cacciaguida is describing a town of perhaps 18,000 citizens as compared to the 90,000–100,000 at the time of Dante's priorate in 1300, a town, therefore, without the appalling urban pressures, the extreme contrasts of wealth and poverty, the clashes between classes and between parties, the dependence on foreign monarchs or on the papacy that the later involvement of Florence in banking was to bring about. Life was probably as simple as Cacciaguida describes and, perhaps, as honourable.

In the course of his praises of the simple bearing of his contemporaries Cacciaguida mentions that, among his contemporaries, Bellincion Berti wore leather and bone, and notables of other families, de' Nerli and del Vecchio, were content to wear skin jerkins.[18] It is a Crusader praising these old-fashioned garments, but it was to a large extent because of the importation of luxury goods through the trade routes opened up by the Crusades that the luxurious tastes he deplores were introduced, especially the great change in fashion brought about by a growing preference for fine cloth. Through the introduction of secret techniques in the treatment and dyeing of woollen cloth, the Florentines seized their chance of providing for this lasting fashion.[19] From the mastery of this and related trades the future wealth and eminence of Florence grew. Pisa, which had played so great a part in the Crusades and whose native industry depended on the older skills in the treatment of leather and furs, was to decline into a staging-post for the export of Florentine goods. The need to supply themselves with what they needed for their trade was, in the course of the thirteenth century, to send Florentine merchants off to the fairs of France and all round the Mediterranean to buy the best cloth or the raw materials for treating and dyeing it and to sell the results of their skill. Thus they built up the international connexions from which derived the later Florentine predominance in banking. From the evidence of expanding city walls—those of Florence were extended in about 1173—there was a population explosion—and it was probably the introduction of improved methods of reclaiming land that enabled the country around the big cities like Florence to produce the surplus of food needed for a greater urban population than had been known since Roman times.

The communes arose in response to one crisis in papal and imperial relations; they were to find their maturity in another. Frederick I Barbarossa, of the Hohenstaufen family, succeeded Cacciaguida's emperor Conrad III in 1152 and he entered Italy on his way to his coronation at Rome in 1154, accompanied by a brilliant court of soldiers, prelates, scholars, and poets. He was determined to restore imperial authority but he came as a foreigner, totally insensitive to the strength and ambitions of the new urban societies that he soon provoked into opposition. Something of his pride and impatience is conveyed in his speech to the representatives of the Roman Senate in 1155 when they had dared to suggest that it was the right of the Roman people to choose and make the emperor. Barbarossa's uncle, Otto of Freising, reports how the emperor castigated them for their presumption both in resembling themselves to their nobler forebears and for attempting to limit his powers, and also how he spoke of the Franks as the true heirs of empire for their prowess in conquest.[20]

In such tones were the arguments of the imperial party newly forged, arguments on which Dante was to draw for his treatise on empire, *De monarchia*. Barbarossa soon clashed both with the papacy and the communes, and was involved in sieges of several recalcitrant towns. The memory of these wars lasted a long time. Dante would mention their horrors in his letter to the Florentines in 1311 summoning them to submit to Henry of Luxemburg and threatening them with Barbarossa's treatment of Milan and Spoleto.[21] After several invasions in the course of which Milan especially suffered, the powerful Lombard League of all the threatened cities was formed against him. When Barbarossa came next to chastise them, he was roundly defeated in the battle of Legnano in 1176. His Italian policy was in ruins and he was forced to agree to a reconciliation with the pope and the communes in a meeting that took place in Venice in 1177. There he had to allow the pope to set his foot on his neck and he had to lead the pope's horse outside St Mark's cathedral—a crushing reversal of his ambitions. The settlement made there was followed by the Peace of Constance in 1183 when the cities of the League, Florence among them, were granted the right of electing their own consuls and of effective self-government within their walls, while they acknowledged Barbarossa as their feudal overlord.

Barbarossa still kept a firm grip on Tuscany until his death on crusade in 1190, a policy followed by his son, Henry VI, who took the Hohenstaufen involvement in Italy a step further by his marriage to Constance, the heiress of the Norman kingdom of Sicily. Their son was to become the last Hohenstaufen emperor, Frederick II.

Though Dante only introduces Frederick II of Hohenstaufen fleetingly in the *Commedia* when he is shown his tomb among the heretics in Hell, his baleful presence broods over many episodes because several characters closely connected with him appear in person. These include his chancellor, Pier della Vigne, the poet, and great stylist who killed himself after Frederick had had him blinded; Frederick's bastard son, Manfred; Michael Scot, his magician; and the empress Constance, his mother. It was popularly thought that Constance was torn from a convent to marry the emperor Henry VI and that she gave birth to Frederick in public in the market-place of the town of Iesi to avoid any suspicion that, because of her age (she was forty at the time), she was not his mother.

Chosen as emperor when an adolescent by the great pope Innocent III, Frederick was to spend most of his life fighting against the papacy, and, although the temporal leader of Western Christianity, he was a sceptic and tended to prefer Islam of the religions known to him. Yet, although a sceptic, he was prey to superstition, keeping magicians and astrologers, notably Michael Scot, at his court, and he would never stay in Florence because of a prophecy that he would die *sub flore*. In the event he died at his small castle of Castel Fiorentino. He would appear to have reconciled these contradictions best in his patronage of the arts. The buildings and sculptures erected under his orders, especially Castel del Monte, Lucera, and the Capua Bridge, reveal a deliberate attempt to achieve a synthesis between varying disparate styles and influences. Under his patronage also, there flourished the Sicilian school of poets who were the first in Italy to express the forms and themes of the Provençal troubadours (see Chapter 7) in an Italian literary language.

Frederick was powerfully supplied with administrators, soldiers, and money for his great object, the creation of a unified national state out of Italy which would link up with his possessions beyond the Alps. Such an object naturally clashed with the aims of papal policy. The popes could not bear the thought of being permanently surrounded by the Hohenstaufen and were forced to engineer alliances with the city states to oppose his ambitions. Frederick was a powerful and resourceful enemy. In 1237 he defeated the Lombard League at the battle of Cortenuova, after which Tuscany fell under his dominance. Again in 1241, the Sicilian and Pisan fleets under his son, the poet-king Enzo, captured a party of bishops sailing to Rome to pack a General Council that Gregory IX had called to raise Christendom against him. Innocent IV did succeed in this aim; after making Frederick agree to a humiliating peace in 1244 he called a General Council the next year at Lyons where Frederick was denounced as an enemy of the Church, guilty of sacrilege and suspected of heresy. Innocent even declared a Crusade against him. A series of further misfortunes hit Frederick: he failed to take the city of Parma in a siege in 1248 when the besiegers made a foray in which they seized his treasury and regalia; he had to deal with a Muslim rebellion in Sicily; his son Enzo was captured and was to be imprisoned till his death in Bologna in 1272. Falling prey to suspicions Frederick believed he was surrounded by plotters, and had his most trusted adviser, Pier della Vigne, blinded by having red-hot brass basins held in front of his eyes. In the *Inferno* Pier describes his downfall in the following words which, with their elaborate wordplay on the theme of flame, evoke the heat of hatred in the minds of those who brought about his physical blindness.

La meretrice che mai da l'ospizio
  di Cesare non torse li occhi putti,
  morte comune e de le corti vizio,
infiammò contra me li animi tutti;
  e li' nfiammati infiammar sì Augusto,
  che' lieti onor tornaro in tristi lutti.
L'animo mio, per disdegnoso gusto,
  credendo col morir fuggir disdegno,
  ingiusto fece me contra me giusto.[22]

The whore that at the house where Caesar is
  Will ever her adulterous glances aim,
Man's common bane, of courts the special vice,
The minds of all against me did inflame,
  And these, inflamed, inflamed my lord august
  Till my glad honours withered to sad shame.
My soul into disdainful temper thrust,
  Thinking by death to escape the world's disdain,
  Made me, the just, unto myself unjust.

On Frederick's death in 1250, his son Conrad inherited his realms but he died in 1254, leaving to the pope's protection an infant, Conradin, who was raised far away in Germany. The southern kingdom fell into the hands of Frederick's bastard son, Manfred, and Innocent IV, who had hoped and schemed to annex the kingdom to the papacy, died as he heard of Manfred's successes.

Every vicissitude of Frederick's fortunes had had an effect on Florence throughout his reign, affecting her constitution and her relations with her neighbour cities. They also increased the divisions in the city; the nobles and great entrepreneurs were divided into parties, the Ghibellines who took their name from a Hohenstaufen castle in Swabia, Waiblingen, and the Guelphs who were called after Welf, the family name of Otto IV, the emperor who preceded Frederick II. The increasing complexity of Florentine commerce had led to the growth of separate organizations or guilds for the separate trades, not only for regulating their specialized operations, but also to act as pressure groups within the city to secure their rights. The first major divisions in the city have been traced back to the attempts led by the noble family of the Uberti in 1177–9 to gain a greater say in the government. The increasing size of the city—the population was about 50,000 in 1200 and had probably doubled by the end of the century—and the presence of so many conflicting interests brought about the end of the rule of the consuls and the first of a long series of constitutional experiments. In 1207 Florence, copying the custom of Lombard cities in the North, appointed its first *podestà* from outside the city, a paid official, generally a nobleman trained as a lawyer, who headed the judiciary and led the commune in time of war. To make sure that he acted without bias towards any factional interest he always came from another city, and to prevent him establishing his own power base in the city, his appointment was generally only for a year.

Dante and his contemporaries all ascribe the introduction of the Guelph and Ghibelline quarrels into the city to the murder of Buondelmonte dei Buondelmonti in 1215.

Buondelmonte, a young nobleman, was engaged to a lady of another noble family, the Amidei, in order to settle a feud between the families. He jilted this lady in preference for a girl of the Donati family and he married her on the day appointed for his marriage into the Amidei. The outraged Amidei gathered together their *consorzeria* which included the powerful Uberti clan and, urged on by Mosca Lamberti whom Dante depicts in Hell with his hands cut off as his punishment for his words,[23] they decided to kill Buondelmonte. They found their opportunity on Easter Day. The Amidei house overlooked the Ponte Vecchio and the statue of Mars. Buondelmonte was riding across the bridge from the other side of the Arno, conspicuously dressed in white, with a white cloak, wearing a garland on his head and riding a white horse. As he reached the end of the bridge five assailants came out. He was clubbed, dragged to the ground and stabbed to death. The Amidei gazed down from their tower with satisfaction at the corpse lying at the foot of the statue of Mars. In their grief and dismay the murdered man's relations were quick to make capital of the killing.

They paraded the corpse with its head cradled in the lap of his beautiful Donati bride through the streets of the city.

This murder polarized the factions to such an extent that each side would only be content with the destruction or permanent exile of the other. Each side in Florence naturally sought outside help, either from the pope or from the emperor, in trying to gain the upper hand. The Uberti, through their skill in war, their wealth, and their ancient birth, became the natural leaders of the Ghibelline magnates. The Buondelmonti and the Donati formed the core of the Guelph party. Because Frederick II was the candidate of the pope, at first it was the Ghibellines who were the papal party. As Frederick broke with the papacy, so the Ghibellines became the supporters of the imperial Hohenstaufen party and the Guelphs the supporters of the pope. In between 1237 and 1250 the bitterness and savagery of the quarrels between the Guelphs and Ghibellines grew in extent, the fortunes of each going up and down with the fortunes of Frederick II. Each side when gaining the upper hand exiled the leaders of the other and destroyed their property. There was, however, another movement of great significance in the city, and a common feature of other Italian cities of the period, thrusting its way into power. This was the movement known as the *popolo*, a vehemently anti-aristocratic grouping of merchants, notaries, and other members of the middle bourgeoisie who banded together in self-protection against the turbulent nobles and who gradually formed their own organization headed by an official known as the captain of the people. Where the *podestà* was the executive of the wishes of the oligarchy ruling the commune, this official performed for the *popolo* the same offices that the *podestà* did for the commune as a whole.

Shortly before Frederick's death in 1250 the *popolo* of Florence overturned the Ghibelline government and established the régime that was to last for ten years and that was later known as the *primo* or *vecchio popolo*. Where Dante had idealized the Florence of Cacciaguida at a time when it was at peace under the acknowledged rule of an emperor, other Florentine writers with a Guelph bias, such as Villani, were to look back on this decade as one of pure republican virtue. Under this régime Florence was ruled by a *podestà* and a captain of the *popolo* with the help of councils drawn from a much wider cross-section of the city than ever before. Linking these two systems and formulating the policies on which they were to act were the men with whom the real power rested, the *Anziani* or ancients. To signify the fundamental break with the past that this régime had wrought, the Guelphs changed the standard of the republic from a white lily on a red field to a red lily on a white field.[24]

Their pride was to be brought low in the disastrous battle of Montaperti in 1260 against what was now the traditional enemy of Florence, Siena. Though Siena had neither the population nor the industry of Florence, she had acquired great riches through her bankers who, until the end of the century, provided the chief bankers of the papacy. In 1258 the Guelph rulers of Florence had exiled numerous Ghibellines who were suspected of a plot against them and these

Ghibellines took refuge in Siena, only thirty miles distant. The Guelphs had weakened their own position by quarrelling with the pope while the Ghibelline exiles had been given new heart by the powerful position which Manfred had built up for himself in the South. Manfred's authority as vicar-general and wielder of imperial power was also recognized in the ring of cities like Siena with Ghibelline allegiances that surrounded Florence (see Figure 2). The Florentine exiles led by Farinata degli Uberti collected at Siena where their presence was a constant source of anxiety to the weakening Guelph alliance in Florence. Hostilities broke out and by June 1260 the Sienese had ravaged the country round Montepulciano and laid siege to the town of Montalcino, which was under Florentine protection. The Florentines were nervous of the extended operation involved in raising the siege. Farinata in Siena, estimating that his party's only chance of return to Florence lay in a battle between Florence and Siena in which Florence should be defeated, managed to enter into secret negotiations with two of the Florentine *Anziani*, with two friars as intermediaries.[25] The friars made the *Anziani* believe that the Ghibelline exiles in Siena were so at odds with the Sienese government that they would betray one of the gates of Siena if only the Florentines would send an army to the Arbia, a stream six miles from Siena. The Florentines were to make it look as though they were going to relieve Montalcino. It was all that the two *Anziani* wanted to hear; they could destroy Siena and since, in doing so, they would remove the Ghibellines' base, they could then fulfil as much of the bargain as suited them later. Unfortunately for them the friars had sworn them to secrecy about the plot and, when the *Anziani* convened the Great Council, they presented the plan of the expedition as having as its aim only the relief of Montalcino.

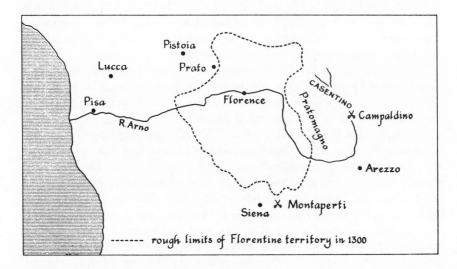

Figure 2 Florence and her neighbouring cities

35

Though warned in debate by experienced soldiers of the dangers of the expedition, the *Anziani* silenced their opposition and went ahead with preparations for war. At the end of August, the Florentine army and its allies moved south to battle.

In Siena preparations went ahead to deal with the attack. King Manfred had sent 800 German men-at-arms or cavalry, under Count Giordano, to their aid. The resolve of the Sienese to resist was strengthened when on 2 September envoys from Florence appeared before the Council of Siena and made the following implacable demands: that the town walls of Siena should be destroyed allowing free passage to Florentines; that governors of the Florentines' choice should govern the three wards of the city; and that a great fortress should be built nearby to dominate the city. Failing their compliance, the Sienese were threatened with siege, conquest, and the sword. They quickly reached a decision to resist, and in moving ceremonies their newly elected leader, Buonguida Lucari, offered their city to the Virgin Mary. Carrying the keys of the city, he led the citizens barefoot and bareheaded to the cathedral where he was greeted by the bishop with the kiss of peace, and where he laid the keys on the altar before the painting known as the 'Madonna of the Great Eyes', asking the Virgin to accept the gift of the city and imploring her protection. After a procession everyone knelt in confession and sought out their enemies for forgiveness. Then they hastened to prepare for war.

The Florentine army had reached the place appointed in the secret negotiations with the Ghibelline exiles, encamping on and below the hill of Montaperti overlooking the plain intersected by the river Arbia. There, in a strange landscape of mounded, breastlike hillocks, they halted the Carroccio, the great red-painted war waggon carrying the standards of the Florentine republic. The Carroccio was the rallying point in battle and the focus of civic pride. News of the impending betrayal had by now circulated in the army but they were even more disheartened by the evidence of the strength of the Sienese resistance, which was quite at odds with what they had expected.

Throughout the night of 3 September the Sienese launched skirmishing attacks on the Florentine camp, and the next morning, the day of the battle, the Sienese army and its German allies advanced on the Florentines, who now found themselves on a battleground of their enemies' choosing. They left their camp and came half-way down the hill with their right wing against the castle of Montaperti. Some of the Ghibellines with the Florentines took advantage of the closeness of the armies and galloped across to the other side. The infantry of the centre had engaged and the Florentine cavalry was about to advance. Their commander had raised the standard when a Ghibelline noble, Bocca degli Abati, slashed off the commander's hand. The cavalry were thrown into some commotion at this treachery, and at that point the German horse charged. A young knight of the house of Steinberg, his horse gorgeously caparisoned with crimson taffeta encrusted with the gold-green dragons of his armorial bearings,[26] led the charge, and the sheer professional skill of the foreigners drove back the Florentines' disheartened advance. The Florentine cavalry regrouped and fought back hard. The issue seemed uncertain until the Sienese carried out a successful flank attack with cavalry and infantry. The Florentine cavalry fled and a desperate hand-to-hand battle centred round the Carroccio, which the Sienese finally captured after killing most of its bodyguard. The battle continued till the evening by which time over half the Florentine army was killed or captured. The Sienese did not pursue but plundered the field and returned in triumph to their city with their enemy's Carroccio and the standards and with one of the Florentine envoys, who had appeared two days before with those outrageous demands, tied head to tail on a donkey.

It was the worst disgrace ever suffered by Florence. Nearly every family must have lost a son or a husband, and the telling of the story reverberated deeply in the young Dante. It was eyewitness accounts, probably from his uncle, Brunetto, who distinguished himself in the battle, that told him of the Arbia red with blood, and when he meets the spirit of Bocca degli Abati in the pit of traitors,[27] he tears the hair from his scalp in rejection of his treachery.

The Guelph leaders, when the news reached Florence, were so shocked at the results of their stupidity that they left immediately for exile, making no attempt to use the considerable defences of the city. The victorious Ghibellines with their allies met at Empoli to discuss what should be done to Florence and, with almost one accord, they decided to destroy the city. At this, Farinata degli Uberti, the man whose cunning and skill had devised the means of victory, opposed them saying that, even if he stood alone, he would defend the city with his sword in his hand. The force of his speech and presence was so great the other leaders abandoned the idea. Instead Florence was given to the Ghibelline Count Guido Novello to rule and great numbers of Guelph families were proscribed and ordered into exile. Dante cannot have known Farinata since he died shortly before his birth, but in the great tenth canto of the *Inferno* one sees Dante meeting him as one of the legendary giants of his childhood, looking as though he held Hell in great despite.[28] The Ghibellines were to hold Florence till 1267. This meant that Dante was born in 1265 under a régime that was aberrant from the Guelph destiny the city was to follow. How the Guelphs won back the city is a story to be told in Chapter 4. First we must turn to some of the wider issues affecting Dante's world, the conflict of pope and emperor, the rise of the mendicant orders, and the new spirit of individuality, already current in many sides of medieval life, to which Dante was to give new expression in his own works.

3

Heraldry, prophecy, and the individual self

As Dante mounts the heavens of the *Paradiso*, so from the sphere of the sun onwards, he sees the souls of the blessed grouped into amazing patterns of light that form great symbols: the double crown or garland of the wise in the heaven of the sun, the cross of the warriors in the heaven of Mars, the eagle of justice in the heaven of Jupiter, and the ladder of the contemplatives in the heaven of Saturn. These great symbols are wonderful examples of the way in which art can delve to the depths of a historical movement and present it in its essence, as its cause reunited with its manifestation and its fulfilment. Just as in heraldry a badge or coat of arms sums up something permanent about the nature of a city or a family, something more than the natures of the individual citizens or family members at any one time,[1] so the poet, forced by the necessities of his art to compress meaning, discovers in such symbols the concentrated experience of centuries. Symbols, because they contain the past and future of what they symbolize, force prophecy upon the poet with a marvellous and intriguing attraction. Boris Pasternak, writing of his unfinished play *The Blind Beauty*, spoke of his desire 'to seize a small part of that obscure and magic thing called destiny, the future'.[2] Though the play is set in the Russia of the last century, Pasternak is concerned with the future because it is there that the meaning of the sufferings he records will be found. Dante, too, found the images arising in his visionary inspirations beckoning him to prophecy because, being symbols of historical processes as yet uncompleted, he still, as an artist, had to treat of them as wholes.

As will be seen in Chapter 20, the originality of Dante's presentation of individual characters is closely linked to the novel interpretation he brought to the symbols at his command. In this he had to hand two popular and widely disseminated symbolic languages: the devices and pictographs of heraldry and the signs, numbers, and patterns of prophecy. The act of the Guelphs in reversing the colours on the standard of Florence when the white lily, drawn from the wild irises that flourished by the banks of the Arno, was made red, was more than an act of defiance to their Ghibelline enemies; it was a recognition of the different spirit of the Guelph *popolo*, printing in the colour of blood their

38

fraternal association and their readiness to die in the cause of their ideal of the commune. When that standard was torn from the Carroccio in the defeat at Montaperti, it was dragged in the mud before the myriad badges of the Sienese, the older Ghibelline standard, and the family arms of the victors. Heraldry was not the prerogative of the noble fighting man; in Florence as in other cities, every family of importance whether noble or bourgeois, every trade association and guild, every ward of the city, had devised its own coat of arms or badge, as a reminder of its particular nature and aims, and in Florence, with her skilled craftsmen in weaving, dyeing, and painting, no opportunity was lost, whether in war or in the celebrations of peace, to emblazon the event with the quarterings of heraldry and the devices of civic and mercantile pride.

The heraldic devices that surpassed all others in honour were the crossed keys of the papacy and the black eagle of the empire. Though much has been said in the last chapter about the strife between these two great institutions, here, taking into account their influence on Dante's thought and his world, we will consider why they occupied their pre-eminent positions, why they attracted their various adherents, and why they caused such divisions in Christendom.

The papal coat of arms derives from Christ's charge to Peter: 'And I will give unto thee the keys of the kingdom of heaven: and whatsoever thou shalt bind on earth shall be bound in heaven: and whatsoever thou shalt loose on earth shall be loosed in heaven.'[3] These keys were later to be surmounted by the triple tiara, probably introduced in Dante's time, signifying the mission of the pope as the father of princes and kings, the ruler of the world, and the vicar of Christ. By the beginning of the twelfth century the papacy had firmly established claims to its rights in these areas of authority. In the spiritual sphere the pope, as the successor of Peter and vicar of Christ, was the arbiter of what men should believe. He controlled the gateway to Death and his judgments were binding on Earth and in Heaven. He could lessen the pains of Purgatory and he could add to the treasury of intercessors by canonizing new saints. All the roads to Heaven went through him. He had power over every altar because Mass could only be celebrated on an altar that contained authenticated relics and only his agents could authenticate those relics. To impose his will he had the weapons of excommunication against individuals and of interdict against cities and nations, and to assert his spiritual authority he had throughout Western Europe the hierarchy of bishops, priests, and deacons, the hundreds of abbeys with their innumerable daughter houses, and later the thousands of mendicant convents, the only literate international body in existence. By these means the papacy exercised control over the consciences of men through the hope of Heaven and the fear of Hell, or intervened in political and economic affairs through the more immediate means of compulsion available through the Church's ownership of so much land and other temporal assets. With the expansion of the penitential system, the popular appeal of auricular confession, and the glorification of the Mass, the Church enhanced her sacerdotal authority and dominated the inner life of humanity.

The making of a poet

The days were gone when the stronger successors of Charlemagne had chosen pliant pontiffs and imposed their will on them. The papacy had emerged very strong from the Investiture Contest of the late eleventh and early twelfth centuries (see pp. 27–9), aided greatly by the Reform movement. At this point the older monarchies were in decline and the future nation states were still to emerge. The real power lay in an alliance between the international government exercised by the Church throughout its hierarchy and the aristocracy of town and countryside which formed the local governments throughout the West. The Church had survived the testing time of the Investiture Contest by making use of everything that was most vital in the various forms of feudal society, through the Normans in their conquest of the two Sicilies and of England, and through the new, late appearance of feudal institutions in the German-speaking areas of the empire, so that 'what led Europe was an inadvertent, rarely conscious, but very real alliance between Europe's aristocracies and the See of Peter'.[4] The success of the alliance drew the Church deeper and deeper into the management and regulation of temporal affairs. In fact every spiritual and moral advance of the Church also implicated her more deeply in current events. This was owed largely to the sensitivity of certain great popes to those popular movements which could be guided to the benefit of the Church and so were taken under her wing. Urban II's promulgation of the First Crusade in 1095, and Innocent III's patronage of the mendicant orders in the early thirteenth century are two notable examples of this particular flair.

The success of the First Crusade not only won the Holy Places for Latin Christendom and created a new kingdom of which the Pope was suzerain but also, through the system of plenary indulgences associated with the Crusades, greatly extended the pope's control of the consciences of men, especially of the ruling classes, because only the pope could release a man from the crusading oath. Another effect was the first laws of the Church against usury, issued partly to protect the Crusader who had to borrow money to fulfil his oath, and this, with the development of the idea of the just price, came to involve the Church in the regulation of the market-place.

The papacy also recognized in Cistercianism and in the great military orders of the Templars and Hospitallers, which were modelled on the constitutional basis of Cîteaux, more movements which redounded to the fame and credit of the Roman See. In this, it responded to the new mood of constitutionalism and the accent on brotherhood that was to be found in the stirrings of the Italian communes as well as in the monastic world, and it therefore found natural allies in many of the communes in its struggle with the Hohenstaufen emperors.

Buoyed up by the great spiritual power of movements such as these, many of the popes gradually came to see themselves as the rightful supreme rulers of Christendom in temporal as well as in spiritual matters. From 1199, with the introduction of the papal tithe, the papacy enjoyed the benefit of the most efficient and highly developed tax-collecting machinery in Europe. Secular governments took their cut from it but they could not hope to rival or supplant it. The pope also had at his command, in the curia, the most highly trained civil service in Europe and the increase in appellate jurisdiction greatly added to the business and income. By 1301 Boniface VIII could speak of Rome as 'the common court of all the nations of the Christian people'.[5] The pope also assumed from the emperor, whose right it had previously been, the power to summon councils of the Church, and the series of councils, from the First Lateran in 1123 up to the Council of Vienne in 1311–12, further illustrate the triumph of the papacy. In the propaganda battle against the emperors the popes marshalled strong arguments, the Donation of Constantine* (then generally thought genuine), and the charge of Christ to Peter, and they adapted to their own political purposes the powerful sun imagery of Christian spirituality. As their power and influence grew, so they adopted the insignia of ancient secular power, the umbrella of oriental princes from Venice in the 1170s and, the final boast before the fall, the triple tiara, introduced by Boniface VIII in about 1300.

As a result of these and other factors the Church was enmeshed in the social and economic fabric of society and it is difficult to blame her for this, given the lack of permanent lay government institutions, and the nature of the alliance the Church formed with the urban and rural governing classes. As these classes prospered with the economic recovery of Europe in the twelfth and thirteenth centuries, so the Church, with her vast lands and her efficient means of collecting taxes, also prospered; to an extent that, in the opinion of many, went far beyond the measure that Christ had allowed his disciples. In the eyes of the laity it was difficult to separate the money the papacy needed for the maintenance of a secular state and of a court of appeal and for its interventions in keeping the balance of power, and the money that seemed to be devoured out of sheer greed and cupidity. The popes came to depend largely on Tuscan merchant bankers for collecting taxes all over Europe and were forced to connive at usury by licensing not only these bankers in the practice, but also all those clerics who had to borrow money to pay the papal fees for confirmation of their benefices. These double standards over usury were hard to justify and

---

*The Donation of Constantine is a document written at a time (about AD 750) when the papacy was working to free itself from the suzerainty of the Eastern emperor and it was forged in order to bolster the papal claims. In this document the emperor Constantine records his conversion to Christianity on being healed of leprosy by Pope Sylvester and his grant of the Western empire to the papacy in gratitude. Its authenticity was sometimes challenged in the Middle Ages, long before Valla proved it a forgery in 1440, notably by the Roman rebels who called it 'this lie and heretical fable' in 1152. Dante did, however, accept it as a genuine document although, to him, its provisions were invalid because the emperor could not alienate the rights of his office. Constantine in Heaven is made to know that the evil derived from his good deed does not harm him though the world is brought to ruin by it (*Par.* XX. 55–60). To Dante the Donation was an appalling fact never enough to be deplored and he returns frequently to lament it.

some of Dante's most biting lines are devoted to the Church and money, none more bitter than the identification of the Church with the she-wolf, whose hunger for gold can never be satisfied.[6]

Nevertheless the Church of Western Christendom was an extraordinary creation, providing for and regulating every part of man's life, directing his belief through doctrine, enriching his emotions with liturgy and music, working on his conscience through the penitentiary system, controlling his warlike impulses by the idea of the just war and the Crusades, and restraining his greed in the market-place within an ethos of brotherly love and of the corporate spirit. She took all this upon herself and frequently failed and, with her failures, more and more men were convinced that she was undertaking tasks for which she was not fitted.

The empire opposes to the crossed keys the older symbol of the eagle, the bird of Jupiter, the emblem of justice, of military power as the standard of the legions and of hierarchy. Under the figure of the eagle one can reasonably include all those who in some way opposed the excessive claims of the Church, not simply those emperors and their followers who descended periodically into Italy and engaged in warfare with the pope's allies. Many layfolk, without rejecting Christianity, saw in the celibate and sterile hierarchy of the Church something strange and unnatural. Others objected to the confusion of functions and the debasement of spiritual aims caused by the Church's involvement in temporal affairs. These included some of the greatest intellects and strongest creative personalities of the high Middle Ages, all the more curious a fact because it was the papacy which had identified its cause with the new movements and the new classes, whereas the emperors had to depend on more hidebound, less articulate traditionalist supporters—but with the significant help of this small number of vocal intellectuals which included Dante. The empire could never claim to aspire to the position the Church occupied in regulating all sides of human experience; in this it did not follow the pattern of Byzantium, where the Eastern emperor was regarded as the vicar of Christ, a belief which the emotional power of the Greek Church enhanced through its architecture, liturgy, and iconography. Nevertheless Byzantine influence can be seen in the high point of imperial claims, the *Liber augustalis*[7] of Frederick II in 1231, in which the imperium is described as the fullness of power and the emperor is the executor of God's will on earth and the living image of justice and law in all lands. This document also reflects the powerful influence of the rebirth of Roman law which derived from the work of the great twelfth-century lawyer Irnerius at Bologna. A vast labour of commentary had been carried out on Justinian's Codex, all of which depended on the essential fact that the emperor was the fount of honour and justice. The work of these lawyers was an essential prop to the imperial cause and men trained in this school of legal thought had provided Barbarossa, for example, with an entourage of clever and educated publicists. When the emperor came with force, nothing could withstand the argument that all titles, rights to jurisdiction, suzerainty, and the imposition of taxes derived from him and could be revoked by him. In the laws and constitutions drawn up for him by Pier della Vigne and his other advisers but which obviously reflect his own views, Frederick II led, by reason of his nature and his supreme rank, a movement which has been called 'a spiritual revolution of immeasurable importance which amounted in essence to a secularization of the whole of human life'.[8]

Other movements, though less obvious in their imperialist bias, certainly supported the trend towards secularization—the troubadour and minnesinger traditions, for example. The Church did not know what to do with women in its hierarchy: they were excluded from confecting and administering the sacraments. Its solution for those women who wished to play a part in the life of the Church was generally monastic. They were shut away. Sexual love was a distraction to the priest or monk who should devote himself to the love of God. Contemporaneously with the growth of the Albigensian heresy in Provence and Northern Italy—the greatest doctrinal threat that the medieval Church had to meet—there arose the school of the troubadours, who, found in the experience of sexual love a new perception of life and a new avenue to the love of God. A similar experience was that of the minnesingers, many of whom, such as Walter von der Vogelweide, were members of the knightly *ministerialis* class particularly devoted to the Hohenstaufen interest. Italian lyric poetry first arises in the milieu of the emperor Frederick II's Southern court, and among Italian poets later in the century the weight of talent including Guinizzelli and Dante is inclined towards the Ghibelline cause. In these literary movements, in the *Roman de la Rose*, and in the Charlemagne and Grail legends, a balance was being regained; the problems of sexuality were discussed instead of being repressed and women were restored to a more equal place in society. Some of these works, notably the Provençal *sirventes*, contained blistering attacks on the Church, and they reflect also the hard core of scepticism, dislike, anticlericalism, and disbelief the Church had to contend with, even among its own clergy, in that age of belief.

The Church had brought chivalry into the Christian fold, enveloping the ceremonials of knighthood with symbolism and liturgy and imposing a code of behaviour through the Pax Dei. The psychological bias of chivalry as seen in the Charlemagne and Arthurian cycles and in heraldry, however, tended towards the imperial cause. In the *Chanson de Roland* the bias is clear because it tells of the heroism of the emperor's paladins. In the Arthurian cycles it is the knight Perceval, the representative of the secular world, who is granted the vision of the Holy Grail and so restores the fertility of the waste land of his soul and his world, not the priests and anchorites, who may advise and prepare him but who cannot act. The great stories of adultery, of Lancelot and Guenevere, of Tristan and Iseult, told of situations in which any man or woman might find themselves. The Church could meet them only with condemnation but, from the popularity of these stories not only in the knightly society of France, Germany, and England but also in the mercantile cities of Italy, it is clear that people felt them deeply and wanted to discuss them. A new awareness of the power and subtlety of love was released and its energy was such that the Church could not control or contain it.

Dante, as prophet of the Christian empire, was to define what was amiss in the relationship of pope and emperor. In the *Monarchia* written in support of Henry VII, the first emperor to visit Italy since the death of Frederick II, he expressed his view of the ideal relations between empire and papacy in relation to the two goals of mankind. Man, he says, was given two guides for these two goals:

> scilicet summo Pontifice, qui secundum revelata humanum genus perduceret ad vitam ecternam, et Imperatore, qui secundum phylo-sophica documenta genus humanum ad temporalem felicitatem dirigeret. Et cum ad hunc portum vel nulli vel pauci, et hii cum difficultate nimia, pervenire possint, nisi sedatis fluctibus blande cupiditatis genus humanum liberum in pacis tranquillitate quiescat, hoc est illud signum ad quod maxime debet intendere curator orbis, qui dicitur romanus Princeps.[9]

> there is the Supreme Pontiff who is to lead mankind to eternal life in accordance with revelation; and there is the Emperor who, in accordance with philosophical teaching, is to lead mankind to temporal happiness. None would reach this harbour—or at least, few would do so, and only with the greatest difficulty—unless the waves of alluring cupidity were assuaged and mankind were freed from them so as to rest in the tranquillity of peace; and this is the task to which that protector of the world must devote his energies who is called the Roman Prince.

He uttered his later views on the relationship of the two powers through the mouth of Marco Lombardo, a Venetian or Lombard courtier who takes the central position in the *Purgatorio* as Brunetto Latini does in the *Inferno* and Cacciaguida in the *Paradiso*. Surrounded by a dense black cloud of smoke in which the angry are purged of their sin but which also symbolizes the confusion and rage in earthly life produced by the confounding of the powers, Marco says:

Soleva Roma, che 'l buon mondo feo,
   due soli aver, che l'una e l'altra strada
   facean vedere, e del mondo e di Deo.
L'un l'altro ha spento; ed è giunta la
   spada

Rome, that the good world made for
   man's abode,
Was used to have two suns, by which
   were clear
Both roads, that of the world and that
   of God.
One hath put out the other; to
   crozier

col pasturale, e l'un con l'altro insieme	Is joined the sword; and going in union
per viva forza mal convien che vada;	Necessity compels that ill they fare,
però che, giunti, l'un l'altro non teme:[10]	Since, joined now, neither fears the other one.

These lines follow the famous description of the issuing of the simple soul, *l'anima semplicetta*, from the hand of God. In his concern for simple souls Dante was able to draw on the work and inspiration of certain great prophets and saints who preceded him in awakening new spiritual possibilities in mankind, notably Joachim of Fiore and the founders of the two chief mendicant orders, St Francis and St Dominic.

As men used the language of heraldry to express their ideals and loyalties, so they also thought it right that the Divine Will should be revealed as the significance behind natural disasters and unusual events. They were imbued with a special way of interpreting the Old Testament in which the stories of ancient Israel were regarded as not only possessing literal historical truth but also as prefigurings of the events of the life of Christ and the Church—so that, for example the old religion could be represented as the blindfold female figure of Synagogue and the Church of Christ as her open-eyed, clear-seeing successor and counterpart, Ecclesia. The denunciatory tones of the older prophets came easily to the tongues of modern reformers and preachers. Astrologers and necromancers, though officially condemned by the Church, were widely consulted even by members of the higher clergy, and the line was thin that divided the legitimate use of foreknowledge granted by God and the wicked delving into forbidden regions. Men and women of every degree expected prophets to rise among them and to give them guidance; they looked for portents and they found them.

It was a matter not only of simple people being taken in by uneducated soothsayers—like the credulous townfolk of Parma who followed the prophesying cobbler Asdente, placed by Dante in Hell[11]—but of hard-headed rulers, clerics, politicians, and businessmen who sought out sages with insight into the future and into the hidden meaning of current events. Those they consulted were frequently of unimpeachable reputation and of great intellectual attainment. Thus Barbarossa consulted the Rhineland prophetess Hildegard of Bingen,[12] and Richard the Lionheart had the Calabrian abbot Joachim of Fiore brought to him at Messina on his way to the Holy Land.[13] When the Ghibelline cardinal Ottaviano degli Ubaldini rejoiced in the presence of the pope at the victory of Montaperti, one of his brother cardinals, gifted with prophetic foresight, demurred. Though unwilling to say more, he was forced at the pope's command to voice his foreknowledge of how the defeated Guelphs would be victorious and would never be conquered again.[14] Though Michael Scot's reputation as a wizard extended from the Scottish Borders to Sicily, and he was Frederick II's astrologer, he was also one of the greatest intellects of his period, the translator of Aristotle and Arabic works and a participator in Frederick's scientific interests. In 1289 when the priors of Florence had gone to sleep after

45

waiting anxiously for news of the Campaldino expedition against Arezzo, they were awoken, long before any message could have come from the field, by a banging on the door and a voice crying out that their enemies were defeated,[15] and no trace could be found of the utterer of these words. Boniface VIII patronized and sheltered the Catalan physician Arnold of Villanova, who made him wear an astrological talisman as part of his cure for the stone and who was the author of numerous prophetic writings.[16] In the midst of the turmoil brought about by Charles of Valois, Boniface's envoy to Florence in 1301, the chronicler Dino Compagni—and others—saw a bright red cross appear in the sky above the Palazzo della Signoria, a sight they not surprisingly interpreted as a sign of divine vengeance on Florence.[17] Dante makes mention of this apparition in the *Convivio*.[18] There were myths current of a mysterious redeemer who would arise in the East, the priest-emperor Prester John, and those myths seemed likely to be realized in fact when the Mongols in the mid-thirteenth century put an end to the caliphate at Baghdad and came close to destroying Islamic civilization. Some have seen in this myth the origin of Dante's great prophetic enigma, the *veltro* or hound who is born between *feltro* and *feltro*, 'felt' and 'felt', as the Mongol khans were consecrated at their inaugurations upon felt.[19] The very name *veltro* may conceal a hidden pun upon *cane*, 'dog', and khan.

Perhaps the most influential of all these prophets was Joachim of Fiore (*c.* 1135–1202), a man so modest that he refused the designation of prophet,[20] regarding his insight into scripture as his special God-granted gift. On his death he submitted his writings to the judgment of the Church, and though his teaching on the Trinity was condemned by the Lateran Council in 1215 in a judgment that specifically excluded him personally from blame, his writings had a profound influence; Dante was echoing widely held opinions in calling him in the *Paradiso*

il calavrese abate Giovacchino
di spirito profetico dotato.[21]

Joachim the Calabrian abbot, great
In gift, through whom the spirit
prophesied.

Joachim received certain remarkable visionary inspirations (mentioned more fully on p. 9 and p. 298) which he interpreted according to his numerological studies of the Bible. Among these inspirations was a vision of the Trinity expressing threeness in oneness through interlaced circles—his expression of this image almost certainly influenced Dante's description of his own vision of the Trinity, the fundamental inspiration of the *Commedia* (see p. 153). Joachim, in interpreting his visions, realized that the history of mankind took on a new comprehensive and unified pattern if seen as the work of God the Father and of God the Son, with, proceeding from them, the work of God the Holy Spirit. Thus history has two strands, the Status of the Father, from Creation to the first Advent, and the Status of the Son, from the

Incarnation to the second coming, each coexisting in time, with the Status of the Holy Spirit brooding over each. The first Status was under the law and was the time of *scientia*, the second Status was under grace and was the time of *sapientia*, and the third Status, which was to be the fulfilment of history, was the realized condition of the fullness of understanding and of liberty. In this third Status, which he expected shortly to dawn and which would be announced by the founding of two great religious orders and the appearance of Antichrist, the Latin Church would be transformed from the active Church into the contemplative Church.[22] These powerful ideas were soon to be interpreted, without Joachim's subtlety of approach, into a succession of three Ages in which the spiritual and psychological revolution he anticipated was substituted by radical political and social upheavals.

Much of Joachim's prestige derived from the widely held belief that he predicted the coming of St Francis and St Dominic as forerunners of the Status of the Holy Ghost. Dante conveys the rise and flowering of the two great mendicant orders in a set of sun symbols, drawing on astronomy, the parables, and heraldry. In Cantos XI and XII of the *Paradiso*, St Thomas Aquinas as a Dominican sings the eulogy of St Francis; and St Bonaventure as a Franciscan praises the life of St Dominic.

Through the mouth of Aquinas, Dante begins St Francis's life with an image he uses throughout the *Commedia*, the equivalence of a man's life with a river on its way to the sea:

Intra Tupino e l'acqua che discende
   del colle eletto dal beato Ubaldo,
   fertile costa d'alto monte pende,
onde Perugia sente freddo e caldo
   da Porta Sole; e di rietro le piange
   per grave giogo Nocera con Gualdo.
Di questa costa, là dov' ella frange
   più sua rattezza, nacque al mondo un
     sole,
   come fa questo talvolta di Gange.[23]

Between Tupino and the dropping rill,
   Blessed Ubaldo's chosen mountain-
     nook,
   A fertile slope hangs from a lofty hill,
Whence cold and heat come to Perugia's
   folk
   Through Porta Sole, and behind it
     weep
   Nocera and Gualdo for the oppressor's
     yoke.
From this slope, where it breaketh most
   the steep,
   A sun was born into the world, as
     this
   Is seen somewhiles from Ganges to
     upleap.

He then proceeds throughout the rest of the description to metamorphose his images. Francis is the sun who rises from this slope. Earth is strengthened by his love for the lady Poverty, who lost her first husband Christ and had remained despised for over a thousand years. The intensity of their love draws Francis's first followers running barefoot after them. Innocent puts his seal on the order

47

and Honorius encircles Francis with a second crown. After the rejection of his mission by the sultan, he returns to the harvest of Italy where

nel crudo sasso intra Tevero e Arno
   da Cristo prese l'ultimo sigillo,
   che le sue membra due anni
      portarno.[24]
	On the rough rock 'twixt Tiber and
	   Arno shore
	He took that final imprint of the rood
	From Christ, which for two years
	   his body bore.

Finally Francis dies after commending his love to his followers as he lies naked on the ground.

The theme throughout this passage is the love for the lady Poverty. Francis is the troubadour, the lover; there is no mention of the miracles he performed, the masses he converted, the lives he transformed, and in this form of history through poetry there is no need. Everything is contained and compressed into the image of the lovers: all the miracles were but the consequences of his love.

St Dominic is praised by St Bonaventure in complementary terms:

In quella parte ove surge ad aprire
   Zefiro dolce le novelle fronde
   di che si vede Europa rivestire,
non molto lungi al percuoter de l'onde
   dietro a le quali, per la lunga foga,
   lo sol talvolta ad ogne uom si
      nasconde,
siede la fortunata Calaroga
   sotto la protezion del grande scudo
   in che soggiace il leone e soggioga:[25]
	In that land where the sweet west wind
	   is stirred
	   To open the fresh foliage to the light,
	   And therewith Europe shows her re-
	      attired,
	Not far from where the waves of
	   ocean smite
	   Behind which, when his weary
	   course he quits,
	The sun at times hideth from
	   all men's sight,
	The fortune-favoured Calaroga sits
	   With the great shield protecting
	   her repose
	Whereon the lion, who
	   subdues, submits.

If St Francis's life begins with a waterfall and is transformed to the sun in the east, St Dominic starts as the new breath of the Spirit and is changed to the sun in the west. There follows the superb heraldic image of Calaroga (more properly Calahorra) sheltered under the arms of Leon and Castile which quarter lions and castles. A similar rapid alternation of images follows. Dominic is *amoroso drudo*, loving vassal, *sante atleta*, holy athlete. His mother becomes a prophetess with the force of his mind in the womb. His baptism is a wedding between himself and the faith. He is the labourer chosen by Christ to help in the garden and again the messenger of Christ's household. After these and many other metamorphoses he is 'quasi torrente ch'alta vene preme' and this torrent strikes on the heretic thickets with greatest force where the resistance is most stubborn.

48

Thence spring from him the various brooks watering the Catholic garden and giving its young trees refreshment. Thus the image of water with which the praise of St Francis began returns again to bring to a close the celebration of St Dominic.

Dante concentrates on the emotional fervour and inner strength of these two great saints, leaving aside the political and social effects of their movements. These, however, were considerable. They affected Italy at a time of great social and economic change, of migration to the cities and of increasing wealth. Many looked on the prospect of wealth opening up before them and turned aside in a kind of abhorrence to sects and orders that repudiated riches. The doctrine of apostolic poverty, in the practice and ideal of St Francis, was an inner poverty of the spirit of which the deprivations and the simplicity of his life were the outward sign. Similarly his visionary inspirations were to Joachim of Fiore the intimations of great spiritual changes.

Once interpreted politically and socially as it was by a large party of the Franciscans, the doctrine of apostolic poverty became the slogan of a radical revolutionary movement, causing great divisions among the Franciscans themselves and struggle and condemnation outside the order. This party seized upon Joachim's works and sought for confirmation of his prophecies in the state of politics about them. Thus the emperor Frederick II was widely regarded as the Antichrist whose imminent coming had been foretold by Joachim, and friars played a great part in rousing the populace of the communes against the Hohenstaufen interest in the cause of Pope Innocent IV. The chronicler Fra Salimbene of Parma was deeply disappointed when Frederick II, by dying too early, proved himself not to be Antichrist.[26] Even more extreme use was made of Joachim's writings by the friar Gerardo di Borgo San Donnino who compiled from them a new gospel, the Eternal Evangel, which he said was to replace the existing canonical Gospels. The new Age of the Holy Ghost he and his followers expected would dawn in the year 1260 and, though his movement was widely discredited by the all too obvious failure of the prophecy, the Spiritual Franciscans still attracted many more reputable and distinguished figures, two of whom, Petrus Olivi and Ubertino da Casale, are discussed in relation to Dante in Chapter 6. Their opponents, the Conventuals, maintained the necessity of possessions and convent houses if they were to found their orthodoxy upon study and settled reflection.

Orthodoxy was the standard under which many friars of both orders led heresy hunts. The Dominicans were prominent in the terrible slaughters of the Albigensian Crusade and Franciscans developed the power of the Inquisition. The Dominican Peter Martyr used to lead gangs of bullies in forays to beat up heretics and, not, surprisingly, was murdered by some of his intended victims. He became a patron of the Guelph cause because one of the easiest ways in which the Ghibellines by their opposition to the papacy laid themselves open to attack was in the matter of heresy—with some reason going by the reputations of Frederick II and Farinata degli Uberti.

The desire to maintain orthodoxy inspired also a far nobler movement. The mendicants became predominant in the universities through the intellectual weight of such great thinkers as Albertus Magnus, Aquinas, and Bonaventure. They determined to press all the new knowledge made available through the new translations of Aristotle, and Islamic and Jewish philosophers, into the service of faith. They believed that they lived in an age of new possibilities of knowledge and they laboured over vast compendia of information, encyclopaedias that would mirror the Divine Will in creation, and *summae*, elaborate, systematic theological treatises in which thought could be refined to the level of the thought of Christ Himself. In their zeal for the faith and their utmost confidence in their new intellectual tools, they made the human soul the subject of investigation, reviving the psychological terms and ideas of Aristotelian philosophy in ways that soon influenced, for instance, the medical profession and the lay culture of Dante's Florence. Every work of Dante's reflects the influence of these scholastic philosophers—many of the most distinguished of whom were members of the mendicant orders—in language, modes of thought, and ideas.

Prophecy was one of the subjects to which the scholastics applied their critical and analytical skills; Aquinas, for example, devoted many fascinating pages to prophecy, evaluating the thoughts of earlier writers on the topic and defining the degrees and types of prophetic revelation. Prophecy is a form of inspiration and Dante employed the categories of prophecy to delineate the levels of inspiration from which he wrote. Treating the characters appearing in his creative imagination as prophetic insights, he introduced a new kind of poetic history—history seen as the drama of the individual. In doing so he transformed the future possibilities of European literature by reviving the ancient and classical presentation of the individual as a unity of body and soul. By revitalizing the technique of the dramatic monologue in which a character creates himself out of his own words, he laid the foundations of Western drama. As Erich Auerbach says,

> he was the first to configure what antiquity had configured very
> differently and the Middle Ages not at all: man not as a remote
> legendary hero, not as an abstract or anecdotal representation of an
> ethical type but man as we know him in historical reality, the concrete
> individual in his unity and wholeness.[27]

No Western writer had dared to take historical characters, many of whom would be vivid in the memories of contemporary readers, and fit them into a literary work. Chrétien de Troyes and Wolfram von Eschenbach, great inventors of character and masters of psychological interpretations that they were, worked upon mythical themes and situations and so, such was the distance in time separating them from their subjects, did the anonymous writers of the *Chanson de Roland* and the Orange cycles. Dante takes real people involved in recent events and makes them reveal themselves at the tragic point when their fates, their characters, and their environment form the unity by which they are judged and appointed their places in the hereafter. This is original not only in relation to earlier secular literature but also in relation to the previous journeys to the Other World, whether Irish, Islamic, or Italian. In these the reader is presented either with a stock figure whose character he is meant to fill in from his own knowledge, or else with humanity divided simply into the good and the bad, as though by the feet of Christ in majesty over the doors of Romanesque cathedrals.

The unity of Dante's characters owes much to his skill in visualizing them in surroundings that convey the mood of their particular qualities; in this he was heir to one of the greatest achievements of the sculptors of the Gothic cathedrals: the new realism, the new understanding of human character, and the new tactile grace they brought to the figures of the prophets of the Old Testament and the saints of the New which they arranged in figural patterns. This new capacity for precision and detail in individual portraiture, which appears for the first time in the extraordinary figures of the west portal at Chartres of about 1150, derives from an appreciation of the history and nature of a man that can be learned from his face in repose, executed with an accuracy unprecedented since the times of the Roman portrait busts. From the labours of these sculptors in bringing living likenesses to the prophets and the saints of scripture grew first the realization that the recently dead could be rendered more realistically in funeral effigies, and then that the living themselves could be so represented. Italy possessed great reserves of classical sculpture to act as a further spur, and in the course of the thirteenth century one can trace the development of a tendency to precise individual portraiture.

The fragmented bust of Frederick II from the Capua gate provides one instance and, by the end of the century, Arnolfo da Cambio's figure of Charles of Anjou and the series of statues of himself commissioned by Boniface VIII prove that a new era in precise and individual portraiture had arrived. Allied to this movement is the great revolution in sculpture achieved by Giovanni Pisano, not only in his tomb sculpture but also in his series of apostles and prophets, where he must frequently have made use of actual models or else drawn composite memories of close observation to create physiognomies that perfectly expressed the characters of the men he had to represent. The contemporary and related revolution in painting brought about by the various talents of Cimabue, Giotto, and Duccio, in which men and women are presented as individuals in the round, set in landscapes, rooms, or cities as three-dimensional as themselves, offer a counterpart to Dante's achievement in his depiction of his characters. Here, especially with regard to painting, one cannot underestimate the Franciscan influence since, almost from the time of the saint's death in 1226, there was an attempt to preserve an exact record of his features; from this there developed the great series of paintings in the upper church at Assisi containing historical figures recognizable as individual actors in the drama surrounding the saint. Similarly, from the solemn archetypal Virgins of his predecessors, such as the *Madonna of the Great Eyes*, Duccio could move to the human tenderness of the Mother of God in his *Maestà*.

Influenced by the lady of the Sicilian poets, unnamed except as the Flower or the Rose of Syria, Guinizzelli and his followers could find the same wonderful manifestation of Divine Wisdom in individual women whom they could name as Lucia, Giovanna, Beatrice, or Selvaggia. It was one of the great benefits of the growth of a vernacular literature, in which both fiction and chronicle could be told, that the barrier between experience and description erected by the use of Latin could be torn down and a new precision was brought to the creation and depiction of an individual's quirks and quiddities. Paradoxically, the same movement can be seen in Latin because the creation of a new Latin style, made necessary by the translation of Aristotle in which words were deliberately freed of association to make the first scientific language, allowed full expression to the great thirteenth-century debates on the immortality of the soul between St Thomas and the Averroists. The question of immortality necessarily involves the individuality of the man who possesses the soul in question. The new ability to body forth the visible world derived from a deeper appreciation of the invisible worlds, worlds invisible because they are hidden in the depths of our natures and as distinct as—to make an analogy of a building finished in Dante's lifetime and built to celebrate the man who most of all made possible this new sense of the worth of the individual—the three levels of the Basilica of San Francesco at Assisi. The lowest and most still level is the crypt, where the saint's body was hidden in a pillar surrounded by a candle-lit chamber of plain stone. Here Francis has returned to the stony earth from which he was formed and the walls of the crypt, in fact, extend out not only to the most massive part of the whole building, the fortress walls of the convent, but also down to the mountainside on which the building rides like a battleship. Here he is 'as flowers that in their causes sleep'. Above the crypt is the lower church, a mysterious place with light looming from side chapels, a dark mirror of dreams dominated by the archetypes of faith that give order to our psychologies. Above it is the light, tall upper church, whose decoration celebrates life in the world made perfect in man rising from the inner illumination of the crypt and the ordering of his psychology in the lower church, through the examples of Christ in the crossing and of Francis in the nave. Perfection is attainable and the walls depict a new sensibility between men as individuals, to creation in brutes and birds and inanimate nature—a sensibility that is the achievement in history of one man's awakening through love his sleeping possibilities.

4

Dante's family and the history of Florence in the later thirteenth century

Of the outstanding individuals of the high Middle Ages who have bequeathed a vivid impression to our day, the one we recognize most immediately is Dante himself. The sight of his aquiline profile, whether in a Botticelli drawing or used on a label to give a bottle of wine the distinction it lacks in all other ways, instantly evokes his name and its associations. The force of this visual impression derives partly from the need of all illustrators of the *Commedia* from its first publication to portray him because he never leaves the scene of the poem.[1] That is, in itself, a result of the autobiographical character of his writings and of the way he makes his readers intimate with the deepest recesses of his nature, a nature that is one of the most remarkable in history.

We cannot conjecture why so imposing a personality emerged from Dante's particular family background, because our information about his parents and his antecedents is so meagre. From his conversation with his ancestor Cacciaguida in *Paradiso* XV we gather that Dante believed that he was descended through Cacciaguida from the Elisei, one of the Roman families who reputedly founded Florence. Cacciaguida married a lady from the valley of the Po, probably from Ferrara, whose family was Alighieri (it has numerous other spellings), and this name was adopted by their descendants. Numerous documents survive which contain references to members of his family but they are legal or business papers with no flicker of personal character.[2] His father Alighiero may have been a notary and was certainly a money-lender, doing well enough out of his transactions to buy property in the city and in the *contado*, the income from which supported Dante without the necessity of his practising a profession up to the time of his exile. After Montaperti the leaders of the Guelph party and their families were exiled; none of the Alighieri are mentioned in the lists of the proscribed though a great-uncle later received damages for the looting of his property by Ghibellines.

From this the comparative lack of significance of the family has been deduced. Apart from what is said of her in the next chapter, almost nothing is known of his mother. She was called Bella, and it has been suggested that she was connected with the Abati family and was the daughter of Durante di Scolaro degli Abati. The exact date of Dante's birth is not known but it took place in May 1265.[3] The traditional day for celebrating his birthday is 14 May (old style) which would make it 25 May. It was certainly at that season of the year because he states that he was born under the sign of Gemini, through whose segment of the zodiac he enters the Primum Mobile in *Paradiso* XXII, and in the *Vita Nuova* he says that he was almost nine on 1 May 1274, the day he met Beatrice. On his mother's death, his father, when Dante was five or six, married a lady called Lapa di Chiarissimo Cialuffi, by whom he had a son and perhaps two daughters. Dante's half-brother was called Francesco. The Alighieri family arms consisted of a shield divided perpendicularly into gold and black and crossed horizontally by a band or fesse of silver,[4] a simple device into whose three elements it is tempting to read one of the earliest influences of the number three on the child's mind.

He was brought up in the ward of the city known as the *sesto* of San Piero (Florence was at that time divided into sixths or *sestieri*). Although his family were of no particular account in city life, they lived in this district surrounded by the houses and towers of many very important families, and they were related to several of them. The Alighieri had two houses near the church of San Martino Vescovo. Neither has survived: the house now shown as Dante's is a reconstruction of the last century. A little to the north at a crossroads on the Corso, there lived on one corner the powerful Donati family who provided Dante with his great friend, Forese Donati, and his great enemy, Corso Donati, and at the other corner the banker Folco Portinari, the father of Beatrice. Nearby was the house of Giano della Bella, the political leader who was to crush his own class, the nobility, as a power with his Ordinances of Justice in 1293. Coming south, next door to the Alighieri house was that of Geri del Bello, Dante's cousin, who was to be murdered by the nearby Sacchetti family and placed by Dante in *Inferno* XXIX among the sowers of discord. A branch of the Donati had another house close at hand where lived Gemma, daughter of Manetto Donati, who was betrothed to Dante when he was twelve. The alignments of party, both outside and within the city, were further complicated by patterns of relationship and intermarriage and by family feuds. Every family group was deeply conscious of its honour and of the shame that might accrue to it by not avenging insult or murder. Vendettas in both noble and merchant families could be pursued from generation to generation, often with much the same cold calculation that the merchants devoted to their business interests.[5] Dante depicts Geri del Bello as avoiding him in Hell as though in reproach for the failure of his relations to avenge him against the Sacchetti, and the feud between the families was only ended in 1342 when Dante's half-brother Francesco was a guarantor in the settlement with the Sacchetti. Old and young lived closely together and, if not in and out of one another's houses, then jostling constantly in the street where knowledge of what every family was up to was quickly exchanged. Dante was an exceptionally sensitive and observant boy, taking in all the quirks of character, good and bad, that abounded so richly in the dense population of the *sesto*. Members of these families appear in the *Commedia* mingling on an equal footing with emperors, saints, classical heroes, and famous whores as befits their republican upbringing. The naturalness with which it is done must owe much to Dante's childhood experience; to him as a child they were far more immediately important than distant kings and popes, and in his eyes they had the same standing.

The city at the time of Dante's birth in 1265 was under the government of the Ghibelline party with Count Guido Novello, the brother-in-law of King Manfred, at its head. Large numbers of Guelph exiles intrigued and fought elsewhere, attempting to make a power base for their return. Their despair was turned to triumph by the success of Charles of Anjou, brother of the king of France, Louis IX, in conquering Southern Italy and Sicily and bringing Manfred's rule to an end. The long-lasting alliance following Charles's victory between the papacy, the Angevin kingdom of Naples he founded, and the Guelphs of Florence was the most powerful factor in determining the events of Dante's life. It arose in the following way.

It was with Manfred's help, as we have seen, that the Sienese and the Florentine Ghibelline exiles triumphed at Montaperti in 1260 when, quite unwittingly, Manfred found himself the master of all Tuscany except for Lucca. He also found himself in possession of Rome and most of the papal states. Once more the papacy was trapped. On Alexander IV's death in 1261, a French pope, Urban IV, revived the anti-Hohenstaufen policy with renewed vigour. He chose his own candidate to replace Manfred as king, Charles of Anjou, who had already been made senator of Rome. Italy had long suffered from the insensitivity of foreigners, largely the Germans; henceforth it was the French who assumed the dominant role as invaders and interferers. Urban found a powerful weapon to bring the bankers of Siena and Florence to heel; he forbade their debtors to repay them. As their cities were firmly Ghibelline at the time, many bankers had to seek exile and papal protection, but still the money was raised for the enterprise which was as much a vast investment as a military campaign and one that, in the event, paid off very well. When Urban died in 1264 preparations for the conquest had begun and these were helped by the election of another Frenchman, Clement IV, as pope. Charles came to Rome, was crowned, withstood attacks on the city, and early in 1266 advanced into Manfred's kingdom over a bridge on the river Verde or Liri. This bridge was neither defended nor destroyed and Dante hints at treachery[6] as the reason. Charles's army consisted of Provençal, Languedoc, and Northern French soldiers with a large body of Guelph horsemen under Count Guido Guerra, then in exile from Florence as a result of Montaperti. The numerous castles guarding the approach to Naples, in which Manfred had trusted, fell easily to Charles, and so Manfred felt himself forced to come out and offer battle. With his German and Lombard mercenaries, his Saracen archers, and the followings of his barons, he grouped at Benevento by the river Calore. On 26 February

1266 the two armies met. An attack by the Saracens was driven off by Provençal horsemen; then the German cavalry, many of whom were the victors of Montaperti, charged the French. The French noticed that their armpits were unprotected by their otherwise impenetrable plate armour and went for them there with their short daggers, which were more effective in the mêlée than the long swords of the Germans. Manfred's cavalry reserve came up too late to support the Germans, and the barons of the kingdom, suddenly judging the day was lost, retreated, leaving Manfred alone on the battlefield with his bodyguard. Manfred exchanged his royal surcoat with a friend and plunged into the fighting where, unrecognized by his assailants, he died. A frightful slaughter of the fugitives, blocked from escape by a narrow bridge and the flood waters of the river, took place. By the evening Charles had won the battle and the kingdom.

Two days later a man led a donkey carrying a corpse through the camp shouting, 'Who wants to bury Manfred?' Charles made three captured nobles identify the body and one of them, Giordano Lancia, who should have kept that bridge on the Liri, covered his face saying, 'Alas, alas, my lord!' Some French knights begged Charles to give this brave enemy an honourable burial. Charles could not agree to a religious ceremony because Manfred had died excommunicate, and so a pit was dug for the dead king's body by the bridge at Benevento. Every soldier of the Angevin army passed by and threw a stone into it so that a high cairn was made. Even this was too great an honour in the eyes of the pope for such an enemy of the Church and, on his orders, the archbishop of Cosenza had the body dug up and reburied outside the borders of the kingdom. Dante did not agree with this judgment of the Church, and in the Ante-Purgatory he is addressed by a soul who asks if he had ever seen him in life:

E un di loro incominciò: 'Chiunque
   tu se', così andando, volgi 'l viso:
   pon mente se di là mi vedesti unque.'
Io mi volsi ver' lui e guardail fiso:
   biondo era e bello e di gentile aspetto,
   ma l'un de' cigli un colpo avea diviso.
Quand' io mi fui umilmente disdetto
   d'averlo visto mai, el disse: 'Or vedi';
   e mostrommi una piaga a sommo 'l
     petto.
Poi sorridendo disse: 'Io son Manfredi,
   nepote di Costanza imperadrice:...'[7]

And one of them began: 'Whoe'er
   thou be,
Turn thy face, as thou goest thus
   beyond:
Consider if ever on earth thou sawest
   me.'
I turned and fixedly looked on him: blond
   He was, and beautiful, of noble mien;
But one eye-brow was cleft by a great
   wound.
I disclaimed humbly ever to have seen
   His person; then 'Look on my breast,'
   he said,
And showed me, above, a scar upon
   the skin.
Smiling he spoke: 'Manfred am I,
   Manfred,
   The grandson of Constantia, the
     Empress;...'

Manfred then begs Dante to tell his daughter, the queen of Aragon, how he died and how, though his sins were horrible, the infinite Goodness had opened its arms to him when he repented at the point of death. Then he speaks of the fate of his body after the battle.

Se 'l pastor di Cosenza, che a la caccia
    di me fu messo per Clemente allora,
    avesse in Dio ben letta questa faccia,
l'ossa del corpo mio sariano ancora
    in co del ponte presso a Benevento,
    sotto la guardia de la grave mora.
Or le bagna la pioggia e move il vento
    di fuor dal regno, quasi lungo 'l Verde,
    dov' e' le trasmutò a lume spento.[8]

And if Cosenza's pastor, who in chase
    Of me was sent by Clement, had but once
    Read well in God the rubric of his grace,
Still at the bridge-head would my body's bones
    Be found near Benevento, as at first,
    Under the guard of the heaped, heavy stones.
Now by the rains they are washed, by winds dispersed
    Forth of the Kingdom, beside Verde tost,
    Whither he had borne them with quenched lights, accurst.

Charles took possession of his conquest. Manfred's wife and children were imprisoned, his sons for life. Otherwise Charles was remarkably lenient though his unattractive legalistic character won him few friends in his new realm and his efficient tax-gatherers provoked resentment and hatred. His authority, though, was great and was soon extended further north. The Ghibelline rulers of Florence, on hearing the news of Benevento, tried to make up to the pope, who nominated two Bolognese as joint rulers of the city. These were the Frati Godenti whom Dante meets among the hypocrites in Hell.[9] They were not liked, and a popular uprising seized power, soon to be followed by the entry of the Guelphs aided by French cavalry in 1267. Four thousand Ghibellines fled and they were never to hold Florence again.

Elsewhere there was still a strong Ghibelline movement and it found a head in the last legitimate Hohenstaufen, the young Conradin, Frederick II's grandson, who had been brought up in Germany. Evading his family's attempts to restrain him, with his friend Frederick of Baden and a small army, he came down through the Brenner Pass and reached the Ghibelline city of Verona in October 1267. There he remained till early in 1268, attracting supporters and winning over the Castilian prince, the Infant Henry, who had become senator of Rome in succession to Charles of Anjou. He then went to Pisa by sea and, joined by his army, he moved down towards Rome. At Rome the handsome sixteen-year-old boy was greeted with feasting and scenes of wild enthusiasm. In mid-August he moved his army south to claim his ancestral rights. Charles was forced to raise the siege of the town and fortress of Lucera, where Manfred's Saracens still defied him, and he marched up to meet the invader. The armies met five miles from Tagliacozzo. On the advice of a veteran Crusader, Erard de Valéry,[10] Charles kept a thousand of his best cavalry hidden in reserve and he remained with them. The Ghibelline army attacked the visible Angevin forces with great ferocity and entirely defeated them. The Infant Henry who led this attack pursued the fugitives and, when Conradin with the Ghibelline reserve came to the battlefield, it seemed as though he had won a total victory. Then on Erard's advice, when only a small group was left, the Angevins attacked and forced Conradin and Frederick to flee. When the Infant Henry returned, he found the battlefield in the enemy's possession. His men and horses were too exhausted to win it back again and once more Charles had gained an astonishing victory which he consolidated by having Conradin and Frederick put on trial, sentenced to death and publicly decapitated in Naples.

The increasing French involvement with Italy, beginning with the entry of Charles of Anjou as the champion of the papacy, was to end in Dante's lifetime with the French monarchy stripping the papacy of all its pretensions and reducing it on occasions to the status of an appanage of the French Crown. French cultural influence in Italy had already been strong for many years; indeed it might be said that if the empire had political sovereignty over Italy, the French had sovereignty where manners, fashion, and civilization were concerned. The songs of Southern and the stories of Northern France were popular throughout all classes in the cities; travelling bands of joglars would regularly come from France and attract audiences. Italian bankers and merchants either travelling to France or else settled there in business houses maintained the lines of communication. The *langue d'oïl* was regarded as an international language—to the extent that Brunetto Latini, the Florentine politician and friend of Dante, wrote his chief work, *Li Livres dou Tresor*, in French rather than in Italian of which he was an early master. Paolo and Francesca were reading the romance of Lancelot in French when their passion seized them and they kissed. The intellectual influence of the university of Paris was also an attraction, drawing there the best intellects of the Church including Thomas Aquinas from Naples and Bonaventure from Bagnoreggio. France's social and political influence was also immense; social, because it was in France that *la chevalerie*, the culture of the knight, originated and the French were still the arbiters of chivalry. The curious mixed society of the communes, however much its burghers disliked the nobles in their streets or in the *contado*, regarded chivalry as something different, a necessary element of style and excitement in life. French political influence derived from the sudden expansion of Capetian power under Louis IX's immediate predecessors and the extent to which Louis himself had increased and pacified their gains, bringing France to a point where it was more unified than it had ever been since the death of Charlemagne. Much of his prestige came from the fact that he had shouldered the responsibility of leading the crusading movement, something the French with considerable justice always regarded as a mission peculiarly their own.

The chief link between the young Dante and the culture and the new influence of France would have been Brunetto Latini who, according to Lionardo Bruni, took notice of Dante's exceptional abilities when Dante was still a boy.[11] The debt Dante owed to Brunetto he repaid in the strangest way. In the seventh circle of Hell, Dante and Virgil find themselves walking along a dyke dividing a stream from a plain of burning sand. The sand is burning because fire, acting against its nature, rains down on the plain and in doing so it raises a cloud of steam from the water. This is the place of punishment for the violent against nature, among them the homosexuals. A band of naked men come running by, squinnying at them like passers-by in twilight when a new moon has risen, and one of them catches hold of Dante and exclaims, 'Qual maraviglia!' Even though the speaker's face is cooked by the fires, Dante immediately recognizes his old friend and instructor, Brunetto Latini. Brunetto cannot stop because the penalty for halting is to lie a hundred years upon the sand and so, as they converse, they have to keep moving. He inquires how Dante has come there and goes on to warn him of the bad blood in Florence that will be inimical to him for the good he will do. Dante pays little attention to the warning but bursts out in gratitude to Brunetto, telling him that his dear and good paternal image has been fixed in his mind from the time when, hour by hour, Brunetto taught him how man eternalizes himself. He speaks proudly of how equal he feels to any future blows of fortune and here Virgil breaks in to warn him to pay attention. Brunetto then describes some of his companions, but at the sight of the sand kicked up by a band with whom he may not mix he takes his leave, entrusting to Dante his chief work, the *Tresor* 'in which I still live; and more I do not ask'.

Poi si rivolse e parve di coloro
    che corrono a Verona il drappo verde
    per la campagna; e parve di costoro
quelli che vince, non colui che perde.[12]

He turned, and seemed like, in the
    field before
Verona, one of those who run the race
For the green cloth; so seemed he
    running, nor
Seemed in the loser's but the winner's
    place.

The simile is with a race run by naked athletes competing for a prize of cloth at Verona on the first Sunday in Lent to celebrate a victory.

What was Brunetto's relationship to Dante? Some have seen in him a teacher and others an older and deeply experienced friend from whose conversation Dante learned and benefited. Though in his own writings Brunetto specifically condemns homosexuality, the vice for which he is punished in Hell, we can only presume either that Dante knew for certain of this side of his character or that it was an insight into his master's nature that accompanied the inspiration in which Brunetto appeared as a personage for the *Commedia*.[13]

Brunetto was recognized as a citizen exceptional for his learning and his eloquence; Villani says that, though he was a worldly man, he was the instigator and master in civilizing the Florentines, making them expert in speaking well, in acquiring judgment, and in ruling the republic according to policy.[14] He was also the author of the encyclopaedia in French, *Li Livres dou Tresor*, two poems in Tuscan, the *Tesoretto*, and the *Favolello*, and of translations from Cicero.

This gifted, charming, and able man was born in 1220 and died in 1294. He was trained as a notary and thus was an early example of the new educated class of officials and politicians who played a vital role in democratizing the communes in the thirteenth century. He first appears in 1254 in Florentine documents as magistrate of the Guelph party and notary to the *Anziani*, the rulers of Florence from 1250 to 1260 during the period of the *vecchio popolo*. The supreme crisis of his life came when he was sent on an embassy to Alfonso X of Castile and on his return he met a scholar from Bologna riding a mule through the pass of Roncesvalles. As he describes in the *Tesoretto*:

> I asked him as politely as I could to give me news of Tuscany, and he courteously replied without delay that the Guelphs through evil providence and force of war were driven from the city and that the losses were great in imprisonments and death.[15]

Thus Brunetto learned of the disaster of Montaperti and knew he had no home to return to. He spent six years of exile in France, probably supported by a rich Florentine Guelph for whom he wrote his *Tresor*, a work that was to be considered a classic by the French for the next two centuries. Charles of Anjou's victory at Benevento in 1266 gave him the opportunity to return and in 1267 he was at the siege of Poggibonsi negotiating with the republic the terms for making Charles vicar of Tuscany. Returning to Florence he continued to hold important offices, becoming secretary of the councils and of the chancery of the republic. This almost continual involvement in political life explains the practical bent of his writings, particularly in the *Tresor* where he devotes much space to the actual problems of government. Most of the fourth book consists of instructions to the rulers of a city. The encyclopaedic nature of the work illustrates an immediate connexion with Dante's own writing and so does a feature noted by Brunetto's most recent biographer, the way in which the author's personality is present and affirmed in the work and is not lost in it.[16]

The full triumph of the popular movement to which Brunetto belonged, announced abortively by the popular uprising of 1266, was delayed for many years by the hold Charles of Anjou and the Guelph party kept over Florence. Charles was appointed vicar-general of Tuscany in the name of the pope and thus was the overlord of Florence. The Guelph party, led largely by nobles, became rich through the sequestration of the property of the Ghibellines and repressed the popular movement. Then in 1271 a new pope, Gregory X, was elected. Alarmed at the dominant position Charles had won in Italy, he sought more independent lines of action that would free the papacy from its too powerful friend.

Gregory had been archbishop of Tyre and his dearest ambition was to organize a Crusade that would finally rescue Jerusalem from Islam. To fulfil this end, he had to pacify the differences between the parties and rival cities of Italy and so he came to Florence with Charles of Anjou, and the claimant to the Latin empire of the East, Baldwin XII, in June 1272, when Dante was seven, with the object of reconciling the ruling Guelphs and the exiled Ghibellines. Dante must have watched these great personages, noting particularly the large bulbous nose of Charles of Anjou by which he later identified him in the *Purgatorio*.[17] A public ceremony took place on a platform erected on piles in the bed of the Arno by the Rubaconte bridge. The populace lined the banks of the river and watched the representatives of each side give the kiss of peace and exchange hostages. That evening all the hopes and efforts of the pope were undone by Charles of Anjou who, unable to restrain the Guelphs' desire for vengeance, sent a message to the Ghibellines telling them they would all be murdered by the Guelphs if they spent another day in Florence. They left as soon as possible, and so did the pope who, furious at the treachery, placed an interdict upon the city, a sentence that lasted until Gregory's death in 1276.

Florence was too important to the papacy to be abandoned to its own devices. Pope Nicholas III (1277–80) of the Orsini family of Rome was even more actively opposed to Charles of Anjou and, as part of his plans to establish an equilibrium of power in Italy, favourable to the papacy, sent his nephew, the able and eloquent Cardinal Latino, to Florence in 1279 to pacify the city and reconcile the Guelphs and Ghibellines. He stayed there until April 1280. Here too the young Dante would have seen the great open-air assemblies at which, under the cardinal's command, the guarantors of the peace from the exiled Ghibelline families and from the ruling Guelphs swore solemnly to keep the treaties laid down and kissed each other on the mouth to seal their promises. The young nobleman and poet, Guido Cavalcanti, soon to be Dante's friend, was one of the Guelph guarantors, and Dante's master, Brunetto Latini, was another. The constitution Cardinal Latino set up was too frail to survive the death of his uncle in the same year and in two years' time there occurred the revolution in which the leaders of the 'arts' or guilds set up their own constitution.

This revolution must be seen against three factors external to Florence, the decline in power and the death of Charles of Anjou, the rise of the despots in Northern and Central Italy, and the history of the papacy in the later thirteenth century. Though Gregory X had failed to launch a new Crusade, the possibility was still there. After the death of his brother Louis in 1270, Charles of Anjou inherited the secular leadership of the crusading movement. He had himself made king of Jerusalem in 1277 and nursed ambitions to re-establish the Latin empire at Byzantium, which had fallen to the Greeks again in 1261. Charles of Anjou's designs on Byzantium were well known and it provoked a conspiracy against him between the emperor, Michael Palaeologus; John of Procida, formerly physician to Frederick II and chancellor to Manfred; and Peter of Aragon, whose wife Constance was the only surviving child of Manfred not in captivity. Pope Nicholas III was privy to this conspiracy. Charles's rule had always been unpopular in Sicily, and on Easter Monday 1282, while his great fleet prepared for the conquest of Byzantium lay at Messina, the riot of the Sicilian Vespers broke out at Palermo leading to a massacre of the French occupiers. The uprising spread to Messina where Charles's fleet was burned, and the Sicilians turned to Peter of Aragon for help. Charles on hearing the news prayed, 'Lord Christ, since it has pleased You to ruin my fortune, let me only go down by small steps!'[18] Neither he nor his descendants were ever to regain Sicily although the papacy remained firmly on his side and a savage war was waged. Further blows were to follow as when in 1284 the Aragonese fleet captured Charles's heir, the prince of Salerno. The following year Charles died and he was soon followed to the grave by the French pope Martin IV, whom he had appointed. Both of them appear in the *Purgatorio*, Charles amongst the negligent rulers and Martin repenting among the gluttons the surfeit of eels from Lake Bolsena and the vernaccia wine of which he died.[19]

Though nothing remained of Charles's wider ambitions in the Mediterranean, his descendants still ruled the South of Italy and the one lasting effect of his conquest was the strength of the alliance between Naples, the papacy, and Florence. Florentine bankers acted for both the Angevins and the papacy, controlling the trade of Naples and ensuring the city's grain imports, and it was in conflict with the aims of this alliance that Dante was to meet the two great political disappointments of his career, the first being the expulsion of his party, the Whites, by the pro-Angevin and papal party, the Blacks, in 1301, and the second, the successful resistance put up by the same alliance to the emperor Henry VII. In the period following Charles's death his Angevin successors tried for twenty years of fruitless war to regain Sicily. The papacy turned again to its old ambitions of creating a strong papal state in central Italy, and Florence was occupied with popular revolutions which spared her from the fate that overtook the liberties of most other Italian cities.

Between 1250 and 1300 nearly every commune of Central and Northern Italy apart from Venice and some of the Tuscan cities surrendered its liberties to a despot and many of these despots founded dynasties.[20] The great and heroic struggles for urban liberty had so exhausted the energies of those who had won them that they had no strength left for its maintenance. These despots had won control in most of the towns where Dante was to live during his exile and they decided the political facts of that period of his life. Some of them, such as Gherardo da Cammino, despot of Treviso, and members of the Scala dynasty at Verona, he admired greatly, although he was to speak harshly of tyranny as a system of government in the *Monarchia* and lashed individual despots in the *Commedia*.[21]

To Dante, in his later thought and experience, there would have been little to choose between the liberty afforded by Florence under the Black faction and the liberty allowed by one of the nastier despots of the Romagna. Both were corrupt forms of government and both needed the guidance of a universal emperor for mankind to achieve its fullest possible experience of liberty.

No emperor, however, came to Italy between 1250 and 1310. The interregnum after Frederick II's death in 1250 ended in 1273 with the election of Rudolf of Habsburg. Rudolf and his successors up to Henry of Luxemburg were too busy settling the problems of Germany, Austria, and Moravia to afford time for Italy, where they were content to cede imperial rights to the papacy in return for advantages at home. The papacy's aim in Italy was to build up a strong central state, but the real advantages the popes could have gained from the extinction of the Hohenstaufens were never fully grasped. One reason for this was the very short average reign of each incumbent of the papacy between 1254 and 1294—less than three and a half years. Nevertheless the energetic and independent Gregory X extracted the promise of the Romagna from Rudolf of Habsburg and Nicholas III completed the transfer. Another problem dogging each pope was that the only political officers he could really trust were his own relations.[22] The frequent conclaves in this period had meant a great growth in the authority of the cardinals, who would pursue policies of their own and were frequently active against the official lines of the papacy. Thus a pope either had to make use of his own relations if he were a member of a great family, as Nicholas III (1277–80) did the Orsini, or else he had to adopt a powerful clan as Nicholas IV (1288–92) adopted the Colonna. Each new pope would find his predecessor's nephews and placemen entrenched in positions of great power, from which he would have to expel them. Thus Boniface VIII was forced by his ambitions for his own Caetani relations to make war on the Colonna cardinals and family who had become so powerful under Nicholas IV. One can understand why the popes had to use these particular means for their aims but the aims themselves were mean when seen in the light of the true mission of the papacy. All the spiritual weapons of the papacy, excommunication, interdict, and the promulgation of crusades, became debased into political manoeuvres. The argument of Innocent III that he could interfere in all business of monarchs and men where sin was involved, *ratione peccati*, was soon to be turned against the popes themselves when Philip the Fair's lawyers could threaten Boniface VIII as a false pope with a General Council to investigate his crimes. And it was not only the French king who felt able to condemn papal practices, but someone far purer in his motives, who sought out and analysed the sin—Dante Alighieri.

Florence was saved from the fate of the majority of the communes which surrendered their liberties to despots by the complexity of her interests and institutions. Her freedom was also achieved at the expense of constant watchfulness against the ever-ingenious aristocrats who tried to take over whatever institutions were devised for the rule of the commune. From 1267, with the return of the Guelphs, until 1282 the city was governed by the Guelph party. This party was increasingly dominated by the aristocrats who could brand any opponents as Ghibellines and who, by the confiscation of Ghibelline property, had put themselves in a position where it was impossible to compromise. The attempts of Gregory X in 1272 and of the Cardinal Latino in 1279–80 to pacify the parties both failed against the obduracy of the Guelphs, and it was not until the institution of government by the priors in 1282 that a régime more thoroughly representative of the city as a whole came to power. The reforms dating from 1282 determined that only members of the seven greater 'arts' or guilds (the medical and legal professions, the bankers, and the entrepreneurial associations of the silk workers, the skinners, and the two woollen institutions) could take part in the government. This was the first stage in the exclusion of the magnates, who either had to become members of a guild and thereby accept that they were part of a corporatist state or else had to surrender any influence on affairs. The supreme government was in the hands of the priors, at first three in number and soon increased to six, who held power for only two months, so that the government actually changed six times in the course of the year. This was the office Dante was to hold in 1300. So greatly did the Florentines fear the effects of intimidation and corruption on their rulers that they not only changed them frequently but kept them almost in conditions of social imprisonment during their term of office, forbidden to accept private invitations and made to live together in special apartments. One of the objects of the construction of the Palazzo della Signoria was to provide them with a state residence in this manner.

It was difficult to repress the magnates. They had wealth and power bases in the *contado*, and they formed an essential element in the city's armed forces. When, after the great victory of Campaldino (described more fully in Chapter 6) in 1289, they tried to assert their strength, they were crushed again by the popular party led by a radical aristocrat, Giano della Bella. By the Ordinances of Justice of 1293, all the greater noble families (those with two or more knights) were excluded from office, and in pursuit of its provisions the ruling party ruthlessly exiled or executed any who gave the slightest hint of trouble, or destroyed their property. In the next two years, 1293–5, members of seventy-three magnate and great popular families were exiled, nearly half the families in these ranks. If the revolution treated these harshly, it also opened participation in government to even wider sections of the community. Over a thousand citizens were called each year to take part in the various councils. There were frequent constitutional experiments and changes. Other guilds forced their way into the offices and councils. There were now twelve major 'arts' or guilds, and thus greatly extending the distribution of power amongst the citizens. In the 1290s, apart from the gonfalonier of justice, an elected official with an army of 1,000 to enforce the provisions of the Ordinances, and the six priors elected by these twelve major 'arts', there were three councils: one, with 100 members, to deal with finance; one, with 300 members, to advise the *podestà*, and one, with 150 members, to advise the captain of the people. Each council was re-elected every six months at different times and no councillor could be re-elected to the council on which he had just served. The system was still oligarchic, but drawing its members from the broad basis of about 400 families. This still excluded the members of many lesser guilds and the artisan and working population, but nevertheless it was a remarkable social and political achievement. It also serves to show how participation in political life was almost inescapable for Dante, even if his ambition and a sense of his abilities had not guided him into it.

The system, with its rapid turnover and its exclusion of some of the richest and ablest members of the community, gave rise to as many grievances as it settled. Guilds were divided internally and family quarrels continued to give a vicious flavour to party feeling. In 1295 Giano della Bella was made the victim of a plot graphically described by his friend, the chronicler Dino Compagni,[23] and he was forced into exile. Members of the nobility were re-admitted to the councils and, as a result of this relaxation, Dante became a member of the apothecaries' guild in that year as his first essential qualification for political life, the consequences of which are described in Chapter 10.

The rise of this mercantile oligarchy to power through constitutional changes and experiments was accompanied in time by a commercial revolution.[24] New and efficient introductions in business management, at which the Florentines were particularly adept, meant that the most important entrepreneurs and merchants no longer needed to travel with their goods to conduct their affairs but that they now became examples of what has been called the 'sedentary' merchant, controlling from their counting-houses distant enterprises through correspondence with agents and outposts of their businesses. Contracts of exchange, one of the most vital introductions, enabled them to transfer credit quickly from one trading centre to another; by this means loans advanced in one currency could be repaid elsewhere in another currency, the process masking the practice of usury and encouraging speculation in exchange rates. With the help of improved book-keeping techniques and a messenger service so good that the papacy employed it for its own correspondence, the great Florentine bankers were able to use funds collected for Church taxes in far-off places such as England to buy raw materials or to lend to monarchs, confident that they would be able to meet claims elsewhere and able to oversee their tentacular operations with the benefit of up-to-date information. All the major banking houses took an active part in industry, trade, and investment in property, thereby putting their operations on a firmer basis than the Sienese bankers who did not take this precaution. It was the failure of the Sienese Buonsignori house in 1298 that finally established the Florentines as the most important of the pope's bankers. The business and banking houses were based on a new kind of partnership, the terminal partnership which lasted a fixed number of years after which profits would be divided and the partnership could be renewed or regrouped. Some firms made God a partner, inscribing Him in the deed of partnership as messer Domenneddio and paying a due portion of profits to charity.[25] One consequence of this commercial revolution was that some of the ablest merchants who formerly had to spend much time away from Florence were now free to play a more active part in the city's life. Another was the dominant position Florence gained in relation to the trade of Europe. The operations of these merchants and bankers covered the Mediterranean world, extending into Asia and Africa and up the line of trade running to Paris, Bruges, and London. Writing in about 1340 but summing up thirty years of commercial experience, the Florentine Francesco Balducci di Pegolotti[26] described in his survey of countries and merchandise, going eastward, trading posts in Byzantium, Anatolia, Armenia, Persia and giving an itinerary for reaching Peking in 270 days. Thus Dante's familiarity with the life, products, and affairs of far-off places must have owed much to the stream of information that constantly poured into Florence; and the new artistic control he exhibited in the *Commedia* in bringing together all the knowledge of the high Middle Ages and the heritage of the classical past, synthesizing them with his interpretation of contemporary events, is paralleled by the new level of control the partners of the great business houses of his city exercised over operations that affected society and politics throughout Western Europe.

Cultural progress in Florence had not kept pace with the great political and administrative advances. Intellectually and artistically, she had been far behind many smaller Italian cities and, while the single-minded devotion of her ruling classes to business had allowed them to accumulate great wealth, they had developed little idea of patronage beyond the founding of hospitals and other charitable gifts to ease the penalties of usury in the future life. Suddenly, in the last years of the thirteenth century, she began to wake up. A series of great public works – the building of the third circuit of walls, the cathedral, and the Palazzo della Signoria – was directed by Arnolfo da Cambio. The Franciscans at Santa Croce and the Dominicans at Santa Maria Novella played a notable part in enlivening the spiritual and intellectual life of the city. And when Dante circulated the sonnet that was to be the first of the *Vita Nuova* at the age of eighteen in 1283, there were many poets or devotees of poetry in that money-grubbing society from whom he could gain a response.

The pride that Florentines felt in their city and their influence was expressed in a sermon by the distinguished Dominican friar Remigio de' Girolami at Santa Maria Novella. In this sermon he counted the seven great blessings that had been granted to Florence: great wealth, a large population, a noble currency, a civilized way of life, the textile industries, armaments, and magnificent buildings.[27] Provided one escaped the stresses of the fight for power in the constitutional battles and was not bound by breaches of family honour to take part in hereditary quarrels, Florence was a delightful place in which to live. The sense of grandeur evoked by Remigio is complemented by Villani's record of simpler pleasures as when he describes the feasts on the first of May when bands of youths paraded, tents of cloth and silk were set up in the squares and streets, girls danced and women in pairs, crowned with flowers and playing instruments, took the air.[28] It was at one of these festal occasions that Dante first met Beatrice.

5

The meeting with Beatrice

Boccaccio says that shortly before Dante was born his mother had a remarkable dream.[1] She dreamt she was in a green field beside a spring and that over her there grew a bay tree. In her dream she gave birth to a boy who fed only on the berries of the tree and the water of the spring. The boy grew up to be a shepherd and struggled to pick the leaves of the bay tree. In doing so, he fell and when he got up he had turned into a peacock. This startled her into waking up and a little time afterwards she gave birth to the boy she and her husband called Dante, the Giver. Boccaccio gives a long interpretation of the dream, saying the berries Dante fed on are the poems of earlier writers, that his growing up to be a shepherd signified his future career in caring spiritually and intellectually for others, that the fall from the tree meant his death, and that his transformation into a peacock foretold the influence of the *Commedia* after his death. The peacock's flesh according to the bestiaries was sweet-smelling and incorruptible, meaning the immortal matter of the poem; its feathers were beautifully various, indicating how the expression of each part of the poem fitted exactly its subject-matter; its feet were ugly, meaning that it was written in the vernacular; and its voice was harsh, befitting the violent condemnations of crime and malpractice the poem contains.

As we have seen, Dante's mother died when he was very young, and his father then married his second wife, by whom he had other children. Premonitory dreams are frequently ascribed to the mothers of saints and heroes in biographies and narratives of the Middle Ages; a somewhat similar story is told of Virgil's mother in early lives of the poet, and so Boccaccio may have introduced this story as a delightful and apposite invention. On the other hand it may have happened and equally the dream, though not of course its interpretation, could have been told to Dante as a child. It is exactly this kind of mysterious message that an orphaned child will seize upon, not just for comfort or for bolstering self-confidence, but in hope of solving what his individual gifts are, of finding the inner strength to deal with the mystery of his deprivation, and of keeping a link between his own living existence and the continuing existence of his parent in the realm of the dead. It raises also the wider point of how a poet learns to think in images. Probably many children do this and then forget through their education how to go on with it. It is to a poet a more reasonable and fruitful method of reflection and it was, perhaps, because of the shock of his mother's death, of the effect of the report of this dream upon him, and of the strain of adjusting to a new stepmother, that the young Dante first started to develop his unequalled imaginative powers in living the private life common to every child.

Another link with this dream is the importance Dante attached to his dreams in later life. Early in the *Vita Nuova* he describes the powerful dream which led him to write 'A ciascun' alma presa', the sonnet that won him the friendship of Guido Cavalcanti (see p. 76). The progress of dreams in that work provides it with an inner structure. There are no dreams described in the *Inferno*, the place of deep sleep and the extinction of consciousness, or in the *Paradiso*, the domain of pure consciousness, but in the *Purgatorio* there are three dreams described in ways that confirm the high estimate he would attach to the messages that dreams can convey. Here again we can presume his active and curious mind as a child working on these experiences at the edge of waking and sleeping, and making the symbols and visions encountered there as much a matter for exploration and investigation as all the bustle of Florentine life as seen from the *sesto* of San Piero.

Of the impressions of his childhood, probably nothing apart from his relations with his family and the meeting with Beatrice had as great an effect on Dante as his attendance in the churches of Florence. However splendid many of the homes of his friends might be, none could compare with the richness of the interiors of many of the churches. Throughout his life and especially in exile, the one that meant the most to him was the baptistery of San Giovanni which at this time was not overshadowed by the great mass of the present cathedral but stood in a wide graveyard of Roman and Lombard sarcophagi used again by the Florentine nobility for their own dead. It was here that his parents brought the infant Dante on the Saturday of Holy Week 1266 to enter the 'faith that makes souls known to God'. He would have been baptized nearly a year after his birth, because the custom of the city was to hold a great ceremony of baptism once a year on that day in San Giovanni. The baptismal water was contained in several deep fonts or wells and when Dante served as a prior and was one of the rulers of Florence, he broke one of these wells to free a child who had got stuck in it and could not get out.[2]

Whether he was taken to the baptistery, the old cathedral, the Badia, San Miniato or his own parish church, he would have been soaked in dramatic impressions, of moving out of sunlight into blackened porches and then into gorgeous gilded interiors where candles blazed on gold, on mosaics, on sculptures and paintings of Christ, the Virgin, and the saints, on the vestments of the clergy, or made recurrent patterns on the wall slabs of polished marble. Dante's *Commedia*, which is like a continuation of the theme of the Gospel of St

John the Evangelist, is an expression of the mystery behind the equation of the Logos with God and of the life of God with light. On a great festival such as Easter, the citizens would forget their quarrels and become one with the Church and the republic. For a short time the intense emotions dissipated generally in civil conflicts would be channelled altogether to a concentration on the resurrection of Christ as the priors and guilds processed through the streets, and after the services and the dismissal, the crowds would pour into the streets, the boy Dante jostled among them, where the girls and young men would dance in the dazzling sunlight, as though prefiguring the rounds and carols of the blessed spirits in Paradise. Then, when Dante was seven, in 1272 came Gregory X's interdict upon the city, a sentence lasting four years that forbade the celebration of any rites apart from the administration of the viaticum to the dying, another kind of orphaning for Dante, through the deprivation of the sacraments in a city full of dark and silent churches.

These churches would have provided the chief stimulus to his visual imagination, but it was probably the social standing of his family that decided that his talents should be developed through literature and words rather than through the visual arts. Painters and sculptors tended either to come from the lower ranks of society like his friend Giotto or else to follow a family tradition like the Pisani. The vital importance of rhetoric and literacy in the ruling and administration of the city states, i.e. the need to put over policies in public assemblies and to persuade their members to a course of action and the attendant need to record decisions, would have decided the training of someone of his social position and would have turned him in the direction of literature. The strength of his visual imagination was such that he was impelled to give it expression in words rather than with the brush or chisel. Earlier writers brought up in the monastic way had the training both in writing and illumination that would enable them to express their visions in both forms (see Chapter 17 for the examples of Joachim of Fiore and Hildegard of Bingen). In Florence literacy and numeracy were the chief elements of the education needed for a thriving community of bankers, merchants, and lawyers while the visual arts were reserved to separate professions.

Not very much is known about the education of children in Florence during the time of Dante's upbringing.[3] Villani, writing of lay instruction in about 1339, says that 8,000–10,000 boys and girls were being taught to read, and the boys then went on to a commercial or literary education.[4] No such details survive for the period of Dante's boyhood. There are references to *doctores puerorum* who taught the elements of Latin to children and a document of 1277 mentions a master called Romanus teaching in Dante's neighbourhood. Whereas Bologna, Arezzo, and Siena already had their universities and even a town as small as San Gimignano engaged masters of grammar to educate its youth, Florence had no centre of higher learning and showed no concern for the acquisition of what, after all, were skills vital to her business interests. Davidsohn[5] could find only one reference to a grammarian before 1300. Florentine parents must have been satisfied with the efforts of small, individually run schools or with private tutors and it was probably in one of these schools that Dante learned the Latin that made Boethius and Cicero so difficult for him to tackle when he started reading them at about the age of twenty-five. It is interesting that Dante, who was to become one of the most powerful influences in the rehabilitation of the classics, only came to them when he was already formed as a poet and committed to the vernacular language as his chief means of expression. Thus it was fortunate for his future development that the educational environment of Florence was impoverished to a degree that prevented him from becoming yet another talented early humanist devoting his life to the production of clumsy hexameters.

From six to eleven Dante would have studied the *Ars grammatica* of Donatus.[6] Then he would have progressed to Priscian whom he has running on the burning sand with Brunetto Latini and the other sodomites. (He apparently got him mixed up with Priscillian, a heretical fourth-century bishop.) He would have gained moral instruction from: the *Disticha* or *Dicta Catonis*, a collection of 144 moral sentences, the work not of Cato of Utica but of Dionysius Cato (third century AD); a collection of Aesop's fables; the *Ecloga Theoduli* which paralleled episodes from classical mythology and scripture; and a work called the *Facetus* which taught polite behaviour.

For all the lack of precise information about his early life and education we can imagine the young Dante as an exceptionally well-endowed boy, observant, intellectually curious, open to instruction and gifted with a remarkable memory.[7] Allied to his gifts was a driving ambition to excel at whatever he touched. This drive, fateful in its effects on him, probably owed something of its force to his early life and circumstances: the loss of his mother and his need to demonstrate to his father and his stepmother by exceptional success that he was still worthy of love. Perhaps from this derive also his faults, his pride, his need to justify himself in all his doings: the hypersensitivity that made him flare with pain at any criticism, the deep capacity for resentment that was to make him so impatient of compromise in any overtures made by Florence for his return when he was in exile. The positive side of this crisis of his childhood can perhaps be seen in the way it forced him to preserve his earliest memories. One of the recurrent images of the *Commedia* is that of the mother, depicted playing with and cherishing her baby, giving the breast to it, and saving it from danger.[8] His return again and again to this image, moving, as it were, from incident to incident in his memory, would suggest that in early childhood he was deeply loved and cherished. These images are nearly always presented from the view of the child rather than of the mother, and this would suggest that he was one of those adults whose memories go back to the breast, and that he could draw on those special memories in which grown self looking back at younger self, while acknowledging the external differences between childhood and adulthood, can find no essential difference in the feeling of individuality. Suddenly the cherishing stopped and he could later remember the contrast when he called Florence a stepmother as bitter to him as Phaedra was to Hippolytus.[9]

These were the wounds of his childhood, wounds inflicted as much by his talents as by the vicissitudes of early life. But there is something as important as memory to take into account in describing the early life of an artist or poet, and that is the growth of his creativeness in the sense his being able to take imaginative control of his surroundings; a child has the ability to take any object he can hold, and christen it as another object and then make all his surroundings part of the game. He takes a brick, he says it is a boat; now the carpet becomes a sea, chair-legs are mountainous islands, a box is a port. All depends on the initial assumption that the brick is a boat; five minutes later the brick may become an aircraft and anything useful in the room to the fulfilling of this new game is renamed as an airport or an enemy fighter. The important part of this process is the creative assumption to which, in the course of the game, everything in his experience can be made to relate. From this assumption he makes a world which he is happy to inhabit and which he is soon as happy to replace with another world of invention. He has the ability to make whole experiences, and what is remarkable about them is the degree to which he has control over them; he can call them into existence and abolish them at his whim in a manner quite different from day-dreaming, for example.[10] Then it happens that through education or parental disapproval this marvellous metaphorical ability is lost. It seems to be lost with another capacity which is also much stronger in children than in adults, that of receiving hypnagogic imagery. In many people, including artists, writers, and scientists, something preserves the genius of childhood so that it can, while keeping its nature, serve the aims and interests of adulthood. One cannot speak generally of what this something is, but, in the case of Dante, there is the well-recorded story of his falling in love, which is, in itself, explanation enough of how he made the life-preserving bridge between his childhood and his grown self and of how he maintained his innate control over image-making.

On May Day, 1274, when he was almost nine, his father took him to a festivity given by the great banker Folco Portinari, who lived in the *sesto* of San Piero. There were many other children at the party, including Folco's daughter, known as Bice (the diminutive of Beatrice), a little girl almost eight years old. After a meal had been served, the children went off to play and it was then that the sight of this child in her bright scarlet dress, with her manners and speech quieter than might have been expected of her years, and her delicate and lovely features, entered his heart 'with such affection, that, from that day forth never so long as he lived, was he severed therefrom'.[11] In the *Vita Nuova*, Dante describes in detail the effect of the shock of love on his psychological and physical state.

> In quello punto dico veracemente che lo spirito de la vita, lo quale
> dimora ne la secretissima camera de lo cuore, cominciò a tremare sì

fortemente, che apparia ne li menimi polsi orribilmente; e tremando, disse queste parole: 'Ecce deus fortior me, qui veniens dominabitur michi'. In quello punto lo spirito animale, lo quale dimora ne l'alta camera ne la quale tutti li spiriti sensitivi portano le loro percezioni, si cominciò a maravigliare molto, e parlando spezialmente a li spiriti del viso, sì disse queste parole: 'Apparuit iam beatitudo vestra'. In quello punto lo spirito naturale, lo quale dimora in quella parte ove si ministra lo nutrimento nostro, cominciò a piangere, e piangendo, disse queste parole: 'Heu miser, quia frequenter impeditus ero deinceps.' D' allora innanzi dico che Amore segnoreggiò la mia anima, la quale fu sì tosto a lui disponsata, e cominciò a prendere sopra me tanta sicurtade e tanta signoria per la vertù che li dava la mia imaginazione, che me convenia fare tutti li suoi piaceri compiutamente. Elli mi comandava molte volte che io cercasse per vedere questa angiola giovanissima, onde io ne la mia puerizia molte volte l'andai cercando, e vedeala di sì nobili e laudabili portamenti, che certo di lei si potea dire quella parola del poeta Omero: *Ella non parea figliuola d'uomo mortale, ma di deo.*[12]

At that moment I say truly (*veracemente*) that the vital spirit which lives in the most secret room of the heart, began to tremble so strongly that it affected dreadfully the least of my pulses; and in trembling it spoke these words: 'Behold the God who is stronger than I and who in his coming will rule over me.' At that moment the animal spirit which lives in the high room to which all the spirits of the senses bear their perceptions, began to marvel greatly and, speaking particularly to the spirits of sight, said these words: 'Now does your blessedness appear.' At that moment the natural spirit, which lives in that part where our nutriment is digested, began to weep and in weeping spoke these words: 'Alas! henceforth I shall be frequently impeded.' From that time, I say, Love so mastered my soul which was married so young to him, and began to exert over me such care and authority through the power my imagination gave him, that I was forced to carry out all his wishes absolutely. He often ordered me to go and look for this youngest of the angels, so that many times in my boyhood I would seek her out and would find her of so noble and so laudable a bearing that in all certainty one could ascribe to her those words of Homer: 'She seemed the daughter not of a mortal man but of God.'

This is the first of the series of visions on which Dante was to draw for his future works. In writing his description of the meeting about twenty years later he imposes on the incident the language he is then accustomed to from scholastic sources. The freshness and the power of the happening, however, survive in his memory so strongly that they surmount his attempts at analysis. The phrases spoken by the spirits are given in Latin in the *Vita Nuova*, and a rather clumsy Latin, based on the language of the psalms, as has been pointed out.[13] It is possible that a child of Dante's precocity heard these phrases coming unbidden into his head at the time of the experience and that he later apportioned them to the spirits that in the psychology current at the time acted as the subtle intermediaries joining body to soul. The boy was in a state of total love, haunting the places where the girl might be seen, not just for a short time but for several years. It was this condition of being in love, of finding something within him to which he could refer every other aspect of his experience, which made the bridge for the preservation of his creative self into adult life. The intensity of the experience also undoubtedly developed his intellectual originality by making him ask innumerable questions of himself about this extraordinary experience. *Amore* or Love is the figure in the *Vita Nuova* who constantly appears in his dreams to rule and guide his life in relation to Beatrice. He is the manifestation in Dante of the way towards the highest level of mental integration, the guide to the experience of pure consciousness that is out of the world and yet explains the world, intensifying the perceptions and refining them.

Some writers have doubted the veracity of Dante's account. They include priests who wish to see Beatrice as the figure of theology and academics to whom she is a formal ingredient in a literary tradition. Against these doubts one can only set the force of the experience as it comes through Dante's words; it is too extraordinary to have been invented. Dante, at the age of almost nine, experienced the same vision that one of the founders of the tradition of the *donna angelicata*, the Sufi poet Ibn al-'Arabī, had expressed in the words, 'It is He [God] who in every beloved being is manifested to the gaze of each lover.'[14]

It was because it was a true and living experience and not a polite social and literary convention that Dante was able to make profound changes in the tradition. T. S. Eliot suggested that the experience took place earlier and adduces the opinion of an unnamed expert that nine years of age is very late for such an experience.[15] Curiously enough Dante, in a *canzone* excluded from the *Vita Nuova*, 'E'm'incresce', says that at the moment of Beatrice's birth he felt the event in his soul so strongly that he fainted—at the age of about one, referring presumably to some extraordinary experience among the early memories already mentioned that had the same emotional quality as his later encounters with Beatrice.[16] There is, on the other hand, the example of the poet and philosopher Vladimir Solovyov, the founder of the Russian Symbolist movement. The direction of his life was determined by three visions of the Divine Sophia or Wisdom, the first of which came to him when he was nine through a girl he met in a Moscow park.[17] Dante's falling in love was undoubtedly mystical in its origin and there are resemblances to the descriptions of similar experiences in the childhood of both Christian and Muslim mystics, notably St Catherine of Siena, who was granted her first vision of her heavenly Bridegroom when she was six,[18] and Shams-i-Tabrizi, the friend of Jalāl al-Dîn Rûmî.[19]

These experiences are not, of course, confined only to childhood. James Joyce drew on such a visionary experience in *A Portrait of the Artist as a Young Man* to describe the meeting of Stephen Dedalus with the girl standing in a stream on the beach at Dollymount[20]—and so must Pierre Teilhard de Chardin have done for the prose poem 'L'Éternel Féminin', written amidst the horrors of the trenches in the First World War and to which, significantly, he attached the dedication 'à Béatrix'.[21]

Love not only reveals the qualities and the soul of the beloved to the lover. It can also launch the beginnings of self-discovery. It did this at the most precocious age in Dante, exalting and changing his perceptions and making to his eyes, as it did to one of his friends and contemporaries when in love, the ramparts of Florence seem of gold and the river Arno flow with balsam.[22]

6

The faithful followers of Love

Nine years after the first meeting with Beatrice, when Dante was almost eighteen, he came upon her walking with two older ladies in a street of Florence. Beatrice was wearing pure white; she looked at him and greeted him with such charm that he seemed to experience the very limits of blessedness. Like a drunkard he went to his room to be alone and to reflect on her courtesy. He fell into a light sleep in which he experienced a marvellous dream. His room filled with a cloud the colour of flame and in the cloud he saw a lordly figure, frightening in his aspect, but nevertheless in an exultant mood. Love—for this is how he named this apparition—spoke to him, but Dante understood only a little of what he said including the phrase 'Ego dominus tuus'. In his arms Love carried a woman asleep, naked but wrapped lightly in a blood-coloured shawl. Dante recognized the woman as Beatrice. In one of his hands Love held something that was on fire and told Dante it was his heart. Then Love woke the woman and forced her to eat the heart which she did unwillingly. Love's joy turned into the bitterest weeping and he disappeared, still holding her, towards the sky. Dante was pierced with such anguish that he woke up. Out of this dream he wrote a sonnet addressed to the *fedeli d'amore*, the faithful followers of Love, which begins:

A ciascun' alma presa e gentil core[1]   To every captive soul and noble heart.

Dante received many replies, the most important of which was one from Guido Cavalcanti, the most accomplished poet of his time in Florence. Cavalcanti drew him into the select circle of the *dolce stil nuovo*, a phrase that Dante invented and which he used to describe his own style in the *Purgatorio*.[2] He wrote this sonnet in 1283 and the story of his relationship with Beatrice up to her death in 1290 is told in Chapter 9. To understand the significance of his contact with Cavalcanti it is necessary first to describe something of the other influences to which he was open in these formative years which include his later education

76

and his first act as a citizen, his participation in the Campaldino campaign of 1289.

Nothing definite is known about his later education. Some have conjectured that he studied at the University of Bologna, then one of the most celebrated in Europe. Florence, for all her wealth and importance, was to possess no university of her own until the fifteenth century. He certainly went to Bologna, because in an early sonnet[3] he mentions the famous Garisenda tower to which he was later to resemble one of the giants ringing Cocytus in *Inferno* XXXII. Much thought has also been given to the nature of the role Brunetto Latini played in his life. Did Brunetto actually teach him or was his influence that of an older, cultivated friend? It has been suggested that Brunetto Latini gave lectures on the *ars dictaminis*, the art of writing rhythmical Latin prose in which formal correspondence was conducted, on Ciceronian rhetoric, and perhaps on astrology.[4] What we can be more certain of is the effect of the interaction of this vigorous society with a young man who had lost his parents, who was strong-willed enough to resist his guardians, who was free from the necessity of earning his living by the possession of property in Florence and in the *contado*, surrounded by many friends, and finding a deserved popularity with his lyrics, which were widely disseminated. He was free to experiment, to dabble in other arts, to satisfy his love for music and the visual arts, and he was probably fortunate in his rank in that he could move easily amongst different classes, observing and yet not becoming involved with any one set of ideas or social attitudes. There would have been many pulls upon his attention, attempts by members of different sects or groups to attract so promising a prize to their particular beliefs, and many would have been deluded by his sympathetic intelligence into believing for a time that they had won him. He preserved himself, however, from all these by two special strengths: one, his poet's eclecticism, which enabled him to enter into the ideas and experiences of others while retaining over his own inner life a control that was essential to his art, and the other, the continuing mystery of his love for Beatrice, which altered and transfigured his perceptions and constantly awoke questions that delved to the depths of his being.

Tuscany at this period was a delightful place for a young man of means, as can be seen in the sybaritic life described in the sonnets of Folgore da San Gimignano.[5] Villani says that the nobles and the wealthy citizens of Florence spent at least four months of each year in the *contado*. The result of this long-standing custom was that, where the ruling classes were concerned the social division between town and country had been practically obliterated in large parts of Tuscany and Lombardy.[6] The delight in country sports and activities that is so clear in the images of natural observation in the *Commedia* appear in the early sonnet, with its pictures and rhythms of hunting:

Sonar bracchetti, e cacciatori aizzare[7]

and it is obvious that, in making his great innovations in the use of concrete imagery, he could draw an immediate response from his readers because of their own familiarity with the countryside surrounding their cities.

Again, something of the quality of the friendships he formed and the easy fantasizing conversations in which he and his friends indulged can be inferred from the mood of a sonnet in which he wishes that Guido Cavalcanti, Lapo Gianni, and he were placed by magic in a boat that would travel wherever they wished, free of the shocks of fortune and evil times. In the boat the kind enchanter responsible for this adventure would also place their ladies, and their conversation would be of nothing but love.[8]

Fortune and evil times were indeed to ruin the pleasures of this delightful time between 1283 and 1288, first by the warfare of the Campaldino campaign and then by the death of Beatrice. From this war and the intrigues and revolutions of power associated with it, Dante was to derive not only first-hand experience of the dangers and excitements of active service, but also some of the most dramatic incidents of the *Commedia*. For involved in these affairs were the Montefeltri father and son, Guido and Buonconte, Count Ugolino, Nino Visconti the judge of Gallura, Vieri de' Cerchi, the future leader of Dante's party, the Whites, and Corso Donati, a leader of his enemies, the Blacks.

All this came about as the result of a serious threat to the Guelph hegemony in Tuscany. Following the victory of the popular party in Florence in 1282, Guelph power had seemed firmly established. Florence's three chief enemies, the traditionally Ghibelline cities of Siena, Pisa, and Arezzo, were now either wholly or partly dominated by Guelph supporters. In 1283 Siena had established a priorate on the model of Florence. In 1284 Pisa was disastrously defeated at sea by Genoa in the battle of Meloria. Genoa, Lucca, and Florence had formed the league partly negotiated by Brunetto Latini to destroy Pisa, and Pisa had only saved herself by submitting to a Guelph administration under Count Ugolino della Gherardesca who concluded a separate treaty with Florence, bribing, it is said, the Florentine ambassadors with wine flasks stuffed with gold florins sent in with a meal during the talks. In Arezzo the two parties were evenly balanced. But the great Guelph alliance soon suffered serious reverses: Charles of Anjou died while his heir was still a prisoner of the Aragonese; Pope Martin IV died in 1285 and his successor, Honorius IV, only ruled until 1287. This gave the bellicose Ghibelline bishop of Arezzo the opportunity to form a strong Ghibelline alliance, driving the Guelphs from the city. Dino Compagni, the contemporary Florentine chronicler, says of him that he was more familiar with the offices of war than those of the Church.[9] Florence was drawn into a war on her southern and western flanks, having to deal with Pisa as well as Arezzo, and, in the course of 1288, having generally the worst of the fighting. The Guelph sympathies of Count Ugolino in Pisa did Florence little good because, in order to rid himself of his nephew, Nino Visconti, the judge of Gallura, he had formed an alliance with another Ghibelline prelate, the archbishop of Pisa, Ruggieri degli Ubaldini, which was successful in driving Nino Visconti from the town. The archbishop now intrigued against Ugolino and in July 1288 had him, two sons, and two grandsons imprisoned in a tower whose door was nailed up and where they died of starvation, a story horrifyingly recreated in *Inferno* XXXIII. Pisa was now once again wholly in the hands of the Ghibellines and her armies were led by the great Ghibelline warlord, Guido of Montefeltro.

The new king of Naples, Charles of Salerno, son of Charles of Anjou, was released after nearly five years of captivity in Aragon. On his progress southwards to his kingdom he stayed in Florence in May 1289 and, in response to urgent requests for help, he gave the services of a young but experienced soldier, Aimeric de Narbonne, to act as general of the republic's forces. Negotiations for peace between the bishop of Arezzo and the Florentines came to nothing, and on 2 June the Florentine army, Dante amongst them, marched towards Arezzo. On 11 June they met the army of Arezzo on the wide plain of the Casentino at Campaldino before the tower and keep of the castle of Poppi, the seat of the Ghibelline Count Guido Novello, who had ruled Florence after Montaperti. Dante was one of the *feditori*, the cavalry under Vieri de' Cerchi, who were given the post of honour in the forefront of the Florentine dispositions. These were supported on the flanks by crossbowmen and infantry. The infantry carried huge body shields, known as *pavois*, painted white and adorned with the lily of Florence in red. The bishop of Arezzo, who was very short-sighted, looking across at the opposing forces, asked, 'What are those walls over there?' and received the reply, 'The shields of the enemy.'[10] The Florentines drew up two other lines and a reserve was kept of Pistoian and Lucchese cavalry under Corso Donati, then *podestà* of Pistoia. Corso was under pain of death not to stir without orders. The fighting began with a charge by the Aretines and the *feditori* were driven back. Vieri de' Cerchi and one of his sons distinguished themselves in the struggle but the Ghibellines pressed on with great confidence, sending in soldiers with knives to disembowel the Guelph horses. The Florentines were driven back to their third line with the baggage and the situation seemed desperate for them. At this point Corso Donati disobeyed his orders and charged with the reserves. The Ghibelline success was turned into a rout. Most of the Aretine leaders were killed, including the bishop and Buonconte da Montefeltro. Guido Novello fled. A great slaughter followed and was only stopped by the torrential downpour of rain described by Buonconte in *Purgatorio* V. The Florentines seized several castles but failed to follow up their advantage in taking Arezzo. Dante described his feelings during the day in a letter now lost but quoted by his fifteenth-century biographer, Lionardo Bruni, who says that Dante drew a map of the battle. Bruni also quotes another letter in which Dante wrote of Campaldino, 'when I found myself no babe in arms, where I felt much fear and in the end the greatest joy because of the varied fortunes of the battle'.[11] Later that year Dante was present at the surrender of the Pisan fortress of Caprona and he compares in *Inferno* XXI his own feelings when confronted with the demons of the eighth circle of Hell with those of the defeated Pisan forces.

così vid' ïo già temer li fanti
ch'uscivan patteggiati di Caprona,
veggendo sé tra nemici contanti.[12]
	Thus did I once the foot-men who
	   marched out
	Under safe-conduct from Caprona see,
	Ringed by so many foemen, fear and
	   doubt.

From Dante's inclusion in the crack squadron of the *feditori* we may deduce something else about his education: he must have been trained in horsemanship and in the use of weapons from early adolescence, because the knightly skills demanded years of exercise and effort for their acquisition. In this he was subscribing to the knightly code to which the citizens of the city republics had such an ambivalent attitude, on the one hand dependent on the aristocrats who were their natural leaders in war (and being also an easy prey to the sheer glamour of chivalry in both fact and story), and, on the other hand, bitterly resentful and mistrustful of the arrogance and brutality of so many of the nobles.

A layman had two ways of escape from the constraints of the knightly code or from the limited horizons of mercantile life: the first and more general was to take lay membership of one of the mendicant orders (these were known as tertiary orders) or at least to frequent the libraries and facilities for study of these orders, as Dante was to do in the years following the death of Beatrice. The second, which was open to a few, was to subscribe to the ideals of the *fedeli d'amore*, to become accepted as Dante was among those rare spirits who were struggling to devise a code of life that retained from chivalry the idea of nobility, while making it depend on personal virtue instead of inherited wealth and breeding, and that preserved spiritual aspirations not unlike those of some mendicants without demanding a life of withdrawal or celibacy. Although it may anticipate something of an influence that only fully affected Dante at a later period, it is necessary first to say something of the role of the mendicant orders in Florence, because he certainly must have come into contact with them throughout his youth.

The mendicant orders had built up a particularly powerful position in Italian cities because their organization was better suited to urban life than the older network of parish priests which had evolved for rural communities. Their skills in preaching and their expertise in the penitential system appealed to a citizenry with a high proportion of literate members; they also offered a spirituality that both accorded with the popular and corporatist movements in politics and business and allowed laymen a fuller place within the framework of the Church, thus keeping them from the various heresies that still abounded. Santa Croce, the Franciscan convent in Florence, was, in fact, the headquarters of the Tuscan Inquisition and there its courts and prisons were sited. Although

Santa Croce was thus the citadel of orthodoxy and was surrounded by the homes of pious laymen and women, members of the tertiary order, there was nevertheless division amongst its friars as to what constituted orthodoxy. This quarrel went back to the time of the death of St Francis and the split among his followers into the Spirituals, who read into the writings of Joachim of Fiore the prophecy that a new era in the life of the Church was dawning and who demanded a literal interpretation of the doctrine of apostolic poverty, and the Conventuals, who rejected the Joachimite message and maintained that possessions and an ordered life were necessary to the study on which the promotion of orthodoxy depended. There were, of course, shades of opinion between the extremes and St Bonaventure, the general of the order from 1257 to 1274, represented a middle way. As was said earlier, the Spirituals had received a set-back when the Joachimite millennium prophesied for 1260 had not been fulfilled. Nevertheless, strong Spiritual currents survived and their hopes were to reach a high point of exaltation when, in 1294, a man thought favourable to the Spirituals became pope as Celestine V. The Spirituals posed, however, the threat of political and economic revolution through their attachment to the doctrine of apostolic poverty, as well as to the hope of spiritual transformation and, although they attracted such courageous souls as the poet Jacopone da Todi, the emphasis they put on the tribulations and sufferings that were necessary for the birth of the new age was not always successful in attracting supporters. For all their radical ideas, the Spirituals were still within the Church at this time (they were not driven out until the 1320s) and it is likely that Dante first came into contact with their ideas between 1287 and 1289, when two of the Spiritual leaders, Petrus Olivi and Ubertino da Casale, were teaching at Santa Croce.[13] Dante may have been influenced by Ubertino's *Arbor vite crucifixe Jesu* and there are correspondences between the two men in their attacks on contemporary popes. He also shares with Olivi the interpretation of the Great Whore of Babylon as the present condition of the Church. What he did not share was Olivi's rejection of the pagan world: 'They handed down to us false beatitude and a false morality.' It seems clear that he felt the impact of these forceful and apocalyptic ideas though the incubation period for them in his creative processes was a long one, and they were only awakened by the apparent fulfilment of them as prophecies in the degradation of the Church under Boniface VIII and Clement V.

The other great intellectual centre in Florence was the Dominican convent of Santa Maria Novella, where one of the most popular and learned preachers was Remigio de' Girolami, a former pupil of Thomas Aquinas. By giving his authority to establishing the basis of philosophy on Aristotle's works, Aquinas had opened the way to a reappraisal of other pagan and classical writers. Charles Davis lists the similarities between Remigio's and Dante's thought: they agree in condemning the Donation of Constantine; they eulogize the rule of Augustus; they look on Cicero as a defender of the *respublica* and as representative of true nobility derived from virtue; they apply Aristotelian

81

principles to contemporary political problems; and they distinguish between the theological virtues which should guide ecclesiastics and the philosophical virtues which should guide secular rulers.[14] It was probably the influence of Santa Maria Novella and of Remigio that awakened in Dante his positive attitude to the classical past and prepared his mind for the vision in which the divine mission of Rome became clear to him as part of the all-embracing synthesis in which history, salvation, and love were revealed as parts of a single unity.

The Dominican influence probably affected Dante most after 1290 and Beatrice's death. Here we must turn back to the strongest and most abiding influence on him, that of the *fedeli d'amore*, the faithful followers of love, as Dante names them in the *Vita Nuova*.

The social ideals of this school were given their fullest expression by Dante in the fourth book of his *Convivio*, though it must be remembered that this was written many years later than the period with which we are dealing. There, at great length, he expounds the idea that nobility is a matter of individual attainment, not of heredity. The virtuous man ennobles his family: the family does not ennoble one of its evil members. Underlying these social and political attitudes was the great theme of the school: the man who possesses a gentle heart is trained by means of Love's instructions to understand the nature of his lady and to surrender all his psychology to the effects of her greeting. What is the gentle heart? Who possesses it and who does not? What is Love? How does he come to dominate his followers? Who is the lady? Is she the wife of a banker living up the street or is she the figure of Sapientia? What is meant by her greeting?

An attempt to answer these questions will be made in the next three chapters, in the course of describing the artistic and intellectual heritage of the poets of the *dolce stil nuovo*. The group of poets whom Dante joined in 1283 largely belonged to important families or were men of law. Their leader was Guido Cavalcanti, who was married to a daughter of the Ghibelline leader, Farinata degli Uberti. The other members included Dino Frescobaldi, a member of a banking family, Lapo Gianni, who seems to have been an imperial notary, Cino da Pistoia, also a lawyer by profession, Guido Orlandi, and Gianni Alfani. Nothing certain is known of these last two. Dante's earliest surviving poems consist of an exchange of sonnets with the obscure Dante da Maiano but, when he wrote the sonnet 'A ciascun' alma presa e gentil core' Dante da Maiano wrote him a rude and slighting reply, quite unlike that of the magnificent Guido Cavalcanti, whose answer tells him that what Dante had seen in his vision was all nobility and all joy. Guido quickly found out the identity of the young poet and drew him into his circle. Guido would have been about twenty-eight to Dante's eighteen. In every way he was made to dazzle and impress Dante. He was the wittiest and cleverest member of one of the wealthiest families in Florence, a family that owned large stretches of property in the city and that provided so many men-at-arms of its name that when Francesco de' Cavalcanti was murdered in the village of Gaville they nearly depopulated the village in revenge.[15] The family was Guelph in sympathy and it was because of its importance that Guido, when young, was betrothed to his Uberti bride and later was a guarantor of the pacification of Cardinal Latino. His great intellectual gifts, his disdain for others, and his love of solitude are recorded by several writers. Boccaccio tells the story of how he liked to muse among the tombs and sarcophagi that then surrounded the baptistery and the old cathedral, and on one occasion a party of young noblemen led by Betto Brunelleschi, rode up to tease and annoy him. They said to him, 'Guido, you reject our company: suppose you discover that God doesn't exist, what good will it do you?' Guido, seeing himself surrounded, replied: 'Gentlemen, since you are in your own house, you may say whatever you like to me.' He then vaulted over a tombstone and escaped out of their reach, leaving them astounded at his extraordinary answer, which Betto had to explain to them. Compared to someone of Guido's understanding they were as dead as the skeletons that lay about them and were as much at home in a graveyard as in their own houses.[16]

Because of his love of speculation and philosophy he was, as the story shows, suspected of atheism or at least of disbelief in immortality, the heresy for which both his father and father-in-law share a tomb in the sixth circle. He was obviously an ardent student of the new knowledge and it was he who showed how the terms of scholastic physiology and psychology could be brought into the language of vernacular love poetry, thus providing an entirely new vocabulary for lovers to describe their inner experiences in verse. He was deeply read in Albertus Magnus and also in Averroes, and it is the influence of the latter that has led many modern writers to believe with his stupider contemporaries that he was indeed an atheist and to mark him as a morbid melancholic. He was a supremely fine poet and, just as it has been shown to be wrong to suppose that Dante was a slavish follower of Thomas Aquinas, so it is dangerous to ascribe to Cavalcanti's inner beliefs the doctrines and ideas from philosophy he was using for the purposes of reaching in poetry a new definition of the effects and nature of love. Much of his verse is delightfully fresh and clear with a resonant gaiety and love of nature: and much is dark and obscure, most notably his *canzone* 'Donna mi prega', which has invited commentaries for centuries, being variously regarded, by Ficino and his circle, as a supreme Neoplatonic statement of love, by Luigi Valli as a document written in a secret language for a secret group devoted to Sapientia, and by others as a manifesto of Averroist ideas. The clearest evidence that he did believe in the immortality of the soul, apart from the angelology of many of his poems, seems to me to lie in the close part he took in the composition of the *Vita Nuova*, whose whole story depends on the certainty of immortal life.

Cavalcanti undoubtedly possessed great authority amongst the *fedeli d'amore*, an authority that seems to have been as much moral as that owed to his rank and riches. Luigi Valli saw him as the leader of a sect communicating in a *gergo* or secret language, made necessary by fear of the heresy hunters of the Inquisition.[17] Valli maintained that the ladies all these poets worshipped under their various names such as Beatrice or Selvaggia were not flesh-and-blood women but, instead, were all masks of the ideal Feminine, Sapientia or Holy Wisdom; that Boccaccio who was a later member of the same sect, deliberately identified Dante's Beatrice with Beatrice Portinari in order to safeguard the secret teaching of the sect, as expressed in Dante's works, from the Inquisition; and that the key words in the poems of these poets had multiple meanings to be interpreted according to the context in which they are placed. *Donna*, for example, can stand for Sapientia or for a member of the sect; it is known that Cavalcanti wrote the *canzone* mentioned above, 'Donna mi prega' ('A lady asks me . . .') in reply to a sonnet written, not by a lady, but by the poet Guido Orlandi; *amore* has amongst its meanings the sect itself; *morte* can mean according to its context the dreaded attentions of the Inquisition or the state of mystical ecstasy; and *pietra* is the carnal and corrupt Church against which these poets formed their secret brotherhood. In stating that the lady adored by these poets was an allegory of Sapientia, Valli was reviving and attempting to revindicate the ideas of Gabriele Rossetti,[18] the liberal Italian exile writing in London in the last century. Rossetti's firmly antipapal interpretation of Dante had aroused the ire of the devout and the learned in his time and, equally, many of Valli's ideas were a source of exasperation to more sober Dante scholars in his day. Many of his ideas have, however, borne interesting fruit, though not always confirming his exact theses. He drew attention to the more openly mystical bent of Sufi love poetry in order to demonstrate that the lady of these poets was indeed an allegory of the Divine Wisdom also sought by the Sufis; but Henry Corbin, whose judgment is the one I adopt in the following chapters, while paying his respects to Valli's insights, points out, on the basis of a profound knowledge of Sufi literature, that Valli had created a false dilemma and that what 'the *fedeli d'amore* saw was at once the Angel Intelligence-Wisdom and some particular earthly figure but this simultaneity was actual and visible only to each one of them'.[19] The resemblances between the Florentine and Sufi poets are frequently remarkable both in their themes and their experience and one of Valli's followers has gone so far as to maintain that the group of poets to which Dante belonged was in fact a Sufi *tarika* or secret conventicle.[20]

Valli also draws attention to a possible connexion of the *fedeli d'amore* with the Templar order. This theory is more fully developed by Robert John and René Guénon who said that Dante was a member of the tertiary order of the Templars known as La Fede Santa.[21] This powerful, aristocratic order had a house in Florence up to the dramatic period of its crushing and condemnation on charges of heresy in 1307–12, and its Rule certainly allowed laymen to be affiliated to the order[22] in the way, for example, that the Franciscans had a tertiary order. The first reference to Dante as a Templar sympathizer is an isolated remark in an ecclesiastical history by a seventeenth-century French bishop.[23] The possible connexion was raised again by Rossetti whose ideas were adopted but done no good service by the ardently Catholic French writer, Eugène Aroux, who set out to prove that, for all his surface orthodoxy, Dante was a wild revolutionary tainted with every heresy current in his period. His chief work on the subject is called *Dante: hérétique, révolutionnaire et socialiste.*[24] Such ideas again raised the hackles of the orthodox to whom the Templars were heretics condemned by a pope at a general council, and there was the added horror that the Freemasons, who were regarded by conservative Catholics as the chief fomentors of revolution and freethinking, believed themselves to be the heirs of Templars who had fled to the Scotland of Robert the Bruce on the crushing of their order. Those quarrels are now long dead; where the question of their heresy as affecting the whole order is concerned, the Templars are now believed to be wholly innocent and the pretended descent of Masonry from the order has never been substantiated. Much is said in later chapters of the history of the downfall of the Templars because of Dante's evident sympathy for them, because his distress at their fate provides the best explanation for his hatred of the two authors of their ruin, Philip the Fair of France and Pope Clement V, and because of his use of symbolism and imagery connected with the order and with the Temple of Jerusalem in the *Commedia*. The question here is whether the Templars could have provided the link which would account for the resemblances between themes and images of the Sufi writers and those of the Florentine poets. On the face of it the Templars, as a celibate military order, strictly forbidden to have any relations with women, would appear to be a most unlikely channel for themes devoted to the praise of beautiful ladies. On the other hand, many Templars were soaked in the culture of the East and some may well have come into contact with Sufi schools and have learned the doctrines of the Perennial Philosophy underlying the symbolism. The same, however, could apply to Florentine and other Italian merchants trading with the East, or it could be laid to a survival of the many contacts with Arab civilization known to have existed at the courts of Frederick II and Manfred. This Sicilian school is mentioned in the next chapter in connexion with the Western tradition of *amour courtois* which, of course, provided the main literary origins of the poetry of the *dolce stil nuovo*.

Whether or not the *fedeli d'amore* possessed these contacts with the East, and whether or not they were connected with the Templars or other bodies at this time, one thing is clear. They formed a closed brotherhood devoted to achieving a harmony between the sexual and emotional sides of their natures and their intellectual and mystical aspirations.

There are constant references in the poems of the Florentine writers to the need for secrecy and discretion and the *Vita Nuova* itself bristles with these injunctions. Erich Auerbach, who was very sympathetic to Valli's ideas, says of Cavalcanti and his friends:

> these men opposed nobility of heart to nobility of birth, and, though actively engaged in political affairs, give the impression of a secret

85

society of initiates. In their poems love mysticism and philosophical and political elements form a unity that is often hard to account for. They appear to have striven more clearly and consciously than the poets of any other country to create a sublime style in their native language. They addressed the élite of the *cor gentile* and it was their endeavour to create a conscious élite.[25]

Guido Cavalcanti drew Dante into this conscious élite. By doing so, he drew him into his own branch of the Guelph party which was later to become the White party, he exercised over him a stern and exacting mastery in the standards of poetic art, he introduced him to the newest and the most thrilling ideas of contemporary philosophy and psychology, and he showed him how these could be made to glow with a new light in the fresh understanding he was bringing to the expression of love through his discovery in his various ladies of the qualities of the one sapiential lady, a unity he expressed in a lovely sonnet: 'Biltà di donna e di saccente core'.[26] Here he lists everything admirable, beautiful, sophisticated, and heart-stirring in his experience: a woman's beauty, a wise heart, noblemen in their armour, birdsong, the conversation of lovers, ships in a high-running sea, the quietness of air at dawn, the falling of white snow without a breath of wind, river banks and meadows of flowers, and jewellery of gold, silver and lapis lazuli. To an observer all these would be worth nothing when set beside the qualities of his lady:

e tanto più d'ogni altr'ha canoscenza
quanto lo ciel de la terra è maggio.

And she surpasses all these in wisdom
As much as heaven is greater than earth.

7

The genealogy of Beatrice

It was Dante's fortune, as the lover of Beatrice and as a poet, to inherit a tradition of lyric verse with a well-developed vocabulary of love that enabled him to interpret and express his own experience of love. He followed that tradition in his poems devoted to Beatrice in the period of her lifetime and after her death. When he turned, after her death, for consolation to philosophy and to other loves, the tradition enabled him to maintain his lyric impulse in the poems devoted to the allegorical figure of philosophy as Sapientia, Divine Wisdom. When in the crisis that preceded the writing of the *Commedia* he realized that Beatrice was the dominant force in his creative life and that she was also the messenger of the Virgin sent for his salvation, again his grounding in the tradition empowered him to describe the life of the blessed spirits and the ascent from earthly love to the love of the Divine that she revealed to him. When Beatrice reappears to him on the summit of Mount Purgatory, she announces her identity to him in the superb lines:

Guardaci ben! Ben son, ben son Beatrice.	Look on me well: I am, I am Beatrice.
Come degnasti d'accedere al monte?	How, then, didst thou deign to ascend
non sapei tu che qui è l'uom felice?[1]	the Mount?
	Knewest thou not that, here, man is in
	bliss?

These lines can be said to contain the inner life of the tradition in their evocation of the power of love, and the life of service it demands, and the permanent happiness that a full understanding of love bestows.

His ability to express this love and to relate it to the transformation of his being and the salvation of his soul, he owed first to the circle of poets surrounding Guido Cavalcanti who sang the praises of their angelic lady, the *donna angelicata*, and then to all those poets, writers, and philosophers who, in the preceding 200 years, had helped to bring about a profound revaluation of the esteem in which women were held.

87

The making of a poet

Through this tradition, Dante was the heir to an immense body of vernacular and Latin literature, lyric, narrative, and didactic whose various authors strove to express the complexity and the psychology of human sexual love. In art was found the means of expressing the special qualities and evolutionary possibilities of the nature of womankind which had been debased in secular society and was ignored by ecclesiastical tradition. Thus art acted as a magic mirror that reveals to men the imbalances in their natures and at the same time effaces or corrects the flaws with a fully formed image of their nature perfected. The Germanic and Norse traditions saw in women breeders of warriors, chanters of victory, and keeners of death; the high position women had won in Roman society had been eroded by the hierarchy of the Church in its exclusion of the female sex from all offices and in its adoption of Greek and Asiatic attitudes to women. In Islam, where there arose a similar movement among poets to counterbalance the inequity, the position of women had been even further debased. Celtic society retained a more reasonable and equitable attitude to the balance of the sexes and from that society derived the first romantic stories of Western European literature. As feudal society continued to develop in France in the eleventh century, and as courts arose around local independent leaders, women recovered their position through their importance in marriage alliances and in the inheritance of property and rights. The origins of courtly love and the social environment in which it flourished have been traced back to the court of Poitiers, where a remarkable lady, Agnes of Burgundy, and her husband, Guilhem the Great, developed links with the Neoplatonic school of Chartres in the early eleventh century.[2] Their descendant, Guilhem VII, count of Poitou and duke of Aquitaine (1071–1127), is the first named troubadour.

Though there is evidence of vernacular songs and lyrics long before Guilhem's time, Dante's lyric art has its most direct origins in the discoveries of the troubadours writing in Southern France from the beginning of the twelfth century. He knew their language so well that he wrote Arnaut Daniel's speech in the *Purgatorio* in Provençal, and he regarded certain of them, as *De vulgari eloquentia* shows, as supreme masters of their craft. The very word 'troubadour' derives from *trobar*, the Provençal equivalent of *invenire*, which signified in classical Latin 'to discover or invent'. One of these discoveries may be illustrated by a stanza from a *canso* of Bernart de Ventadorn.

Non es meravelha s'ieu chan	It is no wonder that I sing
Mielhs de nulh autre chantador,	better than any other singer,
Que plus mi tra-l cors ves amor	for my heart impels me more towards love,
E mielhs sui faitz a son coman.	and I am better made for its command.
Cor e cors e saber e sen	I've given it my heart and body,
E fors'e poder hi ai mes;	wisdom and sense, strength and power;
Si-m tira ves Amor lo fres	this bridle so leads me towards love
Que ves autra part no m'atem.[3]	that I'm attracted by nothing else.

If he sings better than anyone else it is because his experience of love is deeper than anyone else's. The finer the experience, the better the art; or, as Dr Johnson remarked of the resources of good poetry in another context: a man 'can only mint guineas in proportion as he has gold'. It is much the same reason that Dante gives to Bonagiunta (see Chapters 1 and 17) for the superiority of the *dolce stil nuovo*: that its followers reach more deeply into themselves for their inspiration.

Before turning to those troubadours whose works Dante mentions or who played an essential part in the development of the tradition, we must mention other literary movements which also gave voice to the imperative reassertion of the needs of feminine psychology and of the feminine ideal. Among these were the cult of the Virgin in art and the Latin and vernacular literature which grew with the spread of Mariolatry in the twelfth and thirteenth centuries, certain works in Latin inspired by Neoplatonic influences, and the Arthurian romances.

Dante was to say of the Virgin that he always had her name on his lips morning and night.[4] His devotion to her is revealed throughout the *Commedia*. On the seven levels of Mount Purgatory which correspond to the seven deadly sins the souls are purified by contemplation of a separate episode in her life. It is at her intercession that Dante is granted the final vision of the Trinity. In his devotion he was sharing in one of the greatest popular and artistic movements of his time. In the course of the twelfth century Mary recovered her youth and her humanity. From being the distant and solemn Virgin of Romanesque and Byzantine art, she became the young, entrancing girl identified with the flowers of the field, with eyes that sought out her beholders from her depictions in painting, sculpture, and glass, with smiling lips that seemed always about to impart words of grace and comfort. Her mantle was in the air, ready to enfold the roughest soldier and the most sinful monk in their time of need and it was capacious enough to succour cities like Siena at the crisis of Montaperti and crusaders singing her hymn, 'Salve regina', as they faced the infidel. Widely circulating apocryphal stories of her life and miracles[5] brought her closer to the lives of ordinary men and women through descriptions of her earthly existence which revealed how she shared the sorrows and joys of humanity. Just as the Gothic artists had brought a new individuality and realism to their prophets and saints, so on the Virgin they lavished their best talents to convey the immediacy and the joy of her presence. Through her, men remembered the tenderness of their own mothering; through her, women knew that their sufferings were regarded in heaven. Innumerable songs and hymns in Latin and vernaculars were composed in her honour, and throughout Tuscany and Umbria in Dante's time wandering Franciscans would perform *laudi* which included praises of her and also short plays of scenes from the Passion, of which Jacopone da Todi's is the most memorable,[6] in which she is presented as overwhelmed by the crucifixion. The fire of devotion to the Virgin which burnt with such ardour in the breasts of layfolk and of the knightly classes also spread through the monasteries and schools. St Bernard, to whom Dante gives some of his greatest verse to speak in the prayer to the Virgin Mother in the last canto of *Paradiso*, was popularly believed to have received a vision of the Virgin in which she expressed three drops of her milk onto his lips.[7] The bishops and chapters who commissioned the rebuilding of their cathedrals in the new Gothic style frequently rededicated their cathedrals to the Virgin where before they had been under the patronage of lesser saints. Thus she was particularly associated with the flowering of the Gothic and when, in Dante's lifetime, the Florentines pulled down their old cathedral of Santa Reparata, they dedicated their new one to Santa Maria del Fiore.

It was in the ambience of one of the most famous shrines of the Virgin, in the school of the cathedral of Chartres where her mantle is still preserved, that there arose a more abstract and esoteric conception of the essence of womanhood pervading the universe. This influential school, which was one of the most important centres of the development of abstract thought and of the philosophical origins of science before the reintroduction of Aristotle's works, drew from its study of Plato and Neoplatonic writings, most of all from Plato's *Timaeus*, a particular concern with the structure and form of the universe and with their relation to creativity and to man. Its members saw Plato's *Anima Mundi* as an omnipresent intelligence disposed throughout the world by which man can be inspired and instructed. They were also deeply learned in classical writers and in the allegorical interpretation of poets such as Virgil, finding, especially in the imagery of the latter, parallels with the inspiration and visions of the Hebrew prophets. Some of their conclusions were shocking and heretical to orthodox views, especially the identification of the *Anima Mundi* with the Holy Ghost. It has been suggested that it was the attacks of rival theologians that drove them to disguise their new conceptions in allegorical forms.[8] What is fascinating is that the two great poets who derive from this school, Bernard Sylvester and Alan of Lille, both expressed their ideas through women as symbols of the divine and cosmic urges for creation, so that, whereas the trans-valuation of woman achieved through Mariolatry came from a new spirit of religious devotion, and that achieved by the exaltation of the lady by the troubadours arose from a new understanding of sexual love, these poets discovered a related principle of femininity in the universe through the intellect and their researches into cosmology, a discovery which was to lead both of them in their different ways to celebrate sexual generation in man. In this they were both obviously influenced by Boethius' presentation of Philosophy as a sublimely ideal woman. They both reveal an interest in their own creative processes that anticipates Dante. Bernard does so, not by direct autobiographi-cal description for he hardly appears in the main work of his that is discussed here, *De natura universitate*, but because the whole work is suffused with the high intellectual mood from which it was created. There are few works that make the reader as possessed of the intellectual and emotional experience it grew from as this. The first part, 'Megacosmos', describes the coming of Natura to the Divine

Mind, Noys, to beg for the ordering of matter, Silva, which is in a state of chaos. The response of Noys is to create the universe and earth, and all earthly life except for man. In the second part, 'Macrocosmos', other goddesses after a celestial journey by Natura are called upon to take part in the making of man. Bernard read this work to Pope Eugene III in 1142. Alan of Lille, writing later in the century, produced two works with somewhat similar themes, *De planctu Naturae* and *Anticlaudianus*. In the first of these works Alan is instructed in a dream by the ravishingly attractive goddess Natura who laments perversity in mankind both sexual and intellectual and restores him to himself through a sequence of questions and answers. The work closes with her calling on her high priest Genius. Nature appears again in the long epic *Anticlaudianus* when she appeals in an assembly of the virtues for the creation of a perfect man. Phronesis (Prudence) is given the task of ascending to Heaven under the guidance of other beings to receive the soul of this perfect man from God, Himself, and there are many passages, as well as the theme of the celestial journey, which have caused scholars to claim the direct influence of Alan on Dante.[9] His influence is far more clear than that of Bernard Sylvester though Dante may well have used the latter's commentary on the first six books of the *Aeneid*.

Another important literary influence was that of the Arthurian legends. Dante, it is clear, loved these stories, speaking of 'most beautiful legends of King Arthur' in *De vulgari eloquentia*,[10] and comparing Beatrice's reproval of his pride in ancestry with the cough given by the Dame de Malehaut to show that the first kiss Guenevere gave Lancelot had not gone unnoticed.[11] The influence appears most profoundly in the story of Paolo and Francesca, when Francesca in the following lines tells the story of their love:

Noi leggiavamo un giorno per diletto
di Lancialotto come amor lo strinse;
soli eravamo e sanza alcun sospetto.
Per più fiate li occhi ci sospinse
quella lettura, e scolorocci il viso;
ma solo un punto fu quel che ci vinse.
Quando leggemmo il disïato riso
esser basciato da cotanto amante,
questi, che mai da me non fia diviso,
la bocca mi basciò tutto tremante.
Galeotto fu 'l libro e chi lo scrisse:
quel giorno più non vi leggemmo
avante.[12]

One day together, for pastime, we read
Of Launcelot, and how Love held him
in thrall.
We were alone, and without any dread.
Sometimes our eyes, at the word's secret
call,
Met, and our cheeks a changing colour
wore.
But it was one page only that did all.
When we read how that smile, so
thirsted for,
Was kissed by such a lover, he that may
Never from me be separated more
All trembling kissed my mouth. The
book I say
Was a Galahalt to us, and he beside
That wrote the book. We read no more
that day.

No lines in European verse since Catullus had so captured the ardour and passion of physical love. The influence of the Matter of Britain is not just to be seen in the occasion: that the lovers were sitting together reading the story of Lancelot and Guenevere. They themselves played out a story as fated and as tragic as anything in the legends. Her crippled husband, Gianciotto Malatesta, had baited her with the sight of his handsome brother before their marriage, as in a way Mark of Cornwall had baited Iseult with Tristan, and when they surrendered to their passion they were involved in as deep a conflict of duties, she to her husband and he to his brother and the head of his noble family, as was Guenevere to Arthur and Lancelot to his uncle and his feudal lord. In one moment the lovers change worlds, the world of imagination where passion is an exciting but distant possibility to be observed only in fictional characters, for the world of physical contact and desire—a transition marked by the differences in the description of the kisses, Lancelot's on the romantic *disïato riso* and Paolo's on *la bocca*, an almost brutally realized contrast.[13] It is Francesca who tells the story, not Paolo, who can only weep and gesture. Behind her story are also the voices of the Arthurian heroines, the good, the betrayed, and the evil, from Guenevere to Morgan le Fay, and this episode concentrates nearly 200 years' experience in assimilating and expressing the depths of woman's love.

Turning back to the influence of the troubadours on Dante, we must now ask, what lay behind this experience of sexual love and its transformation into a rule of life as service of the beloved? At the turn of the eleventh century, certain poets understood, with the force of spring, that when they fell in love something enchanting happened to them; it was not just that they were sexually attracted to their mistresses and women friends, but that the experience of being in love totally altered their perceptions of the world. They found they could reinterpret their lives, the direction of their feelings, and their surroundings, in terms of this love; and out of the intensity of their emotions, in the swings from exaltation to despair, as they were driven to explore the essence of their sexual beings, so they experienced ever higher levels of consciousness in instantaneous but ever memorable moments of illumination. They discovered in themselves the ability to stand back and watch the contradictions and impulses of their emotional natures and, because they could stand back, they could observe, note, and transmit to others the depth of their experience. They were free to a great extent of the misogyny expressed in so much clerical literature, and even when, like the troubadour Marcabru, they did attack women's faults and vices, it was more to give point to their ideal lady and her virtues than to lambast the female sex in general. Marcabru illustrates how all-embracing the philosophy of love could be, as when he contrasts the broken and fragmented thinking of a man who cannot distinguish false love from true love with the integrated thought of a man who has this power of discrimination and therefore is, through God, one with nature.[14]

The poets borrowed from other traditions to extend the range of their art, drawing on many sources in Latin, on mystical themes from the contemplatives, on Neoplatonic and Aristotelian ideas and definitions, and taking from the Books of Solomon the figure of Sapientia, or Wisdom, the female aspect of divinity that had from earlier days been associated with Christ. Their own movement was strong enough to adopt and adapt these religious and philosophical sources and yet preserve the movement's vigorously secular character, because it affirmed the goodness of sexual love, and because it found a ready audience in the numerous courts of Southern France open, as they were, to the influences of Muslim Spain and the First Crusade. These poets expressed the confidence and vigour of their society and they developed a vocabulary of special words, which came to gather rich associations and in translation were still in use by Dante and his friends. One such word is *jois* (*gioia*) which meant not transient joy but a permanent and positive attitude to life. The almost esoteric knowledge they gained through this cultivation of the emotions they called the *gai* or *ver saber*, and to distinguish the exquisite character of their love from lower forms, they named it *fin' amors*.

They discovered not only the vocabulary, but also the lyric forms in which to set them, and they became wonderfully skilled in inventing new stanzaic patterns. The noblest of these forms, the *canso* (or *canzone* to the Italian poets), presented a particular challenge which drew from them their best. Ezra Pound says of the *canzone* that it was to poets of the time what the fugue was to musicians in Bach's time, being a highly specialized form with its own self-imposed limits.[15] Dante looked upon his *canzoni* as though they too were lovely women whom he had to adorn, and to whom he gave maid servants in the final stanza; the curving, waisted look on the page of some of his *canzoni* is essentially feminine. So the poets, in rendering service to their ladies, made their poems as like the nature of the beloved as possible. The *canzone*, above all, as a form offered a new mode of poetic expression, allowing a special union of intellect and emotion.

The culture of the troubadours grew up in the society surrounding the numerous courts of Southern France in the twelfth century. This society was mixed though basically feudal and therefore allied to the society of Northern France, where chivalry was created. It still had a number of large towns though, unlike those in Italy, only a few had thrown off the domination of their overlords. The people of this society played a great part in the First Crusade and also were in close contact with Spain and its Muslim culture. Power remained in the hands of nobles, dukes, and counts who were too distant from the kings of France and the emperors to fear challenge to their own effective sovereignty. Trade and pilgrim routes passed through their lands, increasing their wealth, and in the halls of their castles and palaces there developed a court culture of great sophistication and style. It was an area where the Church possessed little dominance and, in this exceptionally tolerant atmosphere, not only did the troubadour civilization flourish but also the widespread and powerful religion of the Cathars or Albigensians.

The influence of the troubadours spread far beyond Southern France, so that there were poets writing in Provençal across the Pyrenees in Spain and also in Northern Italy. The troubadours also travelled widely, to England and as far as Hungary and the Holy Land. The names of over 400 poets survive from the twelfth and thirteenth centuries. Although the Albigensian Crusade (1209–18) largely destroyed the society and the courts which had sheltered these poets, sending many into exile in Italy, several notable poets were writing in Provençal after the Crusade and it was still a living tradition in Dante's time.

The lyrics of the troubadours were written to be sung. They were performed either by the poet himself or by professional singers whom he employed. This meant that, although their matter could be based on the deepest personal experience, that experience still had to be projected not only in words and music but virtually as a dramatic presentation. This approach to poetry, essentially one of acting, survived to Dante's day and in the Italian city states it was reinforced by the importance of training in oratory and rhetoric. By his time, too, as we know from his reference to his friend, the poet Gotto of Mantua,[16] poems were recited as well as sung, and he and his contemporaries would have delivered their works with every aid of oratory and expression.

One reason for the wide range of vernacular literature was its importance in the life of the royal and noble courts where the poets found their patrons. The most influential court was that of the Angevin empire after Eleanor of Aquitaine, the granddaughter of Guilhem of Poitou, married Henry II of England. Dante, in *De vulgari eloquentia*, lays down three themes for treatment in the vernacular, war, righteousness, and love.[17] The warlike nature of feudal society and the responsiveness of the knightly classes to reputation, and to the need to preserve standards of right chivalric behaviour in patronage and service, meant that poets, with their widely scattered audiences, could be either dangerous enemies or valuable allies with a power totally beyond their physical resources. The most notable of the poets who became publicists for war was Bertran de Born (*c.* 1140–*c.* 1215) who, in his *sirventes* on war, turns brigandage and murder into a high-spirited but vicious game.

Ie-us dic que tan no m'a sabor	I tell you that I find less pleasure
Manjar ni beure ni dormir	in eating, drinking or sleeping
Coma quant auch cridar: 'A lor!'	than in hearing the cry of 'Charge!'
D'ambas las partz et auch ennir	from both sides, and hearing riderless
Chavals vochs per l'ombratge,	horses whinnying in the shade,
Et auch cridar: 'Aidatz! Aidatz!'	and hearing shouts of 'Help! Help!'
E vei chazer per los fossatz	and seeing the great and small
Paucs e grans per l'erbatge,	fall beside the moat,
E vei los mortz que pe-ls costatz	and seeing the dead with bits of
An los tronzos ab los cendatz.[18]	lances
	and banners protruding from their sides.

Behind his exultation in battle lives his certainty that he felt most alive in this dangerous sport, a feeling that most of his audience shared and to which Dante, by the evidence of the effect of the Campaldino campaign, was not immune. Allied to this was the trust and affection that could grow up between companions in arms and their lord—as is shown in Bertran's beautiful lament for the Young King, Henry Plantagenet, the son of Henry II:

Si tuit li dol e-lh plor e-lh marrimen
E las dolors e-lh dan e-lh chaitivier
Qu'om anc auzis en est segle dolen
Fossen ensems, sembleran tuit leugier
Contra la mort del jove Rei engles,
Don rema Pretz e Jovens doloros
E-l mons oscurs e teintz e tenebros
Sems de tot joi, ples de tristor e d'ira.[19]

If all the grief and tears and sorrow,
and the pain, affliction and misery
known to man in this sad world were brought
together, they would seem as nothing
beside the death of the young English King
which makes Worth and Youth sorrowful
and turns the world sombre, dark and shadowy
void of all joy, full of woe and sadness.

Dante greatly admired Bertran as a poet but, because of his evil influence on the young king in urging him to war against his father, a war graphically described in the Provençal biographies of Bertran, he condemned him to a hideous eternity among the sowers of discord in *Inferno* XXVIII. He sees Bertran as a headless trunk running towards him and swinging his own head by the hair like a lantern. When he reaches Dante, he flings up his arm with the head which says:

Or vedi la pena molesta,
tu che, spirando, vai veggendo i morti:
vedi s'alcuna è grande come questa.
E perché tu di me novella porti,
sappi ch'i' son Bertram dal Bornio, quelli
che diedi al re giovane i ma' conforti.
Io feci il padre e 'l figlio in sé ribelli;
Achitofèl non fé più d'Absalone
e di Davìd coi malvagi punzelli.
Perch' io parti' così giunte persone,
partito porto il mio cerebro, lasso!,
dal suo principio ch'è in questo troncone.
Così s'osserva in me lo contrapasso.[20]

Behold what I have merited!
Thou who still breathing goest the dead to view
See if any suffer punishment as dread.
Know, that thou may'st bear tidings of me true,
Bertran de Born am I, and the Young King
My evil promptings to rebellion drew.
Father and son did I to quarrel bring.
Ahitophel wrought not more on Absalom
And David with the malice of his sting.
Such union since I made asunder come,
I carry alas! dissevered this my brain
From the live marrow it fed its vigour from.
Thus retribution's law do I maintain.

The general name for the literary form employed by Bertran de Born was the *sirventes*, which covered those works more concerned with social comment than with love. The *sirventes* could be used as much for the correction of evil as for its advancement. Some critics have seen in the *sirventes* of Peire Cardenal (*c.* 1180–1278), for example, a source or precedent for Dante's own attacks on the faults and bad guidance of the Church and civil government of his own day. He begins one poem: 'The clergy give themselves out for shepherds, and they are assassins'.[21] Guilhem Montanhagol wrote a savage attack on the Dominican Inquisitors, and Guilhem Figueira's *Sirventes contre Rome*, written between 1226 and 1229 during the Albigensian Crusade, has been called the most virulent satire against Rome dared in the Middle Ages. These poems were also addressed to secular rulers. The Mantuan poet Sordello (*c.* 1200–69), who wrote in Provençal in his *planh* for a dead nobleman, Blancatz, combines the form of the lament with a polemic against the monarchs of Europe, saying they will have to eat the dead man's heart because none of them has heart of his own. It was probably on account of this poem that Sordello in *Purgatorio* has the task of pointing out to Dante the valley of the negligent rulers.

Sordello's work demonstrates the strong hold Provençal literature had in Northern Italy. The appearance of his former mistress, the much married, much loved, and much loving Cunizza in the heaven of Venus helps to remind us of the flesh-and-blood natures of some of the ladies who inspired the tradition of courtly love. Cunizza was the sister of the tyrant Ezzelino da Romano, but she had a temperament as far as possible opposed to his. She eloped with Sordello from her first husband and later acquired three more husbands and other lovers. Her last years were spent in Florence, where she lived in the palace of the Cavalcanti and was renowned for her charity. The fact of her salvation has been contrasted with the damning of Francesca and the difference between Francesca's obsession, which is far more the cause of her fate than the mere act of adultery, and Cunizza's own generous detachment may be read in her words:

Cunizza fui chiamata, e qui refulgo	Cunizza was I called; and here I glow,
perché mi vinse il lume d'esta stella;	Since I was conquered by this burning
ma lietamente a me medesma indulgo	star.
la cagion di mia sorte, e non mi noia;	But for the cause of this my lot I owe
che parria forse forte al vostro vulgo.[22]	No grief, but shrive myself in happiness:
	Hard saying, may-be, to your crowd
	below.

Cunizza then passes Dante on to another soul, who flashes like a ruby struck by the sun and who on earth played a role both in Provençal literature and in bringing to an end the civilization in which it flourished. This is Folquet of Marseilles, the son of a Genoese merchant, who became well known for his poetry and for his ardent love affairs. On the death of one of his mistresses he abandoned the world for a monastery, but later was made bishop of Toulouse. He was said to have played an energetic part in crushing the Albigensians. The contemporary epic on the Crusade accuses him of the death of 10,000 people and says of him that he seemed more like the Antichrist than the agent of Rome. Dante makes no use of these stories. What is interesting about Folquet's speech is that it contains an attack on the corruption of Rome as strong as the complaints made by his enemies in life. Just as Aquinas is made to praise his earthly opponent, Sigier of Brabant, so Folquet in the state of glory redresses the imbalance in his over-vehement support of the papacy.

Accompanying the influence of contemporary Latin literature on vernacular love poetry was the abiding classical influence of Ovid, most notably his *Ars amatoria* and *Remedia amoris*. The *Ars amatoria*, with its heavy, voluptuous mood, so much more erotic than any specific description it contains, preserved the memory of an urban sophistication unattainable anywhere in this period except, perhaps, in the Eastern Mediterranean. It depicted the possibility of a life shorn of all responsibilities except for the single-minded pursuit of love, and, curiously enough, it was this very concentration on love as a way of life that brought out resemblances to the *fin' amors* of the troubadours. This helped to make it so strong an influence on them. Its seemingly cynical tone did not mask from them the vein of devoted feeling it also conveys, the sense of transformation through sexual love that was part of their own experience.

The worldly-wise tone of Ovid imbues the most important treatise on love associated with the ideals of *amour courtois*, Andrew the Chaplain's *De amore*. In this late-twelfth-century work, the author instructs a young nobleman called Walter in the ways of love, with the ultimate object of warning him off it. Few readers paid attention to its final pages, so gripped were they by the witty examples of speeches by lovers of different and equal ranks and by the way it presented a world of rules and behaviour, not so much at variance with the world of conventional Christian morals as existing in another continuum from it. Andrew, through one of his speakers, even describes an afterworld in which ladies receive rewards, corrections, or torture according to the measure in which they showed kindness to their lovers in life. This book was translated into Tuscan[23] and was known in Dante's Florence where it exercised a strong influence on lovers and poets, especially in its insistence on discretion and secrecy: an influence to be detected in Dante's use of the ladies who were 'a screen of the truth' to disguise his love for Beatrice in the *Vita Nuova*.

Another recent work that influenced Florentine literary circles was the long allegorical poem, the *Roman de la Rose*, whose first part was written by Guillaume de Lorris between 1225 and 1237 and which was continued and finished about forty years later by Jean de Meung. In telling the story of a lover who falls in love with the Rose, the symbol of his lady and his love, Guillaume, using allegorical figures to express the courtly virtues and their opposing vices, drew on the ideas of the troubadours. Jean de Meung, a layman deeply influenced by the Aristotelian and Averroist philosophies of the Paris of his time but also owing a great debt to Alan of Lille in his personified characters, introduced long philosophical disquisitions into the poem. His lover is now guided by Reason according to the dictates of Nature and the poem acquired a strong anticlerical—though by no means anti-religious—bias. The *Roman* was the chief inspiration of Brunetto Latini's *Tesoretto* and a skilful translation and adaptation of part of it into 232 sonnets was made in Florence in the 1290s by a Messer Durante. This adaptation, *Il Fiore*, has often been ascribed to Dante, because the author had the same name (Dante is a diminutive of Durante), because of its technical mastery, because the author introduces the name of Sigier of Brabant, the Averroist philosopher whom Dante admired, into his version, and because of resemblances between some of its verses to lines by Dante. Scholarly opinion, headed by Michele Barbi, for long rejected the ascription to Dante but now it seems, tentatively, to be veering in the opposite direction. In any case Dante was probably familiar with the original, and among the influences of the *Roman de la Rose* to be traced in the *Commedia* are the use of landscapes such as that of the garden, the ambiguous island of fortune, and the castle built to protect the Rose against the lover as evocative symbols of mental states, the treatment in the vernacular of philosophical problems hitherto confined to the speculations of the learned, the employment of geometrical imagery to express the mystery of the Incarnation and the Trinity[24] which is the kind of imagery Dante uses in describing the final vision of the *Commedia*, and, last and most important, the image of the Rose itself which is the object of the Lover's desire and the symbol in which Dante sees the true nature of the Empyrean. What left no trace on Dante was Jean de Meung's ambivalent attitude to women, sometimes expressed in passages of the bitterest misogyny.

All these literary works in some way affected and influenced Dante in his writings, but what enabled him to synthesize and purify their influences was the tradition of the lady, through the love of whom all the rest of the universe gains its meaning. And it is in the love lyrics of Provençal and Italian poets that we may trace the genealogy of Beatrice. There is no full description of the philosophy guiding these poets beyond what is to be found in the poems themselves. The subtleties of *fin' amors* probably could not be expressed in any other way; they are as closely tied to the verse as the concentrated descriptions of physical laws are to the equations that express them. The *razos*, the prose descriptions of what occasioned the writing of particular poems, though fascinating, are purely anecdotal and, though Andrew the Chaplain's *De amore* is sometimes seen as a textbook of courtly love, it is too limited in its range, too dependent on jealousy, for instance, as an ingredient of true love to encompass the full experience of service and surrender to the lady that so many of the poems convey.

A recent writer on the troubadours[25] has discerned in the songs of the earlier poets three planes of love: 'a worldly plane of physical love', which suited the general tastes of courtly society; 'a plane of dream-like imaginings', which characterizes, for example, the work of Jaufre Rudel and his love for the distant princess; and a 'transcendental' plane which opens the way to a supreme and unshakeable happiness. These different planes of treatment attracted different audiences and demanded different styles so that the first two were generally treated in the 'open style' of language known as the *trobar leu* and the third in a different, 'closed' style or *trobar clus*. Many poets felt the tension set up by the demands on the one hand of the courtly audience on whom their livelihoods depended and their desire to express the inner aspirations of their love. It was because Marcabru and later poets such as Arnaut Daniel were successful in maintaining and strengthening the ideal of love on the transcendental plane that the tradition of the troubadours survived the destruction of the social order in which it had flourished and could be transplanted to the different environments of Southern and Central Italy.

This fullness of the experience of love is to be found as early as Guilhem of Poitou, whose attitude to women in his surviving poems ranges from that of a practised roué to the tenderest devotion that is conveyed radiantly in the following stanza, with its deep feeling for nature:

La nostr' amor vai enaissi	Our love is like
Com la branca de l'albespi	the hawthorn branch
Qu'esta sobre l'arbre en treman,	which, at night, trembles
La nuoit, a la ploja ez al gel,	beneath rain and ice
Tro l'endeman, que-l sols s'espan	until day comes and the sun spreads
Pel las fueillas verz e-l ramel.[26]	through the boughs and green leaves.

Bernart de Ventadorn brought a new radiance and depth to the theme, and Guiraut de Bornelh, obviously regarded in Dante's time as the supreme craftsman (though Dante himself preferred Arnaut Daniel), encompassed it in verse of great virtuosity. One of Guiraut's works is a *tenzon* or argument in verse with the great lord Raimbaut of Orange in which they argue whether poetry with a secret meaning should be allowed. Raimbaut is for it and Guiraut against it. The argument was a development of one familiar to the troubadours and it centred on the contrast of styles, the *trobar leu* or clear style and the *trobar clus*, the obscure style. Raimbaut favoured a middle way known as the *trobar rics*, which could reconcile the demands of clarity with the obscure quality which is essential to poetry and which satisfied the troubadours' own need for secrecy. Arnaut Daniel was Raimbaut's disciple in using the *trobar rics* and the influence of the style was very important to Dante in the development of his own poetic voice.

Raimbaut once described his ideal style in the following way

Cars, bruns, e teinz motz entre besc	Rare, dark and coloured words I wind
Pensius—pensanz....[27]	In thoughtful thought....

It was Arnaut Daniel who took this instruction and founded his style upon it. His words are unusual, they are obscure, but they also evoke pictorial and spatial images which more than compensate for the difficulty of any of his poems. His sympathy for complex formal patterns appears in another aspect of his originality: his invention of the new form of the *sestina*, a *canso* without rhyme but with the same end words repeated in a different order in seven combinations, and his use of the *canso* in which each stanza as a whole rhymes with all the other stanzas. Though one of his constant themes is of his own frustration in love, the very intensity of expression points to the fact that he is describing something far less banal than mere sexual frustration, but more a state of transition, of excited awareness, that passes from love as a physical desire to love as a state of consciousness under the rule of reason. Something of that flavour may be seen in the last two stanzas of his sestina, 'Lo ferm voler'.

Pois flori la seca verga
ni d'en Adam mogron nebot ni
  oncle,
tant fin' amors cum cella q'el cor
  m'intra
non cuig fos anc en cors, ni eis en arma;
on q'ill estei, fors en plaz', o dins
  cambra,
mos cors no · is part de lieis tant cum ten
  l'ongla.

C' aissi s'enpren e s'enongla
mos cors en lei cum l'escorss'en la verga;
q'ill m'es de ioi tors e palaitz e cambra,
e non am tant fraire, paren ni oncle:
q'en paradis n'aura doble ioi m'arma,
si ia nuills hom per ben amar lai
  intra.[28]

Since flowered the dry rod,
or from Adam came forth nephew and
  uncle,
there never was a love so true as that
  which enters
my heart, neither in body nor in soul.
And wherever she may be, outside or in
  her chamber,
I shall be no further than the length of
  my nail.

As if with tooth and nail
my heart grips her, or as the bark the rod;
for to me she is tower, palace and chamber
of joy, and neither brother, parent or
  uncle
I love so much; and in paradise my soul
will find redoubled joy, if lovers therein
  enter.

Dante had many reasons to admire Arnaut and to learn from him. In his *Pietra* poems (see pp. 169–73) he learnt from him how to preserve the emotional resonances of an experience, at a time when his philosophical studies threatened to turn his *canzoni* into over-cerebral virtuoso pieces. He found in him at the same time someone who not only could create new forms in which to praise and expound his love, but also a new style, composed of what Dante calls in *De vulgari eloquentia* 'combed' (*pexa*) and 'shaggy' (*yrsuta*) words, combining charm and power.[29] Above all, Arnaut taught him how to use his eyes and how to stir his slumbering visual imagination into life. Sir Maurice Bowra said of Arnaut that Dante liked and admired him because he saw that 'the soft Italian tongue might easily become too sweet and need some astringent corrective'.[30] Dante was indeed very harsh on some of the earlier Italian poets but here again it must be partly his poet's eclecticism. Poets read selfishly, to improve their craft, to help them to make their own poems—as well as for pleasure—and their instinct may lead them to neglect work of great merit and beauty because their attention is demanded elsewhere. Nevertheless, the Sicilian poets and their Tuscan successors played a vital part in creating the language and the tradition of the *donna angelicata* which Dante inherited. In being transplanted from Southern France to Southern Italy the tradition moved to a very different society, from the freedom of the many scattered small courts and castles to the imperial court of Frederick II. There it was reinforced by strong Arabic influences. At the same time many of the *sirventes* themes, the political ones, could not be taken up, partly because there was only one policy, the emperor's, and partly because these particular energies were devoted to the development of a new grand style of Latin for the imperial chancery under the direction of Pier della Vigne. This meant there was an almost total dedication to the themes of love and the lady. Though deeply influenced by Provençal writing (the area became one of refuge to troubadours during the Albigensian Crusade) the Sicilian school produced much original work. Neoplatonic influences are clearly strong in the earliest of the school, the notary Jacopo da Lentini, who probably invented the sonnet as a distinct form. This is the third stanza of his *canzone* 'Meravigliosamente':

Avendo gran disio,	When filled with great desire
dipinsi una pintura,	I painted a picture,
bella, voi simigliante	My beauty, of your likeness
e quando voi non vio,	And when I do not see you,
guardo 'n quella figura,	I look on your image,
e par ch'eo v'aggia avante:	And it seems I have you before me:
come quello che crede	Just like a man who believes
salvarsi per sua fede,	He will be saved through his faith
ancor non veggia inante[31]	Although he does not see.

Another characteristic of the school was its debates on the nature of love: was it of demonic or divine origin? This debate was initiated was Jacopo Mostacci,[32] falconer to Frederick II, and it was to continue throughout the century. It is interesting that they could raise such a question without ever imputing to the cause of love, their lady, anything but the best of origins. The lady herself is never named except in general terms as the Flower, the precious stone beyond all others, or the Rose of Syria. They preserved the musical tradition of their Provençal forebears and the corpus of their literature contains an exceptional number of delightful lyrics.

Dante does not go out of his way to praise the Sicilian poets. He quotes some of them approvingly in *De vulgari eloquentia*, drawing on their works for instances of style or technique, but lumping Jacopo da Lentini with Guittone d'Arezzo in his conversation with Bonagiunta da Lucca on inspiration. He also quotes,[33] admittedly as an example of Sicilian dialect spoken by the lower classes, the *Contrasto* of Cielo d'Alcamo, a startlingly witty dialogue between a lover and his girl friend which almost certainly was written for dramatic presentation.

The making of a poet

The Sicilian themes were translated to Tuscany by Bonagiunta da Lucca and they were also added to and extended by Guittone d'Arezzo, a voluminous writer of tedious sincerity. Guittone turned away from writing love poems on joining the confraternity of the Frati Godenti, and he was the first Tuscan poet to treat the moral and ethical themes, which Dante was to develop with infinitely greater skill, and on which he based his self-granted title of the poet of righteousness. It was annoyance at Guittone's bungling of great themes, as well as the wide reputation the older poet enjoyed, that made Dante so sharp in his reflections on him.

Other influences encouraged the poets of Central Italy. The poet-king Enzo, son of Frederick II, was taken prisoner by the Bolognese in 1249 and they refused to let him go, keeping him in the fine palace that still bears his name beside Giambologna's Neptune fountain. In his prison court poetry flourished and it was in Bologna that the first great poet of our period was born and wrote, Guido Guinizzelli, *il saggio*, as Dante called him. In Guinizzelli the currents of art and the tributaries of social life that I have been describing met in a fountain of new and original poetry: the theme of service to the lady from feudal Provence survived but it was, in his urban society, shorn of many of the assumptions of courtly love, among them the idea that the lover should be of noble birth, that the poetic language developed in the southern kingdom was refined and enriched in his hands through his vision of his lady that was at once more individual and more universal than that of the earlier poets. More will be said of his particular achievements in the next chapter, when we consider his work and that of his heirs — Dante, Guido Cavalcanti, Lapo Gianni, and others. Here it is enough to take him as the type of man so purified by his love of the lady that he too grows in his moral being, understanding that his own nobility is totally free of the accidents of birth or wealth and utterly dependent on his own virtue. In such an understanding the lady appears as a vision of womanhood so perfect that only through her service can a man achieve perfection for himself.

8

Convergent worlds: the scientific and symbolic modes of thought available to Dante and his contemporaries

An educated Tuscan of Dante's generation would have gathered together, from his reading and from conversation, a body of information about the world[1] and his relation to it that formed a remarkably coherent whole and, if he were a poet, one that allowed him to express it in terms of his own experience of love. From the Tuscan hills at night, he would gaze up from an earth that he knew to be stationary into the night sky which he knew to be darkened by the cone of the earth's shadow travelling around the earth as the sun whirled about it every twenty-four hours. He would pick out the planets, aware of their contrary motions, and distinguish them from the fixed stars against whose zodiacal band the planets moved. The conjunctions of planets and zodiacal signs would be deciding the characters and fates of those being born at that moment and also working the changes of history, raising up and casting down the fortunes of men. Everything above him was in motion, hurtled round by the incredibly fast impetus of the invisible Primum Mobile, the outermost sphere whose motion was caused by its love for God in the stillness of the Empyrean, a love so great that with every part of its being it longed to touch the Godhead. Everything above him was the work of intelligences and of angels; the brightness of the stars would convince him that they were alive and make him reflect on the intuitively felt bond of kinship between his own understanding and the intelligences of the stars to the point that his own experience of love welled up in him, and he saw his own character, the stars, his lady, and the sapiential wisdom of the angels forming a connected pattern that explained the expansion of his emotions and understanding under the power of love.

The origin of this view of the universe can be traced back to Plato, who in his *Timaeus* described the making of a cosmos whose matter is infused with soul and intelligence and whose heavenly bodies move in circular motions. Circular motion, being the most perfect kind of motion, accorded with the perfection of the heavens. Eudoxus and Callippus, following this last requirement of Plato's, produced the concentric model of the universe, consisting of eight concentric heavens ranging inwards from that of the fixed stars to that of the moon, with

103

the motionless Earth at their common centre. Aristotle, following them, postulated for each planet not one, but a system of spheres, to account for irregular motions of the planets. He was particularly interested in what made the planets move and, though he provided each sphere with a soul, ascribed their motions to the rubbing of each outer crystalline sphere upon each inner sphere, driven ultimately by what, in his system, is the outermost sphere, that of the fixed stars. This is the fastest moving sphere and it communicates its diurnal motion all the way through the inner spheres down to the sluggish moon. The planets, though they rotate each day, being carried by the outermost sphere's motion, have their own motions in the opposite direction.

Aristotle's model was widely followed in the Middle Ages, but by Dante's time it was superseded by that of Ptolemy the astronomer of the second century

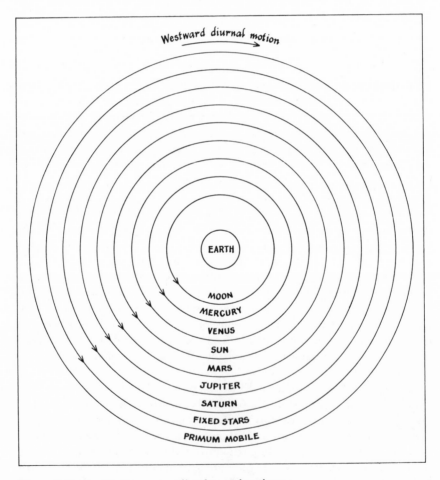

Figure 3 Earth with the surrounding heavenly spheres

AD whose model was more exact mathematically. By using the devices of the moveable eccentric and the epicycle, he was able to give a very accurate description of the movements of the planets. To explain the precession of the equinoxes, the apparent creeping motion of the stars around the axis of the ecliptic, Arab astronomers introduced a ninth sphere outside the stellar sphere, the Primum Mobile, which causes the diurnal motion from east to west. This addition completed the number of spheres in the description of the universe familiar to Dante and his contemporaries. In following Ptolemy rather than Aristotle, Dante aligned himself with most intellectuals of the thirteenth century. Plato's view of the universe suffused with intelligence received a strong backing from the Judaic tradition of angelology, a tradition which became common to both Christendom and Islam. The nine spheres of the heavens were found to tally with the nine orders of angels in the most surprisingly exact way.

Dante refers in the *Inferno*[2] to two men who have made the journey to the Afterlife before him: one was Aeneas and the other St Paul. That St Paul made this journey is assumed from his words:

> I knew a man in Christ above fourteen years ago, (Whether in the body, I cannot tell; or whether out of the body, I cannot tell: God knoweth;) such an one caught up to the third heaven. And I knew such a man (Whether in the body, or out of the body, I cannot tell; God knoweth.) How that he was caught up into paradise, and heard unspeakable words, which it is not lawful for a man to utter.[3]

Many years after St Paul, in the fifth century, an unnamed Syrian monk wrote four books which came to be ascribed to Dionysius the Areopagite whom St Paul converted in Athens (Acts 17:34). It was believed that one of these books, *The Celestial Hierarchies*, with its description of the various orders of angels and their disposition in Heaven, was the result of St Paul describing his vision to Dionysius.* The hierarchies of angels are arranged thus:

Seraphim Cherubim Thrones	1st triad closest to God
Dominions Virtues Powers	2nd triad
Princedoms Archangels Angels	3rd triad

---

*Other arrangements of the angelic orders were possible. Dante followed another arrangement, that given by Brunetto Latini, in *Convivio* II. v. He changed to following the order given by Dionysius when he wrote the *Paradiso*. Gregory the Great put forward yet another system in his *Homilies on the Gospel* and Dante makes the charming remark that Gregory smiled at himself for his mistake on entering heaven (*Par.* XXVIII. 133–5).

It was discovered that these nine orders could easily be related to the heavens of the geocentric model, as in Figure 4. A new and powerful impetus, having at one remove the authority of an apostle, was given to Plato's original statement that the universe is suffused with soul, and to Aristotle's assignment of an intelligence to each sphere.

Throughout Christendom and Islam a great body of the lore concerning the angels was disseminated. It came to be seen that God, in creating the universe, had disposed intelligence in two kinds of being: first in the angelic orders and second in man. The difference between these two orders of intelligence is that the angels receive the revelation of God at once and man only gradually works

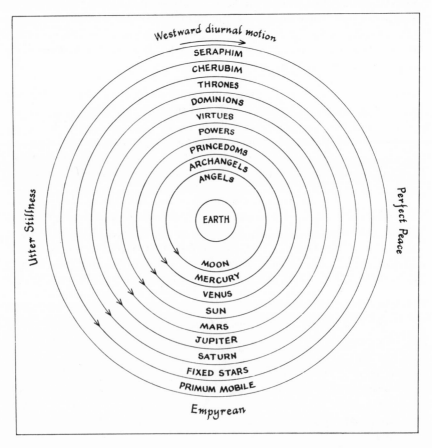

Figure 4 The spheres related to the angelic orders in Dionysius' classification

106

his way towards it. The angelic hierarchy is an image of being; the very spheres of which they are the intelligences revolve not from any action of theirs, but as an effect of their contemplations.[4] Mankind, in contrast, is an image of becoming and man is fated only to reach the truth through the processes of history in ever repeated striving. Both angel and man were involved in the Fall. Lucifer and his followers fell from Heaven to the lowest point in the universe, the centre of Earth, and the lukewarm angels went to Limbo. The good angels remained, as before, devoted to the work of eternal praise and are as perfect as when they were created. Where man is concerned, nature and the universe are there to bring about his perfection: the whole material world exists to support and educate the souls of men.[5]

To many groups of thinkers, both Christian and Islamic, the angels still played a part in the education of man. It was not just that the Ptolemaic-Aristotelian universe received much of its authority from its synthesis with angelology nor that the frequent references to angels in the holy writings of both religions required faith in their existence. To the great Sufi philosopher Avicenna (980–1037), whose works were widely disseminated in the West, they were the means of transmitting spiritual intelligence from God to humanity. Such an idea might offend Augustinian theologians, for example, who were always jealous to defend the direct connexion between the human individual and the Godhead and therefore disliked what seemed to them the interposing of mediating intelligences. The power of the angels was, however, more deeply seated than theological arguments could reach. They accorded with the experience both of the mystics and of the poets. In many accounts, visits to the Other World are nearly always conducted under the guidance of an angel. In Avicenna's recitals and in the writings of Ibn al-'Arabī, the angels or the angel-like figure of Khidr are inner messengers who guide the writer through the world of the imagination and bring order to the universe of symbols.[6] In the poetic revolution brought about by Guido Guinizzelli, the lady who is so indistinct in the works of the earlier Sicilian poets not only appears as an individual woman but also as an incarnate angel. The insistence of these poets on the angelic nature of their ladies bears witness to the depth of an experience forcing them to conclusions that at least varied from orthodoxy. Guinizzelli felt obliged to justify his praise of Lucia to God:

Donna, Deo mi dirà: 'Che presomisti?	My lady, God shall say: 'How did you presume
siando l'alma mia a lui davanti.	
Lo ciel passasti e'nfin a Me venisti,	(When my soul stands before His presence)
e desti in vano amor Me per semblanti;	
ch'a Me conven le laude	To enter Heaven, and before Me come
	To make of Me love's vain resemblance;
	To Me belong the praises

e a la reina del regname degno,	And to the Kingdom's queen,
per cui cessa onne fraude'.	Whose worth all fraud erases.'
Dir Li porò: 'Tenne d'angel sembianza	I can plead of you: 'Of Your realm high above
che fosse del Tuo regno;	She seemed an angel to have been;
non me fu fallo, s'in lei posi amanza.'[7]	I did no wrong, to place in her my love.'

The stanza reflects the need these poets felt to reconcile the two ways of looking at man, one from the point of view of doctrine and the other from the point of view of psychology. Both views were strongly influenced in the thirteenth century by Aristotle and his Arab commentators. First of all, man had to be regarded in the light of the doctrines of the Fall, the Redemption, and the Resurrection. When man fell in Adam, his body, previously perfect and incorruptible, became imperfect and subject to death. Before the Incarnation, all men, except for some of the Jews, were denied salvation. Human nature was in a state of imbalance and, to redeem the balance, as an act of supreme justice and mercy, God took human nature in the second Person of the Trinity. After the crucifixion Christ descended into Hell (this is described in the apocryphal Gospel of Nicodemus), and tore from its grasp certain notables from the past including Adam. Christ ascended to Heaven leaving the possibilities for humanity changed for ever. Man's perfection consists in both body and soul and therefore the soul without the body does not have the perfection of its nature. The souls that Dante meets in the afterworld are therefore in an intermediate state awaiting perfection in the Resurrection.

The four cardinal virtues which shine as a kind of Southern Cross over Mount Purgatory were all that were necessary to man's right living before the Fall. After the Fall they were all that the best of the pagans had to guide them to a life of virtue but with their influence diminished by original sin. Original sin would be wiped out by the sacrament of baptism, and the three theological virtues, faith, hope, and charity, were granted to lead men to salvation, with the added graces of the other sacraments of the Church. Thus if a man died in a state of contrition and having received absolution (or at least having the right intention) he would no longer go to Hell but to Purgatory, where the sins of his life would be erased by punishments eagerly submitted to. After a period of time that varies greatly from soul to soul he is finally admitted to the company of the blessed in Heaven. That is a general statement of the doctrines that defined man's journey through this world and the next.

Man's psychology following the reintroduction of Aristotle's *De anima* was described in relation to the rest of nature. Every living thing has a soul or vital principle that underlies its physical activities. Plants have a vegetative soul whose powers are nutrition, growth, and propagation. Animals have a sensitive soul which adds to the qualities of the vegetative soul those of sentience and movement. Man has a rational soul, which adds the qualities of thinking and free choice to those of the lower souls. These souls were considered to be immaterial and therefore the question was raised of how the body was connected with the souls. This connexion was performed by the spirits which had a subtle and intermediate nature and which were located in different parts of the body. It is these that cry out so forcibly in the opening of the *Vita Nuova* when Dante falls in love with Beatrice.

As it was through drawing on the medical language of physiology and psychology that Cavalcanti and his friends transformed the tradition of love poetry and produced a new school of intellectualized and 'scientific' poetry, something must be said of the theory underlying these ideas. The spirits, the medium of our psychologies, were thought, on the authority of Galen, to arise in the following way. The chyle, which is the product of digestion, travels from the stomach to the liver, and by a second stage of digestion the blood and other humours are produced together with the natural spirit from which the other spirits are evolved. The natural spirit ascends through the veins to the left ventricle of the heart. Through heating in the heart the vital spirit is formed which is incorporated in the arterial system and brings heat to the members of the body. It then moves to the brain where, under further heating, it is changed to the animal spirit, the noblest of the spirits. This, passing through hollow nerves, imparts motion and sensation to the body, and acts as the medium of communication for the perceptive faculties of the soul. The brain has three cells and the animal spirits serve, in the anterior cell, the faculties of common sense, imagination (in the sense of image-making) and *fantasia*, in the middle cell, the faculties of judgment (*aestimativa*) and thought (*cogitativa*) and,

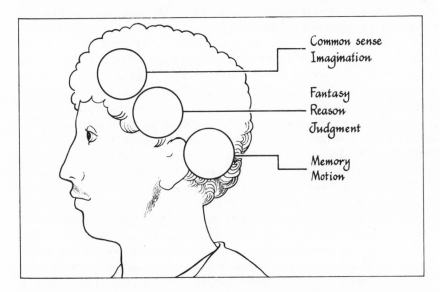

Figure 5 The three cells or ventricles with their faculties, based on various drawings and engravings in Clarke and Dewhurst, *An Illustrated History of Brain Function* (Oxford, 1972)

in the posterior cell, the faculty of memory. There were many variations possible within this basic framework: sometimes *fantasia* as a higher imaginative faculty is placed in the second cell and Albertus Magnus placed motor function in the third cell.[8]

Thus the workings of the animal spirits in the three cells could be shown to demonstrate an orderly process of cognition from the first sight of the beloved to the creation of her image within as a permanently acquired treasure, from the first inkling of a poem to its fully evolved form. The physiological basis of the psychology of spirits has been entirely exploded by modern medicine: the system was ignorant of the circulation of the blood and depended on several physical mechanisms that have been shown not to exist. Although the causal basis of this psychology is without foundation, that should not blind us to the excellence of the system as a way of describing our psychological experiences and as a model on which to base ventures into self-knowledge. The variety and number of the spirits, for example, account for the extraordinary jumble of desires, thoughts, moods, and sensations that constantly fight for supremacy in our natures, and when the *fedeli d'amore* applied this psychological terminology to what happened when they fell in love or when they were inspired to write, they found that it provided them with a whole body of new subject-matter to explore and describe.

It might seem at first that the teaching on the spirits and their dependence on the physiology of the body would lead to a mechanical and deterministic outlook, but this was not so. Where inspiration was concerned Thomas Aquinas explained how an angel could set in motion the physiological processes that led to the conception and interpretation of a vision.[9] The angel would induce the movement of spirits and humours to present a man with the vision and alter his intellect so that it was capable of interpreting it. Similarly, falling in love was initiated by a ray from the third heaven (or by a shadow from Mars in the case of Cavalcanti's 'Donna mi prega'). Falling in love could be explained as the passing of spirits through the medium of light from the eyes of the lady to the heart of the lover, a process described by Cavalcanti in 'Veggio negli occhi' (see p. 118). This movement of spirits would awaken desire in the lover and, if he were of a coarse nature, the desire, as Cavalcanti says in 'Donna mi prega' might have a disastrous effect on him, affecting his rational judgment. In the man possessing the *cor gentile*, the spirits passing from the eyes of the lady and entering into his nature could set in motion a progression that could lead to the creation in him of an intellectual love, and the possession of the *intelletto d'amore*. 'Since the intellectual faculty was considered to be the distinguishing characteristic of the human being, to love humanly was to love intellectually.'[10] The process would seem to involve a transformation of sexual energy, through which the love of the lady's exterior form would dissolve into love of the miraculous revelation of her soul, and, by implication, to a universal love of the Maker of her soul. This process of the transformation of the sensual into rational love, as we know from the laments of the *fedeli d'amore* and from the *Vita Nuova*, would seem frequently to have been extremely painful. It could result, however, in moments of transcendental understanding or ecstasy. It would appear that there were definite stages or degrees in this progression, somewhat like the degrees set out by Diotima in the *Symposium* or by St Augustine in *De quantitate*, a work that was to affect the fundamental form of the *Commedia* (see Chapter 18). Dante says that it would be impossible for anyone to understand the destructive effect of love on his spirits who was not a *fedele d'amore* of a similar grade.[11]

The question of what was the nature of the rational soul in man was also raised. The rational soul has the two faculties of *ratio* and *intellectus*. Aquinas describes the relationship between them thus:

> to understand [*intelligere*] is to apprehend quite simply an intelligible truth, to reason [*ratiocinari*] is to move from one thing understood to another, so as to know an intelligible truth . . . the relation of reasoning to understanding is that of motion to rest, or of acquiring to having; the first is of the incomplete, the second of the complete.[12]

Intellectus is higher than *ratio* and is the form of cognition enjoyed perfectly by the angels and generally only imperfectly by man.

How did a man grasp truth in his intellect? Following Aristotle it was generally agreed that men possessed the potential knowledge of things as they are and that, to varying degrees, they shared in this potential knowledge or possible intellect; the knowledge was actualized by an irradiating force called the active intellect, which came from beyond man and accounted for his understanding of suprasensible things. The active intellect was something far more marvellous than the name might suggest; it was also called the Angel, or Intelligentia, or Sapientia, being in the last case identified with the Wisdom of the Solomonic books. To many of the poets with whom we are dealing, the lady, to whom they were drawn by the love in their hearts, was this same active intellect bringing their latent potentialities into the clear light of understanding. As Corbin says:

> This Figure imposes itself in the imperious manner of a central symbol, appearing to man's mental vision under the complementary feminine aspect that makes his being a total being. The mystical Iranian 'Ushshaq and the *fedeli d'amore*, companions of Dante, profess a secret religion that, though free from any confessionary denomination, is none the less common to them all. . . . The union that joins the possible intellect of the human soul with the Active Intelligence as *Dator formarum*, Angel of Knowledge, or Wisdom-Sophia, is visualized and experienced as a love union.[13]

This description of the workings of the human psyche and how it received communications from higher intelligences was of the greatest value to the poets of the *dolce stil nuovo*. It was dangerous ground, however, because of the use put to the idea of the active intelligence by the Arab commentator on Aristotle, Averroes, and his many followers in the West. Averroes was held responsible for the doctrine of the unity of the intellect according to which each man is enlightened during his life by the active intellect and is deserted by it on his death. Soul is one and, from this, it follows that there can be no personal immortality because there is no means by which man can impress his individual nature upon soul. The idea was a serious threat to doctrine and to man's personal responsibility for his actions, even when maintained by a philosopher such as Sigier of Brabant to whom it was a philosophical conclusion and, as such, independent of the teaching of revealed religion. It was against this idea that Aquinas was to fight some of his fiercest battles. Dante seems to have been aloof from this particular controversy: he gives Averroes an honoured place in Limbo, quotes him in the *Monarchia*, and makes Aquinas praise Sigier in the *Paradiso*.

Curiously enough, whereas the idea of the active intellect when made universal seemed to theologians a threat to the individual and to his immortality, to these poets it was what purified them, under the guise of Sapientia or Madonna Intelligenza, as Dino Compagni called his lady, and made them more individual. In another way these poets preserved the integrity of the individual because, instead of their being absorbed into the unity of the active intellect, it was the active intellect which was made individual in their ladies. Clerics had tried to make the figure of Wisdom in the Solomonic books into a symbol of Ecclesia, the Church. The poets, of course, knew better. The danger, where the Church was concerned, could be that by finding his individual way to divine knowledge through his lady, who was his particular image of Sapientia, the poet was by-passing the necessary mediation of the Church, and indeed declaring his independence of its teachings.[14] In an early poem to Beatrice, Dante says that, when he dies, the love he has experienced will so grip his soul that it will accompany it before God and, even though God sends his soul into torment, it will be so intent on contemplating the image of Beatrice that it will feel no terror nor will it notice any punishment.[15]

The symbol of Sapientia was so all-embracing it could include all the various philosophical and symbolic approaches to truth and understanding that we have been surveying. So, to Guinizzelli, the girl he sees wearing a hat of grey squirrel fur so proudly that she leaves him trembling like a snake's chopped-off head is also the lady with the semblance of an angel—the lady whose very nature justifies his love to God. A poet's 'lady' included in her meanings even the mystery of the Incarnation, so that Dante could parallel the events of Beatrice's life with those of the life of Christ. The Sapientia of the Solomonic books was seen to be the eternally existing Wisdom of Christ, as Sapientia says in Proverbs:

> The Lord possessed me in the beginning of his way, before his works of old.

I was set up from everlasting, from the beginning, or ever the earth was.

When there were no depths, I was brought forth; when there were no fountains abounding with water.

Before the mountains were settled, before the hills was I brought forth:

While as yet he had not made the earth, nor the fields, nor the highest part of the dust of the world.

When he prepared the heavens, I was there: when he set a compass upon the face of the depth:

When he established the clouds above: when he strengthened the fountains of the deep:

When he gave to the sea his decree, that the waters should not pass his commandment: when he appointed the foundations of the earth:

Then I was by him, as one brought up with him: and I was daily his delight, rejoicing always before him;

Rejoicing in the habitable part of his earth; and my delights were with the sons of men.[16]

It was to this Wisdom that Justinian had raised his great church of Hagia Sophia, crying out as he entered it: 'Solomon, I have surpassed you!' It was this Wisdom that poets of Christendom and Islam found individuated in the ladies of their hearts and minds. It was this Wisdom that inflamed the mystics of religious orders to urge others to experience the ascent of the soul through love, as did St Bernard in his sermons on the Song of Solomon. The only words the dying Aquinas wished to hear were those from the same canticles of the espousal of the soul with her beloved. Her divine knowledge illuminated the mystic, instructed the philosopher, and inspired the artist, thus making the poets part of a great and shared tradition of inner understanding so that each could ask with Solomon:

Who is she that looketh forth as the morning, fair as the moon, clear as the sun, and terrible as an army with banners?[17]

and find the answer coming towards him in the girl walking along a street in Florence, about to give him her greeting.

The master of all the Florentine poets in the manipulation of these philosophical and psychological ideas and terms was Guido Cavalcanti, who saw his own nature as a theatre in which the struggles and sorrows of love were played out. He would appear to have been strongly influenced by Averroist teachings, especially in his *canzone* 'Donna mi prega'. He also introduced into poetry, the concept of the spirits, the instruments of the soul in all its vital operations, treating them as divisions of his nature that he would address and that would be transformed or destroyed by the sight of his lady.

113

Like Dante, Guido found Sapientia in several loves, among them two ladies called Giovanna and Mandetta. It is difficult to distinguish between them in his poems, because he devotes his attention so much to the effect of the lady on *him*. What he describes again and again is a process of transformation of his intelligence, the death of his old mind in bewilderment and his surrender to the lady, and his union with her in a new understanding. What has been interpreted as despair and melancholy in, for example, his ballad 'Perch'i' no spero' ends with a triumphant promise to his soul that it will dwell for ever with the lady of the sweet intellect and adore her.

One of the most important characteristics shared by the poets of the *dolce stil nuovo* is the attention they paid to their visions and dreams. They might perhaps differ among themselves in their individual philosophical bent, as Guido Cavalcanti tended towards Averroes and Dante to Platonism, but what really mattered to them was their visions and, by judging the visions that formed the inspiration of their poems, they could estimate how deeply the imagery they possessed in common had entered into an individual's experience. They took care to distinguish those dreams that were based on truth and those that were pathological in origin. Dante's first dream sonnet, 'A ciascun' alma presa', won Guido's blessing as an authentic experience, but Dante da Maiano, following the best medical advice, advised him to wash his testicles frequently to stop vapours rising to his head and causing such dreams.[18] Dante da Maiano had himself issued a dream sonnet in which he described how his lady gave him a green garland; how he found himself wearing her shift; how they embraced; and how his dead mother was standing nearby. This sonnet prompted replies from Dante Alighieri, which are thought to be his earliest poems.[19]

The most powerful expression of a vision in verse before Dante's poems is this sonnet by Guido Guinizzelli.

Lo vostro bel saluto e 'l gentil sguardo	Your handsome greeting, your regard so fair,
che fate quando v'encontro, m'ancide;	
Amor m'assale e già non ha reguardo	Are such when we meet I am quickly slain;
s'elli face peccato o ver merzede,	Then Love attacks me and he does not care
ché per mezzo lo cor me lanciò un dardo	
ched oltre 'n parte lo taglia e divide;	Whether he grants good or wrongful pain.
parlar non posso, che 'n pene io ardo,	Straight through my heart he thrusts a spear
sì come quelli che sua morte vede.	That cuts and divides it into twain
	I cannot speak and suffer the fear
Per li occhi passa come fa lo trono,	Of a man who sees his death made plain.
che fer' per la finestra de la torre	
e ciò che dentro trova spezza e fende:	He strikes through my eyes as lightning brands
remagno como statua d'ottono	Lance through the window of the tower,
	Wasting all within its length and span:
	I stay like a statue made of bronze

ove vita né spirto non ricorre,
se non che la figura d'omo rende.[20]

Where life and spirit never again shall
recur
Except I keep the likeness of a man.

The sestet of this sonnet is nothing short of stupendous. It introduces into vernacular literature a new kind of imagery, imagery that is not just visual but three-dimensionally plastic. The reader becomes the tower through which the lightning strikes and experiences the destruction throughout his own being; he becomes the bronze bust and yet he can walk about it as though it were in a gallery. It is an achievement comparable to that of Giotto, with his introduction of a new experience of volume and the roundedness of bodies and things, but it must antedate Giotto by two decades. It is the achievement towards which Dante was working first most successfully in his prose and finally in the *Commedia*, in such lines as this when, to describe the astonishment of the souls in Purgatory at seeing a living man who casts a shadow, he describes how they gaze:

pur me, pur me, e 'l lume ch'era
    rotto.[21]

At me alone, at me alone, and the light
    that was broken.

The piling up of detail plays almost no part in conveying the immediacy and physical reality of experience. The force of such images derives instead from a moment of integration between the inner dream world and outer experience, a moment actualized by higher intelligence.

The vision poems take various forms. Some follow the tradition of Jaufre Rudel and the *amor de lonh*. Among these are the ideal journey that Dante wishes the kind enchanter to grant him and his companions; and the ideal Florence that Lapo Gianni sees in 'Amor, eo chero mia donna in domino', when the world is at peace and every road is safe and he would be as handsome as Absalom and rule like Samson and Solomon. They include poems with cosmological settings implied, as in the second stanza of 'Donne ch'avete' (see p. 119), and even those that are not particularly graphic in their expression refer constantly to things seen, to the vision of the lady giving her greeting or to the transformation of spirit. It may be that the symbolic language those poets shared was based on a series of pictorial symbols such as was used by the Spiritualist followers of Joachim of Fiore; the manuscript of the *Documenti d'amore* of a Florentine poet writing a few years later, Francesco da Barberino, is full of mysterious emblems depicting love in various stages.[22] Dante, as he tells us in the *Vita Nuova*, was discovered drawing an angel after the death of Beatrice.

It may be that what these poets had in common was a method of contemplation that expanded consciousness in them so that they were made open to the illumination of Sapientia, and that an effect of this expanded consciousness was to open up to them the world of the imagination, the world of symbols, the *alam-al-mithal* of Ibn al-'Arabī, through which Love acted as their guide.[23] I offer this as a conjecture, but the suggestion would help to account for the problem of the secret language mentioned in Chapter 6, page 84. It was a secret language, not so much in Valli's sense of a *gergo*[24] in which one term replaced another to put the Inquisition off the scent of heresy (though their ideas were certainly capable of misinterpretation and suspicion) but a language as highly developed as the poets could make it, drawing on scholastic and biblical language, to express an experience that only they or those possessing the *cor gentile* shared. In a way they were being as open as they knew how; they had the problem of expressing in words not simply the ineffable experience of mystical illumination but that illumination experienced through woman, in whom divine and earthly love were united as one.

To interpret and express their visions and inspirations, the poets drew on two important sources. One of these was numerology, the discovery and use of the objective meanings residing in numbers and patterns of numbers. The other was the rich heritage of symbolism, with its related technique of the transformation of images.

Numerology was particularly linked to the tradition of Sapientia. St Bonaventure says that a man contemplating things in themselves sees in them weight, number, and measure: 'weight, which directs them to a certain location; number, by which they are distinguished from one another; and measure, by which they are limited'.[25] From these a man rises from the traces of creation to the power, wisdom, and goodness of the Creator. Thus number, the principle of individuation, is particularly connected with the wisdom of the second Person of the Trinity. The meaning of numbers was also highly important in the study of cosmology, because one aspect of Plato's statement that creation is suffused with intelligence is that this intelligence proceeds throughout the universe according to mathematical laws and proportions. There is a virtue in numbers far beyond their nature as ciphers or their use for practical purposes in trade, construction, or warfare. Through understanding the virtues of different numbers, the relationship between them, their squares and their cubes, and the process known as mystic addition, not only can we grasp the connexions between our own natures and the universe because they are both built according to the same mathematical laws, but, when we create something ourselves, we must, to make perfect works of art, employ the numerological symbolism best suited to the work in devising its proportions or disposing the relationship of its parts to the whole. The Pythagorean and Platonic doctrines on number were eagerly taken up by early Christian writers, most notably St Augustine, who wrote his *De musica* on music and metre, basing it on numerological principles, and who would arrange the chapters of his other works so that they amounted to numbers that particularly expressed their nature. Classical number lore was preserved for the Middle Ages in Martianus Capella's *Marriage of Philology and Mercury*,[26] a fifth-century work that, with its alternating passages in verse and prose, provided, possibly, a model for the *Vita*

Nuova. The Judaic number symbolism of the cabala was also a potent influence. What made the Christians so receptive to numerology was their own doctrine of the Trinity, which made them search for patterns of three throughout creation as evidence of its Maker. Later Latin poets, such as Bernard of Cluny, would prefer to write in triple or compound rhythms because they did greater honour to their subjects.

It is well known that Dante constructed the *Commedia* on numerological principles, with its three parts comprising ninety-nine cantos plus one, relating throughout to the *terza rima* pattern of its rhyming, and it is also accepted that the *Vita Nuova* is also arranged according to a pattern that brings out the significance of nine, the number of Beatrice, related as the square of three to the Trinity, from whom she proceeds as a miracle. It is possible that the disposition of rhymes and the number of stanzas in the *canzoni* of the *fedeli d'amore* were also based on numerological principles. It would in fact be surprising if it were not so, given that the *canzone* form was based on the musical song form of repeating a melody and then opposing to the first melody another melody and that music itself was analysed for its numerological properties. In any case, the main point to note here is that numerology was part of these poets' technique; it was not an imposed doctrine but a thoroughly practical aid to planning and executing the writing of a poem, and the symbolism of the numbers they used added another dimension of meaning to their readers' understanding.

Numerological thought would also have been familiar to these poets through its use in prophecy by the Spiritual Franciscans. Their predecessor, Joachim of Fiore, derived much of his authority from his skill in finding number patterns in scripture to support his prophecies and in translating them into memorable images or *figurae*.[27] Dante will use the number nine in the *Vita Nuova* in everything to do with Beatrice, showing by its presence at the beginning of their relationship that the events that follow are prophesied in its intrinsic nature.

The heritage of symbolism these poets drew on was also influenced by prophecy, because it underlay the science of typology, a method of interpreting the Old Testament by finding resemblances between the lives and deeds of historical personages and events and the life of Christ. This technique had a profound influence on the range of Christian symbolism available to poets writing in Latin. It enabled them to 'convert' their images in a series of graphic progressions, as, for example, in the well-known hymn of Venantius Fortunatus (*c.* 530–*c.* 610), 'Vexilla regis prodeunt', which Dante parodies in *Inferno* XXXIV. In Venantius' hymn, the cross on the banners transforms into the gallows and then into the victim in the flesh pierced by the spear and dripping with water and blood. David's prophecy is recalled that God will reign from a tree. The ugly gallows now becomes a lovely tree hung with the imperial purple and again it transforms into a scale or balance weighing the ransom of the world. Thus image grows out of image, a technique employed much later by the writers of sequences such as Notker Balbulus. It is a rapid, shorthand way of expressing correspondences and it has its parallel amongst our poets, who would have been familiar with the technique from the liturgy, in those poems in which they listed all the wonders that their ladies surpassed, and in the dynamism of their imagery. Cavalcanti, for example, in the poem 'Veggio negli occhi della donna mia', describes a progression of transformations:

Cosa m'aven, quand' i' le son presente,	When I am in her presence, something
ch' i' no la posso a lo 'ntelletto dire:	happens to me
veder mi par de la sua labbia uscire	that I cannot tell to the intellect:
una sì bella donna, che la mente	I seem to see outgoing from her lips
comprender no la può, ché 'mmantenente	a lady so beautiful that the mind
ne nasce un'altra di bellezza nova,	cannot comprehend her, so that at once
da la qual par ch'una stella si mova	another is born of her, of new beauty,
e dica: 'La salute tua è apparita'.[28]	from whom it seems a star moves out
	and says 'Your salvation has appeared'.

Here his lady appears to him as the active intellect of the heaven of the moon, transforming into the intelligence of the heaven of Mercury and then into the intelligence of Venus, the third heaven.[29] In other poems the stanza structure aids the rapid progression of images because the form acts like a constant frame in which the new pictures appear. Dante was to extend greatly the possibilities of this technique, basing, as I hope to show, the dynamic symbolism of the *Commedia* in it. Mandelstam, in his *Conversation about Dante*, produced this description of it:

As in all true poetry, Dante's thinking in images is accomplished with the help of a characteristic of poetic material which I propose to call its transformability or convertibility. It is only by convention that the development of an image can be called development. Indeed, imagine to yourself an airplane (forgetting the technical impossibility) which in full flight constructs and launches another machine. In just the same way, this second flying machine, completely absorbed in its own flight, still manages to assemble and launch a third. In order to make this suggestive and helpful comparison more precise, I will add that the assembly and launching of these technically unthinkable machines that are sent flying off in the midst of flight do not constitute a secondary or peripheral function of the plane that is in flight; they form a most essential attribute and part of the flight itself, and they contribute no less to its feasibility and safety than the proper functioning of the steering gear or the uninterrupted working of the engine.[30]

How all these strands of knowledge and experience that have been discussed in this chapter were brought together may be demonstrated by a reading of Dante's first great *canzone* in the *Vita Nuova* XIX:

Convergent worlds: scientific and symbolic modes of thought

1

Donne ch'avete intelletto d'amore,
i' vo' con voi de la mia donna dire,
non perch'io creda sua laude
  finire,
ma ragionar per isfogar la mente.

Io dico che pensando il suo valore,
Amor sì dolce mi si fa sentire,

che s'io allora non perdessi
  ardire,
farei parlando innamorar la
  gente.

E io non vo' parlar sì altamente,

ch'io divenisse per temenza
  vile;
ma tratterò del suo stato gentile
a respetto di lei leggeramente,

donne e donzelle amorose, con vui,
ché non è cosa da parlarne altrui.

1

Ladies who possess the intellect of love,
To tell you of my lady I desire,
Not that I claim to show her praise
  entire
But so, by speech, I ease my mind's sad
  plight.

I say, from my reflections on her worth,
Such sweetness now does Love in me
  inspire
That, did I not lose courage, I would
  fire
All men to fall in love through my
  words' might.

I must not pitch my style to
  such a height

That I might fail my theme, betrayed
  by fear.
So I'll portray her gentle nature here
In words that poorly answer to her
  right,
Loving ladies and girls, alone to you;
Others must not learn what is for the
  few.

oda 1

oda 2

concatenatio pulchra the lovely linking

sirma

2

Angelo clama in divino intelletto
e dice: 'Sire, nel mondo si vede
maraviglia ne l'atto che procede
d'un'anima che 'nfin qua su
  risplende.'
Lo cielo, che non have altro difetto
che d'aver lei, al suo segnor la
  chiede,
e ciascun santo ne grida
  merzede.
Sola Pietà nostra parte difende,
che parla Dio, che di madonna intende:
'Diletti miei, or sofferite in pace
che vostra spene sia quanto me
  piace
là 'v'è alcun che perder lei
  s'attende,
e che dirà ne lo inferno: "O mal nati,
io vidi la speranza de' beati".'

2

An angel cries in the divine intellect,
Saying, 'Lord, the world now heeds
A wonder in action that proceeds
From a soul whose splendour even here
  has climbed!'
Heaven, which suffers no other defect
Except her lack, begs God for her and
  pleads;
Each saint shouts for this boon; there
  intercedes
Pity alone for the cause of mankind.
God now speaks with my lady in
  mind:
'My chosen people, as long as I ordain,
Endure in peace that your hope shall
  remain
There where a man lives, to her loss
  resigned,
Who shall say in Hell "O souls accurst,
I have looked on the hope of the
  blest".'

119

3

Madonna è disïata in sommo
cielo:
or vòi di sua virtù farvi savere.
Dico, qual vuol gentil donna parere
vada con lei, che quando va per
via,
gitta nei cor villani Amore un
gelo,
per che onne lor pensero agghiaccia
e pere;
e qual soffrisse di starla a vedere
diverria nobil cosa, o si mor-
ria.
E quando trova alcun che degno
sia
di veder lei, quel prova sua
vertute,
chè li avvien, ciò che li dona, in
salute.
e sì l'umilia, ch'ogni offesa oblia.
Ancor l'ha Dio per maggior grazia
dato
che non pò mal finir chi l'ha
parlato.

3

My lady is desired in the height of
heaven.
Now let me make her qualities clear.
I say: the lady, wishing to appear
As good, should walk with her; she
passes by
And Love throws ice on hearts of
wicked men
So all their thoughts are frozen and
expire.
Whoever stood firm to look and admire
Would be made noble or else he would
die.
When she chances to find a man
nearby
Worthy of seeing her, her power is
displayed.
Out of the happiness she grants, he is
made
So humble he forgets any injury.
Thus God bestowed on her the greater
grace
That none ends ill who greets her face
to face.

4

Dice di lei Amor: 'Cosa
mortale
come esser pò sì adorna e sì pura?'
Poi la reguarda, e fra se stesso
giura
che Dio ne 'ntenda di far cosa
nova.
Color di perle ha quasi, in forma
quale
convene a donna aver, non for misura:
ella è quanto de ben pò far natura;
per essemplo di lei bieltà si
prova.
De li occhi suoi, come ch'ella li mova,
escono spirti d'amore inflammati,
che feron li occhi a qual che allor la
guati,
e passan sì che 'l cor ciascun
retrova:
voi le vedete Amor pinto nel
viso,

4

Love says of her: 'How can a mortal
creature
Be fair and pure to so full a degree?'
He looks and swears to himself that
she
Was made by God portending some-
thing new.
A colour like pearl adorns every
feature,
Extreme in nothing but all as should be.
She is the height of nature's artistry.
Hers is the image Beauty issues
through.
Out of her eyes, whatever they view,
Inflammatory spirits of love dispatch
To strike the eyes of those who
watch,
Passing to the heart within, aimed
true.
You see how Love is painted in
her face

là 've non pote alcun mirarla fiso.	Where none can bear to look for any space.

5

Canzone, io so che tu girai parlando	My song, I know that when I send you out,
a donne assai, quand'io t'avrò avanzata.	You'll speak to many ladies as you fare.
Or t'ammonisco, perch'io t'ho allevata	I warn you since I raised you in my care
per figliuola d'Amor giovane e piana,	As Love's own daughter, young, of modest strain,
che là 've giugni tu diche pregando:	That you enquire in travelling about:
'Insegnatemi gir, ch'io son mandata	'Where should I go? for I must now repair
a quella di cui laude so' adornata.'	To her whose praise as ornament I bear.'
E se non vuoli andar sì come vana,	You will not want to journey on in vain;
non restare ove sia gente villana:	Where the people are coarse, do not remain.
ingegnati, se puoi, d'esser palese	Reveal yourself openly if you can
solo con donne o con omo cortese,	Only to ladies or a courteous man
che ti merranno là per via tostana.	Who'll guide you by a road that's quick and plain.
Tu troverai Amor con esso lei;	You will discover Love beside her found.
raccomandami a lui come tu dei.	Commend me to him there as you are bound.

This *canzone* follows the general rules of its form which is dictated by its musical origins. The first four lines of each stanza are a melody, marked 'oda 1' above; that melody is repeated in the next four lines (oda 2). There is a transition marked by the carrying over of the last rhyme word in the oda, in what was known as the 'lovely linking' or *concatenatio pulchra*, into the second part of the stanza known as the *sirma*. This is not repeated. The *canzone* generally ended with a *tornata* telling the *canzone* to whom it should go. In this case the *tornata* follows the pattern of the preceding stanzas, though it was not always so. There were several other ways in which a *canzone* stanza could be arranged. Dante discusses these in the second book of *De vulgari eloquentia*.[31] The repeated and contrasting tunes form a basic pattern for the stanzas, which provide a constant frame within which the ideas are developed and the images are converted.

There is another aspect of its construction into which Dante goes at length in the *Vita Nuova* (XIX) and that is its formal divisions. The poem has three main divisions: the first part is stanza 1, which is a prologue; the second part consists of the middle three stanzas beginning with 'Angelo clama'; and the third is the

121

last stanza, which is the *tornata*. Part I is subdivided into four; Part II is broken down into a progression of binary subdivisions always proceeding from the second; he does not subdivide the *tornata* because it is clear enough already. Now Dante says he is making the *canzone* more comprehensible by all these subdivisions, though he gives nothing in the way of commentary on the meaning of the poem. He even says he thinks he has revealed too much of its meaning by these subdivisions and it looks as though he is saying something about the poem through the numerological significance of the divisions. His scheme of divisions may be set out as in Figure 6. The divisions of Part I are of an equal standing and come to four, which is the number of wholeness, in this case the wholeness of understanding of love. The four stages of subdivisions in Part II reveal a descent into incarnation which reflects the comparison of Beatrice with Christ (this is dealt with more fully in the next chapter). The numbers of stages descending from and including the first division of Part II makes 9, which is the number peculiarly associated with Beatrice. This part is made up of stanzas 2, 3, and 4, which, by mystic addition $(2 + 3 + 4 = 9)$, also emphasizes the precise numerological connection. If the three main parts are related to weight, number, and measure as described by St Bonaventure, which are in turn reflections of the divine power, wisdom, and goodness, then Part I concerns the location of the *intelletto d'amore* in those worthy to hear about Beatrice and the power that Dante has to keep in check in case all people are made to fall in love. Part II concerns what distinguishes the individual nature of Beatrice from her significance in the cosmos, down to her eyes and mouth, and so demonstrates the manifestation of Divine Wisdom. *Pietà*, translated above as 'pity', can also mean 'piety', a characteristic[32] of the lowest order of angels, those in the sphere of the moon and therefore the diffusers of the active intellect among humanity. This is why only *Pietà* defends our cause. And Part III concerns measure—what limits and what deals with distance and travel—by telling the *canzone* that it must go on a journey, only stopping with those who are good.

The framing effect of the exactly similar stanzas demonstrates the convertibility of images through the device of picking out someone or a group in a crowd, from the apostrophe at the opening to those who among humanity possess the intellect of love. The *donne e donzelle* are transformed in the next stanza into the blessed in the nine spheres of Heaven crying out to the Divine Majesty, to whom the light of Beatrice ascends, while *la gente*, the people of the first stanza, become the *malnati* to whom Dante will speak in Hell. In stanza 3 there is a call to surround Beatrice with ladies and with men who wish to be transformed. In the next stanza she is the touchstone of nature's art and the canon of beauty, and the crowd turns into the flaming spirits that issue from her eyes. In the *tornata* the *canzone* is sent out among people distinguished between the good and the bad and finally makes its way to Beatrice.

The poem contains a great variety of scenes, moods, and incidents, after many readings still astonishing us with the sudden elevation into the heavens of

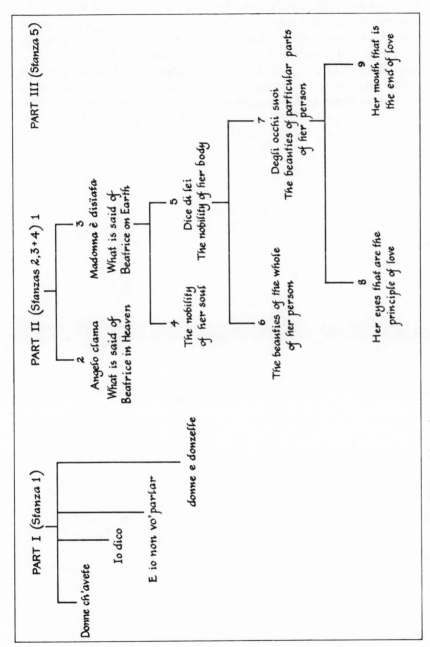

Figure 6 The structure of 'Donne ch'avete'

the second stanza, reaching its climax in the exultant boast of 'Madonna è disïata in sommo cielo', changing its movement in the return to Earth as the ladies surround her and the men stand in amazement, subsiding into the gentle musing of Love on the miracle of her, exploding once more in the spirits darting from her eyes, and passing away in the image of the poem's own journey.

This discussion of the poem has been intended only to relate it to the preceding passages on the intellectual and artistic climate of its time and to demonstrate something of the complex planning that went into its making. The experience that inspired it and made it into the first example of the poetry of praise will be told in discussing the *Vita Nuova* which it also adorns.

9

La Vita Nuova and the poetry of praise

Jacob Burckhardt said of Dante's youthful poems that they marked the boundary between medievalism and modern times and he went on to remark: 'The human spirit had taken a mighty step towards the consciousness of its own secret life.'[1] Many of these poems Dante collected and arranged in his first major work, the *Vita Nuova*; the new life of its title describes the growth in Dante of an expanded consciousness, and it does this in a way no secular writing had ever achieved before. Burckhardt's 'mighty step' may be described as one in the journey of Christianity towards an ever greater realization of man's inner understanding, and of his ability to express his experience as an individual. Christianity had destroyed the mythology by which men of classical times had lived and according to which they interpreted their experience. In doing so, it brought about a gigantic revolution in the symbolism, in the rules governing personal relationships and mores, and in all the preconceptions which give a society its cohesion and which are so much a matter of custom that they are hardly questioned. For explanation of the outer world Christianity replaced mythology with a new and grander view of history based on the Incarnation; for the discovery of the inner world of human psychology it offered a journey to the consciousness symbolized by Christ as the Sun of Righteousness within a man's soul. 'The kingdom of God is within you', says Christ, and in searching inwards for that kingdom men discovered new faculties, new terrors and new treasures of the spirit, aided by the rites and prayers of the Church, the symbolism of the sun, and the faith in, and the hope of, the charity of the kingdom awaiting them. There are two aspects of the Incarnation that relate particularly to the *Vita Nuova*: one concerns the outer world to which Christ comes in the flesh onto an Earth whose matter He redeems even to its densest and most unregenerate forms by His descent into Hell; the other world is the inner one of the human soul into which He may be born by grace and to whose darkest reaches He brings the light of understanding and reconciliation. This is what Meister Eckhart describes as follows:

Thus my text says: 'God sent his only begotten Son into the world'—and by that you should not understand the external world in which he ate and drank with us but you should know that it refers to the inner world.[2]

In both aspects Christ comes to take on Himself the sins of the whole world, and from its earliest days the Church found in the practice of auricular confession a means of cleansing the individual of the burden of guilt. Autobiography grows out of the practice of confession. *The Shepherd of Hermas*, for example, a Christian work of the second century AD, contains a series of visions which have been compared to those in the *Vita Nuova*; what the writer learnt from these visions was a new understanding of doctrine on penitence. The first autobiography of Christendom is the *Confessions* of St Augustine who, using the form of a greatly extended prayer, takes another, earlier 'mighty step' towards individual self-expression by the creation of autobiography as devotional and literary art. It is his life, his experience, his confession that he writes about; the reader will learn from it and be moved by it but he must use the lessons to reinterpret and recreate his own life out of his own experience.

Another work from late antiquity which contains a strong autobiographical element and which had a profound influence on the *Vita Nuova* is the *De consolatione* of Boethius; its influence will be discussed later. During the Dark Ages and the early Middle Ages, biography, especially hagiography, replace autobiography, though occasionally and in intense form autobiography appears in some of the lyrics of monks of the Dark Ages, among them the unfortunate Gottschalk (804–69) and Walafrid Strabo (808–49). It is not until the twelfth century, when Peter Abelard, in his *History of My Calamities*, describes his love for Héloïse, his castration, and his theological battles, that we find a writer telling his story, justifying himself, pitying himself, blaming himself, but at the same time laying open his soul with honesty and abrasive directness.

What is new in the *Vita Nuova*, in the autobiographical sense, when compared with these earlier examples, is that, drawing on the traditions of courtly love and the *donna angelicata*, Dante describes his own experience of the inner life of those traditions. He tells his own love story, and because the poems grew out of this love, the work becomes an autobiographical record of his own creativity at this period of his life. This makes the work quite distinct from the numerous primers on writing poetry extant before his time,[3] and the nearest precedent in medieval literature I can find for Dante's description of his creative processes is the letter that Bernard of Cluny addressed to his abbot with his poem 'De contemptu mundi'. Here, there is a strong resemblance between Dante's description of the inspiration of 'Donne ch'avete' and Bernard's admission that it was only through the Lord filling his mouth with wisdom and understanding that he was able to master the sheer technical difficulty confronting him.[4] Biographies (*vidas*) and prose descriptions of the origins of poems (*razos*) had already accumulated around the poems of the troubadours and Dante was anticipating later commentators by writing his own *vita* and interspersing his poems with passages of prose which he calls *ragioni*. The biographies of the troubadours, for all their charm and interest, are now generally regarded as works of fiction; the *Vita Nuova* may similarly be partly fictional, at least in the order in which certain events are depicted. Dante wrote it primarily for Guido Cavalcanti and his friends, as a means of explaining a particular period of his emotional and creative life. Though it contains many philosophical under-tones, it is not the work of a man faced with death as Boethius was. Nor is it a passionate self-exculpation as with Abelard. It is a description of a miracle and its mystery which gave birth to poems whose verses 'are as spells which unseal the inmost enchanted fountains of the delight which is in the grief of love'.[5] Acquiescing in the miracle, we find ourselves as much at home with the *Vita Nuova*, though we may understand little of its meaning in communicable terms, as we are at home in the inner depths of our own minds, where incom-prehensible thoughts and emotions may arise but where we are accustomed to, and even welcome, the incomprehensible.

Dante wrote the work sometime before 1295, perhaps in 1294, which would have been four years after the death of Beatrice. The book is based on the image of the book of memory;[6] Dante says he will act as a *chiosatore* or glossator commenting on and selecting from what he finds there under the rubric 'Incipit vita nova'. He begins by describing the effect on him of his first meeting Beatrice when he was almost nine and how he used to seek her out when he was a boy. Passing on to when he was eighteen, he describes how one day Beatrice, walking with two other ladies in the street, greeted him. The effect of her greeting was so marvellous that it resulted in the dream already described in which he saw Love carrying Beatrice wrapped in a blood-coloured cloth and giving her Dante's heart to eat. He wrote a sonnet based on this dream which brought many replies and won him the friendship of Guido Cavalcanti. Determined to keep secret his love for Beatrice, he let it be thought by his friends that he was in love with another lady. This lady left the city and, one day, when Dante was out riding in the direction of the place where she had gone to live, Love appeared to him dressed like a pilgrim and told him to take another lady as a 'screen of the truth', or disguise, for his love for Beatrice. Unhappily for him a report reached Beatrice that this second 'screen' lady had suffered from his attentions and Beatrice withheld her greeting from him. He then explains exactly what the marvellous effect of her greeting was on him, how it transformed him with a flame of charity and what a terrible deprivation it was that he now had to suffer.

> Dico che quando ella apparia da parte alcuna, per la speranza de la mirabile salute nullo nemico mi rimanea, anzi mi giugnea una fiamma di caritate, la quale mi facea perdonare a chiunque m'avesse offeso; e chi allora m'avesse domandato di cosa alcuna, la mia risponsione sarebbe stata solamente 'Amore', con viso vestito d' umilitade. E

quando ella fosse alquanto propinqua al salutare, uno spirito d'amore, distruggendo tutti li altri spiriti sensitivi, pingea fuori li deboletti spiriti del viso, e dicea loro: 'Andate a onorare la donna vostra'; ed elli si rimanea nel luogo loro. E chi avesse voluto conoscere Amore, fare lo potea mirando lo tremare de li occhi miei. E quando questa gentilissima salute salutava, non che Amore fosse tal mezzo che potesse obumbrare a me la intollerabile beatitudine, ma elli quasi per soverchio di dolcezza divenia tale, che lo mio corpo, lo quale era tutto allora sotto lo suo reggimento, molte volte si movea come cosa grave inanimata. Sì che appare manifestamente che ne le sue salute abitava la mia beatitudine, la quale molte volte passava e redundava la mia capacitade.

I say that when in any way she appeared, just through the hope of receiving her marvellous greeting, I had no enemies left but was instead possessed by such a flame of charity that I was made to forgive anyone who had injured me; and if at that moment someone had asked me a question about any matter in the world, my answer, with my face clothed in humility, would have been quite simply: 'Love.' Then as she drew near to give her greeting, one spirit of Love, destroying all the other spirits of perception, would cast out the weak spirits of sight and say to them 'Go to honour your lady', while he himself remained in their place. If any one had wished to study Love, he could have done so by watching the quivering of my eyes. When this gentlest source of salvation gave her greeting, Love by no means overshadowed the unendurable blessedness, but indeed grew to such power by a superabundance of rapture that my body, being completely under his domination, often moved like a heavy inanimate thing. From this it is obvious that my blessedness dwelt in her greetings, which frequently surpassed and exceeded my capacity.

Once more Love appeared to him in a dream, as a young man dressed in white vestments, and told him in oblique Latin sentences that he, Love, could see the beginning and end of things while Dante could not and that it was time to put aside the images, that is, to ditch the disguise of his love. Love also told him that Beatrice was now better informed about him and he ordered Dante to write a poem explaining Love's domination over him. This order Dante carried out in a ballad. He also wrote a series of sonnets much influenced by Cavalcanti's use of the conflict of spirits within his soul, including one he wrote after an incident at a wedding when he was so overcome by the sight of Beatrice there that he had to support himself against a wall. Some ladies, including Beatrice, mocked him and he left in shame.

Then, one day, he came upon a group of ladies and dared approach them only because Beatrice was absent. They asked him what was the object of his loving Beatrice since he could not endure her presence. Such a love, they thought, must be very strange. Dante replied that the object of his love used to be the greeting his lady gave him and all his blessedness had been in that, but, since she had withheld it, Love, his lord, had placed it where it could not fail him. They asked him to say where this new, unfailing blessedness resided and he replied 'in those words that praise my lady'. If that were true, they countered, then the poems describing his condition would have borne a very different meaning.

Ashamed of this striking inconsistency Dante went away determined to write something that would indeed praise his lady, and while walking beside a river his tongue spoke as though moved by itself with the words, 'Donne ch'avete intelletto d'amore' (Ladies who possess the intellect of love), and this he used as the opening of his first great poem, the *canzone* given on pp. 119–21, in which he celebrates Beatrice as desired by the blessed in Heaven and expatiates on her miraculous presence on Earth. He followed this with two exultant sonnets in the same vein and then with two inspired by the death of Beatrice's father. Shortly afterwards Dante fell seriously ill and in his fever he experienced a series of terrifying dreams prophesying that Beatrice would die, amidst earthquakes, the darkening of the sun, and the death of birds on the wing, and he was also shown the translation of her soul to heaven and her lifeless corpse laid out. All this he set down in the second great *canzone* of the work, 'Donna pietosa e di novella etate', from which I quote the two central stanzas:

Mentr'io pensava la mia frale vita,
e vedea 'l suo durar com'è leggiero,
piansemi Amor nel core, ove dimora;
　per che l'anima mia fu sì smarrita,
che sospirando dicea nel pensero:
'Ben converrà che la mia donna mora.'
　Io presi tanto smarrimento allora,
ch'io chiusi li occhi vilmente gravati,
e furon sì smagati
li spirti miei, che ciascun giva errando;
e poscia imaginando,
di caunoscenza e di verità fora,
visi di donne m'apparver crucciati,
che mi dicean pur: 'Morra'ti,
　　morra'ti.'

While I was pondering my own frail life
And saw how short was the time it could last,
Love from his home in my heart complained;
　At this my soul was plunged in such strife
That into my mind the thought then passed:
'My lady will die; it has been ordained'.
　Such a delirium at this I sustained
I shut my eyes weighed with infirmity
And so disturbed thereby
Were my spirits, they were scattered in flight.
In my imagined plight
Where nothing of wisdom or truth remained,
Wild with rage, women's faces flashed me by;
'You will die!' they repeated 'You will die!'

Poi vidi cose dubitose molte,
nel vano imaginare ov'io entrai;
ed esser mi parea non so in qual loco,
  e veder donne andar per via
    disciolte,
qual lagrimando, e qual traendo guai,
che di tristizia saettavan foco.
  Poi mi parve vedere a poco a poco
turbar lo sole e apparir la stella,
e pianger elli ed ella;
cader li augelli volando per l'are,
e la terra tremare;
ed omo apparve scolorito e fioco,
dicendomi: 'Che fai? non sai novella?
Morta è la donna tua, ch'era si bella.'

Then I saw many things that doubt
  bedevilled
In the dream I entered so void of sense,
Not even knowing the name of the place.
  I saw women wander, their hair
    dishevelled;
Some of them wept and others shrieked
  laments
That shot out arrows with misery ablaze.
  Then I seemed to see how, with gradual
  pace,
The Sun darkened and the stars shone
  instead;
How he and they wept overhead;
How birds dropped as they flew through
  the air
And the earth quaked there;
And then a man appeared, hoarse, pale of
  face,
Saying 'What's wrong with you? Has
  no-one said?
Your lady, who once was so fair, is dead'.

This apprehensive and gloomy mood was shaken off by a new experience when Love appeared, telling him to bless the day he first possessed him. Beatrice entered, preceded by Guido Cavalcanti's mistress, Giovanna, who was also known as Primavera or 'prima verrà' (she who will come first on the day Beatrice reveals herself 'according to the imagination of her faithful followers'). Dante wrote a sonnet describing this scene, in which Love tells him that Beatrice also has the name Amor, she resembles him so much.

Dante now goes off on a digression on the poet's use of metaphor, dismissing Love as an accident of a substance, not as a thing in himself. He then returns to the poetry of praise in two wonderful sonnets, 'Tanto gentile e tanto onesta pare' and 'Vede perfettamente ogni salute', after describing the extraordinary effect of Beatrice on people as she passed through the streets, how she was crowned and clothed in humility and how people thought she was a miracle and one of the loveliest angels of Heaven. While Dante was engaged on another *canzone* in her praise the news came that she was dead.

Dante does not describe her death for reasons that are discussed later. He says he wrote a letter in Latin, beginning with the quotation from Jeremiah, 'Quomodo sedet sola civitas . . .', but because it is in Latin he does not give it here. Instead he has another digression on the significance of the number nine in relation to Beatrice and to the events surrounding her. When he has recovered a little he gives vent to his sense of loss in the third great *canzone* of the work, the magnificently solemn 'Li occhi dolenti per pietà del core', from which I quote the second stanza:

Ita n'è Bëatrice in l'alto cielo,	Beatrice has gone to the height of
nel reame ove li angeli hanno pace,	heaven,
e sta con loro, e voi, donne, ha lassate:	To the realm where the angels know
no la ci tolse qualità di gelo	peace;
né di calore, come l'altre face,	She stays with them, leaving you behind.
ma solo fue sua gran benignitate;	Neither by heat nor cold was she taken,
ché luce de la sua umilitate	Excess of which causes others' decease
passò li cieli con tanta vertute,	But only by her benignity of mind;
che fé maravigliar l'etterno Sire,	For the light of her humbleness climbed
sì che dolce disire	Through the heavens with such power
lo giunse di chiamar tanta salute;	and direction
e fella di qua giù a sé venire,	That the everlasting Lord was made to
perché vedea ch'esta vita noiosa	wonder
non era degna di sì gentil cosa.	And feel a tender
	Desire to call to Himself such perfection;
	From all below He made her sunder
	Herself, for He saw that this life of
	trouble
	Did not deserve a creature so noble.

He also includes two other poems lamenting her death and then recounts an incident that happened on the first anniversary of her death when some visitors came upon him while he was executing a drawing of an angel. He wrote a sonnet with alternative first quatrains about this incident.

Then there follows the episode of the *donna gentile*, a lady who saw him passing by with such misery in his face that she looked on him with deep compassion. He came to find such comfort in her face that she nearly took him away from the memory of Beatrice. He includes the sonnets in which he describes first the comfort derived from her and then the struggle in which the memory of Beatrice triumphed, through a vision of Beatrice in glory dressed as she had been when he set eyes on her in his ninth year. (He was to give a very different complexion to this episode of the *donna gentile*, as we shall see, in the *Convivio*.)

He then describes an event that inspired another sonnet, the sight of foreign pilgrims travelling through Florence to see the image of Christ preserved at Rome on the veil of Veronica. In this sonnet he addresses the pilgrims who come from so far away that they have not heard of the city's loss, and he tells that the words that can be said of her have the power to make others weep. Two ladies asked him to write something for them and he obliged with what is the last sonnet in the book:

Oltre la spera che più larga gira	Beyond the sphere that turns with widest
passa 'l sospiro ch'esce del mio core:	gyre
intelligenza nova, che l'Amore	Out of my heart a sigh ascends above:
piangendo mette in lui, pur su lo tira.	A new intelligence that weeping Love
Quand'elli è giunto là dove disira,	Bestows on him attracts him ever higher.
	When he attains his aim of desire

vede una donna, che riceve onore,	He sees a lady honoured for her worth
e luce sì, che per lo suo splendore	Who shines so that at the splendour thereof
lo peregrino spirito la mira.	
Vedela tal, che quando 'l mi ridice,	The pilgrim spirit must gaze and admire.
io no lo intendo, sì parla sottile	Such does he see her that, when he repeats this
al cor dolente, che lo fa parlare.	
So io che parla di quella gentile,	I do not understand, so subtly run
però che spesso ricorda Beatrice,	His words to my sad heart that makes him tell.
si ch'io lo 'ntendo ben, donne mie care.	
	I know that he speaks of that noble one
	For frequently he mentions Beatrice,
	Then, dear ladies, I understand him well.

After writing this sonnet he received a vision so marvellous that he decided not to write anything more about Beatrice until he was trained by study to say of her what had never been said of any woman. The work ends with a prayer to God that he may ascend to see the glory of his blessed lady, Beatrice, who gazes into the face of Him 'qui est per omnia saecula benedictus'.

How close the story of the *Vita Nuova* is to the actual events of this period of Dante's life is hard to tell. The first sonnet, 'A ciascun' alma presa' was written when he was eighteen, in 1283, and the death of Folco Portinari, who was celebrated for his charitable actions, took place on 31 December 1289. Beatrice, by this time, was married to Simone de' Bardi and she herself died on 8 June 1290. This means that the anniversary sonnet was written in June 1291 and, at about this time, he found solace for his grief in reading Boethius' *De consolatione* and the *De amicitia* of Cicero. They could have been lent to him by Brunetto Latini. Sometime after this began his attraction to the *donna gentile*. The dating now becomes very confused because of the contradictory statements he makes in the *Convivio* about his first attraction to the *donna gentile*, who there appears as Philosophy. There he says that the new love overcame the memory of Beatrice two epicyclic revolutions of Venus after Beatrice's death—a period of just over three years and two months, which brings us to August 1293. Between late 1293 and spring 1294, when Charles Martel came to Florence, he wrote the *canzone*, 'Voi che 'ntendendo',[7] which expresses the tension between the old and the new loves, and he probably wrote the last sonnet of the *Vita Nuova* at around the same time.[8] In the *Convivio* he says[9] he wrote the *Vita Nuova* when he was a little past adolescence, a period he defines elsewhere in the same work as ending at twenty-five.[10] All this makes it likely that the two visions of Beatrice with which the *Vita Nuova* ends took place in 1294 and were followed soon by the rapid composition of the work.

I say 'rapid' partly because of the shortness of the work and the fact that all, or nearly all, the poetry in it was already composed, and partly because of its exceptional unity of tone. The two visions of Beatrice in glory evoked another experience in him that was the fundamental inspiration of the work as a whole. Suddenly he must have seen that his creative and emotional life up to that date, which was already recorded episodically in his poems, had a pattern, that he himself had been the witness of a miracle, and that by commenting on his own book of memory he could create a work of exceptional originality. With the inspiration of the *Vita Nuova* he saw that his life fell into two parts, the period before Beatrice's death and the period after. Her death became the centre panel of a triptych, a panel which he filled with the *canzone* 'Donna pietosa', the one poem that was probably composed especially for the *Vita Nuova* and not on an earlier occasion.[11] Furthermore, the pattern of three of the triptych could be further broken down into patterns of nine, determining the number and kind of poems he could include in the work. If the first poem is regarded as an introduction and the last as an epilogue the pattern of the poems may be seen as 1; 9; I; 4-II-4; III; 9; 1, where the three main *canzoni* are indicated by Roman numerals and the sonnets and other poems by Arabic, or else as 1; 9; 1; 9; 1; 9; 1, which makes the number nine recur three times.[12] The pattern of three in the triptych enabled him to organize his material with bilateral symmetry in the supporting wings so that, for example, the appearance of Beatrice in his life at the beginning is mirrored by the visions of her celestial nature at the end, the episode of the ladies of the screen is mirrored by that of the *donna gentile*, Love as a pilgrim in 'Cavalcando l'altr' ier' mirrors the pilgrims in 'Deh peregrini', the canzone 'Donne ch'avete' mirrors 'Li occhi dolenti', and the death of Beatrice's father balances the announcement of her own death, all on either side of the central *canzone*, 'Donna pietosa'. The mirror-imaging is also brought out in the way the divisions he makes of the poems in his commentaries follow each poem before Beatrice's death and precede them after it, done in the case of the latter poems to make them seem more 'widowed', but, by the reversal of order, emphasizing the central pattern of the work. The *canzone* 'Donna pietosa' begins with the events with which the prose passage *ends* so that the centre of the book from which the bilateral symmetry radiates may be said to come between the prose introduction and the *canzone* itself. The commentaries on the poems make another lower order of divisions. They have frequently met with criticism, both for being boring and for being no help in understanding the poems they are meant to illuminate. They reflect the influence of the scholastic philosophers, who always divided and subdivided their commentaries with the intention of clarifying exactly what stage their arguments had reached, and this habit of clarification accords well with Dante's description of himself as the *chiosatore* or glossator writing a commentary on the book of memory. Dante believes that he is conveying significant information in these divisions of the poems; and I have already offered the suggestion in relation to 'Donne ch'avete' that the information is conveyed in the numerology of the main divisions and subsidiary divisions. This may also apply to the other poems; a high proportion of the sonnets expressing misery are broken down in the commentaries into two, the number of dualism and division, while the more joyful sonnets are divided into three, the number of creation and happiness, or four, the number of wholeness.

The making of a poet

Even if this last suggestion is unfounded, enough has been said to show that numerology offered Dante a practical aid in planning the work as well as enabling him to find a recurring pattern of symbolic significance in the number nine. It is comparable to the way in which the architects of this and later periods found in the symbolism of number and proportion both a practical guide to the execution of their work and the emotional meaning with which they could infuse it. The relationship of Beatrice with nine shows that she is a miracle with its root in the Trinity, as three is the factor of nine and the square of a number in this symbolism denotes the fulfilment of some purpose related to the significance of the factor. The nine spheres of Heaven were in perfect harmony at the time of her conception and nine can be found returning again and again in the calendar and in all the events of their relationship, binding together the supernatural and the natural.

The inspiration of the *Vita Nuova* not only showed Dante how his experience could be organized and expressed in this numerological pattern, but also conveyed an extraordinarily deep emotional flavour. The period of his life on which he drew for the subject-matter of the *Vita Nuova* arose in his memory as though it were transmuted into music. Nearly all the prose possesses the same integrity of tone as a song in one mode, casting a spell powerful enough to make the reader, while he reads, oblivious of the numerous contradictions and difficulties because he accepts and surrenders to the mood. It is the spell of a voice, the voice of a man, surprised by what his own memory has to show him, distant enough to stand back from his own participation in the events described and moved as though moved by a work of art into which memory had changed this period of his life. The tone of voice of the *Vita Nuova* does not depend on moments of time remembered in a Proustian sense : there is no regret for the time past, the chance not taken, or the misunderstood invitation. The long training amongst the *fedeli d'amore* had taught Dante to be aware of and to respond to the subtlest nuances of his inner nature, so that the response to these nuances became part of his technique as an artist. His first learning to respond to this deep source of memory, to listen to it as though to a guide or a divine messenger, was also his first discovery that he had in fact entered on a 'new life'.

The purified emotion engendered by this memory acted as a kind of conscience, warning him what to include in the work, what, as in the case of the death of Beatrice, to exclude, and what would ensure the fullest possible infusion into the work of the nature of this emotion. It was memory sought so far back into the roots of his nature that it revealed to him a pattern of causes evoked by the miracle of Beatrice, a pattern so still and tranquil, so calm compared with the vicissitudes of his emotions when Beatrice was alive and in the period following her death, that anything in past physical actuality, the order of events, the city of Florence herself, might be altered or changed in order to fulfil his primary object : to secure in the work the truth of this particular pattern of memory. Memory in the depth that Dante reached in writing the *Vita Nuova* is far more than the mental and emotional recovery of experience, though it includes that; it is the conscious apprehension of peace when regret and recrimination are abolished by the establishment in the mind of a firm acceptance of events. It is this peace that informs the prose of the work, granting it its unexampled grace and simplicity. No aim in his artistic, political, and spiritual life was more emotionally charged for Dante than the aim of peace; and in reconstructing the experience on which this work is based we must remember the special kinds of peace to which the artist sometimes attains: the peace of suddenly understanding how he can make a work of art and the peace that comes upon him when he realizes he has done all in his power to make it perfect.

From this it would seem that Dante wrote the *Vita Nuova* in a period of exceptional mental equilibrium, when he had recovered from the shock of Beatrice's death and from the first excitement of his discovery of philosophy. The vision of Beatrice in glory was the culmination of perhaps four years of anxious searching and self-questioning, and its effect was to grant him a short period of calm in which to write the *Vita Nuova*, before he was absorbed into political life. In attaining this state of calm he was greatly helped by the two works already referred to, the *De consolatione* of Boethius and the *De amicitia* of Cicero, and I would like to suggest some of the ways in which these works not only influenced the form and content of the *Vita Nuova*, but also enabled him to penetrate to the depth of experience from which he wrote it.

It used to be thought that Dante wrote the *Vita Nuova* before reading and assimilating these two works,[13] but now their influence has been fully established.[14] It was either from Boethius or from Martianus Capella that Dante got the idea of interweaving prose passages with poems in which the matter of the prose was concentrated. As was said in Chapter 2, Boethius wrote *De consolatione* while unjustly imprisoned by the Ostrogothic king, Theodoric. He had reconciled himself to his certain death by assembling in this book everything of value he had learnt in his days of good fortune. Apart from their similarity of structure, there are many interesting parallels between it and the *Vita Nuova*. *De consolatione* begins with a poem dictated to Boethius by the false muses; this poem does no more than express his self-pity. However, he is suddenly faced with Philosophy, who appears in his prison as a majestic woman. She upbraids him for his fickleness in forgetting her and remains with him until she has restored all his powers of reasoning and has brought back to his memory all that she ever taught him. Dante, too, gives way to self-pity when he writes poems lamenting what he considers Beatrice's unkindness to him. He too is upbraided by the ladies for this self-pity and he goes away in shame to write 'Donne ch'avete'. Memory is also a connecting link between them because Philosophy is concerned first of all with bringing Boethius back to spiritual health by making him remember, and Dante copies out everything of importance he finds in the book of memory. Boethius is taken on a mental journey of return, so that he can understand from a level beyond the stars whence his soul had its origin. Dante's last sonnet tells of the ascent of a sigh to the Empyrean, beyond the sphere of the fixed stars, and he cannot understand the sigh's description of Heaven until it makes him remember Beatrice: 'And then, dear ladies, I understand him well.'

De amicitia does not have the dramatic sense of urgency with which, in his desperate situation, Boethius invested his search for an unshakeable attitude of mind. Cicero set it as a conversation held in the garden of Laelius in about 128 BC, over twenty years before Cicero's birth. Laelius was the chief friend of the statesman and conqueror Scipio Africanus and, at the request of his two sons-in-law, he gives them his views on friendship, notably his reaction to Scipio's death. It is a gentle work, full of admirable common sense and constancy, based on profound reflection and experience. Laelius discusses various ideas about friendship, especially rejecting the thought that true friendship is founded on mutual advantage. He says: 'We believe that friendship is desirable, not because we are influenced by hope of gain, but because its entire profit is in the love itself.'[15] Speaking of the death of a friend he remarks that there is happiness in a good man's death because he ennobles the lives of those he leaves behind. For Laelius, Scipio is still living and his memory keeps the vision alive.[16] This work, made all the more attractive by Laelius' insistence on the immortality of the soul, was much loved in the Middle Ages and inspired several works on Christian friendship. When trying to read it with Dante's eyes as he sought comfort for the loss of Beatrice, we find that certain sentences take on a much sharper and tenser significance, as in the case of this remark, read in the light that Dante believed Beatrice to be a miracle: 'Virtue knits friendship together; if there should be some exhibition of shining virtue to which a kindred spirit should attach and adjust itself, then, when that happens, love must needs spring forth.'[17] Dante had experienced a love that never allowed him to go beyond the bounds of reason and *De amicitia* helped him to explain to himself the possibility of disinterested love. He may also have been familiar with some of the Christian works inspired by *De amicitia*, notably the *De spirituali amicitia* of the Yorkshire abbot, Aelred of Rievaulx (1109–67), and the *De amicitia christiana* of Peter of Blois. Aelred, for example, identifies *amicitia* with *sapientia* and furthermore defines the relationship between reason and attraction in love.[18]

Accompanying these influences are those of the Bible, notably the Psalms, the Song of Songs, the Lamentations of Jeremiah, and the story of Christ, and of the tradition of the troubadours. None of the many influences, however, can detract from the originality of the *Vita Nuova*. I have already dealt with the story; now, to illustrate something more both of its originality and complexity, I will try to show how it may be read as a record of Dante's development as an artist, as a description of his progress along the mystical path, and as the celebration of Beatrice as a miracle. The 'new life' of the title may be understood as Dante's discovery of a new possibility in his art, the poetry of praise that begins with 'Donne ch'avete'; it may also be read in the mystical sense that St Augustine used when, interpreting the psalm 'Sing unto the Lord a new song', he said, 'The new man knows, the old man does not know. The old man is the old life and the new man is the new life [*nova vita*].'[19] And it may also be seen in the light of Dante's love of Beatrice, of his progress, because the book records his training in the degrees of love towards the attainment of a higher consciousness.

There is something curious about the book when taken as a description of the development of Dante's style. It is written for Guido Cavalcanti and yet it describes how Dante underwent Cavalcanti's influence and then escaped from it in his discovery of the poetry of praise. Yet there is no sense of boasting, no rejection of Cavalcanti here. Cavalcanti had developed the new psychological language of the spirits to define the torments and thrills of love still rooted in strong physical attraction, love that depended on appetite. Dante, in the *Vita Nuova*, describes a new and more permanent love that progresses in his experience from being dependent on Beatrice's physical presence to the inner discovery of love as praise and as eternal memory. It is almost as though the two poets had different tasks, tasks of which they were aware and which they respected in one another. Chapters V–XI, describing the episode of the two 'screen' ladies, show the early influence on Dante of the tradition of *amour courtois* both in the poems and in the prose passages, reflecting, perhaps, the influence of Andrew the Chaplain. After the denial of the greeting, Cavalcanti's influence becomes paramount from Chapters XIII to XVI, with the categorizing of conflicting voices in 'Tutti li miei penser' and the depiction of love as a terrifying and death-dealing experience, laying waste amongst the spirits in sonnets 7, 8, and 9. Then, in Chapter XVIII, the new life truly begins with the remarkable scene of the meeting with the ladies who ask him what is the aim of his love, and chide him for the gap between his claim that Love has placed his experience of blessedness where it cannot fail him, that is, in the words that praise his lady, and his failure to live up to this claim. The scene records a rare moment, the moment when a man is stricken in his conscience and when, out of the new understanding that follows, he creates a work of art, transforming the intense but destructive emotion brought about in him by the denial of the greeting into a positive surrender to his love. This immeasurably enlarges the field of his subject from the sufferings of his psychology to a drama in which all humanity, the angelic orders and God Himself are involved. The scene also provokes the question: 'Who are these ladies so wise and so shrewd that they can see straight to the contradiction in a man's soul and effectively make a work of art by asking him the question that resolves the contradiction?' Was it a scene that actually took place, is it another of the visions like those of Love, or is it an example of a waking dream imposed on physical actuality, evoking understanding that on later reflection he dramatized with human voices, as recently he had been dramatizing the spirits of his psychology? The passage also provokes one of the central questions of aesthetics: how does grief expressed in art, as the words of these ladies intermingled with sighs resemble the falling of 'rain mixed with beautiful snow', give such intense pleasure, such a deep awakening of our unremembered emotions, such an impersonal but individual joy? Ibn al-'Arabī wrote of a state of the soul known as the Sadness of the Divine Names, a state founded upon the tradition, 'I was a hidden Treasure and I yearned to be known. Then I created creatures to be known by them.'[20] The speaker is God, explaining His urge in creation, and the same urge to be discovered, to be known, is felt by the angelic orders. The sadness of the ladies is also at the lying in darkness of the full nature of Beatrice, at an urge for praise and discovery that is unfulfilled. Praise is the function of the highest angelic orders, of Cherubim and Seraphim, and it is Dante's mission to create on Earth a new poetry of praise that reflects the continual service of praise in Heaven. Cavalcanti had described sensual love based on appetite as caused by a dark influence from Mars, and in 'Veggio negli occhi' (see p. 118) had described the experience of seeing his spiritual love developing from the level of the active intellect, the sphere of the moon, to an emanation from the heaven of Venus. At the beginning of the *Vita Nuova* Beatrice's nature is related to the nine spheres and at the end she passes above these to the Empyrean, the abode of God.

Though Dante seems to be describing here the way in which he surpassed Cavalcanti, the latter still retains a vivid presence. After the dream of Beatrice's coming death in 'Donna pietosa', there takes place the episode of the appearance of Beatrice preceded by Cavalcanti's mistress, Giovanna. As John the Baptist was the precursor of Christ, so Giovanna is the precursor of Beatrice, and Cavalcanti is the precursor of Dante in the latter's achievement of realizing the poetry of praise. Cavalcanti is also present in the passage which follows, the justification of personification in poetry, where, following Cavalcanti's rigorous example of subjecting psychological experiences to philosophical analysis, he points out that love is only the accident of a substance and speaks sharply of those who use metaphor without being able to lay bare the underlying meaning.

This passage might be thought to call in question the validity of what I have stressed in Dante's creative method, the importance of dreams, visions, and the unexpected gift of phrases as the starting-point of his poems. The digression has a dramatic purpose in unveiling another aspect of Beatrice's nature: that she, herself, is Love. It also demonstrates the degree of Dante's technical control. The dreams are what is given; but they must be worked on, tested against the experience of others, seen in various aspects and subjected to expression in verse, and this passage illustrates the detachment necessary in an artist to develop the full significance of an inspiration in his realization of it. It may also be objected that these visions are reworkings of symbols and stories Dante had come across in his reading. The dream in Chapter IV, when Love appears carrying Beatrice and makes her eat his heart, bears a strong resemblance to a passage in Brunetto Latini,[21] describing a dream of the father of Elijah, and also to the troubadour legends in which a lady is made to eat her lover's heart. The second vision of Love, in which he states that he is at the centre of a circle and that it is not so with Dante, has been variously traced back to the angel in the tomb (Mark 16:5) and to a ninth-century tradition in which God appears to the prophet as a 'beardless youth of great beauty'.[22] The figure of Love here may also be identified with the recurrent dream image Jung calls the 'puer aeternus', who announces change and transfiguration. It is a very poor dream, however, that is entirely original, and the fact that all these examples only partly coincide in detail with the visions in the *Vita Nuova* emphasizes the process of re-creation that Dante's reading underwent in his imagination and dream life, becoming synthesized into his own experience and issuing in his poems as completely assimilated impressions of his own. He accepts every dream and vision recorded in the *Vita Nuova* as being a messenger of truth and genuine prophecy, except in one case, the visions on which 'Donna pietosa' is based, which are described in both prose and poem as *vana* and *fallace*. This is very strange because it is soon followed by Beatrice's death, which it prophesies. It has been explained as a dramatic device to keep up the suspense at this point.[23] It may also be a tacit admission that the poem itself was not written at that time but was made especially for the *Vita Nuova*. The poem is a deliberately dramatic creation in which he drew on the dreams that assailed him *after* Beatrice's death to enable him to present the reader with an account of her death which he was unable, according to his ground rules, to describe directly.

The rest of the book contains further hints about his creative methods and his relationship with Cavalcanti. The episode of the *donna gentile* is presented here as a battle between love based on appetite and love based on reason. The sufferings of love as appetite was Cavalcanti's special theme and is finally overcome by the triumphant memory of Beatrice. But it is beyond Dante's technical capacity to describe these last visions. Even 'Oltre la spera', beautiful as it is in itself and as the concluding poem of the book, is only a series of notes on an experience he has not been able to explain to himself. The book ends with his hope that he will live long enough to say of Beatrice what was never said of any woman and that on death his soul will go to behold her who now in glory looks on the face of Him *qui est per omnia secula benedictus.*

It is clear that each stage of artistic development recorded in the *Vita Nuova* is preceded by an advance made by Dante in spiritual understanding as a lover and as a man. This brings us to the question of the mystical basis of the work.[24] One way of seeing it in this way is to regard the whole story as set in an interior landscape. Whereas Cavalcanti dramatized his own states of mind, Dante enlarges the stage to include Florence, its people and customs as images of the inner secret progress of his soul. The unnamed city is an image of his soul in which he undergoes a trial, passing from lower to higher stages of love, as, for example, Richard of St Victor (d. 1173) had taken the genealogy of Benjamin to describe the passage of the soul to the final stage of ecstasy in contemplation.[25] The various people mentioned as taking part in the drama are aspects of his own soul that hinder or advance his progress. His gradual understanding of the nature of Beatrice is the dawning in him of the consciousness of Christ. Her death is the passing of this consciousness to a higher level, beyond the reach of ordinary intellection which, through memory and the granting of visions, remains permanently part of himself. The abuse of death at the beginning of the work is changed into the welcoming of death because it is understood in the sense of St Bernard who said, in one of his sermons on the Song of Songs:

> I may, then, without any absurdity, call the ecstasy of the Bride death; but it is a death which, far from depriving her of life, delivers her from the snares, so that she is able to say: 'Our soul is escaped even as a bird out of the snare of the fowlers' [Psalms 124 : 7].[26]

When Dante refuses to describe Beatrice's death, he gives as his third reason that he would be constrained to sing his own praises—a remark that has been interpreted as meaning that he had received a mystical illumination, and that may be compared with St Paul's prologue to his description of being taken up to the third heaven: 'It is not expedient for me doubtless to glory. I will come to visions and revelations of the Lord.'[27] On this interpretation many of the difficulties of the work are resolved. The widowing of the city is the widowing of his soul, the writing of the mysterious letter to the princes of the Earth is his announcement to his fellow *fedeli d'amore* of the stage he has reached on the way, the miracle of Beatrice is the miracle of consciousness in his soul, and the recognition of her marvellous nature in the streets of the city is the integration and turning towards her divine light of all the conflicting parts of Dante's own psychology.

It also helps to explain the identification of Beatrice with Christ in the sense of Meister Eckhart's remarks quoted above, that we must understand the Incarnation as concerning the inner world. This identification is carried throughout the work, in the numerological symbolism and in open comparisons, from the quotation from Homer to describe her as a 'daughter of God', as Christ is the Son of God, to the description of the effect of her greeting, which enables him to forgive his enemies, to the earthquake and other portents which plainly refer to the events surrounding the crucifixion, to the way Giovanna precedes Beatrice as John the Baptist, to the pilgrims going to Rome to see the Veronica, the true image of Christ's face, on to the final vision of Beatrice in glory with its associations with the appearances of Christ after the crucifixion and with His Ascension. It even resolves the difficulties of those who refuse a mystical interpretation of the *Vita Nuova* because they point to the fact that the final object of Dante's longings in Heaven is still Beatrice and not God.[28] It can be said in reply that she is what is divine in Dante's soul, she is Christ in him, and her death and ascension to Heaven signify the return of the individual soul to the Universal.

But to be content with this interpretation, because it offers a solution to many of the contradictions and difficulties of the work, would be to limit its richness of meaning and complexity, because, though it identifies the mystical experience within the soul of which the city is the metaphor, it still leaves us with the problem of Beatrice's identity and the nature of Dante's love for her. Some have taken the identification with Beatrice Portinari to have been made far too long after Dante's time to be satisfactory, and have chosen to regard her purely as a symbolic representation of Sapientia[29] or of Theology;[30] others, such as Auerbach,[31] have accepted her as Beatrice Portinari but find her identity so overlaid with Dante's glorification of her that the identity no longer remains of account. In this way, the historical Beatrice becomes a rather pathetic figure, herself a screen of the truth. The *Vita Nuova*, however, bears the trace of contact with great human qualities, showing that in Beatrice Dante had been close to someone of exceptional spiritual qualities.

There are two barriers to accepting Dante's assessment of Beatrice's nature at its face value; one is the dominance of the monastic and conventual traditions of mysticism which at this period overshadowed all secular attempts in that direction. Yet Florence had by this time created a secular society, with the leisure, the education, and the opportunities for cultural interchange that would make it possible for men and women, not practising celibacy, not withdrawn from the world, to cultivate their spiritual lives. The other difficulty is the modern one of being unable to believe that sexual attraction without physical consummation could lead to anything but frustration and neurosis. Petrarch was later to state that the very permanence of his love for Laura was a consequence of her denying him all sexual satisfaction.[32] Dante stresses again and again that he was guided by reason in his love for Beatrice, and Boccaccio, who stresses Dante's ardour as a lover of other women, calls this a chaste love.[33] There is a parallel also in Ibn al-'Arabī, who tells of his love for a Persian girl at Mecca who initiated him into spiritual mysteries. Ibn al-'Arabī, while insisting both on her physical reality as a human being and on the chastity of their love, also allegorizes her as a Greek princess of Rum, making her into a Christian to stress the closeness of her nature to Christ, even calling her by the epithet 'Christ-like'.[34] Turning back to Beatrice, one can say of her that Dante found in her an almost perfect human being, and a permanence of love that was denied to Cavalcanti and others of his fellow poets. It may be that Beatrice was the creation of Dante as every lover makes a new creation of his beloved, interpreting his experience before and after her death in the light of his reading, of his discussions with the *fedeli d'amore*, of the troubadour tradition and of his own artistic and spiritual development. But it was still the goodness and beauty of this girl, from whom wisdom and charity radiated into connexions beyond the cosmos itself, that were stamped on him as the fundamental experience of his life. A colleague reported of Thomas Aquinas that just to be in his presence was to receive the grace of consolation,[35] and Dante's contemporary, the friar Ubertino da Casale, described the effect on him of Angela da Foligno who, when he had experienced the splendour of her virtue, changed the face of his mind and caused the spirit of Christ to be begotten anew in him.[36] So Dante records the miraculous effects of Beatrice on those she greeted and those accompanying her during her life.

141

Questa gentilissima donna, di cui ragionato è ne le precedenti parole,
venne in tanta grazia de le genti, che quando passava per via, le
persone correano per vedere lei; onde mirabile letizia me ne giungea.
E quando ella fosse presso d'alcuno, tanta onestade giungea nel cuore
di quello, che non ardia di levare li occhi, nè di rispondere a lo suo
saluto; e di questo molti, sì come esperti, mi potrebbero testimoniare a
chi non lo credesse. Ella coronata e vestita d'umilitade s'andava,
nulla gloria mostrando di ciò ch'ella vedea e udia. Diceano molti, poi
che passata era: 'Questa non è femmina, anzi è uno de li bellissimi
angeli del cielo'. E altri diceano: 'Questa è una maraviglia; che
benedetto sia lo Segnore, che sì mirabilemente sae adoperare!' Io dico
ch'ella si mostrava sì gentile e sì piena di tutti li piaceri, che quelli che
la miravano comprendeano in loro una dolcezza onesta e soave, tanto
che ridicere non lo sapeano; nè alcuno era lo quale potesse mirare lei,
che nel principio nol convenisse sospirare.[37]

That most gentle lady who is spoken of in the preceding words came
to be held in such esteem by people that, when she passed along the
street, they would run after her to see her; I felt a miraculous joy at
this. When she passed close to anyone, such modesty would awake in
his heart that he would not dare to raise his eyes to reply to her
greeting. Any one who does not believe this can find it substantiated
by many men from their own experience. Crowned and clothed in
humility, she would continue on her way, showing no vanity at what
she saw and heard. After she had gone by, many would say: 'She is
not a woman, but one of the loveliest angels in heaven.' Others would
repeat: 'She is a wonder; blessed be God who can work such miracles.' I say that she showed herself to be so noble and so full of all the
graces that all who saw her experienced in themselves a warm and
modest charm which they could never describe afterwards; nor could
anyone look at her without sighing immediately.

As Laelius maintained that the greatness of Scipio was preserved beyond death
in his memory, so Dante discovered that the Christian greatness of Beatrice was
a living force in his nature, that he was to forget again and again but then to
recover eternally. Though in his presentation of her she is illumined by the
symbols of the sapiential and philosophic traditions, all attempts to explain her
solely as an allegory or as a symbol of virtues detract from her, because no virtue
can be more wonderful to us than in its appearance and working in a human
soul, and no miracle is more marvellous than the awakened consciousness of a
human being.

PART II

POWER, EXILE, AND THE WORKS
OF DANTE'S MIDDLE YEARS

10

The taste of power and the salt
of exile

Towards the end of his life, when writing a passage of the *Paradiso* that particularly referred to citizenship and the diversity of human talents, Dante turned back in his memory to the very period when he himself was about to enter politics. This moment is recalled in the meeting with Charles Martel, titular king of Hungary, heir to the Angevin kingdom and pretensions in Southern Italy, and son-in-law of Rudolf of Habsburg, who reveals himself to Dante in the heaven of Venus. His very joy, Charles explains, hides his identity from Dante with its radiance, as a silkworm is hidden in its cocoon. He reminds Dante of their meeting in former times, speaking of the services he could have rendered the poet had he not died young, and recites the proud series of dominions which he would have ruled. Then he describes the means by which nature imprints men with their individual characters, preceding this with a question:

Or dì: sarebbe il peggio	Now say, would it be worse
Per l'omo in terra, se non fosse cive?[1]	For a man on earth were he not a citizen?

And Dante replies:

'Sì,' rispuos'io, 'e qui ragion non cheggio'[2] 'Yes,' I replied, 'and here I ask no proof'

This episode of Charles Martel recalls a crucial period when Dante was emerging from philosophical studies after the death of Beatrice and was nearly thirty years old, at which age he could enter Florentine political life. At this time, a life close to power and the control of events beckoned with a kind of glamour. Dante had already been the protégé of men like Brunetto Latini and Nino Visconti, and the success of his meeting with Charles Martel probably convinced him that he, too, had the special abilities, the tact, the political sense, that would draw him above his comparatively humble station and lack of means to the abiding attention of the great. For someone like Dante with no power base of his own, the patronage or the support of a great family or institution would be vital for political success. It may be therefore that it was in this way that he became involved with the Templars, who with their international banking connexions would have been of considerable weight in Florence and who would need able and sympathetic laymen to act or influence events on their behalf. If the affiliation began as a matter of mutual political advantage, it was to have remarkable artistic results.

Charles Martel visited Florence in March 1294 for three weeks. He was there to meet his father, the king of Naples, Charles II, who was bringing back his younger son, who had been imprisoned by the Aragonese. The young king was accompanied by 200 knights wearing scarlet and dark green with the cloth trappers of their horses embroidered with gold lilies bordered with red and silver.[3] The Florentines, eager as usual to honour their Angevin allies, laid on splendid entertainments and appointed a body of young citizens, Dante among them, to amuse the young king. It is presumed from Charles's quotation of its opening (in *Paradiso*) that the *canzone* 'Voi che 'ntendendo il terzo ciel movete' was recited or sung before him and that he, sharing his family's love of music and verse, responded to the poet.[4] All Dante's hopes of advancement through him failed because, in August 1295, Charles died of the plague in Naples.

A little while after the meeting in Florence, Charles Martel was involved in the events that had overtaken the papacy. Following the death of Nicholas IV in 1292, the Holy See remained vacant for two years as a diminishing band of cardinals failed to agree on an election from their own number. Finally, on the inspiration of the Cardinal Latino, on 5 July 1294, they chose an outsider, Peter Morrone, a hermit of great age who had founded thirty-six communities but had retired to a cave on Mount Morrone in the Abruzzi, in the Angevin territories. A mission was dispatched to announce the election to the hermit, led by the archbishop of Lyons and soon joined by Charles II and Charles Martel. Charles II was lame and could not make the ascent, and so his son accompanied the clerics, sweating up the mountainside in their richest and heaviest garments. They entered the cave, where the hermit had once spent twenty days glued to the rock wall by ice. There they flung themselves prostrate before the wild old man, who responded by falling flat on his face. Then they bore him off, first to Aquila for his coronation as Celestine V and then to the Castel Nuovo in Naples. The cardinals soon discovered what they had done. Celestine was almost illiterate and would take a day to read through the simplest document. They had appointed a fakir of undoubted holiness, but who was quite incapable of holding the most difficult political office and of managing the most complex bureaucracy in Europe. One cardinal came to the fore in guiding Celestine through the maze of business, and he was Benedetto Caetani, from Anagni, a member of the lesser nobility of the Campagna. After holding his office for just over five months, Celestine abdicated the papacy, prompted, it was later unkindly said, by messages threatening his damnation delivered through a speaking tube to his bedside by Caetani pretending to be an angel. On

The taste of power and the salt of exile

St Lucy's Day, 13 December, Celestine formally divested himself of his papal robes and insignia, having pronounced his abdication before the consistory of cardinals.[5] On 24 December 1294, Benedetto Caetani was proclaimed as the new pope Boniface VIII.

This extraordinary man, whose name Dante has blackened beyond all attempts of outraged clerics to cleanse it,[6] was as practical in worldly affairs as Celestine was incompetent. Trained as a lawyer, by the time of his elevation he had conducted innumerable negotiations for earlier popes. In the course of these negotiations, he had been besieged by Simon de Montfort's supporters in the Tower of London in 1265, he was continuously involved in the diplomatic business following the Sicilian Vespers, and he had taken on in debate and defeated the masters of the Sorbonne in 1290. Numerous statues and paintings of him remain and they all bear witness to one feature of his appearance, his bland, always young and unlined face, untouched by the rigours of a constantly busy and dangerous life, unmarked by the torture he endured from the stone, a complaint that exacerbated his outbursts of violent rage. That bland face concealed a very complex character. A witty man, fond of conversation on a wide variety of topics, from the arts to birth control, he had the most powerful intellect of the popes of his century and was a skilful writer, as the style of his bulls attests. He is recorded at one moment receiving the host with tears in his eyes and, at another, screaming the word 'beasts' at his clerks because they dared to look up from their work when the consecration bell rang in the chapel next door. He was a consummate diplomatist who nevertheless made hordes of enemies by the vehemence of his personal abuse, throwing the Lenten ashes in the face of one bishop who knelt before him and grabbing another by the beard. No one had ever made such claims for the papacy as he was to do and the outward honour of the Church was everything to him.[7] He was one of those very clever men who find contradiction from others an impediment to their own superior lines of thought. He cherished the arts, liked the feel of well-wrought embroideries, and had golden roses sewn onto his slippers.

This was the man whom Dante was to meet face to face in a few years' time. Boniface introduced no new ideas into papal policy; he continued to prosecute the Sicilian War in the Angevin interest; he went on with the efforts to construct a strong papal state with the aid of his nephews, as Nicholas III had done with his Orsini relations and Nicholas IV with the Colonna. What was new was the force with which he implemented his designs and the intellectual clarity with which he made explicit the papal claims to supreme temporal and spiritual authority; it was this that broke the long-standing friendship of the papacy with France. Boniface provoked thereby the supreme crisis of the medieval papacy, and his failure sent his successors into exile for over seventy years. His judgments concerning matters away from Italy and outside his private interests were objective and reasonable. Where conflict arose over his schemes for his family, or the papal revenues, he became thoroughly unscrupulous. Florence, as the greatest city of Tuscany, involved both these interests because, it is thought, he either wished to incorporate her into the papal possessions or else to make her into a hereditary appanage of his family. As by this time, with the collapse of several Sienese bankers, Florence provided the chief bankers of the papacy, it was vital to his interests that no civil disturbances should cause a lasting blow to credit. Boniface had, as cardinal, already formed close links with the Spini through Caetani relations at Pisa, who were also bankers. He was very pleased when Giano della Bella, the author of the Ordinances of Justice, was expelled from Florence in March 1295 and expressly forbade a move later that year to allow him to return. Giano had been planning the nationalization of the property of the Guelph party, the control of whose wealth was one of the chief means by which the magnates could assert themselves in the city's affairs. Boniface approved the modification of the severer enactments of the Ordinances against the magnates and continued to give the magnates his support, chiefly through the understanding he reached with one of their leaders, Corso Donati.

Dante was to enter active politics at a time when the chief dissensions in the city no longer arose from the class warfare that had culminated in the Ordinances of Justice, when the lesser guilds had forced their way into full participation in the city's government, and the nobility had been excluded and depressed. The Guelph party itself split into two alignments soon to be known as the Whites and the Blacks. These labels, according to contemporary chroniclers, came from the nearby small city of Pistoia, where the important family of the Cancellieri had split into two branches known as the White Cancellieri and the Black Cancellieri. A series of minor quarrels between them had exploded into violence when a young man of the Black branch wounded the son of the leader of the Whites. The Blacks, to make amends, sent the young man to the White leader for a token punishment. Gualfredo Cancellieri, the White leader, took him into a stable, cut off his right hand on a manger, gashed his face, and sent him home with an insulting message. Civil war broke out, with members of either side taking refuge with friends or relations in Florence. Eventually the White party dominated Pistoia for a few years, but the conflict proved a model for what was to happen on a far greater scale in Florence.

The White and Black factions in Florence threw up two leaders, the banker Vieri de' Cerchi for the Whites, and Corso Donati for the Blacks. The Cerchi were a new family that had only recently (that is, in the past fifty years) come to wealth and prominence. They had bought the palace of the Conti Guidi, where their numerous members lived ostentatious and self-indulgent lives. The palace was opposite the home of Corso Donati, a nobleman of ancient family and lesser wealth. Corso was a man of great abilities in war and affairs; he had been *podestà* of Pistoia and it had been his charge at Campaldino that had won the day for Florence. He had also been captain of the people at Treviso. Handsome, much married, with an exuberant personality, he had a large popular following in the city and would be greeted with cries of 'il barone'. He was a clever and murderous bully with a practised talent for vituperation—which is partly why Boniface found in him such a fellow spirit. Vieri de' Cerchi's wealth and dull temperament provoked Corso's jealousy and derision and he would go about asking if anyone had heard the braying of 'the donkey of la Porta', his name for Vieri.

Corso had annoyed the Cerchi when he married an heiress to whom they were related, without her family's full consent. Annoyance changed to hatred when some young men of the Cerchi family with two of their friends, who were imprisoned in the courtyard of the *podestà*'s palace for their part in a fight, died after eating a black pudding. Corso was suspected of poisoning the pudding but he was never charged with the crime. On a later occasion both families were present at an open-air meeting before the burial of a lady. On such occasions the women went inside the house and the men stayed outside, commoners sitting on rush matting and knights and doctors on raised benches. Someone stood up from his place on the matting, probably, as Dino says, to adjust his clothes, and the other side immediately drew their swords. A fight was imminent and was only prevented by the other families there. Another bitter enemy Corso made was Dante's friend Guido Cavalcanti. Corso's name for Guido was 'cavicchia' (wooden peg) and, according to Dino, he had tried to have Guido murdered when he was on pilgrimage to Compostela. One day when Guido was out riding with some of the Cerchi and came across Corso, he rode at him, throwing a hunting spear which missed.[8]

The personal hatred between Corso and Vieri provided standards round which more complex and conflicting interests could group. Round Corso Donati gathered the families of the papal bankers and those with interests in the Angevin kingdom and France, keeping up the traditional supports of the Guelph party. Round Vieri gathered new families like his own, whose interests extended to Ghibelline cities and territories such as Verona, Pisa, and the Romagna, and also the ancient Ghibelline aristocrats of Florence. This meant that the nobleman Corso Donati was allied with the wealthy *popolani* of the Florentine greater guilds on the one side, and the *nouveau riche* Vieri de' Cerchi adhered to the Ghibelline axis on the other; and it has been pointed out that it was not class divisions but 'the intense competition brought about by the breakdown of traditional barriers which exacerbated the conflict'.[9]

Dante began his political career in 1295, at the age of thirty, at the time when Boniface VIII started to meddle in the affairs of Florence, and when the exile of Giano della Bella signalled the end of the *popolo* phase of the city's life and the beginning of the new party conflict, which was to lead to Dante's exile. By this time he had married Gemma Donati, who was to bear him four children: Pietro, Jacopo, Giovanni, and Antonia. Boccaccio says[10] that his family married him to Gemma after Beatrice's death in order to console him. If this was so, it was in fulfilment of a contract made when he was only twelve and which is referred to in a later document.[11] In the five years from the death of Beatrice in 1290 up to the start of his political career, he began his philosophical studies, wrote the *Vita Nuova*, and then evolved a new style, characterized by the *canzoni* (later incorporated in the *Convivio*) devoted to the *donna gentile*. Some have suggested that he went through a period of wild living and dissipation. The evidence for this is a sonnet by Guido Cavalcanti[12] chiding him for falling away from his formerly high standards, but this could have been written, for all we know, at almost any time in the seventeen years of their friendship. Another source of conjecture is the *tenzone*, or battle of sonnets, he exchanged with his friend and connexion by marriage, Forese Donati—lively and tasteless productions, in which Dante jeers at Forese for neglecting his wife who never stops coughing and Forese sneers at Dante's father's money-lending activities. These have given much distress to some commentators, who would prefer Dante not to have written them and who deduce from their existence worse excesses.[13] There are, however, numerous examples of similar flyting poems in existence, notably the vehement sonnets of Dante's friend Cecco Angiolieri. This same tough abuse which could be exchanged by friends also characterized Florentine political life. A man like Corso Donati would cultivate his coarseness of expression as part of his political armoury, and a sparring match between friends such as this *tenzone* was a necessary training for the big fights against enemies. It also turned out in Dante's case to be a training for the many passages of invective in the *Commedia*.

How rapidly Dante advanced in politics is shown by the fact that he was elected a prior of the city after only five years of active political life. According to entries in the records of the debates of the councils, he spoke on 14 December 1295 in a council of the captains of the twelve major arts.[14] He is next recorded on 5 June 1296 speaking in the council of the hundred.[15] The next year he is to be found inscribed in the guild of apothecaries singled out as 'poeta fiorentino'.[16] The official documents are lacking for the next two years or so, although there are records of him and his brother borrowing quite large sums of money. This need not be interpreted as evidence of poverty but rather the opposite. Dante's credit and standing were good enough to make it worth while to lend to him.

To appreciate some of the complexities surrounding the crisis in Dante's political career in 1300 and 1301, it is necessary to go back to the early years of Pope Boniface's reign. When Celestine V had abdicated, Boniface kept him under surveillance, but the old hermit escaped and crossed the Apennines. He was arrested as he was awaiting transport to Greece, and Boniface had him imprisoned in the castle of Fumone near Anagni, where he died, almost certainly of natural causes, in 1296. Many of the Spiritual Franciscans contested the validity of the abdication, having hoped for great things from Celestine, and by implication they contested the validity of Boniface's election. Their doubts infected the two Colonna cardinals, James and Peter, especially the former, who was a noted protector of the Spirituals. Both had, in fact, voted for Boniface but they and their family fell under Boniface's displeasure partly because of the support they gave to the French king, Philip the Fair, in the first great quarrel between the papacy and France over the bull, *Clericis Laicos*.

It had been generally accepted for many years that the Church could be taxed on her wealth and income to provide for the needs of the various lay powers. A high proportion of any tax raised by the papacy for its own purposes had always gone to the lay powers, who were glad to benefit from a fiscal and administrative system they had so far been incapable of organizing themselves. The French monarchy, because its interests had been so closely identified with the policies of the papacy and because it regarded the Crusades as its special responsibility, had come to look upon the support of papal taxes as a right. Philip the Fair was now imposing a tax on the French Church for his wars against England and the Flemings. Many complaints were made by French clerics and institutions. In February 1296, Boniface issued *Clericis Laicos* which expressly forbade any tax on Church property that did not have papal sanction and excommunicated all who imposed or paid such forbidden taxes. Philip responded by stopping the export of bullion from France, a severe blow to Italian bankers and to the papacy. Neither side was ready for a full confrontation and Boniface in fact made concessions, without withdrawing the provisions of the bull. The principle of the immunity of Church possessions from lay control was, however, threatened once more, as it had been in the Investiture Contest; this time the battle was not with an emperor but with the creator of a precocious nation state.

One of the conditions of Boniface's temporary settlement with France was that Philip would give no help to the Colonna, against whom Boniface now moved. The Colonna had intrigued with France, they had relations with Frederick of Sicily, and their great possessions marched with many of the estates purchased by Boniface to enrich his family. In 1296 a member of the Colonna family robbed a papal treasure convoy coming from Anagni of 200,000 gold florins. War broke out. Boniface stripped the cardinals James and Peter of their offices. The Colonna issued manifestos denouncing him as a false pope. Boniface's armies ringed the Colonna in their ancient fortress town of Palestrina after seizing numerous other castles and possessions. Boniface gave full crusading privileges to all who fought against the Colonna, who in 1298 finally surrendered Palestrina. According to Dante, they were taken in by a trick suggested by Guido da Montefeltro (see Chapter 20). Palestrina was razed to the ground and the Colonna went into exile to await the chance of vengeance.

Boniface was still involved in another struggle which concerned his family's interests. He had married his great-nephew Roffred to a lady known as the Red Countess, Margherita Aldobrandesca, who brought much of the huge territories of the Aldobrandeschi family into the Caetani family. This lady had been married twice before and had also kept as her lover the sinister Nello de' Pannocchieschi, who had done away with his wife, Pia de' Tolomei, in the castle of Pietra in the Maremma. Pia is the pathetic lady who speaks to Dante with such consideration, asking him to make mention of her when he has rested from his long journey.[17] Roffred's marriage only lasted a short time and Boniface divorced the couple on the grounds that the countess was a bigamist. He still wanted her lands, and it was by voting against a proposal that Florence should continue to give Boniface help in the ensuing wars that Dante, in 1301, also incurred Boniface's displeasure.

By 1300 Boniface had achieved for the papacy and his family many of his objects, and the Jubilee which he proclaimed on 22 February of that year marks the culmination of his power. The Jubilee celebrated the passing of another century since the birth of Christ, and great benefits in the afterlife were promised to those who made the pilgrimage to Rome and visited the basilicas. Dante seems to acknowledge the efficacy of the Jubilee remissions through his friend Casella.[18] Since its proclamation, all the souls of the just, who gathered at the mouth of the Tiber for their journey to Mount Purgatory, had been instantly admitted. It is almost certain that Dante visited Rome in the Jubilee year because he describes the arrangement for the control of the crowds on the Ponte Sant'Angelo.[19]

If the modern traveller, at least up to a few years ago, could still be impressed by the immensity and spread of the remains of ancient Rome finding even in the innumerable works of Christianity merely a reduced and residuary heir of the imperial splendour, how much more amazed would a sensitive visitor then have been by the evidences of fallen power, seeing the medieval town of about 20,000 inhabitants shrunk beneath the great ruins. Dante came having already made great progress, probably under Remigio de' Girolami, in his classical studies; he knew his Virgil, his Cicero, and many of the ancient and early Christian historians. He came, also, with his dislike of the corruption of the Church probably already aroused, and admiring the achievements of the Roman empire. Once there, and partaking of the benefits of the Holy Year, he soaked in the impressions that later were to make him say of Rome that 'her very stones command reverence'.[20] His fellow Florentine, Giovanni Villani, records this of his visit to Rome in the same year:

> And I finding myself on that blessed pilgrimage in the holy city of Rome, beholding the great and ancient things therein, and reading the stories and the great doings of the Romans, written by Virgil, and by Sallust, and by Lucan, and Titus Livius, and Valerius, and Paulus Orosius, and other masters of history. . . . myself to preserve memorials and give examples to those which should come after, took up their style and design, although as a disciple I was not worthy of such a work.[21]

Villani was inspired when in Rome to plan his chronicle. Dante speaks in *Paradiso* as though his journey to Heaven had begun in Florence. This might mean that he visited Rome early in the Jubilee year, that is, between 22 February and 8 April. He returned to Florence in time for Easter and at some point in Holy Week or in Easter Week he experienced a vision infinitely more powerful and searching than anything he had known before. It is frequently supposed that Dante later chose Easter, 1300, as a convenient date round which to group his characters and prophecies. Among the reasons often given for the choice of 1300 are the fact that it was a Jubilee year, or that it marked in popular estimation the beginning of a new century, or, more interestingly, that it was a year of great astrological significance, denoting a quarter cycle of the Platonic Great Year within whose revolution all the works of time are accomplished.[22] If one sees these, however, as incidental to his main object, the expression in human and vernacular terms of his vision of the infinite, the question of why he chose the year 1300 takes on a different perspective. What he experienced was a vision of the Trinity and he only managed to put down an inkling of the vision, with numerous qualifications of how short of the truth his words came, right at the end of his life in the last canto of the *Paradiso*:

Ne la profonda e chiara sussistenza	Within the clear profound Light's aureole
de l'alto lume parvermi tre giri	Three circles from its substance now
di tre colori e d'una contenenza;	appeared,
e l'un da l'altro come iri da iri	Of three colours, and each an equal
parea reflesso, e 'l terzo parea foco	whole.
che quinci e quindi igualmente si	One its reflection on the next conferred
spiri.	As rainbow upon rainbow, and the two
Oh quanto è corto il dire e come fioco	Breathed equally the fire that was the
al mio concetto! e questo, a quel ch'i'	third.
vidi,	To my conception O how frail and few
è tanto, che non basta a dicer 'poco.'	My words! and that, to what I looked
O luce etterna che sola in te sidi,	upon,
sola t'intendi, e da te intelletta	Is such that 'little' is more than is its
e intendente te ami e arridi![23]	due.
	O Light Eternal, who in thyself alone
	Dwell'st and thyself know'st, and self-
	understood,
	Self-understanding, smilest on thine
	own!

He experienced the *excessus mentis*, the passing of consciousness beyond thought, of which the mystics had spoken. At this stage it left him with an overwhelming memory of light, the sense that he had been on a journey and that in some way marvellous creatures had given him instruction. It took him the rest of his life to work out the implications of his vision. Everything he was to write in the next few years was either a preparation for expressing this vision or, as in the case of the *Convivio*, a running away from it. The vision left him haunted by the number three and the memory of light. He could not at this time identify any of the elusive faces whose faint impress remained with him. Boccaccio says[24] that Dante wrote the first seven cantos of the *Inferno* before his exile and that these were saved from the looting of his house and sent on to him a few years later, at which point he resumed the composition. This is highly unlikely (see

Chapter 14). Others have accepted the story of lost manuscripts but said they were of *canzoni*.[25] If this were so, I would suggest they were notes not for the *Inferno* but for what eventually became the *Paradiso*. Dante's difficulty with the *Commedia* was not with how it ended but with how it should begin.

The memory of the vision would have been frequently erased from his mind by the events of the next few months. In May 1300 he was sent as the Florentine ambassador to the small town of San Gimignano, where he spoke to the general council of the commune on a matter concerning the Guelph League, through which Florence maintained her allies in Tuscany. On 15 June he entered office as one of the six priors appointed to rule Florence for two months, a period most out of joint for him and the city.

The Florentines had generally been on good terms with Boniface; they had supported him in the Colonna war and he appreciated the skills and gifts of its citizens. When the ambassadors of the monarchs of Europe had attended him at the Jubilee ceremonies, all the ambassadors were Florentines. Boniface had then made his famous joke that Florentines were the fifth element. The joke underlines the essential part the city played in keeping open the financial and diplomatic chains of communication in Europe. There were, however, clouds in the relationships: rumours that Boniface was negotiating with Albert of Austria for the transfer of imperial rights in Tuscany, the high place Corso Donati had gained in the pope's esteem after he had been exiled from Florence for corruption in a lawsuit, and a quarrel with the pope's favourite bankers, the Spini, all caused tension. In April 1300 the Florentine government had brought charges against Simone Gherardi, an agent of the Spini, and two associates. They were fined 1,000 florins or sentenced to have their tongues cut out if they did not pay. The fact that they were safe in Rome did not allay Boniface's rage. He addressed a bull to the bishop and inquisitor of Florence expostulating at this defiance of his wishes but Dante and his fellow priors as their first act confirmed the sentence.

There was trouble in the city as well. The long-standing hostility between the Donati and the Cerchi broke out into fights. On May Day, 1300, both families were watching a display of dancing. An armed affray started, and Ricoverino de' Cerchi had his nose cut off by a follower of the Donati. 'This blow was the destruction of our city', says Dino Compagni.[26] The Cerchi plotted revenge and in June Boniface sent Cardinal Matthew of Acquasparta to make peace and to settle the matter of the bankers. While the cardinal was there, new riots broke out. On the eve of the feast of St John the Baptist, the heads of the guilds were processing with offerings through the streets when they were set upon and beaten by some noblemen. 'We won Campaldino and you bar us from the offices and honours of our city', was their cry. Dante and his fellow priors decided to banish leaders from both sides in an attempt to calm the atmosphere. Corso and the Blacks were sent to Castel della Pieve and some of the Whites including Guido Cavalcanti, to Sarzana. There Cavalcanti fell ill, and he was allowed to return to Florence, where he died at the end of August.

Cardinal Matthew of Acquasparta had been working too openly on the side of the Blacks to gain the trust of the rulers of Florence. When a crossbow bolt narrowly missed him, shot by someone of 'not much sense', and stuck in the post of a window in the Bishop's palace, the cardinal took umbrage and decided to leave. The Signoria made him a present of 2,000 new florins, which Dino Compagni took to him in a gilt cup. The cardinal looked at the money very hard and would not take it.[27]

Corso broke bounds and fled to Rome, for which he was condemned. He intrigued with the Spini, who asked Boniface to interfere once more in the affairs of Florence. Boniface sent for Vieri de' Cerchi and asked him to make peace with Corso. The meeting was not a success: Vieri refused the peace-making offer and Boniface dismissed him as an old woman. Further disturbances took place in December, and in April 1301 the Blacks met in the church of Santa Trinità to discuss how to get rid of the Whites. The Whites, still holding power, discovered the conspiracy and more punishments followed.

Boniface was now involved in several problems, all of which he tried to settle by one means. The war over Sicily still dragged on and drained energies and money; the government of Florence had to be assigned to a party firmly of papal persuasion, i.e. the Blacks; he needed support to win the Aldobrandeschi territories; and there was a new quarrel looming with Philip the Fair, which might yet be averted. The first quarrel, over *Clericis Laicos*, had concerned the immunity of the clergy from lay taxation; this second quarrel involved the immunity of the clergy from lay jurisdiction.

Once before there had been a fruitful alliance between the papacy and a younger son of the house of France, when Charles of Anjou had defeated Manfred at Benevento. Boniface had had his eye for some time on another member of the same house, Charles of Valois, younger brother of Philip the Fair, and the idea struck him that Charles should be invited to Italy, where he could settle the Sicilian problem and bring Florence over to Boniface. Charles of Valois shared many of his brother's characteristics: his lethargy, his ability to depute unpleasant tasks to others, and his permanent need of money. Like Charles of Anjou, he believed life owed him a kingdom; unlike his great-uncle he never won one. He had been pretender to the throne of Aragon until the peace of Anagni in 1295. Boniface offered him the hand of Catherine of Courtenay, the heiress of the Latin empire of the East. Charles accepted the invitation and in May 1301 he started on his journey to Italy, staying in July at Parma with Azzo d'Este, from whom he borrowed 10,000 florins, then going on to Bologna, where White ambassadors from Florence discovered that the Blacks had preceded them and won his interest. He met Boniface at Anagni in September and then, primed with instructions and 200,000 florins, he turned northwards to Siena, where Corso Donati met him in October with a sweetener of 70,000 florins. The Whites in Florence were growing very anxious.

Though Dante's priorate had only lasted for two months the previous year, he was still used on many matters of business. A document of 28 April 1301 appoints him to take charge of road works in Florence, so that supplies could be brought in more efficiently from the country, and to protect the commune from the attacks of magnates.[28] The implication is of a long-laid plan against a siege. On 19 June he spoke at two debates,[29] first at a gathering of the council of the hundred and other councils and then at the council of the hundred alone. On both occasions he opposed the proposal to send help to Boniface for the war against the Aldobrandeschi. 'Dante Alagherii consuluit quod de servitio faciendo d. pape nichil fiat', says the record of the first of these councils.[30] The motion to send help was carried but Dante was one of thirty-five who voted against it. His last recorded intervention in a Florentine council was on 28 September 1301. It was probably after this date that he was chosen as a member of a special embassy of the Whites from Florence and Bologna to Boniface. Boccaccio reports his cry of dilemma: 'If I go, who stays? If I stay, who goes?'[31] The Cerchi had proved themselves incapable of giving firm leadership to the movement that had thrust them into prominence; Dante was surrounded by allies of inferior intelligence and shifting allegiances. He was probably chosen partly because of his gifts as an orator and, when they reached Anagni, Boniface received the deputation and singled Dante out for special treatment. He sent the others back to Florence and Bologna, while requiring Dante to stay behind. Boniface must have heard mention of Dante, both of his gifts and his opposition to the papal schemes. He probably flattered Dante at first with a display of his own wide-ranging and cultivated conversation, all the time intending to make sure that this potentially dangerous opponent should be kept from thwarting his plans for Florence. As the plans progressed, so Dante, hanging about the papal court, would have realized from the growing chilliness of his reception how deeply he had been tricked.

Because of his detention by Boniface, he was absent from Florence when Charles of Valois entered the city on 1 November. The White priors were still so bound to their Guelph traditions that they could not bring themselves to bar the gates to a member of the French royal house. Instead they asked for guarantees, which Charles cheerfully gave and as cheerfully ignored. He put up at the house of the Frescobaldi across the Arno, bringing up with him 1,200 men-at-arms at his command. The priors, one of whom at this time was Dino Compagni, were highly suspicious and troubled. Charles asked them to dine with him, but they refused on account of their oath of office, which forbade them to accept such invitations. They agreed to meet him instead at Santa Maria Novella where, in a public assembly, they handed the signory of the city over to him. Charles swore to preserve the peace of the city. Immediately he armed his followers and made them stand to. The citizens erected barricades and the priors found themselves powerless. Corso Donati, still an exile and outlawed, broke into the city with the help of Blacks within. Once Corso got within the inner walls, he stood in the Piazza San Piero Maggiore with his men fully armed while supporters, shouting his name, gathered round him. He then broke open the prisons and forced the priors, who still had a month of their legal term to serve, to resign their offices and go home. Corso's mob was now let loose on the city for five or six days, looting shops and warehouses and robbing the houses of the Whites, Dante's among them. Many Whites were killed or wounded. Charles of Valois did nothing to restrain the violence. Dino says that when a house burnt particularly brightly, he would inquire what the fire was and would be satisfied with the reply that it was a hut, when it was in fact some rich palace.[32]

New priors were elected on 8 November and they were all Blacks. A new *podestà*, Cante de' Gabrielli of Gubbio, was also appointed. The Blacks had learnt a lesson from the Whites during their period of exile and exclusion from office—never to relax their hold on power. Matthew of Acquasparta appeared again, making some accord between the leading families on both sides, but when he tried to make the Blacks share the offices of the city with the Whites, he met blank refusal. He left the city under an interdict and in December new troubles broke out. In a scuffle Simone, Corso Donati's favourite son, attacked Niccola de' Cerchi, who was his uncle. He wounded him fatally, but not before Niccola had struck back with a blow from which Simone died that night. The Whites were finally undone when one of Charles of Valois' barons, acting as an *agent provocateur*, promoted a plot amongst them to betray his master. Evidence and forged letters were placed before Charles, and the Whites implicated fled from the city in April 1302.[33]

Many Whites had already come under sentence from the new government. A law had been passed allowing the *podestà* to bring charges against former priors. In a document of 27 January 1302, Dante and three others are accused of trafficking in offices, bribery, causing the expulsion of the Blacks, 'faithful devotees of the Roman Church', from Pistoia, and of other crimes. For not answering these charges in person he was fined, banished for two years, and permanently excluded from office.[34] This decree was followed by another on 10 March, in which he and fourteen other former priors were condemned to be burnt to death.[35]

Dante was in Siena on his way back from Rome when he heard the full extent of the measures against him.[36] Both rumour and true report would have convinced him of the dangers of returning to answer the charges. He was to remain an exile for the rest of his life and, for at least the next eleven years, until the death of Henry of Luxemburg, he never gave up hope of returning. He was separated from his family and deprived of his income. Though he was again to play important political roles, it would always be as a conspirator, a courtier, or as the agent of some lord; he would never possess the rights in any other commune that his citizenship of Florence conferred on him. All his travels convinced him that there was no better city in which to live than Florence. The great lawyer Accursius, a Florentine eminent in Bologna in the early thirteenth century, had described exile as a kind of secular excommunication 'in so much as it excludes from the common good'.[37] It was to be a long time before Dante found a common good from which he could not be excluded.

He soon made contact with his fellow exiles and joined in various attempts to secure their return to Florence. In June 1302 he and sixteen other Florentines had made an alliance with the Ghibelline Ubaldini family, and at San Godenzo in the Mugello he and his fellow conspirators agreed to made good any damage the Ubaldini should suffer in the projected warfare against Florence. In 1303 he went to Forlì, where he was an aide to another Ghibelline leader, Scarpetta Ordelaffi, and the same year he went as an ambassador of the Whites to Verona, where the lord of the city, Bartolomeo della Scala, 'il gran Lombardo', befriended him. The trading connexion between many of the Whites and Verona, already mentioned, would partly explain why they hoped for support from this quarter, and Dante obviously found solace and comfort in his reception there.

New hope must have come to him in 1303 when Boniface VIII died. The quarrel with France, which had begun in 1301 with Philip the Fair's prosecution of the bishop of Pamiers, Bernard Saisset, had flared into a vehement dispute over the question of clerical immunity. The reconciliation with France that Boniface's invitation to Charles of Valois had partly signified never came about. Charles had wrecked the possibilities of a settlement in Florence and, though the papal party of the Blacks had won, the exiles threatened serious reprisals. After his visit to Florence, Charles invaded Sicily, but his army melted away and he was forced to ignominious terms in the Treaty of Caltabelotta, whereby the Aragonese Frederick of Sicily was confirmed in his possession of the island. The hopes of a successful reconciliation between the papacy and the French monarchy were dashed and new strife broke out between them. Boniface found new allies against Philip in the Flemings, who inflicted a great defeat on the French at the battle of Courtrai, and in Albert of Austria, whom he confirmed as the emperor-elect. The war of words continued between the papacy and Philip's lawyers and advisers. In his bulls, Boniface made ever grander claims to the supremacy of the spiritual power, and the French lawyers responded by attacking not the papal claims but Boniface personally. He was a false pope, he had murdered Celestine, he was a heretic, a simonist, he was guilty of every sexual aberration, and he would be deposed by a general council. In June 1303 Philip summoned his council, to which nearly all the French clergy of the higher ranks came, amd Boniface was indicted on twenty-nine heads. Nearly all the clergy supported Philip. Boniface prepared a bull of excommunication against Philip but, before it was promulgated, an attack was made on Boniface in his palace at Anagni. It was an attempt to kidnap him and bear him off to France to face the projected general council. Philip's lawyer, William Nogaret, whose parents had been burnt as heretics, and Sciarra Colonna, exiled like the rest of his family and desperate for revenge, borrowed money from the Florentine bankers, the Peruzzi, for the venture. With 1,000 foot and 300 horsemen they broke into Anagni and captured Boniface. He met the attackers wearing his papal robes and clasping a cross, refusing their terms, answering their jibes with bitter retorts, and inviting them to kill him. The conspirators could not agree what to do with him. After three days an uprising by the townspeople drove them out and freed Boniface. His spirit was broken, however, and he died in Rome on 12 October 1303. For all his hatred of Boniface, Dante was outraged by the attack and several years later condemned it in the lines:

veggio in Alagna entrar lo fiordaliso	I see the fleur-de-lys enter Anagni
e nel vicario suo Cristo esser catto.[38]	And in his vicar Christ made captive.

The new pope, Benedict XI, was quickly elected. A mild man, he worked hard in his short pontificate for peace and he is the only pope of Dante's maturity not condemned in the *Commedia* to Hell. He sent an able negotiator, the cardinal of Prato, to make peace in Tuscany. Dante's earliest surviving letter,[39] written in the spring of 1304 on behalf of the captain and council of the White party, of which Dante was a member, expresses to the cardinal their joy and their expectations of his mission and promises a truce from warfare on their part. The cardinal's mission was a failure; the Blacks were suspicious of him and refused all his attempts to restore the Whites. After several months the cardinal left Florence in June 1304, placing the city under yet another interdict.

It seems to have been soon after this that Dante had his quarrel with the Whites that was to turn him into a 'party of one'. He thought them 'wicked and stupid', and they harboured serious grudges against him. He did not take part in the attack on Florence which the Whites launched in July 1304 and which failed miserably. Another blow hit both Dante and the Whites that same month when Benedict XI died, according to Villani, of eating poisoned figs brought to him by a young man dressed as a nun.[40] The papacy was to remain vacant for eleven months until the election of Bertrand de Got as Pope Clement V, an election that made the papacy a tool of the French monarchy.

Almost nothing is known of Dante's movements over the next period, except that he travelled. He speaks in the *Convivio* of going 'through almost every region to which this tongue of ours extends, a stranger and almost a beggar' and calls himself 'a ship without sail and without rudder, wafted to divers havens and inlets and shores by the parching wind which woeful poverty exhales'.[41] Having quarrelled with the other Whites he now tried to negotiate his return to Florence singly. Lionardo Bruni speaks of his humility, as he sought through good works and good behaviour to be allowed to return to Florence through a voluntary recall by those in power; he wrote more than once, not only to individual members of the government, but also to the people. Among these letters was a very long one which began 'Popule mee, quid feci tibi?'[42] He also wrote the *canzone* on justice, 'Tre donne', with its pathetic *congedo* begging for forgiveness:

Canzone, uccella con le bianche penne;	Song, go hawking with the wings of white,
canzone, caccia con li neri veltri,	Song, go hunting with the hounds of black,

che fuggir mi convenne,	From which I'm forced to flight
ma far mi poterian di pace dono.	Though peace is in their power to bestow;
Però nol fan che non san quel che sono:	Not knowing what I am, they treat me so:
camera di perdon savio uom non serra,	To mercy's room the wise man locks no door,
ché 'l perdonare è bel vincer di guerra.[43]	For mercy is the finest feat of war.

No favourable answer came. His situation was obviously bad; by a decree of 1303 his sons had been sentenced to the same banishment as himself when they reached the age of fourteen. By breaking with the White exiles, he had cut himself off from the source of money that exiled parties pooled for their members. Except for those occasions when he is recorded as living in the courts of great lords, nothing is known of how he supported himself.

After the great quarrel in about June 1304, he probably went to Bologna, the university city which could provide the books and learned conversations he needed for the next stage of his work. There, he met again his friend, the poet Cino da Pistoia, who was also an exile from his native city. Pistoia was still in the hands of the Whites and remained so until 1306, when Cino returned there. The fact that Cino belonged to the Black party seems to have had no bearing on their relationship. They exchanged correspondence in verse[44] though Dante's main literary energies were devoted to the prose treatises *De vulgari eloquentia* and the *Convivio*, discussed in the next two chapters. The *Convivio* occupied him probably up to about 1308, when he broke it off unfinished. He had left Bologna long before then. In October 1306 the Florentine government had persuaded the Bolognese to expel all White exiles who had taken refuge there. Dante had already gone to the court of the marquis Franceschino Malaspina in the Lunigiana. There, acting as the agent of the Malaspina family, he concluded a treaty settling a long-standing quarrel between that family and the bishop of Luni, as a surviving document shows.[45] Part of the time between 1306 and 1308 he seems to have spent in Lucca.

Villani says he went to Paris at this period of his exile,[46] and Boccaccio tells a story of his remarkable debating powers, which astonished the French scholars.[47] A later author, Giovanni da Serravalle, says that he went to Paris and studied there, but in the earlier period after the death of Beatrice, and he also says that Dante studied at Oxford, a thought that was particularly dear to Gladstone.[48] Few have supported Gladstone in this and, indeed, the weight of modern opinion is against the probability of Dante going to Paris at any time. If Dante went there, his visit would have coincided with Philip the Fair's attack on the Templar order and his harrying of Clement V, who was to sacrifice the Templars to prevent the posthumous condemnation of Boniface VIII. The reasons for disregarding the story of his visit to Paris include the lack of direct evidence in the *Commedia* of the experience Dante would have gained, and the difficulty some find in fitting it into the time-scale of Dante's known movements.

This last objection does not take into account the comparative speed of travel across Europe at this period. On the other hand, Boccaccio would seem to have totally invented as a literary exercise a letter, called that of Frate Ilario, in which Dante is described as stopping at a monastery on his way to France; making friends with Brother Ilario, he hands over a copy of the *Inferno* for the monk to send on to Moroello Malaspina.[49]

Given Dante's position as an exile and his hopes of returning to Florence, what was essential to him at this time, apart from the necessities of providing for his food and lodging, was up-to-date information not just about Florence, but about the papacy, and events in France and the rest of Italy. For as we have seen, the international status of Florence made her particularly sensitive to all major external events. Dante had been a ruler of Florence in the Jubilee year, an appointment admittedly of short duration and one to which, according to another lost letter quoted by Lionardo Bruni,[50] he attributed all his misfortunes; he would have acquired both the need for constant revision of information and the ability to interpret it for his own aims and safety. It was an extraordinary moment in European history, one of those times when every accepted notion seems to crack with illogicalities and doubts. Many popes had suffered physical force and imprisonment before but none been accused of heresy and unbelief on the scale of the charges brought against Boniface VIII. The most esteemed fighting force of Christendom, the Templars whose members came from the noblest families of Europe, were suddenly denounced as infidels, pagans, and sodomites. The traditional friendship of Florence with the royal house of France had turned gravely to the city's detriment. Behind all these catastrophes stood the head of that royal house, Philip the Fair of France, a man of exceptional abilities as a ruler but crookedly devout, and illimitably ambitious. Dante detested him as he did his brother, Charles of Valois. To Dante he was the 'mal di Francia'[51] but in his own eyes he was the divinely appointed agent of God. Influenced probably by the Catalan mystic Ramon Lull[52] who, after the fall of Acre in 1291, the last mainland possession of the Crusader kingdom, advocated the amalgamation of the Templars and the Hospitallers as the basis of a new crusading army, Philip saw himself as the 'Bellator Rex', the monarch who would unite the orders and restore the kingdom of Jerusalem, becoming the Roman emperor and ruling the nations of the Earth from the Holy Land. Many of these ambitions were set out in the tract *De recuperatione terra sancte* by the lawyer, Pierre Dubois.[53] There are close similarities on the surface here with Dante's own ideal monarch, but given Dante's knowledge of his character and the means he adopted for his aims, Philip must have seemed like a disgusting parody of that ideal. For all the unification of his kingdom and the efficiency of his administration, he chronically lacked money, not only for these grand ambitions, but merely for the management of France and for his wars. His taxes on the Church in France provoked the first quarrel with Boniface VIII and he was forced to borrow large sums from the Templars who under their Grand Master, Jacques de Molay, had transferred the headquarters of the order to Paris. This move in itself would have been enough to provoke the doubts of a less suspicious ruler because the Templars, being a trained fighting force, with a private navy, owning vast territorial wealth and long established as bankers to Europe and the Middle East, and noted for their arrogance and independence, were answerable to the pope alone. They rejected his proposals for a united military order, thus at the same time affronting his politico-religious ambitions and confirming that, though seated on French soil, they would continue to act as an autonomous body. Philip took a long time to prepare his assault on the order. Then in 1305 a man called Esquiu de Floyran gained access to Philip with details of the dreadful crimes habitually committed by the order which he had learned from a former Templar with whom he had been imprisoned. (Villani tells the same story, making the informant a Florentine money-lender called Onofrio Deghi who was known as Noffo Dei.[54] Noffo Dei was in fact involved in another case, the charges of necromancy which Philip brought against Guichard, bishop of Troyes, as one of the levers to make the pope abolish the Templar order.) Philip passed Esquiu's revelations on to Clement V who determined to set up an investigation. Rather than allow the Templars the chance of answering the charges which a papal inquiry would have permitted, Philip had all the Templars in France arrested on the same day, 13 October 1307. They were accused of abominable practices which were said to be the rule of the order. These ranged from ritually practised sexual perversion to spitting on the crucifix and denying Christ and worshipping an idol called Baphomet. Philip's publicists, aided by Dominican and Franciscan preachers, spread the news of the dreadful discoveries abroad while his investigators either by torture or by its threat extracted confessions from great numbers of the imprisoned Templars. Threats alone were enough to make the Grand Master confess and he and numbers of his colleagues were forced to make public admission of their guilt. To crush the order and to secure its property Philip had to demonstrate that the order as a whole was a heretical sect and, to do so, his investigators employed the inquisitorial methods of extracting confessions which conformed to a stereotype already agreed by the king's advisers.[55] The charges against the order were wholly false; the investigators only obtained confessions in France and those parts of Italy under papal or French influence where they could employ torture. Even in France a majority of the Templars who did confess later retracted their confessions: in 1309 Philip was forced to have fifty-four of the most stalwart burned to death over slow fires to prevent further embarrassments of this kind. They died protesting their innocence and the purity of the order. Whenever the pope, Clement V, tried to stand up to Philip, the king would either produce new witnesses and confessions or else press for the condemnation of Boniface VIII and the burning of his bones, claiming that, where both the Templars and the dead pope were concerned, he was acting for the honour of the Church, and would have to proceed in that cause even against Clement's opposition. The possible condemnation of Boniface had terrible implications for the Church and for Clement; all Boniface's acts and appointments would have become invalid, including the appointments of cardinals who had aided in the election of Clement, so that Clement's own tenure of the Holy See could have been declared void.

Dante knew well that Philip was acting against the Templars quite illegally, for in the condemnation of Philip uttered by his ancestor Hugh Capet in *Purgatorio* he says that Philip, the new Pilate, is so cruel he is not content with making Christ captive in his vicar (the attempt at Anagni), but *sanza decreto*, without papal decree, he directs his greedy sails against the Temple.[56]

Those lines alone are enough to show Dante's sympathy for the order, a sympathy shared by Villani and later expressed by Boccaccio whose father was present at the immolation of Jacques de Molay in 1314, the final scene in this terrible drama.[57] The evidence for Dante's deeper involvement with the Templars or, at least, for the influence on him of the symbolism of the Temple which the order had been founded to protect, is given at greater length in Chapters 16 and 19. What is indisputable is his opposition to Philip the Fair whose life elsewhere in the *Purgatorio* he describes as *viziata e lorda*,[58] wicked and foul, and his belief that not only his own fortunes but those of humanity as a whole were vitiated by Philip's policies. Whether he was present in Paris at the time of the Templar investigations or not, he would have heard and known of the tortures and the burnings which must certainly in his imagination have contributed to the visions of the torments of the damned later to be set down in the *Inferno*.

The other necessary source of up-to-date information for Dante was Florence, and, from Bologna, Lucca or the Lunigiana he would have been kept well informed of the fortunes of his Black enemies in the city. Thus, always attentive to rumour issuing from Florence, hoping for events to turn in his favour, he would have learnt of the notable happenings in the city: the great spectacle beside the Arno, depicting Hell, in 1303 which ended in the deaths of numerous spectators when a stand collapsed;[59] the terrible fire in 1304, which was started by an arsonist and which destroyed much of the Cavalcanti's property and wealth;[60] and most intriguing of all, the dissensions amongst the leaders of the Blacks. These last came to a head in 1308 when Corso Donati quarrelled with another Black leader, Rosso della Tosa. Corso had married the daughter of the Ghibelline warlord, Uguccione della Faggiuola, and his enemies accused Corso of wanting to make himself despot of Florence. By now Corso was ageing and suffering from gout and had lost much of his support. A mob was roused against him and, besieged in his own house, he escaped and fled the city. He was soon captured and, dreading the fate that would meet him in Florence, he let himself fall from his horse. A Catalan mercenary thrust a lance through his throat from which he died.[61]

This ignominious death is elaborated in the *Purgatorio* when Forese Donati, Dante's friend and Corso's brother, prophesies what will happen to Corso in lines that blame him most of all for the miseries of Florence.

'Or va,' diss' el; 'che quei che più n'ha
    colpa,
  vegg' io a coda d'una bestia tratto
  inver' la valle ove mai non si scolpa.
La bestia ad ogne passo va più ratto,
  crescendo sempre, fin ch'ella il
    percuote,
  e lascia il corpo vilmente disfatto.[62]

'Now go,' said he, 'for him who is most
    embroiled
  I see dragged at the tail of a strong beast
  Down towards the vale where sin is
    unassoiled.
The beast goes faster at every step,
    increased
  In speed, until it breaks him on the
    ground
  And leaves his body hideously defaced.

Here the horse that Corso fell from is transformed into a steed of death accelerating its burden to damnation, a horrifying vignette that visits upon the once brilliant *barone* the waste and ruin to which he subjected so many others, a fate foreseen by his own brother and told to the man who, in all the miseries of exile, could still proudly call himself the poet of righteousness.

11

The poet of righteousness: later lyrics and *De vulgari eloquentia*

The early years of exile must have been a time of appalling disorientation for Dante. He was obviously a figure of very great importance in his party and the city by the time of the crisis of 1301. Boccaccio says that nothing was done without his being consulted,[1] and this is attested by his inclusion in the embassy to Boniface. This raises the questions of what his own political programme was, to what extent he looked upon his art as a mouthpiece for those ideas, and how far that programme and his sense of mission contributed to his permanent exile. It is very likely that, by the time of his priorate, Dante had developed his political philosophy quite far, linking together the social ideals implicit in the thoughts of the *fedeli d'amore* with his classical reading. He was never one for superficial aims and he could hardly have been content with the immediate policies of the White party, which centred mainly on securing the independence of Florence from papal aggression. The visit to Rome and the experience of the vision at Easter, 1300, awoke in him a sense of a comparable destiny awaiting Florence, and what drove him so hard in his political dealings may have been his desire to create out of Florence a great civilizing city. This awoke the prophet in him, and both his enemies and partners would have felt the force of a man driven by visionary ideas expressed with eloquence and intellectual vigour. He probably scared the wits out of many of them but he also towered over them because he possessed one of the most essential qualities of a great politician: he loved his fellow men and was deeply interested in them. This quality shines out in the closing passages of the *Monarchia* and throughout the *Commedia*. His despair and his invective are the consequences of that love.

Had Dante's party stood up to Charles of Valois or had he been allowed to return to Florence, we would probably have had no *Commedia*, at least in the form we have it. Carducci thought that a statue should be put up in every Italian town to Cante de' Gabrielli for exiling Dante, and Carlyle makes play with a similar idea.[2] But all that genius and energy would have found other outlets and the insistence of the Blacks in keeping him in exile is a notable contribution to the misery that Florence was to undergo in the fourteenth century until, at its close, Coluccio Salutati rediscovered the Roman theme and gave new heart to her citizens. The Blacks impoverished their city because they would not embrace Dante's wider vision and ideals. Just as the Soviet government, in banishing Alexander Solzhenitsyn, announced its refusal to entertain any relaxation of its tyranny and its ideology, so the Black rulers, in excluding Dante, postponed for nearly a hundred years the fruition of the long labour that had gone into the making of Florence in the twelfth and thirteenth centuries. It was a terrible crime that they committed. Solzhenitsyn says that literature is the living memory of a nation and that a nation whose literature is interrupted by force no longer remembers itself.[3] Dante's enemies were trying to kill the memory of Florence's destiny in attempting to secure his judicial murder. In rejecting him they rejected the greatest man their city had produced.

Deprived of his position in Florence, hated by both Whites and Blacks, he had to make use of the only outlet for his energies and talents that was left to him: his art, through which he made a new discovery of himself as 'the poet of righteousness'. This discovery helped him, not only to come to terms with the injustice and wickedness of his treatment by his enemies, but also gradually to define what justice, nobility, goodness, and the goal of knowledge meant to him in the widest terms. He therefore connected his own situation with the themes that had recently occupied his attention as a poet and turned to commenting on what he now regarded as his greatest artistic achievements, the philosophical and ethical *canzoni* he had written after the death of Beatrice. Writing in Latin, in *De vulgari eloquentia* he used his *canzoni* and those of his friends as a standard for the illustrious vernacular he hoped to establish. The *Convivio*, which is in Italian, was intended to consist of fifteen books (only four were completed), made up of an introduction and commentaries on fourteen of his *canzoni*. To grasp the significance of these two works in Dante's development, it is necessary first to turn to the poems dating from the period following the *Vita Nuova*.

After the writing of the *Vita Nuova*, Beatrice disappears from his poems. It is hardly likely that Dante had forgotten her, but the inspirations no longer came from her. Apart from the explanation in the *Convivio* of how Philosophy triumphed over her memory, she does not reappear directly in his work until the *Commedia*. The promise to study so that he may say of her what had never been said of any woman before, seems to have been lost sight of in the pursuit of study itself and in the excitement of political life. Among the gains of his discovery of the poetry of praise in 'Donne ch'avete' was a new technical mastery and the urge to find themes that would put that mastery constantly to the test. Thus the poems written after Beatrice's death fall into several stylistic and thematic groups: first the poems celebrating the *donna gentile* as Philosophy, then the poems for the *pargoletta* and the lady known as the *donna giovane*, then the *canzoni* on moral themes, on nobility and *leggiadria* (charm), the sonnet exchange with Forese Donati which experiments with the low style, the four poems on the cruel lady, La Pietra, to be followed during his exile by the *canzoni*

166

'Tre donne' and 'Doglia mi reca', and by the sonnet correspondence with Cino da Pistoia. (Some would add the version of the *Roman de la Rose*, translated into 232 sonnets known as *Il Fiore*.)[4] What Dante in exile found most to admire in this body of work were the allegorical and moral *canzoni*, which he had developed to a new pitch of skill and in which he had introduced a new range of themes. It was on account of these that he declared himself the poet of righteousness,[5] leaving the title of 'the poet of love' to Cino. Many of these *canzoni* are remarkable works of art, each as individually constructed as the canopies or baldacchini of contemporary altar-pieces, and, in the same way, enshrining the sacred images which are their subjects, all floriated with ornate expressions and finialed with rhyme. They are all, apart from the two moral *canzoni*, devoted to the theme of love. How far, if at all, were the ladies celebrated in them, the *donna gentile*, the *pargoletta*, the *donna giovane*, real women and objects of genuine sexual desire? In a later sonnet, addressed, with an explanatory letter written between 1303 and 1306, to Cino da Pistoia, who had asked him whether, since he no longer loves one woman, he should give in to his attraction to another, Dante replies that it is useless to resist love:

Io sono stato con Amore insieme
da la circulazion del sol mia nona,
e so com'egli affrena e come sprona,
e come sotto lui si ride e geme.[6]

I have remained with Love and in his
    keeping
Since the sun encircled nine of my years,
And know how he bridles and how he
    spurs,
And under his weight the laughter and
    weeping.

In the letter[7] he places this love firmly in the appetite, acknowledging the nature of strong physical attraction in a way that recalls Cavalcanti's description of this kind of love in 'Donna mi prega'. Against this, one has to put the firm identification of the *donna gentile* with Philosophy in the *Convivio*, and the close similarity between the passages in the poems to her which he interprets allegorically, and those addressed to the other ladies. These are very difficult contradictions to resolve. If there was anything Dante had learnt from the experiences recorded in the *Vita Nuova*, it was that love existed on many levels and that the attainment of a high spiritual love was not, at any rate for him, something that would exclude the resurgence of physical love for someone other than Beatrice. He had learnt to place his love where it could not fail him—in the praise of his lady; he had been torn apart by his sufferings after Beatrice's death and was probably determined never, if he could help it, to undergo such sufferings again. He had recently married and that, too, would have been an incentive to transfer his songs of love to an allegorical plane—even though he continued to have love affairs. The episode of the *donna gentile* obviously disturbed him greatly. He wrote the *canzone* 'Voi che 'ntendendo' to describe how the memory of Beatrice was replaced by this new love, then wrote a sonnet rejecting the *canzone*, followed by another reinstating it.[8] The influence of the vision of Philosophy in Boethius, the continued power of the image of Sapientia, his own studies of philosophy, all combined, however, to show him a way in which he could continue with his new style of praise: retaining the great cosmological framework that Beatrice had opened to him in the *Vita Nuova*, and making poems that at the same time would appeal to the exigent brotherhood of the *cor gentile* and to the other hearers or readers who could, at least, thrill to the beauty of the brilliant cascades of rhymes and their majesty of form, even if the subtler meanings evaded them. He would seem to have found a full acceptance of these possibilities in the *canzone*, 'Amor che ne la mente mi ragiona'.[9] Many poems are now addressed to Love and not directly to the Lady; Love is no longer presented as the visionary youth of the *Vita Nuova*, but as a cosmic light filling the universe in which Sapientia reigns. The source of his inspiration seems to have shifted from the more pictorial dream images and waking visions of many of the *Vita Nuova* poems to experiences of intellectual light. There is little reliance on metaphor, beyond the basic ones of light and of the lady, and none on the evocation of physical reality, though a repeated reading of that *canzone* brings out a succession of images so bright that details of the world only glimmer faintly under the radiance of an understanding that reduces the appearance of sublunary creation to illusion. These later poems are based on the medieval conception of poetry as rhetoric, in which the beauty and the concordance of the whole are paramount. The spell they cast is of an irradiated light that, through synaesthesia, merges into music: every word, every concept and detail, is chosen with exquisite skill to ensure that nothing jars with the harmony of the whole. Even when he draws on his experiments with optics for an image to develop a point, as in 'Amor, che movi tua vertù da cielo' where he is, in fact, describing a lens made by filling a glass bottle with water, he is deliberately vague:

Per questo mio guardar m'è ne la mente	And through this gazing, entering my mind,
una giovane entrata, che m'ha preso,	A young girl, who enslaved me, came
e hagli un foco acceso,	And in me lit a flame
com'acqua per chiarezza fiamma accende;	As water through its clearness kindles fire;
perché nel suo venir li raggi tuoi,	For at her coming your bright rays
con li quai mi risplende,	To whose splendour I aspire
saliron tutti su negli occhi suoi.[10]	Leap upwards all within her eyes.

The sweetness and harmony of these *canzoni* sometimes failed to satisfy him, however proud he might feel of their perfection of style and form. Crueller sides of his nature demanded expression in his art; the world of sticks and stones still existed. So we find in this period the savage, low style of the exchange with Forese Donati, the stiletto-like sarcasm of his sonnet to Betto Brunelleschi, and the plain speaking of the moral *canzoni*. He was at the beginning of an impasse which was to last for many years: until the beginning of the *Commedia*, he became trapped by his own skill with the *canzone*. This skill, by his own rules of style and form, prevented him from combining all these voices and sides of his nature in one work. He was beset by a need for drama, to expand his own nature by living through others, but he was limited by a format which bound him to set the drama within his own psychology. This, at least artistically, would help to explain the background to the crisis which produced the four explosions known as the *rime petrose*, the poems for the *donna pietra*, the lady of stone.

From at least the time when he was writing the *Vita Nuova* to 1297, the earliest possible date of these poems, Dante had been supplementing his philosophical studies with considerable reading and reflection on Provençal poetry. This was also to bear fruit in *De vulgari eloquentia* and in several passages (already noted in Chapter 7) in the *Commedia*. Of all the many poets, he was drawn most to Arnaut Daniel, whom Guinizzelli describes as *il miglior fabbro*, the 'better maker'. In Chapter 7, I described some of the features that so recommended Arnaut to Dante as a model: his technical virtuosity, his refusal to soften either the complexity of his emotions or the obscurity of the concepts to which he married these emotions, his ability to create memorable pictures, and his sense of mystery. We can tell nothing of the experience that led Dante to seize on Arnaut's example and attempt to surpass him in technical accomplishment. But it is obvious that now a flood of phenomena enter Dante's poems for the first time: deliberately rough language used in a *canzone*, observations of landscape, weather, plants, and animals, bright and brilliant colours and, above all, a new directness about himself that enabled him to bring together in one series of works all the various styles in which he had hitherto written. Presumably he had fallen passionately in love with a woman who rejected him and whom he called *La Pietra*; and, as with his previous loves who attracted like magnets his current ideas and preoccupations, so his hopeless love for her took the mood not only of his sexual frustration but also of the impasse he had reached as a poet and, given the time at which they were written, his difficulties as a young politician. There is another dimension in these poems as well, the dramatic one; cosmology had given him the theatre for his poems of praise; now Earth, its weather, and its creatures gave him a scene for works that seem to be full of hatred and self-loathing. This dimension raises the poems beyond their basic theme of frustration in love to an expression of what is almost delight in this state, to a recognition of it as a necessary condition of emotional arousal that signifies a psychological transition into new understanding.

To read the four *Pietra* poems is like reading a tragedy and being shocked and purified in Aristotle's sense. The transformation that his violent and negative emotions underwent through the discipline of art cleansed the poems of all embarrassing or self-pitying traces. This was achieved aesthetically by the new use he made of his eyes; just as the *Inferno* is made bearable to its readers by the constant comparisons and references to the good and healthy world above it, so here the madness of his condition is controlled by its setting in the objective world of nature, whose beauty he expresses as never before. He regains also in these poems, most notably in 'Così nel mio parlar', the visual force of the dream imagery of the *Vita Nuova* but with a new power and erotic urgency. All this makes them not only great and original works in their own right but also essential stages in the process that led to the direct speech and visual qualities of the *Commedia*. The first of the four poems, 'Io son venuto al punto de la rota', is a *canzone* of five stanzas with a *congedo*. It is based on a theme familiar at the time from the Latin song 'De ramis cadunt folia' (dating from about 1200), which includes these lines

Modo frigescit quicquid est,	Everything that is turns to cold
sed solus ego caleo.	But I alone burn with heat.

though Dante took the theme most probably from the beginning of Arnaut's 'Quan chai la fuelha'. In each stanza he contrasts a state of nature with his own state, dealing in descending order with astronomy, meteorology, zoology, botany, and finally the waters and rocks of the Earth. The contrast is brought out from the tenth line in each stanza, beginning with the word *e* ('and'). The stars (a conjunction is described which only occurred once in Dante's lifetime, in December 1296) are at their most unfavourable for Love, yet he himself cannot shake off any of his thoughts of love. A wind drives from Ethiopia, building up the clouds and causing snow to fall, yet Love will not leave him. The migratory birds have fled; those left behind do not sing; the animals are prevented by cold from mating; yet he is more full of love than ever. Leaves, grass, and flowers are dead yet Love does not draw out his thorn. Finally he comes to the water and Earth.

Versan le vene le fummifere acque	The springs belch waters laden thick with smoke
per li vapor che la terra ha nel ventre,	From gases that the Earth within her womb,
che d'abisso li tira suso in alto;	Draws upwards from abyssal riven crack;
onde cammino al bel giorno mi piacque	So that the path that in fine weather woke
che ora è fatto rivo, e sarà mentre	In me such pleasure is now a flood, a doom
che durerà del verno il grande assalto;	Lasting the length of winter's great attack;
la terra fa un suol che par di smalto,	Earth forms a crust that seems to be of rock,
e l'acqua morta si converte in vetro	And deathly waters change themselves to glass
per la freddura che di fuor la serra:	Through cold that locks them well away from thaw:
e io de la mia guerra	And yet to leave my war
non son però tornato un passo a retro,	I have not turned or let the struggle pass,

170

né vo' tornar; ché, se 'l martiro è dolce,
la morte de' passare ogni altro dolce.[11]

Nor do I wish to turn; if pain is sweet,
Death must surpass all else that too is
sweet.

The second poem, 'Al poco giorno' is a sestina, the form invented by Arnaut
(see Chapter 7) in which the six rhyme words of the first stanza are repeated in a
different order in the remaining five stanzas and the *congedo*. There is punning
throughout on the different meanings these words—*ombra, colli, erba, verde, petra,
donna*—can bear, so that *petra* can be read successively as the speaking statue the
lady resembles, the stone of her heart, the stone of masonry, the strength of rock,
stone in its psychological sense as the least changeable of attitudes, the stone of
the mountains, and finally as a precious stone a man loses under grass—the
image, incidentally, on which the English poem, 'Pearl', of the approaching
century is based. The punning affords another example of the convertibility of
images, and the recurrence of the words builds up a dominating picture of a
landscape such as that of the Casentino, with its flat lush plain surrounded by
mountains, whose stony beauty reflect the triumphant unconcern of the lady.
This may be seen from a reading of the whole poem:

Al poco giorno e al gran cerchio
   d'ombra
son giunto, lasso, ed al bianchir de'
   colli,
quando si perde lo color ne l'erba:
e'l mio disio però non cangia il verde,
si è barbato ne la dura petra
che parla e sente come fosse donna.

To the short day and to the great ring of
   shadow
I have come, alas, and to the whitening
   hills,
When all the colour vanishes from grass:
But my desire can never change its green,
It is so rooted in the obdurate stone
That speaks and hears as though it were
   a woman.

Similemente questa nova donna
si sta gelata come neve a l'ombra;
ché non la move, se non come petra,
il dolce tempo che riscalda i colli,
e che li fa tornar di bianco in verde
perché li copre di fioretti e d'erba.

Similarly this miraculous woman
Stays frozen like the snow within the
   shadow;
She is not moved except as is a stone,
By the sweet season that warms again
   the hills,
And makes them turn from whiteness into
   green
In covering them with little flowers and
   grass.

Quand'ella ha in testa una ghirlanda
   d'erba,
trae de la mente nostra ogn'altra
   donna;
perché si mischia il crespo giallo e 'l verde

When on her head she wears a wreath of
   grass,
She draws our mind from every other
   woman;
Because she joins the yellow crest to green

sì bel, ch'Amor lì viene a stare a
    l'ombra,
che m'ha serrato intra piccioli colli
più forte assai che la calcina petra.

So beautifully, that Love stands in the
    shadow,
Even he who bound me in the little hills
More strongly than the mortar locks the
    stone.

La sua bellezza ha più vertù che petra,
e 'l colpo suo non può sanar per erba;
ch'io son fuggito per piani e per colli,
per potere scampar da cotal donna;
e dal suo lume non mi può far ombra
poggio né muro mai né fronda verde.

Her beauty has more power than stone,
No herb can cure her wound nor grass;
So that I have fled through plains and
    over hills,
To find a refuge from this very woman;
Whose light allows me neither rest nor
    shadow
Of knoll or wall or leaf of green.

Io l'ho veduta già vestita a verde,
sì fatta ch'ella avrebbe messo in petra
l'amor ch'io porto pur a la sua ombra:
ond'io l'ho chesta in un bel prato
    d'erba,
innamorata com'anco fu donna,
e chiuso intorno d'altissimi colli.

I have seen her so attired in green,
She would arouse within a stone
The love I bear her very shadow:
Thus I have wished her in a fine meadow
    of grass,
As much in love as ever was a woman,
And closed around by all the highest hills.

Ma ben ritorneranno i fiumi a' colli,
prima che questo legno molle e verde
s'infiammi, come suol far bella donna,
di me; che mi torrei dormire in petra
tutto il mio tempo e gir pascendo l'erba,
sol per veder do' suoi panni fanno
    ombra.

But sooner will the streams return to
    hills,
Before this bough so soft of sap and
    green
Will burst in flames, as should a lovely
    woman,
In love for me; so that I sleep on stone
All my days and wander grazing grass,
Only to seek for where her robes cast
    shadow.

Quandunque i colli fanno più nera
    ombra,
sotto un bel verde la giovane donna
la fa sparer, com'uom petra sott'erba.[12]

Whenever cast the hills their blacker
    shadow,
Under a lovely green there vanishes this
    woman
As might a precious stone be hidden under
    grass.

His pride at equalling Arnaut in the sestina now drove him to an even more difficult technical achievement: the double sestina, 'Amor, tu vedi ben che questa donna'. There are five rhyme words, each of which is repeated five times as a line-ending in one of the five stanzas. The rigidity of its scheme conveys admirably the petrification that Dante is seeking to express and it contrasts strongly with the violence of the fourth and last poem of the series: 'Così nel mio parlar voglio esser aspro'.[13] Here, he wants to be as rough in his words as she is in her behaviour, and he fulfils his promise. The lady becomes constantly more cruel and savage; no weapon can harm her, and no protection can shield Dante from her blows. He cannot hide from her,

ché, come fior di fronda	for like a flower on its stalk
così de la mia mente tien la cima.	so she holds the summit of my mind.

She responds to his misery no more than a ship does to a motionless sea. His love for her is a merciless file rubbing away his life. His senses are ground by the teeth of Love, who strikes him down and stands over him with the sword that killed Dido. If only he could see Love split her heart:

Omè, perché non latra	O why does she not scream for me
per me, com'io per lei, nel caldo borro?	As I for her, in the hot pit?
ché tosto griderei: 'Io vi soccorro';	I'd soon shout: 'I'll help you',
e fare 'l volentier, sì come quelli	And do it willingly
che ne' biondi capelli	So in her blonde hair
ch'Amor per consumarmi increspa e dora	That Love has curled and gilded to devour me
metterei mano, e piacere'le allora.	I'd thrust my hand and give her pleasure.

At this point the whole theme of the four poems is reversed as Dante exults in the imaginary vengeance he will take on her, how having grabbed her blond hair he will be like a bear at play, taking his revenge a thousandfold, forcing her to let him gaze deep into her eyes in payment for her fleeing from him – and then:

e poi le renderei con amor pace	and then with love I would make peace.

The sudden calm of that line is shattered again by the *congedo*, in which the *canzone* is told to send an arrow through her heart, and the poem ends with a final dart of the snake's tongue:

ché bell'onor s'acquista in far vendetta.	for great honour is gained through taking revenge.

After these poems he would seem to have written little verse for perhaps as long as six or seven years, until in 1304 he broke his silence with the *canzone* of exile, 'Tre donne', and another ethical *canzone*, 'Doglia mi reca'. The demands made on him by his political career and the events described in the last chapter would explain a diminution in the rate of poems, but not such a long period of silence after the intense productiveness that had lasted from about the age of eighteen to about his thirty-third year. Even from the period after 1304, when he found, at least for some periods, peaceful places to stay, there exist only a handful of poems, three *canzoni*, including those just mentioned, and some sonnets. It was not that he had written himself out, but that he had written himself into a technical impasse with his mastery of the *canzone*. The ideas and images that came to him could not be contained in the language or in the span of a *canzone*. These new images come up again and again, however, as I hope to show, in the prose of *De vulgari eloquentia* and, especially, of the *Convivio*, both of which were written on the basis of his *past* artistic achievements, the *canzoni*. He was silent because of an immense pride that fixed him in the style and form of what he had already done. He was silent also perhaps—if my suggestion in the last chapter that he did experience the vision in 1300 that led to the *Commedia* is correct—because the new wine fermenting in him since that vision could not be put into the old bottles of the *canzone* form and had to be found temporary storage in passages of prose. He was silent too because of the exhaustion and the wounds of his political and social defeats. If the two *canzoni*, 'Tre donne' and 'Doglia mi reca', are accusations against humanity, the first for neglect of justice and the second for want of liberality, they may also be read as self-accusations, as acknowledgments of what Dante lacked in himself and of what prevented him from organizing and executing the great work growing within him. 'Tre donne'[14] uses the theme of Astraea, the daughter of Jove, the virgin of Virgil's fourth eclogue, who was the last of the immortals to leave Earth and who symbolizes Justice. This theme is one of the ground images of the *Purgatorio*, culminating in the appearance of Matelda after Dante has been crowned and mitred over himself, signifying his moral regeneration. Here, at this earlier stage, there is no such regeneration. Three ladies gather around his heart where Love is. Each is wretched and bewildered. The chief of them, Drittura or Justice, weeps:

E 'n su la man si posa   And on her hand she leans
Come succisa rosa.   Like a rose dissevered.

Her dress is so torn that her private parts are visible to Love. She describes how she gave birth beside the Nile, whose source was in the Garden of Eden, to one of her companions, Larghezza (Generosity), who in turn gave birth to a third, Temperance. Drittura is a symbol of Justice, of divine and natural law, and her daughter and granddaughter represent respectively the law of nations and human law which derive in turn from her.[15] Love rouses them with a speech declaring that it is humanity that should lament, and not they who are of the eternal citadel. He prophesies that, though they are wounded, they will live and that a new race will come to keep his arrow bright. Dante then speaks of his own condition, finding comfort in the thought that, if creatures as noble as these are exiled, then he gains honour from exile, and he concludes by saying that, if he has committed a fault, then this is now expiated—perhaps a reference to his attempts to win a pardon from the Black rulers of Florence after his break with the Whites. The *canzone* has two *congedi*, one obviously political in its references (given in Chapter 10), but the other referring to the sexual symbolism of the *canzone*, warning the *canzone* not to let any man see what a lady keeps secret but to show its virtues to the friend of virtue. The *canzone* creates a strong and memorable picture of Drittura, sitting and mourning like a great statue, all the more memorable for Dante's insistence on what he may not describe, the wide tear revealing her vulva. The picture of a woman weeping while opening wide her legs to give what is a gesture of invitation evokes great sadness; another kind of frustration from that of the *rime petrose* is described here. Justice is frustrated amongst humanity, and Dante is frustrated in his inner and artistic growth as well as in his political life. He may not enter Justice as he may not enter the work awaiting him.

Nevertheless the poem also confirms a new trust by Dante in his inspirations. The ground image of the poem, of three women coming from outside to Love in his heart which, as he says in the *Convivio*, stands for the most hidden part of a man, has deep connexions with the passage of the three Maries coming to the sepulchre in the *Convivio*, and with the three blessed ladies who work his salvation in the *Commedia* (see p. 205). He brings a new depth of interpretation to the dream or waking experience in which this recurring image appears to him and for the first time he states explicitly the wider human connexions of his inner experience of images.

De vulgari eloquentia

De vulgari eloquentia was probably written in the period when 'Tre donne' was composed.[16] In spite of its frequent references to exile it is a much more exuberant work than that poem, remarkable for its originality, its range of subjects, and its compression. The title may be translated as 'The art of expression in the vernacular', but an idea of its scope and importance cannot be grasped from the title alone. Poets love it for the insight it gives into the ideals and technique of their craft. Critics cherish it as the first great work of criticism since antiquity.[17] Historians of language and students of linguistics admire it for the clarity and definition with which Dante enriched their fields of study.[18] It is also a work of moral instruction because, in it, Dante not only describes the nature of the illustrious vernacular and the high style for which it could be employed, but also limits its use to those whose intellectual and moral capacities are equal to its employment. In doing so, he rediscovers for himself Longinus' derivation of the sublime in a poem from the magnanimity of the poet's soul, and so frees his art from the imputation that it is the gratuitous product of half-conscious reverie or that there is no relation between the quality of what a man is and what that man makes.

De vulgari eloquentia begins with a statement of the general service Dante intends to perform by writing about the vernacular, something that has never been done before, and he defines the vernacular as the speech we acquire, without rules, by imitating a nurse. Speech was given to man alone, not to the angels who have immediate apprehension of one another's thought, and not to animals. Man, as the intermediate between angel and beast, possessing both reason and a mortal body, needed an appropriate means of communication. This is language, which combines the two sides of man's nature: it is based on the senses, because it makes use of sound, and it is based on reason, because it communicates meaning. Dante then deals with the origin of language: he speculates on the first word spoken by man and decides that it was 'El' or 'God' uttered by Adam in the Earthly Paradise. The first language was Hebrew, and this was the one language of mankind until the building of the tower of Babel. Then, with the confusion of tongues, each group of labourers working on the towers spoke a different language. Hebrew continued as the language of those who had refused to work on the tower and therefore when Christ appeared on Earth, there was available to Him a language of grace.

Of the languages arising from the confusion of tongues, Dante considers the three main European groups, those spoken by the Greeks, the Teutons, and the Romance-speakers. He divides the Romance languages into Spanish (the language he terms Spanish is what we call Provençal), French, and Italian, remarking on the important words they have in common. All human languages, apart from Hebrew, must change as we change our dress and behaviour. As a partial remedy for this fluctuation, grammar arose as an invariable constant in all the changes of idiom.

He intends to speak only of Italian and describes its principal division into two, made by the Apennines. These two subdivide into fourteen dialects and, were the further divisions of these counted, Dante is certain they would exceed a thousand. From this point to the end of Book I, he searches for an Italian dialect on which he can base his fine vernacular, so as to make of it a worthy instrument of literature. He starts by rejecting all those that are quite impossible. The ugliest dialect is that of the Romans and this suits the nastiness of their morals. The March of Ancona and Spoleto go the same way. So do the dialects of Milan and Bergamo, Aquileia, Istria, the mountain and rural ones of Casentino and Prato, and, finally, that of Sardinia, where they still try to speak Latin but muff their agreements. In Chapter XII, he turns to Sicily, because Italian poetry is called Sicilian, and this goes back to those 'illustrious heroes Frederick Caesar and his happy-born son Manfred', whose prestige attracted to their courts men endowed with noble hearts and divine talents. Those two princes were quite unlike the present royalty and princes of Italy, who are conspicuous only for greed, deception, and avarice. What is called Sicilian, in verse, however, turns out to be not the Sicilian dialect but in tune with the most praiseworthy form of the vernacular.

Dante spoke so warmly of the Sicilian poets because he was familiar with their poems in versions edited to accommodate them to Tuscan readers. He would probably not have been so complimentary about the originals. Though it is now agreed that his ideal vernacular was founded upon Tuscan, nevertheless his harshest words are reserved for the presumption of those Tuscans who delude themselves that they speak and write an illustrious vernacular. Guittone d'Arezzo, Bonagiunta da Lucca, and Dante's own friend, Brunetto Latini, are brusquely dismissed: their language is municipal, not curial, very good for town clerks, but not for courtiers. A few exceptions, Guido Cavalcanti, Lapo Gianni, Dante himself, and Cino da Pistoia—the poets of the *dolce stil nuovo*, in fact—do understand. He ends Chapter XIII with a characteristic witticism at the expense of Genoa, whose inhabitants, he says, would, if they lost the letter 'z', have to be dumb or else find another language.

He then rejects the feminine dialect of the Romagna, the rough 'bristling and shaggy' words of Brescia, Verona, and Vicenza, with a blow in the direction of Venice. He agrees with those who admire the dialect of Bologna, noting the way in which it borrows words from its neighbours, but it cannot be considered illustrious and courtly because its greatest poets, including Guido Guinizzelli, would not have departed from it in composing their works. Having dismissed the claims of any one city to possess the illustrious vernacular, he describes in the last four chapters of this book the qualities of this superior language. In a series of analogies he shows that, in all our actions, there must be a common measure or means of comparison and, therefore, there must be a language common to every region without being tied to any particular one. He has at last found the object of his search: 'the illustrious, cardinal, courtly and curial vernacular language in Italy' is 'that which belongs to all the towns in Italy but does not appear to belong to any one of them . . .'.

Why does he apply these precise adjectives to the vernacular? It is illustrious because it shines forth, like illustrious men who illuminate others by justice and charity as they themselves are illuminated by power, or in the way that men who are well trained, like Numa and Seneca, train others as well. This vernacular is made sublime by majesty and power and raises its followers to the same height. By training, it is purified of all roughness and solecism, as may be seen in the *canzoni* of Cino and his friend, and it is made sublime by power, as can be seen in its power of persuasion. Finally Dante states that it is made sublime by honour, making the heart-breaking boast that those of its household surpass in renown kings, marquises, counts, and all other magnates. This, he says, has no need of proof. How glorious it makes its familiar friends he knows well himself, because he has cast even his exile behind his back for the sweetness of its glory.

Furthermore, the language is cardinal because, as a door moves according to the direction of its hinges, so the herd of dialects of Italian communes moves as this illustrious language does. It is courtly because, if Italy had a court, this is the language that would be spoken there, and it is curial because it is the language of that Italian tribunal which is united by the gracious light of reason, though it is scattered in the body.

These four magnificent epithets, 'illustre, cardinale, aulicum et curiale',[19] with which he describes his ideal vernacular, ring out like coronation bells at the founding of a new *imperium* of reason and the intellect. Difficult though it may be for us to appreciate the style of the *cursus*, this rhythmical, ornate style that mingles barbarisms and classical references and tropes, as the vestments and robes of the clerics and chancery clerks who evolved it were embroidered with a mixed vocabulary of ornament of Gothic, Byzantine, and classical origin, enabled Dante in this first book to achieve an amazing feat of compression. He has revealed language as a depository of history, making possible a history of races drawn from the inner spirit of the words that unite them. He has shown that the forms of language change as social groups change, that a linguistic community may embrace a diversity of vernaculars and dialects, and that a civilized language can be developed as the product of conscious discrimination and taste.[20] It is when we come upon those four adjectives in the culmination of the book that we realize that what Dante has written here is a prose poem and that he had brought into play the superior qualities of poetry in the compression of meaning to make the history of language subserve his definition of style. The choice of four adjectives, each one illuminating the others and none dispensable without damage to the whole, probably has a numerological significance in that four is the number of completeness and wholeness, a connexion to be explored more deeply in describing the four levels of meaning. The definition of each adjective adorns each word with a train of noble associations, as though each word were a poetic image in itself, with its depths of significance to be fathomed. Through them he brings the book to a close, reasserting the claim of the illustrious vernacular to be the language of the whole of Italy.

Reading backwards from this fourfold definition, we can trace the numerological pattern on which this first book is planned. It is based on a series of descending triads each of which is a subset of the one preceding it. The illustrious vernacular, so wholly defined by these four adjectives, resolves the duality of the main division of the Italian language into two by the Apennines. The Italian language is a subset of the threefold division of the Romance languages, which are in turn a subset of the three main language divisions of Europe. Thus we are brought back to the story of Babel and the confusion of tongues, which has been mirrored in the confusing variety of Italian dialects. Babel destroyed the triad of man, his interlocutors, and their means of communicating in the primal language of grace, which is Hebrew. This returns us to the idea of language uniting the physical and intellectual sides of man as the mean in the triad of angels, men, and beasts. This treatment in turn derives from the division at the outset of language into the artificial (grammar) and the natural (vernacular), which is to be harmonized by the honey-water, or hydromel, of Dante's own inspiration, itself a triad of the *Verbum Dei* or Word of God, aiding him in mixing the water of his own wit with the honey of other distinguished writers. There is in this a cyclical pattern, because inspiration at the beginning of the book is brought by the end to connect with the level and style of language most fitted to the level of inspiration. This technique of hierarchical planning is, of course, exactly the same as the one employed in the composition of Dante's *canzoni*, set out most clearly in his analysis of 'Donne ch'avete' (pp. 122–3).

A similar pattern is clear in Book II though its final resolution is missing because it was left unfinished. This pattern can be seen in the following analysis. From a discussion of the illustrious vernacular and those who are worthy of writing in it he proceeds to define three noble subjects, war, love, and righteousness, which alone are the themes to be treated in the noblest form, the *canzone*. Of the three styles of literature, the tragic, the comic, and elegiac, it is the tragic that is suited to the *canzone*. The tragic style is described under four headings that complement the fourfold characteristics of the illustrious vernacular and exhibit the same force of memorability. These headings are *gravitas sententiae* (weight of meaning), *superbia carminum* (stateliness of the lines), *constructionis elatio* (loftiness of construction), and *excellentia vocabularia* (excellence of words). Each of these phrases—apart from *gravitas sententiae*, which applies to the three subjects of war, love, and righteousness—is defined in sets and subsets of increasing complexity, made clear in examples arranged in groups that themselves have numerological significance. Thus, under *superbia carminum*, he deals with the four lengths of lines allowable in a *canzone*, of which the eleven-syllabled line is the noblest. Under *constructionis elatio*, he gives four examples of construction, a sentence that is merely insipid, one that has flavour, one that has flavour and charm, and the one that exhibits flavour, charm, and elevation. This last is illustrated by ten examples from vernacular poets. It is when he gets to *excellentia vocabularia* that we see best of all how this method enabled him to manoeuvre his complexities of image and thought, for here he offers his reader a sieve in which he can shake his words as though they were seeds or grain. Only the best words suited for the *canzone* should be left in the sieve. The mesh of the sieve is another image, as the biblical connexion of grain with men is carried in the description of the three types of words as children, women, and men. Words are of three kinds, *puerilia* (childish), *muliebria* (feminine), and *virilia* (manly). He dismisses the childish words for their simplicity, and the feminine words for their softness, and divides the manly words into two types: the sylvan, characterized by rough 'rs', gutturals, and consonantal combinations, and the urban. He uses the image of four different knaps of cloth to describe what he means by urban words: these are *pexa* (combed-out), *lubrica* (glossy), *yrsuta* (shaggy), and *reburra* (rumpled). Words, having been compared to men, women, and children, are now described according to the texture of their clothing, an image that would spring naturally to the tongue of a Florentine, whose city's wealth depended partly on cloth-making skills. *Pexa* and *yrsuta* refer to fine and strong wool and therefore to the characters of those who chose these cloths, and the rejected *lubrica* and *reburra* refer respectively to the luxurious silk and the coarsest fabric. Choosing only the combed-out words and the shaggy words for the *canzone*, he gives nine examples of the combed-out words which 'leave the speaker with a certain sweetness,

179

amore, donna, disio; vertute, donare, letitia; salute, securitate, defesa', thus providing three examples each for the division of the three noble themes, love, righteousness, and war. He then divides the shaggy words into two types. These are the necessary and the ornamental. The necessary are monosyllables of which he gives ten examples, ten reducing by mystic addition to $1 + 0 = 1$, and therefore emphasizing the quality of the monosyllables he is describing. The ornamental are polysyllables which, combined with the combed-out, give a harmony of structure. He gives eleven examples, increasing in length of syllable from *terra* to *sovramagnificentissimamente* which has eleven syllables itself, recalling by his number of examples the hendecasyllabic line, which is the noblest line.

Figure 7 (opposite) may make the divisions and subdivisions clearer.

Having dealt with the four characteristics of the tragic style, he moves on to the arrangement of the parts of the *canzone*, defining the art of this arrangement into three aspects, the division of the musical setting, the arrangement of the parts, and the number of lines and syllables. We have already drawn on these passages to describe the basis of the *canzone* in Chapter 8. Just as he was describing the number of lines there should be in a stanza he broke off. The reason for this is discussed in the next chapter. There are few indications of how the work might have continued, except that he would have dealt with the sonnet and ballad and with prose as well.

In both this work and the *Convivio*, Dante was calling a new audience for his work into being. Deprived of the closed society of the *fedeli d'amore*, and especially of the company of Guido Cavalcanti, he now sought a wider and more scattered audience, not among groups such as clerics or among the professional classes such as lawyers or doctors, but among individuals throughout Italy who could respond to the philosophical and ethical ideals that were to underlie his political ideas. By writing this difficult technical treatise in Latin, he was appealing to the more educated readership, typified by practising poets such as Cino da Pistoia, and perhaps to the early humanists, such as he would meet in Bologna or Verona, to pay due attention to the great merits and future possibilities of the high style of vernacular literature. In the *Convivio*, written in Italian, he was addressing a far wider audience of educated laity, making them aware of the infinite riches of classical and scholastic learning and philosophy which could still largely only be unlocked by those who could read Latin. The antithesis is brought out by the way in which, at the opening of *De vulgari eloquentia*, he praises the vernacular as being closer in its naturalness to the Creator while, in the first book of the *Convivio*, he proves Latin to be the nobler of the two in respect of its unchangeable nature, its efficiency in communicating thought, and its greater beauty owing to its artificial character. The contradictions here are superficial: he is drawing each of the two groups in his new audience to a greater appreciation of the meanings contained in the other's medium of communication. The philosophers must be at home in the language of the imperial court (which is yet to be established) to make their influence felt, while the classes from which the courtiers will be drawn must be

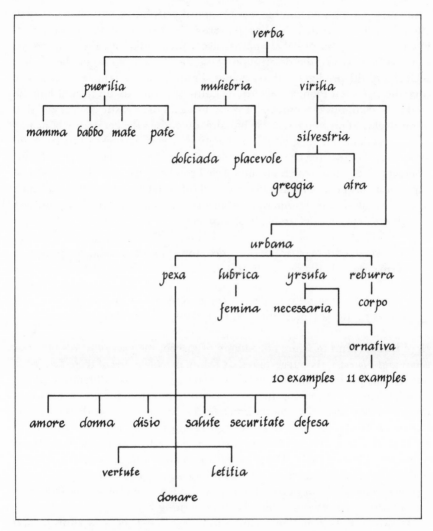

Figure 7 Divisions and subdivisions of words in *De vulgari eloquentia*

responsive to the ideas and vision of the philosophers for the flowering of the new civilization Dante is attempting to create.

In *De vulgari eloquentia* he was defining the standards that should guide this new civilization and it is plain that, to a large extent, these standards were those of the classical writers he was now studying. He says, 'The more closely we copy the great poets the more correct is the poetry we write.'[21] In this and in other aspects of the work's themes and images we can find anticipations of the *Commedia*. The geographical survey of the Italian dialects foreshadows both the deliberate introduction of regional characteristics into the speeches of contemporary persons and also the topographical periphrases with which they so often introduce themselves. The powerful description of the confusion of tongues at the tower of Babel appears like a preparation for the great crowd scenes of the *Inferno*, the description of Limbo, for examples, or the aimless struggles of the prodigal and avaricious. From his four examples of sentence construction, even though they are in Latin, we can gain an idea of how he worked to compress meaning in his verse, using all the stylistic devices and skill in word-play at his command. He has already praised the hendecasyllabic line over lines of different length for its capacity in regard to subject, construction, and words, because the beauty of all these things is multiplied in this line: 'for wherever things that weigh are multiplied so also is weight'. This density of expression may be seen in his fourth example of sentence construction, in which he employs his wit and recriminatory bile to demonstrate a style that in his eyes has flavour, charm, and an exalted manner:

Eiecta maxima parte florum de sinu tuo, Florentia, nequicquam Trinacriam Totila secundus adivit.[22]

Having cast the greatest part of the flowers out of thy bosom, O Florence, the second Totila went fruitlessly to Trinacria.

Here Dante crams in figure after figure of speech, the play of words between *florum* and *Florentia*, the suggestion that Dante in exile is one of these discarded flowers thrown from the bosom of his maternal city, the alliteration of the scornful dental, 't', making the sentence stutter with indignation, the apostrophe to Florence, the comparison of Charles of Valois with the Gothic barbarian Totila, the destroyer of Florence, and the antithetic construction of the sentence in balancing Charles's success in destroying Florence with his miserable failure in Sicily. The passage calls to mind several instances of word-play in the *Commedia*, especially those lines spoken by Pier della Vigne (p. 32), who was responsible for developing to a new pitch of ornateness the elaborate Latin style of the *cursus* in which Dante is writing here.

On two important matters Dante was later to reject the viewpoints he had expressed in *De vulgari eloquentia*. In the *Paradiso*, he makes Adam refute his statement that Hebrew was the language of the Earthly Paradise and hence the original language of mankind.[23] Adam will say that the language he spoke had vanished long before the building of Babel. The other rejection concerns his actual practice in writing, when in the *Commedia* he departed from the *canzone* form and the tragic style, finding both form and style quite inadequate to encompass his new range of themes, characterization, and emotions.

One must not underestimate, however, the importance of the passages in *De vulgari eloquentia* on the construction of the *canzone* for our appreciation of the tradition of poetry in which Dante grew up and for the scale of the revolution in his attitude to his poetry involved in the writing of the *Commedia*. The tradition was a musical tradition and this is borne out by Dante's description of the *canzone* as 'the completed action of one writing words to be set to music'.[24] Something has already been said of the technical construction of the *canzone* in Chapter 8. There it was mentioned that the *canzone* is constructed on the basis of the repetition of tunes and the introduction within the stanza of a contrasted tune. It bears a strong resemblance to sonata form when this is seen as the deliberate offsetting of contrasting emotions and moods. Both forms are therefore related to one of the richest European traditions, already separating by this date into music as the abstract expression of emotion through sound, and poetry demanding the plastic and tactile qualities of the visual arts, a transition already marked in the way Dante categorizes the *sounds* of words, 'combed-out', 'glossy', 'rumpled', etc., in terms of the senses of touch and sight. The development of polyphonic music in which the clarity of words would always tend to be lost and merged in the cross-patterns of sound meant that poets had to turn to visual descriptions if their art were to keep up with the new complexities of experience they wished to express. Thus a great reversal in Dante's style is anticipated in this work; he describes the ornamental words which give grace to a *canzone*, the musically elegant polysyllables, in terms of the very homely images he will later use to supplant those polysyllables for enriching the texture of the *Commedia*. Similarly, though the chapters on the *canzone* reflect his pride in his mastery of technique, the very different form and style of language of the *Commedia* point to a tremendous sacrifice of that pride. He had to jettison that particular mastery from the barque of his inspiration in order to carry the new weight of inspiration; the 'humble' style of the great poem presupposes a humbling of himself as a man and an artist.

De vulgari eloquentia also contains several passages that throw light on Dante's evolving attitude to inspiration, both in his theory and in his practical experience. He writes the treatise with 'the Word aiding us from Heaven',[25] a phrase that shows he is already close to the recognition of the exalted level of inspiration which is his personal point of entry to divine illumination and instruction and which he will build into the *Commedia* as part of the construction and definition of the poem. In proving the *canzone*'s excellence, he brings in a curiously physiological mention of inspiration: 'nam quicquid de cacuminibus illustrium capitum poetantium profluxit ad labia, in solis cantionibus invenitur';[26] 'for all that has flowed from the summits of the heads of illustrious poets down to their lips is found in *canzoni* alone'. He is perhaps remembering here the marvellous moment when his tongue spoke as though moved by itself, the opening line of 'Donne ch'avete'; and just as he has implied various degrees of inspiration in his discussion of what the illustrious vernacular should be used for, so he is also here relating the highest form of inspiration known to him at this time to its neuro-physiological manifestations as he experienced them. *Cacumen* is the summit of a mountain, and the image foreshadows the use of the twin-peaked mountain of Parnassus to symbolize the human and divine levels of inspiration in the *Commedia*. The passage also reflects the psycho-physiological theories on the relations between inspiration, thought, and sensations mentioned in Chapter 8 and is also reminiscent of passages in other poems, notably the sonnet opening:

Due donne in cima de la mente mia
venute sono. . .[27]

Two women have come to the summit of
my mind.

and in 'Così nel mio parlar' where he complains of La Pietra

ché, come fior di fronda
così de la mia mente tien la cima.[28]

for like a flower on its stalk
so she holds the summit of my mind.

Such passages reveal the extent to which Dante was aware of his inner processes of creation, of how he had learned to look inwards and to discriminate between those chance thoughts that arose from the lower levels of his psychology and were to be rejected, and those, like the examples given here, that acted as their own qualification by the precise location in which they excited his mental activity and by the chemical change that flowed from them throughout his body.

He had also acquired through his technical mastery the highest regard for the importance of technique, and this passage looks forward to the way in which classical studies deepened his reflections on the relation between inspiration and interpretation and so revolutionized his practice as a poet:

> Sed cautionem atque discretionem hanc accipere, sicut decet, hoc
> opus et labor est, quoniam nunquam sine strenuitate ingenii et artis
> assiduitate scientiarumque habitu fieri potest. Et hii sunt quos poeta
> Eneidorum sexto Dei dilectos et ab ardente virtute sublimatos ad
> ethera deorumque filios vocat, quanquam figurate loquatur. Et ideo
> confutetur illorum stultitia, qui arte scientiaque immunes, de solo
> ingenio confidentes, ad summa summe canenda prorumpunt; et a
> tanta presumptuositate desistant, et si anseres natura vel desidia sunt,
> nolint astripetam aquilam imitari.[29]

> But it is in the exercise of needful caution and discernment that the
> real difficulty lies, for this can never be attained to without strenuous
> efforts of genius, constant practice in the art, and the habit of the
> sciences. And it is those (so equipped) whom the poet in the sixth
> book of the *Aeneid* describes as beloved of God, raised by glowing
> virtue to the sky, and sons of the Gods, though he is speaking
> figuratively. And therefore let those who, innocent of art and
> science, and trusting to genius alone, rush forward to sing of the
> highest subjects in the highest style, confess their folly and cease
> from such presumption; and if in their natural sluggishness

they are but geese, let them abstain from imitating the eagle soaring to the stars.

Milton, writing in his own defence, produced a comparable argument when he said:

> he who would not be frustrate of his hope to write well hereafter in laudable things, ought him selfe to bee a true Poem, that is, a composition, and patterne of the best and honourablest things; not presuming to sing high praises of heroick men, or famous Cities, unlesse he have in himselfe the experience and the practice of all that which is praise-worthy.[30]

Dante, the poet of righteousness, was seeking to educate a generation of men of genius and knowledge, men who from their experience and understanding had won the right to use the illustrious language. He saw language as something of perfect origin in Eden, before the Fall; the first word Adam uttered was 'God', because language was there the means of expression of joy, the joy that is wholly in God. He was working his way towards the recovery of divine joy in art that was to illuminate the *Paradiso*, and he was stating his certainty that such an art depended first of all on the artist being 'a true Poem'.

12

Invitation to the banquet of knowledge: *Il Convivio*

In nearly every place that Dante travelled in his early days of exile, he came across people who were longing for a new kind of knowledge. If knowledge is a food of the mind, then it was as though the scent of a new intellectual sustenance was passing across the towns of Italy and the enzymes of people's minds were stimulated into the awareness of a new hunger. Dante intended to satisfy this hunger by writing *Il Convivio*, the banquet of knowledge, in the vernacular. Though there had been writers of vernacular works of instruction well before the *Convivio* such as Brunetto Latini or Ristoro d'Arezzo, the author of a work on astronomy, Dante, with a keen educational instinct, realized that people needed to be taught *how* to read. In this he was following a tradition that had been largely limited to monastic and clerical circles and therefore to a culture largely based on Latin and the interpretation of scripture. The most celebrated and influential of such works was the *Didascalicon* of Hugh of St Victor, the twelfth-century scholar whom Dante was later to depict in the heaven of the Sun in the *Paradiso*. In this work Hugh had not only set out for his pupils with clarity and purpose the order and content of their studies but had always kept before their eyes the reasons for each stage in the progression of learning. With the confidence of genius Dante undertook to do for his new secular audience what Hugh of St Victor had done for his readers, not through the interpretation of scripture, but through the act of commenting on the meaning of the most important of his poems, the *canzoni* written after the *Vita Nuova*.

This ambitious project was to have extended to fifteen books, consisting of the first book as an introduction and fourteen acting as commentaries to these *canzoni*. Though he was mainly inspired by this educative purpose in writing the *Convivio*, he had other more personal aims: one was to clear his name of scurrilous gossip circulating about his love poetry and another was to write a work that would soften the hearts of his Black enemies and secure his return to Florence.

The main aim is summed up in the title, *Il Convivio*, the banquet to which he invites all those Italians of goodwill who cannot understand Latin but who should be denied no longer the fruits of philosophy. He calls into being an audience far wider than the closed circle of the *fedeli d'amore*, for whom he had written the *Vita Nuova*, although the *Convivio* too celebrates his devotion to a lady, the *donna gentile*, whom he unveils through allegorical explanation as Philosophy herself. Many ideas implicit in the writings of the school of the *dolce stil nuovo*, ethical, psychological, political, and, above all, the sapiential tradition, are developed here with a clarity and length of exposition that is found nowhere else. As in the *Vita Nuova*, the prose passages reflect on past experience which is encapsulated in poems written at an earlier stage; these passages therefore contain many insights into the inspiration that guided the writing of the *canzoni*. The *Convivio* differs greatly from the *Vita Nuova* in mood and intention, though Dante develops one particular feature of the *Vita Nuova*, the division of the poems into their component parts, into its chief principle of construction because the order in which he takes the topics of each book follows the sections and subsections of the *canzoni*. Its unfinished nature makes it impossible to assess the four books we have as a complete work. Though its intrinsic quality is overshadowed by the pleasure of recognizing, for the first time, ideas and images that will later find employment in the *Commedia*, here in the *Convivio* we gain a picture of Dante the man as he was in his forties. Much of his subject-matter, his concern to eradicate false ideas on social worth, for example, is as alien to us as the scholastic methods he employs to define and set out his propositions and arguments, but here we get hints of what his conversation in his own polished Tuscan must have sounded like. Dante himself notes the difference in style between the *Vita Nuova* and the *Convivio*, attributing the style of the *Convivio* to what is appropriate to the stage of life he had now reached. Almost as a side-effect of his commentary on the *canzoni*, he produced in the *Convivio* a work of intellectual autobiography so that it can be seen as a new stage that Western European man had reached, so confident in his new command of language that he could express, to a degree unknown before, the knowledge of the ancients and the Church in his own vernacular, able to move from subject to subject, constantly making new syntheses of understanding, and finding, in the objectivity that his new conquests in the sciences and mathematics afforded him, a light to direct upon his own stages and processes of reasoning. Towards the end of Book II, he reveals the allegorical meaning of Heaven as Science, an equation that confirms the start of a new age he helps to initiate.

Thus many of the finest passages in the *Convivio* celebrate his own ardour for knowledge, and these, when complemented by Boccaccio's description of his person and habits,[1] enable us to round out our growing picture of Dante as a man. Boccaccio says that Dante was of middling height, stooping slightly as he reached maturity, measured in his movements, and plainly dressed. He had a long face, an aquiline nose, large eyes, heavy jaws with a protruding lower lip, a dark complexion, and curly black hair. His habitual expression was melancholy and pensive. Both at home and in public he was exceptionally composed and polite in his manner. He rarely spoke unless addressed and then with sudden and clear eloquence. He liked solitude where his thoughts would not be interrupted, though he had an exceptional aptitude for concentration, whatever his circumstances. Once in an apothecary's shop in Siena, when handed a book he had very much wanted to read, he propped it up on a counter. Outside a great festival was held, with displays of horsemanship and dancing before a noisy crowd. He was there from midday to sunset, never lifting his eyes from the book, and when afterwards he was asked how he could have missed such a festival, it appeared he had known nothing of it. Like Coleridge, he was obviously 'a library cormorant'. Boccaccio then illustrates his powers of memory and intellect with an anecdote of how at Paris he took on fourteen questions proposed by different masters on various subjects, repeated them, set out the arguments for and against and resolved and answered them, to the amazement of all.

Whether that display took place on the disputed visit to Paris or not, the story exemplifies the intellectual virtuosity that Dante demonstrates in so many passages in the *Convivio*. The emphasis on his powers of memory and of organizing the material retained in his memory help to build up and confirm the picture of his manner of working that has so far evolved. For 'Donne ch'avete', for the *Vita Nuova*, and for *De vulgari eloquentia*, I hope to have demonstrated that before Dante began to write a work, he planned it in his head down to minutest particulars, using numerological patterns linked together in hierarchies of dependent significance. This can be shown equally well to apply to the *Convivio*, the *Monarchia*, and the *Commedia*. It is an abiding feature of his creative life and it gives further meaning to Frances Yates's suggestion in her *Art of Memory* that Dante employed a memory system in the construction of the *Commedia*. Dante could even have met Ramon Lull who incorporated his own art of memory within his system of knowledge, the Lullian Art which first came to him as an inspiration in an illuminative vision on a mountain in Majorca in about 1272. Lull was shipwrecked off Pisa in about 1308, at a time when Dante could well have been there or close by at Lucca or in the Lunigiana, and while in Pisa Lull wrote a short work on memory.[2]

The suggestion would also help to explain how he was able during the vicissitudes of his exile to be so extraordinarily productive. Once he had worked out a complete pattern in his head and committed it to memory, that work or section was secure until he had the leisure to write it down, or dictate it—as, I suspect, was the case with the *Convivio*. An inkling of the form of the work to be executed would accompany the image or gift of words of the original inspiration and a memory technique would have enabled him to draw it out into the pattern of the completed work. In the case of the *Convivio*, in Books II, III, and IV, where he is commenting on *canzoni* written some time before, he makes the form of the commentary follow the division that went into the making of the original poems, as will be shown in the description that follows.

Book I, being an introduction and having no poem to comment on, is based on a series of images drawn from the Gospels, the chief one being that of the parable of the feast, and it is patterned largely on a series of triads.

He begins it with Aristotle's words, 'all men naturally desire to have knowledge'. As knowledge is the ultimate perfection of the soul and in it lies our felicity, we are all naturally subject to the desire for it. Many are deprived of the opportunity for winning this knowledge, for reasons that lie in their natures or in external circumstances. The natural deficiencies include defects of mind or body and the deficiencies of circumstance, the cares of family and civic life and the lack of educational privileges in the place where an individual is raised. These reasons explain why only a few sit at the table, eating the bread of the angels, while the rest have to be content with cattle food. These happy few have pity on those eating grass and acorns. Dante, though he does not sit at the table, but eats the crumbs they let fall, is similarly filled with pity and prepares a banquet in which the meat will be fourteen *canzoni* on love and virtue and the bread will be his commentary on them. The style of this book will be temperate and virile, in contrast to that of the *Vita Nuova*.

Before he enters on the task of commenting on the *canzoni* he has to clear himself of two faults of which he may be accused. The first is that he has to speak of himself, and he calls on St Augustine and Boethius as illustrious examples of men forced to speak of themselves. It is his circumstances as an exile that force Dante to this necessity and he has to clear his name of the charge that he wrote the *canzoni* out of motives of passion and not of virtue. This is why he has to reveal the true meaning underlying his allegory. The second objection to the work is that it is written in the vernacular and not in Latin. His bread is made of rye, not wheat. Three reasons for not writing it in Latin are confirmed by three reasons for writing in the vernacular. These are to avoid 'unmannerly disorder', for the sake of 'spontaneous generosity', and because of the love that is natural for one's own language. The rest of the book is taken up with expositions of these reasons. Dealing first with the question of disorder, he demonstrates how unsuitable Latin, for all its superior qualities, would be for a commentary on *canzoni* written in the vernacular. He explains the three ways in which the vernacular possesses 'spontaneous generosity': it gives to many, it gives something useful, and it gives its gift without being asked for it. Furthermore, Dante writes for those who are noble: most of those who can read Latin have learnt it only for gain and have no noble motives. In the audience he writes for are 'princes, barons, knights, and many other noble folk, not only men but women, numbers of both sexes who use the vulgar tongue and are not scholars'.[3] In his view most members of the clergy, scholars, and lawyers are not noble.

With a quite extraordinary vehemence he denounces the five bad qualities of those who denigrate the vernacular language, and speaks of the benefits he has received from it—he owes even his own existence to it because his conception began with his parents speaking to one another. The bread is now clean enough of its stains for the commentary to begin and he starts Book II with the *canzone* 'Voi che 'ntendendo il terzo ciel movete'. This *canzone*, addressed to the angels or intelligences of the heaven of Venus, describes the conflict in Dante's affections between the thought of the dead Beatrice and the new lady, the *donna gentile*, into whose eyes Love is forcing him to look. His heart is in a strange way; his soul weeps there and a spirit that is conveyed by the rays of Venus argues with his soul. His soul once was so inspired by a thought that ascended to the feet of God, where it saw Beatrice, that his soul desired to join her. A new thought, overmastering the old one, forces him to look at another lady. The thought of Beatrice is destroyed and his soul laments the fact. But a gentle spirit of love reassures him and praises his new lady:

Mira quant' ell' è pietosa e umile,	See how compassionate and gentle she is,
saggia e cortese ne la sua grandezza	how wise and courteous in her greatness
e pensa di chiamarla donna, omai!	and resolve to call her your lady henceforth!

The *congedo* states that there will be very few who will grasp the meaning of the *canzone* and to those who do not understand it, the *congedo* must say, 'At least consider how fair I am.'

This *canzone*, contradicting as it does the final pages of the *Vita Nuova*, where the memory and vision of Beatrice conquer the affection for the *donna gentile*, presents many difficulties. It marks the opening up of a new source of poetic experience, if the memory of Beatrice may be regarded as a setting source of inspiration, and if the *donna gentile*, treated here as pure allegory, as Philosophy, is seen as the newly dawning inspiration before which he must now surrender. The gentle spirit tells him he will see the beauty of such wonders that he will exclaim:

Amor, segnor verace,	Love, true Lord,
ecco l'ancella tua; fa' che ti piace.	behold your handmaid—do whatever you will.

He surrenders to the new inspiration with the words of Mary at the Annunciation.

He divides the five stanzas of the *canzone* into three main parts: the first part covers the first stanza, with its address to the angels of the heaven of Venus; the second part (stanzas 2, 3, and 4) describes the conflict of the two loves and appropriately it is subdivided into two, the number of doubt; the third part consists of the usual address to the *canzone* in the last stanza, the *tornata*. The whole of the commentary that follows is based on these major divisions of the *canzone*, and the fact that Dante could revive and extend a number pattern on which this *canzone* is constructed, and ten years later erect a major work of exegesis upon it, shows the abiding importance of this technique in his creative processes. To it he was able to add a new subtlety of interpretation by drawing on the ancient method of the fourfold interpretation of scripture. This method, of which more is said in Chapter 18, was evolved by Jewish writers and early Church Fathers as a technique of revealing the inner meaning of holy writings and of reconciling apparent inconsistencies in the scriptures, and, in the case of the Church Fathers, of interpreting incidents and events in the Old Testament as figural prophecies and pre-announcements of the story of the New Testament. It came to be accepted that the scriptures had four levels of meaning: the literal or the true story as it is told; the allegorical, which revealed the relation of that story to the requirement of faith, to the history of humanity as a whole and to the coming of Christ; the moral, which revealed the inner psychological truth to be discovered in the story and the right direction of the will by charity, that an understanding of this inner truth would encourage; and the anagogic meaning which is understanding beyond the senses, which concerns celestial things and which reveals the relationship of the soul to God in the expectation of hope. According to Origen and St Gregory, everything that is allegorical can also be moralized: all symbols of the Church are also symbols of the soul.[4] The moral and anagogic meanings were thought to lead naturally from one to the other as the active life should lead to the contemplative.[5] To give an example based on one Old Testament story, Abraham's sacrifice of Isaac had a literal and historical truth from which could be extracted the allegorical truth of the sacrifice of Christ for mankind, the moral truth that sacrifice is necessary in a life devoted to Christ, and the anagogic truth of the surrender of the soul to its Father.[6]

An appreciation of these four levels of meaning brought a wholeness of understanding to a passage such as this and it was thought that only divinely inspired writings contained this perfection of unified meaning. The technique was far more than a rule of thumb for devising a commentary: it was a method for ordering the mind, for bringing thoughts to stillness, and for drawing out symbolic and inner significance, thus making the stories of scripture part of the reader's deepest experience. St Bonaventure said that infinite theories could be elicited from Holy Writ. Its interpretation could never be humanly completed because as new seeds come from plants, so scripture fruited in new ideas and new meanings.[7] Each level of meaning could be used to correct or enhance understanding of the others, and the possibilities of the method when applied to poetry, with its own demands for multiple meanings, were immense. But as it was regarded as a technique for understanding the perfect work of the Divine Artist, few as yet had dared to apply it as a technique of execution or construction in the making of imperfect human art. This is what Dante now proceeded to do. He says that writings can be understood in four senses. The first is the literal which keeps to the strict limits of the letter. The second is the allegorical, the meaning disguised by the fables of the poets and therefore a truth hidden under a beautiful lie. He illustrates this in the following passage after which he goes on to describe the moral and anagogic senses:

. . . sì come quando dice Ovidio che Orfeo facea con la cetera mansuete le fiere, e li arbori e le pietre a sè muovere; che vuol dire che lo savio uomo con lo strumento de la sua voce fa[r]ia mansuescere e umiliare li crudeli cuori, e fa[r]ia muovere a la sua volontade coloro che non hanno vita di scienza e d'arte: e coloro che non hanno vita ragionevole alcuna sono quasi come pietre. E perchè questo nascondimento fosse trovato per li savi, nel penultimo trattato si mosterrà. Veramente li teologi questo senso prendono altrimenti che li poeti; ma però che mia intenzione è qui lo modo de li poeti seguitare, prendo lo senso allegorico secondo che per li poeti è usato.

Lo terzo senso si chiama morale, e questo è quello che li lettori deono intentamente andare appostando per le scritture, ad utilitade di loro e di loro discenti: sì come appostare si può ne lo Evangelio, quando Cristo salio lo monte per transfigurarsi, che de li dodici Apostoli menò seco li tre; in che moralmente si può intendere che a le secretissime cose noi dovemo avere poca compagnia.

Lo quarto senso si chiama anagogico, cioè sovrasenso; e questo è quando spiritualmente si spone una scrittura, la quale ancora [sia vera] eziandio nel senso litterale, per le cose significate significa de le superne cose de l'etternal gloria, sì come vedere si può in quello canto del Profeta che dice che, ne l'uscita del popolo d'Israel d'Egitto, Giudea è fatta santa e libera. Chè avvegna essere vero secondo la lettera sia manifesto, non meno è vero quello che spiritualmente s'intende, cioè che ne l'uscita de l'anima dal peccato, essa sia fatta santa e libera in sua potestate.[8]

. . . thus Ovid says that Orpheus with his lyre made beasts tame, and trees and stones move towards himself; that is to say that the wise man by the instrument of his voice makes cruel hearts grow mild and humble, and those who have not the life of Science and of Art move to his will, while they who have no rational life are as it were like stones. And wherefore this disguise was invented by the wise will be shown in the last Tractate but one. Theologians indeed do not apprehend this sense in the same fashion as poets; but, inasmuch as my intention is to follow here the custom of poets, I will take the allegorical sense after the manner which poets use.

The third sense is called moral; and this sense is that for which teachers ought as they go through writings intently to watch for their own profit and that of their hearers; as in the Gospel when Christ ascended the Mount to be transfigured, we may be watchful of His taking with Himself the three Apostles out of the twelve; whereby morally it may be understood that for the most secret affairs we ought to have few companions.

The fourth sense is called anagogic, that is, above the senses; and this occurs when a writing is spiritually expounded, which even in the literal sense by the things signified likewise gives intimation of higher matters belonging to the eternal glory; as can be seen in that song of the prophet which says that, when the people of Israel went up out of Egypt, Judea was made holy and free. And although it be plain that this is true according to the letter, that which is spiritually understood is not less true, namely, that when the soul issues forth from sin she is made holy and free as mistress of herself.

Dante then goes on to stress the importance of starting with the literal as the sense within the expression of which all the others are included. We cannot reach the meanings without first reaching the outside.

We will find each of the examples he gives here of great significance in the making of the *Commedia*, and when, later, he described the fourfold method in the letter which he sent to the Lord of Verona, Can Grande, with the first cantos of the *Paradiso*, he drew all three allegorical meanings from the example he uses here for the anagogic level, the Exodus psalm. Before he could reach the stage of writing with all four levels of meaning present in his own works, he had to transvalue his own inspiration to that of divinely given prophecy or dictation, and so resolve the conflict he felt between the allegory of the poets and the allegory of the theologians.

Poets use allegory in a different way to that of the theologians, because the allegorical meaning of poetry expresses the truth underlying the *bella menzogna* or beautiful fiction of the literal sense, and the theologians cannot regard the literal sense of scripture as a fiction. Here in the commentary, therefore, Dante is largely concerned with the first two meanings, the literal and the allegorical which he will employ according to the use of the poets. After dividing the *canzone* into its parts he proceeds to its literal meaning, starting with the nature of the beings he addresses in the first line. These are angels or intelligences and he describes the ten heavens of current cosmology, going on to relate the first nine of these to the nine orders of angels, following here the order given by Brunetto Latini. (He was to change to that of Dionysius the Areopagite for the writing of the *Paradiso*.) He returns to his own experience in describing the inner conflict between the memory of his love for Beatrice and the new love for the *donna gentile*. Beatrice, being dead, is beyond the influence of these intelligences and they have directed his attention to the new lady. After an impassioned digression on the subject of immortality, and a discussion of the last stanza and the *tornata*, he turns to the *canzone*'s allegorical meaning. He tells of how, in seeking comfort in Boethius and Cicero after Beatrice's death, he began to see Philosophy as a compassionate lady and he sought her in the schools of the religious and in the colloquies of philosophers. So the *donna gentile* is revealed as Philosophy, and the allegorical interpretation of the heavens reveals these heavens as the sciences of the trivium and the quadrivium and the different kinds of philosophy. In this case the heaven of Venus corresponds to rhetoric. The movers of the science of rhetoric are the rhetoricians and the rays of Venus are writings such as those of Boethius and Cicero.[9] The eyes of the lady are the demonstrations of Philosophy and the anguish of sighs refers to the difficulty of study. What the allegory means, therefore, is that Dante found himself in love with the 'fairest and noblest daughter of the emperor of the universe'.[10]

The ode to which the third book is a commentary is the finest of all Dante's *canzoni* for its combination of the most difficult technique with the smoothest flow, and its marriage of language selected with exquisite discrimination with the perfection of its theme. It begins:

Amor che ne la mente mi ragiona	Love who within my mind discourses
da la mia donna disiosamente,	About my lady so enticingly,
move cose di lei meco sovente,	So often such things of her to me,
che lo 'ntelletto sovr' esse disvia.[11]	My intellect is lost before their meaning.

If he cannot record her praises accurately, the blame is owed to our weak intellect and the shortcomings of our speech. The sun revolving round the Earth has never seen anything as noble as this lady. The intelligences of Heaven gaze at her and all lovers find her in their thoughts when Love shares his peace with them. God pours his divine goodness into her in the same way that He does into an angel in His presence:

Di costei si può dire:	Of her it can be said:
gentile è in donna ciò che in lei si trova,	What ennobles a lady comes from her,
e bello è tanto quanto lei simiglia.	From likeness to her derives the beautiful.
E puossi dir che 'l suo aspetto giova	The sight of her assists us to confer
a consentir ciò che par maraviglia;	Belief in what appears a miracle;
onde la nostra fede è aiutata:	So that our faith is fully sustained:
però fu tal da etterno ordinata.	For this from eternity she was ordained.

The joys of Paradise appear in her aspect. These overwhelm our intellect as a ray of sunlight is too strong for poor vision. Her beauty rains flames of fire and they destroy like a thunderstroke all innate vices. She, who was in the mind of the Creator, restores humility to anyone who has lost it.

The *congedo* refers to another poem, 'Voi che savete', which had spoken harshly of this lady, calling her proud; these words are now explained and retracted. The lady of this wonderful poem owes much to earlier representations of Wisdom, to Boethius' vision of Philosophy, and to the sapiential books, but here she is radiant with Dante's own sense of personal discovery of a new area of poetic material, his emotional delight at the understanding of pure intelligence infused through the higher reaches of creation and revealing itself to man's noblest faculties. The poem bears many resemblances in form and phrasing to 'Donne ch'avete' but, lacking that poem's dark contrasts with the theme of Hell, appears as an even purer and more fully refined example of the poetry of praise. The commentary on it proceeds from the usual noting of the parts into which it divides. Its ease of flow is reflected in these divisions and their subdivisions, which are all triads. Dante defines the nature of the love of which he speaks here. Love is the union of the soul with the *donna gentile*. He describes what he means by the mind in which Love speaks. The lines about the sun circling the Earth lead him into a discussion of various cosmological theories, those of Pythagoras, Plato, and Aristotle, and evoke from him his finest scientific writing.

Having established the movement of the sun, he discusses (III. vi) his praises of the *donna gentile*, showing that the intelligences on high gaze on the lady as a thought existing in the divine mind. God loves her because he has put so much of his own nature into her. Dante praises her soul and says that, as there are gradations amongst men descending to the animal at one end of the scale and rising to the angelic at the other, so she is so noble she could hardly be anything but an angel. She aids our faith through which we escape eternal death. Now (III. viii) he praises her eyes and mouth, in which the soul is most clearly seen, and he describes her power to destroy both innate and acquired vices. He has to explain why, in 'Voi che savete' he spoke of the lady as proud, whereas in this *canzone* she is the opposite, and he does so with extended examples from optics and observations, especially of the time when this poem was written and when he had weakened his eyes by too much study. Just as in III. v we can see the beginnings of the cosmological side of the *Commedia*, so here we get a glimpse of the intense experimental work that would go towards making the imagery of the *Paradiso*. Turning to the allegorical meaning of the *canzone*, he speaks first of the meaning of Philosophy and its origins with Pythagoras, who could not call himself wise but preferred to be a lover of wisdom. An interesting passage follows on love: men should be loved for their worth; wisdom or philosophy for the sake of truth. The growing importance of sun imagery becomes clear in the next chapter (III. xii) when he reveals the allegorical sense of the revolution of the sun round the Earth as the omniscience of God. The closeness of the relationship between the lady and God is stressed:

> Oh nobilissimo ed eccellentissimo cuore che ne la sposa de lo
> Imperadore del cielo s'intende, e non solamente sposa, ma suora e
> figlia dilettissima![12]

> O most noble and excellent heart which is intent upon the bride of the
> Emperor of heaven and not bride alone but sister and most beloved
> daughter.

He identifies (III. xiv) Philosophy with the Wisdom of Solomon and repeats his assertion that she aids faith. From faith comes that hope that longs for things foreseen and from hope comes the workings of charity. 'And by these three virtues men rise to the pursuit of Philosophy in that celestial Athens where Stoics and Peripatetics and Epicureans through skill in eternal truth unite harmoniously in a single will.' In the final chapter of this book (III. xv), he produces one of the finest extended passages of the *Convivio*, in praise of Wisdom-Philosophy, making clear the eternal nature of the *donna gentile*.

Book IV begins with one of Dante's ethical poems, 'Le dolci rime d'amor ch'i' solia', the *canzone* on nobility. He says in the first stanza that he is going to abandon the sweet rhymes in which he had spoken of love and will now in rough and subtle terms refute those who believe nobility depends upon the possession of riches. He quotes the opinion of the Emperor Frederick II, who said that nobility consisted of ancestral wealth and fine manners.[13] Someone else left out the second part of the definition, and made nobility depend entirely on wealth. Dante, in common with earlier Florentine writers on the subject, makes it depend on virtue, and this theme is developed throughout the ensuing commentary of the fourth book, which almost equals the three previous books in length.

In this poem he avoids the use of allegory because he thinks the need to abolish false ideas on nobility is so pressing that he must speak as directly as possible. He wrote the poem at a point when he had reached an impasse in his philosophical studies. The particular problem that caused this impasse was that of whether or not God understood or willed the primal matter of elements. He therefore turned from the themes of the preceding books to deal with a subject of social and ethical importance. He divides the *canzone* as a whole into two parts, the first consisting of an introductory preface, itself divided into two, and the second the main body of the poem, which also has three parts. These consist of the treatment of the emperor's and other people's views on nobility, the true opinion on nobility, and the *tornata*. As he goes through the commentary, so he makes subdivision after subdivision, so long and subtle must be the disentangling of the text of the poem. That is his reason for the length of this book, but it may also be that, with this ethical *canzone*, he had not managed to express half of what he felt and knew about the subject.

In Chapters IV and V he states for the first time his political theory of the just origin of the Roman empire. For the regulation of civic life and of the relations between cities and kingdoms one ruler above all others is necessary; just as a captain is necessary on board ship to secure its safe passage and leaders are needed for religious orders and armies, so an emperor is necessary for men to lead happy lives. Why should this office be lodged in the Roman prince? The Roman people would seem to have acquired power through force not by reason, but this acquisition Dante imputes to Divine Providence. When God desired to bring back to Himself man, who was separated from Him by sin, it was decreed in the consistory of the Trinity that the Son of God should descend to Earth to make this concord. As it was proper for his coming that Earth should be at her best disposition and as Earth is at her best when she is under a single monarchy, Providence ordained Rome to fulfil this condition. The birth of David, the ancestor of Mary, and the birth of Rome took place at the same time. Here Dante begins the first effective challenge to St Augustine's *De civitate dei*, which had denied justice or divine favour to Rome. What is more, Dante then goes on to quote numerous examples of Roman heroes, Fabricius, Mucius Scaevola, Regulus and others that Augustine has already used, for a totally opposite purpose. Augustine set out to show that if these heroes had performed remarkable deeds, it was no thanks to the old gods of Rome, who were in any case demons. Dante has already asserted earlier[14] that the pagan gods may be equated with the angels who are the intelligences of the heavenly spheres, and here he says:

> Surely it should be manifest to us, when we recall the lives of these and all the other godlike citizens, that such wonderful deeds were not done without some light from the divine goodness over and above their own natural goodness.[15]

Of the city of Rome herself he says he has a firm belief 'that the stones of her walls are worthy of reverence, and that the soil on which she is seated is worthy beyond all that men have proclaimed or proved'.[16]

After an excursion defining authority and separating imperial authority from philosophic authority (IV. vi), Dante turns back to the question of nobility. Although it is a commonly received opinion that nobility depends on descent from or relationship to a person of worth, Dante is going to weed this tangled field in order to uncover some of the crop of reason. A man who finds his way across a snow-covered plain with all its paths smothered is nobler than someone coming after him who merely has to follow his footprints. Referring to the lines in the *canzone*,

Ma vilissimo sembra, a chi 'l ver guata,	But worst seems he, to one who values truth,
cui è scorto 'l cammino e poscia l'erra,	To whom the road is plain but then he strays,
e tocca a tal, ch' è morto e va per terra![17]	Resembling one who's dead and walks about the earth!

he speaks of the hierarchy of the life in different forms: of growth in plants; growth, movement, and sensation in animals; growth, movement, sensation, and reason in man. A man without reason is dead as a man but he survives as a beast. These lines, in a generalized way, offer the first formulation of one of the bitterest and most sardonic devices of the *Inferno*, when Dante meets or sees souls in Hell whose bodies are still in the world of the living at the time of the vision but are occupied by demons. They have committed such crimes that their souls have descended to perdition before corporeal death.

Dante's next task (IV. viii) is to clear himself of the charge of lack of reverence both for the emperor and for Aristotle in disagreeing with them, and in Chapter ix he shows that in matters of philosophical definition we are not subject to imperial authority because that is not part of its sway. Having cleared these lesser obstacles out of the way, he now (IV. x) launches into the idea of ancestral wealth as a necessary condition of nobility and he explains the most graphic passage in the *canzone*:

poi chi pinge figura,	Thus he who paints a face
se non può esser lei, non la può porre,	Cannot succeed unless he *is* it first,
nè la diritta torre	Nor may the upright tower
fa piegar rivo che da lungi corre.[18]	Be toppled by a distant river.

Riches cannot bestow nobility; for one thing to breed another there must be some interconnecting similarity. Nor can the removal of riches remove nobility any more than a distant river can bring down a tower.

Riches are vile (IV. xi). They bring great dangers (IV. xii) and the names and words of Boethius, Cicero, Solomon, and others are quoted in serious warning. The desire for them is never satisfied and here Dante separates the boundless desire for knowledge from the boundless desire for wealth. He deals with this here and in the next chapter, introducing a series of illustrations remarkable for their compact psychological illustrations, anticipating the similar observations in the *Commedia*. A pilgrim on a strange road thinks every house is an inn until he finally reaches an inn. A child wants an apple, then a pet bird, then fine clothes, and so on. Merchants carrying money as they travel tremble at the rustle of leaves in the wind. 'A traveller with empty pockets would sing in front of robbers', he quotes from Boethius or Juvenal, and mentions Lucan's story of Caesar and the poor fisherman, Amyclas.

The passage of time is not necessary to nobility either (IV. xiv). He attacks the idea that no one of low birth may become a gentleman and among his arguments is this striking illustration. If Gherardo da Cammino, captain-general of Treviso and one of the most famous despots of the period, had been the grandson of the meanest peasant who ever drank of the rivers Sile or Cagnano and his grandfather had not been forgotten, who would have dared say that Gherardo was not noble? And what about Adam (IV. xv)? Are we to think that men descend in two lines, one noble and one base? This is false according to both Christian and pagan ideas. After castigating those who disagree with him to bring them round to a just awareness of their debased understanding, Dante in Chapter xvi turns to the task of defining nobility. He rejects the idea that noble means well-known or famous and that it derives from *nosco*. If this were so then the obelisk of St Peter's would be the noblest stone in the world, Asdente (the prophesying cobbler of *Inferno* XX) would be the noblest person in Parma, and Alboino della Scala would be nobler than Guido da Castello (Purg. XVI). (Alboino succeeded his brother Bartolomeo in the signory of Verona in 1304 and died in 1311. It is not known why Dante singled out for blame this member of a family he owed so much to.) Noble comes from *nonvile*. (His etymologies, by the way, as in this case, are nearly always wrong.) He quotes Aristotle: 'Everything is in the highest degree perfect when it attains and reaches its proper virtue; and it is then in the highest degree perfect so far as concerns its own nature. . . .' The word 'nobility' means the perfection of their natures in all things and Dante proceeds to define it further through its effects, the moral and intellectual virtues. The moral virtues (IV. xvii) are within our own control and he follows Aristotle in enumerating them: courage, temperance, liberality, magnificence, magnanimity, love of honour, good temper, affability, truthfulness, recreation, and justice. There are two roads to happiness in this life, the active life and the contemplative life. The contemplative life is the better, as Aristotle says, and as may be told from Christ's words to Martha. Why then does Dante deal with the moral virtues, which relate to the active life, and not with the intellectual virtues, which are those of the contemplative life? The moral virtues are more commonly known and much more generally needed than the others; the learner must be led by the path that is easiest for him. All moral virtues come from a single principle, habitual good choice (IV. xviii); this is characteristic of both nobility and virtue and therefore one must derive from the other or both must derive from a third. Which is it? If the virtues are stars, then nobility is the heaven that holds them and more besides, including shame in women and boys (IV. xix). Thus nobility is concerned with the conception of virtue and is divine. The soul, however, must be adapted to receive the divine gift, and nobility is a seed of blessedness placed by God in the soul prepared to receive it. The Uberti of Florence and the Visconti of Milan should never boast, 'Because I am of this race, I am noble'. The divine seed falls on individuals, not on the family tree. Some souls are so badly disposed that the divine light never shines in them.

The next chapter (IV. xxi) contains a disquisition on how nobility enters into us in the processes of generation, a theme Dante will return to in *Purgatorio* XXV. He says with Cicero (IV. xxii) that all creatures begin by loving themselves. This desire is indiscriminate at first but later desires become discriminate. The desires of the mind, those of the will and the intellect, are the best and secure the fullest happiness. He contrasts the practical and speculative employments of the mind and shows, by a figurative interpretation of the appearance of the angel in the tomb to the three Maries, how the speculative use of the mind is more full of blessedness. He then shows how nobility manifests itself at the different stages of life. The life of man is an arch rising to a point and then declining. After further discussion of the standards whereby a family may be judged noble or not, he turns to expound the *congedo* of the *canzone*. The *canzone*, which is called 'Against the erring ones', as Aquinas called his first Summa *Contra Gentiles*, is addressed only to the wise or those who love Wisdom. The nobility spoken of in the poem is the friend of Wisdom, 'whose own perfection is the most secret essence of the Divine Mind'.

There have been various attempts to reconstruct how the *Convivio* might have continued. A recent one is that by Fausto Montanari,[19] who suggests the following arrangement:

Whether it was this or another arrangement, it is clear that Dante knew very well what plan the rest of the work should follow. He never worked blindly. As what we have finishes with a completed book, it is very likely that he had written more, getting far into the fifth book perhaps. The first four books as substantial portions of the whole would have been copied and circulated and the later unfinished portions would have been lost or suppressed during the time of Dante's involvement in the affairs of Henry of Luxemburg.

Why did he leave it unfinished? It is generally thought that he broke it off to begin the writing of the *Commedia* in 1308. Though I think he was frequently occupied by the meaning and significance of the vision of 1300 and kept on trying to plan a work based on it, for reasons which will be developed later, I think he did not start the actual writing of the *Commedia* until 1312 or 1313. It is also thought that he underwent a religious crisis, in which he realized the limitations of human reason unaided by faith, and that this crisis led him to renounce his reliance on philosophy in favour of the revealed teachings of the Church, but this is to treat the *Convivio* as a work of pure philosophy, which it is not. For all his reliance on the methods and analytical techniques of philosophy, the starting-point of each investigation is a poem, and what is discussed in the commentary is the inspiration and meaning of the poem. He starts therefore from the poetic image of the lady as Sapientia or as Nobility and not from a verbal proposition in philosophy. It is in fact more like a work of theology than of strict philosophy but one where the premises of faith are replaced by great poetic images that are discussed and expounded in the manner of the scholastics. The work that is most closely related to Book IV in theme is the *Monarchia*, and the need to study for that is the most likely reason for his not finishing the *Convivio*. Further reasons for this point of view, based on the structure of the *Monarchia* as a further refinement of his skill in constructing his works on a planned hierarchy of number patterns, are given in the next chapter.

Numerous images and themes later to be employed in the *Commedia* do, however, appear in the *Convivio*, and these can be treated as evidence of the stage the great poem had reached in his reflections, a stage I call the proto-

Commedia. First, however, we must look at the *Convivio* as a record of Dante's creative processes in a well-defined period of his life.

The conflict between the presentation of the *donna gentile* at the end of the *Vita Nuova* as the enemy of reason and her celebration here as an allegorical figure of Philosophy will probably never be satisfactorily reconciled in terms of the *Vita Nuova* and the *Convivio* alone. Dante had made such claims for Beatrice in the earlier work, that he trapped himself in an impasse from which there was to be no escape, except to unite the qualities of the *donna gentile* as Sapientia with the character of Beatrice, glorified as she will appear to him in the Earthly Paradise. In seeking consolation for his sorrow at the death of Beatrice he had thrown himself into philosophical studies and these revealed to him a new way of making his creative processes work. This was to tax his intellect to the utmost with such concentration that, when he had driven himself almost to the point of exhaustion, a new level of experience opened up within him, a relaxation that brought clarity both of mind and emotion, creating an experience of intellectual light. The evidence that this is how the poems of this period came to him is supported by his description of how he was tormented by the problem of whether or not God understood first matter,[20] and broke off to write the *canzone* on nobility. The poems, such as 'Amor che ne la mente mi ragiona', that he wrote out of these experiences no longer arose from the dreams and visions from which, *quasi sognando*, he had written the poems of the *Vita Nuova*. They continued the impulse given by the discovery of the poetry of praise, but to Dante, both at the time of writing them and of commenting on them, they marked an advance in his artistic maturity. This helps to explain the way in which he stresses the difference between the styles of the two works and also his fascination with the behaviour appropriate to the different ages of man. He may have sought philosophy at first as a means of forgetting his misery but he continued with his investigations into it in a state of love because it brought him nearer to the possibility of creating poetry when and as he wanted. The poetry of praise had given him a certain poetic freedom by granting him a theme that was independent of the external facts of his situation, of whether Beatrice was kind or unkind to him. The inspiration of Philosophy offered him even greater independence, because his theme was now eternal in its nature, and he could arouse in himself the poetic state of composition by a technique of stretching his intellect to its limits and writing out the condition of relaxed enlightenment that followed. He was to enforce a similar technique on his readers in the *Paradiso*, by making them follow the most demanding and convoluted arguments and then suddenly surprising and delighting them with an image or a description that only fully works on them after they have made the preceding intellectual effort.[21]

He wrote the commentaries of the *Convivio* a decade after the composition of the poems that came to him in this way, and perhaps he hoped to gain from it, as well as the advantages of general esteem and a return to Florence, a repetition of the sense of release he had experienced in writing the *Vita Nuova* and by deciding the conflict in favour of Beatrice. Just as in that work he had overcome that conflict by reorganizing his past work to form a single unified interpretation of his life to date, so here in exile, I would suggest, he hoped to resolve a new conflict. He had his half-understood need to write a work that would express his encyclopaedic knowledge and the new poetic themes, whether derived from his classical reading or original to himself, that were working in him. The idea of this work originated in the vision of the Trinity at Easter 1300. He was, however, fixed artistically in his past achievements with the *canzone*. What he could glimpse of the new work threatened his establishment of the *canzone* as the summit of stylistic and technical mastery. His reputation depended on his achievement in writing *canzoni*. Even though in recent years he had only written two *canzoni* and very little other verse, he could not bring himself to sacrifice his mastery and begin again with a new style and a new form. He therefore tried a compromise, to bring his old *canzoni* together with the long prose passages that could accommodate in some measure the new ideas and images, and this is why the *Convivio* contains so many first sketches, the *sinopie* for the final frescoes of the *Commedia*. The writing of the *Convivio* would demand a further period of intense study and perhaps he hoped that he could recover the way back to the state of composition that the earlier period of study had revealed to him. The thought of making Italian prose express a range of themes and ideas never before attempted beckoned him with all the excitement that a technical challenge aroused in him. A new audience, wider than he had ever written for before, appeared in his imagination to be waiting for what he had to say. The possibility that he might be the man to civilize the ruling classes of Italy aroused a great exultation in him, a taste of didactic fervour that anticipates his later prophetic writings.

He wrote the *Convivio* probably between 1304 and 1308,[22] breaking off, perhaps after completing the first book, to write *De vulgari eloquentia* and returning to it to write Books II, III, and IV. There are differences in the style and type of imagery between the four books and they are partly explained by their subject-matter but more, I think, by the growth of Dante's visual imagination. The imagery of Book I is drawn from the parables and sayings of Christ. The banquet to which his new audience is invited resembles the feast given by the rich man. The clerics and professional people have already refused the invitation and therefore the call is to those in the 'highways and byways' who are feeding on mast, the diet of the Prodigal Son at his lowest ebb. When Dante has cleaned the bread of its stains, he says, 'this commentary shall be that bread mixed with barley with which thousands shall be filled', a reference to the feeding of the five thousand. Here is a foretaste of the use of the language and thought of the Gospels that he will employ for the development of fundamental images in the *Commedia*. Its use here also connects with the homely images of *De vulgari eloquentia*.

It is in Book III that we find the clearest evidence for the way in which Dante's scientific studies forced him into finding graphic expression for the complex ideas he had to grasp. In his explanation of how the movement of the sun ensures an equal period of light and dark for every part of the Earth in the course of a year, he asks his readers to imagine a city at the North Pole called Maria and another city at the South Pole called Lucia. The revolutions of the sun cut through the plane of the Earth's equator when the sun is in Aries and in Libra, rising to a summit in Cancer and descending to give light to Lucia in Capricorn.

Però conviene che Maria veggia nel principio de l'Ariete, quando lo sole va sotto lo mezzo cerchio de li primi poli, esso sole girar lo mondo intorno giù a la terra, o vero al mare, come una mola de la quale non paia più che mezzo lo corpo suo; e questa veggia venire montando a guisa d'una vite dintorno, tanto che compia novanta e una rota e poco più. E quando queste rote sono compiute, lo suo montare è a Maria quasi tanto quanto esso monta a noi ne la mezza terra, [quando] 'l giorno è de la mezza notte iguale; e se uno uomo fosse dritto in Maria e sempre al sole volgesse lo viso, vederebbesi quello andare ver lo braccio destro. Poi per la medesima via par discendere altre novanta e una rota e poco più, tanto ch'elli gira intorno giù a la terra, o vero al mare, sè non tutto mostrandò; e poi si cela e comincialo a vedere Lucia, lo quale montare e discendere intorno a sè allor vede con altrettante rote quante vede Maria. E se uno uomo fosse in Lucia dritto, sempre che volgesse la faccia in ver lo sole, vedrebbe quello andarsi nel braccio sinistro. Per che si può vedere che questi luoghi hanno un dì l'anno di sei mesi; e una notte d'altrettanto tempo; e quando l'uno ha lo giorno, e l'altro ha la notte.[23]

It therefore must needs happen that, when the sun passes beneath the equator of the two first poles, Maria would see this sun at the starting-point of the Ram in circling round the world as he descends on the Earth or the sea, like a mill-stone of which not more than the half is seen; and would see him approach when rising after the fashion of the screw of a press, until he completes ninety-one revolutions and a little more. When these revolutions are completed he ascends above Maria almost as far as he ascends above us in the middle of the Earth at mid-tierce, when day and night are equal. And if a man stood upright in Maria, and always kept his face turned to the sun, it would be seen moving towards his right. Afterwards the sun appears to descend by the same path during another ninety-one revolutions and a little more until he circles entirely round down to the Earth or the sea, only showing part of himself; and afterwards he is hidden, and begins to be visible to Lucia. She then sees the sun rising and descending in the same way round herself, with the same number of revolutions as were seen by Maria. And if a man stood upright in Lucia, always turning his face sunwards, he would see the sun depart on his left. Thus it may be perceived that these two places in the course of the year have a day of six months, and a night of the same length; and that when it is day at one place, it is night at the other.

This description arises as part of the literal meaning of one line in the *canzone*,

Non vede il sol, che tutto 'l mondo gira . . .	The sun that circles the whole world never sees . . .

and it has been called 'the most admirable passage of scientific prose that Italian literature possesses, not inferior to the finest pages of Galileo'.[24] Quite apart from Dante's marvellous skill in putting this most difficult idea in the clearest language, the passage has several points of interest. First it must be remembered that Dante had no royal road to astronomy; he had to piece together his understanding of cosmology mostly from difficult and learned texts and he had to create his own visual and imaginative devices to comprehend the movement of the heavenly bodies. To write this passage he had in his imagination to stand at the south and north poles and to be the sun on its annual corkscrewing gyrations. The phrases, 'if a man stood upright in Maria', 'if a man stood upright in Lucia', are reminiscent of the later addresses to the reader, especially in the *Paradiso*, when Dante is describing similar matters.[25] The effort of conceiving what it is like to be a pure angelic intelligence directly in touch with the pure consciousness of God led him to recreate in his imagination the spheres that revolve as an effect of these angels' contemplations. The thought of these extra-terrestrial intelligences gave him an external viewpoint from which he could present the relations between sun and Earth in all their three-dimensional roundness and, to the extent that he was able to express the literal nature of the spirallings, so he could give greater force to the allegorical meaning he found in this mental picture, in this case, the analogy between the sun and the omniscience of God. That he had conceived at this time the use of an external viewpoint might suggest that he was already thinking of a work describing a journey up to the stars, and this passage has another feature which even more looks forward to the *Commedia*. This concerns the odd names Dante chooses for his cities at the north and south poles, Maria and Lucia. These are the names of two of the persons of the trinity of ladies, through whose mercy and compassion Dante in the *Commedia* is saved, and on whom the whole action of the poem depends. The name of one of them is significantly missing at this stage: it is Beatrice. There is a third lady presupposed in the context of the commentary and that is the *donna gentile*, who is in the allegory revealed as Sapientia, the thought in the mind of God, the daughter of God and the noblest creature on Earth within the divine omniscience. Maria and Lucia are not given an allegorical significance because they are only mentioned in the commentary, not in the *canzone*. This does not mean that Dante used their

204

names in a chance manner: it would have been wholly uncharacteristic of him to do so. I regard this passage as the chief evidence that he had already experienced the vision on which the *Commedia* is based, that his mind was often occupied with the possibility of writing a work describing a journey through the heavenly spheres to the Trinity, and that the Virgin Mary and Lucia were already seen as two of the mediatrices on whom the action of the work would depend. His obsession with the *canzone*, and his unwillingness to depart from it in writing a work of such importance, even though the *canzone* form was quite unsuitable for the range of subjects the new theme demanded forced him to run away from the proto-*Commedia* into writing the *Convivio*, while making use of ideas and workings drawn from the proto-*Commedia*, where they seemed to fit into the scheme of his commentary.

Book III also contains mention of his studies of optics and illustrates his command of the imagery of light as when, following Avicenna, he says:

> Dico che l'usanza de' filosofi è di chiamare 'luce' lo lume, in quanto esso è nel suo fontale principio; di chiamare 'raggio', in quanto esso è per lo mezzo, dal principio al primo corpo dove si termina; di chiamare 'splendore', in quanto esso è in altra parte alluminata ripercosso.[26]

> I say that it is customary with philosophers to call the heaven 'light' insofar as light is here in its original source; to call it 'radiance' insofar as it becomes the medium for conveying light from its source to the first substance by which it is arrested; to call it 'splendour' insofar as it is reflected onto some other region which is lit up.

By contrast, the imagery and examples of Book IV are frequently those of dark places and, in his characterizations of states of mind, of mental confusion. Among these are the buried treasure of silver santelena coins found in a Tuscan mountain by a peasant, and the description of souls bady disposed for the reception of the divine seed of nobility. They are described in an image that foreshadows the ravines of Hell:

> essi siano sì come valli volte ad aquilone, o vero spelunche sotterranee, dove la luce del sole mai non discende, se non ripercussa da altra parte da quella illuminata.[27]

> ... they are like valleys facing towards the North, or underground caves into which the light of the sun never descends, unless it be reflected from some other quarter which is illuminated by it.

The most notable of these images of dark places comes in IV. xxii where, speaking of the speculative use of the mind, 'which is the use of our noblest part, the part which is most of all the object of the love rooted in us . . . the Intellect', he says that in this life we cannot put this part to its most perfect exercise, which is the beholding of God, except insofar as the intellect meditates on God and beholds God through His effects. But that we crave for this perfect exercise of speculation and not for the life of action, he demonstrates from the passage in the Gospel of St Mark where the three Maries visit the sepulchre. They find, not the Saviour, but a young man clothed in white who bids them tell the disciples that Christ has gone before them into Galilee. The three Maries are the three schools of the life of action, the Epicureans, the Stoics, and the Peripatetics, who, in going to the sepulchre, i.e. the corruptible world, fail to find the Saviour, i.e. Beatitude. The angel in white is Nobility, which comes from God, and by telling the disciples, that is those who seek him and those who, like St Peter, have diverged from the path, that Beatitude has gone before them into Galilee, he means that God always goes in advance of our contemplation and that we can never overtake our highest Beatitude.

The passage is remarkable for many reasons; although Dante may have adapted a somewhat similar explanation, in which the tomb is Holy Scripture and the women are scholars wanting to know who will roll away the stone of the difficulty of interpretation,[28] the tone is far more secular. It is as though he had written himself to the point where, losing sight of his original aim in writing the *Convivio*, he rediscovered in himself a vein from the *Vita Nuova*. The angel described here as Nobility bears a strong resemblance to the personification of Love in the earlier work. The identification of Beatrice with Christ already mentioned in Chapter 9 returns repeatedly in the use of the word *beatitudine*, especially in the phrase 'lo Salvatore, cioè la beatitudine'. In the very work he was writing in praise of Philosophy, he found the claims of something beyond philosophy rising up unbidden into the images with which he sought to elucidate and express her charms. As Christ went into Galilee after the Resurrection, so Beatrice has gone to the level of contemplation to await the results of Dante's long training in philosophy, and there she will give her judgment.

Another important feature of this passage is that, although it resembles in some ways the dream descriptions in the *Vita Nuova*, it also bears a marked resemblance to the *canzone*, 'Tre donne', where three ladies present themselves before Love, who is in Dante's heart, which, as he explains in the *Convivio*, can mean the most secret part of his nature, just as the three Maries appear at the mouth of the sepulchre and find the angel. This passage is the third occasion in his writings since 1300 that Dante uses a triad of women to express a powerful emotion or idea, the first being 'Tre donne', and the second being the passage already noted from Book III on the movement of the sun, and it provides further evidence, at least in his thoughts, of the proto-*Commedia*. The recurrence of three women in his dreams or waking visions reveals the working in him of an ancient image of great power, recalling the triple aspects of Hecate with her connexions with the underworld, the three Graces, the three Fates, and the Cucullae, the three hooded women of Celtic mythology. The different guises in which they so far appear in Dante's writings give a hint of the supreme difficulties he had to overcome in reconciling his dream- and vision-based inspirations with an interpretation that would accord with his conscious aims as a Christian poet. The passage on the three Maries has yet another significance, that looks forward to the very title of the *Commedia*. From this same Gospel story and its uses as a performance in the Easter ritual, the theatre in Western Europe was reborn, and with its exegesis here in the *Convivio* the theme of the waiting masterpiece breaks through: the poem that with the rebirth of the dramatic presentation of character, resurrects one of the greatest achievements of Greece and gives new meaning to the heritage and history of Rome.

This and later passages describing the four ages of man illustrate how far Dante had progressed in his grasp of the subtleties of figurative interpretation compared to the clumsier allegorical exegesis in Book II. Though he rejected allegorical interpretation for the *canzone* on nobility, he cannot resist using it on the examples he brings to the *canzone*'s exposition. This again shows the influence and ideas of the proto-*Commedia* breaking through in the skill with which he weaves together passages from four Latin poets, Statius for adolescence, Virgil for youth, Ovid for old age, and Lucan for decline, with examples from three wise men, Solomon, Aristotle, and Cicero. The example of his last poet, Lucan for decline, enabled him to demonstrate for the first time a new and extraordinary synthesis, the use of a pagan hero to illustrate the stages of ascent in Christian mysticism. This is when Dante interprets the story of Marcia's return to Cato in old age from Lucan's *Pharsalia*.[29] It is particularly interesting if one remembers that it is Cato who meets the souls of the saved after death on the shore of Mount Purgatory and who directs them on their return to the Creator. Perhaps borrowing the technique of Richard of St Victor in the *Benjamin minor* of interpreting genealogy as a series of inner births of psychological characteristics, Dante expounds the story of Marcia and Cato. Marcia is a virgin (adolescence). She marries Cato and thus signifies youth. Separated from Cato, she marries Hortensius and her sons by him are the characteristics of old age, the stage she now stands for. On Hortensius' death, she returns to Cato and now she signifies decline, the noble soul turning towards God. 'And what earthly man was worthier of signifying God than Cato? No one, for sure.'[30] The fourfold method of interpretation, which had so excited him but which he was so unused to when he described it in Book II that he had to find a different example for each stage and could not find all the levels in one example, now entered deeply into his preparatory thinking before writing. Then, also, he was trying to apply this method to something written ten years before, most probably before he was conscious of the possibilities of the method in the writing of vernacular or secular works. Here is an example with every level present from the beginning, not imposed in wishful hindsight. In the story of Marcia and

Cato is what we are taught (the literal), what we should believe (the allegorical), what we should do (the moral), and the goal to which we aspire (the anagogic).

By the time, in 1307 or 1308, he left off work on the *Convivio*, it is clear that he was already master of many of the ideas and techniques that were to go into the *Commedia*. Although it is generally thought that he broke off at the end of Book IV to begin the *Commedia*, there is no evidence that at this stage he had realized the part Beatrice had to play in the poem or that he had discovered Virgil as a guide. This point of view will be discussed again in Chapter 14. The announcement by Henry of Luxemburg of his descent on Italy made Dante abandon this work in favour of working for the imperial cause and of preparing himself for his treatise on empire, the *Monarchia*.

13

The descent of Henry of Luxemburg
and the writing of *De monarchia*

E 'n quel gran seggio a che tu li occhi tieni
  per la corona che già v'è sù posta,
  prima che tu a queste nozze ceni,
sederà l'alma, che fia giù agosta,
  de l'alto Arrigo, ch'a drizzare Italia
  verrà in prima ch'ella sia disposta.[1]
	On that great seat thine eyes are drawn unto
	  By the crown hung already over it
	  Ere at this wedding-feast thyself art due,
	The soul, on earth imperial, shall sit
	  Of the high Henry, coming to enforce
	  Right ways on Italy, though she is yet unfit.

With these words Beatrice points out to Dante the vacant throne in the sempiternal rose awaiting the future emperor, Henry of Luxemburg, whose descent into Italy was to cause Dante's most extended involvement in international politics.

The chain of events that brought about the elevation to the imperial throne of Henry of Luxemburg goes back to the period following the unfortunate death of Pope Benedict XI in July 1304. Once more for a long time the cardinals could not agree on a candidate, in this case taking eleven months before choosing someone outside their ranks, the Gascon Bertrand de Got, archbishop of Bordeaux, who took the title of Clement V, the 'lawless shepherd' as Dante was to call him. It came to be widely believed in Italy that Bertrand de Got only obtained the papacy after giving Philip the Fair a number of promises in return for which the king used his influence to secure the election. Villani gives circumstantial details of a meeting between them at which these promises were given and the early commentator on the *Inferno*, Guido da Pisa, tells a similar story when discussing the prophecy of Clement's condemnation to the punishment of the simoniac popes, a passage that indicates Dante's own belief in the story. Guido even says that Clement promised to condemn the Master of the Temple and the Templars as heretics and idolaters and that he would confiscate all the goods and possessions of the Templars.[2] Modern historians have demonstrated the impossibility of Villani's version but, even if Clement

209

did not buy the papacy in this manner, he was, after his election, nearly always to be dominated by the French king except in one major attempt to break away. This was through his initial confirmation of Henry of Luxemburg as emperor-elect. During his coronation procession at Lyons in November 1305 Clement was involved in a serious accident in which numbers of spectators were killed by the collapse of a wall, and Clement himself, from that time onwards, suffered from ill-health that sapped the frail reserves of a constitutionally weak will. He could never bring himself to go to Rome and assume his rightful place at the centre of Christendom but resided at several towns in the South of France and eventually at Avignon, thus beginning the long period of the Babylonian captivity. There he was placed conveniently for Philip the Fair to badger him with requests and demands. Among Philip's many schemes for which he needed Clement's connivance, apart from the great matter of the Templars and the posthumous condemnation of Boniface VIII, was the advancement yet again of the interests of his brother, Charles of Valois, who, this time, was after the empire itself.

The throne was vacant following the murder of Albert of Austria, king of the Romans, in May 1308. Certain cardinals managed to impress on Clement the advantages of a candidate free of French influence, of having someone to whom the papacy could turn in its present dependent position. They chose Henry of Luxemburg, whose younger brother Baldwin had recently become archbishop of Trier and consequently an elector. Baldwin campaigned vigorously and successfully for Henry. Charles of Valois had only obtained the support of one elector, and this elector too swung to Henry when it came to voting. Henry was crowned king of the Romans on 6 January 1309. He was in his middle thirties and came from an ancient family of small distinction. He was French-speaking and owed vassalage to Philip for some of his lands. There is one notable feature about Henry mentioned by both allies and opponents, the fineness of his character, his bravery and magnanimity. He seemed to own already that freedom from cupidity that Dante was to claim as the sign of the monarch who possessed his heritage in full.[3] His first success was a reconciliation with the house of Habsburg, and he followed this with an announcement, published throughout Italy, in July 1309 that he was coming for his coronation and to pacify the rivalries of the peninsula. After long negotiations Clement recognized Henry as the emperor-elect and set aside a date for his coronation in Rome in 1312. There was a plan devised for the marriage of a daughter of Henry's to the son of Robert of Anjou, a pact that would bind Robert as the head of the Guelphs to the new emperor and would heal the divisions caused by the execution of Conradin over forty years before. Many Italians, including those Ghibellines and White exiles who saw in Henry the best chance of restitution to their rights and homes, looked forward with longing to his coming. Clement, after extracting more promises and benefits, sent a letter on 1 September 1310, exhorting all cities and bishops in Henry's territories in Italy to receive him peacefully and obediently as their temporal lord. At the same time Dante addressed his letter, 'Ecce nunc tempus acceptabile'[4], to the princes and peoples of Italy, an ecstatic outburst, greeting Henry as the sun of peace, bidding Italy, whom even the Saracens pity, to welcome him as her bridegroom, requiring the Lombards to put aside their barbarism, and the oppressed to lift up their hearts in hope, and announcing Henry as the instrument of God, 'whom Clement, the present successor of Peter, illumines with the light of the Apostolic benediction'.[5]

Henry entered Italy in October 1310 and delegates and spies from all over Lombardy and Tuscany watched eagerly for what he would do, especially noting whether he was favouring the Guelphs or the Ghibellines. His first appointment as imperial vicar was of a Florentine Ghibelline exile, Ugolino da Vico. Florence had already withheld from sending the embassies that so many other cities had dispatched to Henry and it was appointments such as this that were to strengthen her resolve to resist the new emperor with all the forces at her command. Henry entered Milan, then under the rule of the Guelph Guido della Torre, and there he was crowned king of Lombardy in the church of St Ambrose on 6 January 1311. Dante was probably present at the coronation, for in a letter addressed to Henry he refers to the homage he paid him when his hands touched his feet and his lips paid their tribute, 'Then my spirit rejoiced within me when I said secretly within myself: "Behold the Lamb of God, which taketh away the sins of the world".'[6] Henry's progress south was interrupted by strife between Guido della Torre and his rivals, the Visconti, for the signory of Milan. Guido refused Henry's offices as mediator and rebelled against him. By April 1311 both the French king and Florentine emissaries were working on Clement to weaken his support for Henry, and the Florentines were also pushing Robert of Anjou into becoming the leader of Guelph opposition to the emperor-elect. The Florentines also brought Bologna into the Tuscan League they had formed against Henry and henceforward denied him his imperial titles. Dante was at this time staying with the Ghibelline Count Guido Novello in his castle of Poppi overlooking the field of Campaldino, where Dante had fought on the other side over twenty years earlier. The refusal of Florence to recognize or obey Henry prompted the most vehement and unbalanced of all Dante's writings, his letter addressed to the iniquitous Florentines within the city. He told them that they transgressed every law of God and man and that avarice had driven them to commit every crime. He jeered at their fortifications, the third circuit of walls now hurriedly being completed. 'What shall it avail you to have girt yourself with a rampart, and to have fortified yourselves with bulwarks and battlements, when, terrible in gold, the eagle shall swoop down on you. . . ?'[7] Their buildings will fall to battering rams and will be consumed with flames. The starving populace will turn against its rulers and, in a phrase that must afterwards have singed him with remorse for the damage it did to his authority as a prophet, he foretells the delivery of the city into the hands of the stranger, the death of most of her inhabitants, and the slavery of the remainder. They are not to take comfort from Parma's victory over Frederick II but should rather remember Barbarossa's vengeance on Milan and Spoleto. They are the spawn of Fiesole and barbarians and, even if they repent, their crimes will still merit punishment rather than pardon.

Shortly afterwards, on 17 April, Dante wrote to Henry begging him to leave Lombardy and destroy the root of the opposition, which is Florence. He also wrote at this time three letters, on behalf of the countess of Battifolle, to the empress Margaret of Brabant.

Henry could pay no attention to Dante's exhortations: he was drawn into the long siege of Brescia from May to September 1311. During the siege his brother died and it was with weakened forces that he at last began the journey to Rome by way of Genoa. Nevertheless his successes in Lombardy frightened the Florentines, who offered an amnesty to all exiled citizens in order to swell their armies. In January 1312 Henry, exasperated by the success of Florence in organizing the opposition to him, declared all Florentines, apart from exiles such as Dante, rebels of the empire. Henry had received a deep personal blow in the death of his wife Margaret in December. Rebellions flared up again in Lombardy but slowly he pressed southwards to Pisa, where he was splendidly received. By this time pressure from Philip the Fair, Robert of Anjou, and the Florentines again weakened Clement V's support for Henry: he neglected to arrange for Henry's peaceful reception and coronation in Rome, perhaps, as has been suggested,[8] because he had become worried about the security of his chief vassal in Italy, Robert of Anjou. When Henry approached Rome in May 1312 he found it held by troops of Robert of Anjou. He had to fight his way into Rome across the Milvian bridge but was never able to penetrate to St Peter's, where his coronation should have taken place. Instead, he was crowned on 29 June 1312, in St John Lateran. Next he moved north to Tuscany to strike at Florence, which he besieged for six weeks from mid-September. His troops were never enough to surround the city, whose forces numbered more than twice his own. Nevertheless he gained many successes in battle and in capturing towns and, for all their superiority in numbers, the Florentines could not bring themselves to come out and crush him. (Dante, by the way, is said to have withdrawn from the preparations for the siege of Florence,[9] and this may have been either because he could not bring himself to take part in attacking his own city, or because he had begun the *Commedia* and saw his work on that as a higher duty. This may be the explanation of his letter accompanying the poem known as the *montanina canzone*, in which he excuses himself for apparent negligence in affairs—see pp. 228–31.)

By March 1313, Henry was forced to retire to Pisa, the city that remained constantly faithful to him, to prepare new blows against Florence and against the territories of Robert of Anjou. A propaganda war broke out, with Robert of Anjou's publicists attacking the imperial pretensions and formidable replies being issued by Henry's supporters.

It was, perhaps, at this time that Dante issued *De monarchia*, on which he had probably been working since the announcement of Henry's coronation in 1309.

Henry left Pisa on 8 August 1313 with the intention of marching to Rome and then invading the Southern Kingdom. His hopes that Siena would be surrendered to him were dashed and he fell ill with malaria. He was taken to the town of Buonconvento, and died on 24 August. The expedition was abandoned and the imperial army took his body back to Pisa, where it was interred in the cathedral.

The news must have been a terrible blow to Dante, even if he had withdrawn from an active part in the emperor's cause. For, although in retrospect, Henry's expedition now may seem to have been doomed to failure, the same retrospective viewpoint may make it astonishing that a man of good but inconspicuous family, with meagre financial resources, with a merciful and ingenuous nature, hindered by his foreign background from understanding the complexities and strengths of the Italian city states, accompanied by troops inferior in numbers to those of his enemies, deceived and abandoned by the pope who had at first encouraged him, and dogged by family bereavements, by ill-health, and by great misfortunes, could have achieved as much as he did. But, for all the misfortunes, to Dante and his supporters there was always the hope, and to the Florentines and his enemies, the dread, that he might succeed, that, as in the past, a violent change in the government of the South would cause a violent change in the rule of Florence. Much of the success he did achieve was owed to the still strong recognition of the emperor as the fount of power and honour. In terms of this feeling Dante, in supporting Henry, was not the lonely beater of an antique drum he is sometimes made out to be. The holders of the new signories, such as the Scaligeri of Verona, were desperate for the legitimation of their rule and for the authentic title of imperial vicar that only the emperor could bestow. Nicholas of Butrinto, one of Henry's advisers, reported on the warm welcome he received in Tuscany even from firmly Guelph families in his journey preparing for Henry's reception.[10] Fifty years later Italian communes, including Florence, were to pay Henry's grandson, the Emperor Charles IV, huge sums for the restitution of the privileges Henry had revoked from them. The other element in his success was his own character and the strength of his authority in person, exemplified by an incident when, at the tense moment as he approached Milan, and Guido della Torre was waiting to receive him, Guido had neglected to order the dipping of his standards before the imperial eagles. A German seized the standard and threw it into the mud. Guido dismounted and kissed Henry's foot and Henry, smiling at him, said, 'Henceforth, Guido, be pacific and faithful and recognize as lord him whom it is sinful to deny.'[11]

The incident reminds one of the elegance and forthright speaking of many of the nobler characters portrayed in the *Commedia*, the kind of qualities to which Dante responded warmly. The behaviour of those who had tricked or deserted Henry, notably Clement V, Philip the Fair, and, to a lesser extent, Robert of Anjou, provoked in Dante an obsessive hatred, which he purged himself of in many passages in the *Commedia*. Other events added to his hatred of them. In 1311 Clement had cleared Philip the Fair publicly of all responsibility for the attempt against Boniface VIII at Anagni and in the following year had laid Philip's way open to the fulfilment of his designs on the Templar's possessions by the final dissolution of their order at the Council of Vienne. To Dante, Clement had become the whore, *la puttana*, whose lover was the giant of France, the *drudo* in the pageant of the Earthly Paradise. It is probably this pair that he refers to in the sonnet, 'Se vedi li occhi miei di pianger vaghi'.[12]

In this sonnet he begs God, for the sake of Justice, 'she who never leaves You', to relieve him of his overwhelming desire to weep, to take vengeance on the man who kills Justice and who has taken refuge with the great tyrant. This man sucks the poison that the tyrant has poured over the world. God should repay him for icing the hearts of the faithful with such fear that they are silent. The sonnet ends with the request that this virtue that lies naked and cold should be raised up,

ché sanza lei non è in terra pace.   for without her there is no peace on earth.

This sonnet, the letters already quoted, and *De monarchia* are what remains to us of Dante's activities in this crucial period. Although the letters are dated, we cannot be precise about when the *Monarchia* was composed, though it was between 1309 and June 1312. The last date is when Clement V (under orders from Philip the Fair) forbade Henry to attack Robert of Anjou, and thus reversed the policy of papal encouragement for the emperor. The references to the papacy in the *Monarchia* are respectful, almost ingratiating, and befit the atmosphere of the earlier good relations between Clement and Henry.[13] They differ totally from the tone of the sonnet just quoted and the prophecy of Clement's damnation in *Inferno* XIX. The calm tone of the *Monarchia*, when compared with the exalted language and bitterness of the political letters, would suggest that it was composed at an earlier time and in another mood, probably a little before them if the crisis described in the *montanina canzone* can be dated to 1311 (see pp. 229–30), and if that crisis is related to the start of work on the *Commedia*. Therefore, though it was written long before Henry's expedition ended in failure, it is best seen in the light of that expedition as a whole, as well as for its intrinsic and lasting merit as a discussion of the problem of universal authority, and for its links with the *Commedia*.

If we relate the *Monarchia* both to the method of planning that has been demonstrated for Dante's previous works and to the *Commedia*, we can see in it an essential bridge between the earlier prose works and the return to poetry in the *Commedia*. Like the earlier works, it is built on a series of number patterns and, like the *Commedia*, its construction is founded upon the number three. It is divided into three parts like the *Commedia*, and the dynamic of its argument is provided by the use of the syllogism, with its three parts: major premiss, minor premiss, and conclusion. This logical tool of the scholastics has been seen as one of the origins of Dante's invention of the *terza rima* for the *Commedia*. The main theme of the *Monarchia*, to be developed in much greater richness of detail and significance in the poem, is that mankind has two goals, symbolized by the Heavenly Paradise and the Earthly Paradise, and that mankind needs directors for each of those goals, the spiritual ruler and the temporal ruler united in their purposes by the Divine Will, as in Figure 8.

Dante begins the *Monarchia* by stating that it is a man's duty to enrich posterity as he himself has been enriched by his ancestors. He must, however, produce something original – there is no point in repeating what Euclid, Aristotle, or Cicero have already performed perfectly. He has chosen the theme of monarchy which, for all its worth, has been greatly neglected. He defines temporal monarchy (or the empire) as the single rule over all things in time. Three questions arise about temporal monarchy: (1) Is it necessary for the well-being of the world? (2) Did the Roman people assume the office of the monarch by right? (3) Does the monarch's authority derive directly from God or is it mediated through one of God's ministers or vicars (e.g. the pope)? These three questions decide respectively the subject-matter of the three books of the work.

Dante attempts to answer the first question by demonstrating that mankind as a whole has a special end and purpose. God makes a creature in order that it may perform or serve a particular operation or function. A particular function for mankind as a whole must underlie God's purpose in creating humanity. This function is beyond the capabilities of the individual, the household, the village, the city, or the kingdom to perform. What the function is may be made clear by demonstrating the particular potentiality of humanity.

Man's specific capacity does not consist of being, because the elements have being; nor in compound being, for he shares this with minerals; nor in animate being, for he shares this with plants; nor in apprehension, for he shares this with animals. It consists of his ability to apprehend, through the possible intellect,

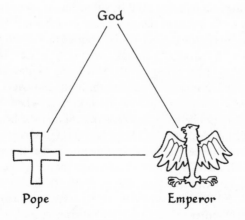

Figure 8 The triad of God, Pope, and Emperor

the quality that separates him from lower and higher beings. Other beings such as the angels possess intellect but their intellect is eternally actualized. Their being and their intellect are one. It is not so with men, whose task is to develop the unrealized potentiality of their intellect and, because the capacity is unrealized, it is called the possible intellect. This task cannot be performed by anyone individual, nor by any section of society, but only by mankind as a whole. Dante brings additional arguments to bear and quotes Averroes. (It was Dante's clear dependence on Averroes[14] here that made the work open to attack by the Dominican friar, Guido Vernani.)[15]

The role of humanity as a whole is, therefore, always to actualize the potentiality of the possible intellect, first through speculation and second by action based on the results of speculation, and in this passage, according to Etienne Gilson, Dante seems to have expressed for the first time our modern conception of humanity.[16] Just as an individual perfects himself in wisdom and prudence through sitting and finding stillness, so it is clear that the human race performs its proper work in the tranquillity of peace. Universal peace is the best of all means ordained for our blessedness.

If universal peace provides the best means for realizing human potentiality as a whole, what is the most direct way of securing this peace? Dante now returns to the first of his three main propositions, that temporal monarchy is necessary for the well-being of the world. He quotes Aristotle to show that when several things have one end, then one of them must rule and the others be the ruled. He takes the same progression of examples as above, individual man, a household, a village, a city, a kingdom, to show how each of these needs a controlling authority, whether it is the intellectual faculty in man or the king in the kingdom. From these examples he derives the necessity of one person to govern or rule mankind and this man should be called the monarch or emperor.

Arguing from the relation of parts to a whole and the order of a part in relation to the order of a whole, Dante shows that (I. vi) all the lesser divisions of society, including kingdoms, should be subordinate to the monarch. In that sense humanity is a whole but in relation to the universe it is only a part. To be brought into unity with this greater whole, it must be unified and in harmony under one prince (I. vii). All things are most perfect when they fulfil the intentions of the first cause, God. Mankind, insofar as it may, most resembles God when it is most unified, and this unity may only occur when it is under one prince (I. viii). A son is most perfect when he imitates the perfection of his father. The human race is the child of the heavens, which are most perfect in all their operations. Therefore humanity's perfection depends upon its reproducing the perfection of the heavens. Just as the heavens have one mover in God, so humanity requires one ruler, the monarch, and one law.

Furthermore a supreme judge is necessary to resolve differences between princes. The world is best disposed when Justice is strongest. He quotes Virgil's fourth Eclogue, 'iam redit et Virgo, redeunt Saturnia regna', where the virgin is

Astraea, or Justice, a figure that will be one of the dominant images of *Purgatorio*.[17] Anticipating the appearance in that cantica of Justice as one of the four stars symbolizing the cardinal virtues, he speaks here of Justice as Phoebe in the rosy dawn. There follows a fascinating but closely argued passage on why the monarch is the mortal most free of cupidity; he has nothing to desire because the ocean is the only limit of his power. In this he is unlike princes such as the kings of Castile and Aragon, whose power is limited by their frontiers. Next he says that the monarch is the purest incarnation of Justice. Just as cupidity clouds the vision of Justice, so charity or rightly ordered love illuminates and sharpens it. He demonstrates that love has this effect. The monarch possesses this rightly ordered love more than all other men; and as all men are nearer to him than to other princes, he loves them more than those others can do.

Other princes derive their power solely from him and, since he is the most universal cause of human well-being, it is clear that he desires most of all the good of man. Justice is most powerfully served by a monarch and therefore, again, monarchy is necessary for the well-being of the world. Dante now brings one of his favourite themes into the next chapter (I. XII), that of liberty, which in the *Commedia* he will enrich with discourses and images, most notably with the figure of Cato. Here he states that the human race is at its best when it is most free. He explains the principle of liberty as free choice. Some people repeat mechanically the idea that free choice is a free judgment exercised upon the will but, to understand this properly, it is necessary to see judgment as the middle term connecting apprehension and appetite. Judgment is free when it directs the appetite. Beasts have no free will because in them judgment is at the mercy of appetite. This explains how angels, in whom will is immutable, and the souls of the blessed do not lose free choice because their will is immutable, but enjoy it in its most perfect and powerful form. Liberty is God's greatest gift to human nature because it makes us happy on Earth as men and happy as gods elsewhere. Mankind is at its best when it uses this principle of liberty to the full and it can only enjoy its fullness under a monarch.

Liberty means to be dependent on oneself and not on others. To be dependent on another is to be bound as a road is bound by its terminating point. Only under a monarch is mankind dependent on itself because all the crooked forms of government, democracies, oligarchies, and tyrannies, which force mankind into slavery, are made straight by monarchy. Under true government, rulers exist for the sake of the people, not the other way round; this is true above all of the monarch, who is the minister of everyone.

Next (I. XIII) he states that the man best suited to rule is the one who draws the best out of others, and he demonstrates that this can only be performed by the monarch. What may be done by one means, should be left to that means, and not be performed through a multiplicity of means (I. XIV). Mankind can be ruled through one prince, the monarch. Dante qualifies this by pointing out

217

that different rules will apply different races, climates, and societies but a common law guiding the characteristics men hold in common should issue from this prince.

A fine passage follows in the next chapter (I. xv) on concord as a harmonious movement of several wills. He says:

> Nam, sicut plures glebas diceremus 'concordes' propter condescendere omnes ad medium, et plures flammas propter coadscendere omnes ad circunferentiam, si voluntarie hoc facerent; ita homines plures 'concordes' dicimus propter simul moveri secundum velle ad unum quod est formaliter in suis voluntatibus, sicut qualitas una formaliter in glebis, scilicet gravitas, et una in flammis, scilicet levitas.

> For just as we should describe several clods which all fell towards the same centre as concordant and say that several flames shooting out towards the same circumference were concordant (if they did so voluntarily), similarly we describe several men as being in concord when their wills are simultaneously directed towards the same formal object (which is present in their wills as the quality of gravity is present in the clods and levity in the flames).

Following this passage he shows how mankind achieves this concord of wills best under a monarch. The last chapter of Book I remarks on the fact that the only time when the whole world was at peace was under the perfect monarchy of Augustus, the fullness of time when Christ was born. This historical fact confirms his earlier arguments and, with a final cry of sorrow at the sufferings of humanity, he closes with the words of the psalmist, 'Behold how good and pleasant it is for brethren to dwell together in unity.' The 'historical fact' of the peace of Augustus makes the link to Book II, whose subject is the Roman empire, which, as Dante seeks to show, was founded by divine ordinance. This was not a question of purely academic interest at the time Dante was writing. The propagandists of King Robert of Naples, the opponent of Henry of Luxemburg, were busy putting it about that the Roman empire was the product of armed force without God's sanction. Dante (in II. 1) admits he once held that opinion but his view was then only superficial. Deeper reflection has led him to the core of the matter and he has recognized the signs of divine providence. The sights of kings and princes resisting the Lord's anointed[18] fills him with contempt and sorrow, but the contempt is dissipated by natural love, just as the sun disperses morning mists, as he determines to rid the kings and princes of their ignorance and to let all men see that they are free of their yoke.

He now states the problem of the second book: 'whether the Roman people acquired the imperial dignity by right'. In a passage anticipating many parts of the *Paradiso* he speaks of nature, like art, having three aspects. Art may be considered under the three aspects of the mind of the artist, the tool he uses, and the matter he invests with form. So nature may be considered as the mind of the first mover, God, the tool He works with, in this case the heavens, and unstable matter. God is perfect, His heavens are the best instrument, and therefore any imperfections lie in matter. What is good in nature must come from God and is the manifestation of His will. Though the will of God is invisible, yet his invisible things may be perceived through his works, and in signs.

Dante's first proof of the right of the Roman people (in II. III) is as follows: it was right for the noblest race to lead all other races; the Roman race was the noblest; therefore it was right that the Romans should lead the others. First he discusses nobility, taking that definition from Aristotle's *Politics* 'that nobility is virtue and ancient wealth', which he had wrongly attributed to Frederick II in *Convivio* IV, and then he proves the exceptional claims of the Roman people to nobility because of their descent from Aeneas. Aeneas' ancestors and his three wives, Creusa, Dido, and Lavinia, came from the three parts of the world, Asia, Africa, and Europe. Here he uses Virgil, 'divinus poeta noster', as an unimpeachable authority in somewhat the same way as he did the four poets in the fourth book of the *Convivio*, happily finding significances far beyond the context of his source.

After arguments showing divine intervention in the history of Rome, the good intention of the Romans in conquering the world, and the fact that they were born to rule other races, Dante comes to his main arguments of the race and the duel. He treats world government as a prize for which several peoples were the contenders. Among these he lists the Assyrians under Ninus and Semiramis, the Egyptians, the Persians under Xerxes, and Alexander the Great. All these lost and the Romans won, triumphing by divine decree and with their victory based on right. Turning to the argument of the duel (II. IX), he says that whatever is won in a duel is won by right. He looks upon a duel as something to which contestants should only have recourse when all other means of deciding an issue are exhausted. It is also something on which they should enter activated solely by the disinterested desire for justice.

That the Roman people won the empire by a duel is attested by many witnesses. He quotes the example of the duel of Aeneas and Turnus, with which the *Aeneid* breaks off; the battle of the Horatii and the Curatii; the Sabine and Samnite wars; and the later examples of the Greek and Punic wars. Warning the decretalists, the commentators on canon law who minimized the power of the emperor, of their misguidedness, he states it as proved that the Roman people won the empire by a duel and therefore by right. Hitherto he has based his arguments on reason, but now he must explain his thesis according to the principles of the Christian faith.

Dante now launches into the boldest argument of the book. If the Roman Empire did not exist by right, then Christ by His birth condoned an injustice. As Luke tells, Christ willed His birth of a Virgin Mother under an edict of Roman authority. The Son of God had Himself made man so that He might be inscribed in that unique scroll of the human race and in doing so He recognized the validity of Roman authority.

Furthermore (II. xi), if the Roman empire did not exist by right, then the sin of Adam was not punished in Christ. If Christ had not made satisfaction for that sin, then we would still be the children of wrath. He quotes Ephesians to prove this is not so. A punishment must be inflicted by someone with the authority to impose it, otherwise it would merely be an injury. Only a judge who had authority over all mankind would have this right because it was the whole of mankind that was punished in Christ. Tiberius, whose officer Pilate was, would not have possessed this authority unless the Roman empire were founded on right. With these and other arguments, Dante brings the book to a close with a final cry against the Donation of Constantine:

> O felicem populum, O Ausoniam te gloriosam, si vel nunquam infirmator ille Imperii tui natus fuisset, vel nunquam sua pia intentio ipsum fefellisset![19]

> O happy people, O glorious Ausonia! If only the one who weakened the Empire had never been born or had never been misled by his own pious intentions!

In Book III, Dante's aim is to discover whether the authority of the monarch comes direct from God or is derived through an intermediary—i.e.. the pope. He is well aware that he is on ground more dangerous than in the earlier books but he is assured of divine help as he enters the arena to throw the impious and the liar from it. He lists the three classes who resist the truth on this issue. They are: (1) the pope, but he is largely excused 'through his zeal for the keys'; (2) the kings and rulers who oppose the empire in whom obstinate cupidity has quenched the light of reason; (3) the decretalists, the canon lawyers who are singled out for exceptional vituperation. These base all their arguments on the decretals, for which Dante has a proper respect. The decretalists are too uneducated, and the rulers are too blind to listen to reason. Therefore his arguments are directed at the pope and his party, with the respect a reverent son owes his father and mother. He now turns to a series of arguments drawn from the Bible, with which the papal publicists fought their cause.

He begins with the argument of the two luminaries, based on Genesis. God made two luminaries, the greater for the day and the lesser for the night. Interpreted allegorically these stand for the spiritual and the temporal powers. Just as the moon derives all its light from the sun, so the temporal power derives all its authority from the spiritual power. Dante says that there are two possible ways of committing an error in the mystical interpretation of scripture, one by seeking it where it is absent and the second by wrong interpretation. Anyone who interprets scripture wrongly should be made aware of his error and forgiven just as we would forgive, Dante says in a charming phrase, someone who was afraid of a lion in the clouds. Those, however, who deliberately commit such errors he compares to tyrants who make the commonwealth serve their own ends. They sin not against Moses and the other writers of the scriptures but against the Holy Ghost, who speaks through them.

The allegorical interpretation of the two luminaries cannot be sustained for two reasons. The first is that the two types of government they are meant to symbolize are accidental to man and do not constitute his essence. God, in making them on the fourth day and man on the sixth, would not have produced the accidents of a substance before making the substance. The second is that the functions of the two governments were made necessary by the Fall; yet the two luminaries were created not only before the Fall but before the existence of man. Having, it would seem, disposed of the analogy between sun and moon and pope and emperor, Dante then seems to accept it for the purposes of his next argument, which is that the moon, though it derives its fullness of light from the sun, does not depend on the sun for its existence, its powers, or its operation. What it receives from the sun, light, enables it to increase its power and, in the same way, temporal government does not owe its existence, power, or operation to spiritual government, though, through the light of grace dispensed by the pope, it is enabled to operate more powerfully.

After dealing with other arguments based on scripture, he turns (III. viii) to Christ's words to Peter: 'Whatsoever ye shall bind on earth shall be bound in heaven; and whatsoever ye shall loose on earth shall be loosed in heaven' (Matthew 18:18). This cannot mean that the successor of Peter is able to bind and loose the laws of the empire because, according to Dante, the loosing and binding refer to the office of the key-bearer of the Kingdom of Heaven. He next takes on the argument of the two swords, based on Luke 22:38, which are taken to symbolize the two forms of government. Dante rejects the allegory because in producing the two swords Peter was acting against Christ's intentions. He goes on to analyse the impetuous nature of Peter with many instances, demonstrating how frequently he misunderstood Christ and yet bringing out his ardour and simplicity. This, apart from the passage on Cato in *Convivio* IV, is the only time Dante discusses at length in a prose work the character of one of the personages in the *Commedia*. The passage is crucial in understanding Dante's creation of character, because of the roundedness with which he sees Peter here, with his faults and his virtues altogether making an individual being. It is also interesting, looking ahead to the function Peter plays in the *Paradiso* of denouncing the corruption of the papacy, because it shows that even in creating a mouthpiece for his views, Dante's dramatic sense could not let character disappear under the polemic.[20] Peter is as impetuous and as vehement as ever he was on Earth; Heaven blushes red with his anger. Though in Heaven he understands the divine intention, no whit of his individuality is removed and, there, the very quirks of his earthly nature exist to further, and not turn aside, the will of God.

He moves now to historical arguments, the most important of which concerns the Donation of Constantine. Dante, as was noted in Chapter 3, accepted the Donation as genuine but he rejected its validity on several grounds. To divide the empire is against the nature of the office the emperor holds, and it is his function to keep mankind in obedience to one will. The foundation of the empire is human justice, and it would be contrary to human justice if the empire were to destroy itself by division. Furthermore, even if Constantine had been right to make the gift, the Church was not right to receive it because of Christ's prohibition: 'Provide neither gold nor silver nor brass in your purses' (Mathew 10:9).

Through many examples, he reaches the conclusion that there is no foundation in natural law or divine law for allowing the Church to grant the empire its authority. It is in fact against the nature of the Church to assume such a power. The form of the Church is the life and words of Christ. Christ renounced this world in saying to Pilate 'My kingdom is not of this world.'

These arguments bring Dante to the climax of the work (III. xv). Though nearly all of these arguments are of no current interest, they played their part in preparing for one of the noblest passages in all the writings of political science. Here Dante transcends the occasion of the work and the limitations of the form of reasoning he has hitherto employed. He no longer argues against his opponents, but sets out his own vision of the two natures of man and his mediate position between the corruptible and incorruptible worlds. Unerring providence has established two goals for man: one is happiness in this life and is figured in the terrestrial Paradise; the other is the blessedness of eternal life, the sight of the Divine Countenance, by which may be understood the celestial Paradise. To reach these two goals, two guides have been appointed: 'the Supreme Pontiff, who is to lead mankind to eternal life in accordance with revelation; and ... the Emperor who, in accordance with philosophical teaching, is to lead mankind to temporal happiness'. The office of the emperor is to give men conditions of freedom and peace as they pass through 'the testing-time of this world'. He will be able to apply the principles of liberty and peace at the right times and in the right measures, because he will receive knowledge of the effect of heavenly bodies in creating earthly change directly 'from the One who sees the whole course of the heavens at a glance'. The emperor is elected and confirmed by God alone: the electors, blinded by their greed from realizing their minor role, are merely the messengers of the Divine Will.

Dante, having answered the last of his three questions by proving that the monarch's authority comes directly from God, ends the book with the qualification that this does not mean the monarch is free of all duty to the pope:

Illa igitur reverentia Cesar utatur ad Petrum qua primogenitus filius debet uti ad patrem: ut luce paterne gratie illustratus virtuosius orbem terre irradiet, cui ab Illo solo prefectus est, qui est omnium spiritualium et temporalium gubernator.[21]

Caesar . . . is obliged to observe that reverence towards Peter which a first-born son owes to his father; so that when he is enlightened by the light of paternal grace he may the more powerfully enlighten the world, at the head of which he has been placed by the One who alone is ruler of all things spiritual and temporal.

Dante's exceptional ability for probing a question to its causal origins enables him to produce a solution for the problem of how a universal authority, once it is established, can be controlled. This he does by dividing the authority according to the two goals of humanity and defining their areas of responsibility. The state, with its tendency to take over and rule all sides of human life, ultimately denying the existence of the spiritual world—a tendency of which the most frightening modern examples in Europe have been Stalin's Russia and Hitler's Germany—should be kept in check by the spiritual well-being of all its subjects who acknowledge through conscience and faith the existence of a spiritual authority external to the state's control. The spiritual authority, with its tendencies either to take over all the functions of the state, as did the medieval papacy, or else to retreat from life, as the Joachimite Spiritual Franciscans wanted and as many modern proponents of an alternative society desire, would influence and be nourished by its contacts with a lively and creative population aware that its life and creativeness depend on the balance it can achieve between the active life and the contemplative life which must be fostered by the spiritual authority. There is a dualism in human society which has to be brought into balance, otherwise it swings to one of the two extremes that in modern terms Arthur Koestler characterized as those of the Yogi and the Commissar. Thus, although Dante was writing in the *Monarchia* against the extreme party of canonists[22] who maintained that the emperor enjoyed only a delegated power from the pope, and against the doctrines of supreme authority claimed by Boniface VIII in *Unam Sanctam*, his division of the powers would also have guarded against the ambitions of Philip the Fair as set out by Pierre Dubois.[23] Philip wanted, amongst other demands, the empire to be the hereditary possession of the French royal house, the possessions of the Church to be transferred to him and his heirs, and the pope to become his pensionary. When Dante writes of the relations between empire and papacy, he has of course very different men in mind as holders of those offices than most of the incumbents in his own and preceding periods. He really requires men who have mastered in themselves the priestly and kingly functions so that, whichever role they are required to play under divine ordinance, each will fully appreciate the functions and duties of the other's part.

It is extremely hard for us now to imagine a supreme ruler, or someone who aspires to supreme rule, as anything but a tyrant and a dictator. Dante forces us, however, to imagine a monarch who is qualified for his office by a unique capacity for love,[24] a monarch who is elected and whose election is secured by Divine Providence, a monarch who allows diversities of government in the various races and societies beneath his sway and keeps peace among them through just and effective international law. The more we reflect on such a paragon the more we realize that he is a new presentation of the legendary great rulers of the past, a Barbarossa about to awake, a Prester John of the Orient, an Arthur sailing back from Avalon, under whose rule the world will achieve rebirth and be renewed. A fuller appreciation of his extraordinary capacities forces us also to reflect on what Dante does not describe, the ideal qualities and nature of the ruler of the spiritual sphere. What seems implicit here is an assumption of two circles of humanity, an inner and an outer that should work in accord, acknowledging each other's spheres, that have a yearning and a need for one another, as Amfortas needs Parzival for the renewal of the Wasteland, and as King Arthur and his court need the benison of the Grail. In fact, given Dante's professed love for the Arthurian legends and the way in which his political ideas and his treatment of Astraea were later taken up and fused with the story of Arthur by English writers and poets to create the great Tudor vision of a new age of empire, it is not too fanciful to seek a contributory influence on Dante's analysis of the necessary division of sovereignty and the equally necessary interdependence in the sharp division between the outer world of Arthur's court and the inner world of the Grail castle in the savage wood. Such a connexion leads us in Wolfram von Eschenbach's *Parzival*, the greatest medieval vernacular poem after the *Commedia*, to the castle of Munsalvaesche, with its Templar guardians, and to the Grail itself, the stone from which the fecundity of all living things on Earth derives, for an inkling of what that other, that undescribed, spiritual power may be. Such a connexion, too, bring us to the opening of the *Commedia*, with its own savage wood of the mind that lies between the outer and the inner world.

Even while the outcome of Henry's descent into Italy was still uncertain, Dante had turned away from the hope of a purely political settlement for the ills of Europe to a rediscovery of his vocation as a poet and a new direction for the prophetic powers that had so coloured the rhetoric of his political letters. This change depended, as we shall see, on his rediscovery of Beatrice and on the revaluation of the ancient world, of which we have already seen many traces in the *Convivio* and the *Monarchia*, through the character of Virgil. It was this change that led to the writing of the *Commedia*. The *Monarchia* had a profound influence in its century: it was revised and used by the supporters of Lewis of Bavaria in his propaganda against the papacy; and it even influenced the Golden Bull of 1356, whereby the emperor Charles IV, the grandson of Henry VII, came to an accord with the electors of the empire; it was so feared by the opposing party that it was condemned by the friar Vernani, was burnt in public at Bologna in 1329, and was placed on the Index when the emperor Charles V used it in his quarrels with the papacy. Its arguments were taken up by Protestant writers in the sixteenth century, most notably by Bishop Jewel and John Foxe, the author of the widely influential *Boke of Martyrs*.[25] Centuries had to pass before the Roman Church could change its attitude towards the work: this came in 1921, when Pope Benedict XV officially described it as a correct analysis of the relations that should obtain between Church and State. Its influence still continues, for it is now seen as the first clear statement of the European ideal,[26] and therefore it may play a part in the creation of a united states of Europe; and it also has wider implications for world government. But all its influence on politics has been far smaller than that of the *Commedia*, with its more profound influences on our civilization and its effects on the very roots of human social intercourse, not to mention the part it played in the making of the Italian nation. The *Commedia* could only be written because Dante realized how the priestly and kingly functions which he analysed and defined for humanity as a whole had to be developed and understood as parts of his own psychology, and it is from that inner understanding that the poem with its greater influence derives.

14

The last years: Lucca, Verona, and Ravenna

Dante's political career did not end with the death of Henry VII. To take a positive view of his involvement in the emperor's affairs, he had probably gained immensely in general respect by his attachment to the imperial court, by the many new contacts he must have made there amongst Italian rulers, by his employment as an envoy, and by the skill he had demonstrated as a publicist in his letters and in *De monarchia*. The example of those letters, together with the report, by 1314,[1] that he was engaged on a great work in which he was portraying his contemporaries with a merciless eye for their faults, also made him someone to be feared and placated, someone who was an adornment to a court, who could be trusted in delicate affairs and could be flattered into such services but, nevertheless, a personage eloquent in invective, savage in retort, and bitter at any affront to his art or his pride. His later years are characterized by his close relations and friendship with three great lords, Uguccione della Faggiuola, the tyrant of Lucca, Can Grande della Scala, imperial vicar and lord of Verona, and, from about 1317 till Dante's death, Guido da Polenta, the ruler of Ravenna. Though he continued to hope to his last days for a completely free return to Florence, he was no longer the suppliant of the time of writing 'Tre donne' and the *Convivio*. His new friends were far more powerful than nobles such as Moroello Malaspina or the conti Guidi; in his art he brought the ideals of the *fedeli d'amore* to a wider public; and in politics he could speak for a large body of Italians in matters of international concern.

This last point is shown by the finest of all his political letters, the letter to the Italian cardinals,[2] written probably quite soon after the death of Clement V on 20 April 1314. Ill throughout his reign, vacillating and greedy for money, Clement had been a disaster as pope. He had sacrificed the Templars in order to safeguard Boniface VIII's reputation and the outward respect in which the papacy was held. He was passionately fond of his family and his native Gascony, creating ten Gascon cardinals, of whom five were his own nephews. He had encouraged Henry VII to enter Italy and then betrayed him and he had made his own ill-health the excuse for keeping the papacy in Southern France, where it was to remain for almost seventy years. Villani tells a story of Clement's death which illustrates how Dante, in basing his *Commedia* on the afterworld and including in it the recently dead, shared a popular vein of speculation. Villani says[3] that, when Clement's favourite among his cardinal nephews died, Clement ordered a necromancer to find out what had happened to his nephew's soul. The necromancer secured that one of Clement's chaplains should be taken by demons to Hell, where he was shown a palace. In the palace was a bed of fire, and on it lay the nephew's soul, punished there for his simony. Next to this palace was another one in the course of construction and this was being prepared for Clement's own soul. When the chaplain told Clement what he had seen, Clement was 'never afterwards glad'. Clement died soon after and his body was left in a church for the night, surrounded by candles. A candle fell on the coffin, setting fire to it and burning Clement's body up to the waist. Dante predicts another form of punishment for Clement among the simoniacal popes in which he will thrust Boniface VIII down into the well of fire and be himself thrust down in his turn. Both stories demonstrate how the great ones of that hierarchical society were made subject to the democracy of gossip and how the transient nature of their elevation gave no protection against judgment on their failings. A much later source credits Dante as the author of the haunting legend that Jacques de Molay, while being burnt alive, summoned Clement V to God in forty days and Philip the Fair to the divine tribunal within the year.[4]

It was to be over two years before the cardinals elected a successor. Dante wrote to the Italian cardinals to urge them to elect a pope who would restore the seat of the papacy to Rome. He began the letter with the quotation from Jeremiah that he had used twenty-four years before to announce the death of Beatrice: 'How doth the city sit solitary that was full of people!' He laments the state of the Church, mocked by Jews, Saracens, and Gentiles. The cardinals, whose task is the guardianship of the Church, have gone astray and they should blush to think that his voice, that of a private individual, is the only one to lament the death of the Church. The cardinals are devoured with avarice, they neglect the study of the Fathers for the decretals and they worship Mammon instead of God. 'Not charity, not Astraea, but the daughters of the horseleech have become thy daughters-in-law.'[5] Dante is not the only one to hold these opinions: 'everyone is murmuring or muttering, or thinking, or dreaming what I cry aloud'. He then turns to the cardinals from Roman families, saying the condition of Rome would arouse the pity of Hannibal, deprived as she is of her two luminaries,[6] and calling on those who knew the sacred Tiber as children to return to their duty. He summons them to fight against the Gascons and for the Bride of Christ, for the seat of the Bride, Rome, for Italy and for the whole of humanity in pilgrimage on the Earth. The letter was much admired and Villani lists it as one of those that men of insight commended.[7] It had no effect on the deliberations of the cardinals, however, who finally on 7 August 1316 chose an elderly member of their conclave, Jacques Duèse, who came from Cahors. He was styled John XXII and the papacy stayed at Avignon. Like his predecessor, he aroused neither respect nor affection in Dante, who would have been amazed by the many benefits to the Church and to Europe as a whole that modern historians have discerned as the consequences of the papacy's long exile at Avignon.

The mention of the symbolism of the two luminaries and the death of Clement V, both of which return or are referred to in the *Commedia*, raises the question of when the *Commedia* was written. If Dante had begun it in 1308 before writing the *Monarchia*, where he still uses the sun–moon symbolism, and before the death of Clement, then we are required to postulate a first draft, which he later altered. If he began it later, between 1311 and 1313, then it is objected that he had far too little time to execute so vast a work. I have earlier suggested the hypothesis of a proto-*Commedia* to reconcile these difficulties and, before advancing this suggestion further, it may help to recapitulate the points already made in earlier chapters about the dating of the *Commedia* and to relate these to another disputed dating, that of the *montanina canzone*, a poem generally thought to have been written about 1308 but here dated to 1311.

1. Dante received a vision of the Trinity at Easter 1300. This released a great burst of energy in him that was, first of all, devoted to his political involvements.

2. His exile made him turn back to his earlier achievements as a poet. He began to see how this vision of the Trinity could be made the basis of a great work in the vernacular, a work that could be constructed on intricate number patterns down to the smallest details. This I called the proto-*Commedia*. He was, however, trapped by his own achievements in the form of the *canzone*. He tried to express something of the new inspiration in the *canzone* 'Tre donne' and the *canzone* on liberality. He wrote *De vulgari eloquentia* almost as a justification of the position on style and form that this proto-*Commedia* was eventually to force him to abandon.

3. At about the same time, because he could not get the new inspiration into the *canzone* form, he started the *Convivio* as a means of relieving the creative pressure, and into the commentary on earlier *canzoni* he inserted themes and ideas taken from his reflections on the proto-*Commedia*. Among these are the examples given in Chapter 12. He left both *De vulgari eloquentia* and the *Convivio* unfinished, perhaps because neither satisfied him in the extent to which the number patterns he was using in them stretched and freed his inventive genius.

4. He had already started to formulate his position with regard to the empire in Book IV of the *Convivio*, when the news of Henry VII's coronation at Aachen in January 1309 reached Italy. A period of intense political activity followed, in the course of which he wrote the *Monarchia* and the two letters of spring 1311.

5. Some time after writing these letters, he received a vision of a lady which bears a great resemblance to the meeting with Beatrice described in the last cantos of the *Purgatorio*. He wrote a *canzone*, known as the *montanina*, in which

Love returns as a dominant character in his verse for the first time for several years, and sent it with a letter which contains his excuses for his inactivity in the imperial cause. Another and more powerful vision and a period of intense striving perhaps convinced him that the lady of the *montanina* vision was Beatrice and that Love was Virgil. One he decided that the lady was Beatrice and that she completed the trinity of ladies which, as a theme, had recurred in his earlier writings, all the scattered themes of the *Commedia* came together and he could begin the work of precise planning that preceded his execution of the work. This planning included not only the main elements of the form and theme but went down to the smallest details so that the imagery of the first two cantos of the *Inferno* foreshadows all the major developments of imagery throughout; the same applies to the cosmological and numerological significances of the poem and to the graded levels of inspiration from which he writes.

This suggested chronology partly depends, from point 5 onwards, on the acceptance of a different date for Letter IV and the *montanina canzone* than that usually followed, because most writers on Dante believe that he broke off the *Convivio* at the end of Book IV to begin the *Commedia* in 1308 or 1309. The letter mentioned in point 5 was one he wrote to Moroello Malaspina, and it bears out that he suffered some great crisis.[8] Although the letter is very obscure, too obscure to enable us to do more than guess at the nature of the crisis, nevertheless it offers some clues to the beginning of work on the *Commedia*. It is addressed in its superscription in the only known manuscript to Moroello Malaspina, with whom he is known to have stayed in October 1306. It is written by the river Arno and in a mountainous region. These facts both point to the Casentino as the place where he had the experience described in it. He was also in the Casentino when he wrote the two political letters of 1311 and it is this later visit to the Casentino that enables us to select a later date for the letter to Moroello Malaspina.[9] This letter is accompanied by the poem known as the *montanina canzone*, which is probably the last *canzone* Dante wrote. He writes to his lordly correspondent to excuse himself from the charge of negligence and to ward against rumours, to explain an extraordinary experience. No sooner had he left the court (*curia*, a word he would be far more likely to apply to the imperial court than to the household of Moroello) and set foot beside the Arno, than:

> subito heu! mulier, ceu fulgur descendens, apparuit, nescio quomodo,
> meis auspitiis undique moribus et forma conformis. O quam in eius
> apparitione obstupui! Sed stupor subsequentis tonitrui terrore cessavit.
> Nam sicut diurnis coruscationibus illico succedunt tonitrua, sic
> inspecta flamma pulchritudinis huius amor terribilis et imperiosus me
> tenuit. Atque hic ferox, tamquam dominus pulsus a patria post
> longum exilium sola in sua repatrians, quidquid eius contrarium fuerat
> intra me, vel occidit, vel expulit, vel ligavit.[10]

Suddenly, alas, descending like a flash of lightning from on high, a woman appeared, I do not know how, delighting me both in manners and appearance. How amazed I was at the sight of her! But my stupefaction ceased at the terror of the thunder that followed. For just as in our everyday experience the thunderclap instantaneously follows the flash, so, at the sight of the flame of this beauty, Love, terrible and imperious, held me. Raging like a Lord, driven from his fatherland, returning to his own soil after a long exile, he killed or expelled or bound whatever in me was opposed to him.

He goes on to say that Love killed his resolve that had kept him from women and songs about women, banished his meditations about things of Heaven and Earth, and bound his free will so that Love now ruled him in the way described in the *canzone* 'Amor, da che convien pur ch'io mi doglia'. He asks Love to give him the art to make his words carry his grief just as he feels it. He cannot stop this woman coming into his imagination and his soul paints her there in all her beauty and malice. When it is possessed by the desire coming from her eyes, it rages against itself for lighting the fire in which it burns. Her image within him drives him to where she is in fact. It may be snow travelling to the sun but he cannot do otherwise. He is then struck as though by lightning.

Così m'hai concio, Amore, in mezzo l'alpi,	Thus have you bound me, Love, amongst the Alps,
ne la valle del fiume	Within the river valley
lungo il qual sempre sopra me se' forte:	Along whose banks you hold me in your strength.
qui vivo e morto, come vuoi, mi palpi,	At your will you press me alive and dead
merzé del fiero lume	
che sfolgorando fa via a la morte.[11]	Thanks to the fierce light
	Which makes a flashing path for Death.

There is no one near who can listen to him. The lady is outside the jurisdiction of Love's court and will never feel his arrows. Then in the *congedo*, calling the poem his 'mountain song', he says the poem may see Florence and can tell his city, 'vota d'amore e nuda di pietate', that he can make war on her no longer because he is bound by such a chain he is no longer free to return.

Who is this lady? In a fourteenth-century life of Dante, it is said that she was a girl of the Casentino Alps who suffered from a goitre.[12] If Dante did fall in love with a flesh and blood girl, this would be all the more shocking to him when he had told Cino off for his affairs in two sonnets, one written on behalf of Moroello Malaspina.[13] The letter emphasizes, however, the inspiration as a vision, a woman like lightning on high, and both letter and poem recall several episodes in the *Vita Nuova*, especially the mention of rivers and their association with Love. The poem also possesses some of the erotic quality of the *rime petrose* and

230

yet its style, as has been pointed out, seems to go back to a much earlier period in Dante's writing, notably the two *canzoni* about Beatrice which were excluded from the *Vita Nuova*. This last resemblance is particularly interesting, because those earlier *canzoni* can be grouped with the poems of self-pity in the *Vita Nuova* that precede his discovery of the poetry of praise. In Chapter 17 I hope to show that the *montanina canzone* stands in the same relation to the writing of the *Commedia* as those poems did to the inspiration of 'Donne ch'avete'. C. G. Hardie, whose later dating for the *montanina canzone* I have followed here, has pointed out also the many resemblances between this poem and the appearance of Beatrice in the Earthly Paradise, not only the general ones of the lady beside the river, the thunder, the lightning, and Dante's fear and tears, but in 'detail and close verbal reminiscences'.[14] Therefore we may see in this poem the first working of the vision that finally turned into the reunion with Beatrice, a scene which in the *Purgatorio* is raised to a mountain top and does not, as in this case, take place in a valley surrounded by mountains. More than that, we can see in it a model of the way in which the *Commedia* itself was worked out: to get to the final form of the vision he had to go by the way of tears and grief, just as to make the lady of the *canzone* have pity on him and speak to him with love, he had to undergo a complete inner conversion. Even while writing the letter, he did not identify the lady of this vision with Beatrice. Beatrice will later upbraid him for not recognizing her in the visions she has sent him.

The *montanina canzone* may also be related to the writing of the *Commedia* in this way: though the identification of the lady of this *canzone* with Beatrice is not affected by whether the poem is dated to 1308 or 1311, an earlier date for the *canzone* would present a strong case for thinking that Dante left off the *Convivio* to begin the *Commedia* then. The earlier date, however, requires the hypothesis of a draft that was altered later to accommodate references such as the death of Clement V in 1314. Paul Renucci makes Dante begin this first draft even earlier, in 1304, to fit his identification of the *veltro* with Pope Benedict XI.[15] There is no evidence that such a draft ever existed, and nearly all the internal evidence from the poem points to the fact that it was conceived and designed as a whole down to very small details, and that the cantos were completed and issued in batches.

To go on the journey Dante needed guides. How he rediscovered Beatrice as one of these guides is discussed in Chapters 17 and 21. How he discovered Virgil as the other guide is included in the theme of Chapter 18. Yet another reason for adopting a later date for the start of work on the *Commedia* is the lack of characterization that is applied to Virgil in the many earlier references to him in the *Convivio* and in the *Monarchia*. In both these works Dante is more interested in Aeneas as a possible character rich in figurative significances, in the same way that he reveals his interest in Cato and St Peter. It may be, therefore, that in his first plans for the poem a far greater role was intended for Aeneas. This would fit with my suggestion that Dante carried round with him in his head the scattered themes of the proto-*Commedia*. This is quite different from saying he wrote substantial portions of the *Inferno* before and during Henry VII's campaign. All that he wrote down, apart from the passages in the *Convivio* and the *Monarchia* and the later *canzoni* I have noted as coming from the proto-*Commedia*, would more likely have been number patterns, geometrical and cosmological figures, and, perhaps, as was suggested in Chapter 10, sketches in *canzone* form for the description of the vision of the Trinity. The best evidence for a preliminary draft comes from the pattern of figures drawn from Ovid (see Appendix), but even this could well have existed largely as notes.[16] Dante could not gather these together until he had finally identified the three ladies who set in motion the action of the poem and until he had found the ideal guide to the infernal regions to whom these ladies could entrust their mission. The moment he recognized that the figure waiting to guide him was Virgil must have been like the moment when Goethe, hearing of the suicide of his friend Jerusalem, found all the scattered reflections of the two preceding years coming together to enable him to start *Werther*. 'At that instant the plan of *Werther* was found; the whole shot together from all directions, and became a solid mass, as the water in a vessel, which is just at the freezing point, is changed by the slightest shaking into ice.'[17]

The earliest independent mention of the *Inferno*, that of Francesco da Barberino dated to 1313–14, is generally taken as evidence for an earlier beginning for the *Commedia* on the grounds that Dante could hardly have reached Canto XIX, where he alludes to the death of Clement V (1314), in the space of twenty odd months if he began the poem, as I think, at the end of 1312. Such a view disregards the immense labour of preparation that preceded actual composition and which would have allowed the verse to flow spontaneously into the prepared mould. It also disregards the speed and efficiency in execution of a mind of genius once it has grasped the true aim of inspiration. Milton, it will be remembered, could compose a hundred lines and then reduce them to a third of that length, all in his head, in the course of one night and have them ready for dictation the next morning, saying to his daughters, 'Come and milk me'[18] — the same image incidentally, as we shall see, that Dante applied to his own processes of creation (see Chapter 17, p. 302). Dante had reached a new height in his technical command and was aware of it. The author of the *Ottimo Commento*, probably Andrea Lancia, who knew Dante, reports him as saying that the use of rhyme never prevented him from expressing exactly what he had in mind to say and, further, that he often made his rhyme words bear different meanings from those they had in other writers.[19] The implications of these remarks denote both speed in composition and a supreme confidence that he could alter the usage of the language with unquestioned authority.

Lionardo Bruni says that Dante withdrew from the imperial preparations for the siege of Florence in 1312, and one likely reason would be his desire to get on with the *Commedia*. This would not mean that he had lost his interest in politics, but that he had found a new and truer direction for himself. After the death of

The last years: Lucca, Verona, and Ravenna

Henry VII in 1313, much happened in Italian politics and abroad to concern Dante. In November 1314, only a few months after he had had Jacques de Molay and his Templar colleague, the preceptor of Normandy, burnt in Paris for publicly affirming the innocence of the Templar order, Philip the Fair of France died while out hunting. The throne of the empire was in dispute between Lewis of Bavaria and Frederick of Austria, and Can Grande was at the beginning of a brilliant military career that made him the most powerful force in Lombardy. Florence, which had escaped with such rejoicings from the threat of Henry VII, was in trouble from a new quarter. This was from the ferocious Ghibelline warlord, Uguccione della Faggiuola, to whom the Pisans had turned for help on the death of the emperor, granting him complete power short of the signory. He transformed the wilting Ghibelline fortunes by seizing the Guelph city of Lucca, thus threatening Florence on her north-western flank. Dante would appear to have been in Lucca after Uguccione's seizure of it in June 1314, and it may have been at this time that he received the hospitality of the lady called Gentucca, mentioned in *Purgatorio* XXIV by her fellow citizen Bonagiunta. The Florentines were extremely anxious, and when, in the summer of 1315, Uguccione laid siege to Montecatini, they begged for help from Robert of Anjou, who sent his brother, the prince of Taranto, with 500 men-at-arms.

In the campaign later that summer the Florentines received their worst military defeat since Montaperti. In the battle of Montecatini on 29 August 1315, Uguccione, his Pisan troops augmented by Lombard Ghibellines and Florentine exiles, together with a large corps of German cavalry who still remained from Henry VII's army, totally routed the Florentines and their Angevin allies. Thousands of Florentines died and the city was in great danger, although what its rulers must have feared most, a repetition of the events that followed Montaperti, when the Ghibellines took over the government of Florence, did not come about.

One result of their fears was another decree against Florentine exiles. Dante had earlier been excluded from the decree of 2 September 1311, known as the Riforma di Messer Baldo d'Aguglione,[20] granting an amnesty to other exiles during Henry VII's campaigns. Now, by a decree of 6 November 1315, he and his sons were named with others as Ghibelline traitors and condemned, if caught, to have their heads struck from their shoulders at the place of public execution.[21] In the following year the Florentines obviously thought better of their threats, and Count Guido of Battifolle, Robert of Anjou's vicar in Florence, issued an amnesty under which the exiles could return home if they underwent a humiliating ceremony. They were to wear mitres inscribed with their crimes and to walk in procession to the baptistery, where they would present themselves as oblates to St John the Baptist. They were also to pay a fine. Several exiles did swallow their pride and accept, but Dante, exploding with scorn, rejected the offer in a letter addressed to someone in the city, perhaps his brother-in-law, the priest Teruccio di Manetto Donati, brother of Gemma. He says that if he may not come back to Florence on honourable terms, then he will never return:

> Non est haec via redeundi ad patriam, Pater mi; sed si alia per vos antecedenter, deinde per alios invenitur, quae famae Dantisque honori non deroget, illam non lentis passibus acceptabo. Quod si per nullam talem Florentia introitur, nunquam Florentiam introibo. Quidni? nonne solis astrorumque specula ubique conspiciam? Nonne dulcissimas veritates potero speculari ubique sub coelo, ni prius inglorium, immo ignominiosum, populo Florentino, civitati me reddam? Quippe nec panis deficiet.[22]

> This is not the path by which I will return to my native city, Father. If some other can be found . . . which does not detract from the fame and honour of Dante, I will accept it with eager steps. But if Florence may not be entered in such a way, then I will never enter Florence again. Can I not gaze upon the face of the sun and the stars anywhere? Can I not contemplate the sweetest truths anywhere under Heaven unless I first return to the city, exposed to abasement and indeed to ignominy before the people of Florence? Rest assured, I will not want for bread!

Uguccione could not have provided a refuge long for Dante because, in the following year, he was stripped of his power and driven into exile at the court of Can Grande della Scala by the rebellion of Castruccio Castracane. Castruccio continued for a long period to threaten and torment Florence, but Dante's remaining years would appear to have been spent on the eastern side of the Apennines and in Lombardy. One of the great attractions for him there was his close and stormy friendship with Can Grande della Scala.

Dante had known Verona since his first refuge in his exile with *il gran Lombardo*,[23] Bartolomeo della Scala. In 1303 Can Grande, Bartolomeo's brother, was eleven years old and Dante was thirty-seven. Can Grande shared the signory of Verona with his brother Alboino from 1308, and in 1311 they were jointly made imperial vicars by Henry VII, an important step in the legitimation of a dynasty that had arisen quite recently from unimpressive origins. Alboino died in October 1311, and Can Grande became the sole ruler of the city when he was only twenty.

He was a brilliant general and a fierce soldier, seizing and, in the course of a short life, adding Vicenza, Padua, Cremona, Mantua, and Treviso to his territories. His military career, up to 1320, when he suffered a reverse at Padua, was one of uninterrupted victory. He was tall, handsome, and extremely clever. He lived in a style that had not been seen on the peninsula since the time of Frederick II and it was his policy to shelter and entertain all the most talented and interesting exiles in Italy. It must have been a strange friendship between the poet, strained with his labours and suffering, who was fifty-two in 1317, and this golden hero of twenty-six. Self-interest explains part of the attraction on both sides. At Verona, Dante found lodging, food, and congenial company among both the other exiles welcomed there and the courtiers, who included Benzo d'Alessandria, Can Grande's chancellor (from 1320) and a noted humanist.[24] Can Grande would have valued him not only as an experienced diplomat and publicist, but also as the greatest poet of his day, whose praise would extend the fame of his court and deeds and help to lay the foundations for his acceptance as the monarch of a united Italy. There was obviously more to the friendship than this because it survived the strains which the differences in their positions and age imposed on it.

Dante was still waiting for the deliverers signified in the *Commedia* as the *veltro* and the DXV. These two symbols may or may not stand for the same person. The interpretation followed in Chapter 16 takes the *veltro* as the spiritual leader and the DXV as the monarch or emperor deliverer. This fits best with Dante's view of the necessity of the division of the powers set out already in the *Monarchia* and emphasized throughout the *Commedia* and also with the symbolism of the cross and the eagle in that work.

Although the puns on the odd name Can-*cane*-dog with the image of the hunting dog, the *veltro*, and the similarity of his name with the Mongol title of 'khan' and its association with Prester John, have suggested to many that Can Grande is signified by the *veltro*, Can Grande is excluded from being a spiritual deliverer. Also, if the phrase 'e sua nazion sarà tra feltro e feltro'[25] points to a deliverer born like Dante between the two felt caps of the Gemini,[26] then Can Grande is excluded because he was born in March under Pisces. On the other hand Dante may have regarded him as a possible vehicle for the prophecy of the DXV. The canting device of the Scaliger arms, a ladder leading to the imperial eagle, revealed the ultimate aim of the dynasty. Dante had already defined some characteristics of the DXV in the *Monarchia*:

Cum ergo Monarcha nullam cupiditatis occasionem habere possit vel saltem minimam inter mortales, ut superius est ostensum, quod ceteris principibus non contingit, et cupiditas ipsa sola sit corruptiva iudicii et iustitie prepeditiva, consequens est quod ipse vel omnino vel maxime bene dispositus ad regendum esse potest, quia inter ceteros iudicium et iustitiam potissime habere potest.[27]

Since the Monarch, then, can have no cause for cupidity (or, of all men, has the least cause for it, as we have already shown), and in this differs from other princes, and since cupidity alone perverts the judgment and compels justice, it follows that the Monarch is in a perfect—or at least the best possible—condition for governing, because he surpasses all others in the power of his judgment and justice.

Power, exile, and the works of Dante's middle years

Something of these qualities, especially the freedom from cupidity, which was noted by other contemporaries about the young ruler,[28] are suggested in Cacciaguida's prophetic praise of Can Grande in these lines:

ma pria che 'l Guasco l'alto Arrigo inganni,
parran faville de la sua virtute
in non curar d' argento né d'affanni.
Le sue magnificenze conosciute
saranno ancora, si che ' suoi nemici
non ne potran tener le lingue mute.
A lui t'aspetta e a' suoi benefici;
per lui fia trasmutata molta gente,
cambiando condizion ricchi e mendici;[29]

Before
The Gascon's guile great Harry have cajoled,
Some sparkles of his virtue shall be shown
In grudging not laborious days nor gold.
Later, shall his magnificence be known,
So that his enemies will not repress
Their tongues from telling what things he hath done.
Look to him; wait his gracious offices!
Through him shall many taste an altered lot,
The beggar and the rich exchanging place.

The bitter experience, though, of his false prophecy of the fate of Florence would have made Dante more than ever wary of committing himself to a positive identification, especially when such an identification, if proved false, might call into question the whole authority and allegorical significance of the *Commedia*. All he was given for the prophecy was a vision and some numerological symbolism, and he had to wait for events to give a name and a character to the deliverer. In the meantime he could wait, with the pleasure of watching Can Grande's precocious brilliance unfold before him.

Can Grande was the greatest patron of the arts in Italy in his day. He was a notable builder of fortresses and churches, he brought Giotto to Verona to paint for him, and he devoted much of his phenomenal energy to ensuring that his court and his courtiers, in the festivities and tournaments that celebrated his frequent victories, presented the most dazzling spectacles in splendour of dress and accoutrements. He would have found a fellow lover of the arts in Dante and would have appreciated the poet's wit and sophisticated conversation, and his experience of men and politics. The rarest experience that Dante possessed, and one that must have contributed to the sympathy between the two men, was that Dante had known what it was like to rule a sovereign state, the peculiar loneliness of high offices and its traps, the temptations of power and the importance of knowing whom and what to trust. Dante had only held such a position for two months as prior of Florence and had shared the responsibility with others. Nevertheless he had been forcibly isolated from the world as a condition of the office, treated as a prince with his fellow priors, and had ruled the most important city in Europe. In return for the elevations and the honours, he had had the task of defying Boniface VIII and of exiling his greatest friend in what had seemed to be the interests of Florence. He could not presume on his short space of office to claim equality of rank with Can Grande, but he could offer the understanding that derived from equality of experience.

On both sides, therefore, there is much to explain how their friendship and respect survived the strains that led to Dante's departure. Can Grande was, in many ways, an admirable and tactful host to the exiles he harboured. He provided them with apartments decorated according to their pursuits: a triumph for soldiers, groves of the Muses for poets, Mercury for artists, Paradise for theologians, and for everyone the device of inconstant Fortune.[30] They all had servants and meals appointed them and Dante was one of those frequently invited to Can Grande's own table. Even prisoners of note were well cared for. Albertino Mussato, the Paduan poet and patriot captured at Vicenza, admits this of his captivity at Verona[31] and he also says that Can Grande wished to be thought crueller than was his nature. He describes him as sharp, intractable, and wanting in self-control, characteristics not surprising in a young ruler accustomed only to success, but ones that, when allied to a streak of coarseness evident in many anecdotes about him, would explain the breach between him and Dante.

Petrarch describes some incidents that led to this split. The court was full of jesters and buffoons; Can Grande, as a great warlord, had to entertain his soldiers and he shared their roughest pleasures. That Dante could look after himself in this atmosphere is shown by the following anecdote. On one occasion a jester received great applause for his dirty jokes and mime. Can Grande, noticing that Dante disliked this performance, said to him, 'I wonder why this stupid fellow knows how to please everyone when you, who are meant to be so wise, can't please them at all.' Dante replied, 'You wouldn't wonder if you knew that friendship is founded on similarity of habits and disposition.'[32] An apocryphal story, much older in its origins than the time of Dante, tells how a practical joke was played on Dante: a boy was hidden under the table to collect the bones thrown down by the guests. He heaped them about Dante's feet and when the table was removed there was revealed the ridiculous spectacle of the poet sitting with a pile of bones at his feet. Can Grande innocently remarked, 'Dante certainly eats a great deal of meat', and Dante replied, 'My Lord, if I had been a dog (a pun on Can Grande's name) you wouldn't have seen so many bones', implying that Can Grande actually ground up the bones as he gnawed them.[33] Though this last story is untrue, Petrarch's evidence is enough to show that the humour was too rough on one side and the retorts too savage on the other. Dante left Verona, probably in 1317, preferring to retain his respect for Can Grande from a distance, repaying him for his many kindnesses with the dedication of the *Paradiso*, in which he is praised so nobly, and with a letter in which he justifies himself for speaking of him as his friend.[34] The connexion between them was not forgotten even when both were dead; phrases from Cacciaguida's speech were translated into Latin and incorporated into the epitaph on Can Grande's tomb, on which he still rides, sword in hand, his helm thrust back on his shoulders, smiling at Death.

According to Boccaccio,[35] Dante was in desperate straits, wandering in the Romagna, when news of his condition reached another ruler, the cultivated lord of Ravenna, Guido Novello da Polenta. Guido sent a message inviting Dante to his city and Dante gratefully accepted. He had probably by this time completed all the *Inferno* and most of the *Purgatorio*, and he left mountainous Tuscany and hilly Verona for the flat plain of the Romagna beside the Adriatic, where the most conspicuous sights are the sky and the play of clouds and light. In Ravenna, where the last emperor of the West had taken refuge and Theodoric, the murderer of Boethius, was buried, he found the energy and the congenial society that enabled him to complete the most difficult and arduous part of the *Commedia*, the *Paradiso*. Every stone and road had some significance that fed back into his writing. The experience of walking in the Pineta, the great forest of pines — then of vast extent and still today an enchanted place with its rides of bright grass, its long plates of water and its interspersed lines of poplars, their leaves brown and purple in spring — enriched and renewed the vision of the Earthly Paradise. The Rubicon, cutting the road to Rimini, lay a few miles south. The funerary stelae of Roman admirals and shipbuilders recalled the role of Classis as the imperial naval base, and the remains of the Ostrogothic kingdom and the Byzantine exarchate sparkled and glinted with the myriad colours of the mosaics that offered a different impression according to the weather and the position of the sun, on whose movements Dante had become such an expert.

In Ravenna Dante was joined by his sons Pietro and Jacopo and by his daughter, Antonia, who was to take the veil in the convent of Santo Stefano delli Ulivi as Sister Beatrice — an obvious tribute to her father's source of inspiration. Dante may also have been joined there by his wife.[36] After their father's death both Pietro and Jacopo were to write commentaries on the *Commedia*. Jacopo's work is confined to the *Inferno* and is of lesser interest in comparison with that of Pietro, who was a man of considerable learning and had a successful career as a judge in Verona. Pietro's immense commentary covers the whole poem and is, of course, of prime importance for the information in it that may have come directly from his father.

In Guido Novello, Dante must have found a congenial host, someone of his own age and a fellow poet in the vernacular.[37] Guido was a nephew of Francesca da Rimini, and his family had ruled Ravenna since 1270. They were Guelphs, and the fact that Dante could take refuge with them reflects the changes wrought by time in the old traditional loyalties rather than any relaxation of Dante's personal beliefs. He may have supported himself there by teaching and lecturing on vernacular poetry: this is what Boccaccio says.[38] Two of his Florentine friends were living there at the same time, Dino Perini, who was apparently also a teacher, and the physician Fiduccio de' Milotti. Dante appears to have corresponded with the astrologer poet, Cecco d'Ascoli, who refers to this in his poem *L'Acerba*. Dante wanted to know how twins who he knew had been brought up separately could turn out completely different in character, when according to Cecco's determinist theories, they should be exactly the same.[39]

Dante still travelled but returned always to Ravenna as his base. In 1320 he was in Verona again and on 20 January he gave a lecture on a subject that had recently been discussed in Mantua. The question was: 'Whether water, in its own sphere, that is in its natural circumference, was in any part higher than the Earth which emerges from the waters and which we call the habitable quarter.' It is a dry little work, except for a dig at those Veronese clergy who, 'burning with excess of charity, will not accept the invitations of others, and who, in the virtue of humility, poor pensioners of the Holy Spirit, lest they should seem to endorse the excellence of others, refuse to be present at their discourses'.[40] Dante set out to prove that water is not higher than exposed or habitable ground and the authority with which he marshals his arguments reflects the labour and dreaming that had gone into the geographical and cosmological basis of the *Commedia*. The demands of the great poem had almost by accident turned him into an expert in many fields, capable of standing up to an audience of doctors in the learned city of Verona.

Another correspondent caused him at first great surprise and then great pleasure. This was Giovanni del Virgilio, a professor at Bologna and 'an ardent disciple of the great Paduan school of Latin poetry, of which Lovato was the founder and Mussato the chief ornament'.[41] Early in 1319 he sent a Latin poem to Dante, an eclogue praising the *Commedia* but chiding him for writing in the vernacular on subjects which are only suitable for the educated and which therefore should be dealt with in Latin. He suggested new themes for Latin poems to Dante, among them the death of Henry VII and Uguccione's victory at Montecatini, and he invited Dante to Bologna to receive the laurel crown. He ends, probably wisely, hoping that Dante will not be annoyed by the goose cackling at the swan.[42]

Dante took the poem in remarkably good humour, especially if we consider that it called into question the basis of his life's work. It tempted him, however, with the one temptation he could never resist: a technical challenge. He responded with an eclogue with the same number of lines as Giovanni's, in which Giovanni and Dante's circle are presented as shepherds. Dante is called Tityrus, Giovanni is Mopsus, Perini is Meliboeus, and Guido Novello is Iolas. Under the device of conversing with Perini, Dante gives his answers to Giovanni. He declines to come to Bologna because his ambition is still to receive the bays in Florence when he has finished the *Paradiso*. To win his correspondent over to a better opinion of the vernacular, he sends ten measures of milk from his best loved ewe, generally interpreted as meaning ten cantos of the *Paradiso*.[43]

Giovanni del Virgilio was delighted and, taking up the pastoral theme, he addressed Dante as a reincarnation of Virgil and begged him nevertheless to

239

come to Bologna. Dante's reply only came to him some time later, sent on by the poet's heirs after his death in September 1321.

The pleasant atmosphere that these poems suggest as being typical of Dante's years in Ravenna was interrupted by a political danger that threatened both the city and Guido Novello. A dispute with Venice had broken out in the summer of 1321; Venetian sailors and sailors from Ravenna had had a fight, in which the Venetians were beaten. The doge, Giovanni Soranzo, and the tyrant of Forlì made an alliance to exterminate Ravenna, securing the support of all Guido's neighbouring rulers. Guido sent Dante with other envoys on the urgent mission to Venice to make peace. Filippo Villani tells the extraordinary story that the Venetians were so frightened of Dante's powers as an orator that they refused to let him address them and, more than that, refused to let him return to Ravenna by sea because his eloquence might turn the Venetian admiral from his duty.[44] The story is probably quite untrue and Dante returned to Ravenna to discuss the terms that were settled by a second embassy to Venice. On the way back, coming back by land across the marshes, he seems to have caught malaria. On 14 September he died.

His head was crowned with laurels and his body, dressed in the robe of a poet and philosopher, was carried to the Franciscan church, beside which it now lies in its later tomb. Guido Novello delivered the funeral oration and planned to make a splendid tomb for the poet. Giovanni del Virgilio wrote an epitaph, but this was never used, because Guido Novello was shortly driven permanently from power by a cousin and the tomb he planned was not built. The epitaph now on the sarcophagus is sometimes ascribed to Dante himself. The sarcophagus was supplied by Bernardo Bembo, father of Cardinal Bembo, who in 1483 commissioned Pietro Lombardi to build a chapel for Dante's tomb. Pietro Lombardi also carved the noble bas-relief of the poet. The Florentines made many attempts from the early fifteenth century onwards to bring the bones of their greatest citizen back to Florence Michelangelo was eager to construct a magnificent tomb in Florence for Dante, and in 1519 emissaries, armed with authority from Pope Leo X, arrived in Ravenna to seize Dante's remains. On opening the tomb they found it empty. Apparently the bones had been removed by the friars of San Francesco, who replaced them once the danger had passed. The bones were removed again and hidden in 1677 during a dispute between the government of Ravenna and the friars over the question of the immunity of the chapel or mausoleum containing the tomb. They were rediscovered only in 1865 during repairs made to an adjoining chapel and restored to the sarcophagus which now stands in the charming small neo-classical temple built for Cardinal Valenti Gonzaga by Morigia in 1780, which incorporates the earlier work of Pietro Lombardi.

The strange fortunes of his mortal remains recalls a story told by Boccaccio of the last cantos of the *Paradiso*. According to this story, which Boccaccio learned from Piero di Giardino, a citizen of Ravenna and a friend of Dante[45], the last thirteen cantos of the *Paradiso* could not be found on Dante's death. His sons

Pietro and Jacopo were persuaded by friends to complete the poem. Jacopo showed more enthusiasm for the task but was stopped when, eight months after his father's death, he had a dream. The dream was shortly before matins (two o'clock in the morning) and in it Dante, wearing white and with an unaccustomed light in his face, appeared to him. Jacopo asked his father if he were alive and his father said, 'Yes, but of the true life, not of ours.' Then he asked him if he had finished the poem and, if so, where the missing part was. Dante in the dream led his son to the room he had used as a bedroom in life and, touching the wall, pointed it out as the place where he should look. Jacopo woke up, fetched Piero di Giardino, and went to the bedroom, which was in another house. At the place indicated in the dream they found a mat fixed to the wall. On removing the mat, they found a manuscript coated with mould from the damp wall and, on brushing the mould off, they discovered the missing thirteen cantos. They were overjoyed and, copying them out, sent them to Can Grande, following the habit of Dante, who had published the other cantos in this way.

The story is not impossible; the dream may have been the only way in which Jacopo's memory could recall seemingly unimportant details of his father's habits and surroundings. Dante, arriving back at Ravenna exhausted after his journey and in a high fever, might not have been in a state to point out where the manuscript lay. The story also complements and rounds off the series of dreams and visions, from the premonitory dream of his mother when she was pregnant, to the dreams and images that, as we have seen, characterized and inspired his work from its earliest stages, and on to the great vision whose origin and form we must now consider, the inspiration of the *Commedia*.

PART III

THE MAKING OF
THE *COMMEDIA*

15
The journey

Mandelstam describes the *Commedia* as a single crystal with 13,000 facets[1] —each line reflecting the essential unity out of which the poem was made. It is an image to bear in mind as a reminder of that unity as, in the chapters that follow, we consider, in order, the possible sources of the cosmology and the historiography of the poem, and the way it was planned, the nature of Dante's inspirations, how he interpreted those inspirations, his imagery, the characters of the poem, and finally the nature of his vision and the effect on our civilization of its expression. First, in keeping with Dante's own injunction to begin with the literal meaning, we describe the story of the *Commedia*—a description that those already familiar with the poem may easily skip but that may be of use to other readers.

Inferno

The poem begins in Holy Week 1300 and opens with the celebrated lines:

Nel mezzo del cammin di nostra vita
  mi ritrovai per una selva oscura,
  che la diritta via era smarrita.
Ahi quanto a dir qual era è cosa dura
  esta selva selvaggia e aspra e forte
  che nel pensier rinova la paura!
Tant' è amara che poco è più morte;
  ma per trattar del ben ch'i' vi trovai,
  dirò de l'altre cose ch'i' v'ho scorte.[2]

Midway life's journey I was made aware
  That I had strayed into a dark forest,
  And the right path appeared not
    anywhere.
Ah, tongue cannot describe how it
    oppressed,
  This wood, so harsh, dismal and wild,
    that fear
  At thought of it strikes now into my
    breast.
So bitter it is, death is scarce bitterer.
  But, for the good it was my hap to find,
  I speak of the other things that I saw
    there.

Dante says that he has no knowledge of how he entered that dreadful wood, but on issuing from it he saw a hill, struck by the rays of the sun, which he tried to climb. As he travelled towards it, a spotted leopard appeared and kept on getting in his way. Suddenly a raging, hungry lion, its head raised high, came towards him, followed by a lean and famished she-wolf. The she-wolf drove him down and back towards the wood, 'where the sun is silent'. Suddenly a man appeared in front of him. Seeing him in that great desert, Dante appealed to him whether he was a shade or a living man. The apparition answers:

'Non omo, omo già fui,
  e li parenti miei furon lombardi,
  mantoani per patrïa ambedui.
Nacqui *sub Iulio*, ancor che fosse tardi,
  e vissi a Roma sotto 'l buono Augusto
  nel tempo de li dèi falsi e bugiardi.
Poeta fui, e cantai di quel giusto
  figliuol d'Anchise che venne di Troia,
  poi che 'l superbo Ilïón fu combusto.'[3]

'Not man; man once I was.
  My parents both were of the Lombard name,
  Of Mantua by their country and by their race.
Sub Julio was I born, though late I came:
  In Rome the good Augustus on me shone,
  In the time of the false Gods of lying fame.
Poet was I, and sang of that just son
  Of old Anchises, who came out from Troy
  After the burning of proud Ilion.'

thus identifying himself, through periphrasis, as the poet Virgil. He asks Dante why he does not climb the delectable mountain and Dante, covered in shame, after acknowledging his debt as a poet to Virgil, points to the she-wolf that prevents his ascent. Virgil tells him he must go by another way because of the vicious and insatiable nature of the wolf, whose career will last until the *veltro* or hound comes to kill her and thrust her back to Hell. The *veltro*, who feeds on wisdom, love, and virtue, will be the salvation of Italy. Dante never directly explained what the three beasts and the *veltro* mean, though they are linked by symbolism and recurring imagery to the form of the poem as a whole. It will become clear, though, that they have a political and historical meaning, a moral and ethical meaning, and a psychological and mystical meaning. Virgil now tells him of the journey he must make to the tormented spirits, then to those who are happy in the fire through which they will join the blessed, and lastly to the blessed, with whom Dante will find a worthier soul as a guide. Virgil himself cannot enter the city of the blessed.

The pair now set out. It is the evening and Dante calls on the Muses to restore his memory of the journey.

O Muse, o alto ingegno, or m'aiutate;
  o mente che scrivesti ciò ch'io vidi,
  qui si parrà la tua nobilitate.[4]

O Muses, O high Genius, strengthen me!
  O Memory, that what I saw hast writ,
  Here shall be made known thine integrity.

The journey

He asks why he, totally unworthy, should be called upon to make the journey that Aeneas, the father of Rome, and St Paul, the bringer of the faith to Rome had made. Virgil rebukes him for faintheartedness and then describes how a heavenly lady descended to him where he was in Limbo, and made a piercing and eloquent plea that he should go to the help of her friend, who was close to perdition. She revealed her identity as Beatrìce and explained, in answer to Virgil's request, why she made this descent. A gracious lady in Heaven (the Blessed Virgin Mary, though unnamed) had pity on Dante and called on Lucia, the enemy of all cruelty, to help her devotee. Lucia came to where Beatrice sat with Rachel and urged her to go to Dante's assistance. Thus Dante's journey is willed in Heaven and Virgil berates him for cowardice:

'Dunque: che è? perché, perché restai,
  perché tanta viltà nel core allette,
  perché ardire e franchezza non hai,
poscia che tai tre donne benedette
  curan di te ne la corte del cielo,
  e 'l mio parlar tanto ben ti promette?'[5]

'What is it, then, keeps thee? Why, why haltest cold?
  Why in thy heart nourishest fear so base?
  Why art thou not delivered, eager, bold,
When three such blessed Ladies of their grace
  Care in the court of Heaven for thy plight,
  And my words promise thee such good to embrace?'

Fired and encouraged Dante submits with the acknowledgment:

'Or va, ch'un sol volere è d'ambedue:
  tu duca, tu segnore e tu maestro.'[6]

'Now it is one will moves us both; thou art Guide, master, lord!'

Over the gate of Hell Dante reads this adamantine inscription:

PER ME SI VA NE LA CITTA DOLENTE,
  PER ME SI VA NE L'ETTERNO DOLORE,
  PER ME SI VA TRA LA PERDUTA GENTE.
GIUSTIZIA MOSSE IL MIO ALTO FATTORE;
  FECEMI LA DIVINA PODESTATE,
  LA SOMMA SAPÏENZA E 'L PRIMO AMORE.
DINANZI A ME NON FUOR COSE CREATE
  SE NON ETTERNE, IO ETTERNO DURO.

THROUGH ME THE WAY IS TO THE CITY OF WOE:
  THROUGH ME THE WAY INTO THE ETERNAL PAIN;
  THROUGH ME THE WAY AMONG THE LOST BELOW.
RIGHTEOUSNESS DID MY MAKER ON HIGH CONSTRAIN.
  ME DID DIVINE AUTHORITY UPREAR;
  ME SUPREME WISDOM AND PRIMAL LOVE SUSTAIN.
BEFORE I WAS, NO THINGS CREATED WERE
  SAVE THE ETERNAL, AND I ETERNAL ABIDE.

LASCIATE OGNE SPERANZA, VOI
CH'INTRATE.[7]

RELINQUISH ALL HOPE, YE WHO
ENTER HERE.

and, passing through the gate, he finds himself in the vestibule for those who lived without infamy and without praise. Dante weeps at the terrible sounds swirling around him like a sandstorm. None of the souls he sees is named and Virgil takes him to the bank of the first river of Hell, Acheron, where the first of the guardians drawn from classical mythology, Charon, is forced to carry Dante across. Dante crosses in a state of unconsciousness because he has fainted at a wind flashing with red light and he wakes on the other side, where he is in Limbo, the place assigned to the good who were never baptized. Passing through a wood thronged with these pathetic souls, men, women, and children, Dante sees a fire making a hemisphere of light in the dark. This is the light of natural reason. Four poets, Homer, Horace, Ovid, and Lucan come to greet the returning Virgil and to make Dante a sixth of their company. Walking towards the light they all enter a castle ringed with seven walls and within, on a green plain, he sees great spirits of antiquity and of Islam. In speaking of this sight, he says he exults within at having seen them and a great catalogue of their names follows, in which his sense of glory imparts a triumphal triple rhythm to the recital of names:

I' vidi Eletra con molti compagni,
  tra' quai conobbi Ettòr ed Enea,
Cesare armato con li occhi grifagni.
Vidi Cammilla e la Pantasilea;
  da l'altra parte vidi 'l re Latino
che con Lavina sua figlia sedea.
Vidi quel Bruto che cacciò Tarquino,
  Lucrezia, Iulia, Marzïa e Corniglia;
e solo, in parte, vidi 'l Saladino.[8]

I saw Electra in a great company
  Among whom Hector and Aeneas were,
  And armèd Caesar with the falcon eye.
I saw Camilla and Penthesilea there
  Over against them, and the Latin
    King;
  Lavinia his daughter sitting near;
That Brutus who drove out the proud
    Tarquin;
  Lucrece, Cornelia, Julia, Marcïa, four
  Together, and by himself the Saladin.

Leaving the light of Limbo, the first circle, they descend to the darkness of the second where they pass Minos, the second guardian, who assigns to the damned the depth of Hell to which they must go. Here they come upon the lovers who submitted their reason to desire, carried on a whirlwind which roars like the sea in a storm. Virgil names some of the souls carried through the air, Semiramis, Dido, Cleopatra, Helen, Paris, and Tristan among them, but Dante is most interested in a pair who turn out to be Francesca da Rimini and Paolo. So overcome is he by pity at Francesca's story that he faints once more. Then the pair continue to the third circle, passing the third guardian, Cerberus, and finding the Florentine glutton Ciacco, pounded by black rain, who gives him the first of many warnings he will receive of the defeat of the White party. In the fourth circle they pass the clucking wolf, Pluto, and see the prodigal and avaricious pushing weights against one another. Coming upon the angry fighting one another in a slough, they reach a watch-tower from whose summit flames signal to another tower in the dim distance. This signal brings the ferryman of the river Styx, Phlegyas, who is to carry them to the entrance of the city of Dis. While Dante is in the boat, he is addressed by the soul of the Florentine Filippo Argenti. Up to this time Dante has expressed nothing but pity and horror at the sufferings of the damned but here he berates Filippo, who is set upon by the other souls. Virgil blesses Dante for this rejection, which announces a great change in the mood of the poem. So far they have passed through the five circles of the sins of incontinence, the sins of the leopard, but, beyond the iron walls of Dis with its ruddy mosques, lie the sins of the lion and of the wolf. Disembarking before the gate of Dis they find entrance denied to them by the Furies and by thousands of fallen angels. The Furies threaten to turn Dante to stone with the sight of Medusa. Virgil is powerless before their opposition and, though he comforts Dante by saying divine help will come, he too is obviously afraid. This episode is the most dramatic and frightening part of the *Inferno*, as the serpent-haired Furies scream threats from the iron ramparts and throngs of demons look down on the bewildered travellers. Virgil covers Dante's eyes with his hands to guard him from the Gorgon but suddenly releases him to watch the amazing sight coming across the Styx.

Come le rane innanzi a la nimica
  biscia per l'acqua si dileguan tutte,
  fin ch'a la terra ciascuna s'abbica,
vid' io più di mille anime distrutte
  fuggir così dinanzi ad un ch'al passo
  passava Stige con le piante asciutte.
Dal volto rimovea quell' aere grasso,
  menando la sinistra innanzi spesso;
  e sol di quell' angoscia parea lasso.
Ben m'accorsi ch'elli era da ciel messo,
  e volsimi al maestro; e quei fé segno
  ch'i' stessi queto ed inchinassi ad esso.
Ahi quanto mi parea pien di disdegno!
  Venne a la porta e con una verghetta
  l'aperse, che non v'ebbe alcun ritegno.[9]

As frogs before their enemy the snake
  Run through the water, scattered at
    his threat,
  Till each squats on the bottom, there to
    quake,
So saw I thousand ruined spirits set
  In flight before one, who at easy pace
  Came and passed over Styx with soles
    unwet.
He waved the gross fumes from before
    his face,
  Moving often his left hand as he went,
  And only of that annoyance showed
    he trace.
Well did I know that he from Heaven
    was sent,
  And turned to the Master, and he
    signed his will
  That I should stand all quiet with head
    down-bent.
Ah, with what scorn his countenance
    seemed to fill!
  He came to the gate, and with a wand
    he held
  Set it wide open, unresisted still.

All opposition collapses before the messenger of Heaven, who departs without a word to the travellers. They are now able to pass into the city and find tombs of the heretics. Here Dante meets the great Ghibelline leader Farinata degli Uberti, who shares his torment with the father of Guido Cavalcanti. Their great and terrible dialogue again connects Dante's fate with the past and future of Florence. To get to the seventh circle of the murderers and tyrants they have to climb down a great scree of rocks that fell in the earthquake at the time of the crucifixion. The circle of the violent is divided into river, wood and plain. The river of blood, Phlegethon, is for the violent against others, the wood is for the violent against themselves, the suicides, and the plain is for the violent against God and nature, the sodomites and usurers. Guided by the centaur, Nessus, past the tyrants and murderers in the river of blood, they pass through the wood of the suicides where Pier della Vigne, the chancellor of Frederick II, bewails his fate. On they move to a plain of burning sand where the sight of a red stream causes Virgil to explain the origin of the rivers of Hell.

Inside a mountain on Crete there stands a great statue of an old man, his back to Damietta in Egypt, his face to Rome; he is made of gold for his head, silver for his arms and chest, brass down to his crotch, and iron for his legs, but clay for his right foot. From his silver part downwards he is split by a fissure that weeps tears, the product of human sin, feeding the rivers of Hell, down from Acheron, to Styx, to Phlegethon and then by this stream to Cocytus. This is another of the symbolic mysteries of the poem, whose mood once more changes in the pathetic and deeply personal scenes of Dante's reunion with Brunetto Latini and then with three noble Florentines. Now they come to the edge of the abyss where, on Virgil's instructions, Dante unlooses his girdle with which he had once hoped to catch the leopard; Virgil takes it and casts it down into the darkness. It attracts the monster Geryon who flies up to hover on the edge of the abyss. Virgil negotiates with Geryon, while Dante is sent off to see some usurers. He returns and, after a terrifying descent spiralling down on the back of Geryon, they dismount into the eighth circle, that of Malebolge, with its ten divisions for various kinds of fraud forming moats like those round a concentric castle. Geryon is the only means of travelling from the sins of violence, the sins of the lion, to the sins of fraud, the sins of the she-wolf. Once alighted they pass the panders, the flatterers sunk in human excrement, the simoniac popes, and the weird sight of the soothsayers with their heads twisted round so their tears fall on their buttocks. After a narrow escape from the demons who torment the barrators in a lake of pitch, they come upon the hypocrites, who wear leaden cloaks painted gold. In the snake-pit of the thieves they watch the bitter transformations of those who no longer command their own physical shape. Among the givers of false counsel swathed in flame, they find Ulysses and Guido da Montefeltro and, when they have looked on the sowers of discord hamstrung by demons and the falsifiers of the last bolgia, they come upon another cliff edge, ringed by the giants who stand with their feet in Cocytus and their bodies above the level of Malebolge.

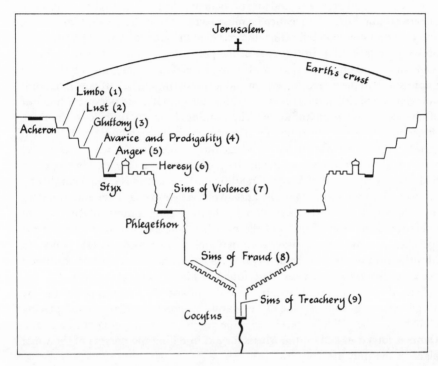

Figure 9 Cross-section of Hell

From the circles of the violent to the circles of Malebolge, a division marked by Geryon's cliff, there is a sharp change in the mood and nature of the poetry. The change is characterized both by the differences in the landscape and in Dante's attitude to the souls he meets. Above the cliff the environs of the sinners still retain some characteristics of human creative endeavour, however perverted: the walls and mosques of Dis make a city, however corrupt; the heated sarcophagi of the heretics recall the great cemeteries of Roman civilized settlements; the dykes across the burning plain are resembled to the dykes of the Flemings and the Paduans; and Dante meets enough noble and pathetic souls to make the journey endurable. In Malebolge, the bare craggy rock sinking into ditches varied with nothing more congenial than boiling pitch or stercoraceous crystals of ordure form a monotonous and repellent background for the armies of naked souls, whose bodies are besmirched, lacerated, cooked, hamstrung, transmogrified, or smitten with pestilence. They suffer within the hideous cachinnation of Hell's mouth, and the characteristic quality of the poetry that describes them exists in a peculiar tension set up in Dante during what must have been the appalling suffering he underwent during the writing of these passages, as he was forced by his theme and his inspiration to visualize these episodes. This tension is between a sardonic humour, visceral, grotesque,

251

vituperative, and mordant, and an ambivalent attitude to the active vengeance he sees around him, a vengeance he must ascribe to the divine wisdom, power, and love that created Hell. The tension is held in balance by what becomes the only sane relationship in this part of the poem, Dante's attachment to Virgil whose intrepid, discriminative, and loving care of his pupil grows all the more impressively in the increasing gloom and terror of the journey. If sane humour is our response to ridiculous contrasts, then to the diabolic and perverted humour of the demiurge licensed to punish, nothing is more ridiculous than the subjection of the most beautiful form in nature, the human body, to the twisted transformations of Malebolge. If vengeance is the Lord's, who is Dante to repine at the mysterious ways in which that vengeance is exacted? But together with the saving sanity of Virgil, a reading of these cantos is made bearable by our wonder at the sheer ingenuity and inventiveness of character and situation, by the images of natural observation, by the increasing command over classical references and associations, and the breath-taking eloquence of many of the speeches, among them Dante's own denunciation of Nicholas III, Guido da Montefeltro's relation of the betrayal of his vows, and, what contains the finest poetry of the *Inferno*, Ulysses' description of his last voyage.

With the descent into Cocytus, the bottommost pit, which is performed by Virgil flattering Antaeus, one of the giants, into picking them up and placing them below the cliff he stands beside, the poetic mood changes once more and Dante is forced to call on the Muses for aid in telling the horrors of the worst place in the universe.

S'io avessi le rime aspre e chiocce,
  come si converrebbe al tristo buco
  sovra 'l qual pontan tutte l'altre rocce,
io premerei di mio concetto il suco
  più pienamente; ma perch' io non l'abbo,
  non sanza tema a dicer mi conduco;
ché non è impresa da pigliare a gabbo
  discriver fondo a tutto l'universo,
  né da lingua che chiami mamma o babbo.
Ma quelle donne aiutino il mio verso
  ch'aiutaro Aufione a chiuder Tebe,
  sì che dal fatto il dir non sia diverso.[10]

If I had rhymes to rasp and words to grate
  Congenial with the grimness of the pit
  Whereon all the other scarps collect their weight,
I should crush out the juice of my conceit
  More fully; but not having them,
    I fall
Into fear, being constrained to tell of it.
For to portray the bottom and core of all
  The world is no feat to essay in sport,
  No, nor for tongues that *Mamma, Pappa*, call.
But may those Ladies now my verse support
  Through whom Thebes rose up to Amphion's note
  So that my words may not the truth distort.

For here the travellers find stretching out before them a vast lake of frozen ice with the heads of traitors sticking out, their tears congealing, as they weep, to form a cup upon their cheeks. As he walks, Dante strikes the face of one of them with his foot. The soul shrieks the question at him as to whether he has come to torture him for Montaperti. Dante tries to find out his name, and as he will not tell it, tears the hair from his scalp. Only when another soul calls out his name, 'Bocca', does Dante learn that he has assaulted the traitor of Montaperti, Bocca degli Abati. This vicious episode is followed by the more terrible story that Dante learns from someone he comes upon who is gnawing the head of another soul. It is Count Ugolino, who eternally bites the head of the archbishop of Pisa, who had Ugolino, his two sons and two grandsons nailed up in the tower to die of hunger. How well the Muses come to Dante's aid may be seen in the descriptive prelude to Ugolino's speech:

La bocca sollevò dal fiero pasto
   quel peccator, forbendola a' capelli
   del capo ch'elli avea di retro guasto.[11]

That sinner raised up from the brute
   repast
   His mouth, wiping it on the hairs left
   few
   About the head he had all behind
   made waste.

But even in his tale of horror there breaks through the redemptive note of human nobility as he describes how his boys showed concern for him in their prison, how they offered their own flesh for him to feed on as they misinterpreted his chewing of his hands for grief, how he crawled about their dead bodies when starvation had induced blindness in him.

Poscia, più che 'l dolor, poté 'l
   digiuno.[12]

Then fasting did what anguish could not
   do.

Leaving Ugolino to resume his gnawing, Dante speaks to another traitor, Fra Alberigo, whose body is still on Earth but occupied by a demon while his soul suffers here. He begs Dante to remove the crust of ice over his eyes for the information he will give him and Dante promises that he will go to the bottom of the ice if he does not do so. But when Fra Alberigo has spoken, Dante refuses his part of the bargain.

e cortesia fu lui esser villano.[13]   And to be rude to him was courteous.

As they progress in this terrible icescape, where whole bodies are embedded below their feet, Virgil points out Satan himself, whom they now approach. The emperor of the wretched realm stands breast high above the ice. He has three faces, the centre one red, the right one yellowish-white, and the left one black. From underneath each chin spread out two bat wings and from the six wings issues the freezing wind that congeals Cocytus. Each mouth champs a traitor, Judas Iscariot in the centre, Brutus on the left, and Cassius on the right.

Virgil now makes Dante clasp him by the neck. As the wings open, with Dante on his back, Virgil grabs the hair on Satan's body and climbs down. When Virgil reaches Satan's thigh, he starts heaving himself around, tugging at the hair so that Dante thinks they are going back to Hell. They come out to a rocky opening and Dante looks up and sees Satan's legs stretching up. He begs Virgil to explain and is told they have passed the centre of the Earth, and Virgil also describes how Satan fell onto the hemisphere they now enter and Earth fled from him to the north. Dante has in fact gone to the bottom of the ice, as he told Fra Alberigo he would, but in another sense. Virgil now makes him climb up a winding road without rest until, through a round opening, Dante sees some of the beauties of Heaven:

E quindi uscimmo a riveder le stelle.[14]   Thence issuing, we beheld again the stars.

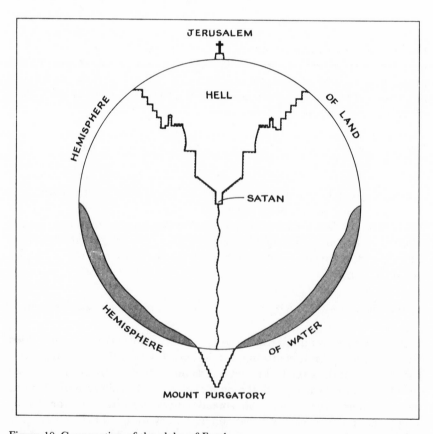

Figure 10 Cross-section of the globe of Earth

Purgatorio

What the travellers have done is to travel many thousand miles to the centre of the great motionless globe of the Earth, through the cone of Hell, and to come out, just before dawn, at the antipodes of Jerusalem on the shores of Mount Purgatory. Dante's huge relief at turning to a theme of hope from one of nightmarish despair resounds through the opening lines of the *Purgatorio*:

Per correr miglior acque alza le vele	Now hoisteth sail the pinnace of my wit
omai la navicella del mio ingegno,	For better waters, and more smoothly flies
che lascia dietro a sé mar sì crudele;	Since of a sea so cruel she is quit,
e canterò di quel secondo regno	And of that second realm, which purifies
dove l'umano spirito si purga	Man's spirit of its soilure, will I sing,
e di salire al ciel diventa degno.	Where it becometh worthy of Paradise.
Ma qui la morta poesì resurga,	Here let dead Poesy from her grave up-spring,
o sante Muse, poi che vostro sono;	O sacred Muses, whom I serve and haunt,
e qui Calïopè alquanto surga,	And sound, Calliope, a louder string
seguitando il mio canto con quel suono	To accompany my song with that high chant
di cui le Piche misere sentiro	Which smote the Magpies' miserable choir
lo colpo tal, che disperar perdono.	That they despaired of pardon for their vaunt.
Dolce color d'orïental zaffiro,	Tender colour of orient sapphire
che s'accoglieva nel sereno aspetto	Which on the air's translucent aspect grew,
del mezzo, puro infino al primo giro,	From mid heaven to horizon deeply clear,
a li occhi miei ricominciò diletto,	Made pleasure in mine eyes be born anew
tosto ch'io usci' fuor de l'aura morta	Soon as I issued forth from the dead air
che m'avea contristati li occhi e 'l petto.[15]	That had oppressed both eye and heart with rue.

Beside the sea, under the glimmering radiance of a late setting moon, they meet the old man who is the guardian of Purgatory and the second of the six guides on the way, Cato. After stern questioning Cato allows them to go on their way, when Virgil has washed Dante's tears away and girded him with a rush. A marvellous vessel sped by its angel helmsman, with his wings as sails, lands a group of souls who have travelled from the mouth of the Tiber, among them Dante's friend, the musician Casella. Cato reappears to upbraid the souls for listening to Casella sing Dante's poem 'Amor che ne la mente', and in confusion they seek their way. The fact that Dante casts a shadow causes constant amazement to the souls in Ante-Purgatory, where they now are. On the first terrace, Dante meets, among those who died excommunicate, the blond and handsome wounded form of Manfred and, on the second terrace, Dante's old friend Belacqua, a maker of musical instruments, and three of a crowd of souls, all of whom died violently: Jacopo del Cassero, Buonconte da Montefeltro, killed at Campaldino, and the gentle lady La Pia. It is now their first evening in the southern hemisphere and the sun has passed behind the mountain. A soul reposing like a lion watches them pass and stirs at Virgil's mention of Mantua. It is the poet Sordello, who takes them to a beautiful valley where various rulers are purged of their negligence. Dante meets his friend Nino Visconti, the judge of Gallura, and Currado Malaspina, to whose family he was indebted. Two angels with swords in their hands and wearing green robes fly in the air above them and drive away a serpent that creeps into the valley. Dante falls asleep and reports the dream that came to him in the morning:

Ne l'ora che comincia i tristi lai
   la rondinella presso a la mattina,
   forse a memoria de' suo' primi guai,
e che la mente nostra, peregrina
   più da la carne e men da' pensier presa
   a le sue visïon quasi è divina,
in sogno mi parea veder sospesa
   un'aguglia nel ciel con penne d'oro,
   con l'ali aperte e a calare intesa;
ed esser mi parea là dove fuoro
   abbandonati i suoi da Ganimede,
   quando fu ratto al sommo consistoro.
Fra me pensava: 'Forse questa fiede
   pur qui per uso, e forse d'altro loco
   disdegna di portarne suso in piede.'
Poi mi parea che, poi rotata un poco,
   terribil come folgor discendesse,
   e me rapisse suso infino al foco.[16]

At that time when the swallow wakes to cheep
   Her sad notes close upon the morning hour,
   Perhaps the record of old plaints to keep,
And when our mind, being a truant more
   From flesh, and with its thoughts less tangled up,
   In vision wins almost prophetic power,
I seemed in a dream to see above me stoop
   An eagle of golden plumage in the sky
   With wings stretcht wide out and intent to swoop.
He seemed above the very place to fly
   Where Ganymede was forced his mates to lose
   When he was snatcht up to the assembly on high.
Within me I thought: Perhaps only because
   Of habit he strikes here, and from elsewhere
   Scorneth to carry up aught in his claws.
Then, having seemed to wheel a little, sheer
   Down he came, terrible as the lightning's lash,
   And snatcht me up far as the fiery sphere.

The journey

On waking up, he finds that while he slept he has been transported by Lucia to the gate of Purgatory itself. This is one of the most crucial episodes of the whole *Commedia*, being part of the intervention of the trinity of ladies in the salvation of Dante, comparable to their act of mercy in sending Virgil to his aid, to the reappearance of Beatrice in the Earthly Paradise, and to the prayer of the Virgin, through whose intercession he gains the vision of the Trinity.

The gate of Purgatory has three steps, one of white marble, one of dark purple stone, and the third of blood coloured porphyry. An angel sits on the threshold of adamant; Dante bows down before him and the angel, with his sword, inscribes the letter 'P' seven times on Dante's forehead. Then he opens the gate

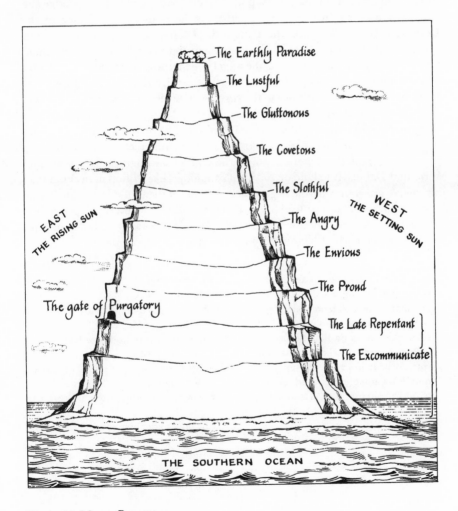

Figure 11 Mount Purgatory

257

and they hear the singing of the 'Te Deum'. They climb up to the first cornice that encircles the mountain and gaze at examples of great humility carved on the cliff, depicting the Annunciation, David dancing before the Ark, the story of Trajan and the widow. In the distance they see approaching a group of the proud, bent under the weight of huge stones. They are saying the Lord's Prayer. Among them are Oderisi of Gubbio, the illuminator, and Provenzan Salvani, the Sienese leader. On the path beneath him Dante sees carved examples of the sin and punishment of pride. An angel brushes his forehead with his wing and the first 'P' is removed. Climbing up to the second cornice, which is bare of sculptures and reliefs, they meet the envious, who sit in sackcloth with their eyes stitched together. He speaks to Sapia, a Sienese lady, expiating a grudge she had harboured against her city. Further on he finds two noblemen of the Romagna, Guido del Duca and Rinieri de' Paolucci da Calboli, and then a splendour of light overcomes him as, turning round a corner of the mountain to face the sun in the west, he meets the angel of generosity, who wipes the second 'P' from his brow. As they climb the stair to the third cornice, Virgil speaks to him of love and at the entrance to the cornice Dante is overwhelmed by the first of a series of waking visions, of Mary seeking Jesus in the Temple, of the clemency of Pisistratus, and of the martyrdom of St Stephen. Virgil jolts him back to himself and they press onward to a black cloud they see before them in the evening light. The smoke contains the souls of the angry. It is so thick and acrid that Dante has to hold on to Virgil's shoulder, like a blind man clinging to his guide. The souls sing the 'Agnus dei' and one of them, the Venetian Marco Lombardo, speaks to Dante of free will and how this, in man, is independent of the planets' influences because it descends from a higher source, and of how his soul needs the curb of legitimate power for its right development.

Esce di mano a lui che la vagheggia
   prima che sia, a guisa di fanciulla
   che piangendo e ridendo pargoleggia,
l'anima semplicetta che sa nulla,
   salvo che, mossa da lieto fattore,
   volontier torna a ciò che la trastulla.
Di picciol bene in pria sente sapore;
   quivi s'inganna, e dietro ad esso corre,
   se guida o fren non torce suo amore.

From the hands of him who wistly loves
   her, ere
She is, forth comes, like a child
   frolicking
That now weeps and now laughs
   without a care,
The little, the innocent soul that knows
   nothing
Saving that, sprung from a Creator's
   joy,
She goes to her own joy and there loves
   to cling.
Ravished at first with good that's but a
   toy,
Still runs she back bewitcht to the fond
   bower
If no guide turn her from delight's
   decoy.

Onde convenne legge per fren porre;
  convenne rege aver, che discernesse
  de la vera cittade almen la torre.
Le leggi son, ma chi pon mano ad esse?
  Nullo, però che 'l pastor che procede,
  rugumar può, ma non ha l'unghie
  fesse;
per che la gente, che sua guida vede
  pur a quel ben fedire ond' ella è
  ghiotta,
  di quel si pasce, e più oltre non chiede.
Ben puoi veder che la mala condotta
  è la cagion che 'l mondo ha fatto reo,
  e non natura che 'n voi sia corrotta.
Soleva Roma, che 'l buon mondo feo,
  due soli aver, che l'una e l'altra strada
  facean vedere, e del mondo e di Deo.[17]

Needs then that law bridle her wayward
  hour
And that she have a king who may
  far-off
Discern of the true city at least the
  tower.
The laws are: but what hand puts them
  to proof?
None; since the shepherd, going before,
  may chew
The cud, but hath not the divided hoof.
Wherefore the people, who see their guide
  pursue
What only his greedy appetite hath
  craved,
Feed upon that nor seek for pastures
  new.
The evil guidance whereto 'tis enslaved
Thou seest is that which doth the
  world corrode,
Not nature, that in you may be
  depraved.
Rome, that the good world made for
  man's abode,
Was used to have two suns, by which
  were clear
Both roads, that of the world and that
  of God.

The Church has confused her functions with those of the temporal monarch and mankind suffers from the evil direction. Marco turns back into the smoke, and Dante asks his reader to draw on his own experiences of the clearing of a mist in the Alps to let the sun through in order to visualize what Dante now experienced as they came out of the smoke. He now received the second wave of waking visions, which again made him oblivious of his outer surroundings, and he exclaims at the power of imagination and at the source of such visions which come without messages from the senses. He comes to and finds himself about to ascend to the fourth cornice, that of the slothful. An angel erases the third 'P' and Virgil speaks again of love while they rest, halted by the law of the mountain, which forbids ascent during the night. What he says explains the disposition of the various groups of souls on the mountain and the different purgations they undergo for the correction of love in them. As the night draws on, Virgil relates the purification of love to reason and free will. A crowd of the slothful come running by. One of them, once abbot of San Zeno in Verona at the time of Barbarossa, just has time to give them directions and to condemn the present holder of his abbacy, and runs on.

Dante sinks into sleep. Near dawn he has a dream in which a woman—stuttering, squinting, lame and with gammy hands and yellow skin—appears to him, and the more he looks at her the more fascinated he becomes; the attention he pays to her allows her to start singing and she reveals herself as the Siren, binding him with the spell of her song. A lady suddenly appears, calling to Virgil, who comes up and, tearing off the Siren's clothes, shows Dante her belly. Such a stench comes from her that Dante wakes up to find Virgil standing over him.

They continue their journey along the fourth cornice, meeting the angel of zeal, and then up to the fifth cornice, where the covetous are chained to the ground and weep. Among them is Pope Adrian V, punished there for his avarice. Dante curses the ancient wolf that claims more victims than any other beast and cries out for the coming of the deliverer. They come upon Hugh Capet, founder of the royal house of France and ancestor of Philip the Fair, who pours the bitterest scorn on his latest descendants, on Charles of Valois, who burst the belly of Florence with the spear of Judas, and on Philip himself, for the attempt at Anagni and the destruction of the Temple. Hugh longs for the vengeance of God on them. As they leave him, the whole mountain is shaken by an earthquake and a great shout of 'Gloria in excelsis' goes up from the souls. Virgil and Dante stand stupefied, like the shepherds at Bethlehem, and then, perplexed, move on. Someone comes up to them, as Christ came upon the travellers to Emmaus. This soul explains the earthquake and the shout as what happens whenever a soul is released from Purgatory. On this occasion the soul is himself. When Virgil asks him who he is, he reveals himself as Statius, who is to be the third guide of the poem. Statius tells of his desire to have seen Virgil, because the *Aeneid* was the nurse and mother of his own art. Though Virgil signals to Dante to keep silent, Dante cannot help smiling. Statius notices the smile and Dante is forced to reveal who his travelling companion is. While Statius tries to embrace his feet, Virgil prevents him:

'Frate, non far, ché tu se' ombra e ombra vedi.'[18]	'Do it not, Brother; thou art a shade, and see'st a shade.'

The angel of liberality erases the sixth 'P' from Dante's brow. As they continue, now on the sixth cornice, Statius describes how he became a Christian and how Virgil's works had first turned him towards the faith. His fear of persecution under Domitian had kept him from declaring his conversion and this cowardice had confined him to the cornice of sloth. Later he expiated his prodigality on the cornice of covetousness. They come upon a tall apple tree tapering down from a flat top onto which a waterfall plays from the rocks above. A voice cries out examples of temperance, the concern of Mary at Cana for the success of the feast, the way in which women of ancient Rome were content with water, and other examples. A band of singing souls draws up, wasted with hunger caused by the scent of the fruit and desire for the water. One of them suddenly recognizes Dante. It is Forese Donati, dead now nearly five years, and expiating here the sin of gluttony. He tells of how his wife Nella, through the efficacy of her prayers, has enabled him to ascend the mountain of Purgatory so quickly. Dante inquires about Forese's sister, Piccarda, and Forese says she is in Heaven. Then Forese points out some of his distinguished companions, one of them the poet Bonagiunta da Lucca, who asks if the man he meets is the author of 'Donne ch'avete'. Dante replies with his celebrated description of himself as one who writes according to Love's inner dictation, and Bonagiunta understands from this the difference between the old and new styles of poetry. The angel of temperance, glowing in his colours, invites them to the next cornice and erases the 'P' of gluttony. As they mount, Statius discourses on the nature of the rational soul in answer to a question of Dante's on how the gluttonous, who now need no food, grow thin as though they are starved. Statius finishes his lecture as they come upon the sheets of flame of the seventh cornice where lovers are refined in their love. The sun strikes Dante from the right, and where his shadow falls it makes the fire red. Some of the souls notice and one addresses him from the flames. Dante's attention is caught by two bands of spirits who approach from different directions and kiss one another as they run on. He compares them to ants nuzzling each other for news or directions. The first soul speaks to him again; it is the poet Guido Guinizzelli, and, at Dante's praise of him, he points out the 'better maker', Arnaut Daniel. As Guido disappears like a fish in a pool, Arnaut speaks in his native Provencal, happily asking for Dante's prayers, and

Poi s'ascose nel foco che li affina.[19]   Then he shrank back in the refining fire.

It is near sunset. Through the sheet of flame Dante sees an angel joyfully singing 'Beati mundo corde' and inviting them to pass through the fire. Dante is very frightened, remembering sights of bodies burning, and Virgil encourages him by mentioning Beatrice and arranging their passage so that he enters the flames between Virgil and Statius. To be thrown into boiling glass would be a refreshment compared to that heat. Once through, they get to the first steps up to the Earthly Paradise but have to halt because night has fallen. Dante gazes at the stars, greater and brighter than ever they were before, and falls asleep. In a third dream he sees two ladies, one gathering flowers who sings out that she is Leah and her sister Rachel who never stirs from gazing in her glass. She is the active life and her sister the contemplative. At daybreak they ascend the stairs and here Virgil halts to discharge his final duty. He can no longer guide:

'Non aspettar mio dir più né mio cenno;   'Expect from me no word or signal
  libero, dritto e sano è tuo arbitrio,   more.
                                 Thy will is upright, sound of tissue,
                                 free:

e fallo fora non fare a suo senno:	To disobey it were a fault;
per ch'io te sovra te corono e mitrio.'[20]	wherefore
	Over thyself I crown thee and mitre thee.'

They are in a beautiful wood, where a fresh breeze blows and the birds sing. Across a river Dante sees a lady by herself, singing and gathering flowers. This lady, known by the name of Matelda answers his questions about the place, describing the breeze as caused by the motion of the heavenly spheres. The soil beneath his feet is packed with seeds of every kind and the waters come not from the Earth's atmosphere but are supplied by the will of God to make the two rivers, Lethe, which now parts them, the river of forgetfulness of sin, and Eunoe, the river of the restoration to memory of good deeds. The three poets on one bank and the lady on the other walk upstream. Light, like continuous lightning, flashes through the forest and they hear singing. Dante calls on the Muses to help him now if ever he endured hunger, cold, or wakefulness for them. Seven gold candlesticks approach them, borne before a company dressed in white. The flames weave spectra on the air over the lily-wreathed heads of twenty-four elders, who are followed by the four beasts of the Apocalypse, crowned with green leaves and with their wings sparkling with eyes. In between these beasts comes a triumphal chariot drawn by a griffin, whose wings rise out of sight, his eagle head and shoulders of gold and his lion body white and red. Three ladies dance by the right wheel, dressed respectively in red, emerald, and snow white, and four others, all dressed in purple, of whom one has three eyes, dance by the left wheel. Bringing up the rear of the procession come two old men, one like a doctor, the other carrying a frightening bright sword, four others of great humility, and one alone moving as in a trance. All these seven are crowned with red roses. The procession halts by Dante at a peal of thunder. To shouts of 'Benedictus qui venis' and 'Manibus O date lilia plenis', a lady appears, wearing a white veil under an olive wreath, a green mantle and a dress the colour of living flame, and Dante instantly recognizes her. He turns to speak to Virgil, but Virgil has disappeared. Shocked into weeping, he is sharply addressed by his name and told he will have other cause to weep. The lady reveals herself as Beatrice and asks how he has dared to climb the mountain where man is happy. The angels plead for pity on him but Beatrice continues with her stern speech, describing how this man of such promise in his new life and so richly endowed has let the harvest of his talents be ruined in weeds. (This scene of Dante's confession, contrition, and absolution is discussed more fully in Chapter 17.) After further reproaches, he falls into a faint, waking to find himself being dragged through Lethe by Matelda, who forces his head down so that he drinks its waters. He comes out of the river first to the group of four ladies (the cardinal virtues) who lead him up to the breast of the griffin, where Beatrice waits, looking into the griffin's eyes. In her eyes Dante sees the griffin mirrored first in one form (incarnate love in its divine nature) and then in the other (incarnate love in its human nature). The other group of three ladies (the theological virtues) now beg Beatrice to unveil her mouth and Dante exclaims at the inability of all poets to describe her as she showed herself then. The procession now moves northward. Matelda, Statius, and Dante follow and, after a distance of three arrowflights, Beatrice stops before a tree totally bare of flowers and leaves. The griffin, after being blessed by the company and replying to them, drags the pole of the chariot up to the tree and ties it to the trunk. The tree breaks into flower and leaf. Dante falls into a sleep and wakes up as the Apostles did at the Transfiguration to find Moses and Elijah gone. Matelda is beside him and Beatrice is sitting on the roots of the tree surrounded by the seven virtues. The griffin and the rest of the company, he is told, have risen to Heaven, and Beatrice tells him that he will stay in the wood a little while and then he will be, with her, an eternal citizen of the Rome where Christ is a Roman. She asks him to note what he will see happening to the chariot and remember it so he may write it down when he returns.

An eagle stoops on the tree, tearing its bark, scattering the new leaves and foliage and giving the chariot a blow that rocks it like a ship in a storm. A thin, starved fox prances and lurks in the chariot till Beatrice drives him away. The eagle descends again on the chariot, leaving on it feathers from its breast. The Earth gapes, as a dragon issues to drive its barbed tail into the chariot's floor and, retracting it as a wasp does its sting, it pulls pieces of the chariot away. The chariot grows feathers all over; four heads with horns growing out of their foreheads sprout at its corners and three heads horned like oxen appear on the shaft. The chariot has now turned into a beast with seven heads. Safe as a castle on a high mountain, a whore sits on the monstrous beast. A giant appears beside her and they embrace and kiss. But because the whore leers at Dante, the giant beats her and drags her and the monster out of sight through the wood.

Beatrice leads her party back and speaks to Dante about what he has seen. She says that the chariot broken by the serpent (the dragon) no longer exists and prophesies that the eagle will not be without heirs because a five hundred, ten and five will come to kill the whore and the giant. Soon historical events will unfold the meanings of her words, though they are now dark. After more instruction from Beatrice they come to the well-head, from which Lethe and Eunoe spring, and at Beatrice's request Matelda leads Statius and Dante through Eunoe. From those waters of the remembrance of good deeds Dante issues like trees clothed with new leaves in spring

puro e disposto a salire a le
    stelle.[21]
	Pure and disposed to mount up to
	    the stars.

The poetry of the *Purgatorio* changes in mood, theme and depth with each major division of the journey, from Ante-Purgatory to the gate of Purgatory and from the last cornice to the Earthly Paradise, just as there were changes with the major divisions of the *Inferno*. The ascent of the mountain brings the travellers not only in touch with souls of increasing purity and understanding, but also recovers for them the beauties of the vegetable and animal worlds. Dante's confusion over light and his shadow in the Ante-Purgatory is settled and given direction by the intervention of Lucia; the significance of his dreams and waking visions that follow her intervention is brought out in the Earthly Paradise where, in the amazing perfection of visible nature, his dream-life is united to his waking perceptions in the sight of the incarnate allegory of the two pageants. The return of Beatrice, the third intervention of the trinity of ladies, brings about an emotional transformation in him, an expansion of his understanding, from which the highest marvel of the *Commedia*, the poetry of the *Paradiso*, derives.

Paradiso

Here he enters a world of light and everlasting praise. Whereas the souls of the *Inferno* are utterly at odds with the crushing rocks that imprison them, and the souls of the *Purgatorio*, although they enter gladly into the punishments that refine them, are limited by the laws of the mountain, the blessed appear as pure light. They are their own environment, free, conscious beings of delight. The canticle begins with a description of its theme and where formerly he invoked only the Muses, he now calls on Apollo:

La gloria di colui che tutto move
   per l'universo penetra, e risplende
   in una parte più e meno altrove.
Nel ciel che più de la sua luce prende
   fu' io, e vidi cose che ridire
   né sa né può chi di là sù discende;
perché appressando sé al suo disire,
   nostro intelletto si profonda tanto,
   che dietro la memoria non può ire.
Veramente quant' io del regno santo
   ne la mia mente potei far tesoro,
   sarà ora materia del mio canto
O buono Appollo, a l'ultimo lavoro
   fammi del tuo valor sì fatto vaso,
   come dimandi a dar l'amato alloro.

The glory of Him who moveth all that is
   Pervades the universe, and glows more bright
   In the one region and in another less.
In that heaven which partakes most of His light
   I have been, and have beheld such things as who
   Comes down thence has no wit nor power to write;
Such depth our understanding deepens to
   When it draws near unto its longing's home
   That memory cannot backward with it go.
Nevertheless what of the blest kingdom
   Could in my memory, for its treasure, stay
   Shall now the matter of my song become.
For the last labour, good Apollo, I pray,
   Make me so apt a vessel of thy power
   As is required for gift of thy loved bay.

Infino a qui l'un giogo di Parnaso
   assai mi fu; ma or con amendue
   m'è uopo intrar ne l'aringo rimaso.[22]

One of Parnassus' peaks hath
   heretofore
Sufficed me; both now shall I need
   forthwith
For entering on the last arena-floor.

Up to now he has been content with one peak of Parnassus but now he needs the other as well. He begs the god to enter his breast and breathe out music like that with which he defeated Marsyas when he flayed him alive. The god must take him utterly so that he may make manifest the shadow of the blessed realm signed on his head, and then Dante will approach Apollo's chosen tree for the bays that are now too rarely plucked for a Caesar's or a poet's triumph. A small spark can raise a great fire and other greater poets following Dante will attain Cirrha, that second peak of Parnassus.

Beatrice is gazing at the sun, now at the spring equinox in Aries, closest to the point at which Creation began. Dante is astonished to find that he too can bear the experience of gazing directly at the sun, even though only for a short period in which the sun seems to spark like boiling iron drawn from the furnace. Suddenly all seems even brighter as though a second sun had dawned. Beatrice

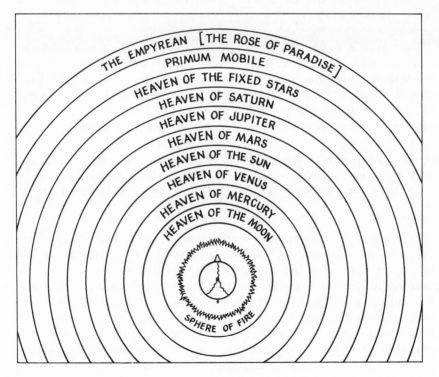

Figure 12 The spheres of Heaven

stands gazing at the wheels of Heaven while Dante, gazing at her, becomes transformed, as Glaucus did in tasting the magic sea herb, and transhumanized, an experience that only those who know it by grace can appreciate. He hears music, sees blazing light, and Beatrice explains that he is no longer on Earth. Dante asks how he in his body can transcend the light bodies, and Beatrice answers with a description of gravitation that moves all things to different ports over the great sea of being. It would be more surprising if Dante, now free of all impediment, should remain on Earth.

Dante warns those readers following him in tiny boats to turn back to port. The sea on which he ventures has never been crossed before. Minerva breathes, Apollo leads him and the Muses point out the constellations of the Bears. The remaining readers who have sought the bread of the angels should chase behind in his wake, and they will be more amazed than the Argonauts were when they saw Jason ploughing with the fiery bulls. Beatrice and Dante rise into the sphere of the moon, where he asks for an explanation of the spots on the moon. Beatrice brushes aside his own explanation, that they are caused by the mingling of dense and rare matter, and puts the argument on a different level, by explaining it as a consequence of the different degrees of power distributed from the angels who move the nine heavens. As the moon is furthest from the Empyrean so it receives less excellence than the other planets; the parts of the moon receive and reflect the light of the sun unequally because they differ so much from one another.

Faces appear, so like reflections in water, and as indistinct as a pearl on a white forehead, that he looks behind him to discover the originals; addressing one of them, Dante discovers that it is the soul of Piccarda, the sister of Forese Donati. The souls here are of those who had been inconstant in their vows and, in answer to Dante's question about whether they do not aspire to a higher place in Paradise, she expresses their happiness within the Divine Will.

'E 'n la sua volontade è nostra pace:	'And in His will is perfected our peace.
ell' è quel mare al qual tutto si move	It is the sea whereunto moveth all
ciò ch'ella crïa o che natura face.'[23]	That it creates and nature makes
	increase.'

Speaking of inconstancy in vows she points to Constance, mother of Frederick II who, like her, was torn from a convent. Singing 'Ave Maria', she disappears. Beatrice is delighted with the clearing of Dante's mind shown by the questions he is asking. In the heaven of Mercury many thousands of souls greet him with the words, 'Ecco chi crescerà li nostri amori'. Amongst them is the soul of the emperor Justinian who gives his great recital of the history of the empire from its earliest days to the time of Charlemagne. According to Justinian, the souls he sees here, for all their good deeds, were tainted with worldly ambition.

As these souls leave, singing 'Hosanna', Dante burns with another question, expressing his state in a tercet studded with 'd's', the consonant of doubt and duality

Io dubitava e dicea 'Dille, dille!'
  fra me, 'dille' dicea, 'a la mia donna
  che mi diseta con le dolci stille.'[24]

A doubt held me; and I said inly 'Tell,
  O tell it to her! Tell my lady,' I said,
  'Who slakes my thirst with sweet drops
    from her well.'

though his reverence for Beatrice prevents him from uttering it. But she, smiling at him, reads his mind. He is perplexed that Justinian should refer to the destruction of Jerusalem by Titus as wreaking 'vengeance for the vengeance on the ancient sin'. Beatrice explains that, though through the Incarnation human nature was united with God and through the crucifixion that human nature paid the penalty for sin, there remained the outrage on the divine nature to be avenged and this was achieved through the destruction of Jerusalem. God gave more of Himself through the Redemption than He would have done by cancelling the debt. Beatrice now goes on to speak of the Resurrection, of how, although all things made of the four elements and the souls of plants and animals are created as a result of the influences of the planets and are seen to decay, the angels and the true country where He is are created for eternity, as life in Dante and in the rest of mankind, and the bodies of our first parents, are the direct creation of God.

They rise into the heaven of Venus where, just as one sees sparks within a flame, or as when, in singing, one voice holds a note and the other performs a roulade, both are distinguishable, so he sees souls bright within the light of that heaven. One of them approaches Dante, quoting 'Voi che 'ntendendo il terzo ciel movete' to him. He reveals himself as Charles Martel and speaks of his family. Dante asks him how wicked or incompetent children come from good and able parents. Charles Martel says that God has provided through the planets the means of differentiating natures. Differences in human nature are essential to the citizenship which is part of every individual's development. Were there no influences from the planets each man would merely be a copy of his father. It is men, not nature, who distort the gifts of providence by placing their fellow men in positions for which they are unsuited. Next appear Cunizza, the generous-hearted lover, prophesying disaster to the inhabitants of the region of Treviso, and Folquet of Marseilles, the troubadour turned bishop, who attacks the avarice of the Church.

Dante now invites his reader to raise his eyes to the high wheelings of the heavens, whose circlings against the zodiac are cut by the plane of the sun at the equinoxes. There, the reader can contemplate the thought of God gazing in love on His own creation and can then sit back on his bench and reflect on this foretaste of the enjoyment awaiting him. They are now in the heaven of the Sun and Beatrice cries

'Ringrazia,
ringrazia il Sol de li angeli, ch'a questo
sensibil t'ha levato per sua grazia.'[25]

'Give thanks, give praise
To the angels' Sun, who to this sun of
    sense
Hath by His favour deigned thy feet to
    raise.'

Dante is consumed with the love of God, even forgetting Beatrice, who smiles with joy at his absorption. They are surrounded by bright lights as with a wreath; the lights, which are souls, swirl round them in a dance and from one a voice issues, identifying himself as Thomas Aquinas and naming the other souls, among them Albertus Magnus, Solomon, Dionysius the Areopagite, Orosius, Boethius, Richard of St Victor, and Sigier of Brabant. The circle comes to rest and Thomas speaks of two princes ordained by providence for the court of the Bride, one seraphic in his ardour, the other a splendour of cherubic light. He sings the praises of the first of these, St Francis, and ends his speech with a condemnation of the greed for offices and preferments shown now by the Dominicans. The circle revolves again and is joined by an outer ring of another twelve souls singing in antiphony to the hymn of the others. A voice from the outer circle proclaims the praises of the cherubic splendour, extolling the life and works of St Dominic, ending with rebukes to the latter-day Franciscans, of whose order he reveals himself to be the former general, with the words

Io son la vita di Bonaventura.[26]   I am the life of Bonaventure.

He identifies the companions of his circle, among them Hugh of St Victor, Nathan, Anselm, and Joachim of Fiore.

Now Dante asks his reader to hold on as to a rock to the comparison he is about to make. If the fifteen stars of the first magnitude, the seven stars of the Great Bear, and the two stars of the mouth of the horn made by the Lesser Bear were grouped into two circles, each like the Corona Borealis but one within the other and rotated, the reader might imagine something of the effect of the two rings of blessed souls revolving about Dante, but even that would only be a shadow, as far from his experience as the motion of the fastest sphere of Heaven, Primum Mobile, exceeds that of the sluggish river Chiana. When the circling stops, further instruction follows on the royal prudence of Solomon, and the effect of the Resurrection on the souls of the blessed when, at the Resurrection, they are reunited with their bodies.

Yet another circle joins the two about him. Beatrice smiles and Dante, looking up, finds himself raised to the heaven of Mars. There in the red heaven he sees a great white cross, from which flashes a vision of Christ. A song he can hardly make out swells in the cross and falls silent: a star shoots from the left-hand bar to the foot of the cross, glowing like flame behind alabaster. This light is Dante's ancestor Cacciaguida, who sings the praises of the Florence of his day when, still confined within her ancient walls, her people lived in peace, sobriety

and modesty. He says something of his own life and of how he followed the
emperor Conrad III, who knighted him, to the Holy Land, where he was killed
in battle. Dante, overcome with pride, asks him at what period he lived.
Cacciaguida answers this and goes on to speak of families illustrious in his day
but now fallen to obscurity, lamenting the strife between the Buondelmonti and
the Amidei which led to the city's troubles. Dante now asks for an explanation
of all the hints he has heard on his journey about his own fate and future.
Cacciaguida hides nothing; as Hippolytus was driven from Athens by the
slander of his stepmother, so Dante will be driven from Florence. When Dante
asks whether he should hold back anything harsh or bitter he learns of his
contemporaries on his journey, Cacciaguida orders him to speak the truth
without concealment and specially never to spare the great; these lines also
explain Dante's choice of characters in the *Commedia*:

'Questo tuo grido farà come vento,
    che le più alte cime più percuote;
    e ciò non fa d'onor poco argomento
Però ti son mostrate in queste rote,
    nel monte e ne la valle dolorosa
    pur l'anime che son di fama note,'
che l'animo di quel ch'ode, non posa
    né ferma fede per essempro ch'aia
    la sua radice incognita e ascosa,
né per altro argomento che non paia.'[27]

'Thy cry shall come with the wind's
    vehemence
That strikes full on the loftiest peaks
    alone;
Honour not small shall be thy
    recompense.
Therefore to thee have on these spheres
    been shown,
And on the Mount, and in the Vale of
    Dread,
Only such souls as have acquired
    renown,
Since the hearer's spirit is not comforted
Nor knits its faith by an example mean
Which hath its roots obscure and darkly
    hid,
Nor by what proof else is not plainly
    seen.'

Beatrice points out other souls in the cross who shoot through it as she names
them, Joshua, Maccabaeus, Roland and Charlemagne, and others.

Gazing at Beatrice he realizes they have moved to another sphere, that of
Jupiter in pure white light. Here the souls, rising like birds, form themselves into
the letters 'D', 'I', and 'L' and then extend them, spelling out the message
'DILIGITE IUSTITIAM QUI IUDICATIS TERRAM'. The 'M' of the last word stands
against the silver planet of Jupiter, and other souls, singing, drop onto the top of
the 'M' which undergoes a transformation into an eagle. This eagle, composed
of the many souls of the just, speaks with one voice. Dante hopes for the solution
of a problem that has long troubled him: an Indian, living far from Christians,
without the opportunity to learn the faith, lives a completely virtuous life. How
can he be blamed for unbelief? Where is the justice in his condemnation? The

eagle, having formulated this question for Dante, explains that human minds are incapable of grasping Divine Justice. Only true believers in Christ reach Heaven, but many who cry out 'Christ! Christ!' will be less near him on Judgment Day than those who never knew his name. The eagle goes on to denounce certain contemporary rulers and then draws Dante's attention to the six souls that make up its eye and eyebrow. David is the pupil of the eye, and Trajan, Hezekiah, Constantine, William II of Sicily, and Ripheus form the eyebrow. On Dante's wondering at seeing Trajan and Ripheus there, the eagle describes the marvellous ways in which they became Christian, and finally he speaks of the mystery of predestination. Dante gazes again at Beatrice, who warns him she may not smile because he would be consumed by her beauty, and also tells him that they have risen to the sphere of Saturn. Here Dante sees a great ladder flashing like gold in the sun and rising out of sight as souls move up and down on it. One of these souls is Peter Damian, who speaks to Dante of his life and denounces the degeneracy of his old monastic settlement at Fonte Avellana and of the lives of luxury of modern bishops. At this a cry of execration goes up from the souls, and Dante turns to Beatrice in terror. She reassures him and he now meets St Benedict, the founder of the Benedictine order. Dante is caught up again, this time to the sphere of the fixed stars and to his own birth sign of Gemini. From this sign, as it revolves, he looks down on the 'threshing floor' of Earth and then returns his gaze to Beatrice's eyes. She bids him watch the triumph of Christ, rising out of sight together with the Virgin Mary. From this canto (XXIII) a new and translucent beauty pervades the poetry as the journey changes from the refulgent luminescence of the lower planets, past the brilliant scintillations of the sun and the higher spheres, to beyond the circlings of the planets, a beauty exemplified in these lines, as Dante looks on a vision of Christ as light:

Quale ne' plenilunïi sereni
   Trivïa ride tra le ninfe etterne
   che dipingon lo ciel per tutti i seni,
vid' i' sopra migliaia di lucerne
   un sol che tutte quante l'accendea,
   come fa 'l nostro le viste superne;
e per la viva luce trasparea
   la lucente sustanza tanto chiara
   nel viso mio, che non la sostenea.[28]

As in a full moon's tranquil brilliance
   Trivia smiles among the nymphs who paint
Eternally Heaven's uttermost expanse,
Over a myriad lamps preëminent
   I saw one Sun which kindled each and all,
As light from our sun to the stars is lent;
And through the living light shone forth the whole
   Irradiated Substance, so intense
   Upon my eyes, I needs must let them fall.

About the Virgin there circles an angel. St Peter appears and questions Dante on faith; St James follows with questions on hope; and when St John takes his turn for questions on love, the light of his soul is so strong that Dante is blinded for a time, a blindness removed when he converses with Adam. St Peter denounces the degeneracy of the modern papacy, and this is what St Peter has to say as the heaven about him blushes red for shame:

'Se io mi trascoloro, non ti maravigliar, ché, dicend' io, vedrai trascolorar tutti costoro. Quelli ch'usurpa in terra il luogo mio, il luogo mio, il luogo mio che vaca ne la presenza del Figliuol di Dio, fatt' ha del cimitero mio cloaca del sangue e de la puzza; onde 'l perverso che cadde di qua sù, là giù si placa.'[29]	'If that I change and flush Marvel thou not; for thou shalt soon divine On all these, as I speak, as deep a blush. He who the place usurpeth that was mine On earth, mine, mine, now vacant in the sight Of the Son of God, has made my grave decline Into a sewer, well-nigh choked outright With blood and filth; wherein the Arch- Renegade, Who fell from here, down there taketh delight.'

The image of the sewer feeding human sin to Satan in the depths thus recapitulates the cosmology of the poem. Once more Dante looks down on the Earth, seeing the parts traversed by Ulysses on his mad voyage, and then Beatrice explains the nature of the heaven of the Primum Mobile, which they have now reached. Here invisible are the roots of Time, and Beatrice denounces cupidity in mankind. Looking into Beatrice's eyes, Dante sees a light reflected in them; he turns around and sees a point of the intensest light, smaller than any known star, about which nine rings of fire circle, the nearest to the point at the fastest rate and the outermost at the slowest. Beatrice says:

'Da quel punto depende il cielo e tutta la natura.'[30]	'From that point of light Dependeth Heaven, and all things that exist.'

She explains that the nine rings of fire are the nine angelic orders, in the relationship described by Dionysius, and to Dante's difficulty in relating his concentric model of the universe, in which the outermost circle (the Primum Mobile) is the fastest, to this vision, where the angels of the Primum Mobile occupy the innermost place to the point, she brings the solution that he is looking at the virtue of the angels, not at their seeming spheres of influence. They are now in the Empyrean. He is blinded with light and then enabled to see another vision, of light streaming like a river between banks adorned with the flowers of a miraculous spring. On bathing his eyes in this he sees, rising in tiers which form the petals of a white rose, the souls of the blessed. Beatrice shows him the empty throne awaiting Henry VII and foretells the doom of Clement V, who will thrust Boniface deeper down among the simoniac popes. Dante now gives a marvellous description of the great white rose, with the angels flying in and out of it like bees. He turns to speak to Beatrice, but she is no longer there; instead an old man, who is St Bernard, says he is there at Beatrice's request to fulfil Dante's last longing. St Bernard, the sixth guide of the poem, shows where Beatrice is seated in the petals of the rose, and then he directs Dante to gaze on the beauty of the Virgin Mary.

St Bernard now explains the divisions of the rose and the place in it of the beatified children. After much instruction he prays to the Virgin that she may intercede for Dante and that he may receive the ultimate vision. Bernard then bids Dante to look, but Dante has anticipated him and his sight enters more and more deeply into the high light. The vision surpasses all language to express it, but he prays for even a little memory of it so that he can give but one spark of its glory to future generations. He beholds the unity of creation bound together by love, like scattered pages into one volume:

Così la mente mia, tutta sospesa,
    mirava fissa, immobile e attenta,
    e sempre di mirar faceasi accesa.[31]
	Thus did my mind in the suspense of
	    thought
	 Gaze fixedly, all immovable and intent,
	 And ever fresh fire from its gazing
	    caught.

With the light he sees three circles, two reflecting each other like rainbow on rainbow and the third seeming of fire breathed out from the other two. As he gazes on them, deep within there appears the image of the Son of man, of Christ. How the image relates to its circle is far beyond his understanding, but a sudden flash overcomes his mind, fulfilling his desire:

A l'alta fantasia qui mancò possa;
    ma già volgeva il mio disio e 'l *velle*,
    sì come rota ch'igualmente è mossa,
 l'amor che move il sole e l'altre stelle.[32]
	To the high imagination force now failed;
	 But like to a wheel whose circling
	    nothing jars,
	 Already on my desire and will prevailed
	 The Love that moves the sun and the
	    other stars.

Those closing cantos, in which every device of imagery, word-play, and rhetoric employed before in the poem is both intensified and made more radiant, like spray thrown up from the rhythmic waves of his verse to catch the light of the noonday sun, are unequalled in literature for their power, profundity, and beauty. In writing them Dante returned to and made secure the vision of the whole, from which the poem had originated. We may be reasonably certain that these cantos were written in the last year of his life. How did he manage to make a work of art so perfect, to achieve such a unity of theme and expression? The answer must lie both in its inspiration and in the way he planned the work.

16

Weight, number, and measure
in the *Commedia*

The galaxy in which we live, according to modern astronomers, contains one hundred thousand million stars (or suns)[1] of which we can see only six thousand with the naked eye. This galaxy, the Milky Way, is just one of a countless series of galaxies, spread out through space. Our understanding of how these macrocosmic entities are born and develop has grown as we have also understood the nature of the infinitesimally small, the sub-atomic particles out of the energy of whose gyrations and dances these galaxies, with their suns and planets, have expanded and contracted. Apart from the evidence on statistical (that is, random) grounds for the existence of planets bearing intelligent life systems comparable to that on Earth, there is no place in this view of the universe for intelligence or consciousness beyond the minds of the men who observe it. Even though we may recall that Ptolemy said that Earth in relation to the Empyrean should be regarded as a mathematical point, if we set the Ptolemaic–Aristotelian system of Dante's day beside this modern view we become aware of the paucity of scale of the older model, a sense that it is too small, too compact, too finished, to convey the marvel and the thrill of creation, the myriad lights of star clusters or the unimaginable devourings of space of the quasars. But once we begin to understand this older model, not as an earlier and less satisfactory mechanical explanation of celestial phenomena, but as a scheme expressing the relation between the highest consciousness and the creation of that consciousness, a creation that in varying gradations contains intelligence diffused through it, then we begin to realize that we have to deal with the presentation of a world of a different order, with a world that is as intrinsically alive in all its aspects as is the film of organic life that covers the Earth.

We have to begin by imagining, not an infinitely extended series of galaxies, but the eternal being, consciousness, and joy of God in the eternity of the Empyrean, the tenth heaven, the heaven of spiritual light, within whose perfect tranquillity all creation is embosomed. Intelligence, whose ultimate source is in the Empyrean, is diffused in creation through the angelic orders, through mankind, and through the animal and vegetable kingdoms. The angels have immediate insight into the mind of God but man, since the Fall, is wounded in his intellect and will. Because of this, God sent His Son to make satisfaction for the fault that man by himself could not redeem. Through the Incarnation, Christ enters into human flesh and, through the harrowing of Hell, He descends into the densest and most unregenerate forms of matter. To the mystics, God, in a definition known to Dante and going back to the twelfth century, is a sphere whose centre is everywhere and whose circumference nowhere.[2] Dante, at a high point in the purification of his vision in the *Paradiso*, sees the whole of creation reversed as the angelic orders revolve about a tiny point of light which is the Divine Intelligence.[3] Men of the Middle Ages could see creation on the hugest and on the minutest scale but manifest as consciousness.

It was the recognition that forms of intelligence other and higher than those of man existed in the angelic orders that, by the thirteenth century, made the Ptolemaic system, with its nine heavens, which could be shown to accord with these angelic orders, the most acceptable of the models then known and thought possible. (See Chapter 8, p. 105.) Thomas Kuhn says of Dante's depiction of the Christian universe, as the world view that took so strong a hold of the late medieval and Renaissance mind, that it was perhaps the first, and certainly the most forceful, of all such depictions, since the earlier scholastic attempts had been too detailed and too erudite for the assimilation of a clear model.[4] This gives a new significance to the importance in the history of science of Dante's visual imagination; it was his ability to give colour, body, volume, light, and shade to this model of the universe that made it so credible a presentation, and it was the universal appeal of the *Commedia* that spread the knowledge of it. He absorbed from philosophers, astronomers, astrologers, and geographers a mass of details, of speculation, ethics, mathematics, symbols, and descriptions of weather and territories, and projected it again in pictorial form with a verisimilitude that imprinted itself on the imaginations of men in the next three centuries, perhaps long delaying the acceptance of the heliocentric theory of the universe—of which, curiously enough, in a spiritual sense he was also a precursor, because he was one of the chief proponents of the Neoplatonic sun symbolism, which played so important a part in the preparations for Copernicus.[5]

Probably the direct influence on him that enabled him to absorb in so united a manner such a mass of heterogeneous facts was that of Dionysius the Areopagite. One of the chief differences between the cosmology of the *Convivio* and that of the *Commedia* is his change in the latter to the orders of angels given by Dionysius in his *Celestial Hierarchies*. That change is but a single aspect of the power of Dionysius' influence on Dante because he was regarded not only as a supreme authority on the angelic orders but also as the wisest guide to the highest states of contemplation, as a subtle definer of those states of waking vision which we have so frequently noted in Dante's experience, and as a man who so obviously in his life had known the yearning of his own soul for the return to its origin and the downpouring of love from that point of origin as the spiritual urge of the cosmos. Dionysius' influence on Dante also includes his treatises on *The Divine Names* and the *Mystical Theology*. To read Dionysius with attention is to be caught into wonderful and rarefied regions of the mind, so drenched in reasonable enthusiasm is his language and so fine are the distinctions with which he preserves the mysteries of which he speaks. Again, he was one of the most convincing expositors of the metaphysics of light, using images of fire and illumination to express the divine hymnody of the angelic beings he describes and impelling his readers on a journey that is at once inward and above.

Dante also went on a journey—a theme that must be as old as story-telling. The purpose of the journey may be to find knowledge or to seek hidden treasure or a beautiful princess, and it may involve descent or ascent into other worlds. It may be disguised in the picaresque novel or transformed into modern science fiction. Whatever form it takes, it begins with some dissatisfaction, some realization that there is a deep lack in the soul and that new experiences, new knowledge, new loves, are needed to expand the soul so that it may find peace in the recognition of its identity with the soul of the universe. The sublimity of the theme can be demonstrated by the *Katha Upanishad*, in which the young Brahmin Nachiketa travels to the king of Death, who grants him three boons for a discourtesy the boy had received on arrival. In his last question Nachiketa asks:

'How, O King, shall I find that blissful Self, supreme, ineffable, who is attained by the wise? Does he shine by himself, or does he reflect another's light?' The king of death replies: 'Him the sun does not illumine, nor the moon, nor the stars, nor the lightning—nor, verily, fires kindled upon the Earth. He is the one light that gives light to all. He shining, everything shines.'[6]

It is characteristic of the theme that it should be concerned with death, and with the invisible world into which the dead disappear. Religious writings from diverse sources either instruct the individual on how to die, as with the manuals on the craft of dying that became popular in the fourteenth and fifteenth centuries,[7] or else, as in the Tibetan Book of the Dead, provide specific advice for the conduct of the soul *after* death, preparing it against the terrors of the next world. The earliest known example in which the guide of the soul is a woman comes from the Zoroastrian writings in which the soul of a good man is met by the dazzling reflection of its own goodness, the virgin Daena,[8] and reaches Paradise by crossing the terrifying knife-edged bridge of Chinvat.

One of the purposes of the classical mystery religions was, through an initiatory ritual taking the character of a journey, to convince the neophyte of the certainty of an afterlife, and enough of these ancient mysteries survived and were revealed in Dante's classical reading, most notably in Book VI of the

Aeneid, to affect the *Commedia* profoundly. Though Dante did not know the greatest expression of the theme in classical antiquity, the myth of Er the Pamphylian in Plato's *Republic*, this work influenced Cicero's *Dream of Scipio* which, with Macrobius' commentary, was probably familiar to him. In the *Dream of Scipio*, Scipio the younger is translated to the heavens in the company of his famous grandfather, Scipio Africanus the elder, who foretells his destiny and political fortunes and then describes and points out the universe with its concentric spheres, in comparison with which Earth is totally insignificant.

> . . . rest assured that it is only your body that is mortal; your true self is nothing of the kind. For the man you outwardly appear to be is not yourself at all. Your real self is not that corporeal, palpable shape, but the spirit inside.'[9]

The eschatology of Christian doctrine demanded the provision of other worlds for the punishment or reward of the immortal soul and provided a rich new source for visions of eternity and of journeys, of which the most notable is the Revelation of St John the Divine. The widely current apocryphal Gospel of Nicodemus described the harrowing of Hell by Christ, and in addition the *Celestial Hierarchies* of Dionysius the Areopagite was taken as the account told by St Paul of the secrets he learnt when he was rapt up to the third heaven; other apocryphal accounts of St Paul's descent to Hell and ascent to Heaven were also current. When monasticism originated in Egypt in the fifth century, rules imposing asceticism and deprivation spurred the imaginations of the monks to create compensating worlds of rich and frequently terrifying imagery. When the forms and organization of Egyptian monasticism were brought to Ireland, the visions coalesced with Celtic mythology, which possessed an already highly developed tradition of stories of journeys and other lands—the voyages of Maelduin and the land of Tir nan Og, for example. This meeting of traditions resulted in a profusion of descriptions of journeys to other worlds and of legends of saints who had made this journey. Thus St Adhamnan, the biographer of St Columba, who lived on the island of Iona in the eighth century, describes the ascent of the soul to Heaven, where he sees the tortures of the damned, and finally comes to the land of the redeemed, where he finds the Tree of Life and the souls of the righteous in the form of white birds.[10] Other visions include those of St Fursey, an Irish saint travelling in England, who received his revelation near Bury St Edmunds, and St Tundal, whose experiences were translated into numerous European languages. So it is perfectly possible that Dante was familiar with some of these Celtic stories.[11]

In other parts of Europe and the East the themes of the journey and the vision of other worlds were current, though masked in other forms. The Arthurian quests and the Alexander epics[12] gave witness to the theme in terms of the chivalric code. Bonvesin da Riva, a tertiary of the Umiliati mendicant order, wrote his account of the punishments and rewards of the three worlds in his

Libor delle Tre Scritture.[13] Great cosmological themes drawing on Neoplatonic ideas were developed in Latin poems and writings of the twelfth century, notably in the *De mundi universitate* of Bernard Sylvester (writing 1145–53) and the *Anticlaudianus* of Alan of Lille (*c.* 1128–1202), and these works and their possible influence on Dante have already been mentioned in relation to the theme of the Eternal Feminine.[14]

Of all the writings more or less contemporary with the *Commedia*, the fullest resemblance comes from Islam. There was a widely diffused legend in Islam based on Sura XVII of the Koran which begins:

> Glorified be He Who carried His servant by night from the Inviolable Place of Worship to the Far Distant Place of Worship the neighbourhood whereof We have blessed, that We might show him of Our tokens! Lo He, only He, is the Hearer, the Seer.[15]

In the development of this story, Mohammed was transported one night from Mecca to the site of the Dome of the Rock in Jerusalem by the archangel Gabriel. Thence, on his mare Burāq, he mounted to Heaven and Gabriel instructed him in the course of his journey. The Spanish Arabist, Father M. Asín Palacios, in a work[16] published in 1919, came to the conclusion, after collating parallels between Islamic descriptions of journeys to the Other World with the *Commedia*, that Dante's subject-matter was drawn to a great extent from Islamic sources. He found these parallels in works by Abu' 1-'Alā al-Ma'arrī (973–1058) and Ibn al-'Arabī, especially the latter's *Meccan Revelations*. What was most remarkable was not only the similarities between the cosmological features, which were, in any case, the common property of intellectuals of both faiths, but also the ethical and moral parallels in the systems of both Dante and Ibn al-'Arabī. Asín's great problem in answering those who remained sceptical was to show how Dante could have gained the detailed knowledge of these works on which Asín's theory depended. He suggested that Brunetto Latini could have provided the link, following his embassy in 1260 to Alfonso X of Castile, whose court was a meeting-place for the two faiths. Some years later an unsuspected key to the link was found in the translation made by an Italian, Bonaventura da Siena, into Latin and Old French of a lost Castilian version of an Arabic *mi'raj*—a popular text describing this very journey of the Prophet to the Other World. Enrico Cerulli, the scholar who found and published the translations, was able to prove that the work was current in early fourteenth-century Italy and was mentioned by followers and imitators of Dante as the *Libro della Scala*.[17] This work, with its fascinating series of bold and almost primitive images, including a giant cockerel which crows at the throne of God and an angel of ice, provided remarkable confirmation of Asín's basic theory, although it turned attention away from Ibn al-'Arabi as a possible source, to Muslim popular literature. Cerulli also suggested that Dante was impelled to create his own poem because he responded to the legend of the *mi'raj* as a challenge to Christianity, a great conception that the West was honour bound to excel.[18] The parallels with Ibn al-'Arabī, which also concern the *Vita Nuova* and the *Convivio*, still remain largely unexplained and probably always will if a direct link is searched for, though there are two possible links, both closely concerned with the site of the Dome of the Rock, from which the Prophet made his ascent and on which the Temple of Jerusalem was built.

These two links are, first, the experiences of pilgrims returning from the Holy Land and, second, the influence of the Templar order which, until the final loss of Jerusalem in 1244, shared the duty of guarding the Temple site. Pilgrims from the West to the site of the Temple would have heard of the Prophet's ascent from the Muslim guides taking them round, and such a connexion brings us to yet another strand of the multitudinous journeys synthesized into the *Commedia*. This is the pilgrimage of the Great Circle, the journey that took hundreds of pilgrims from all parts of Western Europe every year by way of Crete to Egypt, across the desert to Mount Sinai, then to Jerusalem for the visits to the Holy Places, and back across the Mediterranean for the final stage of veneration in the basilicas of Rome. Written accounts of the Holy Land and the places of pilgrimage were popular and many survive.[19] It would appear that Dante was thoroughly familiar with the main stages of this pilgrimage and made his own journey in the poem the figural interpretation of the actual pilgrimage that so many of his contemporaries and acquaintances must have made.[20] The *Inferno* begins with the Exodus theme of the escape from the dark wood and, though Dante cannot climb the delectable mountain, which seems to be Mount Sion, he eventually arrives at the antipodes of Jerusalem to ascend a mountain at whose foot arriving souls sing the Exodus psalm, whose opening phrase is the one which he used twice in his explanations of the fourfold method of interpretation. The mountain of Purgatory is ascended by cornices similar to those of Mount Sinai and it also has marked similarities to other mythical mountains, including Mount Eden, described in reports from pilgrims. Another Jerusalem is entered in the Earthly Paradise, which is itself a figural presentation of the Temple enclosure, whose dimensions and proportions had been copied by the Templar order in their houses throughout Europe, including Florence, and thus would have been familiar to Dante. From that Temple of flowers and trees he continues to the eternal Rome of the celestial Paradise.

This raises once more the question of Dante's possible affiliation to the Templar order,[21] or, at least, of Templar influence on him. The Templars, as a great institution with the need for an international and supranational policy, with their control of banking in the Near East, with an intelligence service that necessitated the deepest knowledge of Islamic society and thought in their long fight to preserve the Latin kingdom, provide one of the best explanations of the line of transmission that could have informed Dante not only of the association of the *mi'raj* legend with the site of the Temple, but also of the myths of world renewal that underlie his prophecies of the *veltro* and the DXV. Many of the most obscure allegorical passages receive their most coherent explanation when related to the crisis of the Templar order. That they are couched in such obscure images, when Dante felt free to denounce the corruption of the Church itself in quite open and uncompromising terms, can be explained by the final suppression of the order in May 1312, after which any attempt to defend them would be seized upon as heresy. The chief evidence for his affiliation lies in the imagery of the poem (see Chapter 19). The order had been founded in 1118, soon winning the guidance and blessing of St Bernard, the sixth guide of the *Commedia*, to guard the Holy Places in Jerusalem, to protect the pilgrim routes, and to fight the infidel. Through long years of proximity with the rival civilization of Islam, the Templars and their adversaries won very high opinions of each other. As was said in Chapter 6, it is possible that, through this proximity, Sufi ideas and practices, founded as they were on many of the same Neoplatonic traditions that nourished Christian mysticism, and with the added appeal of the Perennial Philosophy, infiltrated among the members of the order and thence to the lay members of the confraternity of the order known as La Fede Santa, to which Dante is supposed by supporters of the Templar theory to have belonged.[22] This possibility is, of course, highly conjectural, and if there was a Sufi influence, it would have been confined to small groups within the order—and their beliefs would have borne no relation to the farrago of superstitions devised by Philip the Fair's investigators to which they forced their Templar prisoners to confess. The open aim of the order was still the same in 1300 as in 1118: to contest the infidel; and the connexion may help to explain how Dante could exhibit such a wide knowledge of Islamic lore and tradition and at the same time express such an antipathy to them.[23]

More will be said in this and later chapters about the Templar connexion, notably in dealing with Dante's symbolism of the cross and the eagle in his historiography, with the significance of Lucia, the problems of the *veltro*, the old man of Crete, and the prophecy of the DXV, and in discussing the imagery of the Earthly Paradise. Having described some of the possible sources—ancient classical and oriental, Christian, Celtic, and Islamic—of the themes of journey and of pilgrimage, we must turn to Dante's own contributions to these themes, and to the way in which he brought the new mathematical and scientific outlook of the West to bear on them.

What makes Dante's description different from all earlier versions of the journey that he could have known is his success in constructing a credible reality for his readers. By making himself the traveller, he lost the advantage of the simple faith on which the teller of a miraculous story concerning the Prophet or a Christian saint could depend. He had to replace that faith by another kind of belief, belief in precise facts verified by experience. He gives a mass of details, distances, time references, planetary and stellar dispositions—enough to show that he had worked out in his mind a complete order of events in time and space. That his later commentators have laboured in vain to reach agreement on details such as the dimensions of Hell, the height of Mount Purgatory or the exact day on which the journey begins does not mean that Dante himself was uncertain about these matters, but shows rather the extreme difficulty of recovering the techniques of computation—probably quite simple ones—and of recognizing basic assumptions and premises so generally accepted in his day as not to need mention. This journey took place in a definite week in a definite year. He covers a definite distance to the centre of the Earth, to the antipodes and beyond the Primum Mobile. Here, by frequently mentioning his own exhaustion and the labour of the journey, he points out the reality of the rocks and ravines down which he scrambles and the cornices up to which he has to climb. He emphasizes time and again the plastic and tactile nature of the forms and landscapes he sees, working on his reader's visual imagination with the greatest battery of images that any poet has ever amassed. Even more subtly, he works on his reader through the numerologically decided contrasts and divisions of the poem. Finally, by presenting his reader with human characters as alive and forceful as anyone his reader is ever likely to meet in what is called 'real life', he makes his journey to the ultimate vision of God more acceptable as a depiction of the union of the visible and the invisible sides of life, and closer to human experience than any earlier visionary journey. The precision he gives to his time references, to the particular landscapes he describes, and to the mathematical symbolism of the poem are all related to the new precision he brings to the delineation of human character, the new understanding he gives to the integrity and unique value of every human individual.

His most original contribution to the topography both of this world and the next was the placing of Purgatory on a mountain in light and air. Many earlier Western Christian accounts of the afterworld put Purgatory below the crust of the Earth as an antechamber to Hell proper, and there is little difference between the two abodes—except in the matter of the length of stay.[24] Depictions of Purgatory in painting and sculpture—before the illuminators got to work on manuscripts of the *Commedia*—are extremely rare,[25] in contrast with the numerous representations of Hell whose keener sufferings challenged writers and artists to a morbid rivalry. This is strange when one considers how much doctrinal discussion was devoted to the nature of Purgatory and how much popular religious practice had as an object the alleviation of its pains, through intercession, indulgences, and pilgrimages. As has been suggested, it was through the reports of pilgrims and those guarding the pilgrimage routes that Dante's imagination was fed with legends and descriptions of biblical and mythical mountains. These derived from the ancient Middle Eastern tradition of associating the mountain summit with the place of the propitiation of the gods, a tradition that influenced the design of Hindu, Buddhist, and Muslim religious architecture. It may even be that Dante had heard reports of Adam's Peak in Ceylon.

The first mention of Mount Purgatory is in Ulysses' description of the 'montagna bruna per la distanza', the 'mountain dark in the distance', whose forbidding height rears up before the Greeks on their last voyage and from whose shores they are repelled by a great wave and drowned. The contrast between this first mention and the nature of the mountain as it is revealed by the end of the *Purgatorio* displays a crucial step in the processes of Dante's creative imagination, the conversion of an object of fear and terror into a symbol of blessedness and redemption. Few features of the *Commedia* demonstrate better the authority his inspirations bestowed on him once he had interpreted the waking images or dreams in which a vision, such as that of the *montagna bruna* must have appeared to him, than the boldness with which he converted legends from more alien cultures into a new and acceptable visual realization of Western Christian doctrine.

By removing Purgatory so completely from Hell he devised an environment that gave a new aim and joyfulness to the doctrine of purgation. By placing it in the unpeopled ocean of the southern hemisphere, at the antipodes of Jerusalem, then thought to be the centre of the inhabited world, he gave his audience a fuller sense of the roundedness of the Earth, a quantum leap in understanding of an order best realized by comparing the form of the globe retained after reading the *Commedia* with some of the dull two-dimensional *mappae mundi* of his period. By attributing its creation to the mass thrown up when Lucifer hurtled from the place of the archangels and corkscrewed down to the centre of the Earth and when all the land mass of the southern hemisphere veiled itself with the sea in horror, he made the mountain part of a dynamic cosmography in which the Divine Will provides the place of healing for the consequences of the Fall. If we regard Mount Purgatory, too, as the place of the purification of the imagination, with its bare crags and cliffs signifying the renunciation of the disordered phantasmata of Hell, with its angel guardians, miraculous sculptures, and its cornices benevolently haunted with voices and visions, then, in rearing this prodigious mountain from below the sea-bed into the breath of air and the rays of the sun, he was raising the imagination of our ancestors out of the grasp of sightless rock into the light of conscious awareness. Where before they could only mine for images in their own minds and find nightmare, they could now let their visions grow and flower with new pleasure. At the summit of the mountain, the place of propitiation, he placed the Garden of Eden, reborn in the Temple of Jerusalem.

The events of the poem take place in Holy Week and Easter Week in 1300. The generally accepted order of days runs thus: the evening of Maundy Thursday when Dante enters the dark wood; the entry to Hell on the evening of Good Friday and the descent which takes the night of Good Friday and the whole of Saturday until the evening, when he reaches the centre of the Earth. The change of hemisphere makes a time change from Jerusalem time to Purgatory time, so that his time goes back twelve hours. This means it is again Saturday morning and he spends the day and night of Saturday (Purgatory time) in climbing up to the surface. He appears therefore on the shore of Mount Purgatory on Easter Sunday just before dawn. He spends three days and nights on the mountain, reaching the Earthly Paradise in the morning of the Wednesday of Easter Week. He spends about six hours there, the same length of time Adam will tell him in *Paradiso* XXVI that he spent in Eden before his expulsion. The ascent through the planetary and stellar spheres takes the rest of that day and night, and the final vision occurs on the Thursday, the eighth day of the journey.[26]

It must be said, however, that some have preferred the date of Easter, 1301, because in certain ways this fits better with the dispositions of the planets and constellations Dante describes. Rodolfo Benini has pointed out that many of these difficulties are resolved if one assumes the usual date of Easter, 1300, but starts from the evening of Monday of Holy Week instead of from Maundy Thursday so that Lucia takes Dante up to the gate of Purgatory on Good Friday and Dante is reunited with Beatrice on Easter Day, all of which fits much better with the symbolism of the poem as a whole.[27]

Whatever the exact day on which the action of the poem begins, it is clearly limited to a definite short period in historical time, a week through which all Dante's first adult readers had lived. There are other aspects of time in the poem to which I would like to draw attention. The aim of the poem is to express an experience of eternity, what Boethius described as 'the perfect and simultaneous possession of limitless existence',[28] first revealed to Dante as that minute point of light round which the angelic hierarchies revolve. To grasp a hint of the relationship of time and eternity as expressed by Dante, it is necessary to look at what might be called the planar and solid geometry of the poem. Not only the point, but the straight line, the spiral and the circle all play a part in the *Commedia*. It was Dionysius the Areopagite who, drawing on a long tradition going back to the *Timaeus*, related the three motions of the angelic hierarchies (the circle when they are united to the eternal light of the Lovely and the Good, the straight line when they guide those below them, and the spiral motion in which, while carrying out their duties of guidance, they remain true to their self-identity which is rooted in God) to the three motions of the soul. These three motions in the soul are also circular, spiral, and rectilinear. In the circular motion the soul is withdrawn into a unified concentration of its spiritual powers by a fixed revolution uniting it eventually to God; in the spiral motion it is enlightened by truths of divine knowledge through the exercise of discursive reason and diverse and progressive steps; in the rectilinear motion it goes out to the world around it from which it feels an influence coming 'as from a rich abundance of cunning tokens drawing it into the simple unity of contemplative acts'.[29] From this derived a widespread tradition of the three movements of the mind which St Bonaventure summed up as conversion *extra nos* (rectilinear), *intra nos* (spiral), and *supra nos* (circular).[30] Dante had already applied them to the three operations of the noble soul, animal, intellectual, and divine, in the *Convivio*[31] and it seems clear that he employed the three motions as a guiding idea in the planning of the *Commedia* to bind the microcosm of his life to the macrocosm of the universe. Characteristically he extended and enriched the theme with clusters and cross-associations of imagery. Thus at the outset he tries to make the linear journey straight towards the *dilettoso monte*, but he is hampered by his lame left foot which symbolizes his deficiency of will,[32] and then driven back by the assault of the three beasts. His only escape, under Virgil's guidance, is to make the spiral journey downwards, a journey into the realization of human sin. All the time, however, the world is feeding him 'cunning tokens', impressions and meetings that provide him with the questions by which he advances on the spiral way. Again on the shores of Mount Purgatory he and Virgil are lost on the linear way as they try to climb the mountain, and it is only by the guidance of grace that they reach the gate of Purgatory, and by climbing the cornices they unwind the spiral of Hell turning in the opposite direction.

The extension of a spiral in three dimensions makes a helix and, as a solid figure, a cone. Here again in the recurrence of these figures Dante's visual imagination makes marvellous transformations and memorable images from the abstract and mystical ideas he inherited from the Neoplatonic tradition. First there is the cone of Earth's shadow which extends to the heaven of Venus. Then there is the cone of the *dilettoso monte*, which Dante is prevented from climbing in *Inferno* I. Virgil tells him he must go instead through Hell which takes the shape of a vast inverted cone at whose apex is Satan. Climbing up the helical route to the antipodes, they come upon the great cone of Mount Purgatory, up which, from the gate of Purgatory, travelling only on the sunward side, they trace a spiral journey, and on whose summit Dante sees the Tree of Knowledge, with its extraordinary shape of a wide flat top tapering down to its trunk. Rising with Beatrice through the heavens, Dante reaches the fixed stars in his own birth sign of Gemini and beyond that, seeing a new light in Beatrice's eyes, turns about to see the point of light from which all creation hangs. Thus the journey can be seen as a series of three major helices to the apex of a cone, at which point there is a reversal both physical and psychological, together with numerous minor pointings of the same figure.

The importance of the spiral is that it symbolizes a journey of inner evolution: it is the figure of a man not trapped by his own ego. If one imagines creation, as Dante saw it in *Paradiso* XXVIII, not as a series of concentric spheres round the dark inner world of Hell within the Earth, but as a cone of light depending from that minute point, then one begins to understand something of the complete reversal in his comprehension of reality that Dante experienced, because what is depicted as furthest away, the cherubim who move the Primum Mobile, are on this reversal closest to the point Dante is now approaching, to God, to the truth in himself. All men of good will strive up the spiral of that cone and move in accordance with the divine will. What separates the damned in Hell from the rest of creation is that they cannot move on the spiral. Once they have appeared before Minos and confessed all to him, he wraps his tail around himself as many times as signifies the circle of Hell to which they are assigned (another spiral). Once in their circle they can never move outside it; even the demons of *Inferno* XXI and XXII cannot chase Dante and Virgil beyond their set limits. Those who do move, run like the sodomites in a perpetual circle on the burning sand, or come round endlessly like Mohammed and Ali to be hamstrung by a demon. Only Dante and Virgil, on their spiral journey downwards, are free of this terrifying periodicity which, psychologically, means the infatuation, addiction and hatred of the damned, and the way in which their development has ceased at a certain point. By contrast the repentant sinners, however long their wait on each cornice of Mount Purgatory, know that in time they *will* move up the spiral way, and in Paradise the ability of the blessed spirits to move, to revolve and gyrate by themselves or in carols and dances of groups signifies the freedom of will that they have attained. Thus the highest form of motion—what is in Hell for the sinners a vicious circle—becomes finally for Dante the circle of perfection in which his soul moves as one with God.

Yet another aspect of time in Dante's presentation of the universe concerns what was discussed in Chapter 3, the poet's view of history in which, through symbol and image, historical events are presented in their totality, so that all the men and women responsible for the continuation of a particular crime in history meet together, as do, for example, the simoniac popes in the well of fire. The thirteenth-century forger, Adam of Brescia, can quarrel with the ancient Greek deceiver, Sinon of Troy. Equally, all those of a noble tendency, who, nevertheless, must still be purified, can meet together from several epochs, like the lovers in the wall of flame on Mount Purgatory. History becomes not an endless thread of succeeding events but a gorgeously patterned carpet of emotions in which, remarkably, each thread has the choice of whether it will add to the darkness or the light of the pattern. This gives depth not only to Dante's vision of humanity as a whole but also to his depiction of individual human beings. The dynamism of the poem projects these individuals before us and then withdraws them into the conserved power of a great symbol, as Cacciaguida flashes out of the cross of Mars, speaks to Dante, and returns to the brotherhood of Christian warriors of all epochs, and as the souls in the heaven of Jupiter speak with one voice through the figure of the eagle, which their forms accumulatively present.

An equal power attaches to the numbers according to which the poem is constructed and on which much of its more subtle development depends. The relation of history to eternity is summed up in his image of the tree of Time, whose roots are in the Primum Mobile and extend towards the eternal world of the Trinity, and whose branches extend downwards throughout creation, bearing the numbers of individuation in their divisions. The aim of the journey is the return from the branches of the tree to unity, the union of Dante's soul with its Maker in the vision of God. The journey is developed in a hundred cantos, the number, 100, reducing by mystic addition to $1 + 0 + 0 = 1$. In honour of the Trinity the poem is divided into three parts, each of which has thirty-three cantos except the *Inferno*, whose first canto may be considered as an introduction, and which therefore contains 1 + 33 cantos. Each canto is written in the *terza rima* rhyme scheme, which carries the praise of the Trinity right down into the individual lines of the poem. The nature of this rhyme scheme means that every canto consists of a number of lines divisible by three with one over; in this way there is a return to unity. The saving trinity of ladies is opposed by the three beasts and the ultimate vision of the Trinity is parodied by the sight of the three-headed Satan at the centre of the Earth.

Put another way, the hundred cantos represent the whole of reality as the square of ten, the number of perfection. We have seen from the *Vita Nuova* that Beatrice was a nine, the square of the three of the Trinity. What is created by the symbolic meaning of a number is that number's square. Each afterworld is divided in ways that may be described as tenfold or ninefold, as for example the nine heavens together with the tenth heaven of the Empyrean. The play between the numbers nine and ten is particularly significant where Beatrice herself is concerned, and it demonstrates yet again the rigorous control Dante could exercise over his material. Not only is she mentioned by name sixty-three times in the *Commedia* (6 + 3 = 9) but her name is used as a rhyme word on nine occasions. She reappears to Dante in the thirtieth canto of the *Purgatorio*. This canto is the sixty-fourth of the *Commedia* (6 + 4 = 10) so that it is preceded by 63 cantos (6 + 3 = 9) and followed by 36 later cantos (3 + 6 = 9). The canto itself contains 145 lines (1 + 4 + 5 = 10) and the line in which she announces her identity – 'Guardaci ben; ben son, ben son Beatrice' —is the seventy-third line of the canto (7 + 3 = 10). Her first appearance in that canto dressed in the colours of faith, hope, and charity occurs earlier in lines 31–3. There can be no question that her association with these numbers is a matter of chance. Another example of this numerological planning relates to Christ. The name of Christ is used as a rhyme word (but rhyming only with itself) four times in the *Paradiso*, presumably to signify the four bodies of Christ, the earthly, the mystical, the sacramental, and the glorified.[33]

Ten is the number of perfection and is made up either of 1 + 2 + 3 + 4 or of 9 + 1. Two stands for duality that must be overcome, whether in the division between creation as a whole and its creator, or in the gap between the soul and its origin, or in the division of will and intellect in the individual that must be brought into harmony. Three is the harmonizing force that resolves those dualities, through, for example, the three blessed ladies, the three motions of the soul, and three stages of the mystical way, purgation, illumination, and union. Four, as the number of completeness, may be seen as the universe or what the Trinity acts upon, and, also, as the fourfold method of interpreting scripture. Beatrice as a nine is the light between the truth and the intellect; she contains the ninefold order of reality which must be interpreted by the fourfold method. As we shall see, she is also associated with the number five, the number of love, in the six guides of the poem. These six guides stand for the six stages of the ladder of contemplation which, as I hope to show, is one of the dominant patterns of its construction (see Chapter 18).

Enough has been said to reveal the astonishing extent to which Dante was able to plan the poem from all sorts of viewpoints before he began its writing, and to give added point to what was said elsewhere on the subject of the origin of the poem in the vision of the Trinity. Although recent studies have done much to reveal the invaluable part played by numerology in the creation of literary works of art down to, in our century, Joyce's *Ulysses* and Thomas Mann's *Doktor Faustus*, both of which are heavily indebted to Dante, no other work contains the complexity of number symbolism on such a scale and with such a precision of fine detail as the *Commedia*.

As different and as weighted with their own individual associations as the numbers and their combinations on which the inner coherence of the *Commedia* depends, are the depictions of the dead souls in the poem. Each has been created as a soul by God turning to the brain in the foetus as soon as its articulation is perfect. As the heat of the sun joins with the juice of the grape to make wine, so God breathes into the work of nature a single soul. On death each soul, though parted from the flesh, still keeps with itself its human and divine parts in potency. Memory, intellect, and will become even keener than before. Once the soul reaches its place in one of the afterworlds and is surrounded by space, it imprints the air with its virtual form. It is now a shade and in shade form possesses the organ of every sense.

Quindi parliamo e quindi ridiam noi;	We speak, we laugh, by this, and this alone
quindi facciam le lagrime e' sospiri	By this we liberate the tears and sighs
che per lo monte aver sentiti puoi.[34]	Thou mayst have heard about the mount make moan.

Memory preserves with intense vividness all the events of the earthly life of these souls while, according to the afterlife assigned to them, they lament, expiate, or rejoice in the effects of the uses to which they had put will and intellect.

This brings us to Dante's great overall view of history, the history of the will and intellect in mankind as a whole on which he had already founded the doctrines of the *Monarchia*. These two elements are symbolized by two great sun symbols: the cross for the contemplative life and the purification of the intellect, and the sun eagle for the active life and the right direction of the will. As many as thirty instances of the symmetrical pairings of these symbols[35] have been found in the *Commedia* and in developing their significance Dante, just as he took the themes of cosmology, journey, and pilgrimage and welded them into the original conception of his own individual inspiration, drew upon and transformed the Christian view of history and the long tradition of the symbolism of the sun into the grandest and profoundest historical perspective of the Middle Ages.

Following on their close links with Judaic tradition, the early Christian Fathers and writers had seen history as a linear progression from creation to the second coming. The Incarnation marked a great dividing point in time, allowing this linear progression to be divided into epochs. When this view of history began to prevail, the cyclical theories of classical historians, which went back to the myth of the four ages of man and included the Stoic theories of recurrence and regeneration, fell into abeyance, mentioned only to be dismissed or denounced.[36] Dante not only drew on the Fathers for his evaluation of history but restored and reunited with their view the cyclical ideas of the classical writers, through the image of *Astraea redux* and the promise of the renewal of the world through the return of the Golden Age. In doing so, he was casting a refutation against much of the work of one of the founders of his own civilization, St Augustine.

St Augustine was the most universal of the transmitters of classical knowledge and experience to the Dark Ages and the medieval world and, in the process of transmission through his powerful mind, much of that experience was laid under terrible embargoes. He would explain how men of the past had lived or thought but he forbade any future generations to live or think in that way again. He also drew together and refined for the purposes of the Church in his time whole other areas of past experience, giving them new life and new dimensions.

The most powerful of St Augustine's works of destruction is *The City of God*. Closely linked with this work is the world history of Orosius, written at St Augustine's request. Both of these books were responses to the claim of pagan intellectuals, after the sack of Rome by Alaric the Goth in AD 410, that the decline of the empire was caused by the coming and official adoption of Christianity and the neglect of the old gods and customs. Orosius was given the task of proving from history that infinitely worse disasters had overtaken humanity before the time of Christ and this he set about with gusto and blood-curdling detail. St Augustine himself set out to contrast the *civitas terrena*, in which he included the heathen world, founded by Cain and based on sin, with the *civitas dei*, founded by Christ and growing from justice to grace. In the course of his argument Augustine was impelled to diminish the past glory of the Roman empire, and to demonstrate either the emptiness or the wickedness of the Roman gods. Political societies go against Nature's law; man should rule over beasts and not over men though, because of original sin, men become subject to earthly rulers.[37] Without justice kingdoms are nothing but gangs of criminals on a large scale.[38] It is on the pagan gods that Augustine lavishes his most powerful invective;[39] they are false either because they were of human origin, i.e. they were men or women famous in their time, around whom there gathered the attributes of divinity and to whom was addressed the worship of later, more ignorant generations; or else they are demons, servants of the devil, incapable of acting as mediators between men and the true God, devoted to misleading and corrupting humanity. If the heroes of ancient Rome were advised by these demons, it was generally to their undoing; if the heroes were successful, it was entirely through their own efforts. The demons have the ability to shape the air in which they live in order to appear to men and to form their obscene or corrupting visions.

St Augustine portrayed a very frightening picture of the ancient world, of man unredeemed in a moral wilderness where every attempt to seek help from the gods or religions available to him only plunged him into worse disorder through the evil guidance of the demons. The horror of the picture was reinforced by Orosius, writing, as he jokingly says, as Augustine's dog. Dante owed much to Orosius for enlarging the scope of his historical studies, and Orosius, with his description of the succession of empires, Babylon, Carthage, Macedonia, and Rome, imposed on all later historical writings a powerful and dominant pattern, again emphasizing the horrors of life amongst unredeemed humanity whose history he said, should be examined by the light of the torch of cupidity,[40] the sin to which Dante ascribed the wrongs of the world in his time.

As Dante progressed in his classical studies, the respect in which he held the Roman empire grew into a kind of awe as he began to realize the part it had played in preparing humanity for the mission of Christ. As he soaked himself in the classical poets, so a great emotional change took place in him: a deep and lasting love both for the writers and the nobility of the heroes and heroines they described began to displace the negative or guilty attitude he had inherited towards the pagan past.

In the full development of his themes, Dante was to stand many of St Augustine's and Orosius' ideas on their heads. He took Orosius' succession of empires, Babylon, Carthage, and Macedonia, and showed them as preparations for the divinely ordained Roman empire. The pagan gods that St Augustine had denounced as demons, he described as great members of the angelic hierarchy, totally blameless for the misguided worship that had been devoted to them.[41] It is the influences of the planets at each man's birth that decide his character and thus set him free from the genetic predestination that his parents would otherwise bequeath to him. He even takes over the ability, that St Augustine grants the demons, of imposing their shapes on the air, and makes it the means by which the characters of the *Commedia* are able to manifest themselves in fleshlike forms to his eyes.

It must not be thought that Dante was rejecting outright the traditional interpretation of history, in which, on account of the Fall, all mankind was doomed to Hell before the coming of Christ. There was only one race capable of receiving grace before Christ and this was Christ's own people, the Jews. They alone kept alive the worship of the true God and their prophets had borne witness to the coming of the Messiah. Where the Greeks and Romans had stumbled blindly in search of true standards of righteousness, a pillar of fire had gone before the Jews, leading them to the promised land. The typological interpretation of the Old Testament, which found in Jewish history and its characters presages and prefigurings of the events of the New Testament, constantly reinforced the belief that, up to the Incarnation, the Jews had been the chosen people. This, however, faced Dante with the paradox that the Jews, at the crucial moment of choice, for all the divine guidance they had received, rejected Christ while the pagan world, abandoned by God, had nevertheless managed to institute in the Roman empire the terrestrial order most suited for the Incarnation of God in man.[42] Out of his reflections on this paradox grew his view of the divine mission of the Roman empire, already highly developed by the time he was writing the *Monarchia*, and receiving its fullest expression in Justinian's description of the course of Roman history as the wheelings of the imperial eagle.

Accompanying the rise of Christianity and manifesting in several cults and religions was a new sense of the power of the symbol of the sun as light, heat, and radiance. Christ had said, 'I am come a light into the world that whosoever believeth on me should not abide in darkness.'[43] From this and many similar passages derive the ever revivifying influence of light imagery on Christian thought and art. It is an image expressing joy, life, and the infinite tenderness of Christ to creation, and there is no greater witness of its power in art than Dante's *Paradiso*. The strength of the image is shown from the earliest days of Christianity. St John says, 'This then is the message which we have heard of Him and declare unto you, that God is light, and in Him is no darkness at all.'[44] St James sets the image in a cosmological framework: 'Every good gift and every perfect gift is from above and cometh down from the Father of lights, with whom is no variableness, neither shadow of turning.'[45]

There were a great many currents among Graeco-Roman philosophies and religions tending the same way towards sun symbolism, but it was Christianity, with its exceptional capacity for assimilating diverse influences, which finally channelled them all together. The proliferation of religions in the empire was a consequence of the way in which the Romans not only tolerated but welcomed new cults. One result of this proliferation was the weakening of the old cults based on mythology, and hence the need appeared for a politically sound cult that would support the empire. It was not enough simply to deify the emperor: he had to be supported in his deification by all the panoply of religion. The solution was found in the cult of the sun. It has been pointed out that sun worship is often associated with monarchy as a political institution,[46] and there are examples as far afield as Peru and Mexico and Egypt where the priesthood established around the pharaohs the most impressive example of it in the Mediterranean world before the later Roman empire. The sun had been comparatively weak as Apollo-Helios in Greek mythology, when compared with the god of thunder, Zeus. There were enough points of concord, however, with the new religions, such as Mithraism coming from the East, which infiltrated among the soldiers of the Roman army, to make the sun cult one that fitted in well with the symbolism of most religions, even, on the face of it, with Christianity, whose adherents spoke of Christ as the Sun of Truth, Sun of Resurrection, and Sun of Salvation, however stubbornly they might deny the link. The emperor Aurelian (AD 270–5) established the sun as the supreme deity of Rome and the cult continued among his successors, including

Constantine the Great, who issued a great series of coins celebrating his association with Sol Invictus, the unconquered sun. Then, in 312, on his way to the battle of the Milvian bridge, he received a vision of the sun with a cross imposed on it and he heard the words: 'In hoc signo vinces'. His soldiers put the emblem on their shields and Constantine won the battle, the first stage in the process that led to his deathbed baptism and the establishment of Christianity as the state religion. He was the first Christian emperor and, for a short time in Dante's view of history, mankind was ruled, as it should be, both by an emperor who acknowledged Christ and ruled the active life and by a pope who governed the contemplative life. But it was through Constantine that the disaster known as the Donation came about, when he granted the Western empire to the pope, thereby upsetting the balance that should obtain between the two spheres.

The power of this sun symbolism, associated both with Christianity and with the idea of political supremacy, was never lost throughout the Dark Ages, and it explains why it was so important for later popes, such as Gregory VII and Innocent III, to appropriate it for the glorification of their own office as the heirs of the Western empire under the Donation and in their propaganda battles with the emperors. The symbolism was buttressed by all the ingenuity of clerical pedantry. The pope was the sun and the emperor, as the moon, should always be in subjection to him. As the sun was $7,644\frac{1}{2}$ times brighter than the moon, so the papacy was that number of times more worthy of reverence than the emperor.[47] The wide acceptance of the validity of this kind of reasoning explains Dante's immense efforts to wrest control of the sun symbolism from the supporters of the papacy, admitting the facts but denying the analogy in *Monarchia* III, and substituting for it the idea of the two luminaries in the letter to the Italian cardinals and of the two suns in *Purgatorio* XVI. One possible source of the imagery of the two suns is from Byzantium where it was in use in court poetry in the thirteenth century.[48]

This symbolism is carried throughout the poem through the images of the cross and the eagle. At the outset of the journey Dante refers to his two predecessors, Aeneas who carried the eagle to the founding of Rome, and Paul who carried the cross to Rome. Both received checks on their way to Rome at Crete: Aeneas by his mistaken desire to found a city there and Paul by the refusal of his guardians to heed his warnings of shipwreck. Aeneas bore the principle of just rule that would be the supreme sanction of empire, and Paul the redemptive message of the cross. The significance of the island where their routes cross appears in the story in *Inferno* XIV of the old man of Crete, introduced by Virgil in explaining the source of the rivers of Hell:

'In mezzo mar siede un paese guasto,'
  diss' elli allora, 'che s'appella Creta,
  sotto 'l cui rege fu già 'l mondo casto.

'In the mid sea a country lies, all waste,'
  He therefore now continued, 'Crete by name,
  Under whose king the world of old was chaste.

Una montagna v'è che già fu lieta
d'acqua e di fronde, che si chiamò Ida;
or è diserta come cosa vieta.
Rëa la scelse già per cuna fida
del suo figliuolo, e per celarlo meglio,
quando piangea, vi facea far le grida.
Dentro dal monte sta dritto un gran veglio
che tien volte le spalle inver'
Dammiata
e Roma guarda come süo speglio.
La sua testa è di fin oro formata,
e puro argento son le braccia e 'l
petto,
poi è di rame infino a la forcata;
da indi in giuso è tutto ferro eletto,
salvo che 'l destro piede è terra cotta;
e sta 'n su quel, più che 'n su l'altro,
eretto.
Ciascuna parte, fuor che l'oro, è rotta
d'una fessura che lagrime goccia,
le quali, accolte, fóran quella grotta.
Lor corso in questa valle si diroccia;
fanno Acheronte, Stige e Flegetonta;
poi sen van giù per questa stretta
doccia,
infin, là dove più non si dismonta,
fanno Cocito; e qual sia quello stagno
tu lo vedrai, però qui non si conta.'[49]

There stands a mountain, Ida called,
the same
Which once with green leaf and glad
water shone,
Now desert, like a thing of mouldered
fame.
This for the trusty cradle of her son
Did Rhea choose of yore; and to protect
His infant cries, had clamour made
thereon.
Within the mount a great old man erect
Looks out to Rome as if it were his
glass;
His shoulders Damietta's coast reject.
A head shapen of perfect gold he has;
Of pure silver his arms are, and his
breast:
But to the fork he is of molten brass.
Thence down he is all of iron, proved the
best
Except that the right foot is baked of
clay,
And on this, more than the other, doth
he rest.
All portions of him save the gold betray
Fissures that drop tears, oozing without
end,
Which through the cave, collecting,
force their way.
Their streams cascading in this valley
spend:
Acheron they make, and Styx and
Phlegethon;
Then by this narrow conduit they
descend
To where is no descending more; whereon
They form Cocytus; and what manner
of pool
It is, thou'lt see: words for it now I
have none.'

The figure of the old man is a fusion from Dante's reading of Ovid's description of the cyclic four ages of history, the Golden Age, the Silver Age, the Age of Brass, and the Age of Iron, with the statue that Nebuchadnezzar saw in a dream, which was interpreted to him by Daniel. It is a fusion, therefore, of the cyclic theories of classical history with the linear history of Christian tradition, because the old man represents the stage humanity has reached as a whole,

delayed at Crete on the journey to Rome, with his back to Damietta—a stage
on the journey of the great circle of pilgrimage, depicted on maps of the time as
standing on a straight line between Crete and Sinai, and the scene of two great
crusading triumphs and disasters of the Templars in 1218 and 1249—gazing at
Rome as in a mirror, because in 1300 Rome is the seat of papal power but wants
the presence of the imperial power. Mankind has received the redemptive
power of the cross but lacks the balancing force of the eagle, and therefore the
old man rests more heavily on his right foot of clay, which means the papacy,
than he does on his left foot of iron, which means the empire. The journey of
humanity to redemption may be represented as in Figure 13.[50] The old man, as
the mid-point of the journey, connects not only with the figural interpretation
of the Great Circle of pilgrimage, which ends in the eternal Rome in Heaven,
but also with the prophecies of the *veltro* and the DXV. Virgil, the prophet
of empire, foretells the coming of the *veltro*, a deliverer who will drive the she-
wolf of cupidity, the carnal church, to Hell, and Beatrice foretells the coming of
the DXV. Who are these two mysterious figures and do they represent the same
personage? Pietro Alighieri thought the *veltro* was an emperor to come who
would reign universally as Augustus had done and he compared him to the 'new
man' described by Alan of Lille in his *Anticlaudianus*.[51] In a later version of his
commentary he said that his father was deliberately vague about his identity
but definitely states, as have many commentators since his time, that the *veltro*
and the DXV stand for the same emperor to come.[52] Though this is
considerable authority to go against, the logic of the imagery of the cross and
the eagle, and Dante's stated division of the temporal and the spiritual powers,
both in the *Monarchia* and the *Commedia*, incline me to Robert John's position
according to which these two, when interpreted as redeemers expected in the
future, are not identical but stand for the spiritual and temporal deliverers.
When we come to relate the *veltro* and the DXV to the four levels of meaning in

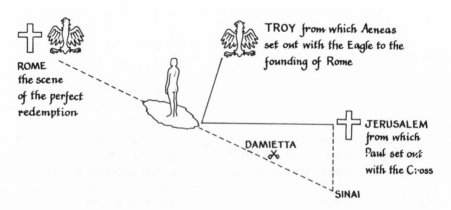

Figure 13 Crete and the pilgrimage routes

292

Chapters 18 and 19 we will see that other interpretations are equally valid, but here we are dealing with the allegorical level according to which the *veltro* is a truly spiritual pope and the DXV is the emperor who will refound the Temple. John explains the mysterious numerals by referring to the apocryphal book of Esdras,[53] from which the date of the completion of the rebuilding of the Temple by Zerrubabel after the Babylonian Captivity was worked out as spring 515 BC. Dante could have found this date in the Chronicle of Eusebius, the chief authority for the chronology of the ancient world.[54] Zerrubabel was one of three young men guarding Darius, king of the Medes and Persians. To win Darius' favour the three youths competed to name the strongest thing in the world. The first said 'wine' and the second 'the king', but Zerrubabel triumphed with his answer: 'Women are strongest: but above all things Truth beareth away the victory.'[55] Darius rewarded him with any request he might make and Zerrubabel reminded Darius of a vow he had made to rebuild the Temple in Jerusalem. As Zerrubabel was the builder of the second Temple so the DXV could be the builder of the third Temple, for which, of course, he would have to lead a successful Crusade, a desire for which Dante expresses several times.[56] The connexion of Zerrubabel with messianic hopes and with future redeemers does not cease there because the most popular and widely accepted prophecy of the end of the world current amongst medieval Jewry was the apocryphal Book of Zerrubabel (*Sefer Zerrubabel*), a firmly anti-Christian work written in the seventh century, which affirmed that Zerrubabel was preserved alive and in secret in Rome, the very seat of the enemy, and that one day he would appear to do battle with the oppressor named as Armilus, who combines the functions of Caesar and pope and is the son of Satan and a stone statue of a woman. After his victory Zerrubabel would rebuild the Temple.[57]

Dante could well have learned of this work from his Jewish acquaintances and contacts, the most likely source being Immanuel ben Zifroni, who introduced the themes of the *dolce stil nuovo* into his own Hebrew poetry and wrote an imitation of the *Commedia* also in Hebrew.[58] If Dante could adapt the *mi'raj* legend from Islam for the honour of Christianity, he could equally well reinterpret a Jewish prophecy that associated a redeemer figure with Rome and Jerusalem, with the destruction of the carnal Church led by an oppressor in whom the two powers are confounded, and with the promised building of the third Temple. He certainly knew of the Christian prophecies of a redeemer known as those of the pseudo-Methodius on which he drew for his letter to the Florentines and which his son Pietro quotes in his commentary.[59] Here, then, we can see once more an example of the process of fusion working in his creative imagination, bringing together the theme of the Christian redeemer and the imagery of the Temple by means of the Jewish legend of Zerrubabel. When the *veltro* and the DXV meet in Rome, the possibilities for humanity will be utterly transformed through the union of the cross and the eagle. Robert John also points out that the seal in use by the grand masters of the Templars, in the later thirteenth century, bore the device of an eagle standing on a cliff surmounted by a cross with two stars on either side,[60] thus drawing new significance from Valli's thirty symmetrical passages of the *Commedia* in which the symbols of eagle and cross occur. Helmut Hatzfeld, who maintains that John's Templar theory 'can solve better than any other theory certain problems of particularly obscure symbolism', gives a 'poetically draped syllogism' to express Dante's philosophy of the two beatitudes.

> Major: the eagle is as necessary to earthly bliss as the cross is to heavenly bliss. Minor: the Earthly Paradise is the necessary passage on the road to Heaven, as actually is the case in the architecture of the *Commedia*. Consequently: the eagle of the world Empire is necessary in order to guarantee a maximum chance for all to reach the celestial Paradise.[61]

The cross and the eagle symbolize at once the means of perfection for mankind as a whole and the healing of the intellect and the will in the individual soul. They recur constantly throughout the poem: first of all in the trinity of ladies; in Lucia, as the eagle of the dream during which he reaches Purgatory; in Beatrice, who in the Earthly Paradise appears as herself and as the Divine Wisdom of Christ; and in Mary, in whom both aspects are harmonized as a citizeness of the just empire and as the mother of God-made-Man. This dual symmetry has been traced in the journey of the two poets: Virgil, who has the power of the eagle but lacks the redemption of the cross; and Dante, who is deprived of the eagle but who enjoys through baptism the saving grace of the cross. The good pagans of the first circle who did not know the cross are paralleled by the negligent rulers of the Ante-Purgatory, who were thwarted by the absence of the eagle. The travellers enter Hell through the first gate, made open by the cross, but cannot enter the second gate, that of the city of Dis, until a messenger of God—perhaps an angel or possibly either the eagle-bearer, Aeneas himself, carrying a *verghetta*, the golden bough, or the god Mercury who commanded Aeneas to leave Carthage for Italy (this last is Pietro Alighieri's identification)—commands its opening. The cross form of the angel with outspread wings at the opening of the *Purgatorio* is paralleled by Lucia as an eagle. In the pageant of the eagle and the tree the two symbols are brought together. In the heaven of the moon are those who were lacking in will, the quality of the eagle, and in the heaven of Mercury are those who went astray through love of glory, a sign of weakness in the intellect, which the cross heals. These two symbols receive their ultimate consummation in the cross of the heaven of Mars and the eagle of Jupiter.

This is one of several major patterns of the *Commedia*. So far we have looked at some of the themes of the poem, at where Dante might have learnt of them and how some of them appear in the poem. Between influences and the finished work, there is a black box: the poet's mind and what happens there to make the golden transmutation of originality. To that we now turn in the search for inspiration as a growth into the light and life of the mind of the Creator.

17

The grace of inspiration

Where does inspiration come from? How does it convey such superhuman powers of understanding and organization? In what way does it infuse language with the light of emotion? These questions underlie all investigations into the origins of civilization and I believe that Dante provided the fullest answers to them of any writer in our Western culture.

True inspiration comes to the artist in a state of enhanced consciousness. The first author I know of to investigate the existence of higher states of consciousness in a scientific way, by collating examples from the lives of men and women from various periods and different cultures, and to look for what was common to their experience was the Canadian doctor, Richard Maurice Bucke, writing at the turn of the century. He included Dante amongst his examples[1] and this seems to have been the first time that Dante's mysticism was treated in the wider context of the Perennial Philosophy rather than as a link in the chain of the Western Christian contemplative tradition. Bucke was led to his investigation by certain remarkable experiences of his own; through collating the examples of others he came to the conclusion that in addition to the states of simple consciousness and self-consciousness, there is a higher state which he called cosmic consciousness. Later writers, influenced by him, have preferred to divide this higher state of consciousness into two. The first may be called subjective consciousness and relates to states of self-awareness in which we experience an exceptional condition of emotional and intellectual unity, with an accompanying deepening of understanding. The term 'cosmic consciousness' is reserved for the second and higher of these states of consciousness, a condition of union with the Divine Self in which there is no division between the Maker of the universe and the individual soul. The supreme examples of this in the *Commedia* is Dante's experience after the vision of the Trinity of being taken up in intellect and will (*disio* and *velle*) into the love 'che muove il sole e l'altre stelle'.

There are of course gradations within each higher state of consciousness just as there are fluctuations in ordinary and lower states of awareness, and in the next chapter we will consider a scale of such steps in relation to the *Commedia*.

The state of subjective consciousness is what Dante experiences in increasing fullness on Mount Purgatory after the intervention of Lucia and with the re-ordering of his inner life. The term 'cosmic consciousness' applies particularly aptly to the return of Beatrice and his ascension with her through the spheres of heaven. As these states are suggested in the poem, however, they must only be approximations of numerous moments of illumination that Dante experienced in the course of his life and which he drew on for the *Commedia*.

We fortunately possess a clear and precise account by a medieval writer of these two higher states of consciousness written before Dante's time. This is in a letter of the Rhineland prophetess and poet, Hildegard of Bingen. Like Dante, she had an intense visual imagination and she experienced numerous visions which she described in writing and in pictures. Copies of certain of her works are known to have been circulating in Italy in Dante's time, for example in the library of Santa Croce. Here, though, I am more interested in the similarity of her experience than with her possible influence on Dante. She says of these two higher states of consciousness:

> From my infancy up to the present time, I being now more than
> seventy years of age, I have always seen this light in my spirit and not
> with external eyes, nor with any thoughts of my heart nor with help
> from the senses. But my outward eyes remain open and the other
> corporeal senses retain their activity. The light which I see is not
> located but yet is more brilliant than the sun, nor can I examine its
> height, length, or breadth, and I name it the 'cloud of the living
> light'. And as sun, moon, and stars are reflected in water, so the
> writings, sayings, virtues and works of men shine in it before me. And
> whatever I thus see in vision the memory thereof remains long with
> me. Likewise I see, hear, and understand almost in a moment and I
> set down what I thus learn. . . . But sometimes I behold within this
> light another light which I name 'the Living Light itself'. . . . And
> when I look upon it every sadness and pain vanishes from my
> memory, so that I am again as a simple maid and not as an old
> woman. And now that I am over seventy years old my spirit,
> according to the will of God, soars upward in vision to the highest
> heaven and to the farthest stretch of the air and spreads itself among
> different peoples to regions exceedingly far from me here, and then I
> can behold the changing clouds and the mutations of all created
> things; for all these I see not with the outward eye or ear, nor do I
> create them from the cogitations of my heart . . . but with my spirit,
> my eyes being open, so that I have never suffered any terror when
> they left me.[2]

This remarkable passage contains many elements that would help to reconstruct Dante's own inspirations. First there are the two orders of inspiration, 'the cloud of the living light' and 'the Living Light itself', which correspond to the twin peaks of Parnassus, as we shall see. The first of these is a subjective state of higher consciousness in which through a clearing of the mind and the purification of the affections, experience is reorganized and understood in a totally new way. This may be compared to the level of inspiration from which Dante wrote before he passed through the rivers Lethe and Eunoe in the Earthly Paradise. The second order of inspiration accords with the objective state of higher consciousness into which Dante enters at the beginning of the *Paradiso* and through which he is drawn to the sight of the spiritual light from which all physical light derives. In both Hildegard and Dante this second order encompasses an expansion of being, far beyond the confines of the Earth, and from her words we gain a hint of an experience similar to Dante's when he looked down on the globe from a high celestial viewpoint.[3]

If it is granted that man is capable of such higher states of consciousness and that these states are frequently the source of artistic inspiration, then the way in which they are expressed will vary according to the talents, education, and environment of the individual experiencing them. There are three main stages, however, within the general framework of artistic creation that can be shown to be part of Dante's experience and that are supported by the experience of others. Inspiration is necessary in all the three stages which I call vision, interpretation, and composition. These stages are described in greater detail below and then related to the journey of the *Commedia* and the reunion with Beatrice.

Vision

In the term 'vision' I include all the various ways in which the initial inspiration comes from states of enhanced awareness. A moment of illumination can affect every side of a man's nature, psychologically and physiologically, both his awareness and the involuntary processes of his dream life. In the case of writers with pronounced visual imaginations such as Dante, it has a particular effect on the dreaming side of their natures, the dreaming condition that recurs throughout the day as well as in sleep (see p. 16), as though the light and nature of that higher consciousness changes the dream in the moment of awareness of it, revealing in the dream image the archetypal image latent in it or impressing on it a symbol that points the eternal significance in the transient picture. Symbol and picture can convey in a flash of time a vast body of thought which can take years to write out because, by their nature, they present all their contents simultaneously. It is as though the mind were melted by emotion and in that moment stamped with a seal. Dante speaks of the prophet Jeremiah receiving the impress of the divine command,[4] and of himself as receiving the shadow of the blessed realm signed upon his head.[5] What makes these dreams and waking visions different from the general flow of mental imagery recurring in the brain at night and during the day are the distinctive features of these states of higher consciousness: pure emotion and intellectual light. As these states endow the artist receiving them with an extraordinary sense of unity and a total reorganization of his mental capacities, so they give him the psychic energy to carry over to the works of art he makes out of these experiences the unity and the organization that impress his audience. A further consequence of the action of states of higher consciousness on the dream levels of the mind appears to be that the experience of conscious unity resonates on those levels to create new symbols and mental pictures, fusing them together from innumerable associations, memories, and images; in the mind of a poet such as Dante, when transformed by a state of higher consciousness, all past symbols, like the elders in Revelation, cast down the crowns of their former dominion and are changed by the voice of the one on the great white throne saying 'Behold, I make all things new'. This is the process in Dante's creative imagination I call 'fusion' and which accounts both for the many sources that can be claimed as influences on particular passages and for the originality of his conceptions.

An essential feature of such dream and mental images is that they are memorable. If the artist does not understand their significance at the time of receiving them, then, because of their memorability, they will recur time and again until he understands both their meaning and what he can make of them. Thus, in an image that evokes the figure of the great pilgrimage to the antipodean Jerusalem, Beatrice tells Dante that though he may not understand the pictorial and numerological riddles of what she has shown him, they will be to him the pilgrim's staff wreathed in palm leaves that he will bring back to ordinary life as evidence of where he has been.[6] The great virtue of this method of composition is that the poet has something fixed to return to so that he can measure his attempts at expression against this memorable and ideal original.

Interpretation

The next stage after the vision is that of interpretation in which reason and powers of discrimination are brought to bear on the memorable experience. Here once more we can take an example from the life of Joachim of Fiore.[7] One Easter morning when Joachim awoke to meditate, he perceived with the 'eyes of the mind' in the clarity of intelligence, a vision concerning the Book of Seven Seals in Revelation, a problem which had been agonizing him for a long time. On reading through his notes afterwards, he suddenly understood that the vision contained the answer to the concordance between the ages of the Old Testament and the New. The stone before the sepulchre was rolled away and the spirit shone forth from the letter of scripture as Christ had issued from the tomb. This experience was one that Joachim expected all men to have in time because the spirit was buried in the letter for all humanity. So Dante thought a great flame of art would follow the tiny spark of his own poetry.[8] The importance of interpretation lies in its scale: on whether an inspiration is interpreted in narrow subjective terms or, as in the examples of Joachim and Dante, from a viewpoint in which as far as possible the personal element is removed.

To understand Dante's own attitude to interpretation we must turn to the long tradition preceding him of prophecy and its meaning. In describing to Bonagiunta da Lucca his manner of writing, he said that his verse was dictated to him. 'Dictation' was an expression previously only used for the means by which the prophets had received their messages. His political letters reveal the powerful influence on him of his study of the Hebrew prophets, and his use and adaptation of their language and style of metaphor reveal his conviction that, as they had in their time, he had a special insight into the historical currents of his epoch and a duty to his fellow men to share his insight, guiding them into the ways that would fulfil the divine purpose. His skill in using Hebraic prophetic language derives from the closeness between his own developed visual imagination and their great pictorial images, the seraphim and cherubim of Isaiah, the widowed city of Jeremiah, the four beasts of Ezekiel, and the angels of the Revelation of St John the Divine. To invest his own work with the authority of these older prophets, he had not only to assume their tone and adapt their imagery but also to reveal the nature of his own inspirations and to incorporate descriptions of his creative processes into the organic nature of the *Commedia*. Since the time of John the Baptist, the role of the prophet had changed from setting out new doctrine to giving guidance in human activities,[9] and here Dante was following a legitimate tradition.

Because it concerned the nature and status of prophecy, the relationship between a visionary apparition and its interpretation had been much discussed by earlier Christian thinkers, especially by St Augustine. Though much of the classical writings on divination, dreams, their interpretation and significance had been preserved in Macrobius' commentary on the *Dream of Scipio*,[10] and these categorizations were widely known, being quoted by Jean de Meung and later by Chaucer, they had lacked the thoroughness and precision of Christian writings on the subject. It was these Christian writings that Dante found agreed best with his own experience. In writing about prophecy, St Augustine defined the three levels of vision by which, progressively, man may apprehend divine truth: corporeal vision, spiritual vision, which mediates between the first and third kinds, and intellectual vision, which is the highest.[11] These three levels of conveying truth seem to correspond to the three parts of the *Commedia*, and to decide the kinds of imagery used in each of those three parts. Just as Dante converted the fourfold method of interpretation from a technique devised for exegesis of Holy Writ into an active means of analysing and reconstructing his own inspirations, so, here, he seems to have adopted a categorization of visions intended primarily for defining the status of the Old Testament prophets, and to have transformed it into practical means of organizing his material, for which his authority was his own conviction that he too was a prophet. The fourfold interpretation depends on this categorization of his inspirations as prophecies because the inspirations provided the basic material of experience on which the method of interpretation was brought to work. St Augustine placed the ability to interpret a vision far above that of receiving a vision. There are many cases in the Old Testament where a dream or vision is seen by one man and its significance is revealed by another. Belshazzar sees the hand-writing, 'Mene, mene, tekel upharsin', but it is Daniel who tells him that it means that his kingdom is numbered by God and finished and that he has been tried in the balance and found wanting.

There is an interesting parallel here with Coleridge[12] who, having been told by a friend of a dream about a ship's company of spectres, made that the starting-point of *The Ancient Mariner*, taking his friend's dream, merging it with the 'ocular spectra' or waking images he derived from his own reading, and making a masterpiece by his superior ability to interpret the experience of others. In his case, as with Dante and Blake, an essential part of that superiority was the way in which the images of others were synthesized and presented as new wholes in their own imaginations, depending on that inner fusion for their intensity of meaning and emotion. Poets are not always so clever in the interpretation of their own inspirations or the insights offered them by others. This is frequently because they devalue them by treating them personally. Rilke writes of the 'ancient curse of poets' ('O alter Fluch der Dichter'): they indulge in self-pity instead of uttering; they sit in judgment on their emotions instead of shaping their emotions; like invalids they use the language of complaint to moan about where it hurts, instead of doing what they ought to be doing: to transmute their selves into words as the masons of the cathedrals carved themselves into the permanent stone.[13] These lines of Rilke's have a direct relevance to what we have already seen of Dante's own practice in the transmutation of self-pity into the poetry of praise. The stages by which Rilke came to write the *Duino Elegies* and the *Sonnets to Orpheus*, the greatest examples of the poetry of praise achieved in our own century, are well documented,[14] and are all the more interesting as objective confirmations of Dante's experience because, unlike Dante, Rilke was a poet unable to accept the Christian revelation. For two modern examples of artists incapable or only partly capable of the imaginative leap necessary to control and transmute their inspirations we can take the fictional account of Thomas Mann's *Doktor Faustus* and the actual experience of the Russian Symbolist poet, Alexander Blok. *Doktor Faustus*, as has already been mentioned, is constructed on numerological principles and bears many marks of the influence of the *Commedia*. (The opening of *Inferno* II appears on its title page.) There, the life of the composer Adrian Leverkühn, the Dionysiac Lutheran, is related after his death by his friend, Serenus Zeitblom, the Apollonian Catholic classicist, writing in secret during the triumph of the German armies in the last war and then, as his tale of spiritual destruction proceeds, against the background of the defeat and collapse of the Nazi régime.

The grace of inspiration

Leverkühn, for all his sympathy and intelligence, withdraws into his private world, believing that his inspiration is granted by a pact with the devil and dying in a state of syphilitic paralysis, rejecting all the help and light his friend, the narrator, could have given him.

Under the pressures of the Russian revolution, Blok—who by the way was deeply influenced by Dante in his cult of the Beautiful Lady—believed he was in contact with the Spirit of Music, the underlying genius of history. He was so much at the mercy of his inspiration that in his poem, 'The Twelve', he found the figure of Christ forcing itself into the poem against all his preconceptions and fixed attitudes, a poem that was shortly followed by complete creative failure till his death.[15] These are only two examples of the many features in an artist's temperament that may limit his powers of interpretation, but perhaps the most damaging is the desire to see the political and historical currents of his age almost entirely in terms of his own ambitions or desire for vengeance. In the dreadful circumstances of his exile there can have been few greater temptations for Dante than to make use of his visions and inspirations for his private and political ends. Later in this chapter we will come upon the extraordinary way in which he escaped from this temptation. It is one of the many ways in which he resembles William Blake. Blake had found the great events of his age, the American and French revolutions and unrest in England, threatening to dominate his imaginative life. Then in a vision by the Sussex coast in 1800,[16] in the course of which he saw particles of light turning into men and women, the very way in which the souls of *Paradiso* appear to Dante, he underwent a lasting change: he believed in the truth of the Apocalypse; the angelic and eternal workings of history came to be of infinitely deeper significance to him; he grasped the inner meaning of the four Zoas (see p. 331) and, as a result, where all his earlier prophetic writings had ended in woe and tragedy, the later and rewritten ones end in the triumph of the good. One of these later works was *Milton*. This, and Wordsworth's *Prelude*, constitute the fullest poetic expressions of the workings of the poet's mind after Dante's own *Commedia*. In Blake's poem the soul of Milton is required to make good the faults of vision and interpretation of his life. Interpretation is made perfect when Milton horrifies the immortals with his announcement of his sacrifice of his ego to the Divine Imagination, using the very imagery of Easter and the resurrection that Dante employed in the *Commedia*.

> I will arise and look forth for the morning of the grave;
> I will go down to the sepulcher to see if morning breaks;
> I will go down to self annihilation and eternal death,
> Lest the last Judgement come & find me annihilate . . . .[17]

Turning back to Dante, having dealt with the stages of vision and interpretation, we will consider the third of the three stages of inspiration.

Composition

There were two occasions in his later works on which Dante described his manner of composition and both describe his surrender to a voice or aspect of his higher nature. The stage of composition is when the Poem becomes the poem, when the words of the dominant hemisphere of the brain fall in love with the rhythms and pictures of the non-dominant hemisphere and the operations of both are married by a unifying source which we may call song. Thus when Bonagiunta da Lucca in Purgatory asks if he sees before him the man who drew out the new verse beginning 'Donne ch'avete intelletto d'amore', Dante replies:

——Io mi son un che, quando
Amor me spira, noto, ed a quel modo
che ditta dentro, vo significando[18]

——I am one who when
Love breathes within me, takes note and
  to the mode
That he dictates within, I go giving
  significance

Here there are three stages: the emotional inspiration of Love, the noting or recording of the inspiration, and the dictation by Love in a particular musical mode which Dante follows in writing. This indicates that he wrote out of a state of music in the mind and, furthermore, as the next example shows, could only write poetry when he was in this state. This passage is from his first Eclogue to Giovanni del Virgilio:

'Est mecum quam noscis ovis gratissima'
  dixi,
'ubera vix quae ferre potest, tam lactis
  abundans.
Rupe sub ingenti carptas modo ruminat
  herbas.
Nulli juncta gregi nullis assuetaque caulis
sponte venire solet nunquam vi poscere
  mulctram.
Hanc ego praestolor manibus mulgere
  paratus.'[19]

'You know,' I said, 'I have a dearest
  ewe
So rich in milk, her udders weight her
  down.
Beneath a massive cliff she chews plucked
  herbs.
Part of no flock, accustomed to no fold,
She comes spontaneously and never
  driven
By force towards the milking pail. I
  mean
To milk her with my hands.'

The plucked herbs (*herbas carptas*) on which the ewe feeds are all the impressions, thoughts, studies, and patterns, that Dante has fed through his imagination, memory and intellect, in the preparatory work for the poem. After this preparation it is simply a matter of settling his thoughts and awaiting her spontaneous coming like a grace from above. The ewe represents the processes in his creative soul over which he has no direct control but which, by long experience, he has learnt to trust; the making of the milk from the plucked herbs represents the resynthesizing of his impressions through the working of dreams and visions and the full udders are the sign that all that preparation is suddenly ready for expression in words.

With Dante, the beginning of the desire to write was associated with an interior landscape, a bare mountain cliff that meant at once the hill of the Muses and the mountain of penitence.[20] Here the dearest ewe that feeds alone beneath the huge cliff may be interpreted as the lost sheep recovered of Matthew 18; in the Vulgate, which was, of course, the version of the Bible used by Dante, the lost sheep is female. So Dante is not just making an interesting revival of the pastoral tradition he knew from Virgil's *Bucolics*; he is uniting that tradition to the teaching of the Good Shepherd—a point that may be further illustrated from a use of similar imagery that comes in the *Purgatorio* after the episode when Cato rebukes the souls for listening to Casella sing Dante's poem 'Amor che ne la mente', thereby implying that there were far higher points of inspiration awaiting him, and before the intervention of Lucia as the eagle of Jove. In this passage Dante shows one group of souls as shy before him as a flock of sheep pressing against the steep cliffs of the mountain:

Come le pecorelle escon del chiuso
  a una, a due, a tre, e l'altre stanno
  timidette atterrando l'occhio e 'l muso;
e ciò che fa la prima, e l'altre fanno,
  addossandosi a lei, s'ella s'arresta,
  semplici e quete, e lo 'mperché non
    sanno;[21]
	As sheep come from the fold where they
	    were penned
	By one, by two, by three; and, eye and
	    nose
	Keeping to earth, timid the others
	    stand;
	And what the first one does the other
	    does,
	All simple and quiet in their ignorance,
	And, if she stand still, huddle to her
	    close;

Each one of these, the late repentant souls, recall the one lost sheep over whose recovery there is more rejoicing than over the ninety-nine which had not gone astray.

To the Christian Dante the inspiration of a truly Christian art depended on practical fulfilment of the precepts of Christ who began his teaching with the words, 'Repent: for the kingdom of heaven is at hand.'[22] The word generally translated as *poenitentia* in the Vulgate and as 'repentance' in the English versions is, in the Greek, *metanoia* which carries none of the associations of guilt and mortification now borne by those translations, but means a complete alteration in the habitual attitudes of the mind—a transformation of the inner man.[23] This theme will be developed more fully in the account of Dante's journey up the mountain of penitence. The sources of his art deepened with his understanding of God as the supreme artist,[24] and though there is no direct record of this I think he prepared himself for writing by spiritual exercises. Such preparation is recorded of other writers,[25] and the emphasis on the *punto*, the point of contemplation in the *Paradiso*, may, in fact, be evidence of such a practice.

How did the words become married to the visions? So far we have concentrated on Dante's intense inner visual experiences, but he was also subject to the audio-hypnagogic phenomena—words, music, sounds—which are described by many mystics and artists. The Franciscan tertiary Angela da Foligno (1248–1304) described many such experiences,[26] and these too are among the means by which the souls of Purgatory are purified. They are there, I believe, because Dante's visual inspirations were often accompanied or followed by inner vibrations of sound, sometimes as music, rhythm, or words.

This is borne out by the use of the word *modo* (mode or pitch) to describe the way Love dictated his inspirations to him. These would come to him not only as an inner hearing of the shrieks of the damned:

Quivi sospiri, pianti e alti guai
    risonavan per l'aere sanza stelle,
    per ch'io al cominciar ne lagrimai.[27]
	Here lamentations, groans and wailings deep
	Reverberated through the starless air
	So that it made me at the beginning weep.

or as the hymns sung on the cornices of Purgatory, or the exultant carols of Paradise. They also conveyed the particular emotion of a scene, and laid on his heart the memory of this emotion, together with an indication of the rhythm that would best preserve and convey this emotion in his hendecasyllabics. It has been demonstrated that the immense variety of rhythmical invention that Dante exhibits within these lines relates in each case to the subject he is describing and differs according to its nature.[28] As form is a function of frequency, the rhythms contained in themselves the numerological significance of the form of the poem as a whole and in its parts. Dante recovered and made part of his practical experience the old Pythagorean view of the universe as harmony analysable into mathematical principles, turning his ear to the sung word of the Logos, in whose resonance space and time appeared and whose continuous reverberations he interpreted to humanity.

Purgatory, repentance, and inspiration

In writing his poetry out of his own mystical experience, Dante lifted yet another embargo laid upon thought by St Augustine. This time it was St Augustine's condemnation of poetry which was taken up with new force in the thirteenth century by the scholastics. Albertus Magnus, for example, defined poetry as the lowest part of logic or rational philosophy.[29] There was one difficulty in the way and that was the frequent use of metaphor in the scriptures. Thomas Aquinas justified it by saying that the symbolic method is common to both poetry and theology. Poetry deals with things that, because of their basic lack of truth, cannot be grasped by reason. Theology pertains to those truths which are above reason.[30]

There was, in fact, a revulsion against this attitude to poetry in Dante's time. Quite apart from Dante's own practice, Albertino Mussato speaks of poets as having been the theologians of ancient times.[31] The movement grew after Dante's death, notably with Boccaccio's praise of poetry as theology in his life of Dante and with other writings.[32] Coluccio Salutati was so convinced of the divine origins of poetry that he tried to convince a sceptical Dominican on this point by saying that if the Dominican denied the authority of inspiration to poets he should deny it also to the scriptures.[33] Landino finally settled the question by placing poetry high above the liberal arts and describing the inspiration of the poet as a divine fury.[34] To him God is the supreme poet and the world is his poem.

Dante did not enter explicitly into this debate; he simply overrode it in practice. He took the technical language of the scholastic theologians and translated it directly into Italian. This scholastic Latin has been called the first scientific language of modern Europe,[35] because it was a language deliberately bared of associations, a language, it was hoped, of total objectivity. By drawing it into the usage of a great vernacular he, at the same time, made that vernacular into a vehicle for intellectual thought and made it subservient to the very purpose from which it was meant to provide an escape, the associative communication which is the nature of poetry. Even though, however, he made it subservient to poetry, he nevertheless preserved its scientific character, not just in his theological disquisitions, but in the objectivity with which it enabled him to describe his own mental and creative processes.

He described these processes in three ways: the imagery of the Muses and Apollo (which is taken up in the next chapter), imagery drawn from the Gospels supported by Dionysius' portrayal of the angels as the singers of divine hymnody and as the ministers of inspiration to men, and in terms of the faculty psychology of his own day. He made, however, notable changes in faculty psychology where the origin and power of the imagination was concerned, for he related depth of inspiration to the growth of spiritual light within him. In his dependence on the technical terms of faculty psychology he was employing the most up-to-date scientific language of his day, but, in modifying it to fit his own observations and experiences, he was acting as a scientist studying the processes of the imagination.

In terms of St Augustine's grades of prophecy, the *Inferno* is on the level of corporeal vision, and this fits with the experiences described there in terms of faculty psychology. The impressions of the senses, of natural observation, of physical effort, of the impact of emotion on physiology, as when Dante faints with terror or weeps in sympathy, are fed through from the seat of imagination in the first cell of the brain to the memory in the posterior cell and are guided and disciplined by Virgil, the *lumen naturale* of reason.

On arriving on the shores of Mount Purgatory, where the light of the heavenly bodies is once more visible, there is a gradual change in the order of inspiration. He is ascending from the corporeal level of prophecy to the spiritual, which is a preparation of his understanding for the experience of spiritual light. Here, he can do what he could not do in the unnatural world of Hell: sleep, dream, see waking visions, and respond to the beauties of nature and art. Cato's assault on him and the other souls for listening to Casella sing 'Amor che ne la mente mi ragiona', the poem which, as was noted above, he probably regarded as the high point of his inspiration in his poetic career up to the *Commedia*, is his acknowledgment that that inspiration of light was a mere shadow of the revelation that is to come. He deliberately shows himself and the other souls in a state of rapture that, as he will soon demonstrate by the effect of divine art in Purgatory, is only a stage in the possibilities of aesthetic delight. As Cato drives them on, Virgil is stung in his conscience while Dante is more worried by the effect of the rebuke on Virgil than on himself. This is another anticipation of what will happen to Dante himself in the Earthly Paradise when he experiences the effect of conscience, directly, in himself.

The succeeding cantos up to the entry into Purgatory show Dante more and more aware of the vacillations of his own mind, vacillations expressed through his worries about his shadow and the effect of it on the souls in Ante-Purgatory. This is an anticipation through uncertainty about corporeal light of the impending revelation through inner spiritual light. Then grace descends in the form of Lucia, the third of the trinity of ladies and the most mysterious of them. In that trinity she is the aspect of the Holy Spirit. Dante knows her only in a dream as an eagle, the bird that, according to the bestiaries, could gaze directly at the sun. Her name is a modified anagram of Aquila —ACUILA. She initiates through grace the process of *metanoia*, the changing or passing beyond of the mind. She bridges the gap between the corporeal and spiritual levels of prophecy and initiates the imagery of the inner light of the inspiration of Christian art. She also initiates the process of the training of Dante's will which in *metanoia* is a change in the inner man, a change that goes so deep that it affects the involuntary processes of the psyche. This is why she appears in a dream, the first of three dreams and two waking visions Dante experiences as he climbs up the mountain. To follow the Templar interpretation and the imagery of the cross and the eagle described in the last chapter: the Templars apparently paid special devotion to her because, in her defence at the trial that preceded her martyrdom, she said that those who live chastely and piously are the Temple of the Holy Spirit[36] —a further link with her identification with the third person of the Trinity. In the dream of Lucia he sees the eagle above him about to stoop. He seems to be on Mount Ida, above Troy, the very place from which Ganymede was taken up to Olympus. As in certain kinds of dream, he is detached enough to comment on what he sees, saying:

Fra me pensava: 'Forse questa fiede	Within me I thought 'Perhaps only because
pur qui per uso, e forse d'altro loco	
disdegna di portarne suso in piede.'[37]	Of habit he strikes here, and from elsewhere
	Scorneth to carry up aught in his claws.'

thus emphasizing the importance of the spiritual stage he has reached. Then the eagle bears him up to the fire whose heat is so intense, that he wakes from the dream to find the sun over two hours risen and his face towards the sea.

St Augustine had said that there was no need for man to be the victim of the impressions falling on him because he has the power of will to master them, to transform them either into fantasies that lead to right conduct or into phantasms leading to damnation. In saying this he freed men from the necessity of believing they were the slaves of their imaginations. By connecting the ability of the imagination to make its own syntheses of sense experience with the freedom of the will, he established the creation of fantasies and therefore of imaginative art as the concern of the inner eye.[38] Dante, on the journey towards the freeing of his will, has to learn to endure the brightness of inner spiritual light because internal vision, like external vision, is blinded unless it is strong enough. Bonaventure, using the same imagery of light for this stage, says, after quoting St Augustine, that 'the light of all who reason truly is kindled at that truth [in eternal art] and strives to return to it', and goes on to say: 'you can see the truth through yourself, the truth that teaches you, if concupiscence and phantasms do not impede you and place themselves like clouds between you and the truth'.[39]

So Dante, on passing through the gate of Purgatory, begins the experience of what souls in that world have to experience: a re-ordering of their imaginative and dream life through the right use of images and through the training to endure the light of spirit. On the first cornice, of the proud, he is exposed to art, to what he has been deprived of since the conversations with the poets in Limbo, in this case the sculptures that would put not only Polycleitus but also Nature to shame. For this is divine art, art of an undreamed-of level of inspiration, as Dante acknowledges in the lines:

Colui che mai non vide cosa nova	He, to whose sight no new thing can appear,
produsse esto visibile parlare,	
novello a noi perché qui non si trova.[40]	Fashioned this visible language, to us new,
	Since such a thing never was fashioned here.

These sculptures carved in marble portray examples of humility, of Mary and the angel of the Annunciation, of David dancing before the Ark, of the justice of Trajan to the widow. From his delighted contemplation of these, Dante turns to meet the proud, staggering under the stones they bear like corbel sculptures, and he bends down to converse with the once-arrogant artist and illuminator Oderisi of Gubbio. As they progress, Dante looks down on the pavement to find it covered with depictions of examples of pride, thirteen examples drawn from antiquity and the Old Testament, set out in four terzains beginning with the word 'Vedeva', four with 'O', four with 'Mostrava', and a final terzain describing the pride of Troy, in which each line begins with the key words of the pattern, thus:

Vedeva Troia in cenere e in caverne;	I saw Troy gaping and in ashes laid.
o Ilïón, come te basso vile	O Ilion, thee how vile and desecrate
mostrava il segno che lì si	The witness of the sculpture there
discerne![41]	betrayed!

The key to the pattern is the word VOM or UOM, emphasizing the moral lesson of the carvings, and Dante drives it home by castigating his readers as children of Eve, daring them to stride on with upright faces and not look down at their evil path.[42] From delight in divine art in the external world, Dante moves to the impress of the divine through the visions of the inner eye. He describes two series of these waking visions on either side of the experience of the black smoke of the cornice of the wrathful.

After Virgil has spoken to him on love, in Canto XV Dante is suddenly caught up into what he calls an ecstatic vision. He sees three pathetic and noble examples of gentleness. In the first he sees many people in a temple and a woman on its threshold uttering the words of Mary to Christ among the doctors. This is displaced by the sight of the tyrant Pisistratus placating a weeping woman who demands vengeance, and turning the edge of her wrath. In the third example he sees people stoning a youth, shouting, 'Kill him! Kill him!' As the youth dies he prays God to forgive them.

As Dante comes to, recognizing what he calls his not false errors, Virgil tells him he has been staggering as though drunk or asleep for over half a league. Walking towards the westering sun they enter the black smoke where Marco Lombardo delivers his great oration on free will and the two suns. Marco ends as he discerns the light of the angel of the cornice beaming through the smoke and the two travellers pass out of the blackness. Dante now calls on his reader's experience of mists in the Alps to understand how he, high on the mountain, met the sunlight coming out of the smoke and then underwent a further series of waking visions, this time of three examples of wrath:

Sì, pareggiando i miei co' passi fidi	So, measuring with my master's faithful tread
del mio maestro, usci' fuor di tal nube	My steps, from such a cloud did I come out
ai raggi morti già ne' bassi lidi.	To rays on the low shore already dead.

O imaginativa che ne rube
  talvolta sì di fuor, ch'om non s'accorge
  perché dintorno suonin mille tube,
chi move te, se 'l senso non ti porge?
  Moveti lume che nel ciel s'informa,
  per sé o per voler che giù lo scorge.
De l'empiezza di lei che mutò forma
  ne l'uccel ch'a cantar più si diletta,
  ne l'imagine mia apparve l'orma;
e qui fu la mia mente sì ristretta
  dentro da sé, che di fuor non venìa
  cosa che fosse allor da lei ricetta.
Poi piovve dentro a l'alta fantasia
  un crucifisso, dispettoso e fero
  ne la sua vista, e cotal si moria;
intorno ad esso era il grande Assüero,
  Estèr sua sposa e 'l giusto Mardoceo,
  che fu al dire e al far così intero.
E come questa imagine rompeo
  sé per sé stessa, a guisa d'una bulla
  cui manca l'acqua sotto qual si feo,
surse in mia visïone una fanciulla
  piangendo forte, e dicea: 'O regina,
  perché per ira hai voluto esser nulla?
Ancisa t'hai per non perder Lavina;
  or m'hai perduta! Io son essa che
    lutto,
  madre, a la tua pria ch'a l'altrui
    ruina.'[43]

O Fantasy, that dost at times so rout
  Our senses that a man stays negligent
  Although a thousand trumpets sound
    about,
Who moves thee, if senses naught to thee
    present?
  There moves thee a light which of itself
    is shaped
  In heaven, or by a will wherefrom 'tis
    sent
The sin of her who from her form escaped
  Into the bird which most delights to
    sing,
  Printed its traces on my fancy rapt;
And here within its own imagining
  So closeted my mind was, it could then
  Receive the imprint of no outer thing.
Within my lofty fancy I next saw rain
  One crucified upon whose visage
    showed,
  In the act of dying so, a fierce disdain.
Beside him great Ahasuerus stood,
  Esther his wife, and Mordecai, he
  Who in speech and act was incorruptly
    good.
And as this image broke spontaneously,
  Like to a bubble when it findeth fail
  The water, under which it came to be,
Rose in my vision, making grievous wail,
  A maiden, saying: 'Queen, why didst
    thou choose
  To become naught, letting thy wrath
    prevail?
Thou hast slain thyself, Lavinia not to
    lose;
  Me now thou hast lost; I am she that
    sadly cries,
  Mother, for no death but thy life's dark
    close.'

This passage is a perfect example of how Dante, trusting to the *ovis gratissima*, brings together the plucked herbs of experience and has them returned to him in the milk of his verse. The complexity of these varied impressions, external and internal, is bound together by the strength of his control over the structure of his sentences: the Dantean syntax evolved through his prose works to woo his readers through the difficulties of his subject-matter into the clarity of his understanding. Here he draws his readers in, not only to the time and place of his position on the mountain, whose size, topography and different states of illumination he recapitulates in the line, miraculously lagging like the turning of a tide at evening, 'ai raggi morti già ne' bassi lidi' but also into the interior experience as he speaks of imagination as snatching 'us' out of 'ourselves'. He is also revealing one of the chief sources of his powers of visual presentation, the synthesis of scattered impressions wrought into the unity of 'ocular spectra' by the hidden artist of his high fantasy. At the same time, by showing how each scene rises in his mind and is displaced by another related in theme and visual content, he is revealing the dynamic of his associative technique, of how his similes and metaphors arise as related mental pictures evoked by their underlying similarity of mood, not as ornaments thought of later and forced upon the subject of his concern at the time of writing. The examples of meekness in the first series of waking visions arose probably in the following way: the figure of Mary, about to enter the Temple (a reminiscence of the three ladies seeking Love in the canzone 'Tre donne') and finding the child Jesus, is probably kneeling, as she is often shown so in depictions of this incident; the scene changes to the woman demanding justice from Pisistratus, again in an attitude of supplication; then the kneeling figure becomes that of the martyr Stephen as he is stoned to death. The people in the Temple in the first scene become the court surrounding Pisistratus and finally the angry crowd shouting out, 'Kill him! Kill him!' This last is reminiscent of the faces of women who appeared to Dante in the *canzone* predicting the death of Beatrice—angry faces telling him he will die. In discussing 'Donne ch'avete' in Chapter 8 it was shown how each succeeding stanza grew out of the *mise en scène* of the preceding one—and here we can see not only the same process of visual punning at work but also the way in which recurrent images tended to attract the same phrases and groups of words.

This process is also evident in the three examples of wrath in the second series. The first example refers to Procne who, in her madness of rage at learning that her husband Tereus had first raped her sister, Philomela, and then ripped out her tongue, murdered her son and served his flesh to Tereus. At this point the gods intervened to turn all three, Procne, Philomela, and Tereus, into birds. Here we can see Procne as a bird with opened wings being transformed into the crucifix of the second example on which Haman dies for wanting in his rage to destroy the Jews, watched from below by the three figures looking at his scornful and fierce expression, Ahasuerus, Esther, and Mordecai. Then comes another transformation, the cross bar of the crucifix turns into the beam from which hangs the body of Amata, the mother of Lavinia who committed suicide on believing that Turnus had been killed and that Aeneas would then marry Lavinia. The three watchers beneath the crucifix become the single distraught figure of Lavinia lamenting her mother's rage and its consequences. The T-shape of bird, crucifix, and beam with its hanging corpse, was the constant in this sequence like the kneeling or suppliant figure in the first.

The grace of inspiration

In describing these two sets of visions and the setting in which they appear, Dante brings together his own version of faculty psychology with the equation of imagination with inner light. He expressly denies a tenet of faculty psychology that there is nothing in the mind that was not in the senses by his rhetorical question:

O imaginativa che ne rube
    talvolta sì di fuor ch'om non s'accorge
    perché dintorno suonin mille tube,
chi move te, se 'l senso non ti porge?
    Moveti lume che nel ciel s'informa,
    per sé o per voler che giù lo scorge.[44]
	O Fantasy, that dost at times so rout
	    Our senses that a man stays negligent
	    Although a thousand trumpets sound about,
	Who moves thee, if senses naught to thee present?
	There moves thee a light which of itself is shaped
	In heaven, or by a will wherefrom 'tis sent.

The origin of such visions is in Heaven or by a will moved from Heaven. This resembles a passage in Bonaventure where, speaking of memory, he says it is not only formed from without by images but 'also from above . . . forms which cannot enter through the doors of the senses and the images of sensible things',[45] and it also connects with Aquinas' discussion of the way in which God may infuse intellectual light in a man's mind. Aquinas says that 'a man can form all manner of images by his natural capacity. . . . Yet a man cannot arrange these forms to represent truths which surpass the mind of man. For this the help of a supernatural light is needed.'[46]

Dante acknowledges, however, the contributory effect of surroundings in inducing or ending such experiences: he is brought out of the second set of visions by an external light, the light of the angel of meekness. There is a somewhat similar experience given to Parzival by Wolfram von Eschenbach[47] when Parzival, parted from his wife and lost in a snow-covered wood close to King Arthur's camp, but unaware of its proximity, gazes at three drops of blood left on the snow left by a wild goose wounded by a falcon. The blood on the snow turns into a vision of his beloved distant wife, Condwiramurs, that transfixes him and makes him entirely oblivious of the Knights of the Round Table who come to challenge him. Only when they interrupt his vision by passing between him and the blood on the snow does he come to enough to fight and defeat them. Gawain alone understands what is wrong and covers the blood with his scarf, freeing Parzival from his stupefaction and leading him to the court on yet another stage in the long journey that will lead to Munsalvaesche and the return of his wife.

Similarly, with these visions Dante is half-way in the process of *metanoia* initiated by Lucia which will receive its fulfilment in the Earthly Paradise. By the way Virgil urges him on after them and after the two remaining dreams of

Purgatory—the dream of the Siren, which warns him of the dangers of unbridled imagination, and the dream of Leah and Rachel, showing the active and contemplative lives—it is clear that such experiences, however wonderful, are stages on the way. They are pavilions providing rest and encouragement, not houses to abide in permanently, and this accords with the warnings in many mystical writings about such experiences.[48]

All these experiences, as described in the poem, are a training for the meeting with Beatrice and the transformation of his imagination. Gradually the involuntary processes of his dream life and his image-making are drawn by example and exposition more and more into the light of consciousness and under the direction of his will. It is only after the declaration by Virgil that his will is free, and he undergoes the shock of his confession, that his dream life and his waking experience coalesce in the living sight of Beatrice. The stricken conscience that he has noted in others is gradually brought nearer and nearer home to him. The significance of the VOM seen in the divine art of the pavement of the first cornice comes closer to his understanding in the sight of his old friend Forese among the emaciated gluttons, with their faces so drawn that Dante says anyone could read the letter 'm' in their faces, signifying man.* This is part of the progression to Dante's own experience of conscience in the reunion with Beatrice. In order to make clear the significance of the emotional transformation that followed, and its relationship to the making of the *Commedia*, we must turn again to Dante's own character.

The poem with the vision as its end offered him a means to a recovery of that state of blessedness, not only as a literary description, but as a constant challenge that his being should be the equal of his subject-matter: that Hell should be the scene of the stripping of his illusions: Purgatory the way of ascent for the purification of his will: and Paradise the circles of transformation where, by gradually being made capable of withstanding the smile of Beatrice, his soul is prepared for the vision of God. To make the poem work, to ensure it awoke in his audience the memory of the union with God that each of them had known when their souls were created, Dante must have experienced in some way the sublimity of which the poem is a shadow. But before he could start on the poem he had to reconcile the glory and joy of that vision with a terrible experience of black despair, loathing, and emptiness, the experience he was to objectify in the cone of Hell. There was a tension set up between the glorious vision and the need to justify the Giver of that vision as the Creator of a world of men who could provoke such loathing in him. The key to the reconciliation was the rediscovery of Beatrice.

I. A. Richards, in his extraordinary *terza rima* quarrel with the *Commedia*, has caught the black side of Dante's nature in these lines:

---

*This is a reference to the familiar medieval monogram representing omo (man) as (ᴼᴹᴼ) which is in itself a simplification of the device 𝕺𝕰𝕴, 'OMO DEI' (Man is of God).

Great hater was this poet, trusting above
A Source of Hate, his hatreds to confirm:
The very warp of the dread web he wove.[49]

but I would rejoin that Dante was saved from making his poem the vehicle of his hatred by the great transformation achieved by the rediscovery of Beatrice and the new depth of interpretation that this brought to his inspirations.

By concentrating on the *Inferno*, it is easy to share I. A. Richards's attitude, but it is an attitude that ignores the greater and the nobler parts both of the *Commedia* and of Dante's own complex character. One obvious feature of his character is the burning need to justify himself that constantly caused him to rewrite the past. A man can rewrite the past in order to hide the truth from himself or others and to create a purely private interpretation of past experience. Or he can be forced to rewrite it because a great emotional reversal reveals that he has not understood the significance of his life and that it has implications far beyond all private concerns. In Dante's case this emotional reversal enabled him to draw on every side of his nature, both good and bad, for the sources of his range of dramatic expression. Earlier, in dealing with his political life, I mentioned his love of humanity which would have been the distinguishing mark of his thwarted career as a statesman; his horror and disgust at humanity is the other side of that love. That hatred of sin receives much of its vehemence, though from the darker sides of his nature, from the sadism so explicit—even if mastered artistically—in the *Pietra* poems and so evident in the letter to the Florentines, from the brooding desire for vengeance and the talent for vicious abuse which were part of his make-up as an Italian politician of his period, and from the sarcasm that derived from his intellectual arrogance. Yet by the time he was writing the *Commedia*, these black aspects of his character are so transmuted by his art from their grosser outbursts in his earlier works that we must see them as parts of his nature that to a certain extent he had mastered in the course of his spiritual development. Rarely does he give any sense of gloating over the punishments of the damned; more often he shows distress and pity, as in the case of Paolo and Francesca or when he weeps at the sight of the soothsayers' distorted bodies. We may be revolted by some aspects of his behaviour, as when he tears hanks of hair from the head of Bocca degli Abati, or by some of the judgments, such as those on Mohammed and Ali, but our distaste is that of another age and a modern sensibility. What is more marvellous is the way in which he could acknowledge these sides of his nature and make use of them for the positive ends of his art.

Through his growth in self-knowledge gained in his progress on the mystical way, he won a mastery over his own emotions that enabled him, instead of being left to the mercy of their swings and vicissitudes, to manipulate them and draw on them for the dramatic effect and intensity of his depiction of other souls. Thus, to give one example, he could draw on his own capacity for hatred as well

313

as his experience of the hatred of others in portraying the sacrilegious thief Vanni Fucci, who exclaims:

'Vita bestial mi piacque e non umana,
  sì come a mul ch'i' fui; son Vanni Fucci
  bestia, e Pistoìa mi fu degna tana.'[50]
	'Bestial life pleased me, not life of men,
	  Mule that I was. For Vanni Fucci I am,
	  Beast! and Pistoia was my fitting den.'

Forced to reveal his name and his crime in robbing a sacristy for which another man was executed, Vanni feels the pain of this confession more than the snake bites that consume him, and in revenge he bursts out with a prophecy of the defeat of Dante's party, the Whites, ending with one of the most shockingly vehement lines of the poem:

E detto l'ho perché doler ti
  debbia[51]
	I've told you this because it will give you
	  pain.

It is incidents such as these that give an insight into the depths of horror that Dante knew at the realization of his own and his fellow men's capacity for evil; at the same time the objective force with which the character is displayed demonstrates the command he had achieved over his emotions in transmuting them into art.

If Lucia initiates the beginning of *metanoia*, the complete change of attitudes taught in the Gospels, then Beatrice marks the entry into the Kingdom of Heaven, which is only open to those who become as little children. Dante meets her in the Earthly Paradise, which is the cradle of the human race, and he says of her:

Così la madre al figlio par superba,
  com' ella parve a me; perché d'amaro
  sente il sapor de la pietade acerba.[52]
	As to a child a mother looks stern-faced,
	  So to me seemed she: pity austere in
	      thought
	  Hath in its savour a so bitter taste.

I would suggest that the fundamental inspiration of this crucial part of the *Commedia*, the rediscovery of Beatrice and her identification with the second figure in the trinity of ladies as the type of Christ, came to Dante late in 1312, after he had already to some extent withdrawn from the imperial party—if the dating and interpretation of the letter to Moroello Malaspina given in Chapter 14 is correct—when he had digested the news of the suppression of the Templars at the Council of Vienne, and when he had refused to take part in the siege of Florence. I also think that this inspiration reflected his deepening understanding of the mystical ideas underlying the philosophy of the *fedeli d'amore*, perhaps aided by Bonaventuran spirituality and the compassion he felt for the Templars (see pp. 413–15). This inspiration, which enabled him to link the vision of the Trinity with the necessity of depicting a journey through Hell, took the form of a waking vision in which he saw the sun of righteousness on a chariot in a wood and in which that sun turned into the lost love, Beatrice. From this was evoked the series of inspirations which turned into the two pageants of the Earthly Paradise, which he depicted as a figura of the Temple at Jerusalem, and which also enabled him to reinterpret and transform the experience already recorded in the *montanina canzone*. This overpowering experience transformed his ability to interpret and mould together all the scattered inspirations that had been accumulating in his memory in the period since 1300 of the proto-*Commedia*. It not only linked the theme of Hell with the final vision of the Trinity, but gave him the experience of 'living light itself', the full realization of the expanded imagination lit by the radiance of the spiritual sun.

This expansion of understanding was achieved in a moment of conscience in which he had an emotional insight into the truth about himself. This connects with his earlier description of his creative processes in the *Vita Nuova*. The new life described in the *Vita Nuova* began with the conscience-stricken realization of the gap that lay between Dante's claim that his blessedness lay in the praise of Beatrice and his actual practice, which bore no relation to this claim. From that moment of conscience came his first great creative achievement, the *canzone* 'Donne ch'avete intelletto d'amore'. There had been in that case a complete reversal in his emotional attitude; his negative self-pity had been transformed into the resounding praise of the miracle of Beatrice. A similar transformation was necessary in Dante before he was capable of understanding the way he had to go about returning to the vision. One of Beatrice's complaints against him in her recital of his misdeeds is that on her death and translation to heaven a great opportunity offered itself to Dante, not only because of the influences of the stars on Dante's birth but also because of an exceptional down-pouring of grace upon him. Beatrice says, expressly referring to the *Vita Nuova*:

questi fu tal ne la sua vita nova
    virtüalmente, ch'ogne abito destro
    fatto averebbe in lui mirabil prova.[53]
	This man was such in natural potency,
	    In his new life, that all the ingrained good
	    Looked in him to have fruited wondrously.

While she lived she led him to the right goal, but on her death, rising from flesh to spirit, although beauty and virtue had grown in her, he gave himself to others, following false images of the good. The inspirations she sent him both in dreams *e altrimenti*, he ignored and the only way to save him was to show him the damned, the *perdute genti*. Even before this denunciation Beatrice had reduced him to the state whereby

lo gel che m'era intorno al cor
    ristretto,
	The ice that round my heart had
	    hardened woke

spirito e acqua fessi, e con angoscia	Warm into breath and water, and from
de la bocca e de li occhi usei del	my breast
petto.[54]	In anguish, through mouth and
	through eyes, outbroke.

and when she commands him to acknowledge the truth of her words, he is so overcome by fear and confusion that it would have been necessary to lip-read in order to tell that his mouth had said 'Yes'. She forces him with further questions to confess that transient things, with their false pleasures, had turned his steps aside as soon as her face was hidden from him; and then, to ensure he is never tempted by the Sirens again, she describes the direction in which her buried flesh should have moved him. Neither nature nor art ever showed him beauty greater than the lovely body in which she was enclosed and which is now scattered in the Earth. If her death removed that delight in the highest beauty, how could any mortal things have attracted him into desiring them? At the first arrow of illusory things, that is, when her mortal body by its death proved an impermanent beauty, he should have risen up to follow her and no girl, no new attraction, should have weighed down his wings to make him a target for other shots. After, these and further reproaches Beatrice turns towards the griffin, whose two natures in one person make him a figure of Christ, and her beauty seems more marvellous than when she surpassed all other women on Earth. Dante is so overcome with contrition he faints and wakes to find himself being drawn through the waters of Lethe by Matelda.

This passage of Dante's confession, contrition, and absolution bears the same relation to the *Commedia* as the interview with the ladies that provoked the writing of 'Donne ch'avete' does to the *Vita Nuova*. In the earlier case it had been the self-pity of a young man in love that was transfigured into the language of praise, leading to Dante's realization of the significance of Beatrice in a cosmic setting. Now it was far more than self-pity that awaited transfiguration; it was the hatred, anguish, wounded pride, thwarted ambition, guilt and doubt of a man in his mid-forties, always aware of his unique combination of gifts of leadership, of expression, of personal authority, that were wasted in the frequently menial and poverty-stricken circumstances of his exile; all these sides of his nature, in the light of the many visions, offered themselves to him as the raw energy that had to be transformed into the finer energy of art.

The connexion of the last three cantos of the *Purgatorio* with the *montanina canzone* has already been noted. That poem blamed and abused the lady mentioned in it, as the poems of the *gabbo*, and the two *canzoni* excluded from the *Vita Nuova*, blamed and criticized Beatrice. There is also the extraordinary feature that this latest of his *canzoni* recalls the style of those two *canzoni* which are among his earliest in that form. What filled the gap between the *montanina canzone* and the realization that the lady described there is Beatrice was the waking vision of Beatrice as the sun of righteousness. Just as the moment of conscience had transformed his ability to interpret his inspirations at the beginning of his new life, so now he understood how he could interpret his inspirations as a new means of praise. Christian art revealed now through Beatrice is an art of praise, as is borne out by his description of the scene when Beatrice is restored to him as the sun veiled at dawn to the sung praises of the escorts of the pageant.

Quali i beati al novissimo bando
　surgeran presti ognun di sua caverna,
　la revestita voce alleluiando,
cotali in su la divina basterna
　si levar cento, *ad vocem tanti senis,*
　ministri e messaggier di vita etterna.
Tutti dicean: '*Benedictus qui venis!*'
　e fior gittando e di sopra e dintorno,
'*Manibus,* oh, *date lilïa plenis!*'
Io vidi già nel cominciar del giorno
　la parte oriental tutta rosata,
　e l'altro ciel di bel sereno addorno;
e la faccia del sol nascere ombrata,
　sì che per temperanza di vapori
　l'occhio la sostenea lunga fïata:
così dentro una nuvola di fiori
　che da le mani angeliche saliva
　e ricadeva in giù dentro e di fori,
sovra candido vel cinta d'uliva
　donna m'apparve, sotto verde manto
　vestita di color di fiamma viva.[55]

As at the last trump shall the saints arise,
　Crying alleluias to be re-attired
　In flesh, up from the cavern where each
　　lies,
Upon the heavenly chariot so inspired
　A hundred sprang *ad vocem tanti senis,*
　Messengers of eternal life, who quired
Singing together *Benedictus qui venis,*
　While from their hands flowers up and
　　down were thrown,
　And *Manibus O date lilia plenis.*
I have seen ere now at the beginning dawn
　The region of the East all coloured rose,
　(The pure sky else in beauty of peace
　　withdrawn)
When shadowed the sun's face uprising
　　shows,
　So that the mists, attempering his
　　powers,
　Let the eye linger upon him in repose;
So now for me amid a cloud of flowers
　That from the angels' hands up-floated
　　light
　And fell, withinside and without, in
　　showers,
A lady, olive-crowned o'er veil of white,
　Clothed in the colour of a living
　　flame,
　Under a mantle green, stole on my
　　sight.

A comparison of this passage and its context with the *montanina canzone* reveals the immense change in Dante's attitude to what he could make of his inspirations. In some way he had broken through to an emotional understanding of what the possibilities of the individual will are in man, and he had seen that the power of direction he possessed over his talents was linked to his own salvation.

　　Out of this inspiration Dante drew a new idea of what his duty was to his imaginative life, and, more, he understood what the consequences of this new understanding could be for humanity. He describes this scene of the renewal of his understanding through conscience as taking place on Easter Saturday. There is a further parallel here with Wolfram von Eschenbach, because the turning-point of the epic *Parzival* is the period that Parzival spends with the hermit Trevizent, who hears his first confession. Parzival, wearing the stolen armour and accoutrements of a Templar knight, comes upon Trevizent on Good Friday. Trevizent melts his heart, which is hardened against God, and reveals to him the dreadful consequences of his thoughtless battles and, above all, of his failure to ask the healing question of the Fisher King.[56] Only after Parzival's purgation does he proceed on the righting of the wrongs that afflict all humanity, and to the restoration of his queen and bride.

What led to this great reappraisal of Dante's inspirations? Beatrice attacks him for not realizing how he could have followed her even after her death, for attachments to other women, for disregarding the visions she sent him, for his connexion with a philosophical school (never identified but probably the learning of the ancients summed up in the figure of the vanished guide, Virgil) that limited his powers of interpretation, and amongst her complaints against him are these lines:

'Novo augelletto due o tre aspetta;
  ma dinanzi da li occhi d'i pennuti
  rete si spiega indarno o si saetta.'[57]

'The young bird waiteth two or three
  indeed;
But in the eyes of the full-fledged in
  vain
The net is spread and the arrows vainly
  speed.'

These lines both quote from, and taunt him with, his own words in his Letter VI to the Florentines when he included himself among the 'full-fledged and undefiled in the way' who will deny all mercy to his wicked fellow citizens in the disaster he foretells for the city. The catastrophe, as we know never fell on Florence and his realization that he had made a fool of himself made him reconsider his whole attitude to his prophetic insights. Just as he had not understood that the source of his visions was Beatrice, so he had not understood that the prophetic insights which he had employed with such violence of expression in his political letters had in fact a far deeper and wider significance, both where his own spiritual development and the spiritual welfare of mankind were concerned, than the aims of his party, his ambitions, and his desire for vengeance. Dante had actually said in the letter,

> And if my prophetic soul be not deceived, which announces what it
> has been taught by infallible signs and incontrovertible arguments,
> your city, worn out with ceaseless mourning, shall be delivered at the
> last into the hands of the stranger, after the greatest part of you has
> been destroyed in death or captivity. . . .[58]

That passage alone is enough to demonstrate how frighteningly close Dante was to paranoia, a state in which all his inner conflicts would have been masked by suspicions of persecution and extreme hostility to the world about him, varied by the worst of all delusions of grandeur: that his wrath worked 'the righteousness of God'. A reading of the scenes in the Earthly Paradise reveal, however, what it was that saved him from that fate, the vision of Beatrice as the rising sun, the insight of conscience that accompanied that vision, and the baring of his own nature made naked to Love.

What Dante is telling us, through the connexion he makes between his inspirations and his spiritual growth, is that we have a choice, when given an inspiration, to let it mirror our own private concerns or to interpret it according to the universal truth it contains. Therefore our ability to create depends upon the quality and freedom of our will, our will to enter the Kingdom of Heaven. On the first cornice of Purgatory, with its examples of divine art, the artists and others of the proud repeat a paraphrase of the Lord's Prayer. For 'Adveniat regnum tuum' (Thy kingdom come), they say:

Vegna ver' noi la pace del tuo regno,
    ché noi ad essa non potem da noi,
    s'ella non vien, con tutto nostro
        ingegno.[59]

May the peace of Thy Kingdom come
    upon us
For we cannot reach it by ourselves
With all our genius if it does not
    come.

Ingegno is one of Dante's terms for genius or the creative imagination, and here the souls depict the possession of the Kingdom of Heaven as a transformation of the imagination made possible only through grace. The approach through Purgatory to Beatrice is a remaking of the imagination and the right use of it in relation to will.

They say in the next petition, 'Fiat voluntas tua sicut in caelo et in terra' (Thy will be done on Earth as it is in Heaven):

Come del suo voler li angeli tuoi
    fan sacrificio a te, cantando *osanna*,
    così facciano li uomini de' suoi.[60]

As of their will Thy angels unto Thee
    Make sacrifice, singing hosanna, so
    May men make of their wills a sacrifice.

Dante not only transposes 'angels' for 'Heaven' and 'men' for 'Earth', thus stressing the psychological meaning of the petition by referring to the working of will in the two highest forms of intelligence in creation, but he also interprets the petition further to show what the consequence of the doing of that will would be. As the angels sacrifice their self-will for the greater cause of praising their creator, so men, by similar sacrifice, would gain the greater reward of spontaneous art, the release of their creativeness in knowing consciously where to direct it. Dante described his creative processes not solely to justify his own procedures, but as an example that he hoped others would follow.

18

The six guides and the four levels of meaning

When, in 1224, St Francis received the stigmata at La Verna through a vision of Christ crucified enwrapped in a six-winged seraph, the whole mountain burnt with flames that lit up all the hills and valleys around as if it had been the sun on Earth.[1] Of all the many visions recorded in the thirteenth century, this was the most famous.

Dante described this event in the lines:

nel crudo sasso intra Tevero e Arno
   da Cristo prese l'ultimo sigillo,
   che le sue membra due anni portarno.[2]

On the rough rock 'twixt Tiber and Arno shore
   He took that final imprint of the rood
   From Christ, which for two years his body bore.

They are spoken, it will be remembered, by Thomas Aquinas, who recites a eulogy of Francis before Bonaventure performs a similar office for Dominic. Some years later, in 1259, when St Bonaventure was minister-general of the Franciscans, he came himself to La Verna, and there he received a similar vision. The form the vision took was again of 'the Winged Seraph in the likeness of the Crucified'.[3] Even while experiencing the vision, Bonaventure understood that it meant the suspension of St Francis in contemplation and that the six wings of the seraph signified the six stages of the ascent of the soul to God. The experience and its interpretation were simultaneous and Bonaventure wrote down his understanding of the vision in his short work, *Itinerarium mentis in Deum (The Journey of the Mind to God)*. This work, a miracle of compression and clarity, consists of a prologue, and seven chapters, one each for the six stages of the ascent and a seventh for the passing of the affections entirely into God. Not only do its main divisions relate to the numbers of the ascent, but every stage of the argument is broken down into subdivisions that are numerologically significant in terms of the subject being discussed. In this way the *Itinerarium* provides the clearest model of the technique that, as I have already tried to show, was employed by Dante throughout his writing career.

The six guides and the four levels of meaning

The resemblances between the *Itinerarium* and the *Commedia* go far deeper than the fact that they are both based on mystical visions and that they are both constructed on numerological patterns. To Bonaventure, the world is a ladder for ascending to God and the mind ascends through three modes: seeing God through the external body, seeing Him within itself, and seeing Him above itself. He describes these three modes through several examples, as the three days' journey into the wilderness of Exodus, the triple illumination of one day, evening, morning, and noon; and the threefold existence of things, in matter, intelligence, and eternal art.[4] Now the Exodus theme is one of the great figural patterns of the *Commedia*: the story of the *Inferno* begins in the evening of Maundy Thursday (or the Monday of Holy Week) and the travellers enter Hell on the following evening; the *Purgatorio* begins at dawn and Dante enters Purgatory itself on the following dawn; and the ascent to Paradise begins at noon from the Earthly Paradise. The three worlds of the afterlife provide the scenes of a journey from external and corporeal things to the ordering of Dante's psychology in Purgatory, and then to the experience of eternal art in Paradise.

These correspondences, though in themselves remarkable, are surpassed in importance by a further parallel which provides the key, in my mind, to the way Dante was able to reconcile his classical heritage not only with his overall view of history, but also with the Christian mystical tradition. Bonaventure then breaks the three modes of experience down into six stages, because each mode is twofold—as when we consider God as Alpha and Omega. As God made the world in six days and rested on the seventh, so man, the small world or microcosm, is led by six successive stages of contemplation to the repose of contemplation. He calls these six stages: (1) sense, (2) imagination, (3) reason, (4) intellect, (5) intelligence, and (6) the apex of the mind.[5]

These six stages were not Bonaventure's own invention but, rather, have a long history. Though Dante does not mention the *Itinerarium mentis*, he was familiar with Bonaventure's works and deeply admired him, as is obvious from the major part he plays in the heaven of the sun. He does, however, mention an earlier classification of the six stages on which Bonaventure must also have drawn and this is in St Augustine's *De quantitate animae*. Dante calls on this book together with works by St Bernard and Richard of St Victor, in his letter to Can Grande in justification of his claim to divine illumination.[6] It was pointed out long ago[7] that St Augustine's classification of the six stages—(1) animation, (2) life of the senses, (3) the Christian rational life, (4) virtue, (5) tranquillity and trust in God, (6) desire of the truth in the highest degree—could be related to the successive moods, scenes, and landscapes of the *Commedia*. In this and later chapters, taking up a suggestion made but hardly developed by Karl Vossler,[8] I hope to show that these six stages are not only expressed in the moods and landscapes, but are summed up in the characters and roles of what I have already called, perhaps mysteriously up to now, the six guides of the poem: Virgil, Cato, Statius, Matelda, Beatrice, and St Bernard. These can be related to St Augustine's and St Bonaventure's classifications thus:

The making of the *Commedia*

	St Augustine	St Bonaventure, who says each stage is	
1 Virgil	animation	sense	implanted by nature
2 Cato	life of the senses	imagination	deformed by sin
3 Statius	the Christian rational life	reason	reformed by grace
4 Matelda	virtue	intellect	purged by justice
5 Beatrice	tranquillity and trust in God	intelligence	exercised by knowledge
6 St Bernard	desire of the truth in the highest degree	apex of the mind	perfected by wisdom
7 The vision of the Trinity	contemplation	repose of contemplation	

We can recall the importance and universality of this sixfold progression leading to a final seventh stage of contemplation, because it goes back at least as far as Socrates' description of what Diotima taught him about the stages of the ascent of love, from the love of the individual to the love of the many, and on to the love of the One, in the *Symposium*. The tradition reached St Augustine through many Neoplatonic sources and he preserved it for Western Christian mysticism in *De quantitate*. Then, a little over a century after Dante's death and in his own city, it was reformulated by Marsilio Ficino and his friends as the stages by which the soul ascends from the Terrestrial Venus to the Celestial Venus. From them Castiglione drew on the tradition to make it, in Bembo's mouth, the climax and finale of *Il Cortegiano*, the chief means, by which, in Hoby's translation, it reached and illuminated the work of Shakespeare and the civilization of Elizabethan England.[9]

In his rediscovery of the inner psychological and mystical meanings of pagan mythology, Dante anticipated and prepared the ground for the makers of the Renaissance. To appreciate his achievement in this we must go on a roundabout journey by way of his use of classical mythology, his use of the legends of Apollo and the Muses, his knowledge of classical philosophies and poetry, the means by which he drew them into his poem through the fourfold method of interpretation, and the relation of the first four guides—the three classical mentors, Virgil, Cato, Statius, and also Matelda—to the first four stages of the ladder of ascent.

The six guides and the four levels of meaning

Pagan mythology is employed throughout the *Commedia*, not just as ornament or allegory but fully integrated into its essential structure. Even in trying to describe the supreme experience of the poem, the direct vision of the Trinity, and to convey its ineffable nature in the last canto of the *Paradiso*, Dante draws on three images from his classical reading. These are the Sibylline leaves, the journey of the Argo, and the personification of the rainbow as Iris.[10] At the outset of the *Paradiso* he had already given notice that he was going to describe what had never been attempted before, calling on Apollo to help him, saying that he now needs the inspiration of both peaks of Parnassus,[11] comparing his own experience of transhumanization to that of Glaucus the fisherman who, by eating a herb, became a sea-god,[12] and telling his readers they will be as amazed at what they hear as were the Argonauts on seeing Jason yoke the oxen and sow the dragons' teeth.[13] How did Dante come to use this imagery, which is drawn from a religion and a mythology that Christianity seemingly had crushed for ever, to picture forth the experience that was reserved by grace for Christians alone?

Many earlier Christian writers had worked on the allegorical interpretation of classical mythology, notably of Virgil and Ovid, but giving them moral or rationalist meanings. The surviving prophecies of the Sibyls and Virgil's fourth Eclogue had long been read as foretellings of the coming of Christ, but these all referred to the historical and external facts of His coming. In all the numerous treatises on mysticism before Dante's time, however, there is no earlier example amongst Christian mystics for his daring juxtaposition of divine theme and pagan images. Dante baptized the ancient gods and called to the task of defining the ineffable the resurrected men, women, and creatures of mythology. The dependence of his predecessors on the Bible for their imagery to describe illumination, however subtle their techniques of interpretation, had limited their means of expression. By seizing on the psychological significance of the classical myths and relating them to the highest of human experiences, Dante was also revealing the identity of his artistic inspirations and his mystical experiences.

In addition to describing his inspirations in terms of faculty psychology and the imagery of the Gospels and of light, Dante also described them in terms of the classical myths of the origins of poetry. He was familiar with the legend of the Muses that goes back to Hesiod, according to which they were the daughters by Zeus of Memory and wandered on Mount Parnassus uttering incoherently, until the god Apollo appeared and gave order to their songs and their dances. He was also familiar with the allegorization of the myth according to which, of the two peaks of Parnassus, Nyssa and Cirrha, the first was the dwelling-place of the Muses and the second the home of Apollo. The peak of the Muses symbolized wisdom attainable by human means and the peak of Apollo symbolized Divine Wisdom. (The peak of the Muses was also sacred to Dionysos so that the twin-peaked mountain symbolized both the Dionysian and the Apollonian modes of inspiration.) This interpretation was widely known in the Middle Ages but it was Dante who, with the revaluation he secured for the heritage of classical antiquity and the role of the poet as the direct recipient of divine inspiration, understood the psychological significance of the myth and gave it new life as an expression of the practical experience he incorporated in the *Commedia*.

Thus to Dante, the writing of the *Inferno* and the *Purgatorio*, the two canticles in which he is accompanied by Virgil, the character symbolizing the *lumen naturale*, the highest that man can achieve under the guidance of reason and the four cardinal virtues, is inspired by the Muses. Their inspirations, their in-breathings, correspond to Hildegard's order of the 'cloud of living light'. At the beginning of the description of their journey he calls on their aid:

O Muse, o alto ingegno, or m'aiutate;	O Muses, O high Genius, strengthen me!
o mente che scrivesti ciò ch'io vidi,	O Memory, that what I saw hast writ,
qui si parrà la tua nobilitate.[14]	Here shall be made known thine integrity.

The nobility of his memory which will appear in his verse is an indication of the authority with which he speaks and even in the profoundest pit of Hell he calls on the aid of the Muses to express the horrors for which his language does not possess rhymes harsh and grating enough.

The pageants of the Earthly Paradise, where Heaven is closest to Earth, make the transition from the parts of the poem where his inspiration is from the Muses alone to those where he is guided by both Apollo and the Muses. There is an anticipation of the Apollonian inspiration in the lifting of Dante from Ante-Purgatory into Purgatory, which he experiences in the dream of Lucia when he is carried by an eagle up towards the sun. Once in the terrestrial Paradise, Virgil resigns his authority over Dante with the words

libero, dritto e sano è tuo arbitrio,	Thy will is upright, sound of tissue, free:
e fallo fora non fare a suo senno:	To disobey it were a fault; wherefore
per ch'io te sovra te corono e mitrio.[15]	Over thyself I crown thee and mitre thee.

Dante's will is now purified to the point where he can make complete confession, and the two great guiding principles of mankind, the imperial and the priestly, have brought him personally to the level of understanding where he can see both their wider historical significance for humanity and their origin in the divine will. Here, in this miraculous wood in whose soil every seed lies buried, he witnesses the procession in which all the most brilliant effects of colour that the Muses grant him are rendered more vivid by the coming splendour of living light eternal, the expression of which he will owe to Apollo. As the procession draws near him he cries on the Muses as holy virgins, reminding them of all the hunger, cold, and wakefulness he has endured for them, to aid him in expressing the 'forti cose a pensar', the hard things to think.[16]

The six guides and the four levels of meaning

With the appearance of Beatrice, who is that 'isplendor di viva luce eterna' the imagery takes on more and more of the radiance of the Apollonian inspiration. The Muses have enabled him to express the tremendous range of human emotion, almost all possible emotions except the highest unifying delight which now breaks through in the reminiscence of the Transfiguration, with which Dante describes his waking from the sleep he falls into between the two visions in the wood:

Quali a veder de' fioretti del melo
    che del suo pome li angeli fa ghiotti
    e perpetüe nozze fa nel cielo,
Pietro e Giovanni e Iacopo condotti
    e vinti, ritornaro a la parola
    da la qual furon maggior sonni rotti,
e videro scemata loro scuola
    così di Moïsè come d'Elia,
    e al maestro suo cangiata stola;
tal torna' io, e vidi quella pia
    sovra me starsi che conducitrice
    fu de' miei passi lungo 'l fiume pria.[17]

As, to behold some flower of the apple-
    spray
Which makes the angels for its fruit
    athirst
And makes in heaven perpetual
    marriage-day,
Peter and John and James were led, and
    first
Quite overpowered, came to themselves
    again
At that word which a greater sleep
    dispersed,
And saw their company diminished then
By Moses and Elias also, and eyed
Their master's raiment altered in its
    grain,
So came I to myself; and I espied
That pitying one bent o'er me, who my
    foot
Had led along the stream and been my
    guide.

He wakes to see Beatrice sitting on the roots of the Tree of Knowledge. As the Muses are the daughters of memory, up to this point he has drawn with their help on his memory of the images and scenes they have presented to him. Beatrice, the *lumen gratiae*, is now his guide to the vision before which memory will be powerless to retain the impressions of the intellect. At the outset of the *Paradiso* he calls on Apollo, because now he will need both peaks of Parnassus to complete the work and his invocation to the sun god is one of the most beautiful descriptions ever penned of the surrender of the artist to his inspiration, begging him to enter his breast and to breathe in him as the god had once drawn Marsyas out of the sheath of his limbs. Apollo the sun god will be his inspiration for the lights of Heaven and for the depiction of the three visions of the unconquered sun that culminate in that of Christ within the Trinity. This doubling of the intensity of inspiration was no late interposition into the *Commedia*, but a necessity of the nature of the work that Dante must have foreseen and planned from the beginning. The promise of this higher order of inspiration lay in the original vision and in the rediscovery of the nature of

Beatrice. The entry of Apollo signifies, with all Dante's brilliance of paradox resolved, the beginnings of a truly Christian poetry whose inspiration derives from the experience of conscious and ecstatic joy, the joy that Beatrice cried her gratitude for, when she exclaimed

> Ringrazia,
> ringrazia il Sol de li angeli . . .[18]

and which Dante has the power to make us feel and remember, whatever our beliefs, whatever our prejudices, as his lines flash through our minds like the fulgurations of lightning.

At certain points Dante mentions individual Muses by name, and it is possible that he employed the classification of the Muses, the three Graces, and Apollo, details of which he could have found in Martianus Capella and Macrobius. Figure 14 shows a late-fifteenth-century frontispiece[19] to a book by the musician Franchino Gafurio, with Apollo at the top and a motto stating that the power of the Apollonian mind moves these Muses everywhere. The three Graces appear on his right and a vase of flowers on his left. Equated respectively with Earth, the heavens and the modes of music, the Muses are depicted rising from the silent Thalia on Earth to Urania, the Muse of the starry heaven. Though this representation is much later than Dante, every element composing it was available to Dante in his reading. Extending downwards from the feet of Apollo is the long body of the snake of Time protruding through the spheres of the four elements to Earth; the snake has the three heads of the god Serapis, the wolf devouring the memory of the past, the ravenous lion of the present, and the fawning and delusive dog of the future.[20] There are certain fascinating parallels here with the main outlines of the *Commedia*. Apollo-Christ, the sun of righteousness, is the ultimate goal of art. The saving intervention of the three Graces relates to Mary, Beatrice, and Lucia, the trinity of ladies. Beatrice herself is a nine, the number of the Muses, so that, as Dante's own Christian muse, she contains in herself all the qualities of the pagan Muses. The work in which they appear is a comedy and therefore the Muse of comedy, Thalia, is especially invoked. Thalia appears twice in this presentation as the silent Muse on Earth oppressed by the three-headed snake of time that destroys memory.

Dante, at the outset of the poem, is driven back from the ascent of the delectable mountain by three beasts, the leopard, the lion, and the wolf, taken from Jeremiah but with their order changed from that of Jeremiah to that of Macrobius if we allow for the substitution of the leopard by the dog. They force him down to the place 'where the sun is silent', to the place of *Thalia surda* where Apollo's influence is unfelt. The dog, replaced by the leopard in this sequence, nevertheless is mentioned as the *veltro*, the mysterious saviour—so that we have here in the fusion of the beasts of Jeremiah and Macrobius yet another example of the hidden marriages of symbols that took place in Dante's dream levels and

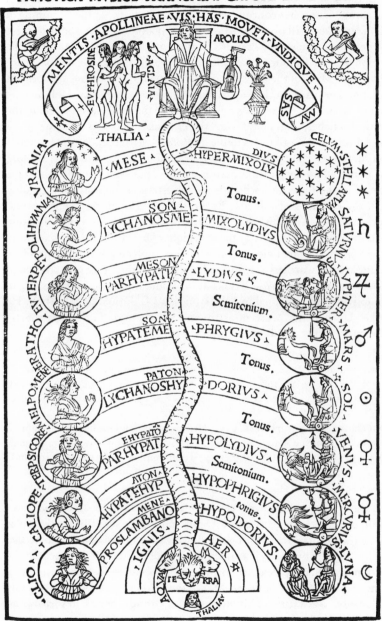

Figure 14 The Muses related to the planets and the fixed stars, frontispiece to Franchino Gafurio's *Practica musice* (Milan, 1496)

were presented to him as the assimilated visions of his inspiration. He is rescued by the greatest poet known to him and taken on a journey through *Memoria*, the recovery of the past, surely under the guidance of Clio, whose association with the moon complements her concern with sublunary affairs. At the beginning of *Purgatorio* he invokes Calliope, the Muse of epic poetry, as he is about to meet Cato, the hero of Lucan's epic, *Pharsalia*, and the guide of souls, as Mercury, the god associated with Calliope, was the psychopomp or herald of the dead. Terpsichore, the Muse of the dance, is one of the two Muses whose art does not use words, and her place is taken up by the intervention of Lucia. Melpomene, associated with the sun, is particularly appropriate for Statius, the singer of the Seven against Thebes, who enters after the enunciation of the doctrine of the two suns. Admittedly Virgil refers to the *Thebaid* as written under the influence of Clio[21] and, though this could be a strong argument against this classification, the Muse under whose inspiration Statius wrote in life need not limit the stage he represents in the *Commedia*, which is the Christian rational life, undergoing purgation, the catharsis of tragedy. Erato, the Muse of erotic poetry, would accompany Matelda, and this is not as strange as might appear at first, because Dante falls in love with Matelda at the very sight of her. Beatrice, for reasons to be discussed later, appears twice in this sequence, replacing Euterpe, the Muse of music, the second wordless art, and as Polyhymnia, the Muse of sacred song, on whom Dante calls in *Paradiso* XXIII at the point of passage from the sphere of Saturn to which she is joined in Martianus' and Gafurio's classification. He also invokes Urania, the Muse of astronomy, in these pathetic lines shortly before the entry of the Apollonian inspiration:

O sacrosante Vergini, se fami,
    freddi o vigilie mai per voi soffersi,
    cagion mi sprona ch'io mercé vi
      chiami.
Or convien che Elicona per me versi,
    e Uranìe m'aiuti col suo coro
    forti cose a pensar mettere in versi.[22]

O Virgins holy and high, if ever fast,
    And cold, and vigil, I for you endured,
    Now am I spurred to claim reward at
      last.
Helicon's founts for me be full out-poured,
    With all her choir Urania me uphold
    To attempt in verse things scarce to
      thought assured.

Some of these correspondences work better than others, but the most remarkable is in the reappearance of Thalia, no longer silent in the Earth as Dante, forgetful or unaware of the continuing creative role of Beatrice in his life, was forced to silence, but placed as the middle figure of the three Graces in the very position occupied by Beatrice in the trinity of ladies, in what is in fact a type of the place of Christ between Mary (the Father) and Lucia (the Holy Spirit). Comedy, says Dante in his letter to Can Grande, begins in sorrow and ends in joy;[23] the lowly humble Muse Thalia is reborn from silence and appears ascended to her rightful place in the Empyrean of Christian poetry.

    Among the new inspirations that had come to him, as a result of his brooding on the proto-*Commedia*, there were dreams or visions of human beings, whom he could frequently identify as historical characters. As, at this time, his reading took him deeper and deeper into classical studies, so it is natural that some of the faces and forms in his dreams and musings should take on the names and attributes of the authors he was studying or the characters they described. What we read with deep attention, undergoes in our minds transformations which will differ according to our trades and natures. In Dante's case, the experience of reading an author or group of authors underwent a transformation into a human being; so that, for example, in his imagination, the experience of reading about the Stoics, Peripatetics, and Epicureans and worrying about their various relationships to the truth, transformed these three philosophical schools into the three Maries before the empty tomb.[24] This means that, in considering the influence of classical ideas and themes upon him, we must also take into account this process of assimilation, whereby they turned into vital souls. This process may be seen at an early stage in Book II of the *Convivio*,[25] where, in his allegorical interpretation, he identifies the movers of the third heaven, to whom he addresses the *canzone* 'Voi che 'ntendendo' with the souls of those writers, such as Boethius and Cicero, who have ushered him on the path of love. This passage also marks the transition from his concentration on angelic and disembodied forms of intelligence to human beings in their full physical and mental unity. Many of his authors, by the nature of their writings, did not of course evoke this response in him, most notably Aristotle who, although quoted and referred to throughout the *Commedia*, is identified by the one famous line 'il maestro di color che sanno'.[26]

Thus, strong as the influence of classical philosophers was on him, they are never presented as speaking characters in the *Commedia*. On the other hand, the poets do speak, either as characters themselves or through their own creations. Quite apart from the influence on him of Virgil, Ovid, Lucan, and Statius where themes, historical subjects, and imagery are concerned, his reading underwent a further transformation in his imagination, as had happened with the philosophers: his experience of reading them turned them into characters demanding expression and a place within the overall allegorical, moral, and mystical interpretation of his vision. Both Virgil and Statius appear as speaking characters in the *Commedia*, and Lucan provided most of the details of the character of Cato. (More is said of these poets and their influence on Dante in the Appendix.)

To understand how the work of these poets and their civilization underwent, in Dante's mind, a revaluation profoundly affecting the *Commedia*, we must now consider his chief means of bringing about that revaluation, the use of the fourfold method of interpretation. Just as the records of ancient history reached Dante through the prism of patristic interpretation and just as he inserted his own correcting lens to readjust the light in which the past was seen, so the writings of the classical poets reached him in texts accompanied by the allegorical commentaries of late classical and Christian glossators. Virgil and

Ovid were almost inseparable in his time from the late classical finders of allegory in their works, such as Macrobius and Fulgentius in the case of Virgil, and the influence of the School of Chartres in the interpretation of these poets had secured for great numbers of their readers that their enjoyment of the characters and stories of mythology pointed them towards greater self-knowledge. It had come to be accepted that poetry had two levels of meaning, the literal and the allegorical, while only the divinely inspired scriptures had higher levels of meaning. Some authorities said there were in scripture three levels of meaning and some that there were four. By the thirteenth century most commentators had settled for four. This technique, although evolved in various schools—including the Judaic-Hellenistic philosopher, Philo of Alexandria—as a means of reconciling the apparent differences between the numerous religions proliferating in the later Roman empire, was taken over by the Christians and reserved by them for their sacred books alone. Though condemned by some authorities for the fantastic interpretations some of its practitioners committed, it had behind it the authority of St John Cassian and St Augustine in earlier days, of Hugh of St Victor in the twelfth century, and of Vincent of Beauvais, St Bonaventure, and St Thomas Aquinas in the thirteenth century.[27] Some writers were regarded as particularly skilful in the interpretation of a particular level of meaning, and Bonaventure summed up their reputations for these skills in the way set out in the following table, placing a modern master beside each of his examples of doctors of the Church:

	Great master
Allegory (faith)	Augustine, followed by Anselm
Tropology or moral meaning (charity)	Gregory the Great, followed by Bernard of Clairvaux
Anagogy (hope)	Dionysius, followed by Richard of St Victor

He also says that Hugh of St Victor is the master who excels in them all.[28] Such an authority, quoting such masters, is enough to demonstrate the universal acceptance of this method of interpretation. In constant use and adaptation over a thousand years, the method had extraordinary vitality and behind such vitality must lie some abiding need and understanding of human psychology.

To Dante's contemporaries there must have been a deep significance in the number of the levels of meaning—four, the number of wholeness, in this case, wholeness of meaning. They accorded with the wholeness of man's experience in the four ages of life, in the four seasons in the cycle of time, the year, in the four ages of history, and in the four elements that made up the matter and envelope of Earth. If we consider man himself, this number accorded with his physical form and existence (the literal), with his place in Christian history (the allegorical), with the state of his soul (the moral), and with the union of his soul with God (the anagogic). Thus, as man is the microcosm of the macrocosm, the four levels may have had their origin either in Neoplatonic doctrines concerning the emanations of the worlds, or in cabbalistic studies. Dante possibly knew several learned Jews who would have been a source of instruction to him not only on multiple interpretations of scripture but also on numerology. It was perhaps also through the influence of the Christian cabbala that William Blake discovered for himself a similar system with his idea of the four Zoas. To him wholeness of vision was fourfold. He prayed:

God us keep
From single vision & Newton's sleep[29]

for to him the world of mechanistic science was a false or partially seen universe wanting the three higher levels of vision. And when he came to illustrate the *Commedia* in his dying years, he executed his drawings in terms of the four Zoas, showing, by symbols and written comments, from which level of vision in any stage of the poem he thought Dante was writing.

The question of how far Dante used and depended on the four levels of meaning in making the *Commedia* has caused much trouble to his modern critics, though it aroused no particular heart-searching in his fourteenth-century commentators, many of whom mention it, drawing on the exposition in the letter to Can Grande. Admittedly, except for one of the earliest and best of them, Guido da Pisa, whose use of the method we will come to in this and the next chapter, for the most part, after mentioning it, they prefer to stick to the simpler interpretations afforded by personification allegory.[30] Cristoforo Landino in the fifteenth century announced his intention of interpreting the *Commedia* according to the four levels, and Tasso mentions Dante's use of the method as a matter of course in his *Discorsi*.[31] Charles S. Singleton has said that, between the writing of the *Convivio* and the writing of the *Commedia*, Dante changed from the twofold allegory of the poets to the fourfold allegory of the theologians.[32] Bruno Nardi said that, because Dante should not have committed the presumption of using the allegory of the theologians, he did not do so.[33] Nardi is also one of the strongest opponents of the authenticity of that part of the letter to Can Grande which contains an exposition of the fourfold method. One of the fullest accounts of how Dante could have used the method is that of Helen Flanders Dunbar,[34] and Joseph Anthony Mazzeo[35] also describes how Dante could have changed the method from a passive means of interpretation into an active means of execution and construction. Erich Auerbach[36] thought the chief principle of allegory in the poem was the method of *figura*, a method which depends on the historicity both of the character or event described and the people or happenings with which it is compared, as the strength and sufferings of Samson were regarded as a type of the strength and sufferings of Christ, or as in Dante's journey the Great Circle pilgrimage is a figure of his own travels from the spiritual Jerusalem to the eternal Rome. But this method can easily be related to the allegorical level of the fourfold method, which relates past and present events in the light of the role of Christ's life in the history of the world. Aquinas, discussing the division of the spiritual sense into three, describes it thus:

> As St. Paul says, *The Old Law is the figure of the New*, and the New Law itself, as Dionysius says, *is the figure of the glory to come*. Then again, under the New Law the deeds wrought by our Head are signs also of what we ourselves ought to do. . . .[37]

One of the difficulties in the way of those commentators who refuse to accept that Dante used the fourfold method with whole-hearted intent is their own inability to understand that poetry must contain multiple meanings as part of its nature. At the most they accept two meanings, the literal and one allegorical meaning. This attitude fixes them into an obsession with one particular interpretation of a crux such as the *veltro* or the DXV, and does not allow them the freedom of the interpretative imagination in ranging over the possibilities of the political or eschatological meanings, the moral and psychological associations, and the essential mystical grounding of the work. If there is such disagreement amongst Dante's commentators on the sources and meaning of so many passages, it is because of the multitude of influences that went into his creative imagination and that were fused there into new amalgams of symbol and expression. This is why there are so many plausible explanations for individual passages and why each explanation can easily be attacked for incompleteness. By bringing the fourfold method into consideration as part of Dante's creative technique we can see that many explanations can be justified as correct when the level of interpretation to which they apply has been established. It may be objected that thus Dante scholarship becomes a Dodo's race in which everyone gets a prize for being partly right, but it is essential to realize that behind any one passage or even behind single lines there may be barrow-loads of reading and decades of visual impressions and conversations. That Dante was aware of this process of fusion may be demonstrated from a comparatively simple example when he compares the four animals in the first pageant of the Earthly Paradise to the four cherubim described by Ezekiel but points out that his animals had six wings like those in Revelation, instead of Ezekiel's four.[38] He had seen his own animals, whole, and with his inner eye, but he knew what in his reading had gone to their making. One great benefit of studying how his creative imagination worked and how it constantly produced new unities out of a myriad diversities, is to realize what a blessing the fourfold method must have been to him in the interpretation of his inspirations and their integration with the vision of the *Commedia*. Another difficulty is that, though these critics accept and admire Dante as one of the greatest of all Western poets, they cannot make the imaginative leap necessary to understand that, in his case, we are not dealing with an art that comes to its executant as a happy chance, a gratuitous gift of his temperament and circumstances, but with art of an infinitely higher order, art with an aim and therefore controlled and directed to that aim, art that takes into consideration all its readers and recipients and that has the intention of leading them to the consciousness of ecstatic joy.

Dante's word for multiple meaning was 'polysemous' and he uses this adjective in introducing his explanation of the four levels of meaning in the letter to Can Grande. He divides the meaning first into the literal, or what is conveyed in the letter, and into the allegorical or mystical meaning. He then breaks this inner meaning down into three, thus:

He then illustrates what he means by the interpretation of the opening of the Exodus psalm that he had formerly used in his different explanation of the method of *Convivio* II. He also used this psalm, as we have seen, as a theme connected with the Great Circle image in the *Commedia*.

> Ad evidentiam itaque dicendorum, sciendum est quod istius operis non est simplex sensus, immo dici potest *polysemos*, hoc est plurium sensuum; nam primus sensus est qui habetur per literam, alius est qui habetur per significata per literam. Et primus dicitur literalis, secundus vero allegoricus, sive mysticus. Qui modus tractandi, ut melius pateat, potest considerari in his versibus: 'In exitu Israel de Aegypto, domus Iacob de populo barbaro, facta est Iudaea sanctificatio eius, Israel potestas eius'. Nam si ad literam solam inspiciamus, significatur nobis exitus filiorum Israel de Aegypto, tempore Moysis; si ad allegoriam, nobis significatur nostra redemptio facta per Christum; si ad moralem sensum, significatur nobis conversio animae de luctu et miseria peccati ad statum gratiae; si ad anagogicum, significatur exitus animae sanctae ab huius corruptionis servitute ad aeternae gloriae libertatem. Et quamvis isti sensus mystici variis appellentur nominibus, generaliter omnes dici possunt allegorici, quum sint a literali sive historiali diversi. Nam allegoria dicitur ab *alleon* graece, quod in latinum dicitur alienum, sive diversum.[39]

For the elucidation, therefore, of what we have to say, it must be understood that the meaning of this work is not of one kind only;

rather the work may be described as 'polysemous', that is, having several meanings; for the first meaning is that which is conveyed by the letter, and the next is that which is conveyed by what the letter signifies; the former of which is called literal, while the latter is called allegorical, or mystical. And for the better illustration of this method of exposition we may apply it to the following verses: 'When Israel went out of Egypt, the house of Jacob from a people of strange language; Judah was his sanctuary, and Israel his dominion. For if we consider the letter alone, the thing signified to us is the going out of the children of Israel from Egypt in the time of Moses; if the allegory, our redemption through Christ is signified; if the moral sense, the conversion of the soul from the sorrow and misery of sin to a state of grace is signified; if the anagogical, the passing of the sanctified soul from the bondage of the corruption of this world to the liberty of everlasting glory is signified. And although these mystical meanings are called by various names, they may one and all in a general sense be termed allegorical, inasmuch as they are different (*diversi*) from the literal or historical; for the word 'allegory' is so called from the Greek *allcon*, which in Latin is *alienum* (strange) or *diversum* (different).

He then goes on to say that the subject of the whole work, taken in the literal sense only, is the state of souls after death. If the work is regarded from the allegorical point of view, the subject is man according to whether by his merits or demerits in the exercise of his free will, he is deserving of reward or punishment by justice. In this way he uses the allegorical meanings to bring the poem back into the world of the present and the living.

Whether Dante was presumptuous or not in adapting the allegory of the theologians to the purposes of his own poetry, I hope to have shown in the last chapter what an exalted view he had of his own inspirations and of his role as a Christian prophet. Just as, to Aquinas, Moses always had Christ before his eyes when writing the Pentateuch and Christ is the unique light Who reveals all prophetic visions, so Dante had received the four visions of Christ he described in the *Commedia*. As those inspirations were divinely given, so he felt it legitimate to bring the fourfold method to bear on them for their interpretation. By applying the fourfold method to the three orders of prophecy, he could bring the imagery of pagan inspiration and characters from the classical past into his depiction of the six stages of ascent in the journey of the mind to God. Those six stages relate, as has been said, to the six guides of the poem and they keep the meaning of the anagogic level, the level of ultimate reality because it concerns the connexion of the soul with God, active throughout the poem's length. Each of these characters in addition has significance on the literal and the two other spiritual levels. Anagogy, as the level of ultimate truth, has two aspects for the Christian soul, as Father de Lubac has pointed out: [40]it concerns what that soul may expect in glory and in this case is speculative, and it also concerns the 'here and now' of the highest reaches of mystical illumination in this life. Thus Abbot Suger could describe the state which he attained through the contemplation of works of art as 'anagogic'.[41] Dante's vision of the Trinity was his practical experience of the anagogic level in this life 'here and now'. This helps to explain why and how the *Commedia* is constructed backwards from that vision. Whereas the student of scripture, applying the method to his reading, worked from the allegorical to the moral and the anagogic meanings, from what Aquinas calls the shadow of truth to the image of truth and then to truth itself,[42] Dante in planning and writing the poem worked the other way round, judging from the ultimate truth of his own experience, the status and placing of the visions and inspirations that were, in their co-ordinated descriptions in poetry, to become the literal level for *his* readers. It would also help to explain the difficulty referred to in Chapter 21 which was felt by some of his early readers when they wondered about the relation of the poem to the truth, the conflict they saw between *visio* and *fictio*. To employ a wholly anachronistic analogy, the *Commedia* is a sandwich with a bottom layer of daily bread (the literal level of the fictional story) and a top level of the bread of the angels (the anagogic level of ultimate truth), filled with the allegoric and the moral meanings.

Dante was an artist and therefore fundamentally close to the many illuminators, painters, and sculptors of the Gothic period, of whom it has been clearly demonstrated that they too drew on mystical experiences for their inspiration.[43] His love of the visual arts, his frequent mention of them, and his practice of them must never be forgotten, but his intellectual capacities were also such as to make him a master of the interpretative techniques evolved by the teachers of the fourfold method. As the artists of his time, in expressing their visions, possessed a common language of design, style, line, and symbolism, so Dante, in making his pictures of words, drew on another common language, that of scriptural interpretation. To demonstrate how Dante could have used the fourfold method to work on the visions and dreams of his inspirations we can look at the technique recommended by Hugh of St Victor. To Hugh of St Victor the method was a means of bringing the human heart, with its instability and restlessness, into a state of peace.[44] The many abuses to which this method of interpretation was open, with the possibilities it offered of wild and extravagant fantasies, had meant that frequently, throughout its long history, from St Jerome to Hugh himself, voices were raised demanding a return to the literal meaning and a concentration on the facts described. To Hugh of St Victor this did not mean that the reader should direct his mind entirely to the literal meaning in the manuscript, but rather that he should follow through a technique of visual contemplation. In doing so, for example, before a student attempted to discover the allegorical meanings of Noah's Ark, he should first visualize in his mind all the physical details of the ark and its building, to the extent that with his inner eye he could see and experience it as a three-dimensional construction.[45] Dante almost certainly knew these passages of Hugh of St Victor because he too used the example of the Ark in describing the literal level of meaning in the *Convivio*.[46] Thus, in studying scripture, the reader first made the literal level in his own mind as a physical reality, rearing landscapes and seasons about biblical characters and then, holding onto this mental picture, he proceeded to draw from it the allegorical levels of meaning. The effort of visualizing a scene in this way would be the first stage of ridding the mind of personal associations and of setting a distance between the reader and the passage to be interpreted, so that the allegorical significances could be allowed to arise and suggest themselves in a more objective manner.

What this would have meant to Dante, given the already developed attention he paid to the imagery of his dreams and visions, was that, once having taken the step of according his visions the status of divine revelation that the scriptures held, he could hold a vision as it came to him in his mind and draw out from it the landscape, the character, or the metaphor its emotional quality demanded. It is a method of controlled dreaming. What gave him the authority to put his own dreams and visions on a level with revealed scripture and adopt this method to his own poetic ends was his rediscovery of Beatrice, who sent him guidance through Virgil, as Venus had guided Aeneas from Troy to Italy. Amongst her rebukes to Dante in the terrestrial Paradise is the charge that she had been sending him visions and dreams to bring him to the right way, which he had not understood as coming from her. She says:

Né l'impetrare ispirazion mi valse
  con le quali e in sogno e altrimenti
  lo rivocai: sì poco a lui ne calse![47]

Nor did it help me to beg for inspirations
  For him through which in dreams and
    otherwise,
  I called him back: so little did he heed
    them!

Beatrice here may be seen as revealed knowledge, and the visions she sends have the same authority as scripture and the same inner base of truth as those his mother grants to Aeneas in order to make him fulfil his divine mission.

As Giovanna had been the precursor of Beatrice in the *Vita Nuova*, so Virgil is the forerunner of Beatrice in the *Commedia*. How did Virgil come to play such a role in the *Commedia*? He is the first human character, apart from Dante himself, to appear in the *Commedia*, and the fact that, on his first appearance and even in his first words, he remains unidentified, or only through periphrasis, suggests that, as Dante held the starting images of the poem in his mind, the dark wood, the desert, the distant hill, and the three beasts who drove him back to sleep, letting each image make its full visual development, so, as the man appeared 'fioco per lungo silenzio', he did not know at first who the man was. He knew him only as someone with obvious authority, clearly sent from Beatrice, as someone who would be a guide, who radiated a highly individual quality of tenderness and the sense of loss. As his writings from the *Vita Nuova* to the letter to Moroello Malaspina show, Dante was already accustomed to the appearance of a guide in his dreams and visions and this guide had been given the name of Love. This unnamed man now appeared at a moment of crisis, as Love had appeared so often in the past, but with the difference that he was a man with a history and an experience of life imprinted on him. In the character of Virgil, Love is gathered into a spirit who has known birth and death.[48] The connexion stresses both the continuity in Dante's creative life and the revolution in his art that followed. Once having acknowledged the presence of this man in his poem, he opens the new understanding of humanity within him that, from his identification with Virgil and the relation of Virgil to Beatrice, enables him to create and give order to the appearance of all the other characters. Just as Love disappears from the *Vita Nuova* after the vision of Beatrice as she appears to her followers, so Virgil will disappear when Beatrice is revealed in the Earthly Paradise. Once Dante recognized the unnamed man as Virgil, by holding the picture of him in his mind and reflecting on the emotional quality that concentrated in it all the experience of reading the *Aeneid*, once he had established his literal identity, then he could apply the test of the allegorical interpretations to him. Allegorically he is right for the task as the prophet of the Christian world order in the fourth Eclogue and as the poet of the empire whose divine mission it is Dante's duty to unfold; at the same time he symbolizes the highest the pagan world could achieve without the redemption of Christ. Morally he is right as standing for reason grounded on the four cardinal virtues that must precede the granting of revelation with the grace of the three theological virtues. On this level, too, he may be seen as the inner conscience of art, the standard and inspiration that in his aspect as Love guided and dictated to Dante. Anagogically he is right, as the symbol of the stage of preparation for the *excessus mentis* and of what must die or disappear in a man before that illumination is bestowed on him, as, earlier, Richard of St Victor, the younger contemporary of Hugh of St Victor, and already quoted as a supreme master of anagogic interpretation, had described how Rachel must die for Benjamin, the youth symbolizing the ecstasy of contemplation, to be born.[49]

The appearance of Virgil signals Dante's new understanding of how he was to present *himself* as a character, at the beginning of the poem, in a state of spiritual weakness that is presupposed by the scene of confession, contrition, and absolution in the Earthly Paradise. It also makes another point in which the creation of the *Commedia* resembles that of the *Vita Nuova*: the understanding of how to reorganize past experience to make a work of art and, in the case of the *Commedia*, to find in past experience examples of different kinds of inspiration which could be graded and arranged so that they should be seen as stages in the approach to ultimate truth. In making himself a character in the poem, Dante is creating a portrait of the poet as a poet, as well as of a Florentine in the year 1300 who is saved from damnation by divine intervention. We must in this case distinguish between Dante the character in the poem, and Dante who is writing the poem with the help of his *alto ingegno* and who is commenting to his readers on the events he describes. For the purposes of the drama that must begin with a tragic situation and end with a happy fulfilment, Dante the writer must present

Dante the character as a man in a state of spiritual disorientation, as the ground of horror that will flourish with the fruits of grace; he depicts himself as a man who, at the beginning of the poem, has woken up to his bad state but whose unaided will and intellect are totally insufficient to prevent his constant return to that state. This, to my mind, is the psychological meaning of his account of coming to himself (*mi ritrovai*) in the dark wood, whose horrors are indescribable, and awakening out of sleep as he attempts to make his way to the *dilettoso monte*. All his efforts are useless because the leopard, the lion, and the wolf drive him back to the dark wood, and at his worst moment of despair a man appears to him. Dante's identification of this soul with Virgil is the third great inspiration of the poem, the inspiration that enabled him to begin the poem and that is a further extension of his new command over the interpretation of his visions. The identification with Virgil enabled him to pull together all the themes he intended to treat in the poem, his ethical, political, and historical ideas, his prophetic mission and his attainment of new altitudes of inspiration. Just as the second great inspiration, that of Beatrice, forced on him a revaluation of his visions, making him understand their inner psychological significations, so he was able to see the three beasts not only as the forces or tendencies in humanity that prevented mankind from attaining its true goal, but also as the recurrent patterns of attachment in himself that cut him off from the vision he hoped to regain and from its attendant benefactions of inspiration, notation, and signification. The cupidity he had denounced in humanity he discovered in his own individual nature as the obsessional greed and infatuation of the she-wolf. The three beasts are the progressive stages by which the intellect is led astray from the truth and by which the will is turned aside from its true direction by false desires. Here, it is not cupidity in the sense of desiring material gains, but the cupidity of the ego, its self-will in desiring to see the world entirely in terms of private satisfactions, in interpreting reality entirely in terms of the hatred, for instance, that Dante is accused of by I. A. Richards. It was this inner personal discovery of the meaning of cupidity that gave Dante the command over the inspirations for the beginning of the work and, as I have demonstrated how he could have used the fourfold method of interpretation to work out the significances of Virgil's character, I will now apply the same method to the three beasts and the *veltro*. The beasts are generally interpreted as allegories of specific sins or as standing for political institutions. As sins they foreshadow the threefold division of Hell into sins of incontinence, violence, and fraud, and form a trinity of illusion that, like the triple-headed Satan, parodies the vision of the Trinity at the close of the poem. It is sometimes said, even by those who maintain the importance of the fourfold method of interpretation, that Dante only intended one of the allegorical senses at a time to be derived from his literal descriptions even though, in the letter to Can Grande, he illustrates the method by drawing all the meanings from the same passage of scripture. In his reflections on the meaning of the three beasts and especially of the *veltro*, I believe he came to the clearest conclusions about what they meant on the anagogic and moral levels and that the political allegory followed from that.

The anagogic level has two aspects, the speculative and the contemplative. Thus Guido da Pisa gives the speculative aspect in his anagogic interpretation of the *veltro* as the second coming of Christ.[50] In the contemplative aspect of the anagogic level the *veltro* is the Christ consciousness, the flash of illumination that transfigures the individual soul and, in driving the she-wolf down to Hell, may be said either to expose as illusion a false view of the self or else to have placed in its proper dwelling an impulse from the lower nature that threatened to usurp and rule the whole psychology. In this case the *veltro* may even be seen as the final vision of the poem. There is a passage in the *Philokalia*[51] which may help to explain on the mystical or anagogic level the progressive decline symbolized by the three beasts into a psychological state in which all spiritual development is impossible. The first stage, *impact*, is when a thought or image presents itself to the mind and it may be related to the leopard; the second stage, *coupling*, when attention is fettered by the object, may be related to the lion; and the third and fourth stages, *merging together*, when the mind inclines with enjoyment to this object, losing all peace, and *passion*, when the mind is passionately attached through repeated association with the object, have a connexion with the she-wolf whose hunger and sexual appetite may never be satisfied.

To take an example from yet another tradition, the three beasts may also be related to the three *gunas* of Hindu philosophy, seen as descending stages of consciousness:[52] *sattva*, the *guna* of balance, charm, and peace but which, according to the *Bhagavad Gita*, may begin to enslave the mind, just as the attractive leopard draws Dante on as an adornment of the spring; *rajas*, the *guna* of rage and energy, which accords with the lion; and *tamas*, the *guna* of fear, terror, inertia and addiction, fully symbolized by the she-wolf.

In drawing attention to these similarities I am not trying to suggest that Dante was influenced by early Greek monasticism[53] or by Hindu sages. Rather, I am trying to show that the *Commedia* may be seen as a heroic attempt to describe the transformed reality that the world presents to a man whose consciousness has been altered by mystical experience, and that Dante had discovered certain truths in his own experience that recur in accounts of the stages of illumination in the literature of various periods and races. By bearing the memory of this inner experience in mind, we can then give greater force to the interpretations of the beasts on the moral and allegorical levels which concern, in the case of the moral meaning, terms over-weighted with associations of guilt and, on the allegorical level, a nexus of historical happenings that no longer concern us directly. Thus, on the moral level, the leopard stands for sensual beauty and, on the allegorical, for the city of Florence; the lion, morally pride, in the allegory is the France of Philip the Fair; and the she-wolf, which is cupidity on the moral level, is allegorically the papacy as the carnal Church. On both levels of interpretation the *veltro* has meaning, as the animal that feeds on wisdom, love, and virtue, morally

correcting and chastening humanity and allegorically, as the spiritual redeemer who will meet the DXV, the saviour emperor, in Rome and ensure that
the right relations between the papacy and the empire enable mankind to
achieve both its earthly and its heavenly goals.

If this view of the fourfold method in Dante's hands enables us to keep a track
of the way he incorporated meanings from different levels of existence and
experience into his poem, it should not be assumed that we should read the
poem in a hyperanalytical spirit. The aim of the method is to bring out the
wholeness of meaning and Dante used the method in order to preserve the
wholeness of the souls who appeared in his creative imagination. Each of these
souls is all the more himself or herself because of the variety of characters and
events among which it appears. Each of them came with a mood signifying his
or her state in the other world, and it was Dante's burning agony at the fate of
the noble pagans that led him to incorporate them among the first three steps of
the ascent of the mystical ladder.

To give a full expression to his sense of what he owed to Beatrice's redemptive
act he had to depict what, by implication and by description of the fate of other
men, would have been his own destiny in the other world, had Mary not had
compassion on him and spoken to Lucia, who sent Beatrice on her mission for
his salvation. Beatrice descended to Limbo, where she implored Virgil to go to
Dante's rescue, and it was in Virgil that Dante discovered the historical
character whose tragic situation best signified Dante's alternative fate. Here, in
Virgil, is the supreme poet, the height of what humanity can achieve without
Christian revelation, and from his character extend the fundamental moods of
the *Inferno*: the elegiac and sorrowful mood of the great pagans in Limbo and
the tragic sense of the waste and bestiality of Hell. For this part of the poem
Virgil is the guide and director of Dante's mind and perceptions; Dante must
see everything through the eyes of Virgil's personal tragedy, from the pagan
structure of Hell to the fact that all the characters whom Dante meets there are
in some sense an extension of Virgil's own character, mood and historical
destiny. In Canto IV of the *Inferno*, just before they meet the good pagans,
Virgil explains that these souls are there not because of sin but because they did
not have baptism and, if they lived before the time of Christianity, they did not
worship God in the right way. He goes on to say:

'Per tai difetti, non per altro rio,   'For such defect and for no other offence
  semo perduti, e sol di tanto offesi   We are lost, and only in so far amerced
  che sanza speme vivemo in disio.'[54]   That without hope we languish in
                                 suspense.'

Then Dante responds with the sympathy that will continually urge him to
question this aspect of divine judgment until the heaven of Jupiter, when he
meets Ripheus and Trajan in the eyebrow of the eagle:

Gran duol mi prese al cor quando lo 'ntesi,	I, when I heard this, to the heart was pierced,
però che gente di molto valore conobbi che 'n quel limbo eran sospesi.[55]	Because I knew men to much virtue bred Whose spirits in that Limbo were athirst.

As Dante is soon to learn, as he descends through the cone of Hell, to be a man or a woman, 'di molto valore', is not enough for salvation. But, because so many characters appear to him with their best qualities preserved, the poignant courtesy of Francesca, the proud patriotism of Farinata, the regal bearing of Jason, the ingenuity and love of knowledge of Ulysses, and even the sheer endurance of Ugolino, their great worth intensifies the horror of their situations and at the same time beckons with a glimmer of hope towards the second coming. When Dante asks Virgil whether the torments of the damned will lessen or increase or be the same at the Judgment, he answers:

'Ritorna a tua scïenza, che vuol, quanto la cosa è più perfetta, più senta il bene, e così la doglienza. Tutto che questa gente maladetta In vera perfezion già mai non vada, di là più che di qua essere aspetta.'[56]	'Turn to thy science and be wise. The more a thing perfected is, the more It feels bliss, and in pain the sharper sighs. Although the state of these accurst at core Never indeed in true perfection ends, They look then to be nearer than before.'

But Virgil feels nothing of that hope. On the shore of Mount Purgatory he refuses to allow that men can understand how their spirit-bodies after death can continue to feel, saying it is one of the matters reserved from human comprehension by God. He bursts out with this adjuration:

'State contenti, umana gente, al *quia*; ché, se potuto aveste veder tutto, mestier non era parturir Maria; e disïar vedeste sanza frutto tai che sarebbe lor disio quetato, ch'etternalmente è dato lor per lutto: io dico d'Aristotile e di Plato	'With the *quia* stay content, children of earth! For if the whole before your eyes had lain, No need was there for Mary to give birth. Ye have seen desiring without fruit, in vain, Men such that their desire had been at rest, Which now is given them for eternal pain. Of Aristotle's and of Plato's quest

341

e di molt' altri'; e qui chinò la fronte, e più non disse, e rimase turbato.[57]	I speak, and many more.' His head he sank Here, and no more said, and remained distrest.

This insight into the centuries-old burden of longing that Virgil carries with him comes after many previous hints at it though never before with such directness, because, for the most part, we have seen Virgil as the kind, brave, and loving guide, lord, and master of Dante's terrifying journey. There is a tragic contrast between his consideration for his pupil, which nearly always takes precedence over his own feelings, and his inner grief and unsatisfied longing which only appears in this outburst after they have met Cato, the second guide on the way, and when some of Virgil's responsibilities are therefore shared. His authority is already diminished from this point: he has been rebuked by Cato; the very problem mentioned above about the spirit bodies will receive an explanation in Cantos XVI and XXV of the *Purgatorio*; and his relationship with Dante alters gradually from that of master to that of friend. There is also an emotional transformation that takes place. The insatiable longing without hope of the good pagans is transformed into the dominant mood of the *Purgatorio*, the homesickness or longing of the soul for its origins in its creator, a longing signified by the nostalgia of the sailors and of the pilgrim at the opening of Canto VIII[58] and which derives graphic emphasis from the refusal of the souls to be deflected from their refining punishments. Virgil has never visited Purgatory before, though he had made the journey to Cocytus. There is one significant moment when he gazes in wonder at the body of Caiaphas who was condemned to his torment after Virgil's first visit. Here, the prophet of the justly ordained government that executed Christ gazes at the unjust priest, who advised that it was better that one man should die than that his people should suffer.[59] Whereas, in the *Inferno*, the characters of Limbo and Hell took their colour from his dominant mood, in the *Purgatorio*, Virgil is still a developing character, but one who takes his colour from the later guides of the poem. Here he is a visitor, not an inhabitant, and he receives great and unexpected rewards—the adoring respect of Sordello and Statius and the sight of the Earthly Paradise, of which Matelda says:

'Quelli ch' anticamente poetaro
  l'età de l'oro e suo stato felice,
  forse in Parnaso esto loco sognaro.
Qui fu innocente l'umana radice;
  qui primavera sempre e ogne frutto;
  nettare è questo di che ciascun dice.'[60]
	'They who in old time dreaming poetized
	  Of the felicity of the Age of Gold
	  On Helicon perchance this place agnized.
	Innocent here was man's first root of old;
	  Here blooms perpetual Spring, all fruits abound:
	  This is the nectar whereof each hath told.'

The six guides and the four levels of meaning

Dante says that at these words he turned round to Virgil and Statius and saw them smile. Virgil's share in preserving the memory of primal innocence here receives its reward in his being allowed to enter the sacred wood of Eden, of which his description had been merely a residual memory. An undercurrent of the *Purgatorio* flows from Virgil's expression of despair in the third canto to this moment, when he is made to smile in recognition of the truth of his past inspiration. Whether he returns to Limbo after his disappearance to enrich with his descriptions the experience of the other worthies of antiquity, or whether he remains a guest in the Earthly Paradise we do not know, but the reason for his disappearance, the paling of the light of natural reason before the light of grace that is Beatrice, can best be understood in connexion with the significance of Dante's psychological and mystical progression as symbolized by the six guides on the way, and with the new ability to interpret his inspirations and convert them into the poetry of praise that he related definitely and clearly to that progression.

If we relate the first four guides to St Bonaventure's classifications of ascent, then what Dante experiences under the first two relates to the external world: to contemplating God through his traces under Virgil's guidance, and then, under the patronage of Cato, to contemplating God in his traces in so far as He is in them by essence, potency and presence.[61] This second stage is particularly linked by Bonaventure to delight in the beauty of creation, the very delight that Dante recovers when he sees the stars again from the southern hemisphere.

There is a special suddenness and wonder associated with the appearances of these guides, related perhaps to the instantaneous changes in consciousness of the mystical experiences which they symbolize on the anagogic level. Thus Cato suddenly appears beside Dante:

vidi presso di me un veglio solo,
   degno di tanta reverenza in vista,
   che più non dee a padre alcun figliuolo.
Lunga la barba e di pel bianco mista
   portava, a' suoi capelli simigliante,
   de' quai cadeva al petto doppia lista.
Li raggi de le quattro luci sante
   fregiavan sì la sua faccia di lume,
   ch'i' 'l vedea come 'l sol fosse
     davante.[62]

Near me an old man solitary I saw,
   In his aspect so much to be revered
   That no son owes a father more of awe.
Long and with white hairs brindled was
    his beard,
   Like to his locks, of which a double list
   Down on his shoulders and his breast
    appeared.
The beams of the four sacred splendours
    kist
   His countenance, and they glorified
    it so
   That in its light the sun's light was not
    missed.

This unearthly description of an old man shone upon by the four stars of a Southern Cross yielding the light of the four cardinal virtues bears all the marks of the vision in which Cato appeared to Dante, containing within himself the results of Dante's earlier reflections on his character, the solution to the problem of liberty set by Dante's own theory of the role of the Roman empire, the key to the moral meaning of the mountain of which he is the guardian, and the second stage of the mystical journey. There is no need for Cato to accompany Dante and Virgil, as the other guides do, up to the point of ascent to Heaven from the earthly Paradise. Cato represents the discovery of God in the traces of His creation and therefore his guidance is all about them on the mountain. Cato, in fact, is the soul of the mountain and others, such as Sordello, can act as runners for him in the omnipresence of his guardianship.

The intervention of Lucia signals the beginning of *metanoia*, which proceeds through the two stages of contemplating God within the mind, first *by* His image—the stage Dante enters into fully with the meeting with Statius—and then *in* His image, which is the stage dominated by the sight and presence of Matelda.

St Augustine said that his third stage was the point of the Christian rational life, and this seems particularly appropriate for Statius, who can teach Dante truths about the soul and the body that were barred to Virgil's comprehension. The fourth stage, which St Augustine called 'virtue', and Bonaventure called 'intellect purged by justice', is linked to Matelda, one of the most mystifying of Dante's characters. In her the Christian and the pagan are joined together. Dante's early commentators, such as his son Pietro, generally identified her as Countess Matilda of Tuscany, who, although aunt of the emperor Henry IV, sided with his enemy, Pope Gregory VII, in the Investiture Contest. She is also held to signify the perfection of the active life that will soon be balanced by the contemplative life in Beatrice. But she is more than these things because she has also been shown to be Astraea, the star maiden, the virgin returned,[63] of whom Virgil had sung in his fourth Eclogue and who is the noble and disconsolate figure of the *canzone*, 'Tre donne', where she is called Drittura or Justice. Bonaventure, as we have seen, called the fourth stage that of the intellect purged by justice. In coming to her, Dante meets again the inviolable innocence of mankind in the wood on the mountain top that is at once the golden Saturnian age returned, the Garden of Eden, and the figure of Jerusalem about the Temple. Bonaventure says of this fourth stage:

> if we wish to enter into the fruition of Truth as into Paradise, we must enter through the faith, hope, and charity of the Mediator between God and man, Jesus Christ Who is as the tree of life in the middle of Paradise.[64]

He also says: 'The image of our soul is purified, illuminated, and perfected, thus the image is repaired and made like the heavenly Jerusalem.' With Matelda, Dante enters just such a Paradise and is led, after the reunion with Christ-Beatrice, to a tree in the middle of Paradise. The three theological virtues dance in the procession of the first pageant. That procession includes the spiritual lives of the books of the scriptures presented as their inspired authors, the prophets, evangelists, and writers of the epistles. As Bonaventure says of this stage, it is one when the inner senses are renewed, so that by faith in the Word one recovers spiritual hearing and vision; by hope in the Word, one recovers spiritual olfaction, and by love of the Word, one recovers taste and touch. It is the stage, in fact, in which the fourfold method of interpretation comes into its own, as Bonaventure particularly stresses, setting out with care the three spiritual meanings, the moral, allegoric, and anagogic.[65] In the elders representing the books of the Bible, Dante actually reveals not only the way in which his experience of reading turned into characters, but characters who are themselves fourfold in meaning.

In the dual nature of Astraea-Matelda, the old classical world of the virgin of renewal is united to the Christian era in the historical character of the countess, who fulfilled herself in the active life by trying to keep the balance between empire and papacy. But she is represented not as an Olympian figure nor as an elderly female aristocrat, but as one of the most delightful of all the ladies and shepherd girls of the *dolce stil nuovo*. She is the girl in love, singing to herself, gathering the red and gold flowers she steps among as though about to break into a dance. And even here, if we follow Bonaventure, she carries an inner meaning of the poets of that school because, again speaking of this fourth stage as that of God's image reformed by the gifts of grace, 'our mind is filled by the *divina Sapientia*, the divine wisdom, as the house of God'.[66] She is also, as she sings, Erato, the muse of love poetry, so that she combines in herself the lyricism of the ancients and the moderns, as she walks beside the 'dark, dark' waters beside which the purest of earthly streams would seem tainted, on the mountain top flashing with lightning in anticipation of the sun about to blaze upon it, the fullness of Sapientia returned to Dante in Beatrice.

19

Change and being: the images of the *Commedia*

The fundamental image of the *Commedia* is light, known in its essence (*luce*) as radiance (*raggio*), and as reflected splendour (*splendore*), creating dramas of colour, shadow, and darkness. Beatrice is called by Virgil 'the light between the truth and the intellect'.[1] If, as I have suggested, Dante used Bonaventure's classification of the six stages of the soul's ascent to God, so that Virgil and Cato stand for the first two stages of contemplating God outside ourselves through and in His traces, and Statius and Matelda the third and fourth stages of contemplating God through and by His image in the mind, then Beatrice and St Bernard stand for the fifth and sixth stages in which God is contemplated above ourselves through and in His light. Bonaventure says of this light, while speaking of the fifth stage, which Beatrice would represent, that 'it has signed upon our minds the light of Eternal Truth, since the mind itself is immediately formed by Truth itself'.[2] It seems almost as though Virgil were quoting Bonaventure directly. After the scenes of confession and the pageants in the Earthly Paradise, Beatrice takes Dante up to the realms of light, where in the increasing clarity of his intellect, as he absorbs knowledge of the being of the universe, she teaches him more and more about the nature of symbolic language until finally he is in the state which is beyond metaphor but to which all his metaphors finally aspire.

It has been said that Dante established a new relationship between author and his reader in the *Commedia*,[3] and he certainly addresses his reader directly on many occasions. He had the object of bringing his readers from a state of misery to a state of bliss.[4] This meant the education of his reader into a fuller awareness of his potential happiness as a citizen of a greater empire and as a member of a church under true spiritual guidance, an education that would awake the reader's memory of his divine origins through Dante's description of his personal journey of recollection as well as through the imaginative depiction of what man may be in the full realization of his possibilities.

As Dante conveyed his message through the medium of poetry, packed with images and multiple meanings, he used symbolic language to work on his readers through surprise and delight, so that they should be elevated by this new awareness into a state where they could remember their lost origins and where their own imaginations might become the equal of his in grasping the true aim and purpose of their own creation. Dante seems to have had two classes of reader in mind: the general audience for literature that decided him to use the vernacular and the development of a style that should be intelligible and attractive even to the uneducated,[5] and those of 'sane intellects'[6] who could see beneath the veil of strange doctrine. For both, he had to plan the development of the imagery, and the range and nature of the experiences and traditions on which he was to draw. If what I have said about the nature of his planning is true, that he worked backwards from the vision of light with which the work ends and created from that a credible cosmology which both reflects the splendour of that light and requires the presentation of the gloom of a world deprived of it, then this would explain how the development of the imagery shares in the coherence and unity that the work possesses in its other aspects. This would account for the way in which the first two cantos of the *Inferno* are the planting-out beds for most of the species of imagery that reach fruition in the last cantos of the *Paradiso*, as, for example, the wild wood of the beginning is converted into the heavenly leaves tended by Christ, the everlasting gardener.[7] One of the features of the poem that caused immediate delight to its readers was the use of simile, or *comparatio* as the device was known. One of the earliest commentators of the *Inferno*, Guido da Pisa, picks out each *comparatio* for special notice[8] and later Landino wrote a lyrical passage expressing his admiration at Dante's superlative skill.[9] The similes and metaphors raise the question of how they are related to the fourfold levels of meaning, if they are related at all. Pietro Alighieri, who describes the four levels at considerable length,[10] says that the literal level itself can be divided into four: the literal, the historical, the apologicetical (meaning the use of fables or legends), and the metaphoric, with the three spiritual meanings following from them. He may well be setting out here what his father told him of his actual practice. Here we will approach the question from another direction: the grading of the imagery according to the cosmology of the poem, in a progression from the images drawn from the nature of man and from his earthly environment to the unfolding of the nature of Beatrice.

The mother-and-child imagery

Numerous images drawing on the relations between a mother and her child characterize the dealings of both Virgil and Beatrice with Dante. As when, for example, Virgil saves Dante from the pursuit of the demons,

Lo duca mio di sùbito mi prese,
   come la madre ch'al romore è desta

My Guide suddenly seized me, hurrying
   As a mother whom the roar and cries
   awake,

347

e vede presso a sé le fiamme accese,	Who sees the flames quite her start
che prende il figlio e fugge e non s'arresta,	and spring,
avendo più di lui che di sé cura,	Snatches her child and flieth, for his sake
tanto che solo una camiscia vesta ;[11]	More than her own, and has no thought to stop
	So long as even a shift on her to take;

These mother-and-child images occur about twenty times in the course of the poem, and the great role of this image is, I feel, a desire on Dante's part to make his readers become as little children, according to Christ's injunction: 'Whosoever shall not enter the Kingdom of God as a little child shall in no wise enter therein.'[12] He wants to make his readers recover through the action of his varied uses of the image on their memories, the state of awareness they frequently possessed as children and have lost as adults, to recover the spontaneity of attention in which the poem's deeper significances can be fully apprehended. Virgil comforts Dante at the entry to Hell as one does a child:

E poi che la sua mano a la mia puose	His hand on mine, to uphold my falterings,
con lieto volto, ond' io mi confortai,	With looks of cheer that bade me comfort keep,
mi mise dentro a le segrete cose.[13]	He led me on into the secret things.

Its use is drawn into the depiction of the *anima semplicetta*, of the soul itself as a little child, and when Dante is about to enter the Kingdom of Heaven he stands as a child before Beatrice, and the image recurs again and again until it reaches its culmination in the Mother of God, the Virgin Mary, at whose intercession Dante enters the kingdom most fully. Even in his closing words he speaks of his inability to describe his vision in terms of this image:

Omai sarà più corta mia favella,	Even for my remembrance now must fail
pur a quel ch'io ricordo, che d'un fante	My words, and less than could an infant's store
che bagni ancor la lingua a la mammella.[14]	Of speech, who at the pap yet sucks, avail;

The images of self-observation

There is a close relation in bringing about a growing degree of awareness in the reader between the images of childhood and the images of self-observation. This is one of Dante's subtlest devices, and one that has been little noted—though T. S. Eliot drew on Dante's example for many of his finest images in both *The Waste Land* and the *Four Quartets*.[15] The first example of it is in *Inferno* I where Dante, to describe what he felt on escaping from the dark wood, compares himself to someone who has escaped from drowning.

E come quei che con lena affannata,
  uscito fuor del pelago a la riva,
  si volge a l'acqua perigliosa e
    guata, . . .[16]

As one, whom pantings of his breath
  exhaust,
Escaped from the deep water to the
  shore,
Turns back and gazes on the danger
  crost, . . .

The comparison of escaping is superficial; the real comparison is with the state of mind. It is the shared relief and terror to which we respond, the quieting of the storms in the lake of the heart, more than the comparison of two kinds of danger neither of which we may have experienced. This imagery has its origins in the efforts of the poets of the *dolce stil nuovo* to describe the psychological effects on themselves of the sight of their ladies, as Guinizzelli, for example, compared himself to the tower struck and wasted by lightning.[17]

Where his readers are concerned, just as the mother-and-child imagery is intended to bring them psychologically to the state of being little children, so the imagery of self-observation is designed to awaken them to a new sense of their adulthood, as men and women with the possibilities of growth through self-knowledge. One of the most telling examples occurs in Dante's conversation with Cacciaguida when, strong enough at last to learn the dreadful future that awaits him, he asks Cacciaguida to expound the baleful hints he frequently was given in Hell. This canto, *Paradiso* XVII, begins with Dante comparing his state of mind to that of Phaethon when he went to his mother Clymene having heard a rumour that his father was Apollo; in this way Dante's apprehension of disaster is linked to the image of a fateful fall through the disarray of the natural order. Cacciaguida explains how the foreknowledge of which, by his blessed state, he is cognizant, does not imply determinism.

All things derived from secondary causes under contingency (which does not stretch beyond the frame of the material world) are plain to the divine sight but they require no more necessity in their actions from that, than a boat is moved by being reflected in a watcher's eye.

necessità però quindi non prende
  se non come dal viso in che si specchia
  nave che per torrente giù discende.[18]

Yet cannot thence Necessity acquire
  More than the eye that is reflecting her
  Can the ship's motion down the tide
    inspire.

This, in my opinion, is one of Dante's most remarkable images. It has a negative function in that it cleaves away a fallacy from Dante's mind and from our own minds; at the same time it has an enlarging positive function in that it creates in two lines a physical world and a cool observer, watching the world, exercising his discrimination in understanding physical events, and knowing his own part in that world as distinct from the ship's, an act that is directly linked to God's observation of the causal workings of the universe and binds the higher consciousness of men to the supreme consciousness of God.

I have placed this discussion of the images of self-observation before the images of natural observation—for which Dante is most generally celebrated—because I believe that his skill in the depiction of natural events and phenomena derives from the same standpoint of detached percipience with which he regarded his inner nature and that what gives the images drawn from nature their precision and realism is the application to the world of nature the clear-eyed vision he learnt to direct upon the motions of his own soul.

The images of natural observation

Dante constantly refers his readers to scenes they may know themselves either directly or by first-hand report, to the descent of Italy's rivers, to her mountain ranges, to seascapes and incidents of marine life, to animal, bird, reptile, and insect life, to the work of the peasant in the country and the gatherings in city squares. In the *Inferno*, for all their variety, these remain within the sublunary limits he has set himself for the imagery of this first part of the poem. He is gradually wooing his readers into an acceptance of the reality of the underworld that opens into an abyss beneath them, but, at the same time, he is using these delightful and forceful reminiscences to impress on them the tragic state of the sinners in Hell, who will never delight in nature again. The use of this imagery is allied to the tragic state of Virgil, who taught Dante to recover for European literature the visual mastery of natural observation in poetry (see the Appendix). It also owes much, I believe, to the influence of the parables, to Christ's employment of the work and incidents of everyday life to reveal the inner needs of man's spiritual development. (See Chapter 17, pp. 303 and 319.)

Here are two examples of the ironic use of this imagery in the *Inferno*. The wood of the suicides is formed by the souls falling on the soil of the seventh circle and growing up as scrubby thornbushes which the Harpies lacerate. Dante, at Virgil's suggestion, breaks a twig from a large thorn and a voice cries in rebuke from the stump, which swells with blood. Dante's description of how the words and blood issue from the stump as he hastily drops the twig is:

Come d'un stizzo verde ch'arso sia
    da l'un de' capi, che da l'altro geme
    e cigola per vento che va via,[19]
	As a green brand that burneth at one end,
	    At the other drips and hisses from the
	    wood
	    Where the escaping wind and fire
	    contend,

This is as fresh an experience as that of a child playing with green sticks by a bonfire. The analogy is so close as to venture on tautology; the difference is all in the experience and the environment. The thorn turns out to be the soul of Pier della Vigne, the chancellor of Frederick II.

Deeper down in Hell the two travellers have been set down in Cocytus by the giant Antaeus. While they are gazing at the cliff past which they have descended, a voice begs them not to tread on the heads of the wretched tired brothers. Turning round Dante sees a frozen lake, frozen more deeply than are the Danube or the Don, and he also sees the heads of sinners sticking out of the ice.

E come a gracidar si sta la rana
    col muso fuor de l'acqua, quando
        sogna
    di spigolar sovente la villana,
livide, insin là dove appar vergogna
    eran l'ombre dolenti ne la ghiaccia,
    mettendo i denti in nota di cicogna.[20]
	Like, when the peasant-woman dreams
	    of of what
	She 'll glean, afield, the frogs that, every
	    one
	With muzzle out of water, croaking
	    squat,
	So livid, up to where men's shame is
	    shown,
	The desolate shades were in the ice
	    confined,
	Setting their teeth to the stork's
	    chattering tune.

The souls he sees are those of the traitors, fixed eternally in this vast sheet of glassy ice, their tears freezing as they weep and building up a crust of ice on their cheeks. Here the image of the frogs, their nostrils just out of water, perfectly describes the physical situation of the sinners, but with the terrible sarcasm that in Cocytus there are no pleasant walks by lakes to observe such things, there is no harvest of which the peasant girl dreams, there is no recurrence of the seasons to bring about that harvest again.[21] There is no movement here at all except for the sullen beat of Satan's wings, whose breezes maintain the frozen state of the lake of human sin.

The beauty of the natural world is not required in the *Purgatorio* as a contrast for here, once again, we are in the world of organic nature at the antipodes. As it is subject to the light of the sun and the stars, as it is the place of Christian purgation where the landscape, however harsh it may seem at times, always promises a fair arrival, so here Dante can revive elements which have been in abeyance since they were first evoked in the first two cantos of the *Inferno*. He can bring in the sight of the open sea with sun and stars shining upon it; he can introduce imagery through his dreams and visions. The function of warders, performed in Hell by the monsters of antiquity, is here taken by Cato of Utica and the angels of the cornices. As the circles of Hell were arranged according to a classical definition of sin, so the cornices of Purgatory rise from one to another of the purgations of the seven deadly sins. Where the colours of Hell were hideous, dark or livid, Purgatory is bright with brilliant clear hues. Here Dante recovers the richness of the Christian and Judaic symbolic traditions with the singing of 'In exitu Israel de Aegypto', resurrecting the theme of *conversio*, and connecting it with the return to the state of innocence under the four stars of the cardinal virtues and the three stars of the theological virtues, who will reappear as nymphs attending the griffin in the pageant of Beatrice. Here, too, he can discover the imagery of the sun, both in its political and ecclesiastical aspects, and in the first training of his mind, he can endure, and rejoice in, the spiritual light of Paradise.

On each succeeding cornice examples of the opposing virtues and sins appropriate to each level are given, either through voices or through visions, so that the souls have their imaginations rightly educated, as Dante does, for the entry into the Earthly Paradise. There, in the two brilliantly colourful Apocalyptic pageants, Dante, by now brought back to a state of innocence, undergoes the terrible experience of his confession and his purification in the waters of forgetting and of remembrance. There follows from these experiences an expansion into another, higher order of understanding, a transformation of the intellect for which Dante needed to prepare his readers from the outset of the poem. One of the ways in which he seems to have done this was through the theory of the elements and their possibility of transmutation. This demonstrates Mandelstam's statement of the convertibility of images as an essential part of the poetic process (see p. 118) and also provides a necessary preparation for understanding how the four levels of meaning relate to the cosmology of the poem.

The elements

The journey to the summit of Mount Purgatory goes through the concentric spheres of the first three elements, earth, water, and air, and approaches the outer sphere of fire. The four elements, it must be remembered, were regarded then as the principles that variously dominated the different aspects of nature in which they were present, and not, as the word is now used in science, as the hundred-odd physical entities that make up matter. They were also linked to the four temperaments of man and therefore had strong psychological significances. According to the alchemists, they were capable of transformation either by degradation from fine to coarse or by purification in the opposite direction. The alchemists who debased their art by deceit are punished in the eighth circle of Hell, but it is possible that Dante was influenced by the mystical ideas underlying alchemy, in his search for the inner transmutation of the soul. The very word 'alchemy' is said to derive from the ancient Egyptian word for the black earth of the Nile delta from which all creatures sprang, and there was the authority of Aristotle, in his *Metaphysics* for the idea of the fifth element, the *hyle*, into which each element could sink and return from it transmuted. This quintessence was the physical explanation of the nature of the heavenly spheres which extend beyond the sphere of fire. Thus there were five elements to be taken into consideration and five is the number symbolizing man, with the four temperaments brought into a unifying balance by the fifth element. Hildegard of Bingen said that man is disposed according to the number five; his height and girth are each made up of five equal parts; he has five senses and five members.[22] This number is also the number of sexual love and of procreation in nature. It is also, I need hardly point out, the number that Beatrice occupies in Bonaventure's classification, so that the stage Dante reaches under her guidance includes the harmonization of his sexual nature through the great love of his life into his highest creative aspirations as a man.

Dante's fascination with the transformations of nature was also fed by his love of Ovid's *Metamorphoses*, with its powerful beginning describing the origin of things out of chaos,[23] and his own delight in the stirrings of his art which led him to objectify his delight in the description of primal chaos as the act of love.[24] All the elements can be shown to play a part in the basic imagery of the poem and display a dualism that is constantly reversed through the processes of transformation.

Earth   This is the first of the elements, the name and nature of the globe through which Dante descends, with all its associations of soil, rock, and the mineral world. The dualism can be seen in stone which exhibits in Hell both the permanence of its construction by Love and the hostile environment in which the damned are imprisoned. The very density of rock expresses the emotional rigidity and obdurate mental attitudes of the sinners, and yet it is through the stony passage that the travellers escape to find themselves on the mountain of stone, at whose top the freedom of man before the Fall is regained.

At that summit the soil contains all the seeds of creation, the matrices of the vegetable world, and there Dante evokes the Transfiguration in the episode dividing the two pageants, the type of illumination on a mountain peak. Earth as an idea is present even in Heaven in the description of Christ as the *ortolano etterno*, in the amazing word-play of Dante's speech to St John:

'Le fronde onde s'infronda tutto l'orto
　　de l'ortolano etterno, am' io cotanto
　　quanto da lui a lor di bene è porto.'[25]

'I love the leaves wherewith is all enleaved
　　The Eternal Gardener's garden, great
　　and least,
　　In the measure of the good from Him
　　received.'

There is one image related to the basic image of Earth whose very name evokes the thought of transmutation: the image of gold. It forms the head of the old man of Crete, whose other parts are of silver, brass, iron and clay. We are shown how desire for it debases men to the point of losing all individuality in the crowds of the prodigal and the avaricious pushing their weights around with their chests as they shout at one another. They are condemned for ever to the hard rocks from which the object of their obsessive desires was mined. Gold coats the leaden cloaks of the hypocrites, burns up the usurers on the hot sands, drives the simoniac popes to their fiery doom, and feeds the she-wolf in the florin pastures of Florence. It is the object of the cupidity that leads mankind astray. It also has strong heraldic connotations; the usurers are only recognizable by the badges on the purses round their necks and the florin is stamped with the lily of

Florence. As heraldry derives from the honours bestowed by their only source, the emperor, so, through the imperial theme, does gold recover the nobility for which it also stands, in the gold background of the eagle-clad banners waving over Trajan as he speaks to the widow[26] and in Statius' confession to Virgil, the poet of empire, that the latter's lines on gold made him repent of his own prodigality. This heraldic connexion appears even in the description of the Virgin as 'the oriflamme of peace'[27] and gold is also developed, as we shall see, in the theme of the Golden Fleece.

The most frightening moment of the *Inferno* is when Dante himself is in danger of being turned to stone by the threatened appearance of the gorgon's head. Thousands of fallen angels throng the ramparts of the city of Dis above the travellers and the snake-haired Furies scream their threats. It is all Virgil can do to preserve his composure as he turns Dante about and covers his eyes:

'Vegna Medusa: sì 'l farem di smalto,'
  dicevan tutte riguardando in giuso;
'mal non vengiammo in Tesëo
  l'assalto.'[28]

'Let come Medusa, and change we him to
  stone!'
  All with one voice, and eyes bent down-
    ward, said.
'Ill made we Theseus his assault
  atone.'

But, at last, with a sound as of wind, the heavenly messenger comes dry-shod across the Styx to abase the pride of the travellers' enemies. Dante has been saved by higher intervention from an encounter that would have left him a block of stone. Dante at this incident appeals:

O voi ch'avete li 'ntelletti sani,
  mirate la dottrina che s'asconde
  sotto 'l velame de li versi strani.[29]

O ye who have sane intellects for guide
  Consider well the doctrines that for
    cloak
  Beneath the strangeness of the verses
    hide!

And at a later stage Beatrice, when Dante is confused and amazed by the meaning of her prophecies, says:

'Dorme lo 'ngegno tuo, se non estima
  per singular cagione essere eccelsa
  lei tanto e sì travolta ne la cima.
E se stati non fossero acqua d'Elsa
  li pensier vani intorno a la tua mente,
  e 'l piacer loro un Piramo a la gelsa,

'Thy wit sleeps if it faileth to discern
  That tree for a special cause to be so
    high
  And at the top to growth inverted turn.
If the vain thoughts thy mind is crusted
    by
  Had not been water of Elsa and not
    made
  Their pleasure a Pyramus to the
    mulberry,

per tante circostanze solamente
   la giustizia di Dio, ne l'interdetto,
   conosceresti a l'arbor moralmente.
Ma perch' io veggio te ne lo 'ntelletto
   fatto di pietra e, impetrato, tinto,
   sì che t'abbaglia il lume del mio
      detto,
voglio anco, e se non scritto, almen
      dipinto,
   che 'l te ne porti dentro a te per quello
   che si reca il bordon di palma cinto.'[30]

By heed to so great circumstances paid
   Thou wouldst have found thy moral
      sense admit
   God's justice in the tree that he forbade.
But since I see dulled into stone thy wit
   And, stony, into stain of colour wrought
   Such that the light of my word dazzles
      it,
I also will that, if not written thy
      thought
Bear it within thee, for the cause
      wherefore
The staff with palm encircled home is
      brought.'

Here she gives the reasons both for his inability to understand and for the necessity of his reporting his visions in images. His vain thoughts have petrified his understanding as the waters of the river Elsa coat twigs and other objects in its bed with a limy crust. We may refer back to her words about his inability to see that his inspirations came from her and to the way in which they languished for want of a true interpretation of their meaning and purpose.

Water A similar dualism may be found in the descriptions of water and other forms of liquid. The way Dante connects creativeness with water and rivers has been noted since the writing of the *Vita Nuova*. The waters of Hell drip down with the perverted creativeness and ingenuity of man to the frozen lake of Cocytus. The gluttonous are lashed by black rain, the tyrants languish in blood, the barrators are sunk in pitch and the traitors are enfixed in ice. Yet even in Hell Dante employs the powerful periphrastic device of connecting a character's life with the stream or river by which he was born. The first example is a short one. Francesca says:

Siede la terra dove nata fui
   su la marina dove 'l Po discende
   per aver pace co' seguaci sui.[31]

The place where I was born sits on the
      strand
   Where Po descends to his peace, and
      with him takes
   All the other streams that follow him
      down the land.

So should her life have found peace if it had not fed the rivers of Hell, and if, instead, her soul had travelled, like all the streams of Italy, to the sea and, like the souls of the saved, over that sea to the mouth of the Tiber, where they gather for the journey to Mount Purgatory in the southern hemisphere.

As the river is connected with birth so it is with death. Manfred's bones are rained and blown upon beside the river Verde, and Buonconte tells how, wounded in the throat, crying on Mary with his last word, he fell by the river

Archiano after Campaldino. The demon, robbed of his prize by the angel of God, causes a storm over the Casentino, and the river in flood rolls Buonconte's body into the Arno.

'Lo corpo mio gelato in su la foce
   trovò l'Archian rubesto; e quel sospinse
   ne l'Arno, e sciolse al mio petto la croce
ch'i' fe' di me quando 'l dolor mi vinse;
   voltòmmi per le ripe e per lo fondo,
   poi di sua preda mi coperse e cinse.[32]

'My frozen body at its mouth the crest
   Of foaming Archian found and bore me down
   Into Arno, and loosed the cross upon my breast
I had made of me when the strong pangs came on.
   It rolled me about its bed from side to side
   Then wrapt me in all the plunder it had won.'

The theme of the river is continued beyond the descriptions of Lethe and Eunoe in the Earthly Paradise up to the heavenly river, with its ecstatic evocation of eternal springtime:

e vidi lume in forma di rivera
   fulvido di fulgore, intra due rive
   dipinte di mirabil primavera.
Di tal fiumana uscian faville vive,
   e d' ogne parte si mettien ne' fiori,
   quasi rubin che oro circunscrive;
poi, come inebrïate da li odori,
   riprofondavan sé nel miro gurge,
   e s'una intrava, un'altra n'uscia fori.[33]

And I beheld, shaped like a river, light
   Streaming a splendour between banks whereon
   The miracle of the spring was pictured bright.
Out of this river living sparkles thrown
   Shot everywhere a fire amid the bloom
   And there like rubies gold-encrusted shone;
Then as if dizzy with the spiced perfume
   They plunged into the enchanted eddy again:
   As one sank, rose another fiery plume.

When Bernard points out where Beatrice has her place in the great rose, Dante says:

Da quella regïon che più sù tona
   occhio mortale alcun tanto non dista,
   qualunque in mare più giù s'abbandona
quanto lì da Beatrice la mia vista;[34]

From the highest sky which rolls the thunder down
   No mortal eye is stationed so remote,
   Though in the deepest of the seas it drown,
As then from Beatrice was my sight;

The final appearance of the imagery of water is in the comparison of the difficulty of recapturing his vision with all the experience of human history since the voyage of the Argo:

Un punto solo m'è maggior letargo
  che venticinque secoli a la 'mpresa
  che fé Nettuno ammirar l'ombra
    d'Argo.[35]

One moment more oblivion has amassed
  Than five-and-twenty centuries have
    wrought
  Since Argo's shadow o'er wondering
    Neptune passed.

But this image also enfolds two other lines of reminiscence that have been evoked earlier in the poem. One is the imagery of seagoing and the other the theme of the Golden Fleece. The *Inferno* is full of mention of ships and storms and wrecks. Pluto collapses like a broken sail and its rigging at Virgil's taunts, and Antaeus raises himself like a mainmast when he has set the travellers down on the ice. Ulysses' great and desperate voyage to the unknown world ends in the wrecking of his ship in sight of the shores of Mount Purgatory to which, when Dante arrives there, comes the angelic skiff with its cargo of singing souls. He compares Beatrice in her chariot in the Earthly Paradise to an admiral directing a fleet from the poop of his ship. Once Dante is launched upon the never before ventured theme of the *Paradiso*, he speaks of the barque of his *ingegno*, the craft of his genius, which the boldest of his readers must follow in the boats of their own imaginations. The image recurs again and again until it culminates in this last metaphor of the Argo.

The Argonaut theme, too, begins early in the poem, and with the same tragic significance that attends much of the classical imagery of the poem, in the sight of Jason among the seducers in the eighth circle. Virgil exclaims:

'Guarda quel grande che vene,
  e per dolor non par lagrime spanda:
quanto aspetto reale ancor ritene!
  Quelli è Iasón, che per cuore e per
    senno
  li Colchi del monton privati féne.'[36]

'Look on that great one who advances
    now
  And seems in all his pain no tear to shed.
How regal still is the aspect of his brow!
  He is Jason, who by courage and by
    guile
  Bore off the Ram's fleece from the
    Colchian bough.'

Even in those dreadful circumstances and that ignominious company Jason keeps his nobility and strikes Dante with the surprise he associates later with the theme, when he tells his readers that they will be more astonished at the sights on the journey he leads them on than were the Argonauts at seeing Jason yoke the fire-breathing oxen at Colchis.[37] This surprise again breaks out in Neptune when he sees the shadow of the first ship darkening the translucence above his head. It was through such cross-associations and the final choice of images in the last canto, which knitted together all the preceding diverse transformations of imagery, that Dante achieved artistically the unity he had experienced spiritually.

Air Air, too, has its dual aspects in the poem. As breath and wind it represents life, and the breathing of the Creator; as the bearer of smoke and mist it sustains the cloud separating the soul from its Maker. It is the medium through which the souls of the dead manifest themselves in the Other World. The souls of the lovers are borne on turbulences of air and they are compared in a series of images to birds, images which will return again in the *Paradiso*. The angry moan:

<table>
<tr><td>

'Tristi fummo
ne l'aere dolce che dal sol s'allegra,
portando dentro accidïoso fummo'.[38]

</td><td>

'We were sullen and wroth
In the sweet air made glad by the Sun's
   fire;
We fumed and smouldered inly, lapt in
   sloth'.

</td></tr>
</table>

The angry in Purgatory live in a cloud of black smoke but for the most part the atmosphere in both senses is clear, letting in the radiance of the sun's beneficence and rustling the tops of the paradisal trees with the motion communicated by the lowest of the heavenly spheres. Air is also connected to the imagery of inspiration, to the breath of Minerva (Beatrice as wisdom) filling out the sail of his singing ship,[39] but the most extended group of images related to air are those of flight. This is an image Dante applies particularly to his own creativity[40] but it has other connotations as well. In the *Inferno* flight is either a symbol of the loss of control as with the lovers in the whirlwind of passion or else a characteristic of the most deformed monsters, of Geryon who does not have wings but moves through the air like a dog paddling in water, of the demons guarding the lake of pitch, so incompetent at flying that two of them collide in mid-air and crash into the lake, and, of course, the bat wings of the fallen Lucifer which beat in vain and never soar. As flight in its positive aspect signifies the delight of freedom and perfect emotional control, so the contrast between its uses in *Paradiso* and *Inferno* brings out superbly Dante's skill in the convertibility of images which, as a technique, he applies also in all the successive images he employs to describe Geryon. Geryon is essential to the travellers' progress on the journey because only he can fly up and down the steep cliff separating the seventh circle from the circles of Malebolge. Attracted by the cord with which Dante had hoped to catch the leopard and which Virgil has thrown down to him, this fearful monster hovers on the edge of the cliff:

<table>
<tr><td>

La faccia sua era faccia d'uom giusto,
  tanto benigna avea di fuor la pelle,
  e d'un serpente tutto l'altro fusto;
due branche avea pilose insin l'ascelle;
  lo dosso e 'l petto e ambedue le coste

</td><td>

His face was as a just man's, and
  expressed
The mildness that its outward aspect
  feigned;
Like to a serpent's trunk was all the rest.
He had two paws, up to the armpits maned
With hair; the neck and breast and
  either flank

</td></tr>
</table>

dipinti avea di nodi e di rotelle.
Con più color, sommesse e sovraposte
  non fer mai drappi Tartari né Turchi,
  né fuor tai tele per Aragne imposte.
Come talvolta stanno a riva i burchi,
  che parte sono in acqua e parte in
    terra,
  e come là tra li Tedeschi lurchi
lo bivero s'assetta a far sua guerra,
  così la fiera pessima si stava
  su l'orlo ch'è di pietra e 'l sabbion
    serra.
Nel vano tutta sua coda guizzava,
  torcendo in sù la venenosa forca
  ch'a guisa di scorpion la punta
    armava.[41]

Were freaked with knots and little
  whorls ingrained.
Never did Turk or Tartar livelier prank
  With colour cloth, inlaid and overlaid;
  Such dyes Arachne's tissue never drank.
As sometimes on the shore a barge is
  stayed,
  That part in water lies and part on
    land;
  And as, where guzzling Germans dwell,
    to aid
His fishery, the beaver takes his stand,
  So that most evil of beasts leant on the
    stone
  Which with its rim encloses the great
    sand.
Out in the void flickered his tail alone,
  Twisting the venomed fork up in the air
  Which armed the point, as in the
    scorpion.

With a man's face, bestially hairy forelegs and armpits, a serpent body but knobbled like a toad, and patterned more richly than Eastern cloths or the weaving of the spiderwoman Arachne, winged and with a tail forked like a scorpion's, that later will manoeuvre like an eel, and compared to a beaver fishing with its tail, Geryon is described in images that recall the earthly extensions of fraud, each image moving into the other to build up a picture of a credible airborne monster. Mandelstam compared him to a 'supertank',[42] and he in fact bears some resemblance to the hideous machines of war which military engineers, then and later, designed to look like monsters.[43] Once loaded with his travellers, he circles down like a falcon to the lure and, having landed them, shoots off like an arrow from the bowstring. Most of his movements are given watery comparisons: he swims through the air as though debasing that noble element, a feature to be dealt with again later in this chapter when we deal with other aspects of his nature.

His ability in flight is nothing to that of the blessed spirits for whom we are prepared by the angels guarding the valley of the negligent rulers, the eagle of Lucia, and the eagle of the empire in the Earthly Paradise. The lights of the blessed spirits wheel and turn and come to rest in a marvellous series of comparisons to birds such as this, when the souls in Jupiter group themselves into the eagle of Justice and, as the eagle pauses in speech, Dante says of that moment:

Quale allodetta che 'n aere si spazia
  prima cantando, e poi tace
    contenta

Like the small lark who wantons free in air,
  First singing and then silent, as
    possessed

de l'ultima dolcezza che la sazia,	By the last sweetness that contenteth her,
tal mi sembiò l'imago de la 'mprenta	So seemed to me the image, deep-impressed
de l'etterno piacere, al cui disio	With the Eternal Pleasure, by whose will
ciascuna cosa qual ell' è diventa.[44]	Each thing in its own nature is ˙ expressed.

Fire   This element can mean torment, purification, or the very source of light. The violent against nature are rained upon by fire and the givers of false counsel walk about in their flame bodies, able to speak only through the flame's summit. In the *Inferno* this element acquires all the fear and terror of volcanic fires, but Dante introduced too much variety into his punishments to make it the sole or main torment that it is in other depictions of Hell. The most marvellous use of it before the *Paradiso* is in the wall of flame on the last cornice, through which Dante has to pass and where he pauses in terror, remembering human bodies (perhaps of heretics) he had once seen burnt.[45] The imagery of fire, the outermost sphere of Earth, is naturally most closely related to that of light. Its transformations where Dante's characters are concerned form part of the next chapter and, before dealing with it as light, it is necessary to turn again to the fourfold interpretation and its relation to the work.

Beatrice and the three allegorical meanings

In the last chapter I tried to show how Dante could have treated the characters and events emerging in his visions and inspirations as coming so close in content and depth of meaning to the scriptures that they were susceptible of interpretation by the fourfold method. I also suggested that he could have drawn out the significances of his characters by interpreting them on the three spiritual levels, and the chief example given was that of the anagogic level relating the first four guides to the first four stages of Bonaventure's *Itinerarium mentis*. The question was also raised of whether the four levels of meaning had in their origins, or in later interpretations, been related not only to man's psychology but also to the macrocosm. This would mean that, at different points in the journey, one interpretation would be more dominant than another, and that the changes in Dante's grasp of reality would be related to a progress through the allegorical and the moral levels to the anagogic level of full contemplation, which is beyond knowledge gained through the senses. His perceptions and what his mind made of the world about him would therefore dictate what he saw according to the dominance of one or other of the levels of meaning. That symbolism should change according to a scale of worlds was not foreign to medieval thought. This is implicit in Hildegard of Bingen's defining of her visions, and Alan of Lille, for example, in a sermon on the Intelligible Sphere, attributes different levels of symbolism to the four spheres he descries in that famous description of the Godhead.[46] Just as the anagogic level is always present, both in the speculative sense because the poem describes the afterlife and in the contemplative sense through the six guides, and just as the moral level is also always present because the symbolism of the cone of Hell, Mount Purgatory, and Heaven relate to the themes of justice, punishment, and reward, what Dante particularly draws attention to up to the end of the scenes in the Earthly Paradise is the allegorical level. Beatrice at this point suddenly mentions the moral interpretation.[47] The pageants in the Earthly Paradise, with their historical and political meanings related to the life of Christ and to the history of the Church and empire, present a culmination of the stage of allegory in the poem ending in the prophecy of the DXV. Beatrice's bringing in of the moral level and her promise not to speak in riddles again would, with the ascent into the heavens, mark a transition to the moral level, but one where the causes of good and evil in man are related to their causes in the eternal world. The sight of the *punto*, the tiny point of light in *Paradiso* XXVIII, would then be the consummation of the moral level and the transition into the anagogic level and the total reversal of Dante's conception of reality. Each stage, both cosmologically and psychologically, would therefore be contained within the other and each could be drawn on singly or in unison at any point of the journey.

The level of allegory on the grandest scale concerns the source of faith, Christ, and the history of humanity centred about the Incarnation. The crises of the Church and of Western Christian society were such in Dante's time that to him, and to others such as Ubertino da Casale, current events could be expressed as figural allegories which would explain their wider significance in the history of humanity, as for example in the linking of the removal of the papacy to France with the Babylonian captivity. Thus there are certain passages linked in allegory with this kind of signification from the beginning of the poem to the second pageant in the Earthly Paradise. These include: the three beasts and the *veltro*, which we have already described as Florence, France, and the carnal Church, which will be defeated by the coming spiritual deliverer, the *veltro*; the failure of Virgil to take Dante into the city of Dis and the threat of Medusa, at which Dante asks those of sane intellects to see behind the veil of the strange verses; the old man of Crete; the monster Geryon himself; the figure of Satan; the hovering of the angels above the negligent rulers where the angels drive away the snake in the grass; and the two pageants, particularly the pageant of Church and empire in the Earthly Paradise. Some of these have been described in relation to the symmetry of the cross and the eagle in the poem, and the connexion of the travels of Aeneas and Paul with the Great Circle of pilgrimage.

Robert John relates the scene in the valley of the negligent rulers to the Templars in the following way. This is an incident where Dante's readers are asked particularly to look for the hidden meaning, when the green-robed angels guard the valley against a mysterious snake. The rulers who, according to Robert John, were sympathetic to the Templars, sing 'Salve regina', a hymn sung all the year round, including at Easter, by the Cistercians (on whose religious practices the Templar rule was founded) and not simply between Whitsun and Advent, as by the rest of the Church.[48] They form a group of thirteen, the number of a Templar cell, again an adoption of a Cistercian practice because it signified Christ and the twelve apostles. John identified the snake, which cannot possibly tempt them in the state of the afterlife they have attained in the literal level of the story, with the bull of Clement V issued from Toulouse on 30 December 1308, instructing the rulers of Europe to institute proceedings against the Templars: the bull began with the words, 'Callidi serpentis . . . .' This explains why the serpent is so cunning, why it is sent specifically to princes, and why the angels in green are sent from the bosom of Mary signifying the help that will come to the Templars.[49] John also finds great significance for his theory in the episode of Geryon—though in what follows I make considerable modifications to his interpretation.

Geryon is one of the strangest beings that ever appeared in Dante's creative imagination. Like the closed doors of the city of Dis he probably derives from a point in the writing or planning of the *Commedia* when Dante seemed to have reached an impasse and had to delve all the more deeply into the dream levels of his mind for a solution. In the story also Dante and Virgil are at a topographical impasse; the cliff descending from the burning sands (the sins of the lion) to the rings of Malebolge (the sins of the wolf) is too sheer for them to climb down. The whole incident vibrates with hidden meanings. Virgil tells Dante to give him the belt or cord Dante wears round his waist, the cord with which Dante says he had thought to tame the leopard, which is Florence in the allegorical interpretation set out earlier. Virgil throws the cord down into the murk below and watches intently for a response. Geryon, with the face of a just man, the body of a beast and the hindquarters and poisonous tail of a scorpion, comes swimming up through the air. Like the old man of Crete, he is a fusion of Dante's classical and biblical reading, of lines in the *Aeneid* with passages from Revelation.[50] Virgil occupies Dante by allowing him to talk to some usurers from Florence, Bologna, and Padua, while he negotiates with Geryon to carry them down. When Dante returns, Virgil orders him to mount Geryon in such a way that he sits in front and Virgil sits behind protecting him from the sting. Thus they circle down to their landing place and Geryon darts off and disappears.

Geryon's immediate symbolism is made clear by Dante who calls him that 'filthy image of fraud', and it is easy to draw out from that the moral and anagogic meanings of the fraud that men practise on themselves when they silence their consciences with lies. Thus the face of a just man hides the poisonous tail which may symbolize the state of envenomed infatuation in which all hope of spiritual development comes to a halt. But what of the allegorical meaning of the cord? Older commentators, following a remark by Francesco da Buti,[51] used to think that Dante belonged to the tertiary order of the Franciscans and that this was the Franciscan girdle, but twice elsewhere in the poem he calls that girdle a *capestro* and not as here, a *corda*.[52] John thinks that it is the Templar girdle, described in the Rule of the Temple, and which played a great part in the accusations brought against the order. On this interpretation, then, the cord with which Dante says he once hoped to capture the leopard might mean that he had wished, while prior, to guide Florence according to Templar ideals and prophecies. Much of John's case here falls to the ground because he identifies the face of Geryon with Noffo Dei, the Florentine agent, who, Villani said, wrongly as it has been proved, was the accuser of the Templars to Philip the Fair.[53] He also says that Dante met the Italian usurers at this point because the Florentine bankers were in league with Philip over the destruction of the order so as to take over their business as bankers. There is no evidence of this, though the advantages to the bankers would have been clear. Others have identified Geryon with Boniface VIII. I would approach my own candidate for the identification of the allegory through the geographical examples given to describe Geryon and the astrological symbolism implicit in his true nature as a scorpion. From the quotations given earlier in this chapter, it will be remembered that in describing Geryon's body there are comparisons made with the cloths of the Tartars and the Turks, the rulers of the lands which it was the aim of the Crusades to bring back to Christianity, and to the dyes of Arachne, a Greek legend which brings in the empire of Byzantium. Then after describing the way Geryon's body from the waist backwards remains in the air like hulks half in and out of water (which might on this interpretation refer to the unused transports that once carried Crusader armies), we come to the final comparison, the beaver which fishes with its tail in the lands of the guzzling Germans, a reference to the main territorial seat of the Western empire. Scorpio is the most fearsome sign of the zodiac; it is a watery sign and this perhaps would account for the way in which Geryon's movements, though airborne, are largely described as swimming. Though the sign under which denunciations, great falsehoods, and tragedies afflict humanity, Scorpio also has a higher aspect, which is symbolized by the eagle.[54] What Geryon symbolizes here, then, is the vast fraud of a false ideal of empire, and we need not look further for what would have been such a fraud in Dante's eyes, than the well publicized ambitions of Philip the Fair for himself and his house as the possessors of a hereditary universal empire, extending over the regions of the Western and Eastern empires and the lands of the Orient. With these ambitions, with the practice of fraud on a gigantic scale in his assault on the Templars and his posthumous vilification of Boniface, all done with the 'face of a just man' and for the honour of the Church, not to mention his frequent debasements of the coinage, Philip the Fair is the most obvious candidate on the allegorical level for the figure of Geryon, a point further confirmed by Geryon as the link between the sins of the lion (France) with the sins of the wolf (the carnal Church). Geryon is made to come by the lure of a cord which, whether it signifies Dante's attachment to the Templars or not, certainly played a major part in the spider's web of lies Philip's advisers constructed about the order. After this the image of false empire carries the two poets of true empire down to the marges of the dolorous realm.

The belt or cord which Templars at all times wore as a reminder of their vows was turned by their accusers into something obscene and pagan.[55] They were accused of touching the image of an idol variously described and sometimes called Baphomet (obviously a corruption of Mahomet) with their belts which thereby acquired some magic power to keep them enthralled. Dante's use of it here is part of the concealed but powerful satire with which he attacked both Philip the Fair and Clement V. Another of the charges against the Templars was the ritual and enforced practice of homosexuality. In the prophecy of the simoniac Pope Nicholas III of the coming of Clement V that follows soon after this episode, Nicholas says of Clement:

Nuovo Iasón sarà, di cui si legge,
 ne' Maccabei: e come a quel fu molle
 suo re, così fia lui chi Francia regge.[56]

A new Jason will he be, of whom we read
 In Maccabees; and as to him his King was soft
 So to this one shall be the ruler of France.

Jason was the high priest who defiled the Temple by introducing Greek practices to curry favour with Antiochus IV Epiphanes. The real savagery of the comparison is generally missed by commentators, though not by Guido da Pisa, who, writing in about 1330, points out that Jason established a homosexual brothel in the Temple precincts for Antiochus.[57] So Clement is represented as a pander to Philip the Fair in the context of the defilement of the Temple, and both have the calumny of homosexuality flung back at them in one of Dante's subtlest and most devastating examples of satirical invective. This passage is preceded by Guido with a hostile account of the character and life of Clement V in which, as already mentioned on page 209, he says that Clement bought the papacy from Philip in exchange for certain promises, among them the condemnation of the Templars.

The connexion with the Templars does not cease there. The prophecy is uttered by Pope Nicholas III, whom Dante taunts for the bribes he received for helping to bring about the conspiracy against Charles of Anjou which led to the Sicilian Vespers and the ruin of the crusading venture in which Charles was acting in alliance with the Templars. We have already seen that Charles himself forms part of a group of monarchs favourable to the Templars. The position Nicholas is in—upside down—is like that in which murderers in Florence were executed. They were put head first into a hole and then smothered by having earth shovelled round their faces. Dante describes himself as having to bend down to talk to Nicholas like a friar confessing one of these murderers. One of the ways in which their torturers extracted their confessions from the Templars was to coat the soles of their victims' feet with fat and set them against blazing fires so that the fat also burst into flame.[58] The punishment that Nicholas suffers is curiously similar; the soles of his feet burn with flames that burn like those on *cose unte*, 'greasy things' or, in this case, rather, basted. In enduring the same punishment as Nicholas when his time comes, so Clement will also suffer eternally what by his betrayal of the Templars he allowed them to undergo.

Dante's depiction of Satan also provides another possible connexion with Philip the Fair's policies, not only in his attack on the Templars but also in the posthumous trial of Boniface VIII. Yet another of the charges against the Templars concerned kisses on certain parts of the body, including the navel, at the reception of new members into the order. It is on Satan's navel that Virgil turns Dante upside down in order to bring him round for the ascent to truth in the southern hemisphere. Satan is the father of lies, and this incident, though necessary in the geography of the poem, together with the further point that Baphomet the idol was sometimes described as having three faces like Satan in the poem, may also be yet another satirical reminiscence of the treachery and lies by which the order was brought low. That is only a suggestion, but there is a wider issue concerning Dante's effect on the course of European history raised by his depiction of Satan. It is easy to see that Dante would have to conceal much of his concern and support for the Templar order under allegorical symbols and comparisons, given the weakness of his political position as an exile, his known opposition to papal and French policy, and his independence and originality of thought that made him so open to charges of heresy, charges that indeed accumulated after his death; but his symbols have a positive worth as well as the negative virtue of concealing some of his most dangerous attitudes and ideals. They are both memorable and mysterious, working on men's minds, like significant dreams demanding interpretation. They have concealed power, preserving civilized ideals and spiritual values in a way that allows them to triumph over the transient setbacks of Dante's immediate political ideals. By advancing new symbols or new presentations of doctrine such as his view of Purgatory as a place of light, Dante was also sapping the power of older and harmful symbols as in the case of Satan. The triple form of Satan, the great illusion, parodies the Trinity of the final vision, and one of the most remarkable features of the *Commedia* is the wholly topographical role that Satan and his legions play in the poem, given the fear and fascination that these embodiments of evil exercised over medieval minds. Dante wholly rejects the customary tendency of men to blame the devil for their own misdeeds and places the responsibility for evil firmly on men themselves. Demons may come to collect the souls of the dead or they may guard them in Hell, but only because of the actions in life of those souls—not because the demons possess any power to limit a man's free will. This is a consequence of his discovery of the worth of the individual and while he, through this discovery, inaugurated one of the most civilizing lines of thought and art in Western history, Philip the Fair and his advisers forged and tempered the techniques of persecution that led to the witch-hunts that were to haunt Europe for centuries.[59] For the purposes of denigrating the dead Boniface VIII they invented a new false religion of ritual magic which they accused Boniface of practising. Great numbers of witnesses were produced to give evidence of the pope's commerce with demons, every word of their evidence a lie, and all set aside and ignored by Philip once he had achieved his greater object of the destruction of the Templars—but remaining as an unholy bequest to future fanatics and unscrupulous politicians and clerics with scores to settle. One of the first to take up the charge of ritual magic against his enemies was Pope John XXII. He believed that there were widespread attempts to practise witchcraft and ritual magic against him: a belief he was ready to substantiate by torture and forgery. Curiously enough, in the false charges brought against one of the Visconti of Milan who was accused of trying to procure John XXII's demise by means of a magic silver statuette of the pope, Dante's name turns up as a likely instrument to consult in fulfilling this aim.[60] Dante was, in fact, in his grave by the time that this investigation was concluded, but it is a chilling reminder of how, in the eyes of the ignorant and the suspicious, his literary conversations with the dead could be translated into criminal commerce with the devil. John XXII's other obsession was to elevate into a kind of negative dogma the impossibility of anyone receiving the beatific vision not only in this life but also in the next until the Resurrection[61]—a thesis which, if it had been generally adopted, would have provided further reason for the condemnation of Dante's work. A corollary of this doctrine was that Hell was empty both of human souls and of devils until the Last Judgment. Dante's only weapons against such men occupying the seats of power and spiritual authority were his pen and the influence he could exert through his command over symbolic language and his ability to renew it.

In the following lines Andrew Marvell was to make Dante into the type of the poet impelled to speak by the very weakness of his position:

> When the Sword glitters ore the Judges head,
> And fear has Coward Churchmen silenced,
> Then is the Poets time, 'tis then he drawes,
> And single fights forsaken Vertues cause.
> He, when the wheel of Empire whirleth back,
> And though the World's disjointed Axel crack,
> Sings still of ancient Rights and better Times,
> Seeks wretched good, arraigns successful Crimes.[62]

Through his writings Dante was able to change and give new values to the symbolism of his civilization. Through the processes of synthesis and fusion of images from various cultures and of the remembered impressions of his life in his creative imagination, he carried out a rite of the reconsecration of symbols.

The greatest example of the reconsecration of a symbol in Dante is, of course, his presentation of Beatrice and, through her, his affirmation that universal love can be experienced in individual and earthly relationships. The fall of Satan displaced the earth that made the mountain on whose summit Dante is reunited with Beatrice. She revealed herself to him in the vision of the rising sun, thereby awakening his conscience to the full implications of the inspirations she had been sending him, and he, in return, to create her living semblance in art, had to treat her with all the loving detachment that a good artist devotes to painting his mistress. To understand this process of reconsecration we must first consider the allegorical, figural, and other meanings of the setting in which she appears to him: the Earthly Paradise.

I have already pointed to the revolution in the symbolism of faith Dante created by presenting Purgatory as a mountain in the light of the sun. In the Earthly Paradise he makes a parallel revolution by revealing Eden, not as something lost for ever by the sin of our first parents, but as an experience every awakened and happy man and woman can recapture in woods on a spring day or as a secret garden of the soul. The trees, the singing birds, the breezes, the way the cresses in the river are bent back by the current of the water, are described with a realism and an intensity of vision that needed more than a century of assimilation before the painters of his own Florence, such as Botticelli, could begin to emulate his example. Such realism derives, however, not just from close observation of nature but from a fusion of a myriad visual memories with his insights into the signatures of natural phenomena and the symbolism of his political, ethical, and spiritual aspirations. Thus, though it is the most magical and yet credible wood ever described in literature, with its dimensions accurately given by the directions, and the distances covered by the travellers and the beings who welcome them there, it is also a transformation into a wooded glade of the enclosure about the Temple of Jerusalem at whose antipodes in the geography of the poem it actually stands. The circular glade in the poem which Dante approaches from the west is paralleled by the depiction in numerous pilgrim maps of Jerusalem as a circle.[63] The red and gold flowers gathered by Matelda may refer to the arms of the city of Jerusalem which were red crosses on a field of gold, and to give a clue to the travellers' whereabouts she quotes a word *delectasti* from a psalm which refers to delight in the works of God but also goes on to say 'Those that be planted in the house of the Lord shall flourish in the courts of our God',[64] a reference to the Temple and its surrounding court, the wooded Haram es Sharif. The nearly a hundred paces which Matelda, guiding Dante from the other bank of Lethe, takes against the current of the river signify the close upon a hundred decades that have passed since the Donation of Constantine. The journey against the current of Lethe is an *unforgetting* leading Dante southwards to a bend and then eastwards to what would be the site of the building then known as the Temple of Solomon, one of the sites formerly in the care of the Templars. It is here that the reunion with Beatrice takes place. These are only some of the parallels drawn by Robert John between the Temple enclosure at Jerusalem and the Earthly Paradise,[65] a thesis largely corroborated, though with modifications, by John Demaray's examination of the pilgrim texts and maps relating to the Great Circle pilgrimage[66] and by Bonaventure's use of Temple imagery for the stages in the journey to

God which Matelda and Beatrice would signify on the anagogic level.[67] The Earthly Paradise is an essential stage on the journey to Heaven just as the earthly beatitude promised in the prophecy of the DXV is a necessary stage for the greatest possible number to achieve celestial beatitude. To these aspects of its symbolism must be added all the allegorical and moral associations with which Christian writers such as St Augustine had loaded the theme of Eden.[68] All these were contributory elements to the brilliant inner vision in which Dante must have seen the *divina foresta*. As with his other great visions, the product was a recreation of ancient symbolism and themes fused together to give a new direction to the creative life of humanity. For in his depiction of the Earthly Paradise as a figure of Jerusalem Dante seems to have preserved all the experience of Western Christians in their relations with the Orient in the previous 200 years—the expansive conquering urge that drove them to win the Holy Land, the piety of the pilgrims with their simple need to touch, see, and walk in the places Christ had sanctified, the long watches, battles, victories and defeats of the military orders—and transferred it to a plane where it was for ever free of the grasp of the Saracens and the cupidity of tyrants. The loss of Acre in 1291 and the crushing of the Templars had brought that age to an end, and although Dante looked for the recovery of the Holy Land he saw that, not as a repetition of the past Crusades, which so often failed because of the dissensions of their leaders, but in the context of the world emperor—a subject which brings us again to the DXV.

The prophecy of the DXV comes as the climax of the second pageant which comes about in this manner. After the first pageant of the elders of the Bible and Dante's confession, Beatrice leads the party in a north-westerly direction and it halts at a withered tree. Demaray points out that on medieval maps of the circular Jerusalem, the Anastasis or Golgotha in the church of the Holy Sepulchre appears as a cross to the north-west of drawings of the Temple.[69] The site of the crucifixion was also said to be the burial place of Adam's skull, and nearby was shown the place where Mary watched the crucifixion. In the poem the angels murmur the name of Adam, Beatrice is compared to Mary before the cross, and she repeats the words of Christ before He was crucified: 'Modicum et non videbitis me . . . .' The tree, then, is the Tree of the Knowledge of Good and Evil to which the griffin attaches the chariot by its pole which is the cross and which by tradition was cut from this tree. The tree breaks into foliage and blossom. Dante falls into a slumber and, awaking in lines that specifically recall the Transfiguration, witnesses the second pageant, a depiction in allegory of the history of the Church, divided into seven parts. In the first scene the bird of Jove, the eagle, like lightning rends the bark of the tree and its new foliage and gives a blow to the chariot, signifying the persecution of the Church by the empire; in the second, a fox (heresy) enters the chariot, but Beatrice drives it away; in the third, the eagle gives a feather from its breast, signifying the Donation; in the fourth, a dragon (possibly Islam) mutilates the chariot; in the fifth and sixth, the chariot degenerates into the carnal Church, sprouting heads like the Beast of the Apocalypse; and in the seventh and last scene, the harlot and giant (Clement V and Philip the Fair) sit on the transformed chariot and embrace, until the harlot leers at Dante and the giant beats her and drags her away into the wood—just as Philip the Fair crushed all Clement's hopes of escape or independence. This ends Canto XXXII and the next canto begins with the opening of a psalm (78 in the Vulgate), which refers to the desecration of the Temple by the heathen.

The pageant over, Beatrice speaks of some of its meanings and says that a clear message in the stars predicts the coming of a five hundred, ten, and five, the DXV sent by God who will kill the harlot and the giant. Many and curious are the solutions proffered for this riddle. My own preference, already described in Chapter 16 for its allegorical interpretation, is the emperor redeemer, the monarch with his infinite capacity for love who is signified by this number because it recalls the rebuilding of the Temple by Zerrubabel and looks forward to the refounding of the Temple by this monarch. That theory has the attraction of linking other lines of imagery, besides that of the Templars and Jerusalem, with the eagle and the cross and with the Great Circle pilgrimage. Zerrubabel's words with which he won the right to rebuild the Temple 'Women are strongest: but above all things Truth beareth away the victory' make the prophecy of the DXV particularly apt in Beatrice's lips for she bears out the good sense of both parts of that statement. Though that analysis provides for a number of the contributory elements fused in this symbol, there are several others which may apply to the moral and anagogic levels of meaning. I suspect that, as well as the marvellously simple solution of it as 515 BC, it also contains a complex numerological meaning on the pattern of the number of the beast 666 in Revelation, but I can make no claim to solve it. The prediction of the DXV by astrology is, however, strongly reminiscent of the closing pages of the *Monarchia* where it is said that the emperor will lead mankind to temporal happiness in accordance with philosophical teaching, and that he will receive knowledge of when to apply the principles of liberty and peace, from God, through harmonizing the conditions on Earth with the movements of the heavens.[70] The moral meaning might therefore refer to a new form of knowledge given out by the philosophers who are to be associated with the monarch. A few lines later Beatrice refers to Dante's 'school', presumably the learning of the ancients which is inadequate to interpret what he has been shown. This new secular knowledge, grounded on a more thorough understanding of the four cardinal virtues in the individual, on a heightened sense of the grandeur and dignity of man and on the reconciliation of classical mythology, doctrines, and symbolism with Christianity implicit in the true ideal of a Christian Roman empire, would point towards a new civilization—the civilization that ultimately appeared in the Renaissance and of which Dante had already spoken in *De vulgari eloquentia* and the *Convivio*. If this is so, then on the moral level of the DXV we can point to at least one of Dante's prophecies that was fulfilled. Where the anagogic level is concerned, there is an interesting theory put forward by R. E. Kaske, admittedly not solely as an anagogic interpretation but as a complete allegorical explanation. He draws attention to the play Dante's visual imagination could have made with the monogram with which innumerable missals began the preface of the Mass:[71] the words *Vere Dignum* were represented by a device that was widely regarded as a symbol of Christ.* This requires the reversal of the order of the initials V, D, and the conversion of the cross joining them into an X, a comparatively simple task amongst all the visual puns Dante's nimble imagination performed, and it is supported by much erudition—enough to lead me to regard it as one of the elements fused into the symbol of the DXV and identified as Christ in His second coming and in a contemplative and mystical sense. This is, of course, much the same meaning as was given to the anagogical level of the *veltro* in the last chapter; and in Christ, who is at once the emperor of Heaven and the high priest, it demonstrates the level on which the two powers which must be separated in their earthly roles become united.

Beatrice, after the prophecy, makes allowances for Dante's mental confusion at the sight of all these marvels, and promises that henceforth she will speak more clearly. She specifically mentions the moral level of interpretation in referring to the Tree of Knowledge, and I think this is done to mark the end of the stage in which the allegorical level predominates and where the moral level begins, in relation to the cosmology of the poem. In the course of these last four cantos of the *Purgatorio* in which she appears, Beatrice displays a number of possible meanings. These begin with the vision of the rising sun greeted with the acclamations of the Palm Sunday crowd, coming like the Palm Sunday processions in Jerusalem which entered the Temple enclosure from the east through the Golden Gate; as if to make no doubt about what she is at that moment, the elders keep the masculine form of the Palm Sunday acclamation 'Benedictus qui venis . . .'. Then Beatrice may be said to proceed out of this vision, the first of the four visions of Christ in the poem, and here she is on a great chariot preceded by the books of the Old Testament and followed by the books of the New as though she is Sapientia, the Divine Wisdom that informs all these holy writings, with her companions making a procession remarkably like the splendid peregrinations performed in the cathedrals and great churches of the Gothic period, especially during Lent and Easter. The olive of Minerva with which she is crowned denotes her possession of all the wisdom of the classical world, another aspect of her as Sapientia. At the same time she is the Beatrice of Dante's past, dead ten years at the time at which the poem is set, and endowed with priestly powers to hear his confession. She reveals herself as the true source of his inspirations, takes him to witness the second pageant, of the history of the Church, and finally becomes a prophetess with her prediction of the DXV. She is the supreme example of the fusion of sources and meanings in the poem and at the same time is indubitably and forcefully alive.

* ⒟

Can she with all these allusive meanings still be the soul of Beatrice Portinari? Robert John, in company with many other writers, refuses to accept this identification. He says that she represents the Templar Gnosis of the Spiritual Church. Others such as Valli see her solely as a symbol of eternal wisdom, pointing to the lateness of Boccaccio's identification of her as the historical Beatrice, to the fact that she speaks of her limbs as scattered in the earth, taking this to refer to the scattered groups or sects devoted to her, and to the part she plays, as revealed knowledge. There is much weight in these arguments. Like many of the early commentators, Dante's sons Pietro and Jacopo both said she was Theology, though Pietro, in a later version of his commentary, identified her as well with Beatrice Portinari but only, it is thought, after reading Boccaccio's life of Dante.[72]

On the other hand, Boccaccio's own father was closely linked to the Bardi family into which Beatrice Portinari married, being one of their business agents, and this would be a likely source of private information. Furthermore there is the opinion of the only one of the early commentators to apply the fourfold interpretation to her, the Carmelite friar Guido da Pisa: though he does not name her he says she must be understood literally as 'a noble Florentine lady who in this life gave out a miraculous radiance by her beauty and the purity of her morals'.[73] He goes on to say that allegorically she is the sacred science of theology, morally the spiritual life, and anagogically—giving both the contemplative and speculative senses of that level—she is divine grace infused in man and the life in glory (*vita beata*) man may expect. He also says that these meanings would be made clearer later in his exposition. Unfortunately he only completed his commentary on the *Inferno* and therefore we lack his exposition of the passages where Beatrice appears directly. Guido's commentary has only recently been published in its entirety and the significance of this passage has therefore been overlooked. He said enough in this one short passage, though, to demonstrate that in the eyes of one of Dante's most intelligent and learned contemporaries, it was perfectly acceptable to recognize that Beatrice was a historical personage and that Dante applied the technique of the fourfold method to her. I think that both these points are correct and an understanding of this enables us to grasp something of the wealth of meaning Dante expressed through Beatrice. (It would be equally fair to speak of the wealth of meaning Beatrice expressed through Dante.)

Let us look first at some further reasons for regarding her as the historical Beatrice. If we consider Beatrice as one of the six guides of the poem, we notice that the five other characters acting as guides have a firm historical past. To regard her purely as a symbol, however magnificent, would make her anomalous in the series. If we apply the four levels of meaning to her, then she must have a literal historical significance for the allegorical levels to depend on for their meaning. If we take into consideration the examples given earlier from the troubadour tradition and from Ibn al-'Arabī, there is much evidence that the poets regarded their ladies as living embodiments of Sapientia. If we think of the records of the many saints who had an effect on their followers remarkably similar to that of Beatrice as recorded in the *Vita Nuova*, then there is even more reason for understanding how Dante's early experience of supreme goodness through her should return to him in redoubled splendour in later life. The best of all reasons for regarding her as the historical Beatrice is that she mirrors the Incarnation of Christ.[74] In making the *Vita Nuova*, Dante took pains to show the parallels between Christ and her. In creating the *Commedia*, he made her the second person of the trinity of ladies, in the position of Christ, as incarnate sapiential wisdom. As these ladies mark the intervention of the divine impulse into Dante's life to initiate and impel each stage of the journey to the vision of God, Beatrice, as the risen sun on the chariot, is Christ in His divine and human natures in one person. The identification is supported by the double nature of the griffin drawing her chariot, the beast, lion-bodied, eagle-winged, and eagle-headed, who, reflected in Beatrice's eyes, reveals to Dante the hypostatic union. Her dual nature is also revealed in that she is the only one of the three blessed ladies to number also in the six guides, her historical character there emphasizing her incarnate being. Where the six guides are concerned, as Lucia bridged the gap between the unbaptized pagans, Virgil and Cato, and the baptized Statius and Matelda, so Beatrice in her divine aspect bridges the gap to carry on the sequence between Statius and Matelda and her historical self and St Bernard.

If those arguments help to establish her historical reality, other questions remain. Why does the reunion with Beatrice take place in Eden? And, what is more, in an Eden that seems to be a figural representation of the Temple enclosure of Jerusalem and that also particularly refers to the Knights Templar? We are so used to the linking of the names of Dante and Beatrice that we need to remind ourselves of the astonishing boldness of all the associations Dante built into his presentation of her. In his description of Beatrice, Dante was destroying the misogyny of Christian monastic civilization; he says in effect, 'If Christ is Holy Wisdom, then Christ is in the woman I love and in whom Holy Wisdom is manifest to me.' As he makes Eden accessible to us again through perceptions purified by art and our imaginations, so in Beatrice he gives us a new Eve who can sit on the roots of the Tree of Knowledge and not be tempted. As he recapitulates and transfers to another plane where they can be satisfied the longings of generations of Crusaders and pilgrims for the true Jerusalem, so he makes his reunion with her take place at the antipodes of the Temple of Solomon to signify her nature as Sapientia. She is preceded by seven candlesticks that at once refer to the seven-branched candlestick of Solomon's Temple and the sevenfold gifts of the Holy Spirit. She is hailed by one of the elders in the procession (probably Solomon himself) as the Bride of Lebanon, and she represents in this context the eternal wisdom who spoke through Solomon in describing her as being with God before the making of worlds. On the allegorical level, therefore, she could well be described as the revealed knowledge of theology—as do most of Dante's early commentators—but it is the theology of a spiritual church, not that of the Church of Boniface VIII, Clement V, and John XXII. She is the wisdom revealed to men of good will in all ages, and is independent of the vicissitudes of the Church as depicted in the second pageant. She evicts the fox of heresy and comments on the other events, but in effect looks more to the future than to the past. She is in herself a prophecy because with the prediction of the DXV and taking other aspects of her nature into account, she points towards what the spirituality of the new age will be, and on what aspects of knowledge and experience her spiritual revelation will throw light. Through her Dante acknowledges that the era of faith most fully symbolized by the Templars and their doom has come to an end, but just as Jerusalem is a stage on the Great Circle pilgrimage for reaching the final goal of Rome, so Beatrice points to the civilization that will appear with the world emperor and the Christianization of the themes of antiquity.

There is another way in which she looks to the future. She is the consummation of the troubadour tradition and she initiates a new understanding of romantic love. It is of the essence of romantic love that for each lover, nothing has true significance except the existence of the beloved, and that consequently the whole of the universe may be discovered in the beloved. As Shakespeare put it in Sonnet 109:

> For nothing this wide Universe I call,
> Save thou, my rose; in it thou art my all.

She is the mistress of the higher and greater worlds that are formed of the fifth element, beyond the four elements of earth, the cosmos of being that I would relate to the moral level of the poem as a whole. This is also the realm of inspiration mediated through the angels and the planets they rule. So that on this moral level Beatrice may be seen as the light of grace presented through poetry and the imagery of light, as Thalia no longer silent but raised to the Primum Mobile as one of the three Graces, and as Polyhymnia, the Muse of sacred song: Guido da Pisa saw her moral sense as signifying the spiritual life. He certainly meant that in a more conventional sense than the implications of a new era of inspiration that I discern in her, but my real justification for this depends on Beatrice's meanings on the anagogic level.

In the speculative sense of the anagogic level she necessarily points to the future for all living readers of the *Commedia* for she is the life of the blessed in Heaven. If we take her as the here and now of the contemplative sense, she is the fifth stage on the journey of the mind to God: the contemplation of God above ourselves through eternal art and in His being. Even here the Temple imagery applies because Bonaventure describes this stage as the entry, with the high priest, into the Holy of Holies 'where above the ark are the Cherubim of glory overshadowing the propitiatory'.[75] Bucke, it will be remembered, identified

Beatrice with cosmic consciousness, the ultimate experience of unity. From such experiences derive the highest works of art, and in the *Paradiso* Dante gives new standards for art by his portrayal of the works of eternal art.

All this interpretation grows out of her nature on the literal level as the blessed soul of Beatrice Portinari—and what a character he depicts in her! A woman of astonishing beauty, with a razor-sharp mind, a cruel eye for all pretension, and a heart-warming grace and charm, she takes Dante up to the world of light in a dizzying alternation of theological lectures and scenes of breathtaking marvels. As she purifies his intellect on this ascent, the meaning of two other strands of imagery relating to the perfection of man, already developed from the beginning of the poem, is made more and more clear in their purpose. These are the imagery of coming face to face and of light and art.

The imagery of coming face to face and the imagery of light and art

The end and consummation of the *Commedia* is the face-to-face meeting of Dante with the vision of the triune God in the Empyrean. In this he drew on an image, familiar to the mystics of both the Christian and the Sufi traditions, founded on one of the most accustomed of human actions: the search for certainty and identity in the features of another. One of the essential doctrines in the mystical writings of St Bernard is the newness of life which will lead men to contemplate the 'glory of the unveiled countenance of the Lord Jesus',[76] a theme especially made clear in his sermons on the Song of Songs. The troubadours and their successors had also drawn on the Sapiential tradition as revealed to them in the Song of Songs and had developed a series of images based on the face of the beloved with special associations devoted to each feature of her face, notably the eyes and the mouth. Dante had drawn on these images for his depictions of Beatrice in the *Vita Nuova* and also in his allegorical explanations of the Lady Philosophy in the *Convivio*. We know also from the *Vita Nuova* the effect of faces appearing in his dreamlife, the angry women of 'Donna pietosa', for example, and also from the same work, at what an early stage the image of the pilgrim journey to see the Veronica, the veil or image imprinted with Christ's sweat, at Rome was rooted in him.[77] He was to use the Veronica again in an image that connects his identification of the Empyrean as the heavenly Rome which he attains on the last stage of his figural Great Circle pilgrimage. The presentation of the *donna angelicata* and her depiction was largely of a woman observed, arousing deep emotions and disturbance in her admirers while herself remaining unmoved. In this she resembled the tradition of the sacred pictures and icons in Italy, the *Santo Volto* at Lucca or the Madonna of the Great Eyes at Siena, for example, or in the Eastern Church the representation of the face of Christ based on the Mandylion, an impression of Christ's features preserved latterly at Byzantium up to the sack of 1204. Such icons played an immense part in popular devotion and inspired many stories of how sometimes they spoke to supplicants who prayed under their gaze, but, with the new dynamic quality brought to religious painting and sculpture by the artists of the Gothic, artists were now intent on delineating personages through capturing a specific and characteristic expression of the features, and as though their lips were poised for utterance. This, as I have already stressed, was one of the most important contributions towards Dante's new mastery of characterization. The experience that enabled him to fuse these and other elements into this new presentation of humanity forms the subject of the next chapter. There may, however, be a further connexion with the Templars that directly affects the present subject of the imagery of coming face to face. This arises from recent speculations on the origin of the Holy Shroud of Turin. Ian Wilson[78] has suggested (a) that the Holy Shroud is identical with the Mandylion (thought lost in the sack of Byzantium); (b) that the Shroud/Mandylion came into the possession of the Templars; (c) that this most sacred relic or copies of it were what the Templars adored in the secret ceremonies that aroused so much suspicion against them. The worship of this image of Christ and of the copies made of it could, on this suggestion, have been the origin of the accusations that they worshipped the idol Baphomet. The arguments supporting these speculations are given in Mr Wilson's book; what is of interest here is the thought that there could have been amongst the Templars, a mystical teaching founded both on the teachings of St Bernard and on the possession of the miraculously preserved features of Christ and a ritual associated with it that could have influenced Dante if he were affiliated to the Templars and which he attempted to preserve and transmit through the alternative medium of his art.

By the very nature of the confrontations and meetings that Dante takes part in, we are constantly prepared for the final vision in the descriptions of the faces of the souls revealing every possibility of human facial expression. There may be delight and pleasure in these confrontations or danger and terror, as in the threat of Medusa's face. There is always curiosity, as in the description of Brunetto Latini's band coming upon the travellers:

e ciascuna	and scrutiny
ci riguardava come suol da sera	Each made of us, as men are wont to do
guardare uno altro sotto nuova luna;	At dusk, when a new moon is in the sky;
e sì ver' noi aguzzavan le ciglia	And at us, puckering their brows, they pried
come 'l vecchio sartor fa ne la cruna.[79]	Like an old tailor at his needle's eye.

Time and again Dante emphasizes what each face looked like, down to the three faces of Satan, and up again to the face of Cato, the wounded brow of Manfred, the stitched-up eyes of Sapia, the emaciated visage of Forese, and then the gradual unfolding of the beauty of Beatrice. How deeply the sight of these souls penetrates his own mind is related to his own growth in self-knowledge and sympathy. In Paradise he has to deal with the paradox of presenting souls so brilliant in their light that he cannot discern their features and yet he is more open than ever to the meeting of their minds with his.

To overcome this paradox he had to extend and transform these strands of imagery in writing the *Paradiso*. After the extraordinary sights in the Earthly Paradise and his drinking of Eunoe, Dante finds himself no longer on Earth. He is ascending into the lunar sphere, transhumanized by the sight of Beatrice and able, to his amazement, to withstand the sight of the sun. Paradise, organized according to the hierarchies of Dionysius the Areopagite, who advocated the constant use of images to correct any false impression that reliance on one image alone would encourage, is the place of freedom from images through the doubled intensity with which they are presented and alternated. Beatrice explains how the souls may appear to Dante in the lowest spheres of Heaven, while their true place is in the Empyrean, with this passage on symbolism:

Qui si mostraro, non perché sortita
　sia questa spera lor, ma per far segno
　de la celestïal c'ha men salita.
Così parlar conviensi al vostro ingegno,
　però che solo da sensato apprende
　ciò che fa poscia d'intelletto degno.
Per questo la Scrittura condescende
　a vostra facultate, e piedi e mano
　attribuisce a Dio e altro intende;
e Santa Chiesa con aspetto umano
　Gabrïel e Michel vi rappresenta,
　e l'altro che Tobia rifece sano.[80]

They showed themselves here, not because they are placed
　In this allotted sphere; rather to show
　The heavenly sphere that is exalted least.
Speech to your wit must needs be tempered so,
　Since but from things of sense it apprehends
　What it makes apt for the intellect to know.
Scripture to your capacity condescends
　For this cause, and a foot and hand will feign
　For God, yet something other it intends.
Thus Holy Church portrays to you as men
　With human look Michael and Gabriel
　And the other who made Tobit whole again.

As Paradise is the dwelling-place of pure intelligences, it is here that Dante's intellect receives its purification and the enlarging of his capacity to conceive the inner truths of creation. Just as the scale on which Dante's questions are answered expands immeasurably from the expositions of Virgil and Statius to those of Beatrice, for example, the way in which the question about spots on the moon is expanded to the way in which higher influences are carried down throughout creation, so the images of the *Paradiso* also expand and find further connexions in all the themes of imagery already introduced. The reader now meets in the *Paradiso* a series of light symbols in which the origins of great movements are made visible. These symbols are no longer the shadows of themselves in dreams or visions, but the effect of illuminated intelligences making themselves manifest; they are the secret life, mind, and love of humanity at its highest.

Dante's journey through Paradise may be described as the entry of a mind into another, higher mind in which it finds so many correspondences that finally the identity of the two minds is mutually recognized and sealed in their union. Among the correspondences are those of numerology and of mathematical species conceived as living intelligences and as having a primary subsistence in the soul. Therefore, among the images new to the *Commedia*, in the *Paradiso* we find examples of geometry, frequently and diversely used for illustrations of astronomy and optics up to the culminating image of the *punto* and the three incomprehensibly linked circles of the Trinity. These images help to bring out Dante's entrance into a world of pure intellect, the noumenal world of ideas which are blissful causes of phenomena. Another group of images, those of dance, song, and ecstatic recitation, bring out the revelation of this world also as one of pure art, or of eternal art, as Bonaventure describes the third mode of the journey to God in the mind seeing Him above itself.[81]

I spoke of the recovery of art at the entrance to Purgatory. There the art, the sculptures, and the hymns had the didactic effect of devotional exercises whereby the purgatorial souls were purified and made ready for the stage of the blessed, of whom every individual soul is an artist. The art of Paradise is truly spontaneous: whatever the souls there speak of or signify is informed by their immediate understanding of their subject's origin in the divine love of creation. Take the example of dancing, which has already appeared in the *Inferno*. The three noble Florentines, stripped like wrestlers, join hands in a circling dance that, perhaps, expresses all they have left of their finer qualities, their sense of community. The nymphs of the Earthly Paradise, transformed from stars in the sky, dance before the chariot. But none of these perform with the exhilaration of the company of Aquinas and Bonaventure or the balletic gyrations of the souls in the heaven of Jupiter, forming the words, DILIGITE IUSTITIAM QUI IUDICATIS TERRAM, with the final M of IUSTITIAM transforming into the eagle of Justice. Where did Dante derive his vision of dancing? Dance as a means of worship had long decayed in the Christian Church; it was revived amongst the Franciscans and other mendicants, but hardly with the sophistication his descriptions imply. On the restoration of the Greek empire at Byzantium in 1261, the sacred dances governing court ritual had been revived with more than antiquarian zeal and in Konya, the capital of the Seljuk Turks, only a few years before Dante's birth the great poet Jalâl al-Dîn Rûmî had instituted the order of the Mevlevi dervishes with its beautiful ceremony of the dance of the turners, designed to bring its participants into ecstatic union with the Divine. Reports from Byzantium and Konya could easily have reached Italy through the numerous trading connexions, but even these would have had to undergo their transvaluation into Dante's visionary experience. Dancing, as I suggested earlier, is the most controlled of human movements and the symbolism of human movements in the poem proceeds from the least individually controlled—the figures in the ice—through the voluntary discipline of Purgatory to the complete physical control and awareness of the blessed, and this symbolism portrays the progression of man from spiritual imprisonment to complete spiritual freedom. This freedom is insisted upon again and again in the repeated use of the related imagery of birds.

Paradise resounds too with music and poetry. The poetry is only a single spark of what he experienced and the music transcends all earthly sounds in beauty. But with their evocation, he manages to make his reader's mind expand to grasp the thought of what it is like to be eternally inspired, eternally creative, eternally an artist, as are the souls he presents before us in Paradise. Thus throughout the poem Dante is building up in his reader a wider and wider conception of what it is to be truly human in the light of grace, a sense of all man's possibilities brought to flower under the sun of love. If, as I have suggested, the aim of the imagery of self-observation is to awaken in the reader limitless possibilities in the growth of self-knowledge, then this group of images is also linked to the parts Virgil and Beatrice play in the development of Dante's own self-knowledge and, by extension, provoke his reader to ask himself, 'What in me is Virgil? What in me is Beatrice?' Dante, while guided by them, is constantly under observation by them, not just his acts and words but also by telepathy. Virgil says:

'S'i' fossi di piombato vetro,
l'imagine di fuor tua non trarrei
più tosto a me, che quella dentro
   'mpetro.
Pur mo venieno i tuo' pensier tra' miei,
con simile atto e con simile faccia,
sì che d'intrambi un sol consiglio fei.'[82]

'Were I of glass and leaden-lined,
Thine outward image were not in me
  shown
Sooner than now is the image of thy
  mind.
Already thy thoughts came among my
  own
With the like motion and the self-same
  face,
So that the two to one resolve have
  grown.'

an anticipation of the mirror imagery of the *Paradiso*, in which the degree of interpenetration of the minds of Beatrice and Dante grows throughout in intensity. As Virgil and Dante progress together, what Virgil knows as the light of natural reason enters more and more into Dante's nature, so that the relationship between them changes from one of authority to one of the closest sympathy and friendship, to the point where Virgil resigns his task and then vanishes. The progress of Beatrice as the light of grace leading him to the light of glory in the Empyrean is unfolded through the transformations of her beauty and the increase in her loveliness, always related to the imagery of light, and this progress symbolizes the stages of Dante's growing understanding. Beatrice unveils her eyes and he sees in them mirrored the two natures of Christ reflected from the griffin. She unveils her mouth and he gasps: 'O isplendor di viva luce eterna'.[83] They ascend to Heaven together, and the sight of her gazing up to eternal wheels transhumanizes him, as happened to Glaucus when he ate the herb that made him a fellow to the gods of the sea. She gazes on him with her eyes full of sparks of love. She even has to tell him at one stage that Paradise is not only in her eyes but all about him. In the heaven of Jupiter she will not smile at him because he will be burnt to ashes, as Semele was at the sight of Jove. In the twenty-third canto she asks him to turn from her face, with which he is so much in love, to see the beautiful garden flowering under the rays of Christ. After he has passed the examination of the three apostles and met his first ancestor, only then does she smile again,

ridendo tanto lieta,	smiling in such a happiness
che Dio parea nel suo volto gioire.[84]	That God's own joy seemed on her lips to dwell.

Then, in the reflection of the eyes of her 'who imparadises my mind', he first sees the *punto*, the infinitely small point of light about which creation revolves, and by turning about to see this he undergoes the reversal in his understanding of reality that takes him to the final vision. So, through the descriptions of the transfiguration of her human beauty, Dante enables us to follow him in imagination to the point where what she experiences of direct participation in the mind of God has so transformed his understanding that he too is ready for that direct experience. The depictions of Beatrice not only preserve the humanity of the poem in this most difficult dilemma, where the very brilliance of the environment precludes the precise physical descriptions of the two earlier canticles, but expands our comprehension of what our own humanity can mean to us illimitably beyond any comparable poem in Western literature. She is the means of our understanding the psychological significance of the imagery of light, leading us to the final sublimity of the last canto, in which all the themes of imagery first played in the beginning of the *Inferno* are resolved in the final chord of love, with which the poem closes.

20

The transformation of man

Through the compact appearances of his characters and through the way in which each one preserves his or her immortal individuality, Dante introduced a new freedom to the imagination of Western man. He changed and enlarged the possibilities of depicting human characters, influencing all future forms of narrative, history, fiction, and drama. In suggesting some of the ways in which he discovered in his own creative imagination this new freedom in depicting men and women, we must consider, first of all, the related paradoxes of why he had to achieve this through describing the Other World and why these depictions, at least to begin with, involve such horrifying and vengeful scenes.

Though William Blake saw the inspiration of the *Inferno* as the gift of Satan,[1] and though critics such as I. A. Richards[2] still raise their voices against the vengefulness of the poem, it is easy to show that, in terms of his own time, both where the interpretation of doctrine and the cruelty of punishments and executions were concerned, Dante was quite remarkably advanced. To large numbers of churchmen, including the great pope Innocent III, who wrote an influential *De contemptu mundi*,[3] the world was an utterly wretched place, and the frequently dreadful means by which people might leave it were part and parcel of its wretchedness. All this was in spite of the fact that it was often considered that very few souls were chosen for Purgatory and therefore eventually for the blessed world, with whose joys the sorrows of Earth were contrasted. A twelfth-century bishop reported that a holy monk had died in the same hour as St Bernard of Clairvaux. The monk appeared to him in a dream and told him that of the 30,000 souls who had departed from earth in that short period only he and St Bernard had gone to Heaven, three had gone to Purgatory, and the rest had gone to Hell for 'everlasting torture'.[4] Let us take examples of punishment, one in the other world, one in this, from two of the most civilized men of the twelfth century, the Anglo-Norman chronicler Ordericus Vitalis and Abbot Suger of St Denis, and see how far Dante is removed from them. There is nothing in Dante's attitude to punishment to compare with the gloating hatred of sex displayed in the account of a vision of the damned, reported by Ordericus and seen by a priest called Walchelin, in which women of loose life are made to ride on side saddles spiked with red-hot nails;[5] nothing to compare with the thorough approval Suger expresses in describing how a man who had murdered a count of Flanders was hanged together with a dog that bit and befouled him in their mutual agony.[6] Dante must have seen or heard eye-witness accounts of, or been threatened with, a great number of the horrors he described himself. Murderers in Florence were executed by being buried alive upside down; Frederick II cloaked his enemies in lead and melted the lead on them; Ezzelino da Romano put thousands to the sword; it was the Pisans who nailed up the door on Count Ugolino, his sons, and their boys, not Dante inventing this episode like a Gothic novelist; one Templar produced before the papal commissioners the bones that had dropped from their sockets in his feet which had been roasted by Philip the Fair's torturers; and of his fellows who like him retracted the confessions obtained by such means, many were put to death by being burnt piecemeal over slow fires. Dante himself would have been burnt at the stake, had the 'Blacks' of Florence caught him. Such sights, thoughts, and fears were the daily food of his imagination and it is no wonder that they should recur in his dreams and visions.

The question of punishment and reward involves the attitudes of men to authority and to one another, not only in their social and political dealings but in the deepest levels of the imagination. Dante was able to build upon the great achievements of the twelfth and thirteenth centuries in discovering a new worth in the Christian conception of the individual and of the goodness of creation. These achievements were made artistically possible by the Gothic sculptors, emotionally possible by the Franciscan ardour of brotherly love and the praise of God through His works, intellectually possible by the Dominicans, with their defence of the immortality of the soul and their attempts to bring all knowledge into the service of faith, and socially and politically possible by the city republics which, for varying periods and to varying degrees, evolved societies in which every man was of account in their government and their defence, and in which the arts were cultivated for the glory of the commune and the delight of all its members. The men of these cities were divided in their attitudes to one another between the paternal and hierarchical attitudes of the Ghibellines, with their feudal tradition of service to a lord, and the fraternal and corporate attitudes of the Guelphs, with their love of equality and their insistence that nobility is a matter of individual worth, not of birth or inheritance. These attitudes are woof and warp of the *Commedia*; the worst crime is the feudal one of treachery to one's lord, so that Satan munches the bodies of Cassius and Brutus, who betrayed Caesar, and of Judas, the betrayer of Christ. As another example of this hierarchical attitude, one of the chief images at the close of the *Paradiso* is the presentation of Heaven as the imperial court where the Virgin Mary is the Augusta, the apostles are barons, and the saints are counts. On the other hand, only a citizen of one of the city republics could have had the confidence to present himself on such terms of equality with the great and famous of every past age, as Dante does, or to depict the damned as excluded from the good of the spiritual commune in which the blessed share a perfect brotherly love, a love they extend through him down to his readers. Through anecdote and reminiscence, the wars of the Ghibellines and Guelphs, with their attendant savagery, are constantly evoked in the poem, but with the underlying contrast of his ideal of the monarch guiding men to happiness in this life—an earthly state through which Hell will receive a smaller tribute of souls and Heaven will be more radiant with the blessed.

If both Guelphs and Ghibellines imposed their political authority by systematic terror, then the Church also used the fear of Hell to secure the submission of believers. In the 'ten dumb centuries' that preceded Dante, many streams of horror-laden guilt had flowed into the imaginations of men to congeal their inner natures with fear, not only in the synthesis of Christian eschatology with classical doctrines of the underworld, but in the Nordic and Celtic inheritance of the grotesque, the memories of man and his world torn apart by wild beasts, the Fenris wolves that devour creation, for example, and whose variants appear repeatedly in Romanesque sculpture and manuscript illumination. By facing up to the doctrine of eternal damnation and portraying it with a totally new definition, he helped to rid the European imagination of some of its worst fears and of its mindless acceptance of cruelty. With his new command of the pictorial and image-making capabilities of language, he took his contemporaries on a tour of their minds, saying to them, 'Look at the visual consequences and realizations of what you believe.' Joseph Campbell describes Dante as one of the medieval writers who brought about a revolution in the uses and purposes of myth, from being a means of maintaining stability in societies as the repository of beliefs and symbols by which each society was guided, to turning myth into a means of changing society through altering emotional attitudes, so that one great individual's rediscovery of the inner meaning of myth became a radical instead of a conservative force.[7] A belief in another world of punishment and retribution was part of Dante's inheritance of myth, as to travel through it was an integral part of the legends of journeys to the afterlife on which he also drew. As a convinced Christian he could not ignore or evade it, agonizing though it was to him to contemplate and write about it, any more than, as a poet, he could ignore the constantly recurring visual inspirations showing him individual souls in states of irremediable sorrow and torment. He could easily have adopted the formula found by Abelard and Aquinas for regarding the great pagans such as Aristotle as saved, but such a course would have run against the insistent authority of his inspirations.[8] Instead of such a purely intellectual solution, he was forced to the emotional solution of the transformation of mood so that, by preserving the earthly reality of his characters, the Hell he depicts has become the most intense description ever penned of the psychological reality of men and women in this life who bind themselves to material things and a material outlook and who destroy their own possibilities of development.

The transformation of man

It was in this way that later writers were most influenced by Dante. Apart from his effect on Milton, his physical interpretation of Hell had a greater effect on artists and sculptors than on writers. What the writers seized on very soon was his new, compact delineation of character, an achievement, by the way, only made possible by the superior qualities of compression of information that poetry has over prose. When Chaucer describes the death of Arcité in *The Knight's Tale*, he says that Arcité's spirit changed house and went off to where Chaucer himself had never been and so he could not describe it.[9] 'I nam no divinistre' (I am no diviner), he jokes at Dante's expense, but he could equally well have said that there was no need for him to be a 'divinistre' because Dante, having shown him and Boccaccio all the new possibilities in the delineation of human character, had rendered unnecessary the account of a character's further progress after death. After the examples of Dante's souls, each depiction of character became a judgment in itself, a judgment made by the writer accumulatively with every gesture and every word of the characters he creates. So Boccaccio was able to make a human *Commedia* out of his *Decameron*, and Chaucer an earthly pilgrimage in his *Canterbury Tales*; Shakespeare, under Dante's influence, it has been suggested, in his later plays, could show the stages of horror, purgation and redemption worked out in dramas of this life;[10] Balzac found in Dante the illuminating key to the series of novels he had embarked upon, so that he christened them *La Comédie humaine*, dedicating two of them, *La Cousine Bette* and *Le Cousin Pons*, to the noted Dante scholar of his time, the Duke of Sermoneta, a collateral descendant of Boniface VIII; and in our own day, bringing the process full cycle whereby the terrors of the afterlife become a symbolic presentation of this life, Solzhenitsyn took Dante's depiction of Limbo as the ground image for life in one of Stalin's special prison camps in his *First Circle*.

The questions of the source of the new freedom of his characters and of the poem's vengefulness both take on new dimensions when the poem is considered as a drama. The *Commedia* is a play made for performance in the reader's mind and for public recitation, far more sophisticated than any of the more conventional forms of dramatic presentation current in his time, and with a range of characters that only the cinema has been able to rival. The nature of drama is to present conflict arising from the clash of characters and the paradoxes of those characters' temperaments, to define the conflict as much by the establishment of an emotional mood as by explicit description, and to show how the conflict is resolved. Just as Dante responded to any technical challenge in his art, so he was spurred on to his greatest poetic achievements by the challenges of the paradoxes implicit in his inspirations. These include the paradox of his hopeless situation in the dark wood, resolved by grace through the intervention of the three ladies, the paradox of the double nature of Beatrice, and the paradox of the damnation of the good pagans. As his intellect is purified by his constant desire to know, expressed in all the questions he asks, so the transformation in his will is conveyed through the transformations of mood conveyed in the three parts of the poem, so that the passage from retribution to redemption is a necessary part of the drama of the poem.

The cast of the *Commedia* consists of nearly 600 named characters. This, as Ernst Robert Curtius points out, is more than any comparable work apart from Ovid's *Metamorphoses*, with its 250 stories.[11] Of these 600-odd characters, about 250 come from Dante's classical studies, about eighty from the Bible, and another 250 from Dante's own and recently preceding periods. This last group constitutes one of Dante's great original gifts to literature, the portrayal of recent historical personages. Of those he meets or sees in Hell, thirty-two are from Florence and eleven are from Tuscany. In Purgatory there are only four Florentines and eleven from Tuscany. In Paradise there are only two Florentines. What determined his choice of classical personages can be accounted for by the part they played in building up his conception of history and of the role of the Roman empire, or by their use in the exemplary catalogues of vices and virtues, or else by their appearances and changes in the transformations of imagery. A similar group of functions explains his use of biblical characters, but no such categorization can account for his choice of many of his contemporaries, whose striking individuality frequently bursts the bounds both of symbolism and of the fate to which the structure of the poem confines them. Sometimes they form part of numerologically significant groups, the seven named pairs chosen out of more than a thousand lovers who precede Paolo and Francesca, the ten tyrants in the lake of blood, the seven homosexuals, and the twenty-four representatives of wisdom that include St Thomas Aquinas and St Bonaventure, the nine warriors in the cross in the heaven of Mars, and the six just men in the eagle's brow.[12] John bases much of his case for the Templar affiliation on the recurrence of groups of thirteen as in the valley of the negligent rulers, and he also points out that the number of persons in the first pageant of the Earthly Paradise comes to 39—3 × 13. Of all these groups the two most significant are the three blessed ladies and the six guides to which we return again in this chapter.

Cacciaguida explains why Dante is shown in the three realms:

pur l'anime che son di fama
    note,[13]

Only such souls as have acquired re-
    nown, . . .

Only those of renown will have the effect on Dante's readers and hearers of attracting their attention and of drawing them into acquiescence with his deeper messages. The fascination of gossip partly explains why Dante made use of recent historical characters. According to Boccaccio,[14] as Dante walked through the streets of Verona a woman remarked on the crisping of his beard and his complexion darkened from the heat and smoke of Hell, and it is clear that certain bands of his audience thought he had actually been there. From his own point of view the use of contemporary characters was a remarkably effective device in winning an audience over. In many cases he was taking recent mysteries and topical subjects and causing the actors in them to relate the truth about the events in which they had been involved. It is as though a modern writer in the same work made Tsar Nicholas II describe the deaths of his family and pronounce on the true status of the claimant Anastasia; forced Lee Harvey Oswald to say whether his killing of President Kennedy was part of a wider conspiracy; caused Claretta Petacci to relate her own and Mussolini's last days beside Lake Como; settled the question of whether or not the *Lusitania* was carrying munitions; dealt with the fates in the afterlife of Himmler and Beria; and, into the bargain, presented Pope John XXIII to comment on his original intentions for the second Vatican Council and on its subsequent effects and to foretell the fate of his successors as pope in the next world. He would not only have to describe all these characters and events, but do it so convincingly that his descriptions would win a wide degree of acceptance and affect all subsequent historical interpretation. This is what Dante succeeded in doing with characters from all levels of society of the twelfth and thirteenth centuries, provided they were of a certain fame and notoriety. The most comprehensive theory that would explain the choice of recent characters that I am aware of is, again, Robert John's identification of them according to whether they were supporters of the Templars or whether they were devoted to the destruction of the order.[15] But this theory works best when related to the allegory and imagery of the poem and one still has to explain the link between the Templars and the originality of Dante's achievement in making use of historical characters as part of the presentation of a cosmic drama. How did these souls force themselves into Dante's awareness, begging for a permanent memorial and recognition, as the dead beg Charon for transport to the further shore? At what point did Dante acknowledge the creative possibilities these souls offered him, the immeasurable extension of the capacities of literature that their interpretation and appearances signified?

I suggested in Chapter 1 (pp. 15–16) the importance, for understanding the origins of Dante's mastery of characterization, of P. D. Ouspensky's observation of the capacity of the hidden artist in our dream levels for impersonation. It raises the question here of what it was in Dante's case that elevated this capacity for impersonation that seems to be a common property of mankind and which is normally exercised only in that most private form of art, our dreams, into an instrument of genius through which he was able to create modern literature by making contemporary events and characters the subject of his universal art. I think that this enhancement of his dream-making capacities into the chief medium of his inspirations is owed first to his experience of states of higher consciousness which can often have the effect of bringing the content and symbols of our inner natures, whether in the daytime as waking visions or on the edge of sleep as dreams, more clearly into awareness. This intensified awareness of the psychic depths was something he had learned to draw on for his inspirations from his earliest days as a creative artist through his association with the *fedeli d'amore*. The second factor in this enhancement is what was being fed into his inner emotional nature from the period from 1307–8, when he broke off work on the *Convivio*, to September 1312; this period covered the attack on the Templars and their final dissolution in 1312 and Dante's active involvement on behalf of the emperor Henry VII up to his withdrawal from the siege of Florence in September 1312. Analysis of episodes such as that of the simoniac popes reveals how deeply Dante was affected by the Templar catastrophe, and it was the repeated shocks of contemporary life in this period, accumulating dramatic stories and events in his mind, that, transformed by the vision of Beatrice as the rising sun, convinced him that he was the prophet ordained to transmit to a new age all that was vital and good in the old. That vision, and the discovery subsequently of Virgil as his first guide, gave him the connexion with the vision of the Trinity that enabled him to start work on the *Commedia*.

This connexion would have made him see that the necessity of using contemporary figures extends back to the poem's original inspiration, to the apprehension that God continues to work creatively in history through the souls and imaginations of men and, therefore, that the mysteries of His workings can be studied in the souls of contemporary men and women. Though the prospect of representing these characters must have beckoned to Dante with extraordinary attraction, and though he must have been well satisfied with the gasps of amazement that would have attended the revelation of these characters during the first public readings of the cantos, it was also an act of great courage, given the danger he courted both from the Church and from some of the great families whose members he portrayed so mercilessly. His sense of mission, illustrated in Cacciaguida's injunction to him to be the wind that strikes the highest summits, convinced him that his insight into contemporary history, as revealed through these souls, was as much a matter of divine inspiration breathing through him as the insights underlying the poetic, philosophical, and theological themes he treats. The impact he had to make with his prophetic message was redoubled with more than ghostly force through the mouthpieces of the recently dead. Many of them had had, in Dante's eyes, roles to play in the right directions of humanity, in which, in various degrees, they had succeeded or failed in the exercise of their individual free will. His making use of their earthly existences to voice his ideas on politics, ethics, the Church and the empire was therefore an extension of the divinely ordained duty of writing the *Commedia*, which he saw as his own individual mission and on which his own salvation and his progress on the mystic way depended.

His understanding of humanity grew with his inner development as a mystic and his progress towards recovering the state of illumination from which the poem arose was intimately linked with the concern he could feel for his fellow human beings. As in the order of his inspirations, the vision of the Trinity preceded and necessitated the sights of Hell, so the appearance in his creative imagination of the souls of the blessed preceded and made necessary by contrast the vision of the damned. Though a concern with the nature of damnation can be traced back to much earlier in his writing career, to 'Lo doloroso amor' and the second stanza of 'Donne ch'avete', his imagination, especially in his later *canzoni*, had been more exercised in the depiction of extra-terrestrial intelligences or of those blessed souls who dwelt among them. Even when he first came to describe his feelings for humanity as a whole in verse, as in the *canzone* 'Tre donne', these feelings were expressed through quasi-divine eternal beings, through Astraea, the last of the Olympians, and her descendants. In the same period he was working out in prose his ideas on a literary vernacular style in *De vulgari eloquentia*, and showing how this high vernacular should act as the medium of culture and serve in place of the court culture that was so signally missing from Italy. In that earlier work the *tour d'horizon* of Italian regional dialects and the characteristics of the people who spoke them acted as a preparation for what seems to have been one of the most influential parts of his design in choosing contemporary characters. In the *Commedia*, through the periphrastic descriptions of mountains, rivers, and cities through which he built up a geographical picture of Italy as a whole as a prelude to its hoped-for political unity under the monarch who will make his seat and court there, he brought in characters from every part of the peninsula, from Constance and Manfred in the South to Marco Lombardo and Sordello in the North. He emphasized their regional natures by including in their speeches elements of the dialects proper to their districts or cities, as in the Mantuan dialogue between Virgil and Sordello, and at the same time won a fuller acceptance for his Tuscan as the literary language of Italy as a whole by means of these references that would touch on veins of local patriotism.

The 'lowly' style of the *Commedia* grew out of the necessity to preserve the local identities of his characters, as well as from the need for a range of language that, bursting the verbal limits formerly imposed on him by the tragic style, could accommodate the variety of emotions and ideas that his great cast of individuals demanded. His style is extraordinary for the directness and clarity that enable him to expound the most complex ideas while rarely losing the poetic nature of the work. As Landino points out, he brought to the vernacular all the devices of the classical tradition of rhetoric, and used them with a skill and on a scale that had not been wielded since the great writers of antiquity. Unlike his classical forebears, however, he was not making use of a special form of Latin that had been created solely for the writing of poetry and that bore little relation to the Latin of everyday work and conversation: the directness of his language, as with his images of natural observation, comes straight from the Italian of the streets and the countryside. He combined the high style of the *dolce stil nuovo* with the low style of such writers as Cecco Angiolieri, making use perhaps of the example of the *sirventes*, the free form that had been evolved by the troubadours for the expression of political and social themes, to develop through his rhymed *terza rima* form a new extension of the Christian tradition of the *sermo humilis*.[16]

Just as he brought a new vividness and life to the Christian concept of the sacredness of the individual, so he created new possibilities for this other

Christian tradition, the idea that a Christian style of language should reflect the ineffable humility of the Son of God in taking on Himself human form. St Augustine contrasted the *humilitas* of Christ with the *superbia* of the Platonists and their contempt for the body,[17] and Benvenuto da Imola, in commenting on the *Commedia*, says that *sermo divinus* is gentle and plain, 'not high and proud like the speech of Virgil and the poets'. Dante unites in the speeches of his souls the sublime and the humble in a manner suggesting that the Incarnation transformed the possibilities of language, the chief distinguishing mark of man, as it did the possibilities of humanity in this life and the next. The descent of Christ into the underworld is a descent into unremembered history, the holding of a lamp to the dark places of the mind and the harrowing of Hell brings to the light of consciousness new and forgotten areas of physical and psychological experience, begging for redemption through language and the transmutation of art. Dante's interest in and changing ideas about the origin of language are an essential part of his searches into his own sources of inspiration and, as they and his ideas on style changed so dramatically between the writing of *De vulgari eloquentia* and the *Convivio* and the beginning of the *Commedia*, we must seek the reasons for his change of mind about language and his sudden mastery of a new, all-embracing, all-expressive style, and his ability to present human characters in a new manner of self-portrayal, in the series of inspirations that preceded the writing of the poem.

Behind the variety of the 600 named characters of the poem there are certain recurring groups and types of character, some of which, like the three ladies and the guide, can be traced back to the *Vita Nuova*. This means that we should look for a connexion between the level of experience that enabled Dante to expand the possibilities of expression in the vernacular and the level of experience from which he drew these characters, who create themselves in recitatives, arias, and cantilenas of autobiography. In both cases there is progression from the general to the particular in Dante's development. In the case of style and language he is limited by his general ideas as expressed in *De vulgari eloquentia* on what words he may or may not use and by the form of the *canzone*. In the case of character, he progresses from the generalized depiction of a type, as in the portrayal of the miser in the *canzone* 'Doglia mi reca', or in the elaborate build-up of the emotions and attitudes appropriate to the four ages of man in Book IV of the *Convivio*, to the named characters of the *Commedia*, who are free to use any word, any phrase, any style of language that will emphasize and bring out their particular individuality. We have already seen how the character of Cato developed from being an example of a general stage in the life of man into the particular historical Cato of Utica, preserving all his individuality in the afterworld and, with the very definition of his character, bringing alive the cosmic drama in which he plays a part. To understand the importance of this progression from the general to the particular in Dante's creation of character, we must relate this both to the way in which the characters first appeared in his awareness and to his deepening capacity for interpreting their significance.

The transformation of man

The very depth and scope of Dante's imaginative feeling for his characters requires us to seek their origins in a place of absolute sympathy, absolute compassion, absolute understanding. Dante discovered within himself the unity underlying all the diversity of human temperaments, experiencing this unity to a depth that is reflected in the progress of the poem from the portrayal of examples of mankind at its worst, encased in the ice of Cocytus, like straws welded in glass, to the appearance of the most perfect example of humanity in the Christ of the vision of the Trinity. The whole poem is not only a revelation to his readers of the amazing variety of human character but, even more, an education in what it is to be a man, conscious, feeling, and capable of development through infinite gradations of intellectual and emotional apprehension. A recurring feature of the poem is that the characters frequently resolve themselves out of patterns, out of groups of bodies or even, a stage before that, out of symbols, such as the cross or the crown. These patterns convey a particular mood, which undergoes transformations similar to those of the characters of which they are made. The patterns develop according to Dante's level of inspiration. If we apply St Augustine's three levels of interpretation to these patterns, we can get an idea of how the growing ability to interpret visions changes the significance and import of these inner perceptions. If we extend Hildegard of Bingen's terminology to what is seen in the cloud, in addition to what is seen in the cloud of living light and what is seen in the living light itself, we can see how a pattern, such as the whirlwind of lovers in Hell, undergoes a visual and emotional transformation into the dancing and whirling of the blessed souls. If we were to try to define the unity underlying Dante's characters in his own terms, we could turn again to his doctrine of memory, the memory of the soul for the moment of its making when it was in direct contact with all the latent possibilities of creation in the divine mind, and to the inspiration of the poem as the recovery by grace of that memory, and to the writing of the poem as an act necessary to its permanent establishment in his nature. After Dante has seen the angelic orders in their true natures revolving about the point of divine light, performing the act of praise through the surrender of their wills, as foretold in his paraphrase of the third petition of the Lord's Prayer,[18] Beatrice speaks of creation in these words:

'Io dico, e non dimando,
quel che tu vuoli udir, perch' io l'ho visto
là 've s'appunta ogne *ubi* e ogne *quando*.
Non per aver a sé di bene acquisto,
ch'esser non può, ma perché suo splendore
potesse, risplendendo, dir *'Subsisto,'*

I ask not what thou long'st to hear,
But tell thee; I can all thy longing name
Here, where is centred every *when* and *where*.
Not increase of His own good to proclaim
(Which is not possible) but that His own
Splendour might in resplendence say
I Am;

389

in sua etternità di tempo fore,	In His eternity, where time is none,
fuor d'ogne altro comprender, come i piacque,	Nor aught of limitation else, He chose
s'aperse in nuovi amor l'etterno amore.'[19]	That in new loves the eternal Love be shown.'

Among the new loves in which the eternal love reveals itself are the souls of men. The resonance of the vision of the Trinity, with its central figure of the Son of Man, the highest realization of human nature, both endowed Dante with insight into what is permanent in humanity, the eternal being through which each one of us can echo the word *Subsisto*, and set up in his deepest memory certain recurring patterns out of which his characters developed and announced themselves.[20]

Within the new loves of the souls of men were created the special gifts of the intellect and the will, the means of knowing and of choosing freedom and the licence of individuality, so that when a soul or group of souls appeared to Dante in one of his dreams or waking visions, they declared through the patterns or landscapes in which they appeared the use to which they had put these gifts. Either in symbols, words, or music, or in combinations of these, they said to him: 'This is what we have done to our souls.' In this way the judgment was part of the inspiration; it was not the result of Dante looking about his contemporaries and choosing the ones he disliked most for the most fiendish retribution. As the inspirations had for him a divine authority, he could not ignore or escape these judgments. Part of Virgil's duties as a guide was to rid him of all sentimentality, as when he berates him for weeping at the sight of the soothsayers, those who had twisted and misused their own gifts of interpretation of prophecies and vision, the very gifts that Dante, through the fourfold method of interpretation and the three grades of prophecy, had to use to work on his inspirations and make them into parts of a coherent pattern. Frequently his surprise, both sorrowful and delighted, at the fates of his friends or those he admired, such as Brunetto Latini, the three noble Florentines, or Forese Donati, survives, from the wonder of the vision in which he first beheld them again, to become part of the drama of their reunion in the story.

As evidence of the great principle of humanity sent out into creation to individuate itself among the new loves, there are certain recurring types of character to which Dante returns time and again as though, if there is not always redemption for the individual souls, there is redemption for the type or principle they may represent. Among these types are what I may call the Wounded Man, the Man of Experience, and the Old Man. Each of these repeats a particular emotional quality that is further and further refined into spirituality as the poem progresses. There is something pathetic and terrible about the Wounded Man, as in the cases of Bertran de Born, of Mohammed and Ali, of Manfred bearing the still fresh wounds of Benevento, of Buonconte da

Montefeltro for whom no one on Earth will pray, something that recalls, for example, the incessant suffering of Amfortas. Dante speaks of humanity as a whole as being wounded by original sin in will and intellect so that these men have a universal significance gradually unfolded in the poem. As with Amfortas healing eventually comes when the right questions are asked, so, in the transformations of Paradise the figure is healed in the once-martyred Crusader, Cacciaguida, and in the appearance of the sublime type of the Wounded Man, Christ, in the final vision.

The second of these types, the Man of Experience, always has something important to tell Dante: souls corresponding to him occupy the centre of each canticle—Brunetto Latini, Marco Lombardo, and Cacciaguida. In *Purgatorio*, both Sordello and Statius can be related to him as well. The emotion developed in him is expressed in the name I have given him, the flavour of having learnt from life, of having known failure and success and how to face both with a brave spirit.

The Old Man, seen in Hell imperiously as Farinata, symbolically as the old man of Crete, nobly as Ulysses, despicably as Guido da Montefeltro, and in terrifying horror as Ugolino, regains his full nobility in Cato, in Cacciaguida, who here mirrors the role of Anchises, and finally as St Bernard. The characteristic of this type is a sense of freedom, freedom that is limited by party spirit in Farinata, that is halted for humanity as a whole in the old man of Crete, that is taken by divine ordinance from Ulysses in his desperate escape to new experiences, that is snatched by the demon at his last hour from Guido, and that is denied Ugolino by treachery and literal imprisonment; from Cato, as political and moral liberty it is elevated, as will be seen, to Christian freedom in St Bernard. It will be noted that Cacciaguida merges the characteristics of all three types, as though he were the funnel for the resynthesis of the soul with its origins that leads from him to the three apostles, then to Adam, and ultimately to the final vision. The three types are familiar from the imagery of dreams, and their recurrence suggests other ways in which the souls in the afterlife can be regarded; they are aspects of the same soul in its unregenerate and regenerating states, the same parts of Dante's deepest nature growing from the hell of attachment to the heaven of consciousness. Within Dante himself are all past and recent history, the three worlds of the afterlife, with all their experience of suffering, purgation, and joy, and all the separate individualities of the new loves that merge with his consciousness into the love that moves the sun and other stars.

Similar patterns of transformation can be seen in the various ways in which the souls are first made manifest to Dante. Often his characters appear first as part of a group: in the *Inferno*, groups sunk in catatonic lethargy or as a nexus of naked bodies. Consider, for example, the relation between the descriptions of the falsifiers in Cantos XXIX and XXX of the *Inferno* and that of the envious in Canto XIII of the *Purgatorio*. In the *Inferno*, Dante sees these souls:

Qual dolor fora, se de li spedali	Pain such as if from lazarets the sick
di Valdichiana tra 'l luglio e 'l settembre	In feverish August from Chiana's fen,
e di Maremma e di Sardigna i mali	And from Maremma and Sardinia, thick
fossero in una fossa tutti 'nsembre,	Were heaped together in a single pen
tal era quivi, e tal puzzo n'usciva	With all their sores, was here: and all so stank
qual suol venir de le marcite membre.[21]	As when they fester do the wounds of men.

Only on approaching these hopelessly incurable souls does he start to distinguish them as individuals, coming upon two leaning against one another as pans are propped up on a stove, who turn out to be Adam of Brescia and Sinon. The physical attitudes of these souls, though not their surroundings, bear a strong resemblance to the description of the envious leaning against one another, their eyes stitched up with iron wire:

Così li ciechi a cui la roba falla,	The blind, to whom is lacking nourishment,
stanno a' perdoni a chieder lor bisogna,	Sit so at Pardons begging for their needs,
e l'uno il capo sopra l'altro avvalla,	And each one's head is on his neighbour bent,
perché 'n altrui pietà tosto si pogna,	So that in others quick may spring the seeds
non pur per lo sonar de le parole,	Of pity, not alone by sound of words
ma per la vista che non meno agogna.[22]	But by the sight, which not less sorely pleads.

The attitudes of the souls and their grouping is very similar to that in the Malebolge. There they are compared to lepers, to the outcasts of society, to those the healthy dare not tolerate in their midst, in contrast to this passage where the souls resemble the unfortunates of society, those who most demand and obtain pity and compassion. The very experience of pity brings into play the hope of mercy, evoked more precisely by the repentance of Sapia. In the *Paradiso*, such groups are utterly transformed into symbols; the symbol of which each blessed soul forms part no longer expresses the lassitude of despair or the inertia of physical trammels, but the realized awareness of joy. The souls stand and dance, and when Dante inquires about the reunion of body with soul at the Resurrection, he is answered by a voice as modest as that of the angel announcing the Incarnation to Mary. The glorified body will keep eternally its lustre and the eyes will be strengthened to endure this lustre.

Tanto mi parver sùbiti e accorti	So quick and eager seemed then either choir

e l'uno e l'altro coro a dicer 'Amme!'
che ben mostrar disio d'i corpi morti:
forse non pur per lor, ma per le mamme,
per li padri e per li altri che fuor cari
anzi che fosser sempiterne fiamme.[23]

To cry Amen, that thus they seemed to announce
Plainly for their dead bodies their desire;
Not only for their own sake, but perchance
For mother and father and others who were dear
Ere they became flames in the eternal dance.

Through transformations of groups such as these, where the physical body goes through stages of depiction from something disgusting and contorted by the debasement of the soul to the ecstatic promise of the reunion and return of the body to the soul, as well as through the recurrent individual types described above, Dante expands our capacity for understanding the infinite variety of our own natures and draws us into his own remembrance of the perfection of our creation.

Another recurrent feature of the presentation of characters is through fire, flame, and light. The episode of Brunetto Latini and his naked companions running on burning sand under a rain of fire combines such a grouping of bodies with this feature but, in the three examples I want to turn to next, the souls only appear to him out of flames or lights which are all he can at first distinguish. These examples are the givers of false counsel in the *Inferno*, the lovers in the *Purgatorio*, and the ladder of the contemplatives in the *Paradiso*. The scene in *Inferno* XXVI that Dante is about to describe overcomes him with such sorrow in remembering it that he has to curb his genius in case it runs away from the guidance of virtue. Virgil and he are standing on a bridge, looking at a scene of flames moving about in the bolgia beneath them. He compares the sight, in one of his most beautiful images of natural observation, to that which a peasant, resting on a hill in the evening in summer, sees in the valley where he has ploughed and where he will harvest the vintage, of fireflies glowing in the crepuscular darkness. Then he compares each flame to that in which Elisha saw Elijah vanishing into Heaven, the prophet, chariot, and horses all indistinguishable in the departing cloud of flame. The very movement into this scene and the emphasis on his inability to see any sign of a soul within the flames suggests one of the most important means in which his creative imagination presented his characters to him. Out of a dream, a mental or hypnagogic vision, accompanied by a mysterious emotion, flames moved about in his mind. As reflection on the vision moves him closer to one of these lights, there is revealed to him a flame body with two summits and containing two men. By holding this astonishing image in his mind and by relating it to the moral scheme he has already drawn up for the structure of Hell, he narrows down their possible identity until Virgil (Love) signifies their names to him. They are Ulysses and Diomedes, bound together in the same flame for eternity because of their part in the fall of Troy. Virgil, at Dante's request, conjures one of them to relate how he met his death, and Ulysses answers, in the finest passage of the *Inferno*, with the description of how he fired his last crew with desire to explore the forbidden seas of the south and how their ship was wrecked within sight of Mount Purgatory. The story is Dante's own invention: there is nothing in classical literature to account for it, because Homer hints at a different death for Ulysses. Dante may have been influenced by the story of the Vivaldi brothers, who sailed from Genoa in 1291 to explore beyond the Pillars of Hercules in search of a passage to India, and were never heard of again.[24] The freedom of the creative method accounts for the feeling of the passage working entirely against the moral scheme of the poem. It is like a prophecy of the part Italians were to play in the discovery of the New World, of the visionary Columbus and the Florentine Vespucci whose Christian name was given to America. Just as Dante was to give the most powerful expression to the Ptolemaic world system and yet prepared the European consciousness for the heliocentric universe through his sun symbolism, so here, while rigidly adhering to a geography framed according to Christian doctrine and biblical references, he voices a new feeling in Europe, the yearning of the old world tired of its small Mediterranean basin, longing, with the longing of age for youth, for rebirth on other shores:

'O frati,' dissi, 'che per cento milia
   perigli siete giunti a l'occidente,
   a questa tanto picciola vigilia
d'i nostri sensi ch'è del rimanente
   non vogliate negar l'esperïenza,
   di retro al sol, del mondo sanza gente.
Considerate la vostra semenza:
   fatti non foste a viver come bruti,
   ma per seguir virtute e canoscenza.'[25]

'Brothers,' I said, 'who manfully, despite
   Ten thousand perils, have attained the
     West,
   In the brief vigil that remains of light
To feel in, stoop not to renounce the quest
   Of what may in the sun's path be
     essayed,
   The world that never mankind hath
     possessed.
Think on the seed ye spring from! Ye were
   made
   Not to life of brute beasts of the field
   But follow virtue and knowledge
     unafraid.'

Dante, by the evidence of the words with which he introduces the episode, curbing his genius in case it led him beyond the guidance of virtue, was obviously shocked by the emotional force of what he found in the vision of flames. Instead of a self-pitying sinner he was faced with a noble being who uttered the finest anticipation of the Renaissance panegyrics on the dignity of man. Here is the freedom that Dante won for human characterization, surpassing the bounds of the doctrine and the interpretative techniques he was employing to extricate that freedom. It is not surprising, therefore, that he turned again to the valley of lights to find another flame-body. This is the old fox, Guido da Montefeltro, the Ghibelline war-lord who, in old age, became a friar and was persuaded by Boniface VIII into advising him how to trick the

The transformation of man

Colonna family into surrendering their fortress of Palestrina in 1297. Here, too, there is a long break before we find out who it is. This flame-body howls and shrieks like the bronze bull made for the Sicilian tyrant Phalaris by Perillus. Phalaris would roast his victims alive in it and the first of them was Perillus. The howling subsides into human speech and the dominating obsession of the character bursts out in the question:

Dimmi se Romagnuoli han pace o guerra.[26]	Tell me if the Romagnuols have peace or war.

Dante, not knowing yet who he is, tells him that war as ever dwells in the hearts of the tyrants of the Romagna, signifying each war-lord by the beasts of their crests—among them, the eagle of Polenta, the mastiff of the Malatesta, and the young lion of Mainardo Pagano. Guido relates his career of deception, in which, unwittingly, he is always deceived himself. He would not tell his story if he thought anyone could bring it back to Earth—and in this too he is to be deceived. Approached by Boniface in order to deceive the Colonna, he tried to avoid giving advice because of his vows and Boniface persuaded him that he had the plenitude of power to absolve him in advance for the sin—and in this he was deceived. When he died St Francis came for his soul, but a black demon claimed him, taunting him with a logical demonstration of why he is damned:

ch'assolver non si può chi non si pente, né pentere e volere insieme puossi per la contradizion che nol consente.[27]	For the unrepentant unabsolvèd dies, Nor can a soul repent and will the sin At once; in this a contradiction lies.

This is the cruellest deception of all, when a man, who lived always by his wits and valued his own ingenuity above all human considerations, has his own stupidity revealed to him. This manipulator of other people is used himself by Dante to erase something of the impression left by Ulysses and, even more, to paint the blackest picture of an even worse manipulator, Boniface VIII.

Guido's character is laid bare in his narration of the supreme crisis of his life, the moment when all the accumulated habits of mind and formed attitudes that make up his inner life are most fully tested in a situation in the outer world. The narration is told in the bitterest tones against Boniface. It is the bitterness of an old man with a grudge, with none of the nobility of age that characterizes Ulysses. But, as all Ulysses' nobility and energy is dwarfed by the dark mountain, the *montagna bruna* before whose shores his vessel is wrecked and which points to the greater theme of purgation in the poem, so the meanness of Guido's soul is a transparency through which we see the soul of the more powerful sinner, still alive at the time when the poem is set and therefore not available for direct appearance in it, who is only able to work the fullness of his malice through the still virulent effect of a great aberration in history, the granting of the Donation.

The Donation is directly referred to here; Constantine gave the Western empire to the papacy when Pope Sylvester cured him of leprosy, and in the same way, Guido says, Boniface sought him out to cure the fever of his pride. Boniface demands his advice and Guido remains silent thinking his words are like a drunkard's. Boniface promises him the false absolution and all Guido's past life comes up in the words with which he disgraces his vows:

> 'Padre, da che tu mi lavi
> di quel peccato ov' io mo cader deggio,
> lunga promessa con l'attender corto
> ti farà triunfar ne l'alto seggio.'[28]

> 'Since, Father, I am cleansed by thee
> Of that guilt into which I now must fall,
> Wouldst thou in the high seat hold triumphant head,
> Make large thy promise, its fulfilment small.'

The next example of flame as the medium in which the souls of the dead exist and appear to Dante is on the last cornice of Mount Purgatory, the circle of the lustful, which consists of a band of flame occupying the whole cornice except for a narrow path on the perimeter of the precipice, along which Dante, Statius, and Virgil have to move. Here again, he notices the flame first of all and then the souls within it, suggesting the same process of the reception of a brilliant fiery image within which he discerns human souls, in this case those in whom the fire of sexual love is refined into the ardour of charity. As bands of the souls run in contrary directions, the heterosexual and the homosexual, they meet and nuzzle one another like ants, another image drawn from the insect world and recalling the fireflies of *Inferno* XXVI. One of these souls, noticing the ruddy glow Dante's shadow makes on the wall of flame, approaches him and reveals himself as Guido Guinizzelli, the founder of Dante's school of poetry. Elegantly and nobly, he accepts Dante's praises of him but passes him on to Arnaut Daniel as the 'miglior fabbro del parlar materno',[29] the better maker of the mother tongue. Theirs is the last punishment Dante has to witness and then, to his terror, he is himself forced to pass through the wall of flame in order to reach the Earthly Paradise and to meet Beatrice once again.

If fire, flame, and light have been one of the fiercest means of punishment and refinement up to this point, they now in the *Paradiso* become both the means of manifestation of the souls of the blessed and their environment of delight. It is the same divinely created element that tortures one soul and irradiates another: thus flame is a permanence both in the cosmology of the poem and in Dante's creative imagination; it is human character that undergoes transformation within its nature. Yet even in the heaven of Saturn, Beatrice refrains from smiling on Dante because he will be burnt to ashes, as was Semele on being granted her wish of seeing Jove's true form, and in that heaven, he sees:

> di color d'oro in che raggio
> traluce

> Coloured like gold which flashes back
> again

vid' io uno scaleo eretto in suso	The sun, I saw a ladder stand, that seemed
tanto, che nol seguiva la mia luce.	So high that the eye followed it in vain.
Vidi anche per li gradi scender giuso	Moreover on the rungs descending gleamed
tanti splendor, ch'io pensai ch'ogne lume	So many splendours that each several star
che par nel ciel, quindi fosse diffuso.[30]	From heaven, methought, collected thither, streamed.

That image of the ladder of contemplation brings me again to the pattern of the six guides which, I believe, was fundamental to Dante's organization of the poem and to his achievement in marrying the experience of his inner spiritual life to the arrangement and delineation of his cast of characters.

St Benedict says of this ladder that it climbs up from the heaven of Saturn (the heaven of abstinence and contemplation) to the highest sphere, which is not in space and has no poles. In that direction Dante mounts, experiencing the vision of Christ and Mary in the amazing Canto XXIII, and meeting in the heaven of the fixed stars the triad of apostles, Peter, James, and John, who question him on the three theological virtues. These apostles accompanied Christ at the Transfiguration and so point to the coming transfiguration of Dante's own mind. The triad becomes a tetrad with the entry of Adam, and then our attention returns to Peter, denouncing the wickedness of the modern papacy. Then, with the sight of the *punto* with the angelic essences whirling about it, Dante is turned about completely towards the true source of all light. Rising towards it, he experiences the white rose of the Empyrean, with the angels flying about it like a swarm of bees:

In forma dunque di candida rosa	In form, then, of a radiant white rose
mi si mostrava la milizia santa	That sacred soldiery before mine eyes
che nel suo sangue Cristo fece sposa;	Appeared, which in His blood Christ made His spouse.
ma l'altra, che volando vede e canta	But the other host which seëth and, as it flies,
la gloria di colui che la 'nnamora	Singeth His glory who enamours it
e la bontà che la fece cotanta,	And the goodness which its greatness magnifies,
sì come schiera d'ape che s'infiora	Like bees, which deep into the flowers retreat
una fiata e una si ritorna	One while, and at another winging come
là dove suo laboro s'insapora,	Back thither where their toil is turned to sweet,
nel gran fior discendeva che s'addorna	Descended into the great flower, a-bloom
di tante foglie, e quindi risaliva	With petal on petal, and re-ascended thence

là dove 'l süo amor sempre soggiorna.	To where its love forever hath its home.
Le facce tutte avean di fiamma viva	Their faces all were as a flame intense,
e l'ali d'oro, e l'altro tanto bianco,	Their wings of gold, the rest so pure a white
che nulla neve a quel termine arriva.[31]	That never snow could dazzle so the sense.

Dante says that, if the barbarians were stupefied on seeing Rome, how much more was he on passing from time to eternity, from Florence to a people *giusto e sano*, thus identifying the Empyrean with the goal of his pilgrimage, as the eternal Rome. He turns aside to question Beatrice and:

credea veder Beatrice e vidi un sene	I thought to have seen Beatrice, and behold!
vestito con le genti glorïose.	An elder, robed like to those glorified.
Diffuso era per li occhi e per le gene	His eyes and cheeks of benign gladness told,
di benigna letizia, in atto pio	And in his bearing was a kindliness
quale a tenero padre si convene.[32]	Such as befits a father tender-souled:

This benign old man points out the place Beatrice occupies in the eternal rose and Dante utters a prayer of burning gratitude. In the distance Beatrice smiles at him and turns to contemplate the eternal fountain. Then the old man, revealing himself as St Bernard, bids Dante to look up to Mary in the height of the rose. Bernard then points out the great division of the rose into the souls of those who believed in Christ to come and those who believed after Christ's coming. With the sternness of doctrine that preserves the poem from all sentimentality, even if it distresses many readers, Bernard insists that, though the souls of children born before Christ's coming and dying before they achieved the age of reason were saved by their innocence and their parents' faith, since the institution of the sacrament of baptism children dying unbaptized have gone to Limbo.

Gabriel sings 'Ave Maria, gratia plena' before the face of Mary. Then Bernard, after pointing out other great souls, including that of Lucia, begins his prayer to the Virgin that Dante, through her intercession, may receive the direct sight of God:

Vergine Madre, figlia del tuo figlio,	Maiden and Mother, daughter of thine own Son,
umile e alta più che creatura,	Beyond all creatures lowly and lifted — high,
termine fisso d'etterno consiglio,	Of the Eternal Design the corner-stone!
tu se' colei che l'umana natura	Thou art she who did man's substance glorify
nobilitasti sì, che 'l suo fattore	So that its own Maker did not eschew
non disdegnò di farsi sua fattura.	Even to be made of its mortality.

Nel ventre tuo si raccese l'amore,
  per lo cui caldo ne l'etterna pace
  così è germinato questo fiore.
Qui se' a noi meridïana face
  di caritate, e giuso, intra 'mortali,
  se' di speranza fontana vivace.
Donna, se' tanto grande e tanto vali,
  che qual vuol grazia e a te non
    ricorre,
  sua disïanza vuol volar sanz' ali.
La tua benignità non pur soccorre
  a chi domanda, ma molte fïate
  liberamente al dimandar precorre.
In te misericordia, in te pietate,
  in te magnificenza, in te s'aduna
  quantunque in creatura è di bontate.[33]

Within thy womb the Love was kindled
  new
  By generation of whose warmth
    supreme
  The flower to bloom in peace eternal
    grew.
Here thou to us art the full noonday beam
  Of love revealed: below, to mortal sight,
  Hope, that for ever springs in living
    stream.
Lady, thou art so great and hast such
  might
  That whoso crave grace, nor to thee
    repair,
  Their longing even without wing seeketh
    flight.
Thy charity doth not only him up-bear
  Who prays, but in thy bounty's large
    excess
  Thou oftentimes dost even forerun the
    prayer.
In thee is pity, in thee is tenderness,
  In thee magnificence, in thee the sum
  Of all that in creation most can bless.

This sublime orison is acknowledged by Mary, who looks into the eternal light. Dante anticipates Bernard's permission to follow her gaze and then experiences what is beyond all capacity of language to express. In images unequalled for their strength and ethereality he describes the binding by Love of all the scattered pages of the universe into one volume, the understanding of all relationships as *un semplice lume*, one simple light. Then in that light appear the three circles of the Trinity, with Christ the Son of Man in the reflected circle. A final question enters Dante's mind, of how the Man is related to the circle. Then suddenly, as his consciousness is taken up in unity with the divine consciousness, his intellect and will turn with the Love that moves the sun and the other stars, and the poem ends in the final, seventh stage of the repose of contemplation.

Here, the sixth guide, St Bernard, who may be seen as the sixth stage, the desire of knowing what is true in the supreme degree, implores the mercy of the first of the trinity of ladies, the Virgin Mary, who began the events of the poem and completes them when she prays to God that Dante may be granted the seventh stage, the vision and contemplation of the Truth. It was to St Augustine's description of this stage, as well as to St Bernard's *De consideratione* and Richard of St Victor's *Benjamin Major*, that Dante appealed in his letter to Can Grande as authorities confirming that such a vision of God as he had experienced was possible.[34]

The resemblances between the last canto and St Bonaventure's description of the sixth stage are even more remarkable, especially if we look for the source of Dante's new conception of humanity within his own vision of the Trinity. Bonaventure says that in this stage the eye of the intelligence must be raised to look upon the most blessed Trinity. In this stage, through the highest communicability of the Good, one sees that a Trinity of Father, Son, and Holy Spirit is necessary. He concludes his description of the stage:

> In this consideration is the perfection of the mind's illumination, when, as if on the sixth day, it sees man made in the image of God. If then the image is an express likeness when our mind contemplates in Christ the Son of God, who is the natural image of the invisible God, our humanity now wonderfully exalted, now ineffably united, by seeing at once in one Being the first and the last, the highest and the lowest, the circumference and the centre, the alpha and the omega, the caused and the cause, the creator and the creature, the book written within and without, it, the mind, arrives at a perfect being in order that it may arrive with God at the perfection of His illuminations on the sixth level, as if on the sixth day; nor does anything more remain save the day of rest, on which, by the elevation of the mind, its insight rests from all work which He had done.[35]

The correspondences between this passage and the passages in which Dante is guided by St Bernard should in no way make one think that Dante is merely copying Bonaventure. The bringing in of the three blessed ladies to bridge the gaps between the three modes of seeing God, the relation of the first four guides to the classical past and the coming of Christianity, and the discovery of the universal experience contained in the particular love of Beatrice, are each enough to show how deeply Dante made the ascension of the six stages part of his own conscious experience.

Like the other guides, Bernard has a past historical existence, as the guardian of the Templar order and the spiritual director of the papacy, which underlies his literal and allegorical significance in the poem. On the allegorical and moral levels also he is Christian liberty, freed of original sin, and on the anagogic level he is the expansion of our humanity, attaining God at the perfection of illumination.

21

The end of the journey

In the last lines of the *Commedia*, Dante records the passing of his consciousness into the conscious Love permeating the universe. These lines express the approaching consummation of the greatest theme of his life, the ardent will to love, so evident from his earliest memories of childhood and recurring as his understanding and knowledge of where his love should be directed grew throughout his experience of life. Boccaccio regretted that he had to record Dante's inclination throughout his life to the sin of *lussuria*, or lechery;[1] yet what this probably means is simply that Dante had a strong sexual drive. Indeed it was the tension between his sexuality and his aspiration towards a perfect, rational, and intellectual love that helps to explain the variety, intensity, and amplitude of his creative powers. There is a constant parallel interaction between his sexuality, his artistic creativeness, and his mystical nature. Often these sides of his character were in conflict, and every now and then they formed a unity of experience, each transvalued and changed in the light of consciousness into major works of art.

His falling in love when he was almost nine with the child Beatrice was a mystical experience of enhanced consciousness that transformed, refined and purified the later and more self-acknowledged sexual attraction and the overwhelming emotions to which he gave vent in his verse. When he fell in love, his general awareness changed, altering his perceptions of the external world, deepening his memory and so making all the impressions of life reveal their inner connexions with the aim of his art. Even though I have no more than sketched the capacity of his mind for absorbing knowledge, ideas, and visual, auditory, and tactile information, I hope to have given some outline of what an efficient and retentive mind it was. True art depends on intensity of experience for the impression and effect it makes : intensity of experience depends in turn on the degree of consciousness in the artist at the moment of experience. The grading of the levels of inspirations shown to relate to the journey of the *Commedia* is equally a grading of the transformations of consciousness from the ordinary waking state to a subjective state of fuller awareness and on to an objective state of higher consciousness. Such a change in the state of consciousness, as shown by the examples Dante gives in the *Purgatorio*, releases the imaginative and dream-making mechanisms of the mind, enabling them to form fuller syntheses and more original creations out of the memory and to draw on the deepest resources of symbols in the psyche. The hidden, forgotten sides of the mind respond with gratitude to the light cast upon them and, though some of their gifts may at first seem strange repayments, monsters wrought in darkness, nightmares of cruelty, succubi riding fearful winds, these have other meanings, made clear by the calm interpretative mind relating them to the pattern of the whole. Gradually this awakening of consciousness expands the understanding of particular events and experiences and reveals their universal significance and the part they play in a hitherto veiled pattern. Then enhanced consciousness unlocks the emotional understanding, showing the link between the love of the individual with the love of the universal and enabling the utterance of the poetry of praise.

Dante's relation of his art to the degrees of consciousness gives one reason for the abiding newness and the inexhaustible richness of the *Commedia* because, although his cosmology, many features of his faith, and the preconceptions of his society have now been totally discarded, the problems and mysteries of human consciousness abide with us still. He contained in himself the whole of a culture that has since become divided into the culture of the scientist and the culture of the artist. By taking over the interpretative techniques devised or handed down through monastics, he saved for literature the multiplicity of meanings that was under serious attack from the scholastics. Again, he took the Aristotelian terminology of the scholastics and used it in the cause of his own Neoplatonic tradition to enrich the vocabulary of poetry. He was intensely alive to the great technological innovations of the thirteenth century, to the yoking of new resources of power and machinery, as the references to dykes, windmills, shipping, and horology show, making the *Commedia* a mirror of the bustle and life and the communications of money and trade of Western Europe, creating in the poem a three-dimensional vision of the globe itself waiting to be explored, and uttering the incipient desire to burst the bonds of experience in exploration.

The scientist in him helped him both to continue and renew the Neoplatonic tradition of which he was an heir. He took the tradition, derived from Plato's *Symposium* of the six stages of ascent which, as I have shown, can be seen to correspond to the anagogic level of his six guides, but submitted it to the criticism, evaluation, and confirmation of his own experience. He also took another tradition deriving from Plato, this time from the *Phaedrus*. In the *Phaedrus* it is said that man has the memory of the good, the beautiful, and the true because he remembers from previous lives his ascent to the plain of truth.[2] In Dante, the memory of that plain becomes the memory of the moment of the soul's creation when it is in contact with the supreme goodness of the Creator, and again it was through the confirmation of this idea, through his own experience in the vision of the Trinity, that he gave new vigour to the tradition.

The end of the journey

Yet another Neoplatonic tradition is that of light-metaphysics, based on the idea that corporeal light is the emanation of a greater, spiritual light and that, correspondingly, the light of our ordinary intelligence depends on the greater light of the divine world.[3] Just as many of the great thirteenth-century students of optics, Bishop Grosseteste of Lincoln and his followers at Oxford, pursued their experimental studies of light in order to find better analogies for their metaphysical ideas about light,[4] so Dante performed similar experiments, as is shown by his famous demonstration of a candle and the three mirrors,[5] to enrich the poetry in which he expressed his own experience of visions of light, radiance, and splendour.

Earlier I suggested that there might be a relationship between the four levels of meaning in the interpretation of scripture and the levels of reality described in the Neoplatonic and cabbalist traditions. In Neoplatonic terms these would relate the One to the anagogic level, the Nous or Mind to the moral level, the World Soul to the allegorical level, and the spheres of creation to the literal level, and in Chapter 19 it was demonstrated how these levels could be seen in connexion with changes of order in the cosmology of the journey. I also quoted Thomas Kuhn in describing Dante's presentation of the geocentric universe as the fullest and most influential of all late medieval cosmological models. Kuhn also says that this model had the added force of allegory to secure its general acceptance.[6] But both the sun symbolism of the tradition of light metaphysics and Dante's allegory worked in completely the opposite direction, preparing for, as much as hindering, the acceptance of the heliocentric theory. Helen Flanders Dunbar says:

> Symbolism of the mystic, when given free play, leads to scientific truth, even though starting from an untrue conception. Medieval astronomy accorded with the Worm at the centre. Yet the mystic maintained the centrality of the Divine Sun because the other laws of his symbolism demanded it.[7]

She also points out that the symbolism of the *Commedia* shows how a man released from the bondage of sin is no longer bound by the gravitational pull of Satan at the centre of the Earth, but is freed to revolve about Christ, the Sun of Righteousness. We can extend this idea further from this example as an inner psychological anticipation of the heliocentric theory, on the plane of allegory in the poem, to remarking on the similarity between the two suns of papacy and empire and the two foci of the planetary ellipses which gave Kepler the clue to his laws of planetary motion. Moving on to the moral level, we can find an anticipation of the idea of the plurality of universes (the idea for which Giordano Bruno died, and which the Kant–Laplace theory reformulated in the idea of the island universes) in the description of the myriads of angels and the essences of the hierarchies revolving about another centre in the consummation of the moral level in *Paradiso* XXVIII and XXIX. Coming to more recent cosmological theories, we can find a parallel, on the anagogic level, between God as the ubiquitous centre of the sphere whose circumference is nowhere, and the views of modern astronomers forced beyond the limits of old thought into new geometrical conceptions. I am not, of course, asserting that Dante willingly or deliberately intended to depart from the geocentric model which he regarded as sanctioned by Catholic truth,[8] but am merely following the logic of an interesting progression from his symbolism, which, if it is not a fancy aroused by a series of chance parallels, points, as does the example of Kekulé's snake biting its tail, to the immense possibilities available both to scientists, if they could grasp the meanings and ideas contained and encoded in their heritage of symbolism, and to artists, if they could understand that the sources of inspiration lead not just to the expression of private vision but to the celebration of greater modes of reality.

In any case, it was the truth and the experience of ultimate reality in Dante's vision that makes the fundamental truth of the poem independent of any cosmological system he could have chosen to enfold it, and it was the change in his consciousness, brought about by the inner transformation of love and mystical experience, that so altered his perception of the outer world that he could look into the heart of the universe, even in Florence at Easter in the year 1300.

The nature of that vision has exercised his readers ever since his first commentators. Dante anticipated the trouble it might cause in his letter to Can Grande where, speaking of himself in the third person, he says:

> Et postquam dixit quod fuit in loco illo Paradisi per suam circumlocutionem, prosequitur dicens se vidisse aliqua quae recitare non potest qui descendit. Et reddit causam, dicens quod 'intellectus in tantum profundat se' in ipsum desiderium suum, quod est Deus, 'quod memoria sequi non potest'. Ad quae intelligenda sciendum est, quod intellectus humanus in hac vita, propter connaturalitatem et affinitatem quam habet ad substantiam intellectualem separatam, quando elevatur, in tantum elevatur ut memoria post reditum deficiat, propter transcendisse humanum modum.[9]

> And after he has said that he was in that place of Paradise which he describes by circumlocution, he goes on to say that he saw certain things which he who descends therefrom is powerless to relate. And he gives the reason, saying that 'the intellect plunges itself to such depth' in its very longing, which is for God, 'that the memory cannot follow'. For the understanding of which it must be noted that the human intellect in this life, by reason of its connaturality and affinity to the separate intellectual substance, when in exaltation, reaches such a height of exaltation that after its return to itself memory fails, since it has transcended the range of human faculty.

The end of the journey

After calling on St Paul, the apostles at the Transfiguration, and Ezekiel, he then refers to more recent authorities.'

> Et ubi ista invidis non sufficiant, legant Richardum de sancto Victore in libro *De Contemplatione*; legant Bernardum in libro *De Consideratione*; legant Augustinum in libro *De Quantitate Animae*, et non invidebunt. Si vero in dispositionem elevationis tantae propter peccatum loquentis oblatrarent, legant Danielem, ubi et Nabuchodonosor invenient contra peccatores aliqua vidisse divinitus, oblivionique mandasse. Nam 'Qui oriri solem suum facit super bonos et malos, et pluit super iustos et iniustos', aliquando misericorditer ad conversionem, aliquando severe ad punitionem, plus et minus, ut vult, gloriam suam quantumcumque male viventibus manifestat.[10]

> And should these not satisfy the cavillers, let them read Richard of St Victor in his book *Contemplation*; let them read Bernard in his book *On Consideration*; let them read Augustine in his book *On the Capacity of the Soul*; and they will cease from their cavilling. But if on account of the sinfulness of the speaker they should cry out against his claim to have reached such a height of exaltation, let them read Daniel, where they will find that even Nebuchadnezzar by divine permission beheld certain things as a warning to sinners, and straightway forgot them. For He 'who maketh his sun to shine on the good and on the evil, and sendeth rain on the just and on the unjust', sometimes in compassion for their conversion, sometimes in wrath for their chastisement, in greater or lesser measure, according as He wills, manifests his glory to evil-doers, be they never so evil.

Then he describes why the experience is beyond his powers of expression:

> Vidit ergo, ut dicit, aliqua 'quae referre nescit et nequit rediens'. Diligenter quippe notandum est quod dicit 'nescit et nequit'. Nescit quia oblitus, nequit quia, si recordatur et contentum tenet, sermo tamen deficit. Multa namque per intellectum videmus, quibus signa vocalia desunt; quod satis Plato insinuat in suis libris per assumptionem metaphorismorum, multa enim per lumen intellectuale vidit quae sermone proprio nequivit exprimere.[11]

> He saw, then, as he says, certain things 'which he who returns has neither knowledge nor power to relate'. Now it must be carefully noted that he says 'has neither knowledge nor power'—knowledge he has not, because he has forgotten; power he has not, because even if he remembers, and retains it thereafter, nevertheless speech fails him. For we perceive many things by the intellect for which language has

no terms—a fact which Plato indicates plainly enough in his books by his employment of metaphors; for he perceived many things by the light of the intellect which his everyday language was inadequate to express.

In the early commentaries on the *Commedia* two questions frequently occur. The first concerned whether the poem was a *fictio*, an invention in every single way, or a *visio*, a vision with a true meaning.[12] If it was a *visio*, then this introduced the second question: can man experience God fully in this life or is it only partial sight? Thomas Aquinas thought it could only be a partial sight, and his viewpoint has been followed by Dante's many Thomist interpreters. That school is the first of three main groups of objectors to taking Dante's own word for the fact of his being granted a vision of the Trinity. The crux of the debate on this issue was whether St Paul, when taken up to the third heaven, received a full or a partial vision of God, and St Paul is one of the two predecessors Dante mentions for his journey.[13] The question of what degree of vision he received in theological terms need not, however, prevent us from acknowledging that he did have a vision and he would have read Dionysius the Areopagite's *Celestial Hierarchies* as an authentic account of what St Paul had experienced. Dionysius also in that work gave a detailed commentary on the vision of Isaiah[14] as the highest angelic illumination, but the passage of Dionysius that best resolves the difficulties for me comes from his *Mystical Theology*. There he says, carefully separating the vision of symbols from the actual experience of union with the Divine, of one pressing forward to the

> topmost pinnacle of the Divine ascent . . . he meets not with God Himself yet he beholds—not Him indeed (for He is invisible)—but the place wherein he dwells. And this I take to signify that the divinest and the highest of the things perceived by the eyes of the body or the mind are but the symbolic language of things subordinate to Him who Himself transcendeth them all. Through these things His incomprehensible presence is shown walking upon those heights of His holy places which are perceived by the mind; and then it breaks forth, even from the things that are beheld and from those that behold them, and plunges the true initiate unto the Darkness of Unknowing. . . .[15]

In this state Dionysius says the initiate belongs wholly to God; through the stillness of his reasoning powers he is united to the wholly 'Unknowable of whom by a rejection of all knowledge he possesses a knowledge that exceeds his understanding'. This passage gives the clue to the total honesty of Dante's closing lines in the poem where he uses all his powers of imagery to disassociate the experience of union from symbol and image. The second objection relies on the vast literature on the theme of the journey and the many similarities in the recorded visions of others, including those of Hildegard of Bingen[16] and the geometrical images in the *Roman de la Rose*;[17] this would mean that he copied and synthesized the experiences of others or, worse, copied and synthesized what they had copied and synthesized in an infinite regress of pretence. One of the most remarkable of these similarities is between the circles of the Trinity drawn and described in a work often given to Joachim of Fiore, the *Liber figurarum*,[18] and the circles of Dante's own vision where both sets of circles have the same colour. If one regards, however, the journey stories as, in their origins, a preparation of the mind of the disciple for the instant of illumination so that he will be equipped to deal with transcendent knowledge and emotion, as in the case of the ancient mystery rituals or Richard of St Victor's earnest care of his novices for such an eventuality, then it would not be surprising that there should be similar effects from similar causes. The same applies to the similarities between Dante's vision and earlier descriptions of visions; a shared faith, a shared heritage of symbolism, a shared emotion would all tend to create, with natural variations for temperament and place, similarities in the descriptions of what is ineffable and therefore by definition beyond the powers of ordinary language to describe. It must be remarked also that the culmination of the journey, the assumption of Dante's consciousness into the unity of the Divine Love, is outside the poem. That vision of the Trinity is still on the sixth step; for the seventh, ultimate stage of the repose of contemplation, he uses the simplest possible geometrical image of a circle rotating about the circumference of the great circle of God, an image that again comes from Dionysius' description of the line, the spiral, and the circle, as the angelic and human approaches to God.[19] Here he is in union, undividedly himself, in the state his contemporary Jacopone da Todi described as 'Love, you are that love: with which the heart loves you'.[20] A third objection is that such visions are mere hallucinations, evidence of pathological states which somehow are a feature of the making of many works of art but cannot be said to convey any truth, or to bear any relation to reality. This has been the attitude of many schools of criticism of Dante in both this and the last century.

Since, in setting out my own approach to Dante, I have so far said little of these or other schools, in searching for the modern lines of thought that accord with or diverge from Dante's own experience of artistic creation, it may be of interest to describe some of them. One of the most influential approaches has been that of modern interpreters and students of scholastic thought. One result of their labours has been to show Dante's independence of Thomism and to free him from being treated as a mere versifier of Aquinas. Bruno Nardi calls Dante one of many Dolomite peaks in the range of scholastic originality.[21] Jacques Maritain, who attempted to fill a major gap in Aquinas' system—the lack of any thorough treatment of the origins and purpose of art—wrote brilliantly on Dante.[22] Kenelm Foster has pointed out the extent to which Dante's philosophical thought revolves around questions of creation.[23]

The first writer that I am aware of to relate Dante's mystical experience to that of mystics of other traditions and religions, in effect to the Perennial Philosophy, was the Canadian doctor Richard Maurice Bucke, a friend of Walt Whitman's (see Chapter 17, pp. 295–7), who, from his own experience, named the state of highest illumination 'cosmic consciousness', and looked for comparable experiences in the lives and works of numerous historical figures, including Dante.[24] Since his time there has been much interest in the parallels that can be drawn between Dante's descriptions of states of mind and his symbols and those of other traditions, for example, the similarity of the *candida rosa* of the last cantos of *Paradiso* to certain mandala designs used by Hindu ascetics for concentrating the attention in contemplation. Studies such as those of Guénon have been invaluable in revealing the universality of Dante's experience, and in helping to define objective standards by which it can be judged and interpreted. Romano Guardini, who has drawn attention to the connexions between the *candida rosa* and the mandala designs, says that one only reaches the profoundest comprehension of the *Commedia* by admitting that Dante had a true vision in which was disclosed the essence of the universe and the meaning both of history and of his own existence.[25]

Amongst those who reject or ignore the mystical basis of Dante's inspiration must be mentioned Michele Barbi, who approached the subject from the point of view that anything that was outside the poet's awareness should not concern us. To him the fundamental inspiration of the *Commedia* was 'politico-religious', an interpretation that led him to disregard any deeper mystical interpretations in favour of seeing Dante as humanity guided from the wood of human error to the terrestrial Paradise, with Virgil symbolizing the emperor of the *Monarchia*, and moving on to the Heavenly Paradise under the guidance of Beatrice, whose function he identifies with that of the pope, also as expressed in the *Monarchia*.[26] This would mean that Dante was inspired and moved to write only by his passionate political beliefs and his concern for the state of the Church, a view that makes Dante into a high-minded propagandist, and ignores completely his own accounts of his poetic processes and his appeals to the mystical experiences of others. Another view totally unsympathetic to the mystical interpretation was that of Benedetto Croce, who, in his iconoclastic *Dante e la poesia* of 1921, made a sharp division between the poetry and the structure of the poem, which he regarded essentially as a theological romance with passages of lyric verse inserted in it.[27]

Dante is also, of course, much discussed in literary histories, often from a viewpoint which sees a literary tradition as the meeting and piling together of influences in the course of which masterpieces may be written. In the course of such histories little or no attention is paid to the process of transformation that these influences must undergo in the individual psychology and by the deliberate exercise of choice by a particular writer. At its best, as in the case of Ernst Robert Curtius, who saw European literature as an 'intelligible unit' which disappears from view when cut into pieces,[28] it provides great insights into the general intellectual climate of a period, but the individual nature of the writer is a black box into whose workings there is no need to inquire. To the positivist and Marxist viewpoints that black box is itself the product of the external environment. As reality is to be found in the correct diagnosis of the class struggles which art, philosophy, and religion, 'the phantasmagorias of the human brain', as Marx described them, promote or disguise, what decides the value of Dante's inspirations are the religious and political elements of his themes, seen as the superstructure of the socio-economic patterns of the high Middle Ages. The psycho-analysts do try to look into the black box, but with eyes coloured entirely by their experiences of clinical and pathological examples, on occasions reducing all symbolism to types of the orifices and protuberances of the human body,[29] and discerning in artistic creativeness only another aspect of the unfulfilled incestuous desires of childhood. This is in spite of Freud's statement of bafflement after many attempts at the problem which art posed to his method: 'Before the problem of the creative artist analysis must, alas, lay down its arms.'[30]

The viewpoint of the Jungian psychologists, who also try to look into the black box, has on the other hand, enriched our understanding of our heritage of symbolism and substituted for the fundamentally hopeless desire for a return to the womb a new conception of the possibilities of the matured human psyche, through the integration of the personality. Among those who have made use of Jung's theories in their writings on Dante are Romano Guardini and Egidio Guidubaldi. Guidubaldi treats the *Vita Nuova* in terms of the personal unconscious, and the *Commedia* in terms of the collective unconscious.[31] I would diverge from their approach in that the most interesting point about artistic creation is its conscious rather than its unconscious origins. The unconscious, by its nature, contains an encyclopaedic store of symbols and images but, like an encyclopaedia, its contents are not arranged in a very attractive manner. It is in studying the effect of awareness in drawing out these symbols into the light of consciousness, in controlling them and in giving expression to them, that we will come closer to understanding the mystery of artistic creation. Here, we can draw upon the work of some of the newer theorists who base their ideas on neuro-physiology and studies of body chemistry. The concentration in these studies on the connexions between mind and body reveal striking likenesses to the psycho-physical outlook that was familiar to Dante, and that he frequently used to describe his creative experiences.

The modern line of investigation into the relation of mind to body that links best with the faculty psychology of Dante's time, and his own refinements and corrections of that school from his own experience, stems from a new understanding of the different roles played by the two cerebral hemispheres of the cortex in the human brain.[32] These two hemispheres are responsible for the two modes of awareness that exist simultaneously within us. The left-hand side of the body is mainly controlled by the hemisphere on the right, and the right-hand side of the body by the left-hand hemisphere. This left-hand hemisphere, in right-handed people, is responsible for our analytical and logical thinking: it is the domain of words, sentence construction, mathematical computation, and linear time. As our Western Society is so dominated by words, our relations with the external world and our activities are ruled to a great extent by this hemisphere, which is called the dominant hemisphere.

The right-hand hemisphere knows only a few words; it can manage nouns but not verbs. Instead, it is concerned with intuitive knowledge, with spatial relationships, with number experienced as proportion and symbol, with visual impressions and images, with visual memory acting on dreams and hypnagogic visions, with rhythm and music. If the dominant hemisphere is concerned with what Michael Polanyi calls 'explicit knowledge', then the other hemisphere enfolds what he has pointed out as our much greater reserve of information, our 'tacit knowledge'.[33] Where the dominant hemisphere proceeds sequentially and in a linear manner, as language, logic, and computation demand, the other hemisphere works in a different manner, creating wholes simultaneously. The voices, music, and mental visions of the *Purgatorio* are examples of the working of this non-dominant hemisphere, revealing how its function, rightly understood and used, seems to lead inward to the repose of contemplation.

Poetry in the most interesting way draws on both the hemispheres. It utilizes the rhythms, forms, and images of the right-hand and the words, syntax, and order of the left-hand. Though the study of the implications of these new investigations into the psycho-physiology of the brain is still in its infancy, the functions of the two modes of awareness can be related both to Dante's poetry and to the ideas and traditions of his time. They relate to his poetry especially in the union between the extended rhythmical passages of verse and his sentence structure, the marriage between complexity of associations and the clarity of his thought. The two modes, one whose function is directed to the outer world and the other whose function is to the inner world, can be related to the ancient distinction between the active life and the contemplative life, to Dante's division of will and intellect, and the earthly and the heavenly paradises. This would mean relating will to what appears to be the more intellectual side, the dominant hemisphere, and intellect to what appears to be the more emotional side and this would seem to be contradictory. But if we remember what Aquinas says of the two kinds of knowing — that the lower, reason, is the active searching for knowledge, and the higher, intellect, is the intuitive possession of it — then we get a glimpse of what that higher knowledge, symbolized by Beatrice as the light between the truth and the intellect, might be when gained through the proper balance between the two hemispheres. Again, words are the most self-willed of conflicting autarchs, enslaving us to attitudes we hardly need, entrapping us in logical boxes, unless they are brought under the command of a more unified will that integrates them with the needs of the opposite hemisphere. What Dante experiences in the purification of his will as he ascends Mount Purgatory, and in the enlightenment of his intellect as he soars into the heavens is, in terms of this theory, a constant interchange between the hemispheres, each correcting and balancing the other.

When he is denied the path to salvation through the active life by the three beasts, he already walks more heavily on his left foot, which, as we have noted, is controlled by the right-hand hemisphere and which is here connected with the contemplative life, the other way to which he is directed by Virgil. The right-hand hemisphere has been connected with the feminine symbolism of night and the left-hand with the masculine symbolism of day.[34] So Dante turns from the sun, denied to him by the three beasts, down to the dark terraces of Hell on the journey that will lead him to the contemplative way. On that descent he is accompanied by Virgil in his aspect as Reason, assured that he will finally reach another kind of light. Bonaventure says that the dark of the inner mind is black night to the outer understanding, but spiritual light to the seer, and it is by passing through the dark hemisphere that Dante experienced those flashing and coruscating patterns which he interpreted into the souls and angels of Paradise. Virgil performs a duty curiously similar to that of the guide in Tibetan writings on the experiences of the soul after death. This guide warns the soul that all the terrors and fearful sounds it experiences are part of the soul's own mind.[35] Virgil names the horrors and gives order to the confusion of nightmare, knows the time and the sequence of the journey, and laments his deprivation of the light necessary to transfigure the patterns of terrors into symbols of joy. But as that hemisphere is feminine, so it provides the pathway to Beatrice, the intuitive knowledge and certainty of the intellect, the gift of memory as the perfect and whole possession of the present. Best of all, this new view of the mind-body organism reveals how, in Dante's case, the marvellous dream, hypnagogic and waking images, appearing as complete wholes through the hemisphere of visual imagination, were controlled and interpreted through the fourfold method in the hemisphere of theory, so that in the balance of the creative mood his words were perfect mirrors to the landscapes and souls of his mind.

The special qualities of the right-hand hemisphere, its connexions with visual-spatial impressions, with music, and with mystical and contemplative experience, bring us to three of Dante's most potent and still continuing influences. For long after his death, his political life and ideas continued to provoke fear and resentment against his works. The cardinal who had the *Monarchia* burnt at Bologna was only just dissuaded from exhuming Dante's bones at Ravenna and burning them as well. In 1335 the Dominicans of the Roman Province, after a chapter held at Florence, were forbidden to read Dante's works,[36] and even in the 1370s, when Boccaccio was giving public readings from the *Commedia* and lectures on Dante in Florence, he came up against opposition from those who remembered Dante as a traitor to his city. Nevertheless the work prevailed over these resentments and soon attracted not only a host of commentaries, but also illuminators, eager to match their skill against the immense challenge the *Commedia* offered them.[37] Many of these are brilliant and ingenious presentations, but it is interesting that neither there nor among the later illustrators, including Botticelli, did anyone appear capable of

411

suggesting the vast spaces implied in the *Commedia* until Gustave Doré executed his designs in the 1860s. The full visual impact of the *Commedia* must be looked for not so much in the manuscript illuminations or even in those frescoes, such as Signorelli's at Orvieto, which draw directly on the *Commedia*, but in the influence of the public and private readings of the rapidly circulating copies of the poem on the youthful minds of artists, their patrons, and their admirers, accustoming them to presentations of the nude, to the naturalness of combining classical motifs and ideas with Christian concepts, and to the imagination of a new and amazing kind of light. Dante's greatest influence was on Michelangelo, who ardently desired to have been Dante—'Fuss'io pur lui!' he says in a sonnet on Dante.[38]

Where music is concerned, again it is not in the works directly inspired by the *Commedia*, among them Lizst's 'Après une lecture de Dante' and his 'Dante Symphony', Tchaikovsky's 'Francesca da Rimini' and, more recently, Luciano Berio's 'Laborintus 2', all significantly drawing on the *Inferno* to a preponderant degree, but in the wider influence of the poem, in its connexion with the drama and therefore with the creation of opera, in its descriptions of a divine and heavenly music, and in the insights it offers into the expression of rapturous joy, that we find it pouring out its fructifying benefits. There are, for example, certain passages in Monteverdi's *Vespers* that are like a recreation of the music of the *Paradiso*.[39]

The third function of the right-hand hemisphere mentioned above is its connexion with contemplation. It was Dante's clear adherence to the Neo-platonic tradition that led Marsilio Ficino and his friends to regard Dante as the rebirth of poetry in Florence, as philosophy was reborn in them. I have already pointed out the similarity between his six guides and their formulation of the ascent to the heavenly Venus. Casting aside the shadow that Petrarch's reputation had cast for decades on Dante's works, they—and especially Cristoforo Landino, who wrote an influential commentary on the *Commedia*—regarded his poetry as the height of modern poetic achievement, and this was not for reasons extraneous to their innermost beliefs, but because his experience related to theirs on the profoundest levels.

The mention of Ficino and his circle, fortunate in their patronage, their period and their surroundings, revives the question once more of the circle of fellow minds with whom Dante was connected and who were not so lucky. It is clear that throughout his career Dante was not alone. It is also clear that in spite of exile and through the recovery of Beatrice he kept true to the ideals implicit in what is known of the *fedeli d'amore*, the 'conscious élite' as Auerbach calls them, to the end of his days. The resemblances that Henry Corbin has drawn between them and Sufi poets demonstrate how they used their experience of human love as the start of their progress on the mystical way and how they saw in their beloved ladies Sapientia individually incarnate. The link between Sapientia and the imagery of the Temple of Solomon together with its associations with the Great Circle pilgrimage lead to the supposition of a connexion between the *fedeli d'amore* and the Knights Templar, even to the extent of regarding them as a lay confraternity of the Templar order. Dante's sympathy with the Templars and their fate has been made abundantly clear: were one to go simply by his reference to Philip the Fair directing his 'greedy sails' against them, one could attribute his sympathy as coming naturally to a Ghibelline who saw the Templars under attack by the traditional leaders of the Guelphs, the papacy and the royal house of France. The depth of meanings, especially on the allegorical level, that can be drawn from so many passages, if the Templar connexion is looked for, go far beyond superficial political allegiances: the way his imagination arranged for Clement V to suffer one of the worst of the tortures practised on the Templars and Beatrice uttering her prophecy of the DXV taken as the refounding of the Temple at the very antipodes of Jerusalem are only two of the most telling indications. There is also the fact—which I can only note with surprise and say no more of here—that the turning points of the two greatest vernacular poems of medieval literature, the *Commedia* and *Parzival*, are both scenes of confession set at Easter with strong Templar connotations.

There is on the other hand the possibility of Dante coming under the guidance of Franciscans in the tradition of St Bonaventure—the middle way of the Franciscan movement—because Dante expressly repudiates the extremes of the Conventuals represented by Matthew of Acquasparta and the Spirituals represented by Ubertino da Casale.[40] The chief evidence, apart from Dante's admiration of St Francis and St Bonaventure, is in the parallels between the *Itinerarium mentis* and the six guides of the *Commedia* set out in Chapter 18. There is a barrier, however, to stating that Dante was a Templar or a Franciscan: the mystical path he followed allowed for sexual love as a way towards mystical experience, something alien to those celibate institutions.

Though I think that the Templars had a profound influence on Dante as did in its different way the *Itinerarium mentis*, I suggest that the reason for the influence on him of both Templars and Franciscan spiritualism can be explained in another way. This is to assume for the *fedeli d'amore* a far more influential role than they are usually given and to say that they saw themselves as having a conscious civilizing mission. Their poetry almost certainly expresses an inner body of spiritual and psychological teaching founded on the Neoplatonic and Sapiential traditions with an absolute insistence on practical experience amongst its members for what they wrote about. They probably already possessed a teaching based on the six stages of the mystical ascent deriving from the same tradition as expressed in St Augustine's *De quantitate* that St Bonaventure drew on for the *Itinerarium mentis*; they certainly had a system of grades related to experience because Dante mentions such grades in the *Vita Nuova*,[41] and probably there was a hierarchy within the group which depended on evidence of spiritual development. The correspondence I have shown between Bonaventure and Dante could therefore be explained by Dante recognizing in Bonaventure's work a different and immensely fruitful exposition of the way that Dante had already been on for several years. This might be part of a deliberate work of synthesis of all that was valuable in contemporary culture carried out by members of the group as well as Dante; this work of synthesis was begun by Guido Cavalcanti with his introduction of current scholastic and psychological theories in his verse. Dante carried on the work by extending it through other branches of scholastic philosophy and also by drawing on the new appreciation of the classics already in the air among the early humanists. As the scholastics aimed at directing all the knowledge of the past to the service of faith, so Dante and his fellow followers of Love aimed at a comparable coordination of cultural and philosophical trends for the making of an art and a civilization founded on the Sapiential tradition. *De vulgari eloquentia* and the *Convivio* are unfinished manifestos of this new civilization. If the school of philosophy which Beatrice calls inadequate for the interpretation of the mysteries she shows Dante is the learning of the ancients, it may well be that in the light of the spiritual crisis of 1312 Dante realized he had departed too far from the ideals of the *fedeli d'amore* in his enthusiasm for the classics. The vision of Beatrice as the rising sun would then have brought him back to the central mission of the *fedeli d'amore* and at the same time initiated him by right of experience into the highest grade of their hierarchy.

If the *fedeli d'amore* shared this civilizing mission with Dante, then they could not escape involvement in politics or at least the development of social attitudes based on their ideal of the *cor gentile*. They were doubtless opposed to the corruption of the Church, and they would have seen, like Dante, the necessity of separating the spiritual from the temporal, if they, based as they were on fundamental spiritual principles that exalted the inner powers of individual inspiration and guidance, were not to fall into the same trap as their enemies in the Church who used all her spiritual authority for political ends. Their eventual adoption of the imperial cause and their support of the emperor Henry VII was an inevitable consequence of the need, implicit in their thought, to separate the powers and to create a lay civilization dominated by the philosophers advising their emperor in order to balance the closed hierarchy of the Church. Mutual interests both spiritual and political may have brought about an alliance between the *fedeli d'amore* and members of the Templar order. The *fedeli d'amore* could have received a new infusion of symbolism and information concerning the Temple as an image of the dwelling-place of Sapientia from this alliance; they may also, if there is any basis for the theory put forward earlier that the Templars had a mystical teaching founded on St Bernard's doctrines concerning the image and likeness of God, have discovered mutual ground where the symbolism of the face was concerned. The Templars, especially after the fall of Acre in 1291, would have needed to establish new alliances in Western Europe, especially, where their banking business was concerned, in Florence; it could have suited them very well to form close bonds with a group of young, talented, well-born men on the verge of great careers in politics. The political benefits would soon have proved illusory, first because of Dante's exile and the dispersal of the *fedeli d'amore*, and then

414

because of the attack on the order. Their hopes revived with the coming of Henry VII, to whom all Dante's known or probable associates amongst the *fedeli d'amore*, Cino da Pistoia, Moroello Malaspina, and Francesco da Barberino, rallied. For a time the emperor seemed to offer the fulfilment of all their hopes, but even before the emperor's death Dante realized that he could do more for the future civilization of Europe through his poem than through his political activity. To change the imaginations and attitudes of coming generations would have an effect of a wholly different order from merely working for a change of contemporary rulers. Art was both the means of prophecy and the ensurement of its fulfilment. What the *fedeli d'amore* learned from the Templars, and what the Order could no longer guard as an institution, could be preserved in the symbols of poetry and in lines of verse that could impose judgment on tyranny and crime more lasting than ever could be handed down from a more conventional tribunal. Dante's innate gifts were giant-like; they were only developed to their full power through the early training begun by the *fedeli d'amore* that taught him to unseal the founts of inspiration. Their influence continued throughout his writing life and among them must have been men and women of exceptional shrewdness and understanding. Their understanding must have extended to an awareness of the creative aspect of sex in helping Dante to realize how the significance of his love for Beatrice, first set out in the *Vita Nuova*, had a continuing and expanding role in the realization of his spiritual possibilities. The transformation of the individual through the service and love of his lady, which is so central to the artistic tradition that Dante inherited is, in his work, made an explicit acknowledgment that the sexual side of man's nature can be brought into harmony with his highest aspiration—the conscious love of the Creator. That tradition had culminated in the poems of Giraut Riquier, in the enthronement of the Virgin in the place of the adored lady; and Meister Eckhart in his sermons asks his hearers to understand that the Virgin who gives birth is man's soul in a state of utmost purity, and in that inner womb Christ, as pure consciousness, is born.[42] Dante's ecstatic and increasing delight at the vision of Beatrice as she draws him up through the heavens brings him to the presence of the Virgin, through whose intercession he is granted the vision of the Trinity with, within it, the sight of Christ in our image, signifying a new birth in his now immaculate soul.

With the help of the *fedeli d'amore*, in the crisis of 1312 Dante made the marvellous discovery that Beatrice was not a matter of the past, a once adored woman whom he had loved and written about *quasi sognando* and who had been expunged from his concerns by the effect of writing the *Vita Nuova*, but a living conscious presence in his life, on whom his creative powers and his spiritual development still depended. She had been a miracle to him from the age of nine to when he was nearly thirty; to his surprise, fleeting torment and lasting delight the miracle proved permanent. From what was said of Beatrice in Chapter 9, it will have been clear that I regard the acceptance of Beatrice as a real living woman as vital to an understanding of both the *Vita Nuova* and the

Commedia, and it is also vital to an understanding of Dante's invention of a new way of presenting human characters. Who Beatrice was and whether she ever existed was a matter of indifference to Erich Auerbach,[43] while, on the other side, Robert Graves represents her as an innocent creature abused and distorted by Dante for his own poetic ambitions.[44] I see her as a woman who, in her earthly existence, realized all her possibilities of goodness and who, after her death, confirmed her saintly nature by appearing to Dante in visions that showed her to be in glory. Through his love of her on Earth he formed an indissoluble union of love with her that transcended the incident of her death. She mirrored to him the Incarnation of Christ and, in purifying his individual nature as a Christian, he found that the only way to the sight of God was through her as the revelation of his soul. Of all the contemporary characters he portrayed, hers was the one in the description of which he had had the longest practice. All the others, in their concrete earthly reality, derive from the experience and labour of portraying her. If Virgil, as an extension of his soul, takes on the earlier role of Love and reflects on a wider scale all the manifestations of history in a Christian universe, so she, as his illuminated soul, represents the search for unity and contains in herself the still causes of history and of creation. Through the love of her his love expands to become the love of God. Through his acknowledgment of her, though dead, as an abiding force in his life, he recovered his powers as a poet which had fallen silent for so long. Turning away from the deceiving ability of philosophy to explain all questions, he regained through her the essential nature of poetry, its preservation of the mystery of things: a theme such as that of the damnation of the virtuous pagans, presented so dramatically in the character of Virgil, may be returned to again and again, until it receives a resolution in the appearance of Ripheus and Trajan in the heaven of Jupiter, but in a manner that leaves the bald question unanswered, a manner that is truly poetic. She is in him the gateway to ecstatic joy, the source both of his inspiration and his salvation, the maker of him as a torch of living flame, and his guide towards the peace which his difficult temperament and the sorrows of his bitter political life so long denied him. Through her guidance he achieved a total transformation in his emotional and intellectual being and in his attitude to creation, so that, no longer at the mercy of created things as he was in the dark wood, he speaks to St John of the way in which love has gripped his heart and turned that dark wood into the leaves of creation tended by Christ the Gardener:

Però ricominciai: 'Tutti quei morsi
   che posson far lo cor volgere a Dio,
   a la mia caritate son concorsi:
ché l'essere del mondo e l'esser mio,

Hence I resumed: 'Those bitings, that incline
   The heart to God by the power that they bring,
   All with the yearning of my love, combine.
For the being of the world, and my being,

la morte ch'el sostenne perch' io viva,
e quel che spera ogne fedel com' io,
con la predetta conoscenza viva,
    tratto m'hanno del mar de l'amor
      torto,
e del diritto m'han posto a la riva.
Le fronde onde s'infronda tutto l'orto
    de l'ortolano etterno, am' io contanto
    quanto da lui a lor di bene è porto.'[45]

The death which He, that I might live,
    endured,
And hope, whereto the faithful, as I,
    cling,
Joined with that living knowledge, have
    secured
That from the sea of the erring love
    retrieved
On the shore of the right love I stand
    assured.
I love the leaves wherewith is all enleaved
    The Eternal Gardener's garden, great
    and least,
    In the measure of the good from Him
    received.'

Through such lines Dante leads our imaginations into the divine imagination which is in the mind of Christ. As we read those last cantos, so his verse awakens visionary faculties in us to perceive, through a perfect beauty of introspection, an infinity of worlds of light, sparkling with the facets of jewels and crystalline forms, alive with forests and gardens whose fronds replicate their radiance where the leaves of earth would cast shadow, and peopled with men and women who know themselves to be among the new loves in which the eternal love is made known. Then, as we reflect on the permanent gift that his poetry has impressed on our memories and that has enriched the possibilities of art for all generations since his time, we too are as struck by amazement that we have followed the craft of his creative imagination as Neptune was at seeing in the waters above his head the portent of a change in the consciousness of man: THE SHADOW OF THE *ARGO*.

Appendix
Ovid, Lucan, Statius, and Virgil

Ovid was probably the first classical poet with whose writings Dante became familiar. Although he knew Ovid's earlier works, the *Ars amatoria* and the *Remedia amoris*, it is the *Metamorphoses*, the brilliantly linked recital of the transformations of the gods and men, that shows Ovid's really powerful influence on the *Commedia*, and it provided Dante with his chief source for Greek mythology. The *Metamorphoses* begins with a description of the transformation of chaos into ordered creation,[1] and takes its story almost up to Ovid's own day with the transformation of Julius Caesar into a star, a climax that would have pleased Dante very much. It gave enormous pleasure to the Middle Ages for its charm, fantasy, and its fascinating stories, and its underlying vein of seriousness had already evoked allegorizing commentaries and the long contemporary French poem, *Ovide moralisé*, in which the description of Deucalion's flood is equated with the flood of sin overwhelming humanity, and Apollo is identified with Christ. Dante found in Ovid's poem constant examples of the convertibility of images, an ever-reflecting mirror of the metamorphoses of history, fashion, and animal and plant life; he even challenges Ovid (as he does Lucan as well) when he describes the metamorphoses in the pit of thieves.[2]

When Dante read the *Metamorphoses*, he did not read a simple unadorned text, but one annotated with allegorical distichs and prose summaries by medieval commentators who, in general, gave rationalist interpretations of the myths. Though he ignored and passed over these explanations in favour of his own psychological interpretations, he drew much from these commentators in other ways and it has been suggested that he used the annotations of one of the most important commentators, John of Garland, to make an earlier draft of the poem in a bipartite division of the myths corresponding to the realms of Virgil and Beatrice.[3]

Yet another aspect of antiquity into which he gained insight from Ovid was its irrational side, its dependence on prophecy and witchcraft. His own practice as a poet and his view of himself as a prophet made him sail dangerously near the attentions of the Inquisition. It may have been this that made him so eager to condemn both contemporary wizards and necromancers, such as Michael Scot, and the ancient prophets and witches he read about in the poets – Tiresias and Manto in Ovid, the Etruscan soothsayer Aruns and the witch Erichtho in Lucan. It was Erichtho who, Dante says,[4] once sent Virgil to the lowest part of Hell to bring up an unnamed soul, and it was this earlier journey, as well as the recording of Aeneas' visit to the underworld, that made Virgil so reliable a guide. Virgil, it must be remembered, was generally considered in the Middle Ages to have been a magician and Dante in this story is acknowledging this tradition, whether he found this particular episode among the many legends circulating about Virgil or whether he invented it himself.

The incident of Erichtho is one of the most blood-curdling episodes in Lucan's hysterical masterpiece, the *Pharsalia*.[5] Dante's reading of the *Pharsalia* demonstrates more than anything else the eclectic and cavalier use he made of his material. It is a virulent attempt to denigrate the memory of one of Dante's heroes, Julius Caesar, in defence of Pompey, a bias Dante ignores as completely as he ignores any mythological story that might show the gods of Olympus in a poor light. He uses the words of Curio, who incited Caesar to attack Rome after crossing the Rubicon, to drive Henry VII to greater activity,[6] and then condemns the same Curio to share the fate of the sowers of discord.[7] He twice uses the story of Amyclas, a fisherman so poor he fears nothing for he has nothing to lose, who carries Caesar from Epirus to Italy, quite out of Lucan's context, which is to contrast the hatefulness of the general with the goodness of the poor man. Dante's greatest debt to Lucan and one where he did not distort the original to his own purposes is in the character of Cato. 'And what earthly man was worthier to signify God than Cato?' he asked in the *Convivio*,[8] and answers his own question: 'No one, for sure.' We have already in that passage seen how the application of the fourfold interpretation to Cato's life and marriage to Marcia prepared for his inclusion in the *Commedia*, but there are three very strong reasons why Cato is wholly unsuitable as the guardian of Purgatory: he was a pagan, he committed suicide, and he opposed Julius Caesar, the creator of the Roman empire. Nevertheless he appeared in Dante's imagination demanding inclusion at this point and, just as a problem of poetic technique had challenged and thrilled Dante in the past, so the problem of justifying Cato as a precursor of Christian liberty, when these three reasons militated against it both on the grounds of doctrine and Dante's own system of history, presented Dante with an irresistible challenge. He was able to continue and even convert the anomaly into justifying the most considerable fault in his view of history. This fault lies in the question why, if the Roman empire was the necessary preparation for the world to receive Christ, did it take three centuries for the emperors themselves to become Christian, and why did the Roman people repeat the crime of the Sanhedrim in rejecting Christ?[9] Cato, in his life and in death, stood for political liberty. Lucan says of him that when the Romans are finally freed from slavery, if that ever happens, Cato will be deified and then Rome will have a god by whose name it need not be ashamed to swear.[10] Just as it was necessary for Christ to die for mankind under the authority of a just government, so it was necessary for political liberty in Cato to be extinguished so that a fuller form of liberty, Christian liberty, could come into being through the long repression of freedom imposed by the empire. The political freedom for which Cato dies is only an *umbra futurorum* of the Christian freedom whose guardian he becomes.[11]

The redemption of Cato leads us to the baptism of the last of our Roman poets, Statius. There is no known source for Dante's story that this Silver Age poet, inspired by Virgil's fourth Eclogue, underwent a conversion he kept secret till his death, for which reticence and for his prodigality he was kept on the mountain for 1,200 years.[12] The certainty that Statius became a Christian probably came upon Dante as a result of his reading of Statius' long epic, the *Thebaid*, as an inspiration accompanying the revelation of Statius as a human soul. It is extremely difficult at first to lay bare the elements of the *Thebaid* that would have convinced Dante of its author's Christianity. It tells the story of the Seven against Thebes and begins with the blind Oedipus praying to Jupiter for vengeance on his sons, who have driven him away and even trampled on his eyeballs as he tore them from their sockets. Jupiter sends Tisiphone, the Fury, to stir up war, and after Eteocles and Polynices have decided to rule Thebes in alternate years Eteocles refuses to surrender the throne when his time is ended. War breaks out, which ends in the death of the seven champions besieging Thebes. For repetitious dwelling on the spilling of blood and descriptions of gratuitous cruelty, Statius exceeds Lucan, as he surpasses him in ridiculous hyperbole. What Dante found in this aspect of the poem was the terrible state of humanity deprived of grace, the aimless savagery of men to one another without the guidance of truth, and Thebes became one of the ground images of the *Inferno*, always implicitly compared to the political life of Florence and the Italian cities and directly compared with Pisa, through the starvation of Count Ugolino and his family. There is an underlying sarcasm in the comparison of the Greeks behaving as they did without the benefit of grace and Dante's contemporaries committing worse crimes even though they are baptized Christians. C. S. Lewis found in Statius the first signs of allegory as a literary form, and ascribed Dante's interest in him to this.[13] There is another aspect of the poem which may have brought about Dante's acknowledgment of Statius as a Christian, and that includes the frequently noble descriptions of Jupiter as a god far apart from fate or destiny and the passage on the altar of Clementia at Athens.[14]

The most important influence of all these poets was that of Virgil. The *Aeneid* is full of dreams and visions. Venus appears to Aeneas in the midst of the sack of Troy, only convincing him he must flee when she removes the scales from his eyes to see the terrifying sight of the gods aiding in the destruction of the city:

Neptunus muros magnoque emota tridenti	It's Neptune's work: he gores and tosses with his great trident

fundamenta quatit totamque a sedibus urbem eruit.[15]	The walls, the foundations, until the whole city is disembowelled.

She guides him on the right way to get help in Carthage after the storm has scattered his fleet, and, only as she leaves, does he realize who she is:

et vera incessu patuit dea.[16]	And in her walk she showed herself true goddess.

Throughout his labours, up to the time when she cures his wound in Book XII, thus making him fit for the duel with Turnus, she is constantly present at moments of crisis or else pleading for him at Jupiter's throne. The true dreams and admonitions do not come only from her, but from the shade of 'maestissimus Hector', waking him up to warn him that the Greeks are in the city, from the voice of Apollo's oracle foretelling the signs that must guide him on his journey, from the moaning of the household gods in the moonlit room on Crete, from Mercury ordering him to leave Carthage forthwith, and from the Sibyl, accompanying him on the descent to the underworld. These are quite different from the nightmares that torment Dido, or the madness of war that enters Turnus in his sleep, which delude and lead to disaster. We may read the visions and dreams of Aeneas as exciting and fabulous adornments to the story, but Dante would have read them as divinely inspired instructions necessary to the creation of an empire worthy enough for Christ to be born within its limits. In the visual power of such a scene as the gods overturning the foundations of Troy, he would have found visions fellow to those in which his own inner life and political fortunes were expressed, and the identity of experience would have gained all the more significance as he came to realize that he must go on the same journey that Aeneas had undertaken before him.

From the confidence in his own visions that he gained from the example of Aeneas, there followed all the other benefactions that the reading of Virgil bestowed on him. The first of these is the strong story-line of the epic form, infinitely superior for conveying dynamic action to the episodic framework of the *canzone*, the longest verse form in which he had hitherto worked. From the epic form also he adapted the monologue and made it the basis on which he revealed his characters. Books II and III of the *Aeneid* are entirely in Aeneas' direct speech and the rest of the work is studded with monologues and conversations. He claims Virgil as the author of 'lo bello stile che m'a fatto onore',[17] ascribing to Virgil the very simplicity and directness in which he, in fact, surpasses his model. Related to Virgil's directness is his supreme gift for epigrammatic compression, such as in the famous sentence,

Sunt lacrimae rerum et mentem mortalia tangunt.[18]	Tears in the nature of things, hearts touched by human transience.

This line, which contains the concentrated emotions of all the lost races that have ever known defeat, Dante seems to emulate with a sublimity of acceptance in

E'n la sua voluntade è nostra pace.[19]

Virgil also possesses the ability to sum up a landscape, a mood, and a duty in a single line:

Sol ruit interea et montes umbrantur opaci[20]	Now the sun sets and the dark mountains are cast into shadow

and here again Dante passes beyond assimilation to a new feeling for landscape, as in the line quoted in Chapter 17:

Ai raggi morti già ne' bassi lidi.[21]

That comparison brings us to the greatest of Virgil's benefactions to Dante after the confidence in his visions: this is the way in which he taught him the merits and beauties of visual expression in poetry.[22] The benefactions are in fact linked; from the trust in the visions came the impulse to figure them with every device of language as living and plastic forms. Arnaut Daniel had awakened the possibilities of visual expression in words in Dante when, under Arnaut's influence, he wrote the *rime petrose*, but a revolution on a far wider scale takes place with the influence of Virgil. A reading of the *Aeneid* leaves our minds glowing with grandiose and glowing images, of the calm bay, like a canvas by Claude in which the battered ships find refuge after the storm, the quivering of the Sibylline leaves, the cutting of the golden bough, and the vision of Lavinia at the altar with the bees swarming in her hair. As well as the example of how to evoke landscape and mood in words, Virgil also taught Dante how to bring his forty-odd years of observation of natural phenomena and country life into his poetry. A great many of Virgil's similes are drawn from personal observation and not from his reading and where Virgil drew from the rural life of his time, Dante followed with his own knowledge of Tuscany. Virgil even gives him a model for his similes of light in the *Paradiso* in the lines:

sicut aquae tremulum labris ubi lumen aenis	As when, in a bronze basin, the quivering water reflects
sole repercussum aut radiantis imagine lunae	A sunbeam or the round of the radiant moon, a light
omnia pervolitat late loca, iamque sub auras	Goes glancing hither and thither, now shooting up from the water
erigitur summique ferit laquearia tecti.[23]	And jigging upon the fretted ceiling over your head.

Appendix

This image is used to describe the perturbations in Aeneas' mind before he falls into a sleep in which Father Tiber appears to him and explains to him the signs by which he will know where to build his city. The use of light imagery as an analogy to describe mental confusion instead of mental illumination is something that would have been quite impossible for Dante who uses darkness or shadow for this purpose, and the contrast between Virgil's and his own practice is another pointer to the immense revolution that had taken place with the triumph of the sun symbolism mentioned in Chapter 16. Just as Virgil makes the savagery of the later books of the *Aeneid* bearable to his listeners by placing the events in the environs of a Rome yet to be built and in the atmosphere of a golden age of dead but deplored rusticity, so Dante makes his descriptions of Hell bearable by his constant reference to natural living things. In the case of Virgil his power of visual evocation encompasses a vast range of human emotions, from the bestial cruelty of Pyrrhus or Turnus to the tenderness and pathos of the dead souls stretching out their hands to the further shore and to the glimpse of the unborn soul of Marcellus. Dante, having learnt from Virgil, adapts his new command of visual evocation to the expression of a different range of emotions that reflect his Christian background, from the despair and misery of those deprived of God to the joy of those who live in the presence of God, and, in the exclusion of Virgil from the fullness of that joy, he bestows on Virgil's character the pathos that the Roman poet has so often evoked in his own creations.

Abbreviations

Aen.	Virgil, *Aeneid*, ed. F. A. Hirtzel, Oxford Classical Texts.
Compagni	*Cronica*, ed. Isidoro del Lungo, in *Dino Compagni e la sua Cronica*, vol. II, Florence, 1879.
Cons. phil.	Boethius, *De consolatione philosophiae*, ed. A. Fortescue, London, 1925.
Conv.	Dante, *Il Convivio*, ed. G. Busnelli and G. Vandelli, intro. Michele Barbi, Florence, 2nd edn, vol. I, 1954, vol. II, 1964.
DDJ	*Deutsches Dante-Jahrbuch.*
De civ. Dei	St Augustine, *De civitate Dei contra paganos*, ed. E. M. Sanford and W. M. Green, Loeb edn, 1955.
DVE	Dante, *De vulgari eloquentia*, ed. Aristide Marigo, 3rd edn, with appendix by Pier Giorgio Ricci, Florence, 1957.
Epist.	*Dantis Alagherii Epistolae*, ed. and tr. Paget Toynbee, 2nd edn, with bibliographical appendix by C. G. Hardie, Oxford, 1966.
Inf.	*Inferno.*
Itinerarium mentis	St Bonaventure, *Itinerarium mentis in Deum*, in *Opera omnia*, vol. 5, Quaracchi, 1891, pp. 295–313.
Landino	*Dante con l'espositioni di Christoforo Landino et d'Alessandro Vellutello. Sopra la sua Comedia dell'Inferno, del Purgatorio, e del Paradiso*, Venice, 1564.
Lyric Poetry	*Dante's Lyric Poetry*, ed. K. Foster and P. Boyde, 2 vols, Oxford, 1967.
Metam.	Ovid, *Metamorphoses*, tr. F. J. Miller, Loeb edn, 2 vols, 1916.
MGH	*Monumenta Germaniae Historica.*
MLR	*Modern Language Review.*
Mon.	Dante, *De monarchia*, ed. Pier Giorgio Ricci, Edizione Nazionale, vol. 5, 1965.

Abbreviations

Muratori	*Rerum Italicarum Scriptores.*
Par.	*Paradiso.*
Phars.	Lucan, *Pharsalia*, tr. J. D. Duff, Loeb edn, 1928.
PL	*Patrologia Latina*, ed. J.-P. Migne, Paris.
Purg.	*Purgatorio.*
ST	St Thomas Aquinas, *Summa theologiae*, Latin text and translation, London and New York, 1964.
Trattatello	Boccaccio, *Trattatello in laude di Dante*, in *Opere in versi: Corbaccio: Trattatello in laude di Dante: Epistole*, ed. Pier Giorgio Ricci, Milan and Naples, 1965.
Villani	Villani, Giovanni, *Cronica*, ed. F. G. Dragomanni, Florence, 1845.
V.N	Dante, *La Vita Nuova*, ed. Michele Barbi, Florence, 1932.

A note on the texts and sources

The text of the *Commedia* used here is taken from the text established by Giorgio Petrocchi in his edition for the Società Dantesca Italiana, *La Commedia secondo l'antico vulgata*, 4 vols, Mondadori, 1966–7.

The verse translations of the *Commedia* are by Laurence Binyon, originally published as *Dante's Inferno*, 1935, *Dante's Purgatorio*, 1938, and *Dante's Paradiso*, 1943, by Macmillan. The translations from *Inferno* used here incorporate the later revisions made by Binyon and now available in *Dante: Selected Works*, ed. Paolo Milano, Chatto & Windus, London, 1972. Other editions and commentaries I have used include the Temple Classics edition (first issued 1899–1901), Charles S. Singleton's recently published edition, in six volumes, with text, translation, and commentary, Princeton University Press (*Inferno*, 1970, *Purgatorio*, 1973, and *Paradiso*, 1975), the Penguin Classics edition, translated by Dorothy L. Sayers and Barbara Reynolds, the editions of the fourteenth-century commentators listed in the bibliography, together with the edition with the commentaries of Cristoforo Landino and Alessandro Vellutello, Venice, 1564 (see Landino, in the Abbreviations).

The text of the *canzoni* and other lyric poems is taken from the edition of K. Foster and P. Boyde (see *Lyric Poetry*, in the Abbreviations).

The prose passages from *La Vita Nuova* are taken from the edition by Michele Barbi (see *VN*, in the Abbreviations).

The edition of *De vulgari eloquentia* is that of A. Marigo (see *DVE*, in the Abbreviations), and the translation used is that by A. G. Ferrers Howell in *Translation of the Latin Works of Dante Alighieri*, London, 1904. (The translation of *De vulgari eloquentia* has recently been reissued separately, with an introduction by Ronald Duncan, Blandford, 1973.)

The passages from the *Convivio* are from the Busnelli and Vandelli edition (see *Conv.*, in the Abbreviations) and the translation used is that of W. W. Jackson, in *The Banquet*, Oxford, 1909.

The passages from *De monarchia* are from the edition by Pier Giorgio Ricci (see *Mon.*, in the Abbreviations) and the translations are by Donald Nicholl, in

Monarchy and Three Political Letters, London, 1954. I have also used the edition by Gustavo Vinay, Florence, 1950.

The edition of *De situ et forma aque et terre* is that of Giorgio Padoan, Florence, 1968, and the translation is by Philip H. Wicksteed, in *Latin Works of Dante Alighieri*, 1904.

The passages from the Eclogues are taken from Wicksteed and Gardner (1902, see Bibliography).

The text and, where indicated, the translations of the letters are taken from Paget Toynbee's edition (see *Epist.*, in the Abbreviations).

The chief sources for Dante's life are the biography by Boccaccio (see *Trattatello*, in the Abbreviations), and the other lives and biographies given in Passerini, ed. (1917, see Bibliography). There are also biographical details given in the early commentaries. There is an anthology of anecdotes concerning Dante in Papanti (1873, see Bibliography). All the surviving documents relating to Dante and his family are collected in Piattoli, *Codice diplomatico dantesco*, 1940.

The main contemporary sources for the history of Florence in Dante's time are Giovanni Villani's Chronicle (see Villani, in the Abbreviations) and the Chronicle of Dino Compagni (see Compagni, in the Abbreviations). A selection from Villani, translated by Rose E. Selfe and edited by Philip H. Wicksteed, was published in London, 1906.

Where a translated passage is not acknowledged in the notes, the translation is mine. On a few occasions I have provided prose or line-for-line versions of passages from the *Commedia* instead of using the Binyon version; where these occur it should be clear to the reader.

Though there are many skilful English versions of the *Commedia* in prose or blank verse, among the most recent being Kenneth Mackenzie's blank verse translation for the Folio Society (1979), I very much wanted to use one that preserved the rhyming *terza rima* form of the original. I therefore chose what many good judges regard as the best complete rhymed translation, which is Lawrence Binyon's version. I prefer it to the other rhymed versions known to me, for his metrical invention which enabled him to respond to the changes of mood and tone in the original, and especially for the way in which, as a poet himself, he knew how to build up a passage to ensure its impact was conveyed as powerfully as possible. If he used a poetic diction that is now out of fashion and that therefore reduces the immediacy of Dante for the modern reader, those who complain of this should reflect on the benefits of that poetic diction and its accompanying syntactical variety.

Notes

1 See *The Stones of Venice* (1898 edn), vol. III iii 67 p. 156. The influence of Dante on Ruskin is as fascinating a subject as Dante's influence on Gladstone (see n. 3 below). Ruskin studded *Modern Painters* with references to Dante and quotations from his works rather in the way that the Venetians incorporated into his beloved St Mark's the plunder and influences of the East.

2 See, for example, the fine passage on Dante by the historian Giuliano Procacci in Procacci (1973), p. 63.

3 J. L. Hammond ascribes both the development of Gladstone's Irish policy and his conquest of the esteem and affection of the English working man to the influence on his mind of Homer and Dante. Writing to an Italian correspondent in 1883 Gladstone said, 'In the school of Dante I have learned a great part of that mental provision . . . which has served me to make the journey of human life up to the term of nearly seventy-three years.' Hammond (1938), pp. 699–700.

4 See Kristeller (1943), p. 23, and Chastel (1954).

5 Lionardo Bruni in Passerini (1917), p. 219.

6 From *Four Quartets*, 'The Dry Salvages', v.

7 *Lyric Poetry*, 69. 52–3.

8 *Epist.* X. 15.

9 A short description of the practice and purpose of *samā* is given in Rice (1964), pp. 97–102.

10 *Mathnawi*, iv. 735, tr. Nicholson, vol. iv (1930), p. 312.

11 Al Ghazzali (1901), pp. 198–9.

12 *Purg.* II. 112–17.

13 *DVE* II. iv. 2.

14 A more genial statement of the problem can be found in Robert Graves's two poems, 'The yet unsayable' and 'None the wiser', in his *Poems 1965–1968*.

15 *Par.* I. 64–72.

16 This is an adaptation of a line of thought expressed in George Wingfield Digby's book on Blake (Wingfield Digby, 1957, p. 96).

17 Thus Livingstone Lowes (1955), p. 394, says, 'Creative genius . . . works through

428

processes which are common to our kind, but these processes are superlatively enhanced.'

18 There is a good survey of the literature on hypnagogic and other forms of 'imaginative imagery' in Richardson (1969), pp. 95–100. See also Sartre (1966), pp. 52–71.

19 See the many confirmations of this in the interviews with fourteen Nobel Prize winners in the sciences in Oliver, ed. (1969).

20 *Milton*, Book I, p. 413, Nonesuch edn.

21 See Foscolo (1825), pp. 10–11. The experience of instantaneous apprehension of a work of art is set out in a letter ascribed to Mozart. '. . . the whole, though it be long, stands almost complete and finished in my mind, so that I can survey it, like a fine picture or a beautiful statue, at a glance. Nor do I hear in my imagination the parts *successively* but I hear them, as it were, all at once . . . What a delight this is I cannot tell!' E. Holmes, *The Life of Mozart* (Everyman edn, London, 1932), p. 256.

22 Both Coleridge and William Blake provide evidence of how these experiences can impose themselves on the waking state. John Livingstone Lowes says of Coleridge: '. . . when Coleridge's imagination was working at high tension, actual pictures seem to have passed before it with the praeternatural vividness of those after-images which the eighteenth century loved to call "ocular spectra" – not spectra as we today understand the term, but impressions retained on the retina of the eye with an independent luminousness and precision after the passing of some flash of vision, as a window, which has leaped at night into dazzling configuration in a blaze of lightning, hangs printed for an instant in sharp definition upon the dark. In the act of metrical composition (so Coleridge wrote Sir Humphry Davy) "voluntary ideas were every minute passing, *more or less transformed into vivid spectra*". "While I wrote that last sentence," he declares in a letter to Southey, "I had a vivid recollection, *indeed an ocular spectrum*, of our room in College Street, a curious instance of association." "I bent down to pick something from the ground," he wrote Godwin in 1801, ". . . as I bent my head there came a *distinct, vivid* spectrum upon my eyes; it was one little picture – a rock, with birches and ferns on it, a cottage backed by it, and a small stream. Were I a painter I would give an outward existence to this, but it will always live in my memory." ' Lowes (1955), pp. 61–2.

There is an anecdote told of Blake by Alexander Gilchrist about a party Blake attended where there was a lady whose children had returned on holiday from school. '"The other evening", said Blake, in his usual quiet way, "taking a walk, I came to a meadow and at the farther corner of it, I saw a fold of lambs. Coming nearer the ground blushed with flowers; and the wattled cote and its woolly tenants were of an exquisite pastoral beauty. But I looked again and it proved to be no living flock but beautiful sculpture." The lady, thinking this a capital holiday-show for her children, eagerly interposed, "I beg pardon Mr. Blake, but *may* I ask you *where* you saw this?" "*Here*, madam," answered Blake, touching his forehead.' Gilchrist (1880), vol. I, pp. 362–3.

23 See Koestler (1964), p. 118.

24 See Reeves and Hirsch-Reich (1972), p. 5.

25 *Par.* XXXIII. 94–6.

26 *VN* XIX. 1–3.

27 Carl Jung discussed this vision in his review 'Brother Klaus' in *Collected Works*, vol. 11 (1958), pp. 316–23, and also in 'The Archetypes and the Collective Unconscious' in *Collected Works*, vol. 9, pp. 8–11. The painting still exists in the Church of Sachseln.

28 C. S. Lewis said that the mental picture from which all his Narnia novels were derived was one he perceived when he was sixteen, a picture of a faun carrying parcels and an umbrella in a snowy wood. It was not until he was forty that he realized what he could do with it and wrote the first novel. Lewis (1966), p. 42.

29 Letter, February 1907, to Stefan Zweig, in *Briefe aus den Jahren 1906–1907* (Insel-Verlag, 1932), p. 190.

30 *Epist.* X. 7.

31 See Chapter 16, pp. 284–6, for the number patterns of the *Commedia*.

32 Pasternak (1956), p. 182.

33 Berenson (1952), p. 122.

34 *Purg.* VIII. 1–6.

35 See Koestler (1964).

36 Armstrong (1946), p. 28.

37 Koestler (1964), p. 317.

38 Yeats, in his essay of 1900, 'The Symbolism of Poetry', reprinted in *Essays and Introductions* (London, 1961), p. 159, also says: 'The purpose of rhythm, it has always seemed to me, is to prolong the moment of contemplation, the moment when we are both asleep and awake, which is the one moment of creation, by hushing us with an alluring monotony, while it holds us waking by variety, to keep us in that state of perhaps real trance, in which the mind liberated from the pressure of the will is unfolded in symbols.'

39 Quoted by Kathleen Raine (1967), p. 126. Muir's description of his waking visions appears in his autobiography (Muir, 1972, pp. 159–66).

40 Ouspensky (1934), pp. 254–5.

41 Ibid., p. 263.

42 See Broughton (1975).

43 *Essays of Elia*, World Classics edn (1901), pp. 255–6.

44 *Purg.* XXIV. 52–4.

45 Guénon (1925), p. 61.

46 See the Penguin edn (1972), p. 364, whose editor, Peter Coveney, draws out the influence of Dante on the novel in his introduction.

Chapter 2   Encounters on the road to Montaperti

1 Villani, I. xxxi–xxxviii.

2 Villani, II. i, got them both mixed up and made them into a composite barbarian, Totila the king of the Goths and Vandals, who sacked the city in AD 440.

3 The inscription is given in Toynbee (1968), p. 279, and discussed in Rubinstein (1942), p. 213.

4 For histories of Florence see Davidsohn (1896–1927), Villari (1908), Gardner (1920), Rubinstein (1968), and the entry by C. G. Hardie, 'Fiorenza', in Toynbee (1968), pp. 267–83; and for works in which the city is treated in the wider context of Italian medieval history see Renouard (1969), Waley (1969), and Hyde (1973).

5 *Par.* X. 121–9.

6 See Lynn White (1968), p. 65, and also p. 63 where he describes St Benedict as the pivotal figure in the history of labour.

7 In *Par.* XXII, and *Par.* XXXIII. 35.

8 *Par.* VI. 1–111.
9 *Par.* XX. 112.
10 *Inf.* XXVIII. 31–6.
11 *Par.* XVIII. 43.
12 Villani, III. I.
13 In 1037 at Milan the *vavassores* or subvassals had won from the emperor Conrad II considerable freedom from the tenants-in-chief, including security in the lands or rights they held and the right to appeal direct to the emperor. J. K. Hyde says that this law 'had wider and more lasting effects on Italian society than any other piece of imperial legislation', Hyde (1973), p. 28. It brought the different ranks of the feudal hierarchy into one legal class.
14 See Chapter 18, p. 344, for a fuller discussion of the identity of Matelda.
15 Renouard (1969), p. 277.
16 Waley (1969), p. 47.
17 The celebration of a vanished Golden Age was a familiar theme among writers in the city republics of Dante's time. See Charles Davis, 'Il buon tempo antico', in Rubinstein (1968), pp. 43–69.
18 *Par.* XV. 112–16.
19 Renouard (1969), p. 287.
20 Otto of Freising (1953), pp. 147–8.
21 *Epist.* VI. 5.
22 *Inf.* XIII. 64–72.
23 *Inf.* XXVIII. 103–11.
24 Villani, VI. XLIII.
25 For these negotiations and the battle see Villani, VI. LXVII–LXX. A contemporary Sienese account is given in T. Burckhardt (1960), pp. 8–18.
26 This story of Walter von Steinberg (see T. Burckhardt, 1960, pp. 15–16) may have suggested to Dante the image of the way in which Forese Donati left him, like a horseman spurring ahead of his squadron to gain the honour of the first encounter (*Purg.* XXIV. 94–6).
27 *Inf.* XXXII. 78–111.
28 *Inf.* X. 36.

Chapter 3   Heraldry, prophecy, and the individual self

1 In this connexion George Mackay Brown, in *An Orkney Tapestry* (London, 1969), p. 27, writes of Edwin Muir's fascination with heraldry: 'Heraldry is the mysterious signs, deeper than art or language, by which a family or a tribe pass on their most precious secrets, their lore of a kingdom lost. It is a stillness into which the torrents of history are gathered, like an unflawed mill pool. In the silence an image out of the past stirs, and illuminates things in our present circumstances, as individuals or as citizens of a country or as members of the human race, that we do not understand. Heraldry is the fury of the human race made wise and formal; from its hands we take at last the wholesome images – the heart's bread – that our ancestors sowed for us in passion and blindness. That quiet pool turns the millstones of religion, and of art, and of the simple graces and courtesies of daily living.'

2 Quoted in Max Hayward's introduction to *The Blind Beauty* (London, 1969), p. 6.
3 Matthew 16:19.
4 Mundy (1973), p. 26.
5 Quoted in Mundy (1973), p. 322.
6 See *Inf.* I. 49, 94–102 and *Purg.* XX. 10–12.
7 See Van Cleve (1972), pp. 257–63 for a discussion of the *Liber augustalis*.
8 A. Brackmann, 'The National State', in Barraclough (1938), vol. II, pp. 297–8.
9 *Mon.* III. xv. 10–11, tr. D. Nicholl, p. 93.
10 *Purg.* XVI. 106–11.
11 *Inf.* XX. 118.
12 See their exchange of letters in *PL*, 197, cols 186–7.
13 Reeves (1976), pp. 22–3.
14 Villani, VI. lxxx.
15 Villani, VII. cxxxi.
16 Boase (1933), pp. 278–83.
17 Compagni, II. xix.
18 *Conv.* II. xiii. 22.
19 Olschki (1949), pp. 20–7.
20 Reeves (1976), p. 24.
21 *Par.* XII. 140–1.
22 See Reeves (1976), pp. 4–22 for an exposition of Joachim's thought.
23 *Par.* XI. 43–51.
24 *Par.* XI. 106–8.
25 *Par.* XII. 46–54.
26 Salimbene (1905–13), pp. 236–41.
27 Auerbach (1961), p. 175. Auerbach's remark loses little of its force when we remember that this is precisely what the thirteenth-century Icelandic writers were doing in their sagas: taking historical figures and setting them at the crises of their fates in an artistically moulded whole. There is no likelihood that Dante would have known of their work and his discovery is his own independent achievement. Jacob Burckhardt had earlier drawn attention to the importance of Dante's innovation. See J. Burckhardt (1955), pp. 81–2. Bernard Bosanquet also drew upon Dante's characters for other aspects of the nature of individuality in his Giffard lectures. See Bosanquet (1912), pp. 380 ff.

Chapter 4   Dante's family and the history of Florence

1 For portraits of Dante see Passerini (1921) and the essay, 'The Smiling Pages' by Millard Meiss in Brieger, Meiss, and Singleton (1970), vol. I, pp. 40–2.
2 All the surviving documents relating to Dante and his family are collected in Piattoli (1940) and there are entries covering different members of the Alighieri family in the *Enciclopedia Dantesca*, vol. I (1970), pp. 125 ff.
3 Boccaccio was told that Dante was born in May by Piero di Giardino who had known Dante (*Comento* I, p. 128). Dante was obviously aware of the details of his own horoscope; Beatrice speaks in *Purg.* XXX. 109–14 of the particularly favourable aspects of the planets on his nativity, and in *Par.* XXII. 112–14 he attributes his genius to the disposition of the stars at that time with the sun rising. I am

informed that the aspects on the morning of 25 May would have confirmed him in this belief. See Benini (1952), pp. 49–50 for more details of Dante's horoscope. Witte (1879), vol. 2, pp. 28–31, suggested 30 May for Dante's birthday because it was the festival of Lucia degli Ubaldini in the Florentine calendar and he thought that this St Lucy was the one to whom Dante showed such attachment in the *Convivio* and the *Commedia*. As will be seen, she is far more likely to have been the more celebrated St Lucy of Syracuse.

4 For the earliest record of the Alighieri arms (in 1302) see Zingarelli (1931), vol. I, pp. 67–8, and also Shankland (1977), pp. 39–40. In the fourteenth century the family adopted another device, that of a doubled eagle's wing (or) on an azure field. Both devices appear at Treviso on the tomb of Dante's son Pietro, who died in 1364. Hugh Shankland, who connects Dante's images of flight with poetic inspiration, suggests that Dante himself may have made the pun on his own name of Alighieri with Virgil's epithet *aliger*, 'winged' or 'wing-bearer'.

5 See Becker (1967), p. 16. 'In a classic instance, a wealthy influential Florentine who had been mortally wounded in a vendetta drew up a testament in favour of his avenger . . . . His immortal soul was set to rest only some twenty-four years later when a stranger did step in to perform the deed and thereby collect the legacy.'

6 *Inf.* XXVIII. 16–17.

7 *Purg.* III. 103–13.

8 *Purg.* III. 124–32.

9 *Inf.* XXIII. 80–108.

10 *Inf.* XXVIII. 17–18.

11 Lionardo Bruni in Passerini (1917), p. 207.

12 *Inf.* XV. 121–4.

13 See Chapter 20, pp. 390–1. A. Pézard has argued that Brunetto is punished, not for the explicit vice, but because he betrayed the language of his birth and wrote the *Tresor* in French. Pézard (1950), pp. 92–130 and 321–5.

14 Villani, VIII. x. 3.

15 See *Il Tesoretto*, lines 152–62, in Contini (1960), vol II, p. 181.

16 Ceva (1965), p. 203.

17 *Purg.* VII. 113, 124.

18 Villani, VII. LXII.

19 *Purg.* XXIV. 20–4.

20 See the account of the rise of the despots in Hyde (1973), pp. 141–52 and also Jones (1965).

21 See *Mon.* III. iv. 10 and *Purg.* VI. 124–5. A recent discussion of Dante's attitude to tyranny appears in Davis (1974), pp. 46–7.

22 See Hyde (1973), p. 130.

23 Compagni, I. xvi.

24 See R. de Roover, chap. II, 'The Organization of Trade', in Postan, Rich, and Miller (1971), pp. 42–118, and also the passages in Renouard (1969), vol. II, pp. 533–40, and Hyde (1973), pp. 158–64.

25 See R. de Roover in Postan, Rich, and Miller (1971), p. 77.

26 Balducci di Pegolotti, ed. Evans (1936).

27 See the article on Remigio, 'An Early Florentine Political Theorist', in Davis (1960), pp. 667–8.

28 Villani, VII. cxxxii.

Chapter 5   *The meeting with Beatrice*

1 *Trattatello*, p. 572 and pp. 647–9. For Boccaccio's possible use of the early lives of Virgil and Virgil's mother's premonitory dream, see Billanovich (1947), p. 60. Dante himself makes use of the story of the premonitory dream experienced by the mother of St Dominic shortly before the saint's birth in *Par.* XII. 58–60. A particularly striking premonitory dream is to be found in Wolfram von Eschenbach when Herzeloyde dreams, before the birth of Parzival, that she is nurse to a dragon that tears her womb and takes suck from her breasts (*Parzival* II, 104, ed. Lachmann). The resemblances of this work to the *Commedia* in certain features are discussed on pp. 311 and 318.
2 *Inf.* XIX. 17–21.
3 See Davis (1965), pp. 415–16.
4 Villani, XI. xciv.
5 Davidsohn (1927), IV. iii. 113–21.
6 These details are taken from Renucci (1954), 'Les années d'école', pp. 22–7.
7 See Boccaccio's description of his character, *Trattatello*, pp. 609–12.
8 See Chapter 19, pp. 347–8, for a discussion of these mother and child images.
9 *Par.* XVII. 46–8.
10 Freud discussed the relationship of play, day-dreaming, and fantasy to creative writing in 'Creative Writers and Day-Dreaming', standard edn, of *Complete Works*, vol. ix, ed. J. Strachey (1964), pp. 143–53, but did not consider the difference in quality of attention and control that I am trying to bring out here.
11 *Trattatello*, pp. 577–8.
12 *VN* II.
13 Renucci (1954), p. 41.
14 Quoted in Corbin (1970), p. 146.
15 Eliot (1929), p. 58.
16 *Lyric Poetry*, 32. 57–70.
17 See his poem 'Tri Svidaniya' ('Three meetings') in Solovyov (1915), p. 192.
18 See Gardner (1913), pp. 7–9 for this and other examples, notably the case of Osanna Andreasi of Mantua, whose vision at the age of six began with a voice saying in her heart, 'Life and death consist in loving God.'
19 See Huart, vol. II (1922), p. 172 for Aflaki's life of Shams, where Shams is reported as saying, 'I was a child, I used to see God, I used to see the angel: I used to contemplate the mysteries of the higher and the lower worlds. I used to think that everyone saw the same. Then I learned that they did not see them.'
20 *A Portrait of the Artist as a Young Man* (London, 1916), pp. 194–6. The resemblance is pointed out in Campbell (1974), pp. 68–9.
21 See Teilhard de Chardin (1965), pp. 249–62.
22 See Lapo Gianni's 'Amor, eo chero mia donna in domino' in Marti (1969), pp. 328–9.

Chapter 6   *The faithful followers of Love*

1 This sonnet and the prose description of the dream appear in *VN* III.
2 *Purg.* XXIV. 57.

3 *Lyric Poetry*, 14.
4 See Davis (1965), p. 417 and the references given there.
5 These are given in Contini (1960), vol. II, pp. 404–19.
6 Hyde (1973), pp. 170–1.
7 *Lyric Poetry*, 16.
8 *Lyric Poetry*, 15.
9 Compagni, I. vi.
10 Compagni, I. x.
11 Lionardo Bruni in Passerini (1917), p. 211. This is the earliest reference to Dante's presence at the battle. The arguments against his having been there are given in Toynbee (1968), p. 130, but Bruni had exceptional knowledge of the Florentine archives and would hardly have been likely either to have forged the letter or to have mistaken its author.
12 *Inf.* XXI. 94–6.
13 See Davis (1965), p. 426, from which these details are taken. See also Davis (1957), pp. 195–235, 239–43.
14 See Davis (1965), pp. 434–5.
15 *Inf.* XXV. 151.
16 *Decameron*, sixth day, ninth story. See Boccaccio (1960), vol. 2, pp. 168–70.
17 See Valli (1928).
18 Rossetti set his ideas out in a series of works in the course of which he changed, where the identity of Beatrice is concerned, from a religio-political interpretation to a Neoplatonic explanation. See Rossetti (1834, 1840). For his last statement on the question of Beatrice see Rossetti (1842).
19 Corbin (1961), p. 269.
20 This is maintained by Philippe Guiberteau (1973), who believes that Dante returned to full Catholic orthodoxy in writing the *Commedia*.
21 See Guénon (1925) and John (1946).
22 See de Curzon (1886), p. 68.
23 Henri de Sponde, bishop of Pamiers, expressly condemns Dante as a hater of the papacy and of France for the Babylonian captivity and for the extinction of the Templars and for what he regards as slanders on Clement V. See de Sponde (1641), vol. 1, p. 534.
24 See Aroux (1854).
25 Auerbach (1965), p. 296.
26 Marti (1969), pp. 131–2.

Chapter 7 The genealogy of Beatrice

1 *Purg.* XXX. 73–5.
2 Topsfield (1975), p. 4.
3 Lavaud and Nelli (1966), p. 64. The translation is from Bonner (1973), p. 96.
4 *Par.* XXIII. 88.
5 Such as those collected in the Golden Legend (see Jacobus de Voragine, ed. Graesse, 1846).
6 Jacopone da Todi (1953), XCIII, pp. 398–401.
7 See Warner (1976), pp. 197–8.

8 See Silverstein (1948–9), p. 92.
9 The question of Alan's influence on Dante was raised by Ernst Robert Curtius (1953), pp. 353 and 360. It is dealt with also by Andrea Ciotti (1960) and Dronke (1968).
10 *DVE* I. x. 2.
11 *Par.* XVI. 14–15.
12 *Inf.* V. 127–38.
13 A point brought out by Renato Poggioli in his article 'Paolo and Francesca' reprinted in Freccero (1965), p. 63.
14 Marcabru (1909), XIX, pp. 10–13.
15 See Ezra Pound's essay on Cavalcanti in *Literary Essays* (London, 1954), p. 168.
16 *DVE* II. xiii. 4.
17 *DVE* II. ii. 8.
18 Lavaud and Nelli (1966), p. 542. Translation in Bonner (1973), p. 142.
19 Lavaud and Nelli (1966), p. 542. Translation in Bonner (1973), p. 147.
20 *Inf.* XXVIII. 130–42.
21 Lavaud and Nelli (1966), p. 795.
22 *Par.* IX. 32–6.
23 See Andrew the Chaplain (1947) for the text of the original and two of these translations.
24 See Guillaume de Lorris and Jean de Meung, ed. Langlois (Paris, 1914), vol. IV, pp. 254–7. *Le Roman de la Rose*, 19171–6 and 19124–40.
25 See Topsfield (1975), pp. 44–5.
26 Lavaud and Nelli (1966), p. 36. Translation in Bonner (1973), pp. 38–9.
27 Pattison (1952), I.
28 Arnaut Daniel (1960), Toja ed., XVIII. v and vi. Translation in Bonner (1973), p. 162.
29 *DVE* II. vii. 2.
30 Bowra (1955), p. 89.
31 Contini (1960), vol. I, pp. 55–6.
32 Nardi (1949), pp. 1–4.
33 *DVE* I. xii. 6.

Chapter 8 Convergent worlds

1 Such an account, written in the vernacular and dealing with many aspects of cosmology, astrology, and the physical world was composed by Ristoro d'Arezzo in his *Della composizione del mondo*, finished in 1282. See Ristoro d'Arezzo (1864). Dante, as a young man, was familiar with the epitome of Ptolemy by the Arab astronomer known in the West as Alfraganus. He used this work in writing the *Vita Nuova*. See Alfraganus (1669).
2 *Inf.* II. 13–33.
3 2 Corinthians 12: 2–4.
4 *Conv.* II. v. 18.
5 See Wicksteed (1913), p. 142, for this view of creation, and also Lewis (1964), especially chaps V and VII.
6 See Corbin (1961), and (1970), pp. 54–62.

7 Marti (1969), p. 62.
8 For descriptions of the various formulations of the cells and their faculties, see the text and illustrations in Clarke and Dewhurst (1972), pp. 10–44.
9 *ST* la. 3. 3.
10 See Valency (1958), p. 224, who also gives an account of the influence of faculty psychology on the poetry of the *dolce stil nuovo*.
11 *VN* XIV.
12 *ST.* la. 79. 8.
13 Corbin (1961), p. 267. Dronke (1968), p. 93, quotes from the same passage and remarks: 'Corbin came to this conclusion by way of Islamic texts, and I have come to accept it by way of Western ones.'
14 Dronke (1968), p. 94.
15 *Lyric Poetry*, 25. 29–42.
16 Proverbs 8:22–30.
17 Song of Solomon 6:10.
18 See Nardi (1959).
19 *Lyric Poetry*, la–5.
20 Marti, (1969), pp. 68–9.
21 *Purg.* V. 9.
22 See Egidi (1902) for examples of these illustrations.
23 See Corbin (1970), pp. 3–4, and the same author's essay 'The Visionary Dream in Islamic Spirituality', in Grunebaum and Caillois (1966), pp. 381–408.
24 Valli (1928), chap. 7: 'Il "dolce stil nuovo". Le parole del gergo'.
25 *Itinerarium mentis*, I. 2. See Hopper (1938) for a general study of numerology in the Middle Ages. One of the best sources for understanding how artists and architects working for the Church made use of number symbolism is the *Rationale Divinorum Officiorum* by the bishop of Mende, Guillaume Durand, writing in the thirteenth century. See Durandus (1592), especially Book I. See also the essays 'Numerological thought' by Christopher Butler and 'Structure as prophecy' by Maren-Sofie Røstvig in Fowler (1970), pp. 1–72.
26 *De nuptiis Philologiae et Mercurii*, Book VII, ed. Dick; Capella (1969), pp. 367–76.
27 Reeves (1969), p. 505.
28 Marti (1969), pp. 181–2.
29 See the discussion of this poem in Dronke (1968), vol. 1, pp. 153–4.
30 From 'Razgovor o Dante', in Mandelstam (1971), vol. 2, p. 421. The translation by Clarence Brown and Robert Hughes is from *Delos*, 6 (1971), p. 81.
31 *DVE* II. xiii. See H. S. Vere-Hodge's introduction to his translation of Dante's *canzoni* (Vere-Hodge, 1963, pp. 1–32) for an excellent account of the variations possible in this form.
32 So St Bonaventure says, *Itinerarium mentis*, IV. 4, adapting a passage of St Bernard in *De consideratione*, V. IV.

Chapter 9 La Vita Nuova *and the poetry of praise*

1 J. Burckhardt (1955), p. 188.
2 From Eckhart (1941), p. 126.
3 Such as those given in Faral (1956).

4 The difficulty was indeed almost superhuman: the task was to write 2,991 lines in dactylic hexameters with internal rhymes within each line, which itself rhymed in couplet with the next. The metre had also been used by St Peter Damian (1007–72). I quote some of the letter to bring out the correspondence with the passage in the *Vita Nuova* referred to: 'when the fire of zeal had burnt brightly in my meditations many days and nights, I finally girded myself up, and spoke with my tongue what I had long kept hidden in my mind. For I had often heard the Bridegroom say, "Let thy voice sound in my ears," but had not obeyed, and again the Beloved cried to me, "Open unto me, my sister." So then I arose to open unto my Beloved, and said: "Lord, that my heart may meditate, my pen write, my tongue proclaim thy praise, pour thy grace into my heart and my pen and my tongue." And he said unto me: "Open thy mouth, and I will fill it." So I opened my mouth, and the Lord filled it with the spirit of wisdom and understanding, that through the one I might speak truly, and through the other clearly. This I say not in pride, but altogether in humility, and only for this reason boldly that, unless the spirit of wisdom and understanding had flowed in upon me, I could not have put together so long a work in so difficult a metre.' Bernard of Cluny (1929), text ed. Hoskier, xxxvii–xxxviii. Translation from S. M. Jackson, *The Source of 'Jerusalem the Golden'* (Chicago, 1919), p. 103.
5 From Shelley's *A Defence of Poetry*, Nonesuch edn, pp. 1042–3.
6 See Singleton (1949), chap. II, 'The Book of Memory', pp. 25–54, for a full discussion of this image and its origins.
7 *Lyric Poetry* 59.
8 See K. Foster's discussion of the biographical problems in 'Voi che 'ntendendo', in *Lyric Poetry*, vol. 2, pp. 341–62.
9 *Conv.* I. i. 16.
10 *Conv.* IV. xxiv. 2.
11 See De Robertis (1961), pp. 152–5, and *Lyric Poetry*, vol. 2, p. 114.
12 Singleton (1949), p. 79.
13 See, for example, Renucci (1954), p. 40.
14 By De Robertis (1961), pp. 18–24.
15 *De amicitia*, IX. 31, Loeb edn, tr. W. A. Falconer.
16 Ibid., XXVII. 102.
17 Ibid., XIV. 49.
18 De Robertis (1961), p. 36.
19 *Enarrationes in Psalmos*, XCVII. *PL* 37, col. 1253. This connexion is pointed out by De Robertis (1961), p. 117.
20 Corbin (1970), p. 114.
21 *Trésor*, I. 46. 3, Brunetto Latini (1948), pp. 51–2. 'Cist Elyas fu de la lignie Aaron. Et quant il vint a sa naissance, Sobi, son pere songa ke hons vestus de blanche robe prenoient Helyas et l'envolepoient en blans dras, et puis li donoient fu a mangier. Et quant il s'esvilla, il enquist des prophetes ke ce pooit estre; et il disent, ne doutes pas, car tes fius sera lumiere et parliers de sciences, et il jugera Israel a fu et a coutel.'
22 Asín Palacios (1926), p. 266.
23 Singleton (1949), p. 18.
24 De Robertis, who has done so much, in his *Libro della 'Vita Nuova'* (1961), to reveal the nature of the work as a description of Dante's artistic progress, strongly denies it a mystical basis, disagreeing on this point (on p. 121) with Singleton (1949). This is a

curious limitation of his own insights because, if ever a work invited interpretation on many levels, it is the *Vita Nuova*.

25 In his *Benjamin Minor*, *PL*, 196, cols 1–64.
26 From Sermon LII on Contemplation, tr. Eales (1895), p. 315.
27 2 Corinthians 12:1. This comparison is pointed out by Auerbach (1959), p. 56.
28 See, for example, De Robertis (note 24 above), P. Boyde, in Limentani (1965), p. 112, and Valency (1961), p. 258.
29 Valli (1928), chaps IV and XI.
30 Mandonnet (1935), p. 39.
31 Auerbach (1961), p. 60.
32 *Secretum*, III, in *Prose*, ed. Carrara (1955), pp. 152–4.
33 *Trattatello*, p. 579.
34 Corbin (1970), pp. 140–5 and p. 165.
35 Quoted in Foster (1959), p. 52, from the life of Aquinas by Bernard Gui.
36 *Arbor Vite*, prologue to Book I, col. 5 (1485 edn).
37 *VN* XXVI. 1–3.

Chapter 10   The taste of power and the salt of exile

1 *Par.* VIII. 115–16.
2 *Par.* VIII. 117.
3 Villani, VIII. xiii.
4 See Benvenuto da Imola, *Comentum* (1887), vol. 4, pp. 484–5, for further details of their meeting.
5 Celestine is the chief candidate for the unnamed soul in Limbo whom Dante calls simply 'colui che fece per viltade il gran rifiuto'. *Inf.* III. 59–60.
6 For example, Monsignor Mann, who says of Boniface that he 'had the misfortune to have as enemies some of the greatest poets of the day', calls Dante's treatment of Boniface and Nicholas III 'impudent'. Mann, vol. XVIII (1932), pp. 22–3.
7 This much is clear but it is difficult to say much about the depth of his personal faith. The depositions claiming that he was an apostate in league with demons and giving evidence of his sceptical attitude which were produced by Philip the Fair's agents for his posthumous trial before Clement V are wholly suspect. See Cohn (1975), pp. 180–5.
8 Compagni, I. xx.
9 Hyde (1973), p. 172.
10 *Trattatello*, p. 582.
11 Piattoli (1940), pp. 41–2.
12 The sonnet is 'I' vegno 'l giorno a te 'infinite volte', in Marti (1969), pp. 228–9.
13 The exchange is given in *Lyric Poetry*, 72–4a. See Gilson (1952), pp. 63–4, for someone who takes the worst possible view.
14 Piattoli (1940), pp. 58–9.
15 Ibid., pp. 62–4.
16 Ibid., p. 87.
17 *Purg.* V. 135.
18 *Purg.* II. 98–9.
19 *Inf.* XVIII. 28.

20 *Conv.* IV. v. 20.

21 Villani, VIII. xxxvi, tr. Rose Selfe (1906), pp. 320–1.

22 See Guénon (1925), pp. 60–5, where the theory of the Great Year is explained in relation to the *Commedia*, and also, for more details, Benini (1952), pp. 57–65.

23 *Par.* XXXIII. 115–26.

24 *Trattatello*, pp. 631–2.

25 Witte (1879), vol. II, p. 52.

26 Compagni, I. xxii. Villani asks his readers to note that the year before, the statue of Mars had been turned to face the north instead of the east, in the course of alterations to the Ponte Vecchio; VIII. xxxix.

27 Compagni, I. xxi.

28 Piattoli (1940), pp. 87–92.

29 Ibid., pp. 92–6.

30 Ibid., p. 95.

31 *Trattatello*, p. 625.

32 Compagni, II. xix.

33 Villani, VIII. xlix.

34 Piattoli (1940), pp. 103–7.

35 Ibid., pp. 108–9.

36 Lionardo Bruno, see Passerini (1917), p. 216.

37 Quoted in Mundy (1973), p. 242.

38 *Purg.* XX. 86–7.

39 *Epist.* I., pp. 4–8.

40 Villani, VIII. lxxx.

41 *Conv.* I. iii. 5, tr. Jackson.

42 Lionardo Bruni, in Passerini (1917), p. 217. The letter is lost.

43 *Lyric Poetry*, 81. 101–7.

44 *Lyric Poetry*, 84a–88a.

45 Piattoli (1940), pp. 118–25.

46 Villani, IX. cxxxvi.

47 *Trattatello*, pp. 611–12.

48 This is stated by Giovanni da Serravalle in the prologue to the Latin translation of the *Commedia* with a commentary which he completed in 1417 at the Council of Constance. He undertook the task for an Italian cardinal and for two English bishops he met at the council, Nicholas Bubwych of Bath and Wells and Robert Hallam of Salisbury. Gladstone's essay 'Did Dante study in Oxford?' appeared in the *Nineteenth Century*, June 1892, pp. 1032–42.

49 See Billanovich (1947), who describes how Boccaccio, when he did not have direct information about episodes in Dante's life, would fill in the gaps from his classical reading.

50 Passerini (1917), p. 211.

51 *Purg.* VII. 109.

52 Hillgarth (1971), pp. 66 and 72–3.

53 Dubois (1891), and see Finke (1907), vol. I, pp. 121–2 and vol. II, p. 118.

54 Villani, VIII. xcii.

55 Norman Cohn in his recent account of the persecution of the Templars demonstrates clearly that the charges brought against them were a variant of those previously

brought against many heretical groups, 'real or imaginary'. See Cohn (1975), pp. 75–98.

56 *Purg.* XX. 91–3.
57 See his account of Jacques de Molay in *De casibus virorum illustrium* in *Opere* (1965), pp. 844–50.
58 *Purg.* VII. 110.
59 Villani, VIII. LXX.
60 Villani, VIII. LXXI.
61 Corso's death is described in Villani, VIII. XCVI.
62 *Purg.* XXIV. 82–7.

Chapter 11   The poet of righteousness: later lyrics and De vulgari eloquentia

1 *Trattatello*, pp. 586–7.
2 *Giambi ed Epodi*, XXVII, 'A Messer Cante Gabrielli da Gubbio, Podestà di Firenze nel MCCCI', and for Carlyle on Dante, see 'The Hero as Poet', in *Heroes and Hero-Worship* (1901), p. 87. 'We will not complain of Dante's miseries: had all gone right with him as he wished it, he might have been prior, podestà, or whatsoever they call it, of Florence, well accepted among neighbours—and the world had wanted one of the most notable words ever spoken or sung. Florence would have had another prosperous Lord Mayor; and the ten dumb centuries continued voiceless, and the ten other listening centuries (for there will be ten of them and more) had no *Divina Commedia* to hear!'
3 In his Nobel speech, 'One word of truth . . .' (London, 1972), pp. 15–16.
4 See Chapter 7, p. 98.
5 *DVE* II. ii. 9.
6 *Lyric Poetry*, 86. 1–4.
7 *Epist.* III. 22–6.
8 *Lyric Poetry*, 62–3.
9 *Lyric Poetry*, 61.
10 *Lyric Poetry*, 67. 24–30.
11 *Lyric Poetry*, 77. 53–65.
12 *Lyric Poetry*, 78.
13 *Lyric Poetry*, 80.
14 *Lyric Poetry*, 81.
15 See the notes by Father Kenelm Foster and Dr Boyde in *Lyric Poetry*, vol. 2, pp. 285–8, for the elucidation of the identity of the three ladies.
16 The first book of *De vulgari eloquentia* was written, on internal evidence, between spring 1303 and the beginning of 1305. The marquis of Monferrat, mentioned as among the living in Book I, died in February 1305. Dante probably first thought of it when he was in Bologna with Cino da Pistoia. It was, perhaps, the originality of *De vulgari eloquentia* that secured it so little notice among Dante's early readers. Both Villani and Boccaccio mention it and the latter says that it was written at the end of Dante's life. This is certainly untrue because of the internal evidence for its dating. Lionardo Bruni appears not to have read it. Its first ardent admirer was Gian

Giorgio Trissino (1478–1550), the Renaissance poet and architect, who saw in it support for his intended reforms of the Italian language and, by introducing it into the debates of his time, secured for it an audience it has never lost.

17 See, for example, the account of it in Saintsbury, vol. I (1900), who (p. 431) claims for it 'not merely the position of the most important critical document between Longinus and the seventeenth century at least, but one of intrinsic importance on a line with that of the very greatest critical documents of all history'.

18 See J. Cremona, 'Dante's Views on Language', in Limentani (1965), pp. 138–62.

19 *DVE* I. xvii. 1.

20 See J. Cremona in Limentani (1965), p. 162.

21 *DVE* II. iv. 3.

22 *DVE* II. vi. 5.

23 *Par.* XXVI. 124–6.

24 *DVE* II. viii. 6.

25 *DVE* I. i. 1.

26 *DVE* II. iii. 9.

27 *Lyric Poetry*, 71. 1–2.

28 *Lyric Poetry*, 80. 16–17.

29 *DVE* II. iv. 10–11, tr. Ferrers Howell.

30 From *An Apology for Smectymnus*, in *John Milton: Selected Prose*, ed. C. A. Patrides (Harmondsworth, 1974), p. 62. Just before this passage Milton speaks of as his models 'the two famous renowners of *Beatrice* and *Laura*, who never write but honour of them to whom they devote their verse . . .'.

Chapter 12   Invitation to the banquet of knowledge:
Il Convivio

1 See *Trattatello*, pp. 610–12, for the details that follow.

2 See Yates (1966), p. 104, for the suggestion of Dante's employment of a memory system in the *Commedia*, and also p. 191 for Lull's stay in Pisa.

3 *Conv.* I. ix. 5.

4 See Lubac (1959), Pt I, vol. II, p. 562.

5 Ibid., p. 632.

6 This example is taken from Dunbar (1929), p. 21.

7 Lubac (1959), Pt II, vol. II, p. 270.

8 *Conv.* II. i. 3–8.

9 *Conv.* II. xv. 1.

10 *Conv.* II. xv. 12.

11 *Lyric Poetry*, 61, 1–4.

12 *Conv.* III. xii. 14.

13 He later corrected this attribution in *Mon.* II. iii. 3, where he ascribes it properly to Aristotle's *Politics*.

14 *Conv.* II. iv. 6–8.

15 *Conv.* IV. v. 17.

16 *Conv.* IV. v. 20.

17 *Lyric Poetry*, 69, 38–40.

18 *Lyric Poetry*, 69, 52–5.

19 Montanari (1968), p. 161. See also Michele Barbi's introduction to the Busnelli and Vandelli edn, vol. I (1954), pp. xli ff.
20 *Conv.* IV. i. 8.
21 Judge, for example, the effect of the atonement passages in *Par.* VII and the comparative relief given by the episode of Charles Martel in the following canto.
22 See Michele Barbi's introduction to the Busnelli and Vandelli edn, vol. I (1954), pp. xviii and xix.
23 *Conv.* III. v. 14–17.
24 F. Angelitti, quoted in the Busnelli and Vandelli edn, vol. I (1954), p. 301, note 16.
25 See Chapter 19, pp. 346–7.
26 *Conv.* III. xiv. 5.
27 *Conv.* IV. xx. 8.
28 By Hugh of St Cher, quoted in the Busnelli and Vandelli edn, vol. II (1964), p. 284, note 9.
29 *Phars.* II. 326 ff.
30 *Conv.* IV. xxviii. 15.

Chapter 13   The descent of Henry of Luxemburg and the
writing of De monarchia

1 *Par.* XXX. 133–8.
2 For Villani's and Guido's accounts see Villani, VIII. lxxx and Guido da Pisa (1974), p. 363. For the impossibility of the story see Mollat (1950), p. 29.
3 *Mon.* I. xiii. 7.
4 *Epist.* V. 46–58.
5 *Epist.* V. 10.
6 *Epist.* VII. 2.
7 *Epist.* VI. 3.
8 Bowsky (1960), p. 156.
9 Lionardo Bruni, in Passerini (1917), p. 218.
10 Nicholas of Butrinto, *Relatio de itinere italico Henrici VII*, in Muratori, vol. 9, cols 909–10, and see Hyde (1973), p. 141.
11 Bowsky (1960), p. 78.
12 *Lyric Poetry*, 82. It may be that Robert of Anjou is intended instead of Philip the Fair, but Dante despised rather than hated Robert and the force of the sonnet fits far better with his other references to Philip.
13 Vinay, however, dated it to a later period, between spring 1312 and August 1313, when Henry died. I am following the arguments used by C. G. Hardie in his 'Note on the Chronology of Dante's Political Works' accompanying Donald Nicholl's translation of the *Monarchia* (London, 1954), p. 117–21. Others date it to Dante's last years on the basis of a reference to *Paradiso* in *Mon.* I. xii. 6.
14 For a discussion of the charge of Averroism, see Gilson (1952), pp. 168–71.
15 See Vernani (1938), pp. 127–8 for his comments on this passage. Vernani who reveals a Dantean talent for derisive abuse in his *De reprobatione monarchiae*, addressed this work to the chancellor of Bologna, Graziolo de' Bambaglioli, who was the author of one of the earliest commentaries in Latin on the *Commedia*. See Bambaglioli (1892).
16 Gilson (1952), p. 179.

17 See Chapter 11, p. 174, and Chapter 18, pp. 344–5, for further discussions of the theme of Astraea in Dante's works.

18 The reference to Henry as 'uncto', anointed, is a vague help in dating the *Monarchia*, vague because he was probably anointed three times, at Aachen on 6 January 1309, at Milan on 6 January 1311, and at Rome on 29 July 1312.

19 *Mon.* II. xi.

20 *Par.* XX. 56 ff.

21 *Mon.* III. xv. 18.

22 For the differences between this hierocratic party of canonists and the moderate party which Dante followed see Kantorowicz (1957), pp. 322 and 456–7.

23 See Chapter 10, p. 161 and note 53.

24 Vernani shrewdly pointed out that only Christ has all the qualities that Dante requires in his emperor. See Vernani (1938), p. 129.

25 See Yates (1975), pp. 41–6.

26 See, for example, Rolf Helmut Foerster's anthology, *Die Idee Europa 1300–1946* (Munich, 1963), pp. 12 and 25.

Chapter 14 The last years: Lucca, Verona, and Ravenna

1 The earliest contemporary reference to the *Commedia* (specifically to the *Inferno*), was made by Francesco da Barberino in the commentary to his *Documenti d'Amore*, dated 1313–14. See Barberino (1905–27), vol. 2, 1912, pp. 375–6, and the discussion of the significance of this reference in Vallone (1971), pp. 288–9.

2 *Epist.* VIII.

3 Villani, IV. lix.

4 See de Sponde (1641), vol. I, p. 534.

5 *Epist.* VIII. 7.

6 Cf. *Purg.* XVI. 106–8.

7 Villani, IX. cxxxvi.

8 *Epist.* IV.

9 C. G. Hardie, in 'Dante's "Canzone Montanina"', *MLR* (1960), vol. 55, pp. 359–70, makes out a strong case for the letter being written in 1311, after the three political letters, that the lady of the *canzone* is Beatrice, that the letter contains Dante's excuse for his inaction in the imperial cause, and that the *canzone* contains the seed of the *Commedia*. This later date for the letter is discussed and rejected by Foster and Boyde in *Lyric Poetry*, vol. 2, pp. 338–40, who prefer the traditional date of 1307–8.

10 *Epist.* IV.

11 *Lyric poetry*, 89, 61–6.

12 So it is said in the short life of Dante adapted from Boccaccio and known as the *Compendio*. See Passerini (1917), p. 21.

13 *Lyric Poetry*, 87 and 88.

14 Hardie (1960), p. 365. The identification of the lady with Beatrice does not depend, however, on his dating of the letter and *canzone* to 1311.

15 Renucci (1954), p. 89.

16 C. A. Robson, 'Dante's Use in the *Divina Commedia* of the Medieval Allegories on Ovid', in Oxford Dante Society (1965), pp. 1–38.

17 *Dichtung und Wahrheit*, XIII (Weimar edn, Abt I, Bd 28, p. 221). Lowes (1955), p. 136, quotes this passage in describing a crucial point in the composition of *The Ancient Mariner*.

18 John Aubrey quoted in *The Life Records of John Milton*, ed. J. Milton French, vol. V, p. 112 (New Brunswick, 1958).

19 Andrea Lancia (*Ottimo Commento*, ed. Torri, 1827), vol. 1, p. 183.

20 Piattoli (1940), pp. 132–44.

21 Piattoli (1940), pp. 155–6.

22 *Epist.* IX. 157–8.

23 *Par.* XVII. 71.

24 For accounts of the prehumanist society of Verona and other aspects of Dante's life there, see the catalogue of the exhibition *Dante e Verona* (Commune di Verona, 1965).

25 *Inf.* I. 105.

26 Olschki (1949), p. 5.

27 *Mon.* I. xiii. 7, tr. Nicholl (1954).

28 Benvenuto da Imola, *Comentum*, vol. 5, p. 197, says that when his father, Alberto, took Can Grande to visit his great treasury, the boy urinated on the gold before him. From this the onlookers prophesied that he would be noted for his munificence.

29 *Par.* XVII. 82–90.

30 These details come from Muratori's introduction to the chronicle of Sagacio Mucio Gazata (Muratori, 23, p. 2).

31 The circumstances of his captivity are described in Wicksteed and Gardner (1902), pp. 33–5.

32 Petrarch, *De rerum memorandarum*, II. iv (Berne, 1610), p. 152.

33 This story is quoted in Papanti (1873), p. 140. Moore (1890), p. 167, points out that the story was first told by Josephus.

34 *Epist.* X. 165–95. The authenticity of this letter has been questioned either in part or in whole since Moore, in his *Dante Studies*, vol. III, pp. 284–369, produced what seemed to be firm reasons for accepting it as genuine, notably by Bruno Nardi, in 'Il punto sull'epistola a Cangrande' (Nardi, 1960), and C. G. Hardie in 'The Epistle to Can Grande Again', *DDJ*, 38 (1960). Many other writers are strongly in favour of its authenticity, among them Mazzoni (1955), Singleton (1954), and Charity (1966). The argument that Boccaccio was uncertain about the status of the letter has been weakened by the recent study by L. Jenaro-MacLennan (1974).

35 *Trattatello*, p. 594.

36 The reference to Phillis in the exchange with Giovanni del Virgilio, Eclogue 1, may refer to Gemma.

37 See Ricci (1921) for an appendix containing Guido Novello's poems.

38 *Trattatello*, p. 595.

39 *Acerba*, II. xii. 1412–47.

40 *De situ et forma aque et terre*, XXIV. 10.

41 Wicksteed and Gardner (1902), p. 121.

42 Ibid., pp. 146–51.

43 Ibid., Eclogue 1, 58–64.

44 F. Villani, in Passerini (1917), pp. 190–1.

45 *Trattatello*, pp. 634–6.

Chapter 15   The journey

1 In his 'Razgovor o Dante' (Conversation about Dante), Mandelstam (1971), vol. 2, p. 415.
2 *Inf.* I. 1–9.
3 *Inf.* I. 67–75.
4 *Inf.* II. 7–9.
5 *Inf.* II. 121–6.
6 *Inf.* II. 139–40.
7 *Inf.* III. 1–9.
8 *Inf.* IV. 121–9.
9 *Inf.* IX. 76–90.
10 *Inf.* XXXII. 1–12.
11 *Inf.* XXXIII. 1–3.
12 *Inf.* XXXIII. 75.
13 *Inf.* XXXIII. 150.
14 *Inf.* XXXIV. 139.
15 *Purg.* I. 1–18.
16 *Purg.* IX. 13–30.
17 *Purg.* XVI. 85–108.
18 *Purg.* XXI. 131–2.
19 *Purg.* XXVI. 148.
20 *Purg.* XXVII. 139–42.
21 *Purg.* XXXIII. 145.
22 *Par.* I. 1–18.
23 *Par.* III. 85–7.
24 *Par.* VII. 10–12.
25 *Par.* X. 52–4.
26 *Par.* XII. 127.
27 *Par.* XVII. 133–42.
28 *Par.* XXIII. 25–33.
29 *Par.* XXVII. 19–27.
30 *Par.* XXVIII. 41–2.
31 *Par.* XXXIII. 97–9.
32 *Par.* XXXIII. 142–5.

Chapter 16   Weight, number, and measure in the Commedia

1 This figure is given in Sciama (1971), p. 15.
2 See the introductory chapter on the origin and influence of this definition in Poulet (1961), pp. iii–xxxi. Translation in Freccero (1965), pp. 151–69.
3 *Par.* XXVIII. 13–45.
4 Kuhn (1957), p. 111. This estimate of Dante's significance in the history of science is far in advance of Pierre Duhem's whose chief praise of Dante's knowledge of astronomy is that 'il n'écrit pas des sottises'; Duhem, vol. IV (1916), p. 22.
5 See Kuhn (1957), p. 129.
6 *The Upanishads*, tr. Swami Prabhavananda and Frederick Manchester, New York (1957), p. 23.

7 See the examples in Comper (1917). See also Collin (1956) for many examples of journeys in the afterlife drawn from a diversity of cultures.

8 See Dhalla (1938), pp. 283–4.

9 Tr. Michael Grant, in *On the Good Life* (Harmondsworth, 1971), p. 353.

10 See Boswell (1908).

11 See Patch (1970).

12 See Cary (1956), pp. 134–5.

13 See Bonvesin da Riva (1901).

14 See Chapter 7, pp. 90–1 and in n. 9.

15 Taken from *The Meaning of the Glorious Koran*, an explanatory translation by Mohammed Marmaduke Pickthall, p. 204.

16 See Asín Palacios (1926).

17 See Cerulli (1949). There is a general review of the current state of informed opinion on the question of Dante and Islam by F. Gabrieli in 'The Transmission of Learning and Literary Influences to Western Europe', *The Cambridge History of Islam*, ed. P. M. Holt, Ann K. S. Lambton, and Bernard Lewis (Cambridge, 1970), pp. 878–80.

18 Cerulli (1949), p. 524.

19 See, for example, Fetellus (1892), Burchard of Mount Sion (1896), and Sanuto (1896).

20 See Demaray (1974), where the importance of the Great Circle route and its relation to the *Commedia* is made clear.

21 See John (1946), and Helmut Hatzfeld, 'Modern Literary Scholarship as Reflected in Dante Criticism', in Clements (1967), pp. 206–8.

22 See the works by Guénon (1925) and Valli (1928).

23 This may explain, though not excuse, the extraordinary bigotry of Western Christians in dealing with Islam. Dante here compares unfavourably with Muslim writers such as Jalâl al-Dîn Rûmî who frequently refers most favourably to Christ, Mary, and to the Christian saints in his *Mathnawi*.

24 Aquinas, for example, speaks of Purgatory as a *locus inferior* joined on to Hell, so that the same fires torture the damned and purge the just. *In IV Lib. Sent.*, dist. XXI qu. I art 1 sol. IIIa.

25 See Boase (1972), p. 49.

26 See Orr (1956), especially the table of time references, pp. 235–44, and 'The assumed date of the vision', pp. 275–88. Earlier attempts to show that the date of the poem was 1301 were weakened by the discovery of a set of tables—that Dante could have used—in which, by mistake, the constellations for 1301 are listed under 1300. All the historical references favour the date of 1300, including the crucial fact that Guido Cavalcanti is expressly referred to as among the living at the time of the journey. As he died in August 1300, this would not have applied a year later. The argument for 1301 has been revived by Walter and Teresa Parri (1956).

27 See Benini (1952), especially pp. 223–47.

28 *Cons. phil.*, V, prose VI, p. 157.

29 *Div. Nom.* III 9, *PL*, 122, cols 1162–3.

30 For this tradition see Freccero (1961).

31 *Conv.* IV. xxi. 9.

32 See Freccero (1959).

33 See Dunbar (1929), p. 466.

34 *Purg.* XXV. 103–5.

35 See Valli (1922b), pp. 258–65.

36 See Collingwood (1946), pp. 49–51, for the division between the Christian and the classical theories of history.

37 *De civ. Dei*, XIX. 15.

38 Ibid., IV. 4.

39 See especially *De civ. Dei*, IV.

40 *Contra Paganos*, I. i. 14–17.

41 *Par.* IV. 61–3.

42 See Renucci (1954), p. 199.

43 John 12:46.

44 1 Epistle of John 1:5.

45 Epistle of James 1:17.

46 Ferguson (1970), p. 44.

47 This was said by the eleventh-century reformer Cardinal Henry of Ostia, quoted in Mundy (1973), p. 27.

48 Ernst H. Kantorowicz (1951) describes the Byzantine tradition of symbolizing both Christ and the emperor as suns in connexion with Dante's use of this imagery. Bruno Nardi (1944), p. 158, thought Dante might have derived it from Albertus Magnus' description of the parhelion. See also Mazzeo (1958), p. 146.

49 *Inf.* XIV. 94–120.

50 This diagram, with details added from Demaray (1974) and one of Marino Sanuto's maps, is adapted from Valli (1922b), p. 279.

51 Pietro Alighieri (1845), pp. 39–48.

52 See Davis (1975), p. 155. Charles Davis (ibid., p. 158) thinks Dante was looking for 'a second Augustus, or rather *the* second Augustus, and not just any righteous Emperor'.

53 John (1946), pp. 217–18. *Encyclopaedia Judaica* dates the completion of the second Temple in the spring of 515 BC.

54 See *Hieronymi Chronicon*, ed. Rudolf Helm in *Werke* 7 (ii), p. 106, Berlin (1956).

55 I Esdras 3:12.

56 *Inf.* XXVII. 85–7 and *Par.* XV. 142–5.

57 This account is taken from the entry 'The Book of Zerrubabel' in the *Encyclopaedia Judaica*, vol. 15, and for the influence of this work see also Salo Wittmayer Baron's *A Social and Religious History of the Jews*, 2nd edn, vol. 5, pp. 140–2 and 354, New York, 1957.

58 Whether Dante was a direct acquaintance of Immanuel ben Zifroni has been much argued over. They certainly had a mutual friend in the poet Bosone da Gubbio. Cino da Pistoia was an admirer of Immanuel who was known to his Italian friends as Manoello Giudeo.

59 For the influence of Methodius see Davis (1975), p. 155.

60 See John (1946), pp. 32–3 and Helmut Hatzfeld's 'Modern Literary Criticism as Reflected in Dante Criticism', in Clements (1967).

61 See Hatzfeld in Clements (1967), p. 206.

Chapter 17   The grace of inspiration

1 Bucke (1972), pp. 116–22.

2 *PL*, 197, cols 17–18. The translation is taken from Singer (1928), pp. 233–4. Charles

Singer, in his essay 'The Visions of Hildegard of Bingen', attributes her visions to attacks of migraine, stressing the similarity between her descriptions and the patterns of light experienced by migraine sufferers at the onset of attacks. He does not explain, however, why migraine patients in general do not create major works of art from these experiences. The connexions between Dante and Hildegard are discussed in Ostlender (1948).

3 *Par.* XXII. 14.

4 *Epist.* VIII. 5.

5 *Par.* I. 23–4. Landino says that here Dante means the posterior cell or ventricle of the brain which is that of memory.

6 *Purg.* XXXIII. 78.

7 Reeves and Hirsch-Reich (1972), p. 5.

8 *Par.* I. 34.

9 *ST.* 2a. 2ae. 174–6.

10 See Macrobius (1963), I, 3, and Macrobius (1966), pp. 87–92.

11 St Augustine, in *De Genesi ad litteram*, VI–XII, 11, 22, *PL*, 34, cols 458–68, describes the three kinds of vision, giving the examples of Exodus 19:19 for corporeal vision, Revelation and Isaiah 6:1 for spiritual vision, and Numbers 12:8 for intellectual vision. See also Bundy (1927), pp. 168 and 233, where he makes the comparison between the three canticles and the three kinds of Augustinian vision. Aquinas drew particularly on St Augustine's writings on prophecy when he was discussing the subject in the *Summa theologiae* (2a. 2ae. 171–4), and it is very interesting to read what he has to say there, bearing in mind how Dante would have read it with his own inspirations to the fore.

12 See Lowes (1955), pp. 155 and 204–5. Aquinas says (*ST.* 2a. 2ae. 173. 2) that God sometimes infuses an intellectual light into the mind of man so that he can pass judgment on those realities which have been seen by others.

13 This passage is in Rilke's poem, 'Für Wolf Graf von Kalckreuth', *Sämtliche Werke* (Insel-Verlag, 1955, vol. 1, p. 663).

14 See, for example, J. B. Leishmann and Stephen Spender's introduction to *Duino Elegies* (London, 1952), pp. 9–21.

15 See Hackel (1975) for a recent study of Blok's last period and the composition of 'The Twelve'.

16 Letter 2, October 1800, to Thomas Butts, Nonesuch edn, pp. 848–54.

17 *Milton* I, Nonesuch edn, p. 391.

18 *Purg.* XXIV. 52–4.

19 *Eclogue* 1, 58–63.

20 See Chapter 11, p. 183, for earlier examples of mountain imagery connected with inspiration.

21 *Purg.* III. 79–84.

22 Matthew 4:17.

23 For *metanoia* in relation to Dante, see Gilles G. Meersseman, O. P., 'Penitenza e penitenti nella vita e nelle opere di Dante', in Branca and Padoan (1967), pp. 224–46. See also Hans Urs von Balthasar's essay *'Purgatorio: Beichte und Inspiration'* for the relationship between repentance and inspiration; Balthasar (1962), pp. 410–22.

24 *Par.* II. 127–32.

25 See the account in Reeves and Hirsch-Reich (1972), p. 52, of how Joachim prepared

himself through spiritual exercises both for his inspirations and his execution of them.

26 See Angela of Foligno's descriptions of the voices instructing her on a journey to Assisi, in her first vision and consolation, in Angela of Foligno (1927), pp. 46–54. See also Evelyn Underhill (1975), pp. 100–8.

27 *Inf.* III. 22–4.

28 See the study of rhythms in the *Commedia* by Martha Amrein-Widmer (1932).

29 Albertus Magnus, *De praedicabilibus*, I, 2, *Omnia Opera*, ed. Borgnet, vol. I (1890), p. 4.

30 Aquinas, *In IV Lib. Sent*, i, prol. V, ad. 3. See also *ST.* 1a. 1. 9.

31 See Lenkeith (1952), pp. 39–42.

32 See *Trattatello*, p. 621, and also *Genealogia deorum gentilium*, Book XIV.

33 See Trinkaus (1970), vol. 2, pp. 555–71, and also Chapter XV, 'From *Theologia Poetica* to *Theologia Platonica*', pp. 683–721, for this whole question.

34 See his *Discorsi* on the poet in the Venice edn, 1564.

35 Auerbach (1965), p. 274.

36 John (1946), p. 190. See also the account of St Lucy's trial and martyrdom in Jacobus de Voragine, *Legenda Aurea*, IV (1846), pp. 30–2. Helen Flanders Dunbar (1929), who also draws out the parallels between the three blessed ladies and the persons of the Trinity, makes Lucia stand for Christ and Beatrice for the Holy Ghost, but the case for the parallel of Beatrice with Christ has been put too cogently by Charles S. Singleton for her interpretation to stand. See the essay, 'The Pattern at the Centre', in Singleton (1954), pp. 45–59.

37 *Purg.* IX. 25–7.

38 *De musica*, VI. XI, XII, *PL*, 32, cols 1179–83, and see Bundy (1927), p. 165.

39 *Itinerarium mentis*, III. 3.

40 *Purg.* X. 94–9.

41 *Purg.* XII. 61–3. The pattern closely resembles the making of a sestina; this passage has the same number of lines, thirty-nine, but with the difference that the repetition is not in the rhyme words but in the beginning of each terzain.

42 *Purg.* XII. 70–2.

43 *Purg.* XVII. 10–39. For a modern account of the experience of waking visions see the reference to Edwin Muir's *An Autobiography* in Chapter 1, note 39.

44 *Purg.* XVII. 13–18.

45 *Itinerarium mentis*, III. 2.

46 *ST.* 2a. 2ae. 173. 2.

47 *Parzival.* VI. 282–302, ed. Lachmann (1854).

48 This is particularly so in the Orthodox tradition. See the warnings of St Gregory of Sinai in *Philokalia*, tr. Kadloubovsky and Palmer (1951), pp. 80–4.

49 I. A. Richards (1975), p. 120, ll. 25–7, 'Whose Endless Jar', on which he comments (p. 132), quoting the words of Lachesis, the daughter of Necessity in the *Republic*, 'Heaven is guiltless': 'Dante's design . . . required that everything that happens be explained as the unquestionable (but incomprehensible) will of Heaven. The argument of my cantos is, in brief, that this makes Heaven very far from guiltless.'

50 *Inf.* XXIV. 124–6.

51 *Inf.* XXIV. 151.

52 *Purg.* XXX. 79–81.

53 *Purg.* XXX. 115–17.

54 *Purg.* XXX. 97–9.

55 *Purg.* XXX. 13–33.

56 This episode forms Book IX of *Parzival.*

57 *Purg.* XXXI. 61–3.

58 *Epist.* VI. 4, tr. Paget Toynbee.

59 *Purg.* XI. 7–9.

60 *Purg.* XI. 10–12.

Chapter 18   The six guides and the four levels of meaning

1 See *The Little Flowers of St Francis*, tr. T. W. Arnold (London, 1903), pp. 191–2.

2 *Par.* XI. 106–8.

3 *Itinerarium mentis*, prologue 2.

4 Ibid., I. 3.

5 Ibid., I. 6.

6 *Epist.* X. 28.

7 See the introduction to Antonio Lubin's edition of the *Commedia* (Padua, 1881), pp. 224–7, and also Gardner (1913), p. 46.

8 See Vossler (1929), pp. 144–5, where, after showing how Richard of St Victor and Bonaventure added intermediate steps to the traditional three stages of knowledge, he says: 'Just as Bonaventure by the insertion of intervening steps sought to give a closer unity to the gradual ascent toward knowledge, so Dante interposed several other persons between the chief representatives of supersensuous knowledge, Virgil and Beatrice. . . . It is clear that Dante intends to assign to these figures tasks similar to that which Richard and Bonaventure ascribed to their intermediaries between understanding, revelation and the highest stage, *apex mentis*. This does not indeed prove that Richard and Bonaventure furnished the direct suggestion for increasing the number of spiritual guides in the *Commedia*. But we may assume with confidence that these figures owe their origin to a mystical intention of the poet.'

9 See Vyvyan (1961).

10 *Par.* XXXIII. 66, 94–6, 118.

11 *Par.* I. 13–36.

12 *Par.* I. 68.

13 *Par.* II. 16–19.

14 *Inf.* II. 7–9.

15 *Purg.* XXVII. 140–2.

16 *Purg.* XXIX. 37–42.

17 *Purg.* XXXII. 73–84.

18 *Par.* X. 52–3.

19 This is discussed by Seznec (1972), pp. 140–2, Wind (1958), pp. 46–7, and Campbell (1974), pp. 99–110. For the Muses in Dante and earlier Latin literature see Curtius (1953), chap. 13, 'The Muses', pp. 228–46.

20 For the figure of Serapis see Macrobius (1963), *Saturnalia*, I, 20, 13–18.

21 *Purg.* XXII. 58.

22 *Purg.* XXIX. 37–42.

23 *Epist.* X. 10.

24 *Conv.* IV. xxii. 13–18.

25 *Conv.* II. xv. 1.

26 *Inf.* IV. 131.

27 See *ST.* la. 1. 10. on whether one passage of scripture can bear several senses. For an account of the history of the method in relation to Dante see Dunbar (1929). See also Charity (1966) and Smalley (1952).

28 *De reductione artium ad theologiam*, 5, in the Quaracchi edn, vol. 5, p. 321. See also de Lubac (1959–64), Part 2, vol. II, p. 269.

29 Letter to Thomas Butts, 22 November 1802, Nonesuch edn, p. 862.

30 See Guido da Pisa (1974) and also Hollander (1969), Appendix I, 'The Fourteenth-Century Commentators on Fourfold Allegory', pp. 266–96.

31 Landino says this in the introduction to his commentary, Venice, 1564, and for Tasso's mention, see *Discorsi del poema eroico*, V, ed. E. Mazzali (1959), pp. 673–4.

32 Singleton (1954), pp. 90–4.

33 Nardi (1944), pp. 23–40 and 55–61.

34 Dunbar (1929).

35 Mazzeo (1958), especially chap. II, 'Dante's Conception of Poetic Expression'.

36 See his essay, 'Figura' in Auerbach (1959), pp. 11–76.

37 *ST.* la. 1. 10, tr. Thomas Gilby, O. P. (Blackfriars edn, 1964), p. 39.

38 *Purg.* XXIX 100–5. The passages he mentions from the Bible are Ezekiel 1 :4–14 and Revelation 4 :8.

39 *Epist.* X. 7.

40 De Lubac (1959–64), Part 1, vol. II, p. 624.

41 Suger (1946), p. 64.

42 *ST.* I. 2. q. 102a. 2 ad 2m.

43 See Chapter 4, 'Art and Mysticism', in Henderson (1967), pp. 143–76.

44 *De Arca Noe Morali*, Prol., *PL*, 176, cols 617–19. See also the translation by a religious of C.S.M.V. (1962), pp. 45–7.

45 Ibid., III, *PL*, 176, cols 62–9. See the translation (1962), pp. 60–72.

46 *Conv.* II. I. 12.

47 *Purg.* XXX. 133–5.

48 The development of the character and role of Virgil from the figure of Love would receive even more significance if we knew that Dante was familiar with a tradition, preserved in Byzantium by Ioannes Laurentius Lydus in his *De mensibus* (IV, 30, 73, 74), of the three names of Rome. When the Romans founded a city they would give it a common name, a sacral name, and a secret name. In the case of Rome herself the common name was Roma, the sacral name was Flora, and the secret name was Amor, an anagram of Roma. Romulus, the fratricide and conqueror, was the founder of Roma, and Dante pays scant attention to him. The sacral name of Flora gives a new origin for the naming of Florence and enhances the Florentines' view of their city as the heiress of Rome; this was an inspiration to Poliziano in the fifteenth century, who was certainly familiar with Lydus.

The founder of Amor was Aeneas, the son of Venus, whom Dante regards as the true creator of the city and the bearer of the mission which Virgil was to inherit and expound. Dante knew no Greek and there is no evidence for his familiarity with Lydus; on the other hand, just as his contemporary Giotto is now thought to have been influenced by the outburst of creative activity in late-thirteenth-century Byzantium, so Dante may, in other ways, have benefited from contemporary Greek sources, most notably the idea of the two suns symbolizing the earthly and spiritual authorities (see Chapter 16, note 48), an idea that of course connects with his thoughts on the origin and mission of Rome. See also note 53 below.

49 *Benjamin Minor*, LXXXVI, *PL*, 196, cols 61–2.
50 Guido da Pisa (1974), p. 33.
51 Philotheus of Sinai in *Philokalia*, tr. Kadloubovsky and Palmer (1951), p. 338.
52 *Bhagavad Gita*, XIV:

The power of sattwa
Enslaves the happy,
The power of rajas
Enslaves the doers,
The power of tamas
Enslaves the deluded
And darkens their judgment.

Tr. Swami Prabhavananda and Christopher Isherwood (1947), p. 142.
53 A Greek Orthodox influence on Dante has been suggested though, by C. A. Trypanis (1950), who drew attention to the Latin translation of a Byzantine work on the virtues and vices that Dante might have used for the scheme of the *Inferno*. This suggestion is discussed and rejected by Agostino Pertusi in 'Cultura greco-bizantina nel tardo medioevo nelle venezie e suoi echi in Dante', in Branca and Padoan (1967), pp. 179–82.
54 *Inf.* IV. 40–2.
55 *Inf.* IV. 43–5.
56 *Inf.* VI. 106–11.
57 *Purg.* III. 37–45.
58 *Purg.* VIII. 1–6.
59 *Inf.* XXIII. 124–6.
60 *Purg.* XXVIII. 139–44.
61 *Itinerarium mentis*, II. 1.
62 *Purg.* I. 31–9.
63 See chaps XI and XII, on the identification of Matelda with Astraea, in Singleton (1958), pp. 184–218.
64 *Itinerarium mentis*, IV. 2.
65 Ibid., IV. 6.
66 Ibid., IV. 8.

Chapter 19   Change and being: the images of the Commedia

1 *Purg.* VI. 45.
2 *Itinerarium mentis*, V. 1.
3 See Erich Auerbach's essay 'Dante's Addresses to the Reader' in Clements, ed. (1967), pp. 637–51.
4 *Epist.* X. 15.
5 *Epist.* X. 10.
6 *Inf.* IX. 61.
7 *Par.* XXIII. 71–2.
8 See, for example, Guido da Pisa (1974), pp. 52–5.
9 See his introductory passages in the Venice edn, Landino (1564).

10 See Pietro Alighieri (1845), pp. 4–8. Robert Hollander (1969), pp. 290–6, draws attention to what he considers the best of all the fourteenth-century discussions of the fourfold method, that of Filippo Villani who in his commentary on the first canto of *Inferno* makes provision for apological and metaphorical symbolism in his sub-divisions of the moral level. See Filippo Villani (1896), p. 25.

11 *Inf.* XXIII. 37–42.

12 Luke 18:16–17.

13 *Inf.* III. 19–21.

14 *Par.* XXXIII. 106–8.

15 See, for example, the images of the theatre and tube train in 'East Coker' III, where the emphasis is on the states of mind of the audience and the passengers rather than on their surroundings.

16 *Inf.* I. 22–4.

17 See Chapter 8, pp. 114–15.

18 *Par.* XVII. 40–2.

19 *Inf.* XIII. 40–2.

20 *Inf.* XXXII. 31–6.

21 Irma Brandeis (1960), p. 137.

22 See the entry 'Man', in Cirlot (1971), p. 197.

23 See the opening lines of *Metam.*, Book I.

24 *Inf.* XII. 41–3. This last passage may also reflect the influence of Bernard Sylvester and his description of *Silva*, matter in a state of primal chaos, in his *De universitate mundi*.

25 *Par.* XXVI. 64–6.

26 *Purg.* X. 79–81.

27 *Par.* XXXI. 127.

28 *Inf.* IX. 52–4.

29 *Inf.* IX. 61–3.

30 *Purg.* XXXIII. 64–78.

31 *Inf.* V. 97–9.

32 *Purg.* V. 124–9.

33 *Par.* XXX. 61–9.

34 *Par.* XXXI. 73–6.

35 *Par.* XXXIII. 94–6.

36 *Inf.* XVIII. 83–7.

37 *Par.* II. 16–18.

38 *Inf.* VII. 121–3.

39 *Par.* II. 8.

40 See Hugh Shankland's article on this question (Shankland, 1975).

41 *Inf.* XVII. 10–27.

42 Mandelstam (1971), p. 419.

43 See some of the examples illustrated in Gille (1966).

44 *Par.* XX. 73–8.

45 *Purg.* XXVII. 17–18.

46 Alan of Lille (1965), pp. 299–302.

47 *Purg.* XXXIII. 72. See p. 355.

48 John (1946), pp. 145–6.

49 Ibid., p. 148.
50 See *Aeneid* VIII. 202, and Revelation 9:7, 10, 19. Dante may also have drawn on descriptions of the mantichora, a mythical composite beast with a scorpion's tail.
51 Francesco da Buti (1858–62), vol. I (1858), p. 439.
52 *Capestro* is the term used by the Franciscan Guido da Montefeltro in *Inf.* XXVII. 92 for his girdle. See also *Par.* XI. 87 and XII. 132.
53 See Chapter 10, p. 162.
54 See M. Bulard, *Le Scorpion* (Paris, 1935), for the eagle-scorpion connexion.
55 See *La Règle des Templiers*, ed. de Curzon (1886), p. 347, and for the use of the belt in the accusations see Lizerand (1923), p. 29, and Cohn (1975), p. 87.
56 *Inf.* XIX. 85–7.
57 Guido da Pisa (1974), p. 364.
58 See Michelet (1841), vol. 1, p. 75, for these details.
59 See Cohn (1975), pp. 180–92, for the significance of the trials of Boniface and of Guichard in this connexion.
60 The episode is described in Zingarelli (1931), vol. II, pp. 740–2.
61 These doctrines and the scandal they aroused are discussed in Mollat (1950), pp. 54–5.
62 See Marvell's poem 'Tom May's Death', 63–70.
63 Such as the often reproduced twelfth-century map now in the Bibliothèque Royale, Brussels. It can be seen, for example, in *Jerusalem: Sacred City of the World* by Teddy Kollek and Moshe Pearlman (London, 1968), p. 174.
64 Psalm 92 (91 in the Vulgate), v. 13.
65 See John (1946), chap. 20, 174–81.
66 Demaray (1974), pp. 169–77.
67 *Itinerarium mentis*, IV and V.
68 See the examples given in Coli (1897), pp. 53 ff.
69 Demaray (1974), p. 174.
70 *Mon.* III. xv 12.
71 See Kaske (1961), pp. 185–254. A shortened version of this article appears in Freccero (1965), pp. 122–40, but without the illustrations that add much conviction to the argument.
72 This does not appear in the printed version of Pietro's commentary but in another manuscript. The relevant passage is given in Toynbee (1968), p. 84.
73 See Guido da Pisa (1974), pp. 31–2.
74 See Singleton (1958), chap. 5, where Beatrice is described as an analogue of Christ.
75 *Itinerarium mentis*, V. 1.
76 See Gilson (1940), for St Bernard's use of this imagery.
77 *Par.* XXX.
78 See Wilson (1978), chap. XIX, pp. 148–64.
79 *Inf.* XV. 17–21.
80 *Par.* IV. 37–48.
81 *Itinerarium mentis*, V and VI.
82 *Inf.* XXIII. 25–30.
83 *Purg.* XXXI. 139.
84 *Par.* XXVII. 104–5.

Chapter 20   *The transformation of man*

1 Blake's Satan is not the Satan of conventional Christianity. Nevertheless he said: 'Whatever Book is for Vengeance for Sin & Whatever Book is Against the Forgiveness of Sins is not of the Father, but of Satan the Accuser & Father of Hell.' This is one of Blake's notes on a diagram of the circles of the *Inferno*, now in the British Museum. He also said of Dante: 'Nature is his Inspirer & not the Holy Ghost.' See Roe (1953), p. 31 and plate 101. His attitude to Dante changed remarkably, however, from his first contact with him through Boyd's translation in about 1785 (see Keynes, 1971, pp. 147–54) to his greater familiarity in his last years when he studied Italian to read him in the original and executed his illustrations of the *Commedia*. He enjoyed quarrelling with Dante.
2 See pp. 312–13, and note 49 to Chapter 17.
3 *PL*, 217, cols 701–46.
4 Quoted in Moore, *Studies in Dante*, third series (1903), p. 135, note 2.
5 See Ordericus Vitalis (1968–75), Book VIII, vol. IV, 1973, pp. 236–51, for the account of the priest Walchelin, who saw these women in a hell rout.
6 Suger (1929), pp. 240–50.
7 See Campbell (1974), pp. 6–7, where he says, 'Creative mythology . . . springs not, like theology, from the dicta of authority, but from the insights, sentiments, thought, and vision of an . . . individual, loyal to his own experience of value.'
8 See Lenkeith (1952), pp. 144–5.
9 *Knight's tale*, 2809–12.
10 For Shakespeare's use of the theme of love's pilgrimage which Dante introduced, see Vyvyan (1961), p. 152.
11 Curtius (1953), p. 365.
12 Ibid., pp. 368–72.
13 *Par.* XVII. 138.
14 *Trattatello*, p. 608.
15 See John (1946).
16 See Auerbach (1965), p. 65.
17 *De civ. Dei*, X. 29.
18 *Purg.* XI. 10–12.
19 *Par.* XXIX. 10–18.
20 I cannot help wondering whether this passage influenced Coleridge in his statement of the primary imagination in Chapter XIII of *Biographia Literaria*: 'The primary imagination I hold to be the living power and prime agent of all human perception, and as a repetition in the finite mind of the eternal act of creation in the infinite I AM.' Everyman edn, p. 167. See also Olivero (1936), p. 135, for a comparison of Dante with Coleridge.
21 *Inf.* XXIX. 46–51.
22 *Purg.* XIII. 61–6.
23 *Par.* XIV. 61–6.
24 See Nardi (1949), pp. 153–4.
25 *Inf.* XXVI. 112–20.
26 *Inf.* XXVII. 28.
27 *Inf.* XXVII. 118–20.
28 *Inf.* XXVII. 108–11.

29 *Purg.* XXVI. 117.
30 *Par.* XXI. 28–33.
31 *Par.* XXXI. 1–15.
32 *Par.* XXXI. 59–63.
33 *Par.* XXXIII. 1–21.
34 *Epist.* X. 28.
35 *Itinerarium mentis*, VI. 7, tr. Boas, p. 42.

Chapter 21   The end of the journey

1 *Trattatello*, p. 627.
2 *Phaedrus* 247. For the influence of the *Phaedrus* tradition on Dante, see Nardi (1949), pp. 1–92, and Mazzeo (1958), pp. 1–24, and for the diffusion of Platonic influence, see Gregory (1958).
3 For this tradition see the studies of E. de Bruyne (1946), vol. III, chap. 1, pp. 3–29, and Guidubaldi (1966), *Dante Europeo*, II, especially Parts II and III.
4 See Crombie (1953), p. 131.
5 *Par.* II. 97–105.
6 Kuhn (1957), p. 111.
7 Dunbar (1929), p. 460, note 14.
8 *Conv.* II. III. 8–10.
9 *Epist.* X. 28.
10 Ibid. The work by Richard of St Victor, which Dante calls *De Contemplatione*, is more generally known as *Benjamin Major*.
11 Ibid.
12 This is discussed by several contributors in the conference report, *Lectura Dantis Mystica* (1969), notably by Mariano Welber, in 'Visio e Fictio nel *Comentum super Dantis Comoediam* di Benvenuto da Imola', pp. 188–226.
13 *ST*. 2a. 2ae. 175. 1, and see Mazzeo (1958), chap. IV, 'Dante and the Pauline Modes of Vision', pp. 84–110.
14 *De caelesti hierarchia* XIII, *PL*, 122, cols 1061–2.
15 *De mystica theologia* II *PL*, 122, cols 1173–4, tr. C. E. Rolt in *The Divine Names and the Mystical Theology*, pp. 193–4, 1940 edn.
16 *Scivias*, II, Visione II, *PL*, col. 499, and ibid., III, Visione I, cols 565–6. See Hildegard of Bingen (1954), plate II.
17 See Chapter 7, p. 98 and note 24.
18 Reeves (1976), pp. 65–6.
19 See the discussion of this image in Freccero (1964).
20 Jacopone da Todi (1953), LXXXI, l. 54, p. 335.
21 Nardi (1949), p. xiv.
22 In his *Creative Intuition in Art and Poetry*, Maritain (1954), pp. 370–400, writes of Dante's 'creative innocence', his phrase for the fact of poetic intuition taking shape in the inaccessible recesses of the soul, and of his 'luck' which 'had to do with the grace of God and the virtues of Dante the man, with centuries of culture and with a unique moment in time'.
23 See his 'The Mind in Love: Dante's Philosophy', reprinted in Freccero (1965), pp. 43–60, where, speaking of the focal point of all Dante's thought, 'which all turns

and converges upon an insight in the *causal nexus*, the relation between cause and effect', he says, on p. 60, 'The poet's eye saw making—*poesis*—everywhere: and this idea guided his particular expression of the Christian mystery.'

24 See the passage on Dante in Bucke (1972), pp. 116–22.

25 Guardini (1958), p. 15.

26 Barbi (1955), pp. 26–7.

27 There is a recent survey of Croce's thought in relation to Dante in Kirkpatrick (1978), pp. 8–15.

28 Curtius (1953), p. 14.

29 For an account of the *Inferno* in terms of oral deprivation, see Francesco Fornari, 'Fantasmi originari e teoria psicoanalitica dell'arte', in *Lectura Dantis Mystica* (1969), p. 113.

30 In his essay, 'Dostoevsky and Parricide' (1928), standard edn, ed. James Strachey, vol. 21 (1961), p. 177. See also Burnshaw (1970), p. 3, for the difference between Freud and Freudians on this point.

31 See the chaps '*Vita Nuova* e "inconscio personale" ' and 'Poema sacro e "inconscio collettivo" ' in Guidubaldi, *Dante Europeo*, III (1968), pp. 100–1.

32 For recent studies on the functions of the two cerebral hemispheres, see the articles by R. W. Sperry, Donald E. Broadbent, and G. Berlucchi, in Schmitt and Worden (1974). In writing this passage, I have also drawn on Robert E. Ornstein (1975), especially chap. 3, 'Two Sides of the Brain', pp. 49–73. There are interesting applications of these theories to the study of musical expression in Critchley and Henson (1977).

33 See Polanyi (1959) and (1967).

34 Ornstein (1975), pp. 65–7.

35 Evans-Wentz (1935), p. 242.

36 *Monumenta ordinis fratrum praedicatorum historica*, Vol. XX. *Acta capitulorum provinciae Romanae (1243–1344)*, ed. T. Kaeppli and A. Doudaine (Rome 1941), p. 286.

37 See Brieger, Meiss, and Singleton (1970).

38 In his sonnet 'Dal ciel discese'.

39 Monteverdi quotes the opening of *Inferno* III in his *Orfeo*, and one of his immediate predecessors, the composer and theorist Vincenzo Galilei, set the 'Lamento' of Count Ugolino (now lost). See Schrade (1951), pp. 38–46.

40 *Par.* XII. 124.

41 *VN* XIV.

42 Eckhart (1941), pp. 207–9.

43 Auerbach (1961), p. 60.

44 See the poem 'Beatrice and Dante', in Graves (1972), p. 50, where he speaks of Beatrice frowning at the way Dante imposed on her love and beat out a new world in her image 'For his own deathless glory'.

45 *Par.* XXVI. 55–66.

Appendix   Ovid, Lucan, Statius, and Virgil

1 *Metam.* I. 5–20.

2 *Inf.* XXV. 94–9.

3 See note 16 to Chapter 14.

4 *Inf.* IX. 22–7.
5 *Phars.* VI. 507–830.
6 *Epist.* VII. 4.
7 *Inf.* XXVIII. 94–9.
8 *Conv.* IV. xxviii. 15.
9 This point is made by Renucci (1954), p. 297.
10 *Phars.* IX. 601–4.
11 Auerbach (1959), p. 65.
12 *Purg.* XXII. 64–93.
13 Lewis (1936), p. 49.
14 *Thebaid*, XII. 481–505. This is suggested by J. H. Mozley in his introduction to the Loeb edition of Statius, vol. I, pp. xvi–xvii.
15 *Aen.* II. 610–12, tr. Cecil Day Lewis (London, 1952), p. 48.
16 *Aen.* I. 405.
17 *Inf.* I. 87.
18 *Aen.* I. 462, tr. Cecil Day Lewis (1952), p. 23.
19 *Par.* III. 85.
20 *Aen.* III. 508.
21 *Purg.* XVII. 12.
22 Ulrich Leo, pointing to the frequent references to Virgil in Book IV of the *Convivio*, maintains that it was a re-reading of Virgil during the composition of the *Convivio* that awoke Dante's visual imagination to the new intensity and precision he exhibited in the *Commedia*. This re-reading of Virgil made him abandon the *Convivio* and begin work on the *Commedia*. See Leo (1951). Though I agree that a re-reading of Virgil would certainly have had a profound influence on Dante's visual imagination, for the reasons given in Chapters 14 and 18, I think this effect was delayed until (1) he had understood the role Beatrice should play in the poem and (2) Virgil had appeared in his visual imagination as a character.
23 *Aen.* VIII. 22–5, tr. Cecil Day Lewis (1952), p. 166.

Bibliography

ALAN OF LILLE (1965), ed. M.-T. d'Alverny, *Textes inédits*, Paris.

ALFRAGANUS (1669), *Elementa Astronomica*, Amsterdam.

ALGHAZZALI (1901), 'On Music', tr. Duncan B. MacDonald, *Journal of the Royal Asiatic Society*, 66, London.

AMREIN-WIDMER, MARTHA (1932), *Rhythmus als Ausdruck inneren Erlebens in Dantes Divina Commedia*, Zurich.

ANDREW THE CHAPLAIN (1947), *Trattato d'Amore, Andreae Capellani regii Francorum de amore libri tres*, ed. Salvatore Battaglia, Rome.

ANGELA OF FOLIGNO (1927), *Le Livre de l'expérience des vrais fidèles*, ed. and tr. M.-J. Ferré and L. Baudry, Paris.

———— (1909), *The Book of Divine Consolation of Angela of Foligno*, tr. Mary G. Steegman, London.

ANONIMO FIORENTINO (1866–74), *Commento alla Divina Commedia d'anonimo fiorentino del secolo XIV*, ed. Pietro Fanfani, 3 vols, Bologna.

ARMSTRONG, EDWARD A. (1946), *Shakespeare's Imagination: a Study of the Psychology of Association and Inspiration*, London.

ARNAUT DANIEL (1960), *Canzoni*, ed. Gianluigi Toja, Florence.

AROUX, EUGÈNE (1854), *Dante, hérétique, révolutionnaire et socialiste: révélations d'un catholique sur le Moyen Age*, Paris.

ARTHOS, JOHN (1963), *Dante, Michaelangelo and Milton*, London.

ASÍN PALACIOS, MIGUEL (1926), *Islam and the Divine Comedy*, tr. Harold Sunderland, London.

AUERBACH, ERICH (1953), *Mimesis: the Representation of Reality in Western Literature*, Princeton.

————(1959), *Scenes from the Drama of European Literature*, tr. R. Manheim *et al.*, New York.

————(1961), *Dante, Poet of the Secular World*, tr. R. Manheim, Chicago.

————(1965), *Literary Language and its Public in Later Latin Antiquity and in the Middle Ages*, tr. R. Manheim, London.

————(1967), *Gesammelte Aufsätze zur Romanischen Philologie*, Berne and Munich.

BALDUCCI DI PEGOLOTTI, FRANCESCO (1936), *La Practica della mercatura*, ed. A. Evans, Cambridge, Mass.

460

Bibliography

BALTHASAR, HANS URS VON (1962), *Herrlichkeit: Band 2 Fächer der Stile*, Einsiedeln.

BAMBAGLIOLI, GRAZIOLO DE' (1892), *Il commento più antico e la più antica versione latina dell' Inferno di Dante*, ed. Antonio Fiammazzo, Udine.

BARBERINO, FRANCESCO DA (1905–27) *I Documenti d'Amore*, ed. Francesco Egidi, 4 vols, Rome.

BARBI, MICHELE (1953), *Dante: Vita, Opere e Fortuna*, Florence. Tr. Paul G. Ruggiers as *Life of Dante*, Berkeley and Los Angeles, 1954.

————(1955), *Problemi fondamentali per un nuovo commento della Divina Commedia*, Florence.

BARRACLOUGH, GEOFFREY (1938), ed. and tr., *Medieval Germany 911–1250; Essays by German Historians*, 2 vols, Oxford.

BECKER, MARVIN B. (1967), *Florence in Transition: Volume one; the Decline of the Commune*, Baltimore.

BENINI, RODOLFO (1952), *Dante tra gli splendori de' suoi enigmi risolti ed altri saggi*, Rome.

BENVENUTO DA IMOLA (1887), *Comentum super Dantis Aldigherij Comoediam*, ed. J. P. Lacaita, 5 vols, Florence.

BERENSON, BERNARD (1952), *The Italian Painters of the Renaissance*, 2nd edn, London.

BERGIN, THOMAS G. (1965), *An Approach to Dante*, London.

BERNARD OF CLUNY (1929) *De Contemptu Mundi*, ed. H. C. Hoskier, London.

BERNARD SYLVESTER (1876), *De Mundi Universitate*, ed. C. S. Barach and J. Wrobel, Innsbruck.

————(1973), *The 'Cosmographia' of Bernardus Silvestris*, tr. Winthrop Wetherbee, New York.

BILLANOVICH, G. (1947), *Prime Ricerche Dantesche*, Rome.

BIONDOLILLO, FRANCESCO (1948), *Poetica e Poesia di Dante*, Messina.

BOASE, T. S. R. (1933), *Boniface VIII*, London.

————(1972), *Death in the Middle Ages: Mortality, Judgment and Remembrance*, London.

BOCCACCIO, GIOVANNI (1918), *Il Comento alla Divina Commedia e gli altri scritti intorno a Dante*, ed. Domenico Guerri, 3 vols, Bari. (Appendix in 4th vol., 1926.)

————(1960), *Il Decamerone*, ed. Vittore Branca, 2 vols, Florence.

————(1965), *Esposizioni sopra la Commedia di Dante*, ed. Giorgio Padoan, Milan.

————(1965), *Opere in versi: Corbaccio: Trattatello in laude di Dante: Epistole*, ed. Pier Giorgio Ricci, Milan and Naples.

BONNER, ANTHONY (1973), ed. and tr., *Songs of the Troubadours*, London.

BONVESIN DA RIVA (1901), *Il Libro delle Tre Scritture e il Volgare delle Vanità*, ed. Vincenzo de Bartholomaeis, Rome.

BOSANQUET, B. (1912), *The Principle of Individuality and Value* (Gifford lectures for 1911), London.

BOSWELL, C. S. (1908), *An Irish Precursor of Dante: a Study on the Vision of Heaven and Hell, ascribed to the 8th century Saint Adamnan, with Translation of the Irish text*, London.

BOWRA, C. M. (1955), *Inspiration and Poetry*, London.

BOWSKY, W. M. (1960), *Henry VII in Italy: the Conflict of Empire and City-State, 1310–1313*, Lincoln, Nebraska.

BRANCA, VITTORE, and PADOAN, GIORGIO, eds (1967), *Dante e la cultura veneta*, Florence.

BRANDEIS, IRMA (1960), *The Ladder of Vision: a Study of Dante's Comedy*, London.

BRIEGER, P., MEISS, M., and SINGLETON, C. S. (1970), *Illuminated Manuscripts of the Divine Comedy*, 2 vols, London.

461

Bibliography

BROUGHTON, ROGER (1975), 'Biorhythmic Variations in Consciousness and Psychological Functions', *Canadian Psychological Review*, vol. 16, no. 4.

BRUNETTO LATINI (1948), *Li Livres dou Tresor de Brunetto Latini*, ed. F. J. Carmody, Berkeley and Los Angeles.

BRUYNE, EDGAR DE (1946), *Etudes d'ésthetique médiévale*, 3 vols, Bruges.

BUCKE, RICHARD MAURICE (1972), *Cosmic Consciousness: a Study in the Evolution of the Human Mind*, Philadelphia, 1905, reprint 1972.

BUNDY, M. W. (1927), 'The Theory of Imagination in Classical and Medieval Thought', *University of Illinois Studies in Language and Literature*, XII, pp. 183–472.

BURCHARD OF MOUNT SION (1896), *A Description of the Holy Land*, tr. Aubrey Stewart, Palestine Pilgrims Text Soc., XII.

BURCKHARDT, JACOB (1955), *The Civilisation of the Renaissance in Italy: an Essay*, tr. S. G. Middlemore, London, reprint.

BURCKHARDT, TITUS (1960), *Siena: the City of the Virgin*, tr. Margaret McDonough Brown, London.

BURNSHAW, STANLEY (1970), *The Seamless Webb*, London.

BUTI, FRANCESCO DA (1858–62), *Commento di Francesco da Buti*, ed. Crescentino Giannini, 3 vols, Pisa.

CAMPBELL, JOSEPH (1974), *The Masks of God: Creative Mythology*, London and New York.

CAPELLA, MARTIANUS (1969), *De Nuptiis Philologiae et Mercurii*, ed. Adolf Dick, Leipzig.

———(1977), *The Marriage of Philology and Mercury*, vol. II, *Martianus Capella and the Seven Liberal Arts*, tr. W. H. Stahl and R. Johnson with E. L. Burge, New York.

CARY, GEORGE (1956), *The Medieval Alexander*, ed. D. J. A. Ross, Cambridge.

CAVALCANTI, GUIDO (1957), *Rime*, ed. G. Favati, Milan and Naples.

CERULLI, ENRICO (1949), *Il Libro della Scala e la questione delle fonti Arabo-Spagnole della Divina Commedia*, Vatican City.

CEVA, BIANCA (1965), *Brunetto Latini: l'uomo e l'opera*, Milan and Naples.

CHARITY, A. C. (1966), *Events and their Afterlife: the Dialectics of Christian Typology in the Bible and Dante*, Cambridge.

CHASTEL, ANDRÉ (1954), *Marsil Ficin et l'Art*, Geneva and Lille.

CHIMENZ, S. A. (1960), 'Dante Alighieri', *Dizionario Biografico degli Italiani*, vol. 2, Rome.

CHYDENIUS, J. (1958), 'The Typological Problem in Dante: a Study in the History of Medieval Ideas', *Societas Scientiarum Fennica: Commentationes Humanorum Litterarum*, XXV 1, Helsingfors.

———(1966), 'The Theory of Medieval Symbolism', *Societas Scientiarum Fennica: Commentationes Humanorum Litterarum*, XXVI, 2, Helsingfors.

CIOTTI, ANDREA (1960), '*Alano e Dante*' *Convivium*, 28, pp. 257–88.

CIRLOT, J. E. (1971), *A Dictionary of Symbols*, tr. Jack Sage, 2nd edn, London.

CLARKE, EDWIN, and DEWHURST, KENNETH (1972), *An Illustrated History of Brain Function*, Oxford.

CLEMENTS, ROBERT J., ed. (1967), *American Critical Essays on the Divine Comedy*, New York and London.

COHN, NORMAN (1975), *Europe's Inner Demons: an Enquiry Inspired by the Great Witch-hunt*, London.

COLI, EDOARDO (1897), *Il Paradiso Terrestre Dantesco*, Florence.

Bibliography

COLLIN, RODNEY (1956), *The Theory of Eternal Life*, London.

COLLINGWOOD, R. G. (1946), *The Idea of History*, Oxford.

COMPER, FRANCES M. (1917), ed. and tr., *The Book of the Craft of Dying, and other Early English Tracts concerning Death*, London.

CONTINI, G., ed. (1960), *Poeti del Duecento*, 2 vols, Milan and Naples.

CORBIN, HENRY (1961), *Avicenna and the Visionary Recital*, tr. Willard R. Trask, London.

————(1970), *Creative Imagination in the Sufism of Ibn 'Arabi*, tr. R. Manheim, London.

COSMO, UMBERTO (1950), *A Handbook to Dante Studies*, tr. David Moore, Oxford.

CRITCHLEY, MACDONALD, and HENSON, R. A. (1977), *Music and the Brain: Studies in the Neurology of Music*, London.

CROMBIE, A. C. (1953), *Robert Grosseteste and the Origins of Experimental Science, 1100–1170*, Oxford.

————(1956), *From Augustine to Galileo: the History of Science, A.D. 400–1650*, London.

CURTIUS, ERNST ROBERT (1953), *European Literature and the Later Middle Ages*, tr. Willard R. Trask, New York.

CURZON, HENRI DE (1886), *La Règle des Templiers*, Paris.

DAVIDSOHN, ROBERT (1896–1927), *Geschichte von Florenz*, 4 vols, Berlin.

DAVIS, CHARLES TILL (1957), *The Idea of Rome*, Oxford.

————(1960), 'An Early Florentine Political Theorist', *Proceedings of the American Philosophical Society*, CIV.

————(1965), 'Education in Dante's Florence', *Speculum*, XL.

————(1974), 'Ptolemy of Lucca and the Roman Republic', *Proceedings of the American Philosophical Society*, CXVIII, no. 1.

————(1975), 'Dante's vision of history', *Dante studies*, XCIII.

DEMARAY, JOHN G. (1974), *The Invention of Dante's Commedia*, New Haven and London.

D'ENTRÈVES, A. P. (1952), *Dante as a Political Thinker*, Oxford.

DE ROBERTIS, DOMENICO (1961), *Il Libro della 'Vita Nuova'*, Florence.

DE SANCTIS, FRANCESCO (1945), *Storia della Letteratura italiana*, ed. B. Croce, Milan.

————(1957), *De Sanctis on Dante*, essays ed. and tr. Joseph Rossi and Alfred Galpin, Madison.

DHALLA, MANECKJI NUSSERVANJI (1938), *History of Zoroastrianism*, New York.

DRONKE, E. P. (1965), 'L'amor che muove il sole e l'altre stelle', *Studi medievali*, 6, pp. 384–422.

————(1968), *The Medieval Lyric*, London.

————(1968), *Medieval Latin and the Rise of the European Love Lyric*, 2nd edn, 2 vols, Oxford.

————(1968), 'Boethius, Alanus and Dante', *Romanische Forschungen*, 78, pp. 119–25.

————(1972), *Poetic Individuality*, Oxford.

DRYDEN, JOHN (1962), *Of Dramatic Poesy and Other Critical Essays*, ed. G. Watson, 2 vols, London.

DUBOIS, PIERRE (1891), *De recuperatione Terre Sancte*, ed. C. V. Langlois, Paris.

DUHEM, PIERRE (1913–59), *Le Système du Monde: histoire des doctrines cosmologiques de Platon à Copernic*, 10 vols, Paris.

DUNBAR, H. FLANDERS (1929), *Symbolism in Medieval Thought and its Consummation in the Divine Comedy*, New Haven, Conn.

DUPUY, PIERRE (1654), *Traittez concernant l'Histoire de France: Sçavoir la Condamnation des Templiers*, etc., Paris.

Bibliography

DURANDUS, GUGLIELMUS, Bishop of Mende (1592), *Rationale Divinorum Officiorum*, Lyons.

ECKHART, MEISTER (1941), *Meister Eckhart: a Modern Translation*, tr. R. P. Blakney, New York.

EGIDI, FRANCESCO (1902), 'Le Miniature dei Codici Barberiniani dei "Documenti d'Amore" ', *Arte*, V, pp. 1–20 and 78–95.

ELIOT, T. S. (1929), *Dante*, London.

————(1944), *The Four Quartets*, London.

Enciclopedia Dantesca (1970–6), ed. Umberto Bosco, 5 vols, Rome.

EVANS-WENTZ, W. Y. (1935), *Tibetan Yoga and Secret Doctrines*, London.

————(1949), *The Tibetan Book of the Dead*, 2nd edn, Oxford.

FARAL, E. (1956), *Les Arts Poétiques du XIIe et du XIIe siècles*, Paris, 1924, reprint 1956.

FERGUSON, JOHN (1970), *The Religions of the Roman Empire*, London.

FERGUSSON, FRANCIS (1953), *Dante's Drama of the Mind: a Modern Reading of the Purgatorio*, Princeton.

————(1966), *Dante*, London.

FETELLUS (1892), *Description of Jerusalem and the Holy Land*, tr. J. R. Macpherson, Palestine Pilgrims Text Soc., VIII.

FINKE, HEINRICH (1907), *Papstum und Untergang des Templerordens*, 2 vols, Münster.

FLETCHER, JEFFERSON B. (1921), *Symbolism of the Divine Comedy*, New York.

FOSCOLO, UGO (1825), *Discorso sul Testo e su le opinioni diverse prevalenti intorno alla storia e alla emendazione critica della Commedia di Dante*, London.

FOSTER, KENELM, O. P. (1959), *The Life of Saint Thomas Aquinas: Biographical Documents*, London.

————(1977), *The Two Dantes, and Other Studies*, London.

FOWLER, ALASTAIR, ed. (1970), *Silent Poetry: Essays in Numerological Analysis*, London.

FRECCERO, JOHN (1959), 'Dante's Firm Foot', *Harvard Theological Review*, LIII, pp. 245–81.

————(1961), 'Dante's Pilgrim in a Gyre', *Publications of the Modern Language Association*, 76, pp. 168–81.

————(1964), 'The Final Image: *Paradiso* XXXIII 144', *Modern Language Notes*, 79, pp. 14–27.

———— ed. (1965), *Dante: a Collection of Critical Essays*, New Jersey.

FUBINI, M. (1962), *Metrica e poesia—Lezioni sulle forme metriche italiane: i. Dal 200 al Petrarca*, Milan.

FULGENTIUS, F. B. (1898), *Opera*, ed. R. Helm, Leipzig.

GARDNER, EDMUND G. (1913), *Dante and the Mystics*, London.

————(1920), *The Story of Florence*, London.

GHYKA, MATILA C. (1952), *Le nombre d'or: rites et rhythmes pythagoriciens dans le dévéloppement de la civilisation occidentale*, vol. 1, *Les Rhythmes*, vol. 2, *Les Rites*, Paris.

GIANNANTONIO, POMPEO (1969), *Dante e l'allegorismo*, Florence.

GILCHRIST, ALEXANDER (1880), *Life of William Blake*, 2 vols, London.

GILLE, B. (1966), *The Renaissance Engineers*, London.

GILSON, ÉTIENNE (1940), *The Mystical Theology of Saint Bernard*, tr. A. H. C. Downes, London.

————(1952), *Dante the Philosopher*, tr. D. Moore, London.

GRANT, EDWARD, ed. (1974), *A Sourcebook in Medieval Science*, Cambridge, Mass.

GRAVES, ROBERT (1972), *Poems 1970–1972*, London.

Bibliography

GREGORY, TULLIO (1958), *Platonismo medievale: studi e richerche*, Rome.

GRUNEBAUM, G. E. VON, and CAILLOIS, ROGER, eds (1966), *The Dream and Human Societies*, Berkeley and Los Angeles.

GUARDINI, ROMANO (1951), *Der Engel in Dantes Göttlicher Komödie*, Munich.

————(1958), *Landschaft der Ewigkeit*, Munich.

GUÉNON, RENÉ (1925), *L'Ésotérisme de Dante*, Paris.

GUIBERTEAU, PHILIPPE (1973), *L'Énigme de Dante*, Paris.

GUIDO DA PISA (1974), *Commentary on Dante's Inferno*, ed. Vincenzo Cioffari, New York.

GUIDUBALDI, EGIDIO (1965, 1966, 1968), *Dante Europeo I: Premesse metodologiche e cornice culturale; Dante Europeo II: il Paradiso come universo di luce; Dante Europeo III: Poema sacro come esperienza mistica*, Florence.

HACKEL, SERGEI (1975), *The Poet and the Revolution: Alexsandr Blok's 'The Twelve'*, Oxford.

HAHN, H. (1961), *Hohenstaufenburgen in Süditalien*, Munich.

HAMMOND, J. L. (1938), *Gladstone and the Irish Nation*, London.

HARDIE, C. G. (1960), 'Dante's "Canzone Montanina" ', *MLR*, LV, pp. 359–70.

————(1960), 'The Epistle to Can Grande Again', *DDJ*, 38, pp. 51–74.

HASKINS, CHARLES H. (1927), *Studies in the History of Medieval Science*, Cambridge, Mass.

HENDERSON, GEORGE (1967), *Gothic*, Harmondsworth.

HILDEGARD of BINGEN (1954), *Wisse die Wege: Scivias*, ed. and tr. Maura Bočkler, Salzburg.

HILLGARTH, J. N. (1971), *Ramon Lull and Lullism in fourteenth century France*, Oxford.

HOLBROOK, RICHARD THAYER (1902), *Dante and the Animal Kingdom*, New York.

HOLLANDER, ROBERT (1969), *Allegory in Dante's Commedia*, Princeton.

HOPPER, VINCENT FOSTER (1938), *Medieval Number Symbolism: its Sources, Meaning and Influence on Thought and Expression*, New York.

HUART, CLAUDE (1918–22), *Les Saints des Derviches Tourneurs*, 2 vols, Paris.

HUGH OF ST-VICTOR (1939), *Didascalicon*, ed. Charles H. Buttimer, Washington.

————(1961), *The Didascalicon of Hugh of St. Victor*, tr. Jerome Taylor, New York.

————(1962), *Hugh of Saint-Victor: Selected Spiritual Writings*, tr. by a Religious of C.S.M.W. with an introduction by Aelred Squire, London.

HYDE, J. K. (1973), *Society and Politics in Medieval Italy: the Evolution of the Civil Life, 1000–1350*, London.

IMMANUEL BEN SOLOMON (1921), *Tophet and Eden (Hell and Paradise) in Imitation of Dante's Inferno and Paradiso*, tr. Hermann Gollancz, London.

JACOBUS DE VORAGINE (1846), *Legenda aurea*, ed. T. Graesse, Dresden and Leipzig.

JACOPONE DA TODI (1953), *Laudi, Trattato, e Detti*, ed. F. Ageno, Florence.

JENARO-MACLENNAN, L. (1974), *The Trecento Commentaries on the Divina Commedia and the Epistle to Can Grande*, Oxford.

JOHN, ROBERT (1946), *Dante*, Vienna.

————(1959), *Dante und Michelangelo: das Paradiso Terrestre und die Sixtinische Decke*, Krefeld.

JONES, P. J. (1965), 'Communes and Despots: the City State in Late-Medieval Italy', *Transactions of the Royal Historical Society*, V, 15, pp. 71–96.

KADLOUBOVSKY, E. and PALMER, G. E. H., tr. (1951), *Writings from the Philokalia on Prayer of the Heart*, London.

KANTOROWICZ, ERNST H. (1951), 'Dante's "Two Suns" ', *Semitic and Oriental Studies*

Bibliography

Presented to William Popper, ed. Walter J. Fischel, in University of California Publications in Semitic Philology, XI, pp. 217–31.

————(1957), *The King's Two Bodies: a Study in Mediaeval Political Theology*, Princeton.

KASKE, R. E. (1961), 'Dante's "DXV" and "Veltro" ', *Traditio*, XVII, pp. 185–254.

KEYNES, SIR GEOFFREY (1971), *Blake Studies: Essays on his Life and Work*, 2nd edn, Oxford.

KIRKPATRICK, ROBIN (1978), *Dante's* Paradiso *and the Limitations of Modern Criticism*, Cambridge.

KLIBANSKY, RAYMOND (1939), *The Continuity of the Platonic Tradition during the Middle Ages*, London.

KLINE, MORRIS (1964), *Mathematics in Western Culture*, New York.

KOESTLER, ARTHUR (1945), *The Yogi and the Commissar*, London.

————(1964), *The Act of Creation*, London.

KRISTELLER, PAUL OSKAR (1943), *The Philosophy of Marsilio Ficino*, tr. Virginia Conant, New York.

KUHN, THOMAS (1957), *The Copernican Revolution: Planetary Astronomy in the Development of Western Thought*, Cambridge, Mass.

LANA, JACOPO DELLA (1866), *Comedia di Dante degli Allagherii col commento di Jacopo della Lana bolognese*, ed. Luciano Scarabelli, 3 vols, Bologna.

LANCIA, ANDREA (1827–9), *L'Ottimo Commento della Divina Commedia: testo inedito d'un contemporaneo di Dante*, ed. A. Torri, 3 vols, Pisa.

LAVAUD, R., and NELLI, R., eds (1966), *Les Troubadours*, vol. II: *Le trésor poétique de l'Occitanie*, Paris.

Lectura Dantis Mystica: il Poema Sacro alla luce delle conquiste psicologhiche odierne. Atti della Settimana Dantesca 28 luglio–3 agosto 1968 (1969), Florence.

LEIGH, GERTRUDE (1929), *New Light on the Youth of Dante*, London.

————(1932), *The Passing of Beatrice: a Study in the Heterodoxy of Dante*, London.

LENKEITH, NANCY (1952), *Dante and the Legend of Rome: an Essay*, London.

LEO, ULRICH (1951), 'The Unfinished *Convivio* and Dante's Re-reading of the Aeneid', *Medieval Studies*, Toronto, XII, pp. 41–64.

LEWIS, C. S. (1936), *The Allegory of Love*, Oxford.

————(1964), *The Discarded Image*, Cambridge.

————(1966), *Of Other Worlds*, London.

LIMENTANI, U., ed. (1965), *The Mind of Dante*, Cambridge.

LIZERAND, GEORGES (1910), *Clément V et Philippe IV le Bel*, Paris.

————(1923), *Le Dossier de l'affaire des Templiers*, Paris.

LOWES, JOHN LIVINGSTONE (1955), *The Road to Xanadu: a Study in the Ways of the Imagination*, Boston, 1927, reprint 1955.

LUBAC, HENRI DE (1959–64), *Exégèse médiévale: les quatre sens de l'écriture*, 4 vols, Paris.

LUBIN, ANTONIO (1881), *Commedia di Dante Alighieri preceduta dalla vita e da studi preparatori illustrativi*, Padua.

MACROBIUS (1963), *Saturnalia & Commentariorum in somnium Scipionis*, ed. J. Willis, Leipzig.

————(1966), *Commentary on the Dream of Scipio*, tr. W. H. Stahl, New York.

MALAGOLI, LUIGI (1960), *Linguaggio e Poesia nella Divina Commedia*, 2nd edn, Pisa.

————(1962), *Saggio sulla Divina Commedia*, Florence.

MÂLE, ÉMILE (1913), *Religious Art in France: XIIIth century*, tr. Dora Nussey, London.

MANDELSTAM, OSIP (1971), *Sobranie sochinenii*, ed. G. P. Struve and B. A. Filippoff, vol. 2, New York.

MANDONNET, PIERRE (1935), *Dante le Théologien*, Paris.

MANN, HORACE K. (1902–32), *The Lives of the Popes in the Middle Ages*, London.

MARCABRU (1909), *Poésies complètes du troubadour Marcabru*, ed. J.-M.-L. Dejeanne, Toulouse.

MARITAIN, JACQUES (1930), *Art and Scholasticism*, tr. J. F. Scanlan, London.

————(1942), *St. Thomas Aquinas: Angel of the Schools*, tr. J. F. Scanlan, London.

————(1954), *Creative Intuition in Art and Poetry*, London.

MARTI, MARIO, ed. (1969), *Poeti del Dolce stil nuovo*, Florence.

MAZZEO, JOSEPH ANTHONY (1958), *Structure and Thought in the Paradiso*, Ithaca, NY.

MAZZONI, F. (1955), 'L'Epistola a Cangrande', *Rendiconti dell'Accademia Nazionale dei Lincei*, X, pp. 157–98.

MICHELET, J. (1841–51), *Le Procès des Templiers*, 2 vols, Paris.

MOLLAT, G. (1950), *Les Papes d'Avignon (1305–1378)*, 9th edn, Paris.

MONTANARI, FAUSTO (1968), *L'esperienza poetica di Dante*, 2nd edn, Florence.

MUIR, EDWIN (1972), *An Autobiography*, London.

MUNDY, JOHN H. (1973), *Europe in the High Middle Ages 1150–1309*, London.

NAPIER, HENRY EDWARD (1846–7), *Florentine History*, 6 vols, London.

NARDI, BRUNO (1944), *Nel mondo di Dante*, Rome.

————(1949), *Dante e la cultura medievale: nuovi saggi di filosofia dantesca*, 2nd edn, Bari.

————(1959), 'L'amore e i medici medievali', *Studi in onore di Angelo Monteverdi*, vol. II, Modena, pp. 517–42.

————(1960), *Dal Convivio alla Commedia*, Rome.

————(1960), 'Il Punto sull'Epistola a Cangrande', *Lectura Dantis Scaligera*, Florence.

NASR, SEYYED HOSSEIN (1968), *Science and Civilisation in Islam*, Cambridge, Mass.

NATHAN, PETER (1969), *The Nervous System*, Harmondsworth.

OLIVER, H. P. H. (1969), *The Way of Discovery* (Nuffield chemistry background book), Harlow and Harmondsworth.

OLIVERO, FEDERICO (1936), *The Representation of the Image in Dante*, Turin.

OLSCHKI, LEONARDO (1949), *The Myth of Felt*, Berkeley and Los Angeles.

ORDERICUS VITALIS (1968–75), *The Ecclesiastical History of Orderic Vitalis*, ed. Marjorie Chibnall, 5 vols, Oxford.

ORNSTEIN, ROBERT E. (1975), *The Psychology of Consciousness*, London.

OROSIUS, PAULUS (1936), *Seven Books of History against the Pagans*, tr. I. W. Raymond, New York.

ORR, M. A. (1956), *Dante and the Early Astronomers*, London, 1914, reprint 1956.

OSTLENDER, H. (1948), 'Dante und Hildegard von Bingen', *DDJ*, 27, pp. 166 ff.

OTTO OF FREISING and RAHEWIN (1953), *The Deeds of Frederick Barbarossa*, tr. C. C. Mierow, New York.

OUSPENSKY, P. D. (1934), *A New Model of the Universe*, 2nd edn, London.

OXFORD DANTE SOCIETY, MEMBERS OF THE (1965), *Centenary Essays on Dante*, Oxford.

PALGEN, R. (1953), *Ursprung und Aufbau der Komödie Dantes*, Graz.

PAPANTI, GIOVANNI (1873), *Dante secondo la tradizione e i novellatori*, Leghorn.

PARRI, WALTER and TERESA (1956), *Anno del viaggio e giorno iniziale della Commedia*, Florence.

Bibliography

PASCOLI, GIOVANNI (1912), *Sotto il velame*, 2nd edn, Bologna.

PASSERINI, G. L., ed. (1917), *Le Vite di Dante scritte da Giovanni e Filippo Villani, da Giovanni Boccaccio, Leonardo Aretino e Gianozzo Manetti*, Florence.

———(1921), *Il ritratto di Dante*, Florence.

PASTERNAK, BORIS (1956), 'Notes on the Translation of Shakespeare's Tragedies', *Soviet Literature*, 7.

PATCH, HOWARD ROLLIN (1935), *The Tradition of Boethius*, New York.

———(1970), *The Other World*, New York.

PATTISON, W. T. (1952), *The Life and Works of the Troubadour Raimbaut d'Orange*, Minneapolis.

PÉZARD, ANDRÉ (1950), *Dante sous la pluie de feu*, Paris.

PIATTOLI, RENATO, ed. (1940), *Codice diplomatico dantesco*, Florence.

PIETRO ALIGHIERI (1845), *Super Dantis ipsius genitoris Comoediam commentarium*, ed. Vincenzio Nannucci, Florence.

PLUMPTRE, E. H. (1903), *The Life of Dante*, London.

POLANYI, MICHAEL (1959), *The Study of Man: the Lindsay Memorial Lectures, 1958*, London.

———(1967), *The Tacit Dimension*, London.

POSTAN, M. M., RICH, E. E., and MILLER, EDWARD, eds (1971), *The Cambridge Economic History of Europe. Vol. III. Economic Organization and Policies in the Middle Ages*, Cambridge.

POULET, G. (1961), *Les Métamorphoses du cercle*, Paris.

PRAZ, MARIO (1970), *Mnemosyne: the Parallel between Literature and the Visual Arts*, Oxford.

PROCACCI, G. (1973), *History of the Italian People*, tr. A. Paul, Harmondsworth.

RAGG, LONSDALE (1907), *Dante and his Italy*, London.

RAINE, KATHLEEN (1962), *Blake and Tradition*, 2 vols, Princeton.

———(1967), *Defending Ancient Springs*, Oxford.

RALPHS, STELLA (1959), *Etterno spiro*, Manchester.

———(1972), *Dante's Journey to the Centre*, Manchester.

RAYNAUD DE LAGE, GUY (1951), *Alain de Lille, poète du XIIe siècle*, Paris and Montreal.

REEVES, MARJORIE (1969), *The Influence of Prophecy in the Later Middle Ages: a Study in Joachism*, Oxford.

———(1976), *Joachim of Fiore and the Prophetic Future*, London.

———and HIRSCH-REICH, BEATRICE (1972), *The Figurae of Joachim of Fiore*, Oxford.

RENAUDET, AUGUSTIN (1952), *Dante Humaniste*, Paris.

RENOUARD, YVES (1969), *Les Villes d'Italie de la fin du Xe siècle au début du XIVe siècle*, ed. P. Braunstein, 2 vols, Paris.

RENUCCI, PAUL (1954), *Dante disciple et juge du monde gréco-latin*, Paris.

RICCI, CORRADO (1921), *L'ultimo rifugio di Dante*, 2nd edn, Milan.

RICE, CYPRIAN (1964), *The Persian Sufis*, London.

RICHARD OF ST VICTOR (1957), *Selected Writings on Contemplation*, tr. Clare Kirchberger, London.

RICHARDS, I. A. (1975), *Beyond*, London.

RICHARDSON, A. (1969), *Mental Imagery*, London.

RISTORO D'AREZZO (1864), *Della Composizione del Mondo*, Biblioteca rara vol. LIV, Milan.

Bibliography

ROE, ALBERT S. (1953), *Blake's Illustrations to the Divine Comedy*, Princeton.

ROSSETTI, GABRIELE (1834), *Disquisitions on the Antipapal Spirit which produced the Reformation; its secret influence on the literature of Europe in general and of Italy in particular*, tr. Miss Caroline Ward, 2 vols, London.

————— (1840), *Il Mistero dell'Amor Platonico*, 5 vols, London.

————— (1842), *La Beatrice di Dante: ragionamenti critici*, London.

RUBINSTEIN, NICOLAI (1942), 'The Beginnings of Political Thought in Florence', *Journal of the Warburg and Courtauld Institutes*, V.

————— ed. (1968), *Florentine Studies: Politics and Society in Renaissance Florence*, London.

RÛMÎ, JALÂL AL-DÎN (1926–34), *The Mathnawi of Jalalu'ddin Rūmi*, tr. Reynolds Nicholson, 6 vols, London.

RUNCIMAN, STEVEN (1960), *The Sicilian Vespers: a History of the Mediterranean World in the Later Thirteenth Century*, Harmondsworth.

SAINTSBURY, GEORGE (1900–4), *A History of Criticism and Literary Taste in Europe*, 3 vols, Edinburgh and London.

SALIMBENE (1905–13), 'Cronica Fratris Salimbene de Adam Ordinis Minorum', ed. O. Holder-Eggar, *MGH SS XXXII*.

SANTAYANA, GEORGE (1910), *Three Philosophical Poets: Lucretius, Dante and Goethe*, Cambridge, Mass.

SANUTO, MARINO (1896), *Secrets for True Crusaders to Help Them Recover the Holy Land*, tr. Aubrey Stewart, Palestine Pilgrims Text Soc., XII.

SARTRE, JEAN-PAUL (1966), *The Psychology of Imagination*, New York.

SAYERS, DOROTHY L. (1954), *Introductory Papers on Dante*, London.

————— (1957), *Further Papers on Dante*, London.

SCHMITT, FRANCIS O., and WORDEN, FREDERIC G., eds (1974), *The Neurosciences: Third Study Program*, Cambridge, Mass., and London.

SCHÖKEL, LUIS ALONSO (1967), *The Inspired Word: Scripture in the Light of Language and Literature*, tr. Francis Martin, London.

SCHRADE, LEO (1951), *Monteverdi: Creator of Modern Music*, London.

SCIAMA, D. W. (1971), *Modern Cosmology*, Cambridge.

SERRAVALLE, GIOVANNI DA (1891), *Translatio et Comentum totius libri Dantis Aldigherii*, ed. Marcellino da Civezza, O. M., and Teofilo Domenichelli, O. M., Prato.

SEZNEC, JEAN (1972), *The Survival of the Pagan Gods: the Mythological Tradition and its Place in Renaissance Humanism and Art*, tr. Barbara F. Sessions, Princeton.

SHANKLAND, HUGH (1975), 'Dante "Aliger"', *MLR* 70, pp. 764–85.

————— (1977), 'Dante Aliger and Ulysses,' *Italian Studies* XXXII, pp. 21–40.

SILVERSTEIN, THEODORE (1948–9), 'The Fabulous Cosmogony of Bernardus Silvestris', *Modern Philology*, 46, pp. 92–116.

SINGER, CHARLES (1928), *From Magic to Science: Essays on the Scientific Twilight*, London.

SINGLETON, CHARLES S. (1949), *An Essay on the Vita Nuova*, Cambridge, Mass.

————— (1954), *Dante Studies I: Commedia, Elements of Structure*, Cambridge, Mass.

————— (1958), *Dante Studies II: Journey to Beatrice*, Cambridge, Mass.

SMALLEY, BERYL (1952), *The Study of the Bible in the Middle Ages*, 2nd edn, Oxford.

SOLOVYOV, VLADIMIR (1915), *Stikhotvoreniya*, Moscow.

SPOERRI, THEOPHIL (1966), *Introduzione alla Divina Commedia*, tr. Marco Cerruti, Milan.

SPONDE, HENRI DE (1641), *Annalium Emin^{mi} Cardinalis Caes. Baronii Continuatio, ab anno MCXCVII quo is desiit ad finem MDCXL*, 3 vols, Paris.

Bibliography

STATIUS (1928), *Opera*, ed. and tr. J. H. Mozley, London and New York.

STEINEN, WOLFRAM VON DEN (1966), 'Les Sujets d'inspiration chez les poètes latins du XII siècle', *Cahiers de civilisation médiévale*, 9, pp. 165–75, 363–83.

SUGER (1929), *Vie de Louis VI le Gros*, ed. and tr. Henri Waquet, Paris.

———— (1946), *Abbot Suger on the Abbey Church of St. Denis and Its Art Treasures*, ed., tr. and annotated Erwin Panofsky, Princeton.

TEILHARD DE CHARDIN, PIERRE (1965), *Écrits du temps de la Guerre (1916–1919)*, Paris.

THORNDIKE, LYNN (1923–58), *A History of Magic and Experimental Science*, 8 vols, New York.

TOPSFIELD, L. T. (1975), *The Troubadours and Love*, Cambridge.

TOYNBEE, PAGET (1968), *A Dictionary of Proper Names and Notable Matters in the Works of Dante*, revised Charles S. Singleton, Oxford.

TRINKAUS, CHARLES (1970), '*In our Image and Likeness*': *Humanity and Divinity in Italian Humanist Thought*, 2 vols, London.

TRYPANIS, C. A. (1950), 'Dante and a Byzantine Treatise on Virtues and Vices', *Medium Aevum*, XIX, pp. 43–9.

UBERTINO DA CASALE (1485), *Arbor Vite Crucifixe Jesu*, Venice.

UNDERHILL, EVELYN (1975), *The Mystics of the Church*, Cambridge, 1925, reprint 1975.

VALENCY, MAURICE (1961), *In Praise of Love: an Introduction to the Love-poetry of the Renaissance*, New York.

VALLI, LUIGI (1922a), *L'Allegoria di Dante secondo Giovanni Pascoli*, Bologna.

———— (1922b) *Il segreto della Croce e dell'Aquila nella Divina Commedia*, Bologna.

———— (1928), *Il linguaggio segreto di Dante e dei fedeli d'amore*, Rome.

VALLONE, ALDO (1953), *La Critica Dantesca contemporanea*, Pisa.

———— (1971), *Dante*, Milan.

VAN CLEVE, THOMAS CURTIS (1972), *The Emperor Frederick II of Hohenstaufen: Immutator Mundi*, Oxford.

VERE-HODGE, H. S., intr. and tr. (1963), *The Odes of Dante*, Oxford.

VERNANI, GUIDO (1938), *De reprobatione monarchiae composita a Dante*, ed. Thomas Käppeli in 'Der Dantegegner Guido Vernani O. P. von Rimini', *Quellen und Forschungen aus italienischen Archiven und Bibliotheken*, XXVIII, pp. 107–46.

VERONA, COMMUNE DI (1965), *Dante e Verona per il VII centenario della nascita*, Verona.

VILLANI, FILIPPO (1896), *Il Comento al primo canto dell'Inferno*, ed. Giuseppe Cugnoni, Città di Castello.

VILLARI, PASQUALE (1908), *The Two First Centuries of Florentine History: the Republic and Parties at the Time of Dante*, tr. Linda Villari, London.

VOSSLER, KARL (1929), *Medieval Culture: an Introduction to Dante and his Times*, tr. W. C. Lawton, 2 vols, London.

VYVYAN, JOHN (1961), *Shakespeare and Platonic Beauty*, London.

WALEY, DANIEL (1969), *The Italian City-republics*, London.

WARNER, MARINA (1976), *Alone of all her Sex: the Myth and the Cult of the Virgin Mary*, London.

WEDEL, THEODORE OTTO (1920), *The Mediaeval Attitude toward Astrology*, Yale Studies in English LX, New Haven.

WETHERBEE, WINTHROP (1972), *Platonism and Poetry in the Twelfth Century: the Literary Influence of the School of Chartres*, Princeton.

Bibliography

WHITE, LYNN H. (1968), *Dynamo and Virgin Reconsidered* (originally published under the title *Machina ex deo*), Cambridge, Mass.

WICKSTEED, PHILIP H., and GARDNER, EDMUND G. (1902), *Dante and Giovanni del Virgilio*, London.

————(1913), *Dante and Aquinas*, London.

WILKINS, ERNEST HATCH (1961), *Life of Petrarch*, Chicago.

———— and BERGIN, THOMAS GODDARD (1965), *A Concordance to the Divine Comedy of Dante Alighieri*, Cambridge, Mass.

WILLIAMS, CHARLES (1943), *The Figure of Beatrice*, London.

WILSON, IAN (1978), *The Turin Shroud*, London.

WIND, EDGAR (1958), *Pagan Mysteries in the Renaissance*, London.

WINGFIELD DIGBY, GEORGE (1957), *Symbol and Image in William Blake*, Oxford.

WITTE, KARL (1879), *Dante – Forschungen*, 2 vols, Heilbronn.

WOLFRAM VON ESCHENBACH (1854), *Parzival*, ed. Karl Lachmann, Berlin.

YATES, F. A. (1966), *The Art of Memory*, London.

————(1975), *Astraea: the Imperial Theme in the Sixteenth Century*, London.

YEATS, W. B. (1961), *Essays and Introductions*, London.

————(1962), *A Vision*, London.

ZINGARELLI, NICOLA (1931), *La Vita, i Tempi, e le Opere di Dante*, 2 vols, Milan.

Index

472

Index

Bologna, 70, 77, 102, 160, 163, 177, 211, 239, 411

Bonagiunta da Lucca, 17, 89, 101, 102, 177; in *Purg.*, 261, 299, 302

Bonaventura da Siena, 277

Bonaventure, St, 47, 50, 58, 81, 116, 122, 191, 282, 320, 413; and fourfold method, 330, 345; in *Par.*, 47, 48, 268, 320, 384; Works, *see Itinerarium mentis*; *De reductione artium*

Boniface VIII, Pope (Benedetto Caetani): attempt of Anagni and his death, 158–9; 'Blacks' of Florence and Corso Donati, relations with, 148–9, 154, 155–7; bulls of, *see under Clericis Laicos* and *Unam Sanctam*; and Caetani family, 63, 147, 151; and Celestine V, 146–7, 150–1, 158; character of, 147; and Charles of Valois and his plans for Sicily and Florence, 146, 155–6; Church and his claims for temporal power, 41; in *Commedia*, 159, 227, 271, 363, 394–6; D. and, 81, 147, 159, 227, 237, 373, 439 n. 6; D.'s embassy to, 156; diplomatic and business experience, 147; and Florence, 147–8, 149, 151, 154, 155, 223; Geryon, suggested identification with, 363; Jubilee of 1300, 152; Philip the Fair, quarrels with, 147, 158–9; portraits of, 51, 147; posthumous charges against, 162–3, 210, 226, 363, 365–6, 439 n. 7; superstition of, 46

Bonvesin da Riva, 276–7

Borgo San Donnino, Gerardo di, 49

Born, Bertran de, 94–5, 390

Bornelh, Guiraut de, 99

Botticelli, Sandro, 367, 411

Bowra, Sir Maurice, 100

brain, hemispheres of, 15, 16, 17, 302, 409–11

Brescia, 177, 212

Brown, George Mackay, quoted, 431 n. 1

Brunelleschi, Betto, 83, 168

Bruni, Lionardo: his life of D. quoted and referred to, 4, 59, 79, 157, 159, 161, 212, 232, 435 n. 11

Bruno, Giordano, 403

Brutus, 253, 381

Bucke, Richard Maurice, 295, 373–4, 408

Buondelmonte dei Buondelmonti, murder of, 33–4, 269

Burckhardt, Jacob, 125

Buti, Francesco da, 362

Butrinto, Nicholas of, 213

Byzantium, 23, 24–5, 290, 363, 374, 375; sacred dances of, 377

Cabala, 331

Cacciaguida: ancestor of D., 29, 53; as

character synthesizing types of Wounded Man, Man of Experience, and Old Man, 390–1; crusader, 29; in *Par.*, 29, 34, 53, 236, 237, 268–9, 284, 349, 384, 386, 390–1

Caesar, Julius, 21, 198, 418, 419; in *Commedia*, 248, 381, 419

Caetani family (*see also* Boniface VIII), 63, 148

Caetani, Roffred, 151

Caiaphas, 342

Calahorra (Calaroga), 48

Calboli, Rinieri de' Paolucci da, 258

Calliope, Muse of epic poetry, 255, 328

Callippus, 103

Caltabellotta, treaty of, 158

Camaldoli, 24

Camilla, 248

Cammino, Gherardo da, despot of Treviso, 62, 198

Campaldino, battle of, 46, 64, 78–9, 148, 154, 211, 256

Campbell, Joseph, 382; quoted, 456 n. 7

Cancellieri family of Pistoia, 148

Can Grande della Scala, *see* Scala

Canossa, 28

Canterbury Tales (Chaucer), 383

canzone form: D.'s love and employment of, 93, 121–4, 166, 167–8, 174, 182–3, 202; its musical origins, 93, 117, 121; technical impasse imposed on D. by, 174, 182–3, 202, 388, 421; in *DVE*, 179–80, 182–3

Capella, Martianus, 116, 135, 326, 328

Capet, Hugh, 163, 260

Caprona, siege of, 80

Cardenal, Peire, 96

Carducci, Giosuè, 165

Carlyle, Thomas, 165; quoted, 441 n. 2

Carroccio, 36, 37, 39

Carthage, 288, 421

Casella, 7, 152, 255, 303, 306

Casentino, 79, 171, 176, 229, 230

Cassero, Jacopo del, 256

Cassino, Monte, 23

Cassius, 253, 381

Castello, Guido da, 198

Castiglione, Bernardo, 322

Castruccio Castracane, 234

Catherine of Siena, St, 74

Catiline, 21

Cato of Utica (*see also* Lucan; *Pharsalia*): in *Commedia*, 255, 303, 306, 328, 329, 342–4, 351, 375, 388, 391, 419–20; in *Conv.*, 207–8, 217, 221, 231, 388, 419; and liberty, political and moral, 217, 344, 391, 419–20; as second of six guides of *Commedia*, 321, 322, 342–4, 346, 372

Catullus, 92

Cavalcanti, de', Florentine family, 82–3, 163

476

Index

Index

X), 6, 346; D.'s originality in treatment of journey theme, 278–80; D.'s two classes of reader for, 347; dating of, 200, 212, 226, 228–32, 386; debate on whether based on invention (*fictio*) or experience (*visio*), 335, 406; as drama and comedy, 207, 337–8, 383–4; the elements, and imagery and cosmology of the poem (*see also* Elements), 352–60; form and numerology of, 111, 117, 232, 236, 280, 284–6, 369, 377, 384; fourfold allegory in, 246, 292, 329–45, 360–74; geometrical imagery in, 282–3, 407; Guelphs and Ghibellines in, 24, 381–2; importance and influence of, in European civilization, 3–4, 380, 383, 411–12; compared with Indian philosophy, 18, 339; influence of, on the arts, music, drama, and opera, 3–4, 380, 383, 411–12; and Islam, 25–6; John of Garland's annotations of Ovid as suggested basis of early draft, 232, 418; journeys and accounts of Afterlife that may have influenced it, 275–9; Andrea Lancia's report on his skill in rhyme, 232; language of, and 'lowly style', 387–8; mood, transformations of, 249, 251, 255, 263–4, 272, 383–4; noble pagans in, 248, 340–2, 383; pagan mythology in, 323, 418–23; prophecies in (*see also* DXV, *veltro*), 46, 235–6, 246, 263, 292–3, 338–40, 368–9; proto-*Commedia*, theory of, 200–1, 202–8, 228, 231–2, 315, 329; retribution and vengefulness in, 249–54, 380–2; and scientific and technological development of its period, 402; six guides of (*see also* Bonaventure; *Itinerarium mentis*; Contemplation), 285, 321–2; story and journey of, 245–72, 279–84; timing of journey and dispute over 1300 or 1301, 152–3, 281–2; topography and cosmology of, 274, 279–81, 352–3, 360–1, 403–4, 447 n. 26; truth of the poem independent of its cosmological setting, 404; visions and its inspiration, 11, 46, 152–3, 228, 296, 315; word play in, 32, 182, 267. Commentaries on: Jacopo Alighieri, 238, Pietro Alighieri, 238, 292, 293, 294, 344, 347, Benvenuto da Imola, 388, Francesco da Buti, 362, Guido da Pisa, 331, 339, 347, 364, 371, 373, Cristoforo Landino, 331, 347, 412, *Ottimo Commento*, 232. Illustrators of, and artists inspired by: Blake, 331, Botticelli, 367, 411, Doré, 412, Michelangelo, 412, Signorelli, 412

Convivio, Il (*Conv.*) (*see also* D. works: lyrics: 'Amor che ne la mente'; 'Le dolci rime'; 'Voi che 'ntendendo'): Al Ghazzali

and, 6; allegory in, 193–4, 329; apparition of red cross in Florence, 46; audience for, and D.'s civilizing mission, 186–7, 202, 369, 413; Beatrice in, 190, 193; clearing of D.'s name one of its objects, 186, 189; and *Commedia* (*see also* D. works: *Commedia*, proto-*Commedia*), 187, 193, 195, 197, 198, 200–1, 202–8, 221, 228, 232, 331, 369, 388; content of, 188–99; cosmology in, 105n, 190, 193–4, 195, 202–5, 274; dating of, 160, 201–2; and *Didascalicon*, 186; and *DVE*, 160, 166, 180–1, 202; exile, D.'s references to, in, 159, 189; as intellectual autobiography, 187; Florence, and D.'s attempts to return to, 186, 226; four ages of man and fourfold allegory, 207–8, 219, 388, 419; fourfold interpretation in, 191–3, 207–8, 336; imagery in, 189, 198, 202, 208, 374; Love (Amore) in, 175, 190, 194, 206; *Mon.*, connexions with, 200, 219; nature of, 186–7; nobility, theme of, in, 196–9; Philosophy, Lady (*donna gentile*), in, 131, 132, 150, 190, 194–6; political thought in, 196–7; quoted, 152, 159, 191–3, 197, 203–4, 205; reasons why D. did not finish, 200, 228, 386; reconstruction by F. Montanari of how it might have continued, 199–200; riches, condemnation of, in, 198; and Rome, 152, 196–7, 198; D.'s scientific studies, evidence of, in, 202–4; and social ideals of *dolce stil nuovo*, 82; the soul, three motions of, in, 282; structure of, 186, 188–9, 190, 195, 196, 200; and vernacular, 166, 180, 186–7, 189; *VN*, connexions with, 132, 189, 190, 201, 206

De situ et forma aque et terre, 239

De vulgari eloquentia (*DVE*): Arthur, 91; D.'s attitude to art revealed in, 175, 183–5; audience of the work and D.'s ideal of civilization, 180, 369, 387, 413; *canzone* form discussed in, 121, 179, 180; and *Commedia*, 181–2, 228, 369, 387, 388; contents, 175–80; and *Conv.*, 180–1, 202; dating, 160, 202, 441 n. 16; imagery in, 179–80, 183, 202; importance of, in history of criticism and study of language, 175–6, 442 n. 17; inspiration, discussed in, 178, 183–5; language, and study of, 178; moral instruction, as work of, 175; poets' and scholars' attitudes to, 175, 441–2 nn. 16 and 17; poets, troubadours, Sicilian and Italian, in, 88, 101, 169, 176; quotations from, 7, 177, 183, 184–5; sentence construction, four examples of, 182; structure based on numerology, 178–80, 181, 188; and tragic style, 180, 387; three themes of vernacular

481

Index

Empire, Western, 21, 26, 42–5, 363
empires, succession of, 219, 288, 289
Empyrean, 103, 104 (Fig. 3), 106 (Fig. 4),
138, 266, 273; in *Par.*, 271–2, 285, 328,
374, 376, 397, 398
Enarrationes in psalmos (St Augustine),
quoted, 136–7
Envy, sin of, and envious, 258, 391, 392
Enzo, King, son of Frederick II, 32, 102
Epicureans, 195, 206, 329
Er the Pamphylian, 276
Erato, Muse of erotic poetry, 328
Erichtho, 419
Esther, 309, 310
Eteocles, 420
Euclid, 215
Eudoxus, 103
Eugene III, Pope, 91
Eunoe, river, 262, 263, 297, 356, 376
Europe, D.'s influence on the civilization of,
3–4, 394, 402, 411–12
Eusebius, 293
Euterpe, Muse of music, 328
Eve, 372
Exodus psalm, 192, 193, 278, 321, 333,
351
Experience, Man of, 390–1
Ezekiel (*see also* Bible, O.T.): in *Commedia*,
332; in *Epist.* X, 405
Ezzelino da Romano, 96, 381

face to face, imagery of coming, 374–9
faculty psychology, 83, 108–9 (Fig. 5),
110–11, 137, 311, 409
Faggiuola, Uguccione della, 163, 226, 233,
234
Fall of man, 108, 281, 288
false counsel, givers of, 393–6
falsifiers, 391–2
fantasia, 109, 110, 272, 309, 310
Farinata degli Uberti, 35, 37, 49, 82; in
Inf., 37, 250, 341, 391
Fates, three, 207
fedeli d'amore (*see also dolce stil nuovo*):
Auerbach on, 85–6; Corbin on, 84, 111;
their code, philosophy, and system of
grades, 80, 82–6, 110–13, 114–17, 413–15;
D.'s association with, and the importance
of their influence, 76, 111, 114, 115, 134,
140, 141, 187, 226, 314, 385, 412–15;
and Sufism, 84, 85, 111; and Templars,
possible links with, 84–5, 412–15; their
training in dreams and visions, 114–16,
134, 385; Valli on, 83–4, 116; in *VN*, 76,
111, 134, 140, 187
Fede Santa, La, 84, 279
Felix Holt (George Eliot), 18 quoted,
430 n. 46

Ficino, Marsilio, 83, 322, 412
Fiesole, 21, 30, 212
Figueira, Guilhem, 96
figura, 117, 331–2
fin' amors, 93, 97, 98
Fiore, Il, 98, 167
Fiorinus, 21
Fire (*see also* Light, symbolism of): and the
way characters appeared to D. out of,
301, 393–7; as one of four elements
related to imagery of *Commedia*, 352, 360;
paradoxical use of in *Commedia* as means
of torment and expression of state of
bliss, 396; sphere of, 254 (Fig. 10), 352
First Circle, The (Solzhenitsyn), 383
Five, numerology of, 285, 352–3
Flight, images of, 358–60
Florence: amnesties to exiles, 233–4;
Angevin dynasty and, 55, 57, 62, 132, 146;
bankers of, 30, 65–6; and Boniface VIII,
147–8, 149, 151, 154, 155, 223;
Cacciaguida's description of, 29–30;
cathedrals and churches of, 69, 70, 90,
109–10; Charles Martel's visit to, 132,
146; Charles of Valois and, 155, 156–7,
158, 161, 165; citizens of, in *Commedia*,
55, 384; and cloth trade, 30, 65–6, 179;
in *Commedia*, 30, 55, 260, 268–9, 339,
353–4, 364, 381, 398; commercial
revolution in, 65–6; constitutional
changes in, 29, 33, 34, 100–2; *contado* of,
29, 35 (Fig. 2), 77; in *Conv.*, 46, 186,
199; cultural life in, 66–7; D.'s exile
from, 157, 159, 163–4, 165–6;
D.'s priorate of, 64, 150, 153–5, 236–7;
D., and resentment of Florentines against,
in, 411; D.'s love of, and ambivalent
attitude to, 71–2, 157, 165, 182, 230,
233–4, 269; effect on D. of technology
and commercial relations of, 66, 402;
in *DVE*, 179, 182; despotism, preserved
from, 63–4; in *Epist.* VI, 31, 211–12, 228,
313, 318; education in, 70–1; and
European trade, 30, 66, 154; fire of 1304,
163; florin, gold, 21, 353–4; Ghibelline
rule of, 34, 37, 55; Gregory X's visit to,
and interdict, 61, 70; Guelph rule of,
34–7, 57; Guelph and Ghibelline
quarrels in, 33–7 (*see also* Guelphs;
Ghibellines); guilds (*arti*) of, 33, 64–5;
and Henry VII, 211–12, 386; heraldry
and insignia of, 21, 34, 38–9; and
leopard, symbolized allegorically by,
339, 361, 362, 363; magnates and *popolo*
in, 64–5; and Countess Matilda, 28, 29;
mendicant orders in, 80–2; Montaperti,
defeated at, 35–7, 39; Montecatini,
defeated at, 233; murderers executed in,

485

Index

487

Index

Index

Index

the imperial and the priestly guiding principles of, 324

Mann, Thomas, 286, 300–1

Manto, 419

Mantua, 234, 246, 256

Marcabru, 92, 99

Marcellus, 423

Marcia: in *Commedia*, 248; in *Conv.*, 207–8, 419

Margaret of Brabant, Empress, 212

Maria, imaginary city in *Conv.*, 203–4

Maries, three, 175, 199, 206, 207, 329

Mariolatry, *see* Mary, Blessed Virgin

Maritain, Jacques, 407; quoted, 457 n. 22

Mars, planet and heaven of, 104 (Fig. 3), 105, 106 (Fig. 4), 110, 138; in *Par.*, 38, 268–9, 384

Mars, statue of, 26, 33

Marsyas, 265

Martin IV, Pope, 62, 78

Marvell, Andrew, quoted, 366

Marx, Karl, 409

Mary, Blessed Virgin (*see also* Trinity of blessed ladies), 36, 87, 89–90, 415; in *Commedia*, 89, 205, 247, 257, 258, 260, 270, 272, 294, 307, 308, 310, 340, 341, 348, 354, 355, 362, 368, 381, 392, 397, 398–9, 415; in *Conv.*, 190, 196, 205

Matelda: and Astraea, 174, 344; in *Commedia*, 262, 263, 316, 328, 342, 344–5, 367–8; and Erato, 328, 345; as fourth of six guides of *Commedia*, 321, 322, 344–5, 346, 367–8, 372; and Countess Matilda of Tuscany, 28, 344, 345

Mathnawi (Rûmî), 6 quoted, 447 n. 23

Matilda of Tuscany, Countess (*see also* Matelda), 28, 29, 344, 345

Mazzeo, Joseph Anthony, 331

Mecca, 277

Meccan Revelations (Ibn al-‘Arabī), 141, 277

Medusa, 249, 354, 361, 375

Meloria, battle of, 78

Melpomene, Muse of tragedy, 328

Memory: in *Commedia*, 246, 323, 325; and creative process, 134–5, 298, 410, 411; and D.'s adaptation of Platonic doctrine of reminiscence, 346, 348, 389, 393, 402; D.'s evocation of, in his readers, 5, 346–7 in *Epist.* X, 404–6; in faculty psychology, 109–10, 449 n. 5; Lullian art of, and D., 188; Muses as daughters of (Mnemosyne), 323, 325; and *VN*, 127, 133, 134–6

mendicant orders (*see also* Franciscans; Dominican order), 37, 40, 45, 80–1

Mercury, god, 294, 328, 421

Mercury, planet and heaven of, 104 (Fig. 3), 106 (Fig. 4), 118, 266, 294

Metamorphoses (Ovid), 353, 384, 418

metanoia: in Gospels, 303, 314; as an explanation of D.'s experience in Purgatory, 303, 306, 311–12, 314, 344, 449 n. 23

metaphor: D.'s discussions of, in *VN*, 138, in *Commedia*, 346, in *Epist.* X, 405–6; implicit and explicit, 13–15; origins of, 15, 72; in scripture, use of, 304–5

Metaphysics (Aristotle), 352

Meung, Jean de, 97–8, 299

Michael Palaeologus, Emperor of Byzantium, 97

Michelangelo, 240, 412

Milan, 31, 176, 212

Milotti, Fiduccio de', 238

Milton, John, 16, 185 quoted, 232, 383, 442 n. 30 quoted

Milton (Blake), quoted, 8–9, 301

Milvian bridge, battles of: Constantine's, 290; Henry VII's, 212

Minerva, 266, 370

Minos, 248, 283

Mirror, imagery of, 378

Mithraism, 289

Mohammed, Prophet, 25–6; in *Inf.*, 24, 25–6, 284, 390; legend of the *mi'raj* and possible influence on *Commedia*, 25, 277–8

Molay, Jacques de, last Grand Master of the Temple, 162, 163, 227, 233

Monarch and monarchy, *see* Emperor; Dante, works: *Monarchia*

monasticism: Egyptian and Celtic, and views of Afterlife, 276; Greek, 339; Western, and civilization, 23–4, 372; and revival of Florence, 24

Mongols, 46

Montanari, Fausto, 199–200

Montanhagol, Guilhem, 96

montanina canzone, see under Dante, works: lyrics, 'Amor da che'

Montaperti, battle of, 34, 36, 37, 39, 45, 55, 60, 89, 233, 253

Montecatini, battle of, 233, 239

Montefeltro, Buonconte da, 78, 79; in *Purg.*, 256, 355–6, 390–1

Montefeltro, Guido da, 78, 79, 151; in *Inf.*, 250, 251, 391, 394–6

Monteverdi, Claudio, 412

Moon, planet and heaven of, 103, 104 (Fig. 3), 105, 106 (Fig. 4); in *Commedia*, 7, 266; question of spots on, 266, 376

moral level of interpretation (tropology) (*see also* Fourfold method): in *Commedia*, 330, 361, 369; in *Conv.*, 192–3; related to cosmology and to Nous in Neoplatonic tradition, 403

Mordecai, 309, 310

490

Index

Morrone, Pietro, *see* Celestine V

Moses, 334; in *Commedia*, 325; in *Epist.* X, 333–4

Mostacci, Jacopo, 101

mother and child imagery: in *Commedia*, 71, 314, 347–8

Mozart, W. A., quoted, 429 n. 21

Muir, Edwin, 15

Munsalvaesche, 224, 311

Muses, nine, 246, 252, 253, 255, 264, 305, 322–8 and Fig. 14, 451 n. 19

Music: and *canzone*, 93, 117, 121, 179–80; D.'s love of, 77; and singing in *Commedia*, 7, 14, 255, 258, 260, 262, 267, 268, 269, 304, 317, 378; and poetry, effects of, 6–7

Mussato, Albertino, 237, 239, 305

Mystical Theology (Dionysius the Areopagite), quoted, 406

mythology: classical and gods, 230, 287–8, 289, 330, 418–23; Nordic and Celtic, 382; as radical and transforming force, 382; D.'s use of, 322–9, 334

Nachiketa, 275

Narbonne, Aimeric de, 79

Nardi, Bruno, 331, 407

Nathan, prophet, 268

Nebuchadnezzar, 291; in *Epist.* X, 405

negligent rulers, episode of, in *Purg.*, 14–15, 256, 361–2, 384

Neoplatonism and its influence, 89, 90–1, 93, 101, 116, 274, 276, 279, 283, 322, 402–3, 412, 413

Neptune: in *Aeneid*, 420–1; in *Commedia*, 9–10, 357, 417

Nessus, centaur, 250

Nicholas III, Pope, 61, 62, 63; in *Inf.*, 252, 364–5

Nicholas IV, Pope, 63, 146

Nicodemus, Apocryphal Gospel of, 108, 276

Nile, river, 174, 352

Noah's Ark, 335–6

Nobility: ideas of, amongst *fedeli d'amore*, 8, 80, 82, 85–6; D. on, 5, 180–1, 184, 196–9, 206

Nogaret, William, 158

Normans, in southern Italy, 38, 61

Notker Balbulus, 117

numerology, 111, 116–17, 133–4, 178–9, 320, 330–1; in *Commedia*, 284–6, 369, 377, 384

Nyssa (twin peak of Parnassus), 323 (*see also* Cirrha)

observation, images of natural, 24, 77–8, 350–2, 393, 422

observation, images of self-, 348–50, 378

Oderisi of Gubbio, 258, 308

Oedipus, 420

Old Man, type of, 390–1

Olivi, Petrus, 49, 81

optics: D.'s studies of, 168, 195; in medieval science, 403; used in imagery of *Commedia*, 377, 403

Ordericus Vitalis, 380–1

Ordinances of Justice, 54, 64, 148

Origen, 191

Orlandi, Guido, 82, 84

Orosius, Paulus, 152, 268, 287, 288

Orpheus: in *Conv.*, 191–2

Orsini family, 63, 268

Ottimo Commento, 232

Otto III, Emperor, 27

Otto IV, Emperor, 33

Otto of Freising, 30

Ouspensky, P. D., 15–16 quoted, 385

Ovid, 97, 232, 291, 329, 353, 384, 418; in *Commedia*, 248, 418; in *Conv.*, 207; medieval allegorical interpretations of, 327, 329–40, 418; Works, *see Ars amatoria*; *Remedia amoris*; *Metamorphoses*

Ovide moralisé, 418

Oxford, 160, 403, 440 n. 48

Padua, 234

pagans, noble, 248, 340–2, 383, 416, 419

Palestrina, 151, 395

Pannochieschi, Nello de', 151

Paolo and Francesca episode, 58, 91–2, 96, 248, 313, 348

Papacy: alliance with aristocracies of Europe, 40; Christ's charge to Peter, 39, 41; and city states, 31, 32; in *Commedia*, 24, 44–5, 271, 339; in D.'s period, 62–3; and Empire (*see also* Henry VII), 26, 27, 32, 40–5; finances, taxes, and banking, 34, 40, 41–2, 65, 150–1; and French monarchy (*see also* Boniface VIII; Clement V; Philip the Fair), 58, 151, 155, 161; heraldry and insignia of, 39, 41; in *Mon.*, 44, 222–3; and papal states, 25, 55, 62, 63, 148; and Reform movement, 27–8, 40; spiritual and temporal claims of, 34–40, 147

Paradise: Celestial, 215, 222, 294, 404, 410; Earthly, 3, 176, 215, 222, 231, 257, 261–4, 278, 279, 294, 297, 314, 315, 319, 324, 336, 337, 342, 343, 344–5, 346, 352, 356, 359, 361, 367–70, 376, 384, 396, 410

pargoletta, 166, 167

Parma, siege of, 32, 212

Parnassus, Mount (*see also* Nyssa; Cirrha), 183, 265, 297, 323, 324, 342

Parzival (Wolfram von Eschenbach), 224, 311, 318, 413

Index

Pasternak, Boris, 13 quoted, 38
Paul, St (*see also* Bible, N.T.), 105, 140, 276, 332, 407; in *Commedia*, 105, 247, 361, 407; in *Epist.* X, 405
Penthesilea, 248
Perillus, 395
Perini, Dino, 238, 239
Peripatetics (*see also* Aristotle), 195, 206, 329
Peter, St (Apostle): Christ's charge to, 39, 41, 221; in *Commedia*, 227, 231, 270–1, 325, 397; in *Conv.*, 206; in *Mon.*, 221
Peter Damian, St, 27, 270
Peter Martyr, St, 49
Peter of Blois, 136
Petrarch, 141, 237, 412
Phaedrus (Plato), 402
Phaethon, 349
Phalaris, 395
Pharsalia (Lucan), 207–8, 328, 419–20
Philip IV (the Fair), king of France: ambitions of, 161, 223, 363; and Boniface VIII, 150–1, 155, 158–9, 162–3, 210, 226, 363, 365–6; and Clement V, 160, 162–3, 209–10, 214, 226, 236, 361, 364–5; in *Commedia*, 161, 163, 213, 260, 339, 363–5, 369; death of, 233; as Geryon's allegorical interpretation, 363–4; and Templars, 160, 161–3, 209–10, 214, 227, 279, 363, 381
Philo of Alexandria, 330
Philokalia, 339
Philosophy, Lady, 87, 132, 166, 167, 187, 193, 194, 195–6, 201, 374; in Boethius, 90, 135, 168, 194
Philosophy, Perennial, 85, 279, 295, 408
Phlegethon, river of Hell, 250, 291
Phlegyas, 248
Pia, La (de' Tolomei), 151, 256
Piero, San (*sesto* of), 54
Pietra, La, 166, 169–74, 184
Pilate, Pontius, 161, 220, 222
pilgrim and pilgrimage, images of, 14–15, 131, 298, 342, 355, 374
Pilgrimage of Great Circle, and its influence on *Commedia*, 278, 292, 331–2, 333, 361, 367, 368, 369, 370, 373, 374, 412
Pisa, 27, 30, 78, 127, 149, 188, 212, 213, 420
Pisa, Guido da, 209, 331, 339, 347, 364, 371, 373
Pisano, Giovanni, 51, 70
Pisistratus, 258, 308, 310
Pistoia, 148, 287, 314
Plato, 90, 103, 105, 106, 116, 276, 402; in *Commedia*, 341; in *Conv.*, 195; in *Epist.* X, 405–6; Works, *see under Phaedrus*; *Republic*; *Symposium*; *Timaeus*
Pluto: in *Commedia*, 248, 357
Po, river, 355

podestà, office of, 33, 34
poetry: and the brain (two hemispheres), 410–11; form and, 17; metaphor and, 18–21; multiple meanings in, 12–13, 304–5, 332–3, 346–7, 402; rhythm and, 17; scholastic objections to, 304–5; two levels of meaning in, as opposed to fourfold meaning, 191–3, 330
Polanyi, Michael, 410
political thought: evolution of D.'s (*see also* Dante, works: *Mon.*), 165, 365–6; influence of D.'s, 3–4, 223–5
Politics (Aristotle), 219, 442
Polyhymnia, Muse of sacred song, 328, 373
Ponte Sant'Angelo, 152
Ponte Vecchio, 26
popes, simoniac, 209, 252, 271, 284, 353, 364–5, 386
Popolo, 34; Captain of, 34; *Primo Popolo*, 34–5
Poppi, 79, 211
Portinari, Florentine family, 54
Portinari, Folco, 54, 72, 129, 132 (*see also* Beatrice)
Pound, Ezra, 93
Poverty, Lady, 47, 48
praise, poetry of, 124, 136–7, 194, 201, 231, 315, 316–19, 343, 402
Prato, Cardinal Nicholas of, 159
predestination, 270, 288
Prelude, The (Wordsworth), 301
Prester John, 46, 224
Primum Mobile, 103, 104 (Fig. 3), 105, 106 (Fig. 4), 268; in *Par.*, 271, 283, 284
Priscian, 71
Procida, John of, 62
Procne, 304, 310
prodigality, sin of, 248–9, 260, 353, 354
Prophecy: Aquinas on, 50, 449 n. 11; St Augustine on, 299–300, 305, 306, 334, 449 n. 11; in Bible, 117, 299–300; D.'s application of fourfold method to, 334; D. as prophet and his thoughts on, 38, 44, 50, 165, 299–300, 305–6, 334, 369, 386, 390, 418–19; and D.'s failure in *Epist.* VI, 211, 318–19; and Joachim of Fiore, 46, 298; medieval attitude to, 45–6, 299; implicit in heraldry and poet's use of symbolism, 38
proto-*Commedia*, *see* Dante, works: *Commedia*
pseudo-Methodius, 293
Ptolemy and Ptolemaic system, 104, 105, 273, 274, 394, 403–4
puer aeternus, 39
punto of light (*Par.* XXVIII), 271, 274, 303–4, 379, 389–90, 397, 403
Purgatory, in doctrine and general belief, 108, 281, 304, 380

492

Index

Purgatory, Mount, 7, 87, 89, 108, 152, 207, 255, 257 (Fig. 11), 258, 264, 278, 280–1, 283, 284, 296, 303–4, 306, 307, 310, 341, 344–5, 355, 357, 365, 394, 395, 410
Pyramus, 354
Pyrrhus, 423
Pythagoras, 195, 304

Rachel: in *Commedia*, 247, 261, 312; in Richard of St Victor, 337
Raimbaut of Orange, 99 quoted
Ravenna, 23, 25, 226, 238, 239, 240, 241
Redemption, 108, 267, 333–4
Reform Movement, eleventh-century, 27, 40
Remedia amoris (Ovid), 97, 418
Remigio de' Girolami, Fra, 66–7, 81–2, 152
Renaissance: 4; D.'s thought and work as a preparation for, 322, 369, 394
Renucci, Paul, 231
Reparata, St, 21; Cathedral of, 21, 90
Republic (Plato), 276
Resurrection, 108, 206–7, 267, 268, 366, 392
Richard of St Victor: as master of anagogic interpretation, 330; in *Epist.* X, 321, 405; in *Par.*, 268; Works referred to (*see also Benjamin Major* and *Minor*), 139, 207, 337, 407
Richards, I. A., 312–13, 338, 380; quoted, 313, 450 n. 49
Rilke, Rainer Maria, 12, 300; Works, *see Duino Elegies*; *Sonnets to Orpheus*
Rimini, 238
Rimini, Francesca da (*see also* Paolo and Francesca), 238, 248, 341, 355
Ripheus, 270, 340, 416
Riquier, Giraut, 415
Ristoro d'Arezzo, 186, 436 n. 1
river, imagery of (*see also* water): in *Commedia*, 47, 355–6
Robert of Anjou, King of Sicily, 210, 212, 213, 214, 218, 443 n. 12
Roland, paladin (*see also Chanson de Roland*): in *Commedia*, 26, 269
Romagna, 149, 177, 238; included in papal states, 99; tyrants of, 98, 395
Romance languages, D.'s division of, 176
Romanesque art and sculpture, 51, 382
Roman de la Rose, 43, 97–8, 167, 407
Roman Law, 43
Romanus, teacher in Florence, 70
Rome (*see also* Empire, Roman; Papacy): Barbarossa and, 30; classical and imperial, 21, 22, 32, 152, 165, 196–7, 218–20, 288–9, 419–20, 423, 452–3 n. 48; in *Commedia*, 24, 246, 247, 259, 263, 292,

332, 374, 381, 398; in *Conv.*, 152, 196–7; and coronation of Western Emperors, 26, 30, 212; dialect of her inhabitants, 176; in *Epist.* VII, 227; and Florence, her founding and traditions, 21–3, 452–3 n. 48; and Great Circle pilgrimage, 278, 292, 332, 374, 381, 398; in *Mon.*, 218–20; papal and medieval, 34, 152, 212, 227; and *VN*, 131
Romulus Augustulus, Emperor, 23
Rose, image of, 97, 98; in *Par.*, 272, 397–8, 408
Rossetti, Gabriele, 84, 435 n. 18
Rubicon, river, 238, 419
Rudel, Jaufre, 98, 115
Rudolf of Habsburg, Emperor, 63, 145
Rûmî, Jalâl al-Dîn, 6, 74, 377, 447 n. 23
Ruskin, John, 3, 428 n. 1

Sacchetti, Florentine family, 54
St Peter's, Rome, basilica of, 198, 212
St Victor, *see under* Hugh of; Richard of
Saints: doctrine of treasury of intercession, 25, 39; shrines of, as foci of local patriotism, 25, 27
Saintsbury, George, quoted, 442 n. 17
Saladin, 248
Salimbene, Fra, 49
Salutati, Coluccio, 166, 305
Salvani, Provenzan, 258
'Salve regina', 89, 361–2
samâ, 6
Samson, 115, 331
San Gimignano, 112, 154
San Marco (Venice), 31, 428 n. 1
San Miniato, 21, 69
Santa Croce, 66, 80–1, 296
Santa Maria del Fiore, Cathedral of Florence, 66, 90
Santa Maria Novella, 66, 81, 156
Santo Volto, 374
Sapia, 258, 375, 392
Sapientia (Divine Wisdom), 82, 83, 84, 86, 87, 93, 103, 111–13, 115, 116, 168, 194, 195–6, 199, 201, 204, 294, 345, 370, 371, 372, 374, 412, 413, 414
Saracens, 26, 27, 368
Sardinia, 176
Satan, 253–4, 271, 338, 351, 358, 361, 365–7, 375, 381, 403; in *Commedia*, 293, 380
Saturn, planet and heaven of, 104 (Fig. 3), 106 (Fig. 4); in *Par.*, 38, 270, 396
Scala, Alboino della, 198, 234
Scala, Bartolomeo della, 158, 198, 234
Scala, Can Grande della, 6, 12, 193, 226, 233, 234–8; as possible candidate for *veltro* and DXV, 235–6; his character,

493

Index

234–5, 236–7; D.'s letter to, *see* Dante, works: *Epist.* X; as a patron, 235, 236–7

Scaligeri dynasty of Verona, 62, 213, 234; arms of, 235

scholastic philosophy, 50, 407; and creation of an objective scientific language, 52, 305, 402

Science: D.'s studies of, and influence on development of, 187, 402–3; language of, compared to compression in poetry, 12

Scipio Africanus, 136, 276

Scipio the younger, 276

Scorpio, sign of Zodiac, 363

scorpion, symbolism of, 359

Scot, Michael, 31, 45, 419

sea and seafaring, images of: in *Commedia*, 14–15, 255, 266, 342, 349, 357; in *Conv.*, 159

Selvaggia, 52, 84

Semele, 379, 396

Semiramis, 219; in *Commedia*, 248

Seraphim, 105, 138, 320

Serravalle, Giovanni da, 160, 440 n. 48

sestina form, 100, 450 n. 41

Shadow, imagery of (*see also* Light imagery of), 115, 255–6, 306

Shakespeare, William, 13, 15, 322, 383; quoted, 373

Shams-i-Tabrizi, 74; remark ascribed to, 434 n. 19

sheep, imagery of, 303–4

Shepherd of Hermas, The, 126

She-wolf (*lupa*), 246, 260, 292, 326, 338, 339, 353, 362, 363

Shroud, Holy, 375

Sibyl, 421

Sibylline leaves, image of, 323, 422

Sibyls, prophecies of, 323

Sicilian school of poetry, 32, 81, 85, 101–2, 176

Sicilian Vespers, 62, 147

Sicilian war, 62, 155, 158

Siena, 34, 35, 36, 37, 78, 89, 155, 157, 188, 374; bankers of, 34, 103, 148

Sigier of Brabant, 97, 112; in *Par.*, 268

Signorelli, Luca, 412

Signoria, Palazzo della, 64, 66

sin, original, 108; in relation to will and intellect, 294, 295, 383–4, 391, 410, 411

Sinai, Mount, 278, 292

Singleton, Charles S., 331

Sinon of Troy, 284, 392

Sion, Mount, 278

Siren (*Purg.*), 312, 316

sirventes form, 95–6, 387

Socrates, 322

Solomon, 113, 195, 198, 207, 372; in *Par.*, 268; for Solomonic books *see under* Bible, O.T.

Solovyov, Vladimir, 74

Solzhcnitsyn, Alexander, 166, 383

Sonnets to Orpheus (Rilke), 300

Sordello, 96; in *Purg.*, 256, 342, 344, 387, 391

soul: in *Commedia*, depiction, nature, and destiny of, 17–18, 45, 197, 282, 285, 286, 342, 348, 355, 358, 376, 390–7; in *Conv.*, 189, 191, 192–3, 197; in faculty psychology, 108–11; immortality of, 52, 83, 112, 381; perfection of, in reunion with the body, 108, 267, 268, 392–3; three kinds of (vegetative, sensitive, rational), 108, 197; three motions of (circular, spiral, rectilinear), 282, 285

Spini, Florentine bankers, 148, 154, 155

spiral, pattern and symbolic meaning of, 283–4

spirits (in faculty psychology and poetry of *dolce stil nuovo*), 72–3, 109–10, 122, 124, 128, 137

Spoleto, 31, 212

Stalin, Joseph, 223, 383

stars, heaven of fixed, 103, 104 (Fig. 3), 105, 106 (Fig. 4); in *Par.*, 270

Statius, 329, 420; in *Commedia*, 260–1, 263, 328, 329, 342–4, 354, 376, 391, 396, 420; in *Conv.*, 207; and prodigality, 354; as third of six guides of *Commedia*, 321, 322, 344, 346, 372

Stephen, St, proto-martyr, 258, 308, 310

Stoics, 195, 206, 287, 329

stone, imagery of (*see also* Earth); in *Commedia*, 353–5; in *Conv.*, 192; in *rime petrose*, 169–74

Styx, river of Hell, 249, 250, 291, 354

Sufis, mystics and poets, 6, 74, 374, 412; possible influences on West, 84, 85, 279

Suger, Abbot of St Denis, 335, 380–1

suicides, wood of, 18, 250, 350

Summa contra gentiles (Aquinas), 199

Summa theologiae (Aquinas), quoted 110, 111, 332, 335

Sun, heaven of, and as planet, 103, 104 (Fig. 3), 106 (Fig. 4); in *Commedia*, 267–8; in *Conv.*, 203–4

Sun symbolism (*see also* Luminaries, two; Light, imagery of), 44–5, 195, 274, 289–90, 320, 394, 403, 423; in *Commedia*, 44–5, 47–8, 259, 265, 268, 290, 315, 316, 317, 325, 326, 378–9, 403; in *Conv.*, 194, 195, 203–4; in *Epist.* VII, 227–8; in *Mon.*, 220–1, 290

Sylvester, Pope, 64, 396

Index

Index